# American Defense Policy in Perspective

# American Defense Policy in Perspective

FROM COLONIAL TIMES TO THE PRESENT

Raymond G. O'Connor, Editor
Temple University

---

John Wiley & Sons, Inc., New York / London / Sydney

Library of Congress Catalog Card Number: 65-21436
Printed in the United States of America

# Preface

This generation of Americans faces a new challenge in national security. Leadership of the Free World in its struggle against Communism and the immediate vulnerability of the continent to the most devastating weapons of destruction ever devised by man have led to a greater appreciation of military power. But with the future of mankind in the balance and over half of every federal tax dollar going for defense expenditures, Americans lack an understanding of military policy and the responsibilities of civilian and military leaders.

Much of the confusion over defense policy is due to America's geographical isolation from other powerful nations and an alleged anti-militarist tradition. For more than one-hundred and fifty years the United States sat smugly behind its ocean moat and usually fought wars only when it chose to do so. Moreover most Americans are not aware of the decisive role played by the armed forces in the development of the nation, and they think of themselves as peace-loving people in contrast to the warlike populations of other countries. Yet it was through the force of arms that the nation won and maintained its independence, displaced the Indians, and rounded out its territory. In time of peace the existence of sufficient armed forces often preserved America's integrity and protected and promoted her interests. By failing to understand that military institutions and their consequences are essential elements of the American past, the public came to regard the armed forces as an alien element in society, a necessary evil in time of peace, and of some value only during periods of war. A knowledge of this aspect of American history would eliminate much of the present confusion over the role of military power.

A familiarity with previous policies also provides insight into the basic ingredients of national defense. Military expenditures have increased phenomenally, and with annual appropriations approximating $50 billion there is a strong incentive for citizen interest. But here again the public is confused, for there seem to be no clear criteria for determining the extent or nature of America's investment in defense items. A nation's security is dependent on many factors, including economic, social, cultural, psychological, and geographical. Then, too, military policy is shaped by other considerations, such as the strength of the probable enemy, technological changes in weapons systems, domestic problems, and world responsibilities. Today the United States has been placed in what is, for the country, an unprecedented position. The nation is committed to resist Communist aggression anywhere in the world by whatever means are necessary, and it is under the threat of immediate attack on the homeland. It has been extremely difficult, if not impossible, for the nation to adjust its thinking and its actions to encompass this new responsibility and frightening vulnerability. But much of the current confusion stems from a failure to understand the role of military power in American national development and recognize the fundamentals of defense policy.*

The selections in this book are designed to acquaint the reader with past and present American defense policies, both what they were and why they took the form they did. In emphasizing the broader aspects of policy, tactical or "battle history" has been to a greater extent ignored, although overall strategy is treated especially when dealing with war. Also the selections do not cover all aspects of each topic or the same aspect of every topic. At times certain factors are emphasized to the subordination or exclusion of other factors. But every major consideration that has affected military policy is dealt with in sufficient depth to provide an understanding of the complexities of policy formulation and execution. These selections include articles, excerpts from books, official documents, and speeches. Some are contemporary with the events, others are written or uttered in retrospect. My aim has been to choose materials that will best reveal the nature of defense problems and the way they were faced by those bearing the responsibility.

*April 1965*

RAYMOND G. O'CONNOR
EDITOR

* Portions of the foregoing paragraphs are from Raymond G. O'Connor, "Force and Diplomacy in American History," *Military Review*, XLIII (March 1963), 80–89.

# Contents

# *Introduction*

## The Value of Military History

According to General Charles L. Bolte, former Vice Chief of Staff, Department of the army: "The past must be studied as the basis for, and a guide to, the study of the future. To make a sound prediction one must project the past into the future. If the past is ignored . . . there is no firm foundation for sound forecasting, sound planning, sound apportioning of the limited means . . . available or to become available." If the limited means of manpower, industrial capacity, and resources are squandered, even inadvertently, the nation will suffer accordingly—perhaps disastrously.

General Bolte further points out, "A close examination and study of the period immediately prior to and following the outbreak of a war" will prove of great value to all those responsible for long-range planning. It is in these periods that the effect of past policies and plans or lack of plans becomes most evident, because errors quickly and decisively influence the course of events. Such errors are particularly serious because they can be overcome, if at all, only at great expense and with the loss of precious time.

History shows conclusively that weapons have a decisive influence upon military operations. The development of weapons should therefore be of particular concern to planners, for it takes years to improve or make new weapons and to insure their proper integration into an organization.

One of the most important lessons a military student can learn from history is the necessity of quickly recognizing the changes in tactics and techniques which are indicated during the course of a war, and especially during the meeting engagement. It is at these times that secret weapons and differences in tactics and techniques show up most clearly and require immediate adjustment to conditions on the battlefield. History teaches that commanders must react quickly to the new conditions and at the same time transmit information to higher commanders concerning the circumstances and occurrences on the battlefield which indicate a need for changes in equipment, tactics, and techniques.

---

From *The Writing of American Military History: A Guide*, Department of the Army Pamphlet No. 20–200, Washington, 1956.

The study of the initial phases of military operations deserves special attention. These are periods that mark the introduction of new weapons, new tactics, or inexperienced troops; that involve a sudden shift in type of terrain, in defensive arrangements, in weather, or in seasonal conditions. It is during these periods that faulty organization, inadequate or impractical training, inefficient weapons, failure of leadership and communications, inadequate logistical support, faulty coordination of the various arms, unforeseen effect of weather and terrain, rumors, and many other factors, some almost intangible, create a state of confusion which should challenge every military student. Knowledge gained through a study of the initial phases of past operations will pay untold dividends to those who may be involved later in similar situations.

A military student should not allow personal experience on the battlefield to limit his point of view but should add to it the experiences of others. Conclusions and principles based on a single personal experience or an inadequate preparation in military history are very dangerous. Ardant du Picq, a profound student of combat, has expressed the matter in another way. In a questionnaire submitted to contemporaries he said "Whoever has seen, turns to a method based on his knowledge, his personal experience as a soldier. But experience is long and life is short. The experiences of each cannot therefore be completed except by those of others." In short, a careful study of objective military history with an open mind and with the determination of learning from the experiences of others will be of great benefit to any military student.

The principles of strategy have been evolved from an analytical study of many wars. They are, therefore, based on a great many experiences of the past and are immutable. "Consequently," as General Douglas MacArthur has said, "the Army extends its analytical interest to the dust-buried accounts of wars long past as well as to those still reeking with the scent of battle" with the object of the search dictating the field for its pursuit.

In the field of tactics and techniques, doctrine based on personal experience or the experience of others is apt to lead to error, for, as General MacArthur has also said: "In every age these (tactics) are decisively influenced by the characteristics of weapons currently available and by the means at hand for maneuvering, supplying, and controlling combat forces". Leadership, organization, communications, training, morale, terrain, weather and climatic conditions, and the enemy will also differ as well as many other things. Peacetime tactical doctrine, therefore, can be determined only by a process of reasoning, by studying experiences of others in the most recent wars, and by experimentation. When doctrine has been subjected to test in actual battle it should be quickly readjusted to conform to reality and kept in step with conditions during the entire course of operations.

Upon the conclusion of a war the victors decide how they should organize and equip for the future. They base their conclusions on their own experiences, which, no matter how great, are limited. It might be said that the victors reorganize on the basis of considerable self-esteem, attributing their success to better organization, equipment, training, and leadership, while the vanquished reorganize on the basis of considerable humility, analyzing events and determining and eliminating weaknesses with the intention of defeating the recent enemy. Military progress is therefore slow among the victors because conceit and complacency too often have the upper hand. The vanquished, however, looking further ahead, build new organization and new equipment. This lesson should be carefully heeded by the United States: having won all the wars in which it has engaged it is in a certain degree of danger because history reveals that military victory has frequently contained the seeds of weakness, deficiencies in coordination, training, discipline, and leadership, inefficiencies in organization and logistical arrangements, inadequacies of intelligence, and shortcomings of equipment and supply.

The most convincing lessons can be learned from defeats. But it is infinitely better to learn from the defeats of others. It is, therefore, advantageous to study and analyze the records of the vanquished. The student of military history should give careful consideration to the writings of the leaders of defeated nations who have been allowed to express themselves unhampered by censorship. Frequently, much more can be learned from them than from the leaders of victorious nations who are apt to pass over the unfavorable matters and leave the impression that few mistakes were made. The veil of censorship usually continues in victorious nations where the proprieties are at least insisted upon and military regulations and discipline are at hand to enforce them.

The American Revolution was but the prelude to the era of peoples' wars, the wild and desperate struggles that have grown in intensity and destructiveness down to the present time. As Marshal Foch has said: " . . . they (the peoples) were to set themselves the goal, not a dynastic interest, not of the conquest or possession of a province, but the defence or the propagation of philosophical ideas in the first place, next of principles of independence, of unity, of immaterial advantages of various kinds. Lastly they staked upon the issue the interests and fortune of every individual private. Hence the rising of passions, that is elements of force, hitherto in the main unused."

In the United States, the direction of the armed forces is vested in the civilian Chief of State or President and the policy matters in the Congress. The Executive and the Congress are elected to office and have not often been trained or soundly experienced in military affairs. The President must of necessity coordinate the vast executive agencies of the government in both peace and war. He must understand the various agencies, the contributions they can make to the national security, as well as their requirements. He must also be capable of convincing the policy-making body or Congress of the necessity for these requirements. At the same time he must be capable of decentralizing the execution of tasks to subordinates.

As General Maurice has pointed out, much of the difficulty in the relations between statesman and soldier has arisen in the past because of a misconception of what is meant by the conduct of war. Too many military men have thought of it as the direction of the armed forces in actual operations. Today, however, it implies the direction of the entire power and resources of the nation in pursuit of national objectives and their coordination with those of allies. This is certainly not the responsibility of the highest ranking military commanders even though they are intimately concerned in them because of their bearing upon the preparation and organization of the nation for war. On the civilian side the statesmen are generally even less prepared for their role in a national emergency because the civilian educational system in the United States has long neglected the study of war. Those who have aspired to high government positions have had to prepare themselves on their own initiative and without satisfactory guidance.

The soundest preparation for an understanding of the delicate relationship of statesman and soldier and of their mutual problems in the conduct of military affairs in peace and war can be made by studying history—particularly American history of the periods preceding, during, and following national emergencies. Unfortunately, future statesmen are rarely sure of their place in sufficient time to make the necessary preparation. Personnel of the armed forces are in much better positions to foresee their future roles in war than those unknown ones who will someday be their superiors. They should, therefore, conscientiously prepare themselves for the supporting roles of advisers to the paramount civilian authorities and of instructors to the American people. Both roles will require great moral courage if the public interests are to be best served. An improperly prepared individual or a base flatterer may rise to the position of chief adviser on the basis of personality and lead his superiors and the country to ruin. The bloody pages of history are replete with examples of this kind.

Today, every element of national strength—ideological, spiritual, psychological, political, financial, economic, technological, and military—is involved in war and in the preparation for war. Even worse, imperialistic communism has made conflict a continuing and continuous activity among the people in every land in the world. The very name *war* has become too restrictive. *Universal conflict* better describes the relations of man to man, of people to people, and of state to state in the shrunken world of the twentieth century.

Now, less than ever before, can responsible military leaders ignore the broad fields of knowledge involved in this concept of *universal conflict*. Accordingly, military leaders who are responsible for advice on strategy should be versed in the broader aspects of all of these matters and should bring to their task a balanced judgment capable of giving to each the correct value it deserves in solving problems that arise in a rapidly changing world.

Above everything else, however, American military leaders should have a knowledge of their own land and its people and of its military history. Without this fundamental knowledge decisions might sooner or later transcend the practical and realistic. This could result in a national catastrophe.

After long and distinguished service, Lieutenant General John M. Schofield concluded that general military education is essential in a country having a popular government. "No man (he wrote) can be fully qualified for the duties of statesman until he has made a thorough study of the science of war in its broadest sense. . . . (Otherwise) he is liable to do almost infinite damage to his country." Although this lesson was pointed out even earlier and the Morrill Act of 1862 was designed to improve the situation, military education is still woefully neglected in American educational institutions and the people give little consideration to the military qualifications of those who seek their support for important positions in the government.

Thus it can be seen that military students can render an important service to the people of the United States and to government officials by clarifying the causes and characteristics of war, the principles underlying the conduct of alliances, the coordination of domestic, foreign, and military policy, and the conditions governing the conduct of operations and the men who fight them.

As Burchardt has pointed out, the history of our country should be considered in parallel with that of other nations and in relation to world history and its laws—a part of a greater whole. This will require not only an understanding of the histories of existing nations but of those, once powerful, but now gone forever.

# A List of United States Wars

1775 The Revolution
1782 Wyoming Valley Insurrection
1786 Shay's Rebellion
1790 Northwest Indian War
1791 Whiskey Insurrection
1798 War With France
1799 Fries Rebellion
1801 Tripolitan War
1806 Burr Conspiracy
1806 Sabine Expedition
1807 Chesapeake Bay Affair
1808 Lake Champlain Affair
1811 Northwest Indian War
1812 Great Britain
1812 Seminole War
1813 Peoria Indians
1813 Creek Indians
1817 Second Seminole
1819 Yellowstone Expedition
1823 Blackfeet Indians
1827 Lefevre Indian War
1831 Sac and Fox Indians
1832 Black Hawk War
1832 South Carolina Nullification
1833 Cherokee War
1834 Pawnee Indians
1835 Third Seminole
1836 Second Creek Indians
1837 Osage Indians
1838 Heatherly Indian War
1838 Mormons
1838 New York-Canada Frontier
1846 Doniphan's Mexican Expedition
1846 Mexican War
1846 New Mexican Expedition
1848 Cayuse War
1849 Navajo
1849 Comanche Indians
1850 Pitt River Expedition (California)
1851 Yuma Expedition
1851 Utah Indian
1851 Oregon and Washington Indians
1855 Snake Indians
1855 Sioux Indians
1855 Yakima Expedition
1855 Cheyenne Indian
1855 Florida War (Seminoles)
1856 Kansas Border Troubles
1857 Gila Expedition
1857 Sioux Indians
1857 Mountain Meadow Massacre
1857 Utah Expedition
1858 Northern Indian Expedition
1858 Puget Sound Expedition
1858 Spokane Indian Troubles
1858 Navajo Expedition
1858 Wichita Expedition
1859 Colorado River Expedition
1859 Pecos Expedition
1859 Antelope Hills Expedition
1859 Bear River Expedition
1859 San Juan Imbroglio
1859 John Brown Raid
1859 Cortina Troubles
1860 Pah Ute Expedition
1860 Kiowa and Comanche Indians
1860 Carson Valley Expedition
1860 Navajo Expedition
1861 Apache Indians
1861 Civil War
1862 Indian Massacres (Minnesota)
1862 Sioux Indians

Announced by Secretary of War Weeks in 1922.

1863 Cheyenne War
1865 Northwestern Indian War
1865 Fenian Raid
1867 Mexican Border Indian War
1868 Canadian River Expedition
1871 Yellowstone Expedition
1871 Fenian Troubles
1872 Yellowstone Expedition
1872 Modoc Campaign
1873 Yellowstone Expedition
1874 Indian Territory War
1874 Sioux War
1874 Black Hills War
1875 Nevada Expedition
1876 Sioux War
1876 Powder River Expedition
1876 Big Horn Expedition
1876 Sioux War
1877 Nez Perces Campaign
1878 Ute Campaign
1878 Snake Indian
1890 Sioux
1891 Mexican Border (Tin Horn War)
1895 Bannock Indian Trouble
1898 Spanish-American War
1898 Chippewa Indians
1899 Philippine Insurrection
1900 Boxer Insurrection
1912 Nicaraguan Expedition
1913 Haitian and San Domingo
1914 Vera Cruz
1916 Punitive Expedition in Mexico
1917 Germany—World War I
1919 Punitive Expedition into Mexico

I.

# The Colonial Background of American Military Policy

There is seldom a satisfactory period in which to begin a history, for events, like people, rarely emerge without antecedents. The British colonies in America inherited most of their military practices from the mother country, whose experience had been somewhat different from that of continental European nations. England capitalized on its insular position by avoiding large standing armies, and the bloody wars against political usurpers created a tradition of hostility to a professional military caste which was transmitted to the colonies. In the late fifteenth century the ocean, which had been an awesome and formidable barrier, became a highway that linked a luxury-hungry Europe with the treasures of Asia and the New World. England, as an island nation, perceived the value of a navy for defense and the control of trade routes to the unexploited riches of non-Western countries. During the glorious Elizabethan Age, Sir Walter Raleigh proclaimed that he "who rules the sea, rules the commerce of the world, and to him that rules the commerce of the world belongs the treasure of the world and indeed the world itself." The sixteenth, seventeenth, and eighteenth centuries were dominated by a series of wars in which the European powers competed for control of the newly discovered lands of other continents. The prize was the wealth that determined national greatness, and England finally emerged from the struggle as master of the North American continent and its vast resources.

The colonists found themselves embroiled on two fronts. As British subjects they participated in the conflicts with European nations, whose victory might well deprive them of their home and livelihood. As settlers in a savage territory they had to defend themselves against the native inhabitants, who often resented the appropriation of their lands by the foreign interlopers. Thus a colonial military establishment was imperative. In New England, as Herbert L. Osgood observed, "The Puritan belonged to the militant type of humanity and considered the defence of his inheritance, by force of arms if necessary, as nothing less than a religious duty." Yet a singular lack of enthusiasm for military service characterized the thirteen colonies, and it became even more noticeable as the distance increased from troublesome neighbors or hostile Indian tribes.

The loosely knit militia organization, whereby men were called up for duty when imminent danger threatened, prevailed in the colonies. Borrowed from England, where the sea furnished an excuse for leisurely mobilization, the militia system in America had serious shortcomings. Campaigns, begun without warning by the Indians, were often inaugurated by what has been called "the opening day massacre." In the following article Professor Louis Morton reveals the nature of colonial defense policy and the ways in which it was perpetuated when the colonies became a nation.

# The Origins of American Military Policy

## BY LOUIS MORTON

ALL TOO OFTEN those who write about the American military tradition start with the Revolution, or with the beginning of the Federal government. They would have us believe that the founders of our nation created and formulated out of thin air a military policy at once complete and perfect.

To represent the origins of American military policy in this way is of course a distortion. The roots of our military policy, like the beginnings of our representative government and political democracy, are to be found in the early settlements at Jamestown, Plymouth, and elsewhere —in the arrangements the settlers made for their defense. The seeds of our policy go back even further in time—to the experience of the English people.

In this three hundred and fiftieth anniversary year of the founding of Jamestown, it is perhaps not out of place to review some of the origins of our national defense establishment. Not only will we understand better why certain things are as they are today. We will also be struck by the fact that many of the problems and solutions of those earlier days are still with us in different form.

Before the new world settlers left their homes in the old world, they provided for their defense on the unknown continent of America. The businessmen who financed the colonizing ventures had invested too much money to risk the destruction of their property. The religious leaders were practical men, not visionaries, and their hope of attaining freedom from persecution was too strong to allow them to be negligent of their military strength. The British crown, which authorized the expeditions and granted lands, but which took no risks, empowered the colonists to take whatever measures were required (in the words of the Massachusetts Charter of 1628) "to incounter, expulse, repell, and resist by force of armes, as well by sea as by lands" any effort to destroy or invade the settlement.

Weapons and military stores were therefore included in the cargo of the ships that came to Virginia and Massachusetts. Among the settlers were experienced soldiers, men specifically engaged to train the colonists in the use of arms, organize them into military formations, and direct them in battle if necessary. Such a man was Captain John Smith, an adventurer and veteran of the religious wars on the Continent. Such a man was Captain Myles Standish, hired by the Pilgrims to accompany them to Plymouth.

Not even a John Smith or a Myles Standish could fight off an Indian attack by himself. The settlers had to do that together, and every able-bodied man became in times of military emergency a front-line soldier. There was never any question about this. The obligation of every male who could carry arms to perform military service in the defense of his community was an ancient English tradition dating back to Saxon

Louis Morton, "The Origins of American Military Policy," *Military Affairs*, XXII, No. 2 (Summer, 1958), 75–82. Reprinted by permission.

times. Such documents as the Assize of Arms (1181), the Statute of Westminster (1285), and the Instructions for General Musters (1572) rooted the obligation of military service firmly in English law. As late as 1588, when the Grand Armada threatened invasion, "the rugged miners poured to war from Mendip's sunless caves . . . and the broad streams of pikes and flags rushed down each roaring street" of London to defend the nation against the approaching Spanish fleet.

According to this tradition, which became organized into the militia system, every able-bodied man was considered a potential soldier. He had to train and drill in military formation at stated intervals. By law, he was required to possess arms and equipment and to have them ready for immediate use.

The system was local in character and organized on a geographical basis. It was administered by county and town officials who had full authority to impose punishment and collect fines. Yet English law also restricted the use of the militia to inhibit the crown from using it as an instrument of despotism and from employing it outside the kingdom. The militia, thus, was a military system for emergencies of short duration in defensive situations.

Since this was the military tradition of the colonists, this was the basis of the military system they employed in the New World. It was admirably suited to their needs. But there was an important difference. In England there had been but a single militia organization; in America there were as many militias as there were colonies. No man would serve in any but his own. "Let the New Yorkers defend themselves," said a North Carolinian of a later day. "Why should I fight the Indians for them?"

Arrived in the New World, the colonists were as much concerned with preparations for defense as with food and shelter. Acting in accordance with instructions from home, the original settlers of Jamestown—100 men and 4 boys—split into three groups upon landing. One group provided fortifications for defense, another furnished a guard and planted a crop, the third explored the nearby area. Within a month after their arrival, they had built a primitive fort, a triangular stockade of "Planckes and strong Posts, foure foot deepe in the ground."

The Puritans, similarly instructed in England, were also militant in defense of their property. As one of their number remarked, "they knew right well" that their church "was surrounded with walls and bulworks and the people of God, in re-edifying the same did prepare to resist their enemies with weapons of war, even while they continued building."

Probably the first military legislation in the English colonies was the code of laws proclaimed in Jamestown by Sir Thomas Dale in 1612. On military leave from his post in the Netherlands, Dale assumed the governorship of Virginia at a time when the colony was in danger of extinction, its inhabitants on the verge of starvation. The strict regime he imposed, based on existing military regulations and on "the laws governing the Armye in the Low Countreys," was even more severe than the English laws of the period. But it accomplished its purpose. Order was restored, crops were planted, and peace was made with the Indians. "Our people," wrote John Rolfe, "yearly plant and reape quietly, and travell in the woods a-fowling and a-hunting as freely and securely from danger or treacherie as in England."

Martial law soon outlived its usefulness. As soon as the colony ceased to be a military outpost, the Virginians wrote into civil law the requirements for military service. The Massacre of 1622, which almost destroyed the colony, was still fresh in mind when the General Assembly in 1623 required all inhabitants "to go under arms." Three years later, Governor Yeardley specified that all males between 17 and 60 years of age were to serve when necessary and perform military duty when required. Changes were afterwards made in the law, but the obligation of universal service was never abandoned. Failure to comply subjected the offender to punishment and fine, as one John Bickley discovered when, for refusing to take up arms, he was sentenced to be "laid neck and heels" for 12 hours and pay a fine of 100 pounds of tobacco.

A local official known as the Commander

controlled the militia in each district. He was charged with responsibility for seeing that his men were properly armed and supplied with powder and shot. Later, as the population grew and his duties increased, a lieutenant commander was appointed to assist him. The Commander's duties were so varied and extensive as to make him the most important person in the community, its chief civilian as well as military official. Not only did he supervise the construction of defenses, drill his units, and have custody of the public gunpowder, but he also saw to it that everyone attended church services and observed the laws relating to the tobacco trade. Though the commissioning of officers remained in the hands of the governor, the commander appointed his own subordinates. Once a man acquired a military title he retained it. So numerous were the officers produced by this system and so fond were the Virginians of their titles that a visitor in a later period, struck by the abundance of military rank, remarked that the colony seemed to be "a retreat of heroes."

The Pilgrims too lost no time in organizing their defenses. Captain Standish was designated military commander of the colony. Under him were formed four companies, each with its own commander and designated area of responsibility. A visitor at Plymouth in 1627 noted approvingly the defensive works and the careful preparations to meet an attack. "They assemble by beat of drum," he explained, "each with his musket or firelock in front of the captain's door; they have their cloakes on and place themselves in order, three abreast, and are led by a sergeant without beat of drum. Behind comes the governor in a long robe; beside him, on the right hand, comes the preacher with his cloak on, and on the left hand the captain with his side-arms and cloak, and with a small cane in his hand; and so they march in good order, and each sets his arms down near him. Thus they are constantly on their guard night and day."

By the middle of the seventeenth century Plymouth had established a military system based on universal service. Each colonist was required to own and maintain his own weapons, and the governor was authorized by law to prescribe military training. As new towns grew up along the frontier, they were brought into the defensive organization by the requirement to maintain their own companies under the central control of the government at Plymouth. The local companies elected their own officers, subject to approval of the government, and the officers appointed subordinates, selected training days, and drilled their units. Regulations were enforced by fines, collected by the clerk of the company or the local constable, and these fines often supported the military activities of the community. If the General Court (the legislature) required it, each town provided a quota of men for military expeditions.

The military system of the Puritans was much like that of Plymouth and Jamestown. According to a law of 1631, all males between 16 and 60, whether freemen or servants, were to provide themselves with weapons and to form into units for training. A council was established for the specific purpose of supervising military matters, for, declared the General Court, "the well ordering of the militia is a matter of great concernment to the safety and welfare of this commonwealth." Additional regulations were issued from time to time and in 1643, after the Pequot War, the entire militia system was overhauled. One of the results was the selection of 30 soldiers within each company "who shall be ready at halfe an hour's warning upon any service they shall be put upon." Here in essence are the Minutemen of the Revolution, more than a century later.

As in the other colonies, provision was made in the law to excuse from military service those with "natural or personal impediment" such as "defect of mind, failing of sences, or impotence of Limbes." Certain professions were also exempted—public officials, clergymen, school teachers, and doctors—as were those who practiced critical trades.

The companies established in Massachusetts numbered from 65 to 200 men, two-thirds of whom were musketeers and one-third pikemen. When the number exceeded 200, a new unit was formed; when it was less than 65, several towns combined to form a single unit. The officers elected by the men consisted of the captain, a lieutenant as his principal assistant, an ensign, sergeants, and corporals. The company clerk kept the roster of men liable for military service, checked attendance at drills, and collected the fines.

At an earlier date than any other colony, Massachusetts formed the militia into regiments. The Act of 1636 divided the military companies then in existence into three regiments and required regimental training at first once a year and then every three years. Commanded by a sergeant major, who was assisted by a muster master, the regiment came ultimately to comprise all the units in a county and its strength consequently varied. Plymouth adopted the regimental organization in 1658 when Josiah Winslow was given the rank of major and designated "chief officer over the military companies of this jurisdiction." "All Captains, inferior officers and soldiers," read his orders, "are hereby required to be in ready subjection to you during your continuance in the said office."

Training was the primary activity of the militia, and regular training periods were an integral part of the system. The first drills at Jamestown were held shortly after the colony was founded. Captain Smith, when he became President of the Council, held drills and target practice on a level stretch of ground within plain view of the Indians, who could see for themselves the effect of cannon shot on the trunk of a tree.

Training exercises in Virginia were initially held, by custom, on holy days. In 1639, when a muster master-general was appointed to enforce the militia regulations, even though the captain remained immediately responsible for training his men, no specific time was set by law for drills. In some districts they were held monthly, in others every three months. Failure to attend brought a fine, but absence was apparently so common that the General Assembly finally set a stiff penalty of 100 pounds of tobacco, declaring that the offenders were bringing about the "ruin of all military discipline." By the end of the seventeenth century the militia regulations in Virginia required an annual drill for the entire regiment and quarterly exercises for companies and troops.

Training in New England was put on a regular basis earlier than in Virginia. In Plymouth drills were held six times a year to assure, in the words of the General Court, "that all postures of pike and muskett, motions, ranks and files . . . skirmishes, sieges, batteries, watches, sentinells, bee always performed according to true military discipline." The first military law of the Puritans called for weekly training periods, held every Saturday. In 1637, when conditions had become more settled, the number of training days per year was fixed at eight, and this number remained in effect for the next forty years.

From the weekly training of the first settlers to the monthly sessions a few decades later can be measured the decreasing threat of Indian attack. Before the century was out, the number of drills per year had dropped to four, with provisions for two extra days if the unit commander thought them necessary. Regimental drills, when held, were deductible from the total. But during times of emergency, interest in military matters revived phenomenally; during King Philip's War drills were held as often as twice a week.

The military code of the day enforced a strict discipline. A militiaman in Virginia guilty of three offenses of drunkenness had to ride the "wooden horse," an ingeniously uncomfortable and ignominious seat; if drunk on post he was liable to the death sentence. Drunk or sober, if he lifted his hand against an officer, he lost the hand; if he raised a weapon, the penalty was death. Should he express discontent with his lot during a march, complain about the ration, or sell his gun, he was treated as a mutineer.

Imposed freely, fines provided one of the sources for defraying militia expenses. All the colonies had laws fining those who failed to supply themselves with arms or to maintain them properly. Failure to attend drill as well as quarreling, and drunkenness during the drill were also punishable by fines.

The drill was usually held in a public place, such as the commons in Boston, and began early in the day. After roll call and prayer, the men practiced close order drill, the manual of arms, and other formations to the accompaniment of drums. Then followed a review and inspection by higher officers and public officials. After that, the units might form into smaller groups for target practice and extended order drill. Training closed with a sham battle and final prayers. By now it was early in the afternoon and the militiamen retired for food and other refreshment. The rest of the day was spent in visits, games, and social events.

The manuals provided for a remarkably complicated series of motions for forming troops, marching, fixing the pike, and firing the musket. These were standard in European armies, where the perfection of mechanical motions governed warfare, but they bore no relation to Indian fighting in the forests of North America. Nevertheless, the militiamen in the New World had to go solemnly through the prescribed movements on each training day. Fifty-six separate motions were required to load and fire the matchlock musket; only eleven for the pike, a fact which may account in part for its retention as a weapon and its popularity among troops. It was also a case, not altogether unusual in a more recent day, of the failure of training to keep pace with changing conditions.

The militia was not limited to foot soldiers; horsemen too were included. From the start, cavalry was the favored arm, and cavalrymen acquired special privileges that gave them higher status. Few men could afford to supply the horse and equipment required, a fact that limited membership to the well-to-do. Massachusetts, for example, restricted service in the cavalry to those with property valued at 100 pounds sterling.

Many advantages accrued to members of a horse unit. The trooper was exempted from training with the foot companies and from guard duty. He enjoyed special tax privileges; he could not be impressed into another service; he did not have to pay the customary fees for pasturage on common grounds.

The number as well as the quality of militia units varied widely in different periods and among the various colonies. Governor Berkeley of Virginia estimated in 1671 that he could put 8,000 horse in the field if needed, and the following year the militia of the colony consisted of 20 foot regiments and 20 horse, a proportion marking clearly the southerner's preference for cavalry.

Second only to Virginia was Massachusetts, which in 1680 had about the same number of foot companies but fewer companies of horse. Since the number of men in the companies varied so widely, exact comparisons are impossible. For Connecticut exact figures appear in the report made by the governor in 1650. "For the present," he wrote, "we have but one troope settled, which consist of about sixty horse, yet we are upon raysing three troopes more. . . . Our other forces are Trained Bands. . . . The whole amount to 2,507."

Though the militia was organized into units, it rarely fought that way. It was not intended to. The system was designed to arm and train men, not to produce military units for combat. Thus, it provided a trained and equipped citizen-soldiery in time of crisis. In this sense it was a local training center and a replacement pool, a county selective service system and a law enforcing agency, an induction camp and a primitive supply depot.

The forces required for active operations against the Indians came usually from the militia. The legislature assigned quotas to the local districts. Volunteers usually filled them. But if they did not, local authorities had the power to impress or draft men, together with their arms and equipment (including horses), into service. The law on this point was specific. The Virginia Assembly in 1629 gave the commanders power to levy parties of men and employ them against the Indians. In Plymouth during the Pequot War, when each town was required to furnish a quota, some of the men volunteered only on the understanding that if they did not, they would be conscripted.

Service was usually limited to expeditions within the colony, but there were numerous occasions when militiamen were employed outside. This right was specifically recognized in the law. Thus, in 1645, the Massachusetts General Court empowered the governor and council "to raise and transport such part of the militia as they shall find needful" outside the

Commonwealth "without their free and voluntary consent" for a period of six months. When the term of service was over, the forces thus raised were dissolved and the men returned to their homes where they resumed their place in the militia.

There was no central command for the militia of all the colonies; each had its own organization and its own commander. Supreme authority within each colony rested usually with the legislative body and was based on the charter. In practice, however, the legislature left the administration of the militia system to other groups, sometimes the Upper House and at other times to various committees or commissions on military affairs or martial discipline.

The utmost care was exercised to maintain civilian supremacy. The General Court of Massachusetts repeatedly asserted its authority over military officials and representatives of the crown. The establishment of the Artillery Company of Boston in 1638 caused some suspicious officials to liken it to the Praetorian Guard in Roman times and to the Knights Templar; care was taken to make certain that the Artillery Company would not become "a standing authority of military men, which might easily in time overthrow the civil power."

The actual management of war was delegated to the governor and a small group of advisers usually, but the legislature in almost every case retained control of the funds and watched expenditures with a suspicious eye. When an expedition was formed, it was the legislature that gave approval, furnished the money—and later appointed a committee to look carefully into the conduct of operations.

The principal officer of the militia and the only single individual who could be considered to exercise supreme command was, in Massachusetts, the sergeant major-general; in Virginia, the governor. When New Hampshire, New York, and Massachusetts came under royal authority late in the century, command of the militia there passed to the governor also.

The office of sergeant major-general—later shortened to major general—was an elective post and carried with it extensive powers and excellent opportunities for personal profit. In addition to general supervision of the militia, the sergeant major-general mobilized the militia, moved units to threatened areas, and procured arms and supplies. He commanded one of the regiments and had the unique privilege of training his own family. In wartime he commanded the colonial forces in the field, which, on occasion, he himself had raised and equipped.

To overcome the absence of a single unifying military authority in the New World, the colonies of New England formed a confederation in 1643. Representatives of Massachusetts, Connecticut, New Haven, and Plymouth came together in Boston and agreed that "inasmuch as the Natives have formerly committed sundry insolencies and outrages upon several Plantations of the English, and have of late combined themselves against us . . . we therefore doe conceive it our bounden duty to enter into a present Confederation among ourselves, for mutuall help and strength." Two commissioners from each colony met as a body, which had authority to declare war, call on the member colonies for funds and troops, select commanders, and unify in other ways the military efforts of the colonies in time of emergency.

Though it lasted 42 years, the Confederation ran into trouble immediately and foundered finally on the rocks of jealousy and conflicting interest. From the outset, Massachusetts contested the right of the Confederation to declare war or draft Massachusetts troops. The dispute came to a head in 1653 when Massachusetts refused to obey a Confederation ruling. There was considerable feeling also about the choice of commander, for no colony was agreeable to placing its troops under an outsider. Like sovereign powers of a later day, each colony was jealous of its prerogatives and quick to object to seeming encroachment on its authority.

In no colony was there a group that resembled a military staff. The need did not exist. In peacetime the various officials of the militia system sufficed; in war the Assembly and the Council of War exercised control over military operations and procured the equipment and supplies needed by the troops. The commander was always adjured to take counsel of his assistants, and he was expected to abide by their advice. In this sense the various councils were policy-making bodies rather than staffs.

Supplying the military forces of the colonies was a comparatively simple matter. The first procurement agencies were the joint stock companies that had financed the original settlements, but by the middle of the century responsibility had devolved upon the colonists. The procurement of individual arms and equipment was, in general, the responsibility of each militiaman. Every colony required each householder to provide for himself and his family weapons and equipment, and specified the type and condition of both. The community itself provided for the poor who served out the cost of their arms in labor. In addition, most colonies required the local authorities to keep on hand a supply of weapons and powder for emergencies, to be paid for by the town or county.

Normally there was no need for commissary or quarter-master in Indian warfare. Operations were of brief duration and the militiaman provided his own weapons, ammunition, clothing, and provisions, for which he was usually recompensed.

Extended operations, though uncommon, could hardly be supported in so informal a manner and there were in each colony various regulations and officials to provide the materials of war. In Massachusetts there was from earliest time an officer—variously known as surveyor of ordnance, overseer of the arms, or surveyor general—who had charge of weapons and ammunition. The officer was responsible for making certain that the towns had a supply of powder and ammunition; he also kept records and made purchases for the colony. Commissaries were appointed when required and were given authority to collect provisions. Two such officers designated for a force numbering 200 men sent against the Indians in 1645 were directed to procure bread, salted beef, fish, flour, butter, oil, cereals, sugar, rum, and beer. Only occasionally were such officials required to purchase arms.

When the colony needed funds for an expedition, it could fix quotas for the counties, borrow from private individuals, or impose special taxes. All methods were followed. The General Assembly in Virginia customarily set levies on the counties and imposed taxes payable in tobacco. In 1645 the expense of an expedition of 80 men to Roanoke was met by a levy of 38,000 pounds of tobacco to pay for the hire of boats, the purchase of provisions, powder and shot, and the payment of surgeons' salaries. The pay of the men alone amounted to 8,000 pounds of tobacco. Those suffering injuries received special compensation. The levy was made against three counties, each tithable person paying about 30 pounds of tobacco.

Even in that era war was a costly business and a fearful drain on the economy. In the greatest Indian war of the century—against King Philip—Massachusetts spent 100,000 pounds sterling, an enormous sum for that day. And though the legislature fixed prices and dealt harshly with profiteers, the war debt at the close of hostilities was larger than the aggregate value of all the personal property in the colony.

By the end of the seventeenth century, the militia system was firmly established in the American colonies. Though the training it afforded was less than adequate and the number of training days had steadily declined as the frontier moved westward, the system had become deeply imbedded in the traditions and laws of the colonists. Under this system they had defended their settlements, driven back the Indians, and pre-empted the most desirable lands along the Atlantic seaboard. A century of military experience had made little impression on the method of instruction, but it had demonstrated to the colonists that a military system based upon the obligation of every able-bodied citizen to bear arms provided a practical solution to their defense needs. Other problems would arise later that could not be solved by this method alone, but the militia system, in one form or another, remained an integral part of the nation's military policy for almost two more centuries. The obligation of universal service on which it was based, though often ignored, has never been abandoned. It constitutes yet today the basis of our military organization.

# 2.

# The War for Independence

Following the momentous victory in the Seven Years' War (known in America as the French and Indian War), the British government began to impose a series of decrees that angered many of the colonists, who previously had enjoyed the advantages of Empire membership with few of the disadvantages. Dissension finally erupted into war, the final arbiter of disputes between men and nations, as the thirteen colonies sought to preserve the substance if not the form of local self-government.

The initial objective of the revolt, in the minds of most colonial leaders, was not independence but a redress of grievances. The Continental Congress tried desperately to create an effective military force, and eventually a complex arrangement evolved that divided jurisdiction and responsibility among the local, colonial, and congressional authorities. As the conflict continued, feelings hardened against the mother country and the need for allies became more apparent. When the Congress adopted the resolution for independence the conflict ceased to be a domestic struggle and became a war against Britain. The new nation was thus able to openly solicit aid from other countries, and France, anxious to regain her international position lost in the Seven Years' War, entered into a military alliance with the American government. Thus the very nature of the conflict changed its initial objective and provided the means whereby the modified objective could be achieved.

The obstacles encountered by the colonists in waging war against Great Britain were enormous. Some were overcome, some were circumvented, and others were ignored. As one authority has observed, "It must always be a source of wonder to the scientific soldier, and of mystery to the historical student, how the Revolutionary War could have been carried through." However, it was largely due to Burgoyne's surrender at Saratoga that France was persuaded to enter into an alliance, and it was as the result of the coalition warfare of the alliance that Britain was induced to grant independence on such favorable terms. In the following selections Colonel Matthew Forney Steele analyses the strategy, planned and actual, of the campaigns in America; and General Emory Upton appraises the military policy of the revolutionary government.

# The Strategy of the War

## BY MATTHEW FORNEY STEELE

THE GENERAL PLAN which the British Ministry proposed, but never could get carried out, was as follows:

To occupy such portion of the territory as would effectually break up the union of the patriots, and prevent intercourse among them; to blockade the coast and prevent supplies from entering by the sea; to destroy any organized armies the colonists might form; and then to suppress by degrees the guerrilla warfare into which an unsuccessful insurrection usually degenerates.

The strategy (of the British) as it gradually unfolded itself, was, first of all, to occupy New York City, and make that the headquarters of British control. From New York City the line of the Hudson Valley all the way to Canada must be secured, which would immediately isolate New England, the hotbed of sedition, from the other colonies, and cut off not merely the interchange of ideas, encouragement, and reinforcements of troops; but also the provisions and supplies which New England drew from the more fertile agricultural communities to the south.

In New England itself they finally decided to hold only one point, Newport, because it was the most convenient harbor south of Halifax for vessels to enter and take shelter in.

South of New York the strategic position was the line of Chesapeake Bay, with strong positions in Maryland and Virginia, as at Alexandria and Annapolis, with, perhaps, part of the Susquehanna River. This line, if well held, would isolate the middle from the southern colonies and stop communication. As for the South, the best method of controlling it was found to be by occupying Charleston, Georgetown, and two or three points on the Santee River in South Carolina.

It is easy to see that, if this strategy had been vigorously carried out with sufficient force, aided by the blockade of the coast, there was every probability that the patriot party would soon have been driven to mere guerrillaism, and from that to a retreat beyond the Alleghanies. . . .

As the war developed, only part of the British plan could be carried out. Newport was held during most of the war, as was also New York, until after the treaty of peace. But . . . the vital line of the Hudson to Canada could not be secured. The position on Chesapeake Bay was not seriously attempted. It would have required a larger force than could be spared from more important places.

The plan of the Americans was the simple defensive—to oppose the British as best they could at every point, and to hold fast the line of the Hudson. About the only offensive movement made by them, was the joint expedition of Montgomery and Arnold to Canada, in 1775. Montgomery went up by way of Lake Champlain with the main force, and Arnold with 1,100 men marched through the forests of Maine. Montgomery defeated a British force under Carleton and captured Montreal. When the two American columns joined in front of Quebec, "there were but a thousand Americans in all, for at the end of their term of enlistment Montgomery's men had left for home in troops." They nevertheless invested the town. Carleton held the citadel with 1,600 men. On the last day of the year the Americans attacked

From Matthew Forney Steele, *American Campaigns* (Washington, 1909), 1, 26–28, 36–41, 53–55.

the town and were repulsed. Montgomery was slain. Arnold with the remnant of the force, some 800 men, continued the siege. It did not much incommode Carleton, whose men were well housed and well fed; he patiently allowed the winter's cold and sickness to defeat his courageous foe. In the following spring Washington dispatched eight regiments of reinforcements; a little later a large reinforcement of British also arrived. The Americans then began a retreat, which was turned into a rout by a sortie of the enemy. Early in July the remnant of the Americans were back at Crown Point.

The double purpose of this expedition was to forestall and prevent an advance of the British southward through the Hudson Valley, and to incite a rebellion against the British among the French Canadians. Neither end was achieved.

The Americans could not keep the British from getting possession of New York City; but, by holding the Highland Passes and the forts near West Point, and by defeating and capturing Burgoyne's army when it came down from Canada, they effectually "prevented the British from securing control of the line of the Hudson Valley. This was the great contention and controlling motive of the first three years of the war. . . . West Point and the Highland Passes constituted the most important American strategic positions." If Benedict Arnold's treachery had succeeded in delivering West Point to the British, the war might have ended sooner and otherwise.

General Howe's conduct of the operations in the American Revolution is still an unsolved mystery; and when we study that war, we can but congratulate ourselves that he, and not Sir Henry Clinton, was in command of the British forces for the first three years; and that Lord George Germain was Colonial Secretary, and not John Chamberlain of the next century.

Judged by the reputation he had already won, General Howe was probably the best general in the British service. He had fought with Wolfe in Canada, and had proved himself a brilliant, courageous, and active soldier. He was still young for his rank, being not yet fifty years old. So his inactivity, his sloth, his apparent timidity, his lack of persistence, make one marvel for an explanation.

When he took command at Boston, he had a splendid little army of 10,000 British regulars; yet he sat there besieged by a motley aggregation of undisciplined Americans; and, in nearly a year, made not a single effort to break the siege. All the while, too, he had full command of the sea. He knew that Dorchester Heights and Nooks Hill commanded the town, yet he never occupied them. When the Americans put a few guns on them, after months of waiting, he evacuated the town, leaving the Americans a large number of cannons and muskets, and vast quantities of ammunition and supplies, which he might just as easily have destroyed.

Howe was a good tactician, too—he knew how to fight a battle. We saw how prettily he turned Putnam's flank on Long Island, and Washington's at Brandywine; but there it ended. He never pushed his victory. He could easily have killed or captured every American soldier on Long Island, if he had tried; and possibly have ended the rebellion then and there. But he gave Washington plenty of time to take his army back across the East River.

General Howe constantly exemplified the worst fault that a soldier or an army can have—the fault of inactivity, of moving and doing things, slowly. He landed on Staten Island, June 28, with his whole army; but it was not till August 27 that he attacked the Americans on Brooklyn Heights. Then he waited two weeks and crossed to Manhattan Island; then waited till September 16, before attacking Washington at Harlem Heights. Then he rested again, till October 16, to move his army to Throgs Neck; then, till October 28 before attacking Washington at White Plains. When Washington retreated into New Jersey, instead of pursuing his demoralized little band to its destruction, Howe followed it slowly a short way, and then stopped and gave it time to recruit and reorganize. So it was throughout the time that Howe commanded the British troops. He made no attempt to do anything at all during the winter months but riot in the fleshpots and frivolities of social life in New York or Philadelphia.

The explanation of it all may be that General Howe did not care to punish the Continental army too severely. He kept hoping all the while that the colonists would come to their senses, see the hopelessness of their struggle, and lay down their arms. He and Admiral Howe were Whigs, and their sympathies were with the Colonies. "As a member of Parliament he had pledged himself to his constituents not to fight against the Americans, and he must have been fettered by that pledge." In America the brothers published proclamations offering amnesty to all who would lay down their arms. It is too much to say that he was unfaithful to the trust imposed upon him, although the evidence certainly points to that verdict.

The plan of capturing the line of the Hudson River, in 1777, by three converging columns was poor strategy. Especially so, because the two columns from Canada had such long lines of march, over such bad roads, and through country in which supplies were so hard to get. It gave the Americans an opportunity to unite their forces and meet the columns one at a time, and defeat them separately—the advantage of "interior lines." Yet, considering that the Americans were but poorly organized insurgents, the British Ministry was probably excusable in adopting such a plan. And the plan probably would have succeeded, if General Howe had marched his army up from New York, to join the other two, as he was expected to do. Instead of which, he took his army to Philadelphia, and let Burgoyne be captured. There was a time when Burgoyne could have made good his retreat to Canada; but he felt he must push on to form a junction with Howe, who, he supposed, was advancing to meet him.

No doubt the object of St. Leger's expedition was to get the assistance of the Indians and Sir John Johnson's loyalists. But it cannot be seen what advantage the British Ministry hoped to gain by two converging columns with independent lines of operation, and independent bases hundreds of miles apart—the columns of Burgoyne and Howe—which they would not have gained by a single column, equal in strength to both of these, advancing up the Hudson from New York. Burgoyne's troops might better have been sent round from Canada to New York by water. The British Ministry was, doubtless, influenced by the fact that every invasion made into New York in the past, during the French and Indian Wars, had gone by way of the Richelieu River and Lake Champlain; but the case was different now, in that the British held New York City as a base, while the French never had done so. Another purpose of Burgoyne's column was, of course, to cover Canada.

The British Ministry was a Tory ministry, but so large a part of the British people was opposed to the war and in sympathy with the colonies, that the Ministry undoubtedly wanted to bring about peace with as little bloodshed, and as much conciliation as possible. Otherwise it would not have tolerated the two Whig Howes as long as it did. It is certain, in fact, that the Ministry instructed General Howe as to the manner of conducting the operations, enjoining conciliatory measures; just as, according to common belief, our Administration at Washington enjoined conciliatory measures upon our commander at Manila, in his early dealings with the Philippine insurgents. The consequences were unfortunate in both cases.

The lesson the British Government learned by the war, was, not to hold out the sword and the olive branch to rebellious colonies at the same time. The sword first and the olive branch afterwards—this has been the British policy since; and we have seen how well it succeeded in the South African War.

The lesson that the American people might have learned, but did not, is the impossibility of carrying on successfully, sustained operations, extending over many months of time, and many miles of distance, with undisciplined, short-term militia. Washington's complaints of his militia were pathetic. It is not so much the strife of battle that tires the discipline of soldiers, as it is the fatigue of long, hard marches; the dreariness of prolonged, uncomfortable encampments; the disappointment of defeat; the discouragement and hardship of retreat.

Our history has chosen well in making Washington the hero of the war and the times. It was only his unswerving sense of duty, his patience, tact, strength of purpose, patriotism, and tenacity, that held his little army together during those trying years of defeat and constant retreat. Those qualities of the man and the commander were even more marked in Washington than were his brilliancy and skill as a general. Yet he quickly learned strategy; his attack at Trenton, and his escape from Cornwallis there, afterwards, and his combat at Princeton, and his occupation of Morristown on the flank of the enemy's line of communication, were after the manner of Stonewall Jackson. They were brilliant little feats of strategy; they recovered New Jersey from the British and revived the hopes of the people. His position at Morristown, on the flank of Howe's line of operations from New York to Philadelphia, also thwarted the British commander's overland advance against the Continental Capital in June, 1777, and forced him to take his army round by sea.

It is not hard, however, to point out mistakes made by Washington; it is strange that he made no more. Where is the surgeon that can perform a capital operation without previous study, and training in a hospital? The science of strategy is more complicated than that of surgery, and the masters of strategy have been fewer by hundreds than the masters of surgery. The little actual experience that Washington had gained in the French and Indian War, was no more than the experience of surgery gained by the nurse in a hospital. He was not a student of military history; he had certainly never studied "again and again the campaigns of Alexander, Hannibal, Caesar, Gustavus Adolphus, Turenne, Eugene, and Frederick," like Napoleon. If he had, he would not have divided his little army between New York and Brooklyn, thus giving Howe the opportunity to beat it in detail. Nor again would he have split his army into pieces, when Howe, finding it impregnable at North Castle, transferred his own command to Dobbs Ferry. Washington ought to have kept his force intact at North Castle, not so much with the view of covering his line of communication with Connecticut, because he could live off the country; but because his strength and his chance of beating the enemy depended upon his keeping his troops in a single body under his own immediate command. When he divided his force, and led a part of it across the Hudson to stand between Howe and Philadelphia, he did precisely what Howe wanted him to do. He also wholly lost control of the larger part of his army, the part left at North Castle under Lee, and he saw his own detachment become so reduced, as no longer to attract Howe's pursuit. It no way barred Howe's march to Philadelphia, if he had wished to take the city at that time. What it did, incidentally, was to lead the enemy away from New England, and to leave that favored soil free from the ravages of hostile armies, as it has been in every other war the United States have waged. But Washington did not lead Howe's army into New Jersey on purpose; in truth, he wholly neglected to make use of what von der Goltz declares to be the most effective lever that the leader of a retreating army has to guide matters according to his own wishes; namely, "the power of attraction."

Another lesson that American statesmen might have learned from the Revolutionary War, is how not to finance a war. That they did not take this lesson to heart, was evidenced later, in the Civil War, when both the United States and the Confederate governments followed the same fiscal method as that of our Revolutionary fathers; namely, the manufacture of paper money. The people of the colonies, as a whole, were rich and prosperous; yet the Continental Congress was too weak in authority or in courage to tax them. It preferred to borrow all it could from France, and to make paper money for the balance; which immediately began to depreciate, and soon became a byword for worthlessness. Not to be worth a "continental" was not to be worth anything at all. With such currency the Government paid its troops; and to this cause alone most of Washington's trouble in keeping his ranks filled may be charged. In respect of its finance, the short-lived insurgent government of Aguinaldo was far ahead of that of our forefathers of the Revolution. It manufactured no paper promises-to-pay; but paid its soldiers in silver coin. Hence there was never a time when there were not thrice as many insurgent soldiers in the

Philippine bosque as there were arms for them. The government collected its revenue from the people according to their means. The rich were made to contribute hard cash. Such was not the case in America during the Revolution.

There is no more shameful page in all our national history than the page that relates that Washington had to pledge his own fortune to sustain his barefooted army in the winter of 1776–1777. John Stark and a few other patriots of the pocket, rather than of the lip, followed his example; and Robert Morris collected five hundred dollars from his friends, and, a few days later, raised fifty thousand dollars in cash, by a house-to-house inquest, and placed it at the disposal of the commander-in-chief.

The battle of Bennington shows how well the American farmer, without any previous service or training, can fight, when he has to do so to defend his own hearthstone. He will not, without training and discipline, fight a long way from home—he cannot be counted upon for distant and enduring campaigns; but for single battles, with his own church spires in sight, he makes a dangerous foe to meet.

There was practically no American navy during the Revolutionary War; but much damage was done to British commerce by privateers manned by "hardy seamen of New England, and Paul Jones in his *Bonhomme Richard* made himself the terror of the English coasts."

General Greene's operations in the Carolinas were more brilliant, from a strategic point of view, than any other operations of Americans or British in this war. True, Washington's sudden and secret transfer of his army from New York to Yorktown resembled very much, on a small scale, Napoleon's march from the English Channel to Bavaria in the Ulm campaign of 1805. Neither movement could be repeated in America or Europe today, with the electric telegraph and enterprising newspaper reporters to contend with; though they might be achieved under a Japanese or Russian censorship. Both depended upon secrecy and swiftness for their success; which, after preparedness—the preparedness that can only be attained in time of peace—are the highest essentials of strategy.

If Greene had failed when he divided his little army in front of Cornwallis, in the winter of 1780–1781, he would have been condemned by the critics for dividing his command in the presence of the enemy, and allowing the two parts of it to be defeated in detail. But General Greene was right, as results proved. There are two cases in which it is safe to divide one's force; first, when either part of the divided force is strong enough to defeat the enemy by itself; and second, when each part of the divided force is so small that it has no intention of fighting—the smaller the detachment the faster it can get out of the way of the enemy. This was General Greene's case. If Cornwallis had kept his army together, it would never have caught either Greene's or Morgan's detachment. Yet by dividing his force, Cornwallis made conditions more nearly equal for the American commanders, and gave Morgan his chance at The Cowpens.

Cornwallis either did not understand and appreciate the policy of Sir Henry Clinton, or, in his eagerness to win victories and laurels for himself, he wilfully failed to carry out the wishes of his chief. A long and bitter controversy was afterward carried on between these two noblemen.

With France and Holland and Spain fighting her in Europe and the West Indies, and Hyder-Ali in India, and all the rest of Europe unfriendly and threatening, England could not furnish Clinton troops enough to enable him to conduct the war as he would have liked to conduct it. So Clinton knew he could not destroy the organized forces of the Americans, and, at the same time, so garrison the conquered territory as to keep down the rebellion. Hence his reason for adopting a "wearing-out" policy —the policy by which he purposed holding New York as a principal base, and establishing one or two smaller bases, like Charleston, from which raids could go out, to make it uncomfortable for the people that were carrying on, or encouraging, the rebellion. He did not intend that the raiding expeditions should go dangerously far from their landing places, or from the posts held in the interior, like Camden and Ninety-Six. As for example, the raiding forces sent to Connecticut seldom spent the night on shore; but they wrought a lot of destruction.

Cornwallis never should have followed Greene up into northern North Carolina; but Greene showed his strategic skill, in drawing his adversary farther and farther away from his base. General Greene put the "power of attraction" of his little army to its fullest use. Cornwallis defeated Greene in every fight, but gained nothing by his victories. It would have been better for the British cause, if Cornwallis had been defeated, and driven back to Charleston at the start; it would have saved him the mortification, and England the misfortune, of Yorktown.

A remarkable thing about Greene's operations is, that, although he was defeated tactically in every battle, his campaign was a strategic success from start to finish; and it resulted in expelling the British from every post in the Carolinas and Georgia, except Charleston. It was, also, a direct factor in the capture of Yorktown.

Cornwallis had no business to go to Virginia. When he retreated to Wilmington, he should have gone back to his base, Charleston, by sea, and made a new start. His movement to Virginia disappointed and offended Sir Henry Clinton. No plausible reason can be assigned for it, except that Cornwallis thought a return to Charleston would be an acknowledgment of defeat. General Greene did right to desist from pursuing him, and to return to South Carolina, whether Cornwallis went to Charleston, as Greene expected him to do, or marched to Virginia, which was the last thing Greene thought he would do.

After all is said, it was the presence of de Grasse's fleet in the Chesapeake that compassed the surrender of Cornwallis's army. And if the British fleet had succeeded in gaining a decisive victory over the French fleet, when it attacked it at the entrance to the Bay, Washington's march to Virginia would have been in vain —more than likely his army would have been sunk or captured by the British fleet in Chesapeake Bay, where it would have been caught in its transports without naval escort; the surrender of Cornwallis would not have taken place; Clinton's "wearing-out" policy would have gone on; the war might have lasted several years longer; and—who knows but we might still be British subjects today?

That was the darkest period of England's history; at war with America, France, Holland, Spain, and her subjects in India; without a friend in all Europe; and, worst of all, with a lot of men at home that were worse enemies than those in foreign lands. Fiske says, and seems to say it with pride rather than contempt,

> There were many people in England, however, who looked upon the matter differently from Lord North. This crushing defeat was just what the Duke of Richmond, at the beginning of the war, had publicly declared he hoped for. Charles Fox always took especial delight in reading about defeats of invading armies, from Marathon and Salamis downward; and over the news of Cornwallis's surrender, he leaped from his chair and clapped his hands. In a debate in Parliament four months before, the youthful William Pitt had denounced the American War as most accursed, wicked, barbarous, cruel, unnatural, unjust, and diabolical.

Precisely this kind of language has been used by men in America concerning our war in the Philippines; and all such men, whether Englishmen or Americans, deserve a place in the same pillory of universal scorn as that occupied by Benedict Arnold.

# The Defective Military Policy of the Revolution

BY EMORY UPTON

ON OCTOBER 3 it was resolved that after January 1, 1781, the Army should consist of:

Four regiments of cavalry, each of 6 troops of 64 noncommissioned officers and privates.
Four regiments of artillery, with 9 companies of 65 noncommissioned officers and privates.
Forty-nine regiments of infantry, with 9 companies of 64 noncommissioned officers and privates.
One regiment of artificers, with 8 companies of 60 noncommissioned officers and privates.

The officers of each company consisted of a captain and 2 lieutenants. . . .

Referring to the reduction of the Army, Washington, on October 11 (1781) wrote to the President of Congress:

I must confess, also, that it would have given me infinite pleasure if Congress had thought proper to take the reduction and incorporation of the regiments under their own direction. The mode of leaving it to the States is contrary to my sentiments, because it is an adherence to the State system, and because I fear it will be productive of great confusion and discontent; and it is requisite the business in contemplation should be conducted with the greatest circumspection. I fear also the professing to select the officers retained in service will give disgust both to those who go and to those who remain. The former will be sent away under the public stigma of inferior merit, and the latter will feel no pleasure in a present preference when they reflect that at some future period they may experience a similar fate. I barely mention this, as I am persuaded Congress did not advert to the operation of the expressions made use of, and will readily alter them.

In making the reduction, Congress provided that the officers made supernumerary, as well as those who remained in service, should receive half-pay for life.

In the same letter, Washington refers to detached service, an evil from which our Army has suffered since its foundation to the present time. Speaking of the organization of the regiments and of the number of officers needed in each, he writes:

I would therefore beg leave to propose that each regiment of infantry should consist of 1 colonel, where the present colonels are continued, or 1 lieutenant-colonel commandant, 2 majors (a first and second), 9 captains, 22 subalterns, 1 surgeon, 1 mate, 1 sergeant-major, 1 quartermaster-sergeant, 45 sergeants, 1 drum major, 1 fife major, 10 drums, 10 fifes, 612 rank and file. Fifty regiments, at 612 rank and file each, will amount to 30,600 rank and file, the force I have stated to be requisite.

The number of officers to a regiment by our present establishment has been found insufficient. It is not only inconvenient and productive of irregularities in our formation and maneuvers, but the number taken for the different offices of the staff leaves the regiments defective in field officers, and the companies so unprovided that they are obliged to be intrusted to the care of sergeants and corporals, which soon ruins them. To obviate this, I ask three field officers to a regiment besides a captain and two subalterns, to do the duty of each company, three supernumerary as paymaster, adjutant, and quartermaster, and one to reside in the State as a

---

From Emory Upton, *The Military Policy of the United States* (Washington, 1904), 48–54, 59–63, 66–67.

recruiting officer. . . . These field officers will be thought necessary when we consider the great proportion employed as adjutant-general, inspectors, brigade majors, wagon master, superintendent of hospitals; in addition to whom I would also propose a field officer to reside in each State, where the number of its regiments exceeds two, and a captain where it does not, to direct the recruiting service and transact with the State all business for the line to which he belongs, which I think would be a very useful institution.

The provision of an extra field officer to conduct the recruiting service and to transact all business with the State was an approach to the depot system now adopted throughout Europe. To lessen the evil of detaching enlisted men, a resolution was passed in March, 1779, organizing a wagoners' corps, similar in its object to the "military trains" of Europe. This resolution was repealed in April, the commander in chief being authorized to enlist for nine months, or for the next campaign, all the wagoners he might deem necessary.

The military policy during the Revolutionary period was so strongly influenced by the depreciation of the currency that a brief statement of its progress would seem necessary.

The Continental Congress, without power to raise a dollar by taxation and only able to pledge the public faith for the redemption of its currency, began to emit bills of credit a year before the Declaration of Independence. In June, 1775, it issued $2,000,000; in July a third million, followed by three more in November. Three more issues of five millions each took place in February, May, and July, 1776.

The waste, incident to the employment of large bodies of raw troops now began. At the end of 1778 the issues amounted to a hundred millions; in September of 1779 they reached one hundred and sixty millions, and finally overran by a million dollars the two hundred millions which Congress in a pledge to the people had fixed as the limit.

After nine millions had been issued, the depreciation was scarcely discernible, but with each subsequent issue, and each reverse to our arms, it steadily increased.

In January, 1777, paper currency, as compared with specie, stood one and a quarter for one; in January, 1778, four to one; in January, 1779, seven, eight, and nine to one. From this time till November it advanced to twelve, twenty, thirty, forty, and forty-five for one. In April, May, June, and July, 1780, it ranged at sixty, reached one hundred in November, and finally, in May, 1781, ceased entirely to circulate.

When this fatal result could no longer be averted, Congress, in March, 1780, tried to set on foot a new scheme of finance, and with five millions of specie sought to redeem, at the rate of forty for one, the two hundred millions of currency which represented the labor and privations of a patriotic people during five years of war.

The same confusion of ideas which prevailed in the organization of the line of the Army during the Revolution appears in the legislation pertaining to the supply department.

Taking the Quartermaster's Department as an illustration, the Journals of Congress show that the first resolution, on June 16, 1775, looked no further than to the appointment of "one Quartermaster-General for the grand army and one for the separate army."

July 19, by a resolution passed, in all probability after the receipt of a letter from General Washington in regard to this subject, the appointment of the Quartermaster-General, Commissary of Musters, and the necessary officers, was left to his discretion. Under this authority he appointed Major Mifflin, of Pennsylvania, Quartermaster-General, and later in the year (December 22) Congress gave him the rank of colonel.

In May, 1776, Colonel Mifflin resigned the office of Quartermaster-General, having been elected by Congress a brigadier-general of the Army, and on June 5 Stephen Moylan was chosen by that body to succeed him. Colonel Moylan having tendered his resignation, Congress by resolution of October 1, 1776, requested General Mifflin to resume the duties of the office, with the continuance of his rank and pay as a brigadier-general.

December 26, Washington was authorized to appoint a clothier-general, whose duties were entirely distinct from the Quartermaster's Department.

In October, 1777, on account of ill health, Mifflin resigned the office of Quartermaster-General as well as that of major-general, to which Congress had elected him in the preceding February. His resignation as Quartermaster-General was accepted, but his rank of major-general was continued without pay until the further pleasure of Congress. Subsequently, November 8, 1777, this body again requested him to take the office of Quartermaster-General, though he does not seem to have accepted.

March 2, 1778, Congress named General Nathaniel Greene, Quartermaster-General, and authorized him to select two assistants and to appoint all the agents of the department. Under the organization which prevailed up to 1780, it will be observed that all the purchasing agents of the departments were citizens without military rank; they had no fixed salary, but were allowed to indemnify themselves by a commission or percentage of the funds they disbursed.

The temptation thus offered to corruption was constantly increased by the fluctuations of the currency. As early as September, 1778, oats sold in Boston at $4 a bushel, and hay at $80 a ton. In October, 1778, Quartermaster-General Greene in a letter to Washington, estimated the cost of each team per day at $14, and the cost of transporting a barrel of flour at $6 for every 10 miles.

The advance in provisions and clothing was scarcely less ruinous. In 1780 the cost of a hat was $400, a suit of clothes $1,600, while the year's pay of a captain would not buy a pair of shoes.

As a result of increasing prices and commissions, charges of corruption against government agents soon became universal. Under such a system all efforts to protect the national treasury were in vain. With no other power than to lessen its own authority and increase the general confusion, Congress at last passed a resolution in July, 1779, earnestly requesting—"the executive powers of each State to make the strictest inquiry into the conduct of every person within such State respectively employed, either in the Quartermaster-General's or purchasing or issuing Commissary-General's Departments."

The State authorities were further empowered to remove or suspend persons or agents "in case of any kind of misbehavior or strong suspicion thereof," and also to discharge and appoint in the above departments such persons as they might "judge necessary."

The above resolution was the first step toward the reorganization of the Quartermaster's Department, which took place in July, 1780. The new system was adopted in opposition to the report of a Congressional committee which had perfected a plan after full consultation with Washington and Greene. It established no check to corruption, but rather increased it by recognizing the paramount authority of the States, under the Confederation, in every matter pertaining to the supply of men and means for the prosecution of the war.

The new organization consisted of a Quartermaster-General and an Assistant Quartermaster-General, appointed by Congress, one Deputy Quartermaster for the main Army and one for each separate army, to be appointed by the Quartermaster-General. The latter officer was further authorized to name a deputy for each State, subject to the approval of the chief executive of the State, and the deputy in his turn was to select such storekeepers, clerks, contractors, artificers, and laborers as might be necessary within his jurisdiction.

Greene was so much opposed to the new organization that he resigned his position in August, and on the fifth of this month Congress elected Colonel Pickering to succeed him. This officer, who still remained a member of the board of war, discharged the duties of the office until the end of the Revolution.

From this time forward Congress lost all control of national expenditures, which were now made to depend on the honesty and economy of the agents of the States. Grave as were the defects of the army supply system devised by Congress, they were small in comparison with the difficulties imposed upon the departments by a depreciated currency. So long as the Continental paper money remained at par, provisions and forage were not wanting, but as soon as depreciation set in the supplies of all kinds were gradually cut off.

A consideration of the various expedients adopted during the Revolution to prevent the dissolution of the army from cold and hunger brings before us a vivid picture of those evil days. Let us not forget that the maintenance of the same general system of military policy may expose us hereafter to similar ills, and that during the rebellion, in the brief space of four years, it forced upon us a debt of almost three thousand million dollars.

When Congress saw that its credit was declining through the too free emission of an irredeemable paper currency it sought to replenish the Treasury by taxes levied by the States, and when these were not forthcoming, either in money or in kind, its next alternative was to make requisition upon the States for the supplies actually needed. The responsibility was thus shifted upon the States, whose credit with the people was but little better than that of Congress.

When both the Continental and State currencies failed to induce our citizens to part with their property, the next measure was forcible impressment, sanctioned by resolution of Congress and State laws. In the first grant of dictatorial powers to Washington he was authorized, in the language of the resolution—"to take, wherever he may be, whatever he may want for the use of the Army, if the inhabitants will not sell it, allowing a reasonable price for the same."

He was further empowered to arrest and confine any person who refused to take the Continental currency or was disaffected to the American cause.

In the second grant he was authorized within a circumference of 70 miles from his headquarters—"to take wherever he may be, all such provisions and other articles as may be necessary for the comfortable subsistence of the army under his command, paying or giving certificates for the same."

The injustice of the impressment laws was their least objectionable feature. They legalized violence, and, worse still, tended to expose unprotected citizens to cruelty and outrage. The correspondence between Washington and Greene, in 1780, shows the influence of these laws in relaxing the bonds of discipline and forcing officers to resort to illegal and summary punishment as the only means of protecting the life and property of our citizens. On August 26 Greene, who commanded a detachment sent to cover a foraging party near the enemy's lines, wrote as follows:

There have been committed some of the most horrid acts of plunder by some of the Pennsylvania line that have disgraced the American arms during the war. The instances of plunder and violence are equal to anything committed by the Hessians.

Two soldiers were taken that were out upon the business, both of which fired upon the inhabitants to prevent their giving intelligence. I think it would be a good effect to hang one of these fellows in the face of the troops, without the form of a trial. It is absolutely necessary to give a check to the licentious spirit, which increases amazingly. The impudence of the soldiers is intolerable. A party plundered a house yesterday in sight of a number of officers, and even threatened the officers if they offered to interfere. It is the opinion of most of the officers that it is absolutely necessary for the good of the service that one of these fellows should be made an example of, and if your Excellency will give permission, I will have one hung up this afternoon when the army are ready to march by.

There is also a deserter, taken three-quarters of the way over to New York, belonging to the Seventh Pennsylvania Regiment, which the officers not only of the regiment, but several others, wish may be executed in the same way that I propose to execute the other in. Several deserters are gone off yesterday and last evening. . . .

I wish Your Excellency's answer respecting the two culprits, as we shall march at five this evening.

In a postscript he adds:

More complaints have this moment come in, of a more shocking nature than those related.

Washington's reply was as follows:

I am this moment favored with your letter of this day. I need scarcely inform you of the extreme pain and anxiety which the licentiousness of some of the soldiery has given me. Something must and shall be done, if possible, to put an effectual check to it. I entirely approve of the prompt punishment which you propose to have inflicted on the culprits in question. You will, therefore, please to order one of the soldiers detected in plundering, and also the deserters you mention, to be immediately executed.

The summary execution of American soldiers without trial, by order of the "Father of his Country," the plundering of our citizens, and the seizure of their property without payment were only a few of the evils springing from unwise legislation.

Toward the close of the war one or more of the States, regardless of the general welfare, made the seizure of supplies for the army a penal offense.

The opinions held by Washington as to our military policy, after an experience of five years, are thus stated in a letter to the President of Congress, dated August 20:

Had we formed a permanent army in the beginning, which, by the continuance of the same men in service, had been capable of discipline, we never should have had to retreat with a handful of men across the Delaware in 1776, trembling for the fate of America, which nothing but the infatuation of the enemy could have saved; we should not have remained all the succeeding winter at their mercy, with sometimes scarcely a sufficient body of men to mount the ordinary guards, liable at every moment to be dissipated, if they had only thought proper to march against us; we should not have been under the necessity of fighting Brandywine, with an unequal number of raw troops, and afterwards of seeing Philadelphia fall a prey to a victorious army; we should not have been at Valley Forge with less than half the force of the enemy, destitute of everything, in a situation neither to resist nor to retire; we should not have seen New York left with a handful of men, yet an overmatch for the main army of these States, while the principal part of their force was detached for the reduction of two of them; we should not have found ourselves this spring so weak as to be insulted by 5,000 men, unable to protect our baggage and magazines, their security depending on a good countenance and a want of enterprise in the enemy; we should not have been the greatest part of the war inferior to the enemy, indebted for our safety to their inactivity, enduring frequently the mortification of seeing inviting opportunities to ruin them pass unimproved for want of a force which the country was completely able to afford, and of seeing the country ravaged, our towns burnt, the inhabitants plundered, abused, murdered, with impunity from the same cause.

Nor have the ill effects been confined to the military line. A great part of the embarrassments in the civil departments flow from the same source. The derangement of our finances is essentially to be ascribed to it. The expenses of the war and the paper emissions have been greatly multiplied by it. We have had a great part of the time two sets of men to feed and pay—the discharged men going home and the levies coming in. This was more remarkably the case in 1775 and 1776. The difficulty and cost of engaging men have increased at every successive attempt, till among the present lines we find there are some who have received $150 in specie for five months' service, while our officers are reduced to the disagreeable necessity of performing the duties of drill sergeants to them, with this mortifying reflection annexed to the business, that by the time they have taught these men the rudiments of a soldier's duty their services will have expired and the work recommenced with a new set. The consumption of provisions, arms, accouterments, and stores of every kind has been doubled in spite of every precaution I could use, not only from the cause just mentioned, but from the carelessness and licentiousness incident to militia and irregular troops. Our discipline also has been much hurt, if not ruined, by such constant changes. The frequent calls upon the militia have interrupted the cultivation of the land, and of course have lessened the quantity of its produce, occasioned a scarcity, and enhanced the prices. In an army so unstable as ours order and economy have been impracticable. No person who has been a close observer of the progress of our affairs can doubt that our currency has depreciated without comparison more rapidly from the system of short enlistments than it would have done otherwise.

There is every reason to believe that the war has been protracted on this account. Our opposition being less, the successes of the enemy have been greater. The fluctuation of the army kept alive their hopes, and at every period of the dissolution of a considerable part of it they have flattered themselves with some decisive advantages. Had we kept a permanent army on foot the enemy could have had nothing to hope for, and would in all probability have listened to terms long since.

Further confirmed in his convictions by the defeat of General Gates, he wrote to the President of Congress on September 15:

I am happy to find that the last disaster in Carolina has not been so great as its first features indicated. This event, however, adds itself to many others to exemplify the necessity of an army and the fatal consequences of depending on militia. Regular troops alone are equal to the exigencies of modern war, as well for defense as offense, and whenever a substitute is attempted it must prove illusory and ruinous. No militia will ever acquire the habits necessary to resist a regular force. Even those nearest to the seat of war are only valuable as light troops to be scattered in the woods and harass rather than do serious injury to the enemy. The firmness requisite for the real business of fighting is only to be attained by a constant course of discipline and service. I have never yet been witness to a single instance that can justify a different opinion, and it is most earnestly to be wished that the liberties of America may no longer be trusted in any material degree, to so precarious a dependence. I can not but remark that it gives me pain to find the measures pursuing at the southward still turn upon accumulating large bodies of militia, instead of once for all making a decided effort to have a permanent force. In my ideas of the true system of war at the southward, the object ought to be to have a good army rather than a large one. . . .

When extravagance and disaster had ruined the credit of the Government so that Congress no longer felt able to carry on the war successfully, the project of a confederation of the States was brought forward as the only means by which the contest could be prolonged. Fortunately for our country when this change in its form of government actually took place, complications in European politics had given us powerful allies, first in France and afterwards in Spain.

Under the confederation, authority to arm and equip troops being left wholly to the States, they necessarily became more or less independent of Congress. In May, 1779, without consulting the Commander in Chief, the people of Boston fitted out a military and naval expedition of nearly four thousand men for the purpose of capturing a British force, seven to eight hundred strong, which had established a post near the mouth of the Penobscot. The garrison was besieged until August 13, when the arrival of a British fleet compelled its assailants to destroy their transports, take to the woods, and make their way home through the wilderness as best they could. Congress having assumed later the expense of this ill-advised undertaking, its sole effect was to deplete the national treasury.

Still graver complications were liable to occur under the system of confederation, as was strikingly illustrated by the action of the governor of Virginia. General Greene, while operating near Fort Ninety-Six, in South Carolina, and impatiently awaiting the militia ordered by Congress, was apprised that Governor Jefferson had detained the Virginia contingent and ordered it to remain for the defense of the State.

In a letter dated June 27, Greene represents the confusion and danger to which such an interference gave rise:

The tardiness and finally the countermanding of the militia ordered to join this army has been attended with the most mortifying and disagreeable consequences. Had they taken the field in time and in force we should have completed the reduction of all the enemy's outposts in this country, and for want of which we have been obliged to raise the siege of Ninety-Six after having the town closely besieged for upward of twenty days, and where four more would have completed its reduction. For want of the militia the approaches went on slow and the siege was rendered bloody and tedious. . . .

The high respect which I ever wish to pay to the prerogatives of every State induces me to question with all due deference the propriety of your excellency's order for countermanding the militia which were directed to join this army. No general plan can ever be undertaken with safety when partial orders may interrupt its progress. Nor is it just to the common interest that local motives should influence measures for the benefit of a part to the prejudice of a whole. I conceive it to be the prerogative of a governor to order the force belonging to a State as he may think necessary for the protection of its inhabitants. But those that are ordered out upon the Continental establishment are only subject to the orders of their officers. Without this just and necessary distribution there would be endless confusion and ruinous disappointments. I only mention these things to avoid a misunderstanding in future. I have no wish for command further than the interest and happiness of the people are concerned, and I hope everybody is convinced of this, from my zeal to promote the common safety of the good people of these Southern States. I feel for the sufferings of Virginia, and if I had been supported here in time I should have been there before this with a great part of our cavalry.

The wretched condition of the Army during the later years of the war was another baleful effect of the quasi independence of the States under the new system.

Though in many parts of the country supplies were abundant, in spite of the ravages of war, yet from the north to the south hunger and nakedness everywhere prevailed in the Continental garrisons and camps.

General Heath on May 6, 1781, wrote to Washington reporting the distress of the garrison at West Point:

> I hoped I should not have been compelled again to represent our situation on account of provisions, but supplies of meat have not arrived. All the Irish beef in the store has been gone for some days; we are at last forced in upon the reserves. That in Fort Clinton has all been taken out this day. The pork which was ordered to be reserved is all issued, except about 16 barrels. The boats are now up from below for provisions, with representations that they are out; the reserves will be gone in a few days if relief does not arrive, and hunger must inevitably disperse the troops. If the authority will not order on supplies, I will struggle to the last moment to maintain the post; but regard to my own character compels me to be thus explicit—that if any ill consequences happen to this post, or its dependencies, through want of provisions, I shall not hold myself accountable for them.

With no general government to which appeal for relief could be made, Washington replied on the eighth:

> Distressed beyond expression at the present situation and future prospects of the Army with regard to provisions, and convinced with you that, unless an immediate and regular supply can be obtained, the most dangerous consequences are to be apprehended, I have determined to make one great effort more on the subject, and must request that you will second and enforce my representations to, and requisitions upon, the New England States by your personal application to the several executives, and even assemblies, if sitting, as I suppose they will be in the course of this month.
>
> From your intimate knowledge of our embarrassed and distressed circumstances, and great personal influence with the Eastern States, I am induced to commit the execution of this interesting and important business to you, and wish you to set out on this mission as early as may be convenient. . . .

The next day Washington sent General Heath the following instructions:

> You will be pleased to proceed immediately to the several eastern States with the dispatches addressed to the governors of Connecticut, Rhode Island, Massachusetts Bay, and the president of New Hampshire, on the subject of supplies for the Army. . . .
>
> The great objects of your attention and mission are, first, an immediate supply of beef cattle; second, the transportation of all the salted provisions in the western part of Connecticut and Massachusetts, and, third, the establishment of a regular systematic, effectual plan for feeding the Army through the campaign. Unless the two former are effected, the garrison of Fort Schuyler must inevitably, that of West Point may probably, fall, and the whole Army be disbanded; without the latter, the same perplexing wants, irregularities, and distress, which we have so often experienced, will incessantly occur, with eventual far greater evils, if not final ruin.
>
> With regard to the particular mode of obtaining and transporting supplies I will not presume to dictate; but something must now be attempted on the spur of the occasion. I would suggest whether it would not be expedient for a committee from the several States, consisting of a few active, sensible men, to meet at some convenient place, in order to make out, upon a uniform and great scale, all the arrangements respecting supplies and transportation for the campaign. In the meantime, to avoid the impending dissolution of the Army, the States must individually comply precisely with the requisitions of the quartermaster and commissary upon them. . . . Previous to your departure you will obtain from the quartermaster-general and commissary with the Army, the proper estimates of supplies and transportation to be required of the several States, together with all the light and information concerning their department, which may be requisite to transact the business committed to you.
>
> After having delivered the dispatches with which you are charged, and made such further representations as you may judge necessary, you will not cease your applications and importunities until you are informed officially whether effectual measures are or will be taken to prevent the Army from starving and disbanding. . . .

These instructions incidentally set forth the difficulties of making war through the combined action of thirteen distinct governments. The only method by which Washington could prevent the dispersion of an important garrison was to order its commander to quit his post, go as a suppliant before the New England assemblies, and beg them for food.

To their honor be it said that they afforded relief, and through the joint action of committees from each State, as suggested in Washington's letter, devised measures by which the Army was thenceforth regularly supplied.

An attentive consideration of the behavior of the regular, or Continental, troops during the Revolution ought to convince every American citizen that a standing army is among the least of the perils to which our freedom is exposed.

From the very beginning of the war the depreciation of the currency practically compelled the officers and men to serve without pay. Weary, naked, foot-sore, and hungry, they made long marches, endured the hardships of winter quarters, and fought their country's battles without the hope of reward. During this long period the want of food, pay, and clothing —usual causes of mutiny—were at all times pressingly felt; and yet, with the exception of a few regiments and the troops of one or two States, the Continental Army was ever true to its trust.

Even the mutiny of the Pennsylvania and New Jersey Line served to illustrate the difference between raw and regular troops. To the former, desertion was the simple and obvious remedy for discontent and ill treatment. Among the latter, a redress of grievances was coupled with loyalty to the cause. They did not mean to desert. Overpowered by a sense of their hardships and wrongs, they momentarily forgot their duty and sought to lay their sufferings before the highest tribunal of the country that it might give them relief. They did not seek to subvert the authority of Congress, but appealed to it as the fountain of justice and law.

The army could point with pride to its subordination to civil authority and to its devotion to liberty. More than this, it could justly claim that the dictatorial powers conferred upon its commander—arbitrary arrests, summary executions without trial, forced impressment of provisions, and other dangerous precedents of the Revolution—were the legitimate fruits of the defective military legislation of our inexperienced statesmen.

Great as was the devotion of the private soldier, the patriotic record of the officer was even more brilliant. Once only did the officers of a Continental regiment combine for relief, and in this case they were under orders to march not against the British but against the Indians.

In 1779, the officers of the First Regiment of the New Jersey Brigade demanded their pay from the legislature and threatened to consider themselves as out of the service if their application was not granted within three days. This summary demand was necessarily regarded as an invasion of the privileges of the assembly, but through the good offices of Washington it was withdrawn, when the legislature made haste to pay both the officers and men.

The position taken by the officers was explained to Washington as follows:

> We are sorry that you should imagine we meant to disobey orders. It was and is still our determination to march with our regiment, and to do the duty of officers until the legislature shall have a reasonable time to appoint others, but no longer. We beg leave to assure Your Excellency that we have the highest sense of your ability and virtues; that executing your orders has ever given us pleasure; that we love the service, and love our country; but when that country gets so lost to virtue and justice as to forget to support its servants, it then becomes their duty to retire from its service. . . .

From this time forward until the end of the war the whole body of officers joined hands in repressing the spirit of discontent among the soldiers, and during the mutiny of the Pennsylvania Line some of them laid down their lives in attempting to quell the insubordination of the men.

Toward the close of the war, in December, 1782, the officers of the Army addressed Congress in reference to arrears of their pay, and as to the security for their half pay for life.

The inability of Congress to meet any of its obligations and the knowledge that several of the States had opposed the half pay for life induced the officers to propose a commutation instead.

When information reached the camp at Newburg that their proposals had not been accepted, an anonymous writer, presuming upon the discontent of the officers, circulated an address, setting forth the wrongs of the Army. With a view to induce the officers to carry their appeals "from the justice to the fears of the Government," he requested the general and field officers—one officer from each company and a delegate from the medical staff—to meet on March 11, 1783, and consider "what measures (if any) should be adopted to obtain that redress of grievances which they seem to have solicited in vain."

To neutralize the effect of this address Washington, on March 11, requested the general and field officers of the army—an officer from each company and representatives of the staff—to assemble on the fifteenth "to hear the report of the committee of the Army to Congress."

He also directed the officers to "devise what further measures ought to be adopted as most rational and best calculated to attain the just and important object in view." That nothing might be done without his sanction he ordered the senior officer present to preside and report the result of the deliberations to the Commander in Chief.

The day after the publication of this order appeared, a second anonymous address by the same author (afterwards General Armstrong), urging energy of action at the meeting sanctioned by the commander in chief.

At the time appointed, the officers convened, and were addressed by Washington, who received the unanimous thanks of the assembly. The address from the Army to Congress in December, the report of the committee from the Army, and the resolutions of Congress of January 25, referring to the pay of the officers, were then read, when a committee was appointed consisting of a general, a field officer, and a captain, with instructions to report in half an hour "resolutions expressive of the business" before the meeting.

The patriotism of the officers, their fortitude in distress, their confidence in the justice of Congress, their devotion to discipline—the only bond that can hold an army together in the hour of disaster—were all expressed in the following resolutions, prepared by the committee consisting of General Knox, Colonel Brooks, and Captain Howard. The report of the committee having been brought in and fully considered:

*Resolved unanimously*, That at the commencement of the present war the officers of the American Army engaged in the service of their country from the purest love and attachment to the rights and liberties of human nature, which motives still exist in the highest degree, and that no circumstance of distress or danger shall induce a conduct that may tend to sully the reputation of glory which they have acquired at the price of their blood and eight years' faithful services.

*Resolved unanimously*, That the Army continue to have an unshaken confidence in the justice of Congress and their country; and are fully convinced that the representatives of America will not disband or disperse the Army until their accounts are liquidated, the balance accurately ascertained, and adequate funds established for payment. And, in this arrangement, the officers expect that the half pay, or commutation of it, should be efficaciously comprehended.

*Resolved unanimously*, That His Excellency the Commander in Chief be requested to write to His Excellency the President of Congress, earnestly entreating the more speedy decision of that honorable body upon the subjects of our late address, which was forwarded by a committee of the Army, some of whom are waiting upon Congress for the result. In the alternative of peace or war this event would be highly satisfactory, and would produce immediate tranquillity in the minds of the Army, and prevent any further machinations of designing men to sow discord between the civil and military forces of the United States.

*Resolved unanimously*, That the officers of the American Army view with abhorrence, and reject with disdain, the infamous propositions contained in a late anonymous address to the officers of the Army, and resent with indignation the secret attempts of some unknown persons to collect the officers together in a manner totally subversive of all discipline and good order.

*Resolved unanimously*, That the thanks of the officers of the Army be given to the committee, who presented to Congress the late address of the Army, for the wisdom and prudence with which they have conducted that business, and that a copy of the proceedings of this day be transmitted by the President to Major-General McDougall, and that he be requested to continue his solicitations at Congress until the objects of his mission are accomplished. . . .

These proceedings were signed by General Yates, and were forwarded by Washington to

Congress, which, in lieu of half-pay for life, gave to the officers full pay for five years, and to the soldiers full pay for four months.

On April 18, 1783, Washington proclaimed the cessation of hostilities, and tendered his congratulations to a patient army. . . .

Exclusive of bounties paid by individuals, towns, and counties, and of provisions seized by impressment for the use of the Army, the debt of Congress and of the States, at the close of the war, amounted to $170,000,000. If to this sum be added the two hundred millions of currency, for the redemption of which the faith of the Continental Congress and the Confederation was twice solemnly pledged, the debt actually incurred by the war amounted to $370,000,000.

Small as this sum may appear when compared with the Rebellion war debt of three thousand millions, investigation will show that the indebtedness of the Revolution was greater in proportion to population.

Assuming three millions as the total number of our people at the beginning of the Revolution, the whole cost of this war to each man, woman, and child, was $123, while, upon the basis of a population of 31,000,000 in 1861, the total cost per capita of the War of the Rebellion was but $96.

Both of these wars were waged upon the same extravagant system, and so long as we blindly adhere to it similar pecuniary sacrifices are sure to follow in the train of every great military contest of the future.

The lessons to be drawn from the Revolution are:

1. That nearly all of the dangers which threatened the cause of independence may be traced to the total inexperience of our statesmen in regard to military affairs, which led to vital mistakes in army legislation.

2. That for waging either an offensive or a defensive war a confederation is the weakest of all forms of government.

3. That in proportion as the general government gives the States authority to arm and equip troops, it lessens the military strength of the whole people and correspondingly increases the national expenditures.

4. That the war resources of a nation can only be called forth and energetically directed by one general government to which the people owe a paramount allegiance.

5. Admitting the poverty of the colonies, their want of credit, their inability to provide proper clothing, food, arms, ammunition, and other supplies for the Army; also the possibilities of a confederation which might deprive Congress of the power to enforce its requisitions—all of these considerations, instead of being accepted as reasons for adopting a feeble military policy, called for wise legislation looking to a vigorous prosecution of the war with the least expense in men and money.

6. No matter what reasons may be given for the adoption of an unwise military policy, that these are powerless to diminish or modify the disastrous effects which inevitably follow.

7. That when a nation attempts to combat disciplined troops with raw levies, it must maintain an army of at least twice the size of that of the enemy, and even then have no guarantee of success.

8. That neither voluntary enlistments based on patriotism, nor the bounty, can be relied upon to supply men for the army during a prolonged war.

9. That the draft, connected or not connected with voluntary enlistments and bounties, is the only sure reliance of a government in time of war.

10. That short enlistments are destructive to discipline, constantly expose an army to disaster, and inevitably prolong war with all its attendant dangers and expenses.

11. That short enlistments at the beginning of a war tend to disgust men with the service, and force the government to resort either to bounties or the draft.

12. That regular troops, engaged for the war, are the only safe reliance of a government, and are in every point of view the best and most economical.

13. That when a nation at war relies upon a system of regulars and volunteers, or regulars and militia, the men, in the absence of compulsion, or very strong inducements, will invariably enlist in the organizations most lax in discipline.

14. That troops become reliable only in proportion as they are disciplined; that discipline is the fruit of long training, and cannot be attained without the existence of a good corps of officers.

15. That the insufficiency of numbers to counterbalance a lack of discipline should convince us that our true policy, both in peace and war, as Washington puts it, "Ought to be to have a good army rather than a large one."

# 3·

# Military Problems of the New Nation

In 1784 Congress, observing that "standing armies in time of peace are inconsistent with the principles of republican governments," authorized the retention of only eighty troops to guard stores at West Point and Fort Pitt. George Washington, writing to Alexander Hamilton in 1783, outlined a proposed "peace establishment" based on a small standing army and a universal militia system. But neither Congress nor the states were willing to jeopardize hard fought for liberties by establishing a national military institution that they believed might become dictatorial. Geographical isolation from European powers and a belief that local units could master the Indians stiffened resistance to a continuance of the quasi-centralized organization that emerged during the Revolutionary War.

But the movement of settlers westward created friction with the natives and the British and Spanish colonies that bordered the new nation. Domestic crises demonstrated further inadequacies of the Articles of Confederation, and a movement began to replace the loosely-knit government with a more national body. Among the motives that provoked the Constitution of 1787 was the desire to provide a more efficient defense establishment, and the following excerpt from the Federalist Papers, written by John Jay, Alexander Hamilton, and James Madison to secure the adoption of the proposed Constitution, reveals the concern for an adequate army and navy. This document furnishes a profound analysis of the considerations that dominated the thinking of these founding fathers.

Under the Constitution, the President, as Commander-in-Chief, came to exercise leadership in the formulation and execution of military policy. Yet he was limited by the control given Congress over legislation and appropriations, and even the prestige of George Washington could not prevail over the recalcitrance of the legislative branch. The Militia Act of 1792 created a huge although unwieldy organization for army mobilization in time of crisis, and the outbreak of the wars of the French Revolution stimulated the creation of a navy as American commercial interests were threatened. Howard White reveals the tortured course of defense policy during the administrations of Washington, Adams, and Jefferson, as the new nation and the new government sought security in a troubled world.

# What American Defense Policy Should Be

BY JOHN JAY

AMONG THE MANY OBJECTS to which a wise and free people find it necessary to direct their attention, that of providing for their *safety* seems to be the first. The *safety* of the people doubtless has relation to a great variety of circumstances and considerations, and consequently affords great latitude to those who wish to define it precisely and comprehensively.

At present I mean only to consider it as it respects security for the preservation of peace and tranquillity, as well as against dangers from *foreign arms and influence*, as from dangers of the *like kind* arising from domestic causes. As the former of these comes first in order, it is proper it should be the first discussed. Let us therefore proceed to examine whether the people are not right in their opinion that a cordial Union, under an efficient national government, affords them the best security that can be devised against *hostilities* from abroad.

The number of wars which have happened or will happen in the world will always be found to be in proportion to the number and weight of the causes, whether *real* or *pretended*, which *provoke* or *invite* them. If this remark be just, it becomes useful to inquire whether so many *just* causes of war are likely to be given by *united America* as by *disunited America*; for if it should turn out that United America will probably give the fewest, then it will follow that in this respect the Union tends most to preserve the people in a state of peace with other nations.

The *just* causes of war, for the most part, arise either from violations of treaties or from direct violence. America has already formed treaties with no less than six foreign nations, and all of them, except Prussia, are maritime, and therefore able to annoy and injure us. She has also extensive commerce with Portugal, Spain, and Britain, and, with respect to the two latter, has, in addition, the circumstance of neighborhood to attend to.

It is of high importance to the peace of America that she observe the laws of nations towards all these powers, and to me it appears evident that this will be more perfectly and punctually done by one national government than it could be either by thirteen separate States or by three or four distinct confederacies.

Because when once an efficient national government is established, the best men in the country will not only consent to serve, but also will generally be appointed to manage it; for, although town or country, or other contracted influence, may place men in State assemblies, or senates, or courts of justice, or executive departments, yet more general and extensive reputation for talents and other qualifications will be necessary to recommend men to offices under the national government—especially as it will have the widest field for choice, and never experience that want of proper persons which is not uncommon in some of the States. Hence, it will result that the administration, the political counsels, and the judicial decisions of the national government will be more wise,

---

From Federalist Paper No. 3.

systematical, and judicious than those of individual States, and consequently more satisfactory with respect to other nations, as well as more *safe* with respect to us.

Because, under the national government, treaties and articles of treaties, as well as the laws of nations, will always be expounded in one sense and executed in the same manner—whereas adjudications on the same points and questions, in thirteen States, or in three or four confederacies, will not always accord or be consistent; and that, as well from the variety of independent courts and judges appointed by different and independent governments, as from the different local laws and interests which may affect and influence them. The wisdom of the convention, in committing such questions to the jurisdiction and judgment of courts appointed by and responsible only to one national government, cannot be too much commended.

Because the prospect of present loss or advantage may often tempt the governing party in one or two States to swerve from good faith and justice; but those temptations, not reaching the other States, and consequently having little or no influence on the national government, the temptation will be fruitless, and good faith and justice be preserved. The case of the treaty of peace with Britain adds great weight to this reasoning.

Because, even if the governing party in a State should be disposed to resist such temptations, yet, as such temptations may, and commonly do, result from circumstances peculiar to the State, and may affect a great number of the inhabitants, the governing party may not always be able, if willing, to prevent the injustice meditated, or to punish the aggressors. But the national government, not being affected by those local circumstances, will neither be induced to commit the wrong themselves, nor want power or inclination to prevent or punish its commission by others.

So far, therefore, as either designed or accidental violations of treaties and the laws of nations afford *just* causes of war, they are less to be apprehended under one general government than under several lesser ones, and in that respect the former most favors the *safety* of the people.

As to those just causes of war which proceed from direct and unlawful violence, it appears equally clear to me that one good national government affords vastly more security against dangers of that sort than can be derived from any other quarter.

Because such violences are more frequently caused by the passions and interests of a part than of the whole; of one or two States than of the Union. Not a single Indian war has yet been occasioned by aggressions of the present federal government, feeble as it is; but there are several instances of Indian hostilities having been provoked by the improper conduct of individual States, who, either unable or unwilling to restrain or punish offences, have given occasion to the slaughter of many innocent inhabitants.

The neighborhood of Spanish and British territories, bordering on some States and not on others, naturally confines the causes of quarrel more immediately to the borderers. The bordering States, if any, will be those who, under the impulse of sudden irritation, and a quick sense of apparent interest or injury, will be most likely, by direct violence, to excite war with these nations; and nothing can so effectually obviate that danger as a national government, whose wisdom and prudence will not be diminished by the passions which actuate the parties immediately interested.

But not only fewer just causes of war will be given by the national government, but it will also be more in their power to accommodate and settle them amicably. They will be more temperate and cool, and in that respect, as well as in others, will be more in capacity to act advisedly than the offending State. The pride of states, as well as of men, naturally disposes them to justify all their actions, and opposes their acknowledging, correcting, or repairing their errors and offences. The national government, in such cases, will not be affected by this pride, but will proceed with moderation and candor to consider and decide on the means most proper to extricate them from the difficulties which threaten them.

Besides, it is well known that acknowledgments, explanations, and compensations are often accepted as satisfactory from a strong united nation, which would be rejected as unsatisfactory if offered by a State or confederacy of little consideration or power.

In the year 1685, the state of Genoa having offended Louis XIV, endeavored to appease him. He demanded that they should send their *Doge*, or chief magistrate, accompanied by four of their senators, to *France*, to ask his pardon and receive his terms. They were obliged to submit to it for the sake of peace. Would he on any occasion either have demanded or have received the like humiliation from Spain, or Britain, or any other *powerful* nation?

# Military Policy during the Administrations of Washington, Adams, and Jefferson

BY HOWARD WHITE

IN ASCERTAINING THE VIEWS of a proper military policy which were held in this precedent-forming period, it seems desirable to make three inquiries. (1) What were the main features of a military policy which the President and his advisers wished Congress to adopt? In accordance with the custom of the Federalist members of Congress to look to the executive for legislative plans, it may be assumed that the answer to this question will indicate the character of the measures which the Federalist leaders in Congress presented and defended. (2) Did the parties divide upon these measures? (3) If so, what did the opposition regard as a proper policy?

For a statement of the main features of the administration's military policy, it will be necessary to rely principally upon the views expressed by the department heads, Hamilton and Knox, and upon the plans submitted by the latter. Washington's messages and addresses indicate the interest which he took in military matters but they usually pertained to ends upon which all were agreed and rarely mentioned means by which these ends were to be attained. As to what should be the size of the army, how many ships should be built and how the militia should be organized, on these "as on most things," Washington's ideas "are locked up in his remarkable reticence." It may reasonably be inferred, from the support he gave his secretaries, and from his pronounced Federalist sympathies, that departmental plans and views met with his approval. It is nevertheless true that the wording of his messages transmitting reports of the secretary of war was often such that those opposing the secretary's recommendations could plausibly argue that the President had not endorsed them.

It was doubtless the wise thing for Washington to do. It did not subject him to attack for every detail in the plans suggested by his subordinates. But it produced a situation which those opposing the administration's military policy turned to their advantage. So great was Washington's prestige in military affairs that the opposition would have been more hesitant in attacking administration measures had it been impossible to assume that these measures did not meet with his unqualified approval. As it was those who professed to be acting in defense of congressional prerogative in determining military policy attacked the proposals on the ground that they originated with the secretary. In reply, their defenders, tacitly admitting the Federalist practice of looking to the executive for the legislative impulse, asserted, seemingly without evidence other than the general statements in his addresses to Congress and his noncommittal messages transmitting the war department's plans and reports, that the President was responsible for the military system which had been created by law.

For a definite enunciation of the military policy which the administration would try to

---

From Howard White, *Executive Influence in Determining Military Policy in the United States* (Urbana, University of Illinois Press, 1924), I, 87–96, 153–172.

persuade Congress to adopt, it will therefore be necessary to rely mainly on the statements of Hamilton and Knox. These will be considered in their relation to the three arms of the national defense: the military establishment, the militia, and the navy.

The President and his subordinates devoted more effort to securing legislation for the military establishment than for the others. Their interest centered here rather than in legislation for the militia, since any force of regular troops which Congress might authorize would be entirely and at all times directly under the control of the executive as commander in chief, while such power could be exercised over the militia only when it was in the service of the United States.

This fact may have had something to do with the form which executive proposals for legislation took in each instance. It appeared so to Senator Maclay, a persistent opponent of centralizing tendencies and of standing armies, for he wrote: "General Knox offers a most exceptional bill for a general militia law which excites (as it is most probable he expected) a general opposition. Thus the business of the militia stands still, and the Military Establishment bill, which increases the standing troops one-half, is pushed with all the art and address of ministerial management."

The direct and constant control of a military force was not desired merely as an end in itself. Hamilton regarded an army of considerable size as essential to the maintenance of a national government. A report which he submitted to the Congress of the Confederation in 1783 recommended a peace establishment of six regiments, a much larger force than the Congress saw fit to authorize. It is true that he discounted the possibility of extensive military establishments, when urging the ratification of the Constitution, but even then he spoke of "the constant necessity of keeping small garrisons on our western frontier. . . . These garrisons," he said, "must either be furnished by occasional detachments from the militia or by permanent corps in the pay of the government. The first is impracticable, and if practicable, would be pernicious. . . . The latter . . . amounts to a standing army in time of peace; a small one indeed, but not the less real for being small."

Even after the new government was established, it was not strong enough for him. "It is to be lamented," he wrote to Washington, "that our system is such as still to leave the public peace of the Union at the mercy of each state government." Though the duties of his department, which involved placing the nation's credit upon a firm basis, were "enough to occupy any man," as he himself said, his active interest in other governmental affairs seems frequently to have been directed toward the discovery of means for increasing the small regular army. Maclay wrote, in February, 1791, that "a war in some shape or other seems to have been the great object with Hamilton's people. At first they would have war with the Northern Indians. That failed. They have succeeded in involving us with the Northwestern Indians. Britain at one time seemed their object. Great efforts were made to get a war with Algiers. That failed. Now it seems to be made a point to differ with the French."

In his efforts to secure a larger armed force, Hamilton was ably supported by Knox. The similarity in their views has led some writers to conclude that Knox was merely a pliant tool of Hamilton's. Parton denied that Knox was "a man of capacious and inquisitive mind," and added that "in the cabinet of Washington, he was the giant shadow of his diminutive friend, Hamilton." This characterization appears unfair in the light of letters which Knox wrote to Washington in 1787, when his relations with Hamilton were not so intimate as to support the view that Hamilton was the author of the ideas therein expressed. In outlining his plan for a general government, Knox gave his idea as to the place which force should occupy in it. He wanted "one government instead of an association of governments; . . . the laws passed by the general government to be obeyed by the local governments, and, if necessary, to be enforced by a body of armed men, to be kept for the purposes which should be designated."

While the convention was in session, he wrote to Washington that "although I frankly confess that the existence of the state governments is an insuperable evil from a national point of view, yet I do not well see how in this stage of the business they could be annihilated; . . . the frame of government proposed . . . is so infinitely preferable to the present constitution, and gives such a bias to a proper line of conduct in the future, that I think all men anxious for a national government should zealously embrace it."

These views are indeed similar to Hamilton's. But it seems reasonable to account for their general agreement, even while recognizing Hamilton's primacy in the cabinet, on the ground that Washington selected them because he knew the similarity of their fundamental convictions as to what should be the character of the national government and as to the part that force would have to play in giving it this character. The selection of these two men may therefore be taken as a good indication of Washington's views. The theory that Knox was merely a figurehead may have been invented by the opponents of standing armies who utilized the fact of general agreement between the two men to attract to their side those inclined to be friendly to Knox's projects, but who could be counted on to oppose them if Hamilton could be associated in their authorship.

The foregoing exposition of views indicates that the influence of the executive departments most directly concerned would be exerted for obtaining a military establishment considerably larger than that which the new government inherited from the Confederation, not only as a means for securing adequate protection of the frontiers but also for giving more prestige and energy to the national government, thereby lessening the importance of the state governments.

Executive interest in legislation for the militia, that branch of the national defense in which all able-bodied, adult, male citizens were liable for service, was real, although not so great, since the purpose of such legislation was mainly to provide for the utilization of the nation's man power in those great emergencies when its existence would be imperiled. In this period neither within the government nor generally among the people did there appear to be any sustained conviction that such danger was imminent. What the Federalist leaders most wanted was not legislative provision for such remote contingencies, but the creation of a force immediately available to aid in asserting the authority of the new government. They hoped, moreover, to provide for the expansion of this force when needed, so that the national government would never need to rely upon the militia of the states.

Until this could be accomplished, and it was not long before difficulties appeared, some provision should be made for organizing, arming, and disciplining the militia. Washington perhaps stated the most impelling reason for "some uniform and effective system for militia of the United States" in one of his early messages. It was that "it is now in our power to avail ourselves of the military knowledge disseminated throughout the several states by means of the many well-instructed officers and soldiers of the late army." Characteristically, this did not indicate the form the organization should take. The form which his secretaries favored, and which he seems to have endorsed, was entirely in keeping with their intention to establish a strong government. But because their interest in the militia was not of such immediate concern, efforts to induce Congress to provide for the desired system were mainly confined to occasional reminders in presidential communications that this duty had not been performed.

From the foregoing outline of what the Federalists considered a proper policy for the military establishment and for the militia, there could be little doubt but that these policies would become party issues. Opposition to a standing army in time of peace was one of the main articles of Republican faith. In the constitutional convention, an effort had been made to place a limit on the size of the army Congress could raise in time of peace. In the state conventions, the fact that no limit had been provided was frequently urged as a reason against adopting the Constitution. Though Madison favored its adoption, he was opposed to the maintenance of standing armies. While its ratification was pending, Jefferson wanted incorporated in a bill of rights some check "to keep the number of standing troops within safe bounds." As to what was a safe number, "more than magazine guards will be useless if few, and dangerous if many."

The Republicans agreed with the Federalists that an armed force was one of the most effective means for imparting energy to the new government. This end which the latter sought to accomplish, the former strove to prevent, particularly denying its right to employ this means. Foremost in the minds of extremists of both parties was the idea that the military machine "might be used for domestic as well as foreign purposes." To this idea they reacted oppositely. As Henry Adams has put it, "to crush democracy by force was the ultimate resource of Hamilton. To crush that force was the determined intention of Jefferson."

Opposition to the maintenance of a regular army in peace time was facilitated by the constitutional provisions for the militia. To the charge that, if not allowed to keep up an army at all times, the national government would be unable to provide for the common defense, the Republicans, in reply, could point to its power over the militia, "the natural strength of the country." They did not, however, approve the Federalist plan to give the national government the maximum control over the militia. In their view, the grant of certain powers over the militia, which had previously existed as a state institution, gave the central government only those powers which had been clearly conferred. For instance, it was denied that the power of Congress to provide for organizing the militia extended to deciding who should compose it. This attitude doubly accorded with their point of view. It would hinder the growth of centralizing tendencies: first, by depriving the national government of a standing army in peace; and second, by retaining for the states a major share in the control of the militia which, at the same time, they offered to the national government as a substitute for standing troops.

With respect to a navy, the attitude of each party cannot be so easily found by reference to the views of their respective leaders. The Federalists were generally agreed upon the eventual desirability of a navy. Hamilton's argument that the adoption of the Constitution would contribute in various ways "to this great national object, a navy," and his statement that "we must endeavor, as soon as possible, to have a navy," were doubtless acceptable to the party that wanted the new form of government put into operation. Those desiring centralization of power did not regard a navy as the immediate necessity that an army was. It would be quite reasonable to hold that government must be made secure at home before attempting to assert its dignity abroad.

But Hamilton seems to have held back when members of his party in Congress, encouraged by Knox and perhaps by Washington, introduced and, with the aid of several votes from the Republican majority in the House, finally passed an act providing for six frigates for protecting American commerce from the Algerian pirates.

At the most, Hamilton differed with his party only as to the time when a navy should be begun. Jefferson's views were contrary to those of most of his party. As early as 1784 he had urged the establishment of "a naval force sufficient to keep the Barbary States in order." Aside from this use, he then favored a navy "to coerce the states that were behindhand in the payment of their requisitions." He did not anticipate the danger from a navy that he feared from a standing army. He continued to advocate the creation of a marine force after entering Washington's cabinet. Perhaps it was out of respect to his views that enough Republican votes were obtained for passing the act of 1794.

But most of the Republicans in Congress supported Madison, Giles, Nicholas, and Clark in opposing the measure. Madison objected principally on the ground that this expedient would be unlikely to accomplish the purpose. While also questioning its efficacy, Giles took a more pronounced stand against the measure. Although it provided that "no farther proceeding be had under this act" if peace were made with Algiers, he declared that it was "the foundation of a permanent naval establishment," an assertion that subsequent events confirmed. To this he was opposed because "a navy is the most expensive of all means of defense, and the tyranny of Governments consists in the expensiveness of their machinery." In the next Congress, Gallatin's argument materially strengthened the Republican position. He declared that "if the sums to be expended to build and maintain the frigates were applied to paying part of our national debt, the payment would make us more respectable in the eyes of foreign nations than all the frigates we can build." "I think there are means of protection which arise from our peculiar situation, and that we ought not to borrow institutions from other nations, for which we are not fit."

The divergent views of the two parties upon what constituted a proper military policy cannot perhaps be summed up better than in the words of Henry Adams: "The Hamiltonian doctrine was that the United States should be a strong government, ready and able to maintain its dignity abroad and its authority at home by force of arms. Mr. Gallatin maintained that its dignity would protect itself if its resources were carefully used for self-development, while its domestic authority should rest only on consent."

The determination of military policy during the presidency of John Adams was distinguished by lack of harmony in the executive branch. Consequently its influence did not produce results commensurate with the opportunities which the difficulties with France provided. Although Adams was chosen by the Federalists, he did not become the undisputed leader of the party by virtue of his election. Prominent Federalists, including the cabinet, whose members were continued from Washington's administration, looked to Hamilton for decisions as to party policies, supporting Adams usually when so advised by Hamilton.

The Hamilton faction which had, under Washington, been most active in advancing projects for strengthening the military arm of government, took advantage of the strained relations with France to demand war. As in the difficulties with England three years earlier, it may be questioned whether they wanted war or only a larger military and naval force. Although "the military group distrusted Adams," to attain either object they had to have his cooperation. He lent himself to their purposes for a time; summoned a special session of Congress soon after his inauguration; and delivered an address whose belligerent tone convinced Jefferson that "the executive temper was for war; and that the convocation of the Representatives was an experiment on the temper of the nation, to see if it was in unison."

Little legislation in conformity with the President's recommendations was passed during the special session. Congress did not consider the French refusal to receive Pinckney a sufficient cause for war; trusted to the further attempts at negotiation which Adams insisted on making; and in the meantime authorized but minor preparations for war.

Consideration of military measures was resumed in the next session of Congress in response to a brief reference in the President's first annual address to his earlier recommendations. But the military group was able to make little headway until the arrival of word from the envoys to France revealing the insults which they had received. Adams held back from recommending the immediate declaration of war demanded by members of his cabinet and others of the war party. He aided them in the accomplishment of what may have been their main purpose by urging preparations for hostilities.

Adams' conduct met with the approval of the moderates in Congress, who with the military group were more than a majority in each house. This combination resulted in the passage of twenty acts for strengthening the national defense between March 27 and July 16, 1798. These accorded with the general suggestions made in presidential addresses and messages and most of the subjects of legislation were proposed more specifically in reports of the secretary of war.

Conforming to the general tendency, opposition to executive recommendations centered upon the proposal to increase considerably the size of the army. The bill detaching 80,000 militia which were to be held in readiness was passed with little opposition soon after difficulties with France began. But to secure authorization for an increase of 20,000 in the regular army required the persistent effort of the administration and of its supporters in Congress through most of two sessions.

Even then the increase was obtained in two diverse installments. The first, originating in a Senate bill introduced four days after Secretary McHenry had recommended it, authorized the President to raise a provisional army of 20,000 men. Upon reaching the House, it became the center of a long and bitter controversy, emerging with the size of the army reduced one-half and with the conditions under which the President could raise it more definitely stated. There was probably a net gain, for the same act empowered the President to accept an unlimited number of volunteers, in addition to the troops for the provisional army. The second installment was obtained by the passage of a House bill, introduced after the enactment of the first bill, this one authorizing an immediate increase of about 10,000 in the regular army. The ultimate passage of these measures, even after making due allowance for the state of relations with France, is an indication of the importance attaching to executive recommendations. It will be recalled that in 1794, without open executive endorsement, Hamilton instigated the various proposals to enlarge the army, presumably to prepare for war with England. As soon as the prospect of war with France appeared in 1797, he proposed to Pickering and McHenry the organization of a provisional army of 25,000. This was probably where Adams' brief reference to a provisional army in his first address to Congress originated. Without waiting for more explicit executive recommendation, Hamilton's followers in the Senate made an unsuccessful attempt to pass a bill to enable the President to raise a provisional army. Such a bill did not pass until after the secretary of war specifically recommended it to the next session.

Its eventual passage seemed to convince the military group that open executive endorsement was a necessary preliminary to legislative ratification of their program. Upon obtaining an appointment second only to that of the aged Washington in the army that was to be organized, Hamilton was in an even better position to direct executive relations with Congress in military affairs. He, with others of the military group, wanted a still larger army. The general principles on which this desire was based have been considered. Some immediate objectives will be suggested below. Here it is significant to note that the movement was launched by Secretary McHenry's report on the reorganization of the army which President Adams sent to Congress on the last day of 1798. In it he recommended "a revival and extension of the power to raise a provisional army," suggesting 50,000 as a desirable number.

Congress responded by passing two bills which Hamilton had prepared. The first gave the President eventual authority to augment the army to slightly more than 50,000, including the troops previously authorized. In addition to these, 75,000 volunteers might be accepted upon conditions resembling those previously authorizing detachments from the militia, except that the officers of volunteers were to be appointed by the President. The second, "for the better organizing of the troops of the United States," differed in few respects from the form of organization in McHenry's report.

The passage of those measures indicated that the executive rather than Congress was in control. The congressional committees had relinquished their function of preparing bills for whatever the military situation might require, giving that privilege to the war department. The department's recommendations, previously reported to Congress, were therefore incorporated in bills which, without essential change, were duly passed.

The result was a triumph for the military party. Congress had at last yielded to their demands. The executive branch, whose influence had apparently been a decisive factor, was presumably in their control, although even before the passage of these measures President Adams had given several indications that he did not attach to them the same importance that they did.

It seems desirable at this point to examine in some detail why the military party had worked for this legislation, in order to bring out certain features of executive influence over legislation.

It is hard to believe that any intelligent person thought that there was much danger of a French invasion, although this reason was given in the House. Why then did Hamilton and his supporters take the lead in urging a larger army at that time?

In the first place, they hoped by this legislation to increase materially the central government's control over the armed forces of the nation, thereby strengthening that government and of course making more complete their control over the military machine which they had been constructing. This was to be accomplished by supplanting the control over the manpower of the nation which the states retained through their rights in the militia. Steps had already been taken by provisions in various acts since 1791 authorizing the President to accept companies of volunteers and to appoint their officers. By 1799 the military nationalists were more confident. Not only were the volunteers assigned to distinctively militia duties and approximately the same number allowed to each state as had formerly been ordered detached from the militia, but a bill authorizing such a detachment was rejected. The intention to create a national force which should supersede the militia was quite obvious. The Republican friends of the militia and of states' rights unsuccessfully attacked the provisions for volunteers as "an infringement of the Constitution," and "as destructive of the militia, and as going to the establishment of a Presidential, instead of a National militia."

There are indications that the Federalists felt that there was an immediate need for such a force, directly and completely under the President's control, for the enforcement of the alien and sedition laws of the preceding session. Having yielded to the temptation to make an illiberal and extreme use of the power which their predominant position in the government and the popular excitement of the moment gave them, it was but natural to take another step to maintain that already taken. This was all the more likely because of their high regard for force as an element in stabilizing government.

Increased national control over the military resources of the nation was desired, not only for insuring obedience to its laws but also for extending the boundaries of the United States. Hamilton wrote that his own policy would be "to maintain a regular army and navy, then to get possession of Louisiana and Florida, and all the time 'to squint at South America.' "

That these purposes were not realized, that even the troops for which legislative authorization had been obtained were only in small part recruited, seems mainly to have been due to President Adams whose aid had probably been the decisive factor in obtaining congressional approval of their program. His aid was given apparently because he believed that such legislation might facilitate negotiations with France.

The military group probably assumed that he was in sympathy with their plans, or at least would not oppose them. They seemed for a time to forget what Revolutionary experience should have made plain, that "Adams personified the opposition to militarism in any form—standing armies, or the existence of an official or semi-official military clique." If they did not forget it, they underestimated the power of his office; they were too optimistic as to their ability to force him to accept their plans.

They had opposed his election to the presidency because "he was not a good party man: they never knew what he was going to do." After his conduct in connection with the execution of the military legislation, they could hardly again forget that characteristic. He had practically turned over to Washington, Hamilton, and the other leaders of the military group the task of putting into effect the military legislation passed in the spring and summer of 1798. When friction developed over the question of rank between Hamilton and Knox, his attitude encouraged it. When it became evident that McHenry's inefficiency in the war department was an almost insuperable obstacle to recruiting and organizing the regiments that had been authorized, Adams made no move to replace him. Finally, after his annual message had recommended legislation upon which the military group counted for the realization of their plans, on February 18, 1799, he sent to the Senate the nomination of a minister to France.

"This nomination fell on the Federalist

leaders like a thunderbolt." Sedgwick, one of the group, wrote: "Had the foulest heart and the ablest head in the world been permitted to select the most embarrassing and ruinous measure, perhaps it would have been the one which has been adopted."

Nevertheless, the war party pushed their legislation through Congress in the closing days of the session. They were able to postpone the sending of the peace commissioners for several months. In the meantime, they sought to recruit and assemble the authorized troops. But the public generally had been pleased with Adams' move, and the war spirit, so necessary to raising an army, could not be kept alive.

This extended review of some of the important events affecting the military policy of Adams' administration brings out two important features of executive influence over legislation. First, it may be exerted to accomplish results other than those which appear on the surface. It is one illustration of the fact that legislation may result from combinations of interests which support it for radically different reasons.

Second, it serves to emphasize the strategic importance of the President. The subordinate officials may take the most active part in securing legislation from Congress. Their objects may differ entirely from those of the President when he makes known to Congress his approval of the projects for which they are working. If, however, it affects the formation of an important policy, the subordinate executive officers can rarely if ever carry out their designs, even with congressional authorization, unless the President gives them his active support.

The study of this period impresses one with the necessity for electing to the presidency only individuals of unquestionable integrity, so that the enormous influence upon the determination and execution of public policies which the occupant of that high office exercises may not be abused. It is perhaps not far from the truth to say that the American people entrust each of their Presidents in turn with the responsibility for maintaining their democratic institutions intact. There has probably not been a time since then, however, when the decision as to whether a government of force should supplant one primarily of suasion has depended so completely upon the character of the man in the presidential office.

The closing months of Adams' presidency witnessed the collapse of the military Federalists' dream. The army was reduced to slightly over 4,000 men and, in accordance with the recommendation of Secretary of the Navy Stoddert, Congress ordered the sale of all public vessels except thirteen frigates, six only of these to be maintained in actual service.

One of the early acts passed by Congress after Jefferson and his party came into power measurably put into effect one of the cardinal Republican principles, the reduction of the standing army. But the method of its enactment violated another principle, perhaps equally fundamental. The Republican theory, as has been repeatedly pointed out, was that "the Executive received its instructions from the Legislature. Upon no point had the Republican party, when in opposition, laid more stress than on the necessity of reducing Executive influence."

In this instance, however, the reduction was first suggested in the President's annual message. Oblivious to the former criticisms of executive formulations of policy, Jefferson informed Congress that "a statement has been formed by the Secretary of War, on mature consideration, of all the posts and stations where garrisons will be expedient and of the number of men required for each garrison. The whole amount is considerably short of the present military establishment. For the surplus no particular use can be pointed out."

Not only did the House make no protest against this infraction of its prerogatives, but it adopted a resolution directing the secretary of war to lay before it the statement to which Jefferson had tactfully referred. The bill which eventually passed, reducing the military establishment about one-fourth, provided the number and organization of troops which the secretary had recommended.

Jefferson had soon begun to use the powers of his position to secure the enactment of legislation. Before he left the presidency, the matured force of his influence was put forth to secure what the Republicans had probably criticized the Federalists most severely for authorizing, an increase of the regular army when the nation was at peace. They had contended that, except for a small number of troops for garrison duty, a regular army should only be authorized when war had actually been begun. Militia should serve until the regular army was raised and ready for duty.

Jefferson's seventh annual message warned that events might necessitate an increase in the army. This, as well as subsequent special messages, transmitting letters and dispatches from various sources, emphasized the precarious condition of relations with the warring European powers and with the Indian tribes. Various bills to increase the military and naval forces were proposed, usually without apparent executive instigation.

The debate was similar to that on former occasions except that each party was beginning to shift to the position formerly held by the other. The Federalists complained of the oppressive influence of the executive which was demanding legislation without furnishing adequate information. They ridiculed the variety and inconsistency of the proposals. While defending the executive as best they could, some of the Republicans for a time reasserted their customary opposition to increases in the standing army. Eppes, a son-in-law of Jefferson, declared: "I have never yet voted for a regular army or soldier in time of peace." He vowed that as long as he lived he would vote down a regular army.

A week later, Jefferson asked for an augmentation of the military force, submitting the secretary of war's suggestion that six thousand regular troops be raised. The opposition, including John Randolph who had turned against the administration, caustically reminded the Republicans of their inconsistency. Besides, the number asked for was too small for war and too large for peace. It could hardly be intended for war because the executive had presented the embargo policy as the alternative for war and had forced it through Congress on the strength of that plea. To increase the army in time of peace was contrary to a venerable Republican principle.

But the tendency to obey the definite requests from the executive prevailed over their aversion to standing armies; Eppes recanted in a long speech attempting "to place before the people of the country our real situation with foreign nations"; by a vote of 95 to 16 the House passed the Senate bill conforming both in number and organization to the executive suggestion; and "the Republican party found itself poorer by the loss of one more traditional principle."

The foregoing are but examples of congressional subservience to the executive, sufficiently, though by no means invariably typical of the relations between the two branches in this period that some inquiry should be made into the causes for this about-face from the position maintained by Jefferson and the members of his cabinet, as well as by other Republicans, before they came into power.

One explanation attributes executive supremacy to pre-eminent ability. According to Henry Adams, "in ability and in energy the Executive overshadowed Congress, where the Republican party, though strong in numbers and discipline, was so weak in leadership, especially among the Northern democrats, that the weakness almost amounted to helplessness. . . . As long as this situation lasted, Jefferson could not escape the exercise of executive influence even greater than that which he had blamed in his predecessors."

Another explanation, or perhaps a consequence of this superiority, emphasizes the methods by which Jefferson and his cabinet controlled. Hamiltonian precedents were followed with at least one important improvement. "From 1801 to 1808 the floor leader was distinctly the lieutenant of the executive. . . . They were presidential agents, appointed by the executive, and dismissed at his pleasure."

Jefferson's interest in Congress did not cease with the selection of a floor leader. "Conferences with his agents were fully as important as cabinet meetings themselves." He drafted some bills which were subsequently laid before Congress. Gallatin attended committee meetings. His house was the customary meeting place of the party leaders. In general, he was as active and as successful in managing Congress as Hamilton had been. Finally, the caucus was regularly used to secure concerted party action with respect to the policies which the executive branch wished to see adopted.

In addition to these factors, the unsettled situation in international affairs gave the executive branch, as the official organ for intercourse with other governments, opportunities to interpret those affairs favorably to the policies for which it was seeking congressional approval. This was particularly true with military policies.

Any account of the relations between the two branches which stops at this point is seriously incomplete. Undoubtedly a majority of the policies formulated by the executive were adopted by Congress. That branch never became so unruly as to oblige Jefferson to use the veto. Yet, one may wonder why, if the executive controlled Congress as completely as the writers quoted seem to infer, several phases of military policy which were strongly recommended by the President and his secretaries, individually or severally, were not adopted.

One of these related to the militia. In six of his annual messages Jefferson asked Congress to provide a more effective organization for the militia. At least one of the bills to accomplish this object had been prepared by Jefferson. Though in accord with the party policy, the attitude of Republican legislators was well expressed in the thirty-three word report of a House committee, concluding that "it would not be proper, at this time, to make any alteration in the militia system of the United States." In short, "the Republicans believed in a militia but neglected it." Jefferson's letters indicate that he was not disposed to neglect it. But with all his influence, congressional inertia triumphed.

Jefferson was no more successful in obtaining authority to build a dock "within which our present vessels may be laid up dry and under cover from the sun." This recommendation, accompanied by elaborate drawings, was favorably reported by a committee of the seventh Congress, but no appropriation for that purpose passed the House.

A third failure is especially noteworthy because Congress accepted the other recommendation which was made at the same time and in the same manner—that there should be an immediate increase of 6,000 in the regular army—although this meant a reversal of the Republican attitude toward standing armies. The proposal which Congress did not adopt demanded no such violent departure from traditional principles. The secretary of war suggested that 24,000 volunteers be enlisted for service less onerous than that in the regular army, apparently in order to give them somewhat more training than they would receive as members of the militia.

The suggested plan was referred to a committee, but nothing was done until the next session. By that time, the executive branch wanted 50,000 volunteers and a bill conforming to the detailed suggestions of the secretary of war was steadily advanced with plenty of supporting votes until it reached the final stage in the House. Then the opposition, which had been contesting its progress with objections strangely similar to those raised by the Republicans in 1798 and 1799, succeeded in tabling the bill.

The failure, at the last, could readily be attributed to that decline in the President's influence which may be expected shortly before his retirement. In addition to that general tendency, tired and discouraged by his inability to bring England and France to terms by peaceable coercion, Jefferson had practically abdicated the duties of his office as soon as the election had decided his successor. As a result, "early in January the House broke away from executive control, and assumed for itself the responsibility of deciding upon the wisdom of various measures." In the Republican caucus it was decided to give up the volunteer army bill.

This may explain why the policy proposed by the executive was not adopted in the final session. It does not explain why it failed in the previous session when the army increase bill was passed, nor why the repeated suggestions with respect to the improvement of the militia system were disregarded. If it be true that the "triumvirate ruled," they ruled by knowing how to give in when Congress refused to obey.

In summary, Jefferson and his subordinates in the executive branch seem to have recommended the military policies which Congress adopted. With Republicans in control, the legislature was almost, if not quite, as dependent on executive initiation of policy as it had been in the days of Federalism. At executive behest, the party reversed its attitude toward standing armies. On the other hand, not every executive proposal was favorably received. However, until shortly before Jefferson's retirement, the executive branch was at least as influential in determining military policy as it had been at any previous time. This result was favored by the general regard for Jefferson as party leader, the executive's close attention to legislative procedure, its more intimate knowledge of what legislation was needed, by the state of relations with foreign nations, and by the inexperience of many of the majority members of Congress.

# 4.
# The War of 1812

The struggle between Great Britain and France, which began in 1793, lasted until 1815 with only two brief interruptions. During the course of the conflict the military genius of Napoleon enabled France to dominate the continent of Europe, and the British had to rely on their control of the seas to continue the war. The United States, as a neutral nation, found its rights being violated as the two powers battled for survival. As pointed out in the previous chapter, American military power fluctuated in response to threats to the national interest posed by the contestants. It also varied depending on the strategic theory and the objectives of a war with either protagonist embraced by the administration in office and the individual members of Congress. Partisan political advantage and financial concerns also affected the defense posture of the country and complicated the efforts of the Chief Executive to secure an acceptance of the American position on neutral rights. It was apparent that hostilities with either Great Britain or France would require more than a frontier police force and a pirate-fighting navy, but few effective preparations were made.

The causes of the War of 1812 were numerous and each had its special pleaders. President Madison has been criticized for leading a dividing nation into war and for his direction of the military effort. In the following selections Colonel Matthew Forney Steele assesses the strategy of the war; and Henry Adams describes some of the political paradoxes involved in the activities of the civil authorities as the government sought first to achieve victory and then to avoid defeat.

# The American Performance

## BY MATTHEW FORNEY STEELE

THE ACHIEVEMENTS OF OUR NAVY during the War of 1812 were such that they will always be a subject of just pride to us; but the management and behavior of our land-forces were in many cases so unhappy, so discreditable, so bad, so burlesque, that a contemplation of them arouses in us mingled feelings of disappointment, shame, disgust, and amusement.

The war was, nevertheless, full of lessons for the military student, but especially for the American citizen—the man that votes and makes the legislators that make the laws. He is the one primarily responsible; for all the failures of this war, like the failure to end the Civil War in a single month, fifty years later, were due to lack of preparedness—to bad legislation.

George Washington by sad practical experience had learned the hopelessness of trying to conduct war with men that had been taught nothing about the business of war. Raw militia were the burden of his complaint from the beginning to the end of the Revolutionary War; and in his very last message he admonished the people that "timely disbursements to prepare for danger, frequently prevent much greater disbursements to repel it." But Mr. Jefferson, who never saw a battle, and during whose administration our regular army was reduced almost to zero, said, in his last message, while war with England was threatening: "For a people who are free and who mean to remain so, a well-organized and armed militia is their best security."

The lesson that the War of 1812 held out above all others, was that our militia furnished no security at all, and that a reliance upon it only resulted in a vast expense to the Government and an immortal national shame. The men that went out with our militia regiments certainly had as much natural courage as any other Americans—all they lacked was military training and educated leaders. They were just as good in battle as regulars with no more training; as was shown by the equally bad behavior of newly enlisted regulars under newly appointed officers, on several occasions.

As we all know; it is the discipline that is instilled into soldiers in garrison and camp and march, under qualified officers, which counts in campaign, far above mere excellence in the manual of arms and the movements of the drill-book. These latter are useful mainly as an aid to discipline. The value and importance of training is shown by a comparison of the conduct of Scott's and Ripley's brigades, at Chippewa and Lundy's Lane, with that of our troops in other battles of the War of 1812.

The disadvantage of short terms of enlistment, which resulted in the discharge of men, and the melting away of whole regiments, just about the time when they became fit for campaign, early became apparent; and the term was changed from one to five years for the regular troops.

The difficulty of recruiting the regular

---

From Matthew Forney Steele, *American Campaigns* (Washington, 1909), I, 75–80.

regiments in time of hostilities was shown in this as in all our later conflicts; and the importance of maintaining a standing army of a size proportionate to our needs and to the population of the country, to serve as a training school for officers, and as a nucleus and a first line, in case of war, was made very evident.

General Upton says that with a standing "army of 15,000 men, so organized as to have been capable of expansion by the aid of voluntary enlistments and obligatory service to double or triple its numbers, there is little reason to doubt that Canada would have been ours, and the war brought to a close on a single campaign."

The Administration was, during the first two years, greatly at a loss for higher commanders. The trade of a general has to be learned; and our army was so small in 1812 that it contained no officers that had had any experience in commanding considerable bodies of men. So the Administration was forced to select its generals from among the territorial governors and other civil officials, like Hull and Dearborn, some of whom had seen a little service in the Revolutionary War, more than thirty years before. Not until they had gone through two years of training in the actual school of war, the best of all military schools, were Jacob Brown and Andrew Jackson and Winfield Scott able to show that they knew how to command men in battle and campaign. The chief qualities of these generals, the qualities that achieved success, were their energy, activity, and readiness to fight.

In its prosecution of the war the Administration was greatly hampered by the opposition of the New England States. The governors of some of those States refused to let their militia leave the States, and took so little pains to enforce the laws of war, that the British army in Canada was fed and supplied by New Englanders, and paid with money furnished by New England banks. The British army also purchased supplies in New York.

From the beginning to the end of the war, there were called out on the American side 56,032 regulars and 471,622 militia and volunteers; while "the largest force of British regulars opposed to us was 16,500"; and the British regulars were probably never at any one time aided by more than 800 Canadian militia and 2,500 Indians.

When we remember that the British government sent upwards of 450,000 troops to South Africa rather than submit to defeat there, we must congratulate ourselves that England had her hands full with her war on the Continent of Europe; that the American war was no more in favor in England than it was in America; that the British really had no cause to fight us, except to keep us out of Canada; and that the causes for which we were fighting ceased with the cessation of hostilities between Napoleon and the British government.

Of strategy and tactics there was not an example worthy of emulation shown by either Americans or British in any campaign of the entire war; unless it was in General Brock's operations. The campaigns are valuable as professional studies only on account of their blunders; and these are so apparent, it should seem that no officer that has passed the primer of his military education could be guilty of repeating them.

In 1812 we saw an invasion of Canada planned for three separate columns between which there could be no cooperation nor concert of action. Each moved, or tried to move, without any regard to the others. So the British met them, and repelled them one at a time, and with the same troops.

General Hull's invasion of Canada by way of Detroit, while Lake Erie was still controlled by a British fleet, was doomed to failure from the start. His only line of communication was by a road 200 miles long, exposed to attack from the British at Malden, exposed for many miles along the lake-shore to fire from the British fleet, and passing through more than a hundred miles of forest and swamp, filled with hostile Indians. The chances of keeping a wagon-train going and coming with supplies along such a route, were very slim.

General Wilkinson's line of communication, also, was in peril when he moved his army down the St. Lawrence with Kingston still in possession of the British in his rear. The Secretary of

War saw the importance of the capture of Kingston, and urged it; but both General Dearborn and General Wilkinson, and later, also, General Brown, were dissuaded by Commodore Chauncey, who commanded the American fleet on Lake Ontario, from undertaking the capture. Then Chauncey, who was to guard the entrance to the St. Lawrence with his fleet, performed his duty so badly as to allow the British gunboats to slip by him and fall upon the rear of Wilkinson's flotilla.

The disasters at the Raisin River and Stony Creek were both due to the failure of the American commanders to secure their camps by outposts.

Even where our troops achieved victory, their success was not due to good tactics, but rather to valor, marksmanship, good discipline, or courageous leading. At Chippewa Scott "tempted destruction by quitting his secure position behind Street's Creek," and marching his little command across the bridge over the creek with the British twenty-four pounders playing on it. Again at Lundy's Lane Scott charged a British force about twice the strength of his own, when he was only out on a reconnaissance, and might better have fallen back, or taken up a defensive position and waited for Ripley's brigade to come to his assistance. Still the fault of attacking superior numbers, and attacking vigorously, as General Scott always did, is one seldom to be censured in a leader. Scott, like all courageous, dashing leaders, had the quality of inspiring his men with something of his own spirit.

In the battle of New Orleans, one of the most remarkable in all history, General Jackson, although two-thirds of his troops had not fired a shot, failed to complete the destruction of the British by a counter-attack. This, however, was probably not practicable with raw, undisciplined, heterogeneous troops, such as his were.

In the first two years of the war the British government had no thought of taking the offensive. With its army engaged in Europe, it only undertook to defend Canada, and to blockade the American coast from New York to Georgia. To maintain the friendship of New England, the ports of that section were not subjected to the blockade. But in 1814, with its armies set free, Great Britain began a more vigorous campaign.

The expedition of Prevost against Plattsburg was undertaken for the purpose of cutting off the Eastern States from the rest of the Union, with the hope of regaining them for the British crown in the treaty of peace. The avowed objects of the expedition to New Orleans were two: "first, the command of the mouth of the Mississippi so as to deprive the back settlements of America of their communication with the sea; second, 'to occupy some important and valuable possession by the restoration of which we may improve the conditions of peace, or which may entitle us to exact its cession as the price of peace.'" The purpose of General Ross's expedition, as shown by his instructions, was "to effect a diversion on the coasts of the United States in favor of the army employed in the defense of Upper and Lower Canada" . . . and not "for any extended operation at a distance from the coast." This explains why Ross did not follow up General Winder's fleeing militia at Washington.

The capture of Washington rather than Baltimore or some other city, had no strategic significance, and might not have been undertaken at all, had not its defenseless condition invited capture. Being the capital of the country, its capture was of some political importance, and was very humiliating to American pride. The excuse for the destruction of the public buildings, as well as for other burning and plundering done by the British, was, to quote from their instructions, to make the Americans "sensible of the impropriety as well as of the inhumanity of the system they have adopted." This referred to the destruction of villages and buildings by American militia in Canada.

# The Struggle to Control Policy

BY HENRY ADAMS

WHILE DALLAS STRUGGLED WITH CONGRESS to obtain the means of establishing a currency in order to pay the army, Monroe carried on a similar struggle in order to obtain an army to pay. On this point, as on the financial issue, Virginian ideas did not accord with the wishes of Government. The prejudice against a regular army was stimulated by the evident impossibility of raising or supporting it. Once more Jefferson expressed the common feeling of his Virginia neighbors.

> We must prepare for interminable war, (he wrote to Monroe, October 16). To this end we should put our house in order by providing men and money to an indefinite extent. The former may be done by classing our militia, and assigning each class to the description of duties for which it is fit. It is nonsense to talk of regulars. They are not to be had among a people so easy and happy at home as ours. We might as well rely on calling down an army of angels from heaven.

As Jefferson lost the habits of power and became once more a Virginia planter, he reverted to the opinions and prejudices of his earlier life and of the society in which he lived. As Monroe grew accustomed to the exercise and the necessities of power, he threw aside Virginian ideas and accepted the responsibilities of government. On the same day when Jefferson wrote to Monroe that it was nonsense to talk of regulars, Monroe wrote to Congress that it was nonsense to talk of militia. The divergence between Monroe and Jefferson was even greater than between Dallas and Eppes.

> It may be stated with confidence (wrote Monroe to Congress), that at least three times the force in militia has been employed at our principal cities, along the coast and on the frontier, in marching to and returning thence, that would have been necessary in regular troops; and that the expense attending it has been more than proportionately augmented from the difficulty if not the impossibility of preserving the same degree of system in the militia as in the regular service.

In Monroe's opinion a regular force was an object "of the highest importance." He told the Senate committee that the army, which was only thirty-four thousand strong on the first of October, should be raised to its legal limit of sixty-two thousand, and that another permanent army of forty thousand men should be raised for strictly defensive service. In the face of Jefferson's warning that he might as well call down an army of angels from heaven, Monroe called for one hundred thousand regular troops, when no exertions had hitherto availed to keep thirty thousand effectives on the rolls.

The mere expression of such a demand carried with it the train of consequences which the people chiefly dreaded. One hundred thousand troops could be raised only by draft. Monroe affirmed the power as well as the need of drafting. "Congress have a right by the Constitution," he said, "to raise regular armies, and no restraint is imposed on the exercise of

---

From Henry Adams, *History of the United States* (New York, 1889–1909), VIII, 263–282.

it. . . . It would be absurd to suppose that Congress could not carry this power into effect otherwise than by accepting the voluntary service of individuals." Absurd as it was, such had been the general impression, and Monroe was believed to have been one of the most emphatic in maintaining it. "Ask him," suggested Randolph, "what he would have done, while governor of Virginia and preparing to resist Federal usurpation, had such an attempt been made by Mr. Adams and his ministers, especially in 1800. He *can* give the answer." Doubtless the silence of the Constitution in respect to conscription was conclusive to some minds in favor of the power; but the people preferred the contrary view, the more because militia service seemed to give more pay for less risk.

The chance of carrying such a measure through Congress was not great, yet Monroe recommended it as his first plan for raising men. He proposed to enroll the free male population between eighteen and forty-five years of age into classes of one hundred, each to furnish four men and to keep their places supplied. The second plan varied from the first only in the classification, not in the absence of compulsion. The militia were to be divided into three sections according to age, with the obligation to serve, when required, for a term of two years. A third plan suggested the exemption from militia service of every five militia-men who could provide one man for the war. If none of these schemes should be approved by Congress, additional bounties must be given under the actual system. Of the four plans, the secretary preferred the first.

The Senate committee immediately summoned Monroe to an interview. They wished an explanation of the failure in the recruiting service, and were told by Monroe that the failure was chiefly due to the competition of the detached militia for substitutes. The military committee of the House then joined with the military committee of the Senate in sounding the members of both bodies in order to ascertain the most rigorous measure that could be passed. According to the report of Troup of Georgia, chairman of the House committee, they "found that no efficacious measure, calculated certainly and promptly to fill the regular army, could be effectually resorted to. Measures were matured and proposed by the (House) committee, but were not pressed on the House, from the solemn conviction that there was no disposition in the Legislature to act finally on the subject."

Yet the issue was made at a moment of extreme anxiety and almost despair. In October, 1814, the result of the war was believed to depend on the establishment of an efficient draft. The price of United States six-per-cents showed better than any other evidence the opinion of the public; but the military situation, known to all the world, warranted deep depression. Sir George Prevost, about to be succeeded by an efficient commander—Sir George Murray—was then at Kingston organizing a campaign against Sackett's Harbor, with an army of twenty thousand regular troops and a fleet that controlled the Lake. Another great force, military and naval, was known to be on its way to New Orleans; and the defences of New Orleans were no stronger than those of Washington. One half the province of Maine, from Eastport to Castine, was already in British possession.

To leave no doubt of England's intentions, despatches from Ghent, communicating the conditions on which the British government offered peace, arrived from the American commissioners and were sent, October 10, to Congress. These conditions assumed rights of conquest. The British negotiators demanded four territorial or proprietary concessions, and all were vital to the integrity of the Union. First, the whole Indian Territory of the Northwest, including about one third of the State of Ohio, two thirds of Indiana, and nearly the entire region from which the States of Illinois, Wisconsin, and Michigan were afterward created, was to be set aside forever as Indian country under British guaranty. Second, the United States were to be excluded from military or naval contact with the Lakes. Third, they had forfeited their rights in the fisheries. Fourth, they were to cede a portion of Maine to strengthen Canada.

These demands, following the unparalleled insult of burning Washington, foreshadowed a war carried to extremities, and military preparations such as the Union had no means ready to repel. Monroe's recommendations rested on the conviction that the nation must resort to extreme measures. Dallas's financial plan could not have been suggested except as a desperate resource. Congress understood as well as the Executive the impending peril, and stood in even more fear of it.

Under these circumstances, when Troup's committee refused to act, Giles reported, on behalf of the Senate committee, two military measures. The first, for filling the regular army, proposed to extend the age of enlistment from twenty-one to eighteen years; to double the land-bounty; and to exempt from militia duty every militia-man who should furnish a recruit for the regular service.

The second measure, reported the same day, November 5, purported to authorize the raising of an army of eighty thousand militia-men by draft, to serve for two years within the limits of their own or an adjoining State. The provisions of this measure were ill-conceived, ill-digested, and unlikely to answer their purpose. The moment the debate began, the bill was attacked so vigorously as to destroy whatever credit it might have otherwise possessed.

Of all the supporters of the war, Senator Varnum of Massachusetts was one of the steadiest. He was also the highest authority in the Senate on matters pertaining to the militia. When Giles's bill came under discussion November 16, Varnum began the debate by a speech vehemently hostile to the proposed legislation. He first objected that although the bill purported to call for an army of eighty thousand men, "yet in some of the subsequent sections of it we find that instead of realizing the pleasing prospect of seeing an ample force in the field, the force is to be reduced to an indefinite amount—which contradiction in terms, inconsistency in principle, and uncertainty in effect, cannot fail to produce mortification and chagrin in every breast." Varnum objected to drafting men from the militia for two years' service because the principle of nine months' service was already established by the common law. If the nation wanted a regular force, why not make it a part of the regular army without a system of drafting militia "unnecessary, unequal, and unjust"? The machinery of classification and draft was "wholly impracticable." The limit of service to adjoining States abandoned the objects for which the Union existed. The proffered bounties would ruin the recruiting service for the regular army; the proffered exemptions and reductions in term of duty left no permanency to the service. The bill inflicted no penalties and charged no officers with the duty of making the draft. "I consider the whole system as resolving into a recommendation upon the patriotism of the States and Territories and upon the patriotism of the classes."

The justice of Varnum's criticism could not fairly be questioned. The bill authorized the President "to issue his orders to such officers of the militia as he may think proper," and left the classification and draft in the hands of these militia officers. Every drafted man who had performed any tour of duty in the militia since the beginning of the war was entitled to deduct a corresponding term from his two years of service; and obviously the demand created for substitutes would stop recruiting for the regular army.

Hardly had Varnum sat down when Senator Daggett of Connecticut spoke.

"The bill," said the Connecticut senator, "is incapable of being executed, as well as unconstitutional and unjust. It proceeds entirely upon the idea that the State governments will lend their aid to carry it into effect. If they refuse, it becomes inoperative. Now, sir, will the Executives, who believe it a violation of the Constitution, assist in its execution? I tell you they will not."

Every member of the Senate who heard these words knew that they were meant to express the will of the convention which was to meet at Hartford within a month. The sentiment thus avowed was supported by another New England senator, whose State was not a party to the Convention. Jeremiah Mason of New Hampshire was second to no one in legal ability or in personal authority, and when he followed Daggett in the debate, he spoke with full knowledge of the effect his words would have on the action of the Hartford Convention and of the State executives.

> In my opinion (he said), this system of military conscription thus recommended by the Secretary of War is not only inconsistent with the provisions and spirit of the Constitution, but also with all the principles of civil liberty. In atrocity it exceeds that adopted by the late Emperor of France for the subjugation of Europe. . . . Such a measure cannot, it ought not to be submitted to. If it could in no other way be averted, I not only believe, but I hope, it would be resisted.

Mason pointed to the alternative—which Massachusetts was then adopting, as the necessary consequence of refusing power to the government—that the States must resume the powers of sovereignty:

> Should the national defence be abandoned by the general government, I trust the people, if still retaining a good portion of their resources, may rally under their State governments against foreign invasion, and rely with confidence on their own courage and virtue.

At that time the State of Massachusetts was occupied for one hundred miles of its sea-coast by a British force, avowedly for purposes of permanent conquest; and the State legislature, October 18, refused to make an inquiry, or to consider any measure for regaining possession of its territory, or to cooperate with the national government for the purpose, but voted to raise an army of ten thousand men. The object of this State army was suggested by Christopher Gore, the Federalist senator from Massachusetts who followed Mason in the debate. In personal and political influence Gore stood hardly second to Mason, and his opinions were likely to carry the utmost weight with the convention at Hartford. With this idea necessarily in his mind, Gore told the Senate:

> This (bill) is the first step on the odious ground of conscription—a plan, sir, which never will and never ought to be submitted to by this country while it retains one idea of civil freedom; a plan, sir, which if attempted will be resisted by many States, and at every hazard. In my judgment, sir, it should be resisted by all who have any regard to public liberty or the rights of the several States.

These denunciations were not confined to New England. Senator Goldsborough of Maryland, also a Federalist, affirmed that the sentiment of abhorrence for military duty was almost universal:

> Sir, you dare not—at least I hope you dare not—attempt a conscription to fill the ranks of your regular army. When the plan of the Secretary of War made its appearance, it was gratifying to find that it met with the abhorrence of almost every man in the nation; and the merit of the bill before you, if such a measure can be supposed to have merit at all, is that it is little else, as regards the militia, than a servile imitation of the secretary's plan.

Nevertheless, when Goldsborough took his seat the Senate passed the Militia Bill by a vote of nineteen to twelve—Anderson of Tennessee and Varnum of Massachusetts joining the Federalists in opposition. The Regular Army Bill, which was in effect a bill to sacrifice the regular army, passed November 11, without a division. Both measures then went to the House and were committed, November 12, to the Committee of the Whole.

Ordinarily such a measure would have been referred to the Military Committee, but in this instance the Military Committee would have nothing to do with the Senate bill. Troup, the chairman, began the debate by denouncing it. The measure, he said, was inadequate to its object. "It proposed to give you a militia force when you wanted, not a militia, but a regular force . . . You have a deficiency of twenty-odd thousand to supply. How will you supply it? Assuredly the (Regular Army) bill from the Senate will not supply it. No, sir, the recruiting system has failed." On the nature of the force necessary for the next campaign Troup expressed his own opinion and that of his committee, as well as that of the Executive, in language as strong as he could use at such a time and place. "If, after what has happened, I could for a moment believe there could be any doubt or hesitation on this point, I would consider everything as lost; then indeed there would be an end of hope and of confidence." Yet on precisely this point Congress showed most doubt. Nothing could induce it to accept

Troup's view of the necessity for providing a regular army. "The bill from the State," remonstrated Troup, "instead of proposing this, proposes to authorize the President to call upon the States for eighty thousand raw militia; and this is to be our reliance for the successful prosecution of the war! Take my word for it, sir, that if you do rely upon it (the military power of the enemy remaining undivided) defeat, disaster, and disgrace, must follow."

The House refused to support Troup or the President. Calhoun was first to yield to the general unwillingness, and declared himself disposed to accept the Senate bill as a matter of policy. Richard M. Johnson, though sympathizing with Troup, still preferred to accept the bill as the only alternative to nothing: "If it was rejected, they would have no dependence for defence but on six months' militia." On the other hand, Thomas K. Harris of Tennessee protested that if the British Government had it in their power to control the deliberations of Congress, they could not devise the adoption of a measure of a military character better calculated to serve their purposes. The people, he said, were in his part of the country prepared to make every sacrifice, and expected Congress, after the news from Ghent, to do its share; but Congress was about to adopt a measure of all others the best calculated to prolong the war.

While the friends of the government spoke in terms of open discouragement and almost despair of the strongest military measure which Congress would consent to consider, the Federalists made no concealment of their wishes and intentions. Daniel Webster used similar arguments to those of his friend Jeremiah Mason in the Senate, affirming that the same principle which authorized the enlistment of apprentices would equally authorize the freeing of slaves, and echoing pathetic threats of disunion. Other Federalists made no professions of sadness over the approaching dissolution of government. Artemas Ward of Massachusetts spoke December 14, the day before the Hartford Convention was to meet, and announced the course which events were to take:

> That the Treasury is empty I admit; that the ranks of the regular army are thin I believe to be true; and that our country must be defended in all events, I not only admit but affirm. But, sir, if all the parts of the United States are defended, of course the whole will be defended. If every State in the Union, with such aid as she can obtain from her neighbors, defends herself, our whole country will be defended. In my mind the resources of the States will be applied with more economy and with greater effect in defence of the country under the State governments than under the government of the United States.

Such avowals of the intent to throw aside Constitutional duties were not limited to members from New England. Morris S. Miller of New York made a vehement speech on the failure of national defence, and declared the inevitable result to be "that the States must and will take care of themselves; and they will preserve the resources of the States for the defence of the States." He also declared that conscription would be resisted, and echoed the well-remembered declamation of Edward Livingston against the Alien Bill in 1798, when the Republican orator prayed to God that the States would never acquiesce in obedience to the law.

"This House," replied Duvall of Kentucky, "has heard discord and rebellion encouraged and avowed from more than one quarter." Indeed, from fully one fourth of its members the House heard little else. Under the shadow of the Hartford Convention the Federalist members talked with entire frankness. "This great fabric seems nodding and tottering to its fall," said Z. R. Shipherd of New York, December 9; "and Heaven only knows how long before the mighty ruin will take place." J. O. Moseley of Connecticut "meant no improper menace" by predicting to the House, "if they were determined to prosecute the war by a recourse to such measures as are provided in the present bill, that they would have no occasion for future committees of investigation into the causes of the failure of their arms." The latest committee of investigation had recently made a long report on the capture of Washington, carefully abstaining from expressing opinions of its own, or imputing blame to any one, and Moseley's remark involved a double sneer. None of these utterances were resented. Richard Stockton of New Jersey was allowed unanswered to denounce in measured terms the mild Militia Bill then under debate, from which the committee had already struck the term of two years' service by substituting one year; and Stockton concluded his fine-drawn arguments by equally studied menace:

> This bill also attacks the right and sovereignty of the State governments. Congress is about to usurp their undoubted rights—to take from them their militia. By this bill we proclaim that we will have their men, as many as we please, when and where and for as long a time as we see fit, and for any service we see proper. Do gentlemen of the majority seriously believe that the people and the State governments will submit to this claim? Do they believe that all the States of this Union will submit to this usurpation? Have you attended to the solemn and almost unanimous declaration of the legislature of Connecticut? Have you examined the cloud arising in the East? Do you perceive that it is black, alarming, portentous?

The Resolution of the Connecticut legislature to which Stockton referred was adopted in October, and authorized the governor in case of the passage of the Militia Bill to convoke the General Assembly forthwith, to consider measures "to secure and preserve the rights and liberties of the people of this State, and the freedom, sovereignty, and independence of the same." Stockton's speech was made December 10, and "the cloud arising in the East," as he figured the Hartford Convention, was to take form December 15. The Republican speakers almost as earnestly used the full influence of these national fears to rouse the energies of the House. They neither denied nor disguised the helplessness of government. All admitted dread of approaching disaster. Perhaps C. J. Ingersoll was the only member who declared that the war had been successful, and that Americans need no longer blush to be Americans; but Ingersoll disliked the Militia Bill as cordially as it was disliked by Troup or Varnum, and voted for it only because "something must be done."

"When our army," said Samuel Hopkins of Kentucky, in closing the debate, "is composed of a mere handful of men, and our treasury empty so that it cannot provide for this gallant handful; when an enemy, powerful and active, is beating against our shores like the strong wave of the ocean; when everything is at stake . . . surely such is not the moment for parsimonious feelings in raising taxes, or for forced constructions to defeat the means for raising men."

Notwithstanding every effort of the war-leaders, the opposition steadily won control over the House. Daniel Webster during his entire lifetime remembered with satisfaction that he shared with Eppes the credit of overthrowing what he called Monroe's conscription. December 10, at Eppes's motion, the House voted by a majority of sixty-two to fifty-seven to reduce the term of service from two years to one. A motion made by Daniel Webster to reduce the term to six months was lost by only one voice, the vote standing seventy-eight to seventy-nine. The bill passed at last, December 14, by a vote of eighty-four to seventy-two, in a House where the true war majority was forty-six. When the Senate insisted on its provision of two years' service, Troup, in conference committee, compromised on eighteen months. Then the House, December 27, by a vote of seventy-three to sixty-four, rejected the report of its conference committee. The next day, December 28, in the Senate, Rufus King made an unpremeditated motion for indefinite postponement. Some members were absent; no debate occurred. The question was immediately put, and carried by a vote of fourteen to thirteen. The effect of this action was to destroy the bill.

With this failure the attempt to supply an army was abandoned, and Congress left the government to conduct the war in 1815, as in 1814, with thirty thousand regular troops and six months' militia. Monroe's effort to fill the ranks of the army ended in doubling the land-bounty; in authorizing the enlistment of minors, who had till then been enlisted without authorization; and in exempting from militia duty such persons as should furnish a recruit for the regular army. The prospect was remote that such inducements could do more than repair the waste of the actual force; but the government was unable to pay a larger number even if the force could be raised, and Monroe was obliged to prepare for the next campaign with such slight means of defence as remained to him. The last effort to induce the House to consider a serious method of raising troops was made February 6, and was referred to the Committee of the Whole, with a tacit understanding that the ordinary process of recruiting was not to be disturbed. According to the returns in the adjutant-general's office, the whole number of men—non-commissioned officers, privates, musicians, and artificers, present or absent, sick or well—in the regular army February 16, 1815, was thirty-two thousand one hundred and sixty. During the previous two months it had remained stationary, the returns of December, 1814, reporting thirty-two thousand three hundred and sixty men. Nothing showed a possibility of greatly increasing the force by the means prescribed by Congress.

The navy requiring little new legislation, readily obtained the little it asked. Almost the first Act of the session, approved November 15, 1814, authorized the purchasing or building of twenty sixteen-gun sloops-of-war. Another Act of February 7, 1815, created a Board of Commissioners for the navy to discharge all the ministerial duties of the secretary, under his superintendence.

This legislation, with the various tax-bills, comprised all that was accomplished by Congress between the months of September and February toward a vigorous prosecution of the war. For the navy the prospect of success in the coming year was sufficiently fair, and privateering promised to be more active than ever; but the army was threatened with many perils. The most serious of all dangers to the military service of the Union was supposed by Federalists to be the establishment of armies by the separate States. The attempt to establish such an army by Massachusetts in time of peace had been one of the causes which led to the Constitution of 1789; and at the close of 1814, when Massachusetts voted to raise an army of ten thousand men, the significance of the step was more clearly evident than in the time of the Confederation.

# 5·
# Between the Wars

Although the almost disastrous War of 1812 provided a number of lessons for the nation, they were perceived by few statesmen and heeded almost not at all. Secretary of War John C. Calhoun proposed an extensive reorganization of the army, placing more reliance on a professional force and strengthening its administration. While moderately successful in securing administrative reform, Calhoun was not able to overcome the traditional predilection for a dependence on the militia, and the regular army declined steadily in size and prestige. Calhoun was able to establish forts along the major rivers west of the Mississippi, which contributed to the exploration and settlement of the frontier. But he never secured the troops necessary to subdue the Indians, much less the military organization to permit a rapid and effectual mobilization in the event of war with a major power. In the following selection Leonard White discusses the management problems that plagued the army until the outbreak of the Civil War.

The navy had emerged from the war with considerable glory, although its efforts on the high seas had little effect on the outcome. As Mahan observed, "Never was there a more lustrous example of what Jomini calls 'the sterile glory of fighting battles merely to win them.' " Repeated efforts were made to reorganize the Navy Department, and President Monroe's message, which transmitted a more detailed report by the Secretary of the Navy, revealed his organizational plans and his version of the peacetime role of the service.

# Plan for a Naval Peace Establishment

## BY JAMES MONROE

WASHINGTON, *January 30, 1824*

*To the House of Representatives of the United States:*

In compliance with a resolution of the House of Representatives, of the 15th of December last, requesting the President of the United States "to communicate a plan for a Peace Establishment of the navy of the United States," I herewith transmit a report from the Secretary of the Navy, which contains the plan required.

In presenting this plan to the consideration of Congress, I avail myself of the occasion to make some remarks on it, which the importance of the subject requires, and experience justifies.

If a system of universal and permanent peace could be established, or if, in war, the belligerent parties would respect the rights of neutral Powers, we should have no occasion for a navy or an army. The expense and dangers of such establishments might be avoided. The history of all ages proves that this cannot be presumed; on the contrary, that at least one-half of every century, in ancient as well as modern times, has been consumed in wars, and often of the most general and desolating character. Nor is there any cause to infer, if we examine the condition of the nations with which we have the most intercourse and strongest political relations, that we shall, in future, be exempt from that calamity within any period to which a rational calculation may be extended. And as to the rights of neutral Powers, it is sufficient to appeal to our own experience to demonstrate how little regard will be paid to them, whenever they come in conflict with the interests of the Powers at war, while we rely on the justice of our cause and on argument alone. The amount of the property of our fellow-citizens, which was seized and confiscated or destroyed, by the belligerent parties in the wars of the French revolution, and of those which followed, before we became a party to the war, is almost incalculable.

The whole movement of our Government, from the establishment of our independence, has been guided by a sacred regard for peace. Situated as we are, in the new hemisphere; distant from Europe, and unconnected with its affairs; blessed with the happiest Government on earth, and having no objects of ambition to gratify; the United States have steadily cultivated the relations of amity with every Power. And if, in any European wars, a respect for our rights might be relied on, it was undoubtedly in those to which I have adverted. The conflict being vital, the force being nearly equally balanced, and the result uncertain, each party had the strongest motives of interest to cultivate our good-will, lest we might be thrown into the opposite scale. Powerful as this consideration usually is, it was nevertheless utterly disregarded, in almost every stage of, and by every party to, those wars. To these encroachments and injuries, our regard for peace was finally forced to yield.

---

From *American State Papers,* XIV, *Naval Affairs* (Washington, 1834), 906–907.

In the war to which at length we became a party, our whole coast, from St. Croix to the Mississippi, was either invaded or menaced with invasion; and in many parts, with a strong, imposing force, both land and naval. In those parts where the population was most dense, the pressure was comparatively light; but there was scarcely a harbor or city, on any of our great inlets, which could be considered secure. New York and Philadelphia were eminently exposed; the then existing works not being sufficient for their protection. The same remark is applicable, in a certain extent, to the cities eastward of the former; and as to the condition of the whole country southward of the latter the events which marked the war are too recent to require detail. Our armies and navy signalized themselves in every quarter where they had occasion to meet their gallant foe, and the militia voluntarily flew to their aid with a patriotism, and fought with a bravery, which exalted the reputation of their Government and country, and which did them the highest honor. In whatever direction the enemy chose to move with their squadrons and to land their troops, our fortifications, where any existed, presented but little obstacle to them. They passed those works without difficulty. Their squadrons, in fact, annoyed our whole coast, not of the sea only, but every bay and great river throughout its whole extent. In entering those inlets and sailing up them with a small force, the effect was disastrous, since it never failed to draw out the whole population on each side, and to keep it in the field while the squadron remained there. The expense attending this species of defence, with the exposure of the inhabitants, and the waste of property, may readily be conceived.

The occurrences which preceded the war, and those which attended it, were alike replete with useful instruction as to our future policy. Those which mark the first epoch, demonstrate clearly, that, in the wars of other Powers, we can rely only on force for the protection of our neutral rights. Those of the second demonstrate, with equal certainty, that, in any war in which we may be engaged hereafter, with a strong naval Power, the expense, waste, and other calamities, attending it, considering the vast extent of our maritime frontier, cannot fail, unless it be defended by adequate fortifications and a suitable naval force, to correspond with those which were experienced in the late war.

Two great objects are, therefore, to be regarded in the establishment of an adequate naval force: The first, to prevent war, so far as it may be practicable; the second, to diminish its calamities, when it may be inevitable. Hence, the subject of defence becomes intimately connected, in all its parts, in war and in peace, for the land and at sea. No Government will be disposed, in its wars with other Powers, to violate our rights, if it knows we have the means, are prepared, and resolved, to defend them. The motive will also be diminished, if it knows that our defences by land are so well planned and executed, that an invasion of our coast cannot be productive of the evils to which we have heretofore been exposed.

It was under a thorough conviction of these truths, derived from the admonitions of the late war, that Congress, as early as the year 1816, during the term of my enlightened and virtuous predecessor, under whom the war had been declared, prosecuted, and terminated, digested and made provision for the defence of our country, and support of its rights, in peace as well as in war, by acts, which authorized and enjoined the augmentation of our navy, to a prescribed limit, and the construction of suitable fortifications throughout the whole extent of our maritime frontier, and wherever else they might be deemed necessary. It is to the execution of these works, both land and naval, and under a thorough conviction that by hastening their completion I should render the best service to my country, and give the most effectual support to our free republican system of Government that my humble faculties would admit of, that I have devoted so much of my time and labor to this great system of national policy, since I came into this office, and shall continue to do it, until my retirement from it at the end of your next session.

The navy is the arm from which our Government will always derive most aid in support of our neutral rights. Every Power engaged in war will know the strength of our naval force, the number of our ships of each class, their condition, and the promptitude with which we may bring them into service, and will pay due consideration to that argument. Justice will always have great weight in the cabinets of Europe; but, in long and destructive wars, exigencies often occur which press so vitally on them, that, unless the argument of force is brought to its aid, it will be disregarded. Our land forces will always perform their duty in the event of war; but they must perform it on the land. Our navy is the arm which must be principally relied on for the annoyance of the commerce of the enemy, and for the protection of our own; and also, by co-operation with the land forces, for the defence of the country. Capable of moving in any and every direction, it possesses the faculty, even when remote from our coast, of extending its aid to every interest on which the security and welfare of our Union depend. Annoying the commerce of the enemy, and menacing, in turn, its coast, provided the force on each side is nearly equally balanced, it will draw its squadrons from our own; and, in case of invasion by a powerful adversary, by a land and naval force, which is always to be anticipated, and ought to be provided against, our navy may, by like co-operation with our land forces, render essential aid in protecting our interior from incursion and depredation.

The great object, in the event of war, is to stop the enemy at the coast. If this is done, our cities, and whole interior, will be secure. For the accomplishment of this object, our fortifications must be principally relied on. By placing strong works near the mouths of our great inlets, in such positions as to command the entrances into them, as may be done in many instances, it will be difficult, if not impossible, for ships to pass them, especially if other precautions, and particularly that of steam-batteries, are resorted to in their aid. In the wars between other Powers, into which we may be drawn in support of our neutral rights, it cannot be doubted that this defence would be adequate to the purpose intended by it; nor can it be doubted, that the knowledge that such works existed, would form a strong motive with any Power not to invade our rights, and thereby contribute essentially to prevent war. There are, it is admitted, some entrances into our interior which are of such vast extent that it would be utterly impossible for any works, however extensive or well posted, to command them. Of this class, the Chesapeake bay, which is an arm of the sea, may be given as an example. But, in my judgment, even this bay may be defended against any Power with whom we may be involved in war as a third party, in the defence of our neutral rights. By erecting strong works at the mouth of James river, on both sides, near the capes, as we are now doing, and at Old Point Comfort and the Rip Raps, and connecting those works together by chains, whenever the enemy's force appeared, placing in the rear some large ships and steam-batteries, the passage up the river would be rendered impracticable. This guard would also tend to protect the whole country bordering on the bay and rivers emptying into it; as the hazard would be too great for the enemy, however strong his naval force, to ascend the bay, and leave such a naval force behind; since, in the event of a storm, whereby his vessels might be separated, or of a calm, the ships and steam-batteries behind the works might rush forth and destroy them. It could only be in the event of an invasion by a great Power, or a combination of several Powers, and by land as well as by naval forces, that those works could be carried; and, even then, they could not fail to retard the movement of the enemy into the country, and give time for the collection of our regular troops, militia, and volunteers, to that point, and thereby contribute essentially to his ultimate defeat and expulsion from our territory.

Under a strong impression, that a peace establishment of our navy is connected with the possible event of war, and that the naval force intended for either State, however small it may be, is connected with the general system of public defence, I have thought it proper, in communicating this report, to submit these remarks on the whole subject.

James Monroe

# Management Problems in the War Department

BY LEONARD D. WHITE

CONGRESSIONAL PARSIMONY and Republican distrust of an armed force kept the army and the War Department in a constant state of frustration from 1829 to 1861, excepting only the years of the Mexican War. The same kind of problems vexed the army as disturbed the navy, although the War Department had the asset of the Military Academy and a professionally trained officer corps. This advantage was achieved by the navy in 1845, but both armed forces had many and similar complaints to make about their organization and resources.

The morale of the army declined during the years from 1829 to 1845, but was restored during the campaigns of the Mexican War. The *Army and Navy Chronicle* spoke in 1837 of "the contempt in which the military service is held by Congress in time of peace—the smallness of pay, and the slowness of promotion." In 1839 it declared, "The military profession in this country has been so poorly encouraged, that but little incentive is held out to devote exclusive attention to it. . . . The distrust of military men, so prevalent among politicians who hold out the idea that they are dangerous to the safety of a republican form of government, it might be supposed would long since have yielded to the light of reason and experience." The army suffered not only from democratic distrust but from the complete absence of any obvious external enemy. An army without a calculable major mission is per se under a grave handicap.

An army without legislative support also operates under severe limitations. For years prior to 1861 Congress failed to make adequate provision either for the army or for weapons for the militia. The armories were equipped to turn out 40,000 stand of arms a year, but appropriations allowed production of only 18,000. Congress appropriated exactly the same amount for arming the militia in 1860 as it had authorized in 1808, although the population had increased fourfold.

## Military Policy

The military policy of the country from 1829 to 1861 was a projection of that which had obtained in earlier years, i.e., distrust of a standing army, parsimony in military expenditures, and reliance upon the militia or volunteers in an emergency.

In the *North American Review* for 1832 it was written, "A large standing army has no advocates among us, and is wholly adverse to the spirit of our Government and to public sentiment." Twenty years later the Board of Visitors at West Point, an annual committee of inspection, declared, "The militia will constitute the great bulwark of defence; and as in past warfare, so again in that of the future, their strong arms and brave hearts are ample guarantees against entire subjugation." President Polk agreed. "A volunteer force," he told Congress in 1846, "is beyond question more

Reprinted with permission of The Macmillan Co. from *The Jacksonians* by Leonard D. White. Copyright 1954 by The Macmillan Co., pp. 187–196.

efficient than any other description of citizen soldiers." All this echoed the convictions of that great citizen-soldier Andrew Jackson, who in his first inaugural address asserted that "the bulwark of our defense is the national militia, which in the present state of our intelligence and population must render us invincible." However great were such illusions, it was nevertheless true that the militia was an organization truly democratic in its character, and that a standing army was still the support of monarchy in most parts of the world.

In conformity with these views the United States Army was held at a minimum strength. Its size had been fixed at the close of the War of 1812 at 10,000, but as a consequence of the post-war depression it had been reduced in 1821 to 6,183 officers and men. The Seminole War in Florida caused a temporary increase, but in 1842 on the occasion of the general retrenchment drive it was reduced from something over 12,000 to 8,613 authorized strength. At the close of the Mexican War, President Polk informed members of the Senate Committee on Military Affairs that all the land forces raised to serve during these campaigns should be discharged and that the "old army" with authority to fill each company to one hundred men would be sufficient. Congress reduced the authorized strength to 10,320. On December 11, 1860, the Senate asked its Committee on Military Affairs whether the expenses of the War Department could not be further reduced.

In 1860 the nation was "nearly destitute of military force." The authorized strength of the army had risen to slightly over 18,000 but the returns showed only about 16,000 officers and men in service. The militia were so lacking in instruction and training, with the exception of a few city regiments, that they could hardly be called a military force. Equipment was poor and uncared for. The Indiana militia had been abandoned in 1834 and its arms lost. "An extravagantly fancy uniform for the commanding officer was often sufficient for an entire company. . . ." Congress had never been able to agree on legislation to introduce order, system, and efficiency into these bodies of citizen soldiers, nor had the states responded to their own immediate responsibilities.

Except for a few detachments assigned to man coastal fortifications, and the officers attached to headquarters in Washington, the army was seldom seen by citizens. This was in full harmony with the settled convictions of Albert Gallatin who had said privately that the best place for soldiers was in distant garrisons where few other inhabitants were to be found. "I never want," he said, "to see the face of one in our cities and intermixed with the people." The army was indeed in distant garrisons, scattered along the western and southern frontiers in small posts where the sparse civilian population comprised traders, trappers, and settlers in their small clearings.

Public policy was committed to employment of the militia and volunteers for emergencies rather than to the expansion of the regular army. The legislation of 1821, indeed, gave no authority to the executive to fill up the companies (set at sixty-one men) as a means of increasing military manpower. During the Seminole War in Florida in the late 1830's the militia and volunteers were the principal means of enlarging the armed forces. When the Mexican War broke out, Polk's first move was to call for 50,000 volunteers and to authorize calls on the state militia. The regular army was increased also, but the volunteers and militia outnumbered the regulars.

## The War Department, the Commanding General, and the Military Bureaus

To control and command these scattered detachments and to equip them with arms, supplies, and subsistence were the major peacetime functions of the War Department and the top command—the General Staff and the general field officers. The department also had civilian duties—responsibility for Indian affairs and, until 1849, for the Pension Office. It also included the bounty land office to discharge land claims of former soldiers. The army built forts and constructed roads in addition to keeping the Indians away from the pioneer settlements.

*The War Department.* The civilian components of the War Department were not impressive. They included the Secretary of War, his chief clerk, and a few clerks working in his office. Other civilian employees worked in the military offices of the General Staff, but they were nothing more than clerks. There was no assistant secretary of War; there were no administrative assistants; there was in fact only a single civilian officer of authority, the Secretary himself. The civilian structure was as simple and undeveloped as it had been in the days of Secretary McHenry under Washington and Adams.

The department had twelve Secretaries from 1829 to 1861, a record that compared favorably with other departments. Only Lewis Cass served more than four years (1831–36). He and Marcy had had some early military experience, and Jefferson Davis (1853–57) was a West Point graduate with several years' service in the regular army. During this same period, the army had two commanding generals, Major General Alexander Macomb (1828–41) and Major General Winfield Scott (1841–61). The frequent changes in the office of the Secretary of War during the Harrison-Tyler administration (four Secretaries in four years) prompted Henry Whiting to declare: "Fortunately, the welfare of the army does not depend for its stability upon this high functionary. He may go out and come in with each season; he may be as deciduous as the leaves; and yet the military establishment, and the national defence . . . remain the same. There is a permanency in the command of the army, and in all the subordinate departments connected with its administration, that makes it nearly independent of these fluctuations."

The Secretary in fact found his immediate assistants and advisers in the person of the commanding general and in the General Staff, an institution established during the War of 1812 and brought into full vigor by John C. Calhoun. The General Staff consisted of the heads of the "housekeeping" departments and auxiliary services, such as the adjutant general, inspector general, quartermaster general, commissary general of subsistence, and paymaster general. It did not act as a collective body and was not the equivalent of the General Staff as organized in 1903.

*The Commanding General.* The subordination of the army to the civil authority in the person of the Secretary of War was not disputed, but there was much ambiguity and difference of opinion concerning the relationships of the one to the other, and the proper organization of military leadership.

By a fortunate combination of circumstances, a commanding general was recognized in 1821 by authorization of the rank of major general, in gratitude for the services during the War of 1812 of General Jacob Brown. This gentleman died in 1828, and a movement developed in the Senate to abolish the office, leaving two brigadier generals as the officers with highest rank. Senators argued that the army (then about 6,000 enlisted strength) was overstocked with officers: "there are now, in this mere shadow of an Army, officers enough for one of 50,000 men"; that no inconvenience would ensue; and that retrenchment was due. Senator Nathaniel Macon of North Carolina asserted, indeed, that it was bad to have too many officers. "When war came, the kind of character you want will come out, nor was it necessary to be seeking it out when it was not wanted."

The central issue in the discussion was seized upon by Senator William Henry Harrison, viz., the need for one commanding officer. He succeeded in sending the matter to committee and brought in an able committee report defending the necessity of unified military command. The alternatives, he pointed out, would be either that direct command would be exercised by the President or Secretary of War, or by the staff officers who surrounded him. Any one of these choices, he argued, would be fatal to the energy and effectiveness of the army. The Senate was satisfied and authorized continuance of the rank and office of major general.

Another attack was launched against the office in 1834. Secretary of War Lewis Cass defended it before the House.

> I consider the office of major general essential to the unity of command. He is stationed at this city to superintend and direct those parts of the

administration of the army which are strictly military in their character, and which, to be properly conducted, require not only the advantage of military experience, but of a military connexion with the army. If the office of major general should be abolished, and but two brigadier generals retained, they must either remain in command of separate districts, and this department thus be deprived of the assistance and advice of an officer of high rank, in the management of those concerns which peculiarly affect the army, or one of them must be stationed here exercising an authority over the whole service. The latter arrangement would certainly be liable to objection, and would be inconsistent with the established principles of the military service.

Cass apparently convinced Congress that a two-headed army was an error in military organization. The office of major general was continued, and its occupant remained the commanding officer of all the military bodies. This issue was now settled.

*The Military Bureaus.* Another difficulty was to persist, the subordination of the staff officers at the head of the great military bureaus to the commanding general and the Secretary of War. This problem reached no crisis, but there were indications that it existed. The rule of seniority brought officers to these positions, and guaranteed them tenure therein, short of a court-martial. They were consequently well placed to develop their own routines and work procedures. Henry Whiting observed that when the bureaus were established during the War of 1812, there was no commanding officer and they were all placed in immediate communication with the Secretary of War. This arrangement was terminated in principle in 1821, but in 1845 Whiting still found it necessary to argue that all the military bureaus should be subordinated to the commanding general. In 1857 Secretary of War Floyd confirmed Whiting's criticism. In his annual report he declared that one of the greatest errors of organization was "the separate, independent character of our staff corps," a status which, he said, "removes them from their proper position as aids or assistants to the commander and constitutes them his equals. . . . He is bound, as they are, by the law, and his construction of it should govern them, not theirs him."

We have already observed the difficulty experienced by Secretary of War Marcy in his dealings with these bureaus. His troubles were compounded by reason of the disfavor into which General Scott fell, both with Marcy and Polk, in the early months of the Mexican War. During the war Polk maintained direct contacts with the heads of the military bureaus. After Scott left Washington to lead the Vera Cruz expedition, there was indeed no alternative. The commanding general, the symbol of unity of the army and the principal adviser to the civilian authority, was in the field, days or weeks distant by the best means of communication.

When peace returned and General Zachary Taylor became President, another awkward situation developed. Scott and Taylor were political as well as professional rivals and the former (as commanding general) could not endure to live in the same city with his Commander in Chief, the President. He consequently moved his headquarters to Governor's Island in New York harbor and remained there most of the time for ten years.

*Feuds and Disputations.* The War Department and the army were torn by quarrels in circles high and low. In 1839 the Charleston *Patriot* complained: "It is most deplorable to perceive the many quarrels which occur between the officers both in the naval and military service of the United States. . . . They have multiplied of late in the American army and navy to a discreditable, if not an alarming degree. Some remedy must be found for this degeneracy, or the service will become a theatre of wrangling and vituperation. . . ."

Among the leading characters involved in these unfortunate affairs was General Winfield Scott. In addition to high qualities as a military officer and student of the art of warfare, Scott had a sharp temper and a too ready pen and tongue. As a young officer he declared that General James Wilkinson was as great a traitor as Aaron Burr, an indiscretion that cost him a year's suspension from the army. In 1817 he criticized a military order of General Jackson as mutinous, and Jackson in turn called him a hectoring bully. In 1828 he resigned his commission in disgust when Alexander Macomb was preferred as commanding general. His resignation was not accepted, but for some time he and General Macomb were not on friendly terms. In 1837 a court of inquiry set up to inquire into the causes of the Seminole campaign reprimanded both Scott and General Edmund P. Gaines for their intemperate language.

Scott's most extraordinary quarrel occurred after the Mexican War and involved no less an antagonist than Secretary of War Jefferson Davis. Bad feeling began in 1851 when Davis, then in the Senate, opposed a resolution to grant the rank of lieutenant general to Scott. This step was finally taken in 1855. Scott thereupon claimed back pay of $30,000, and Davis, now Secretary of War, resisted the claim. Davis also opposed some of Scott's claims for transportation and servants, and for a percentage on certain moneys involved in the Mexican campaign. Furthermore he accused Scott of rank insubordination in refusing to observe an order to cancel a leave of absence for General Ethan Allen Hitchcock.

The temper of the two parties can be disclosed only by excerpts from their voluminous correspondence. By 1855 it had descended to extraordinary levels on both sides. On July 25 Davis wrote Scott, "I leave unnoticed the exhibition of peevish temper in your reply. . . ." Scott retorted that Davis seemed to consider it his special mission, by repeated aggressions on Scott's rights and feelings, to goad him into some perilous attitude of official opposition, and to crush him into servile obedience. He asked Davis to show President Pierce the letter. Davis answered the charges in a letter he considered unofficial, whereupon Scott replied that he would treat all of Davis's communications, "whether designed as private and scurrilous, or public missives of arrogance and superciliousness," as equally official.

After further interchange of long arguments tinged with insults, hot war broke out again early in 1856. Davis poured out his indignation over the "gratuitous and monstrous calumnies" that he alleged he had received from Scott, and concluded a lengthy letter by declaring, "Your petulance, characteristic egotism and recklessness of accusation have imposed on me the task of unveiling some of your deformities," adding that Scott's military fame had been "clouded by grovelling vices" and his career marked by "querulousness, insubordination, greed of lucre and want of truth." Scott told Davis that his letter was merely a new example of "chicanery & tergiversation." After another exchange, Scott declared, "My silence, under the new provocation, has been the result, first, of pity, and next, forgetfulness. Compassion is always due to an enraged imbecile, who lays about him in blows which hurt only himself, or who, at the worst, seeks to stifle his opponent by dint of naughty words."

All of this vituperation was utterly foreign to proper communication between a Secretary of War and a commanding general, and even in the perspective of nearly a century can only cause wonder at the character of the two participants. On the matter of salary claim, Scott apparently was justified by the letter of the law. Pierce sustained this claim although he decided against others. Davis, however, properly accused Scott of insubordination in failing to obey an order to cancel the leave of General Hitchcock. He informed Pierce of Scott's "persistent disobedience," and recommended that his headquarters be removed from Governor's Island to Washington, and that all orders affecting the army generally should be communicated by the War Department (i.e., by Davis) directly through the office of the adjutant general. So wide was the gulf between the Secretary and the commanding general!

Despite much loyal cooperation within officer ranks, it could not be said at any time from 1829 to 1861 that the War Department and the army comprised such a team as that which Calhoun had constructed when he was Secretary of War. These eight years remained as the epitome of good relations between the Secretary of War, the General Staff, and the army. This was due certainly in large measure to Calhoun; but it may have been due in part to the fact that the army appeared to have a significant and large-scale mission: the planning and construction of internal improvements.

# 6.

# The Mexican War

James K. Polk took office officially obligated to protect the boundaries of the recently annexed Texas territory and secretly determined to acquire California. When diplomatic negotiations failed to achieve either objective he ordered American troops to occupy land claimed by Mexico, and an armed clash furnished him with the evidence to persuade Congress to declare war. Virtually no preparations had been made in anticipation of the conflict, in part because the President did not want to be vulnerable to accusations of war-mongering.

Polk's tenure as Commander-in-Chief was complex and frustrating. In planning he miscalculated the nature and duration of the war. His two leading generals were prominent in the opposition party and each had presidential ambitions. Partisan opposition hampered his every move as the Whigs accused the administration of seeking to acquire land for the expansion of Southern slavery. As a final indignity, the House of Representatives, controlled by a Whig majority after the election of 1846, censured the President for his conduct of the war. Nevertheless, the objectives of the war were achieved, and it served to prepare the nation and the officer corps for the domestic struggle to come.

In the following selections General Upton reveals the shortcomings of a military policy that gave every evidence of success on the battlefield; and Louis Smith acutely portrays the troubles that beset the President in Washington as two branches of the government differed on the conduct of the war.

# Military Policy During the War

## BY EMORY UPTON

PALO ALTO, RESACA DE LA PALMA, MONTEREY, BUENA VISTA, the siege and capture of Vera Cruz, Cerro Gordo, Contreras, Churubusco, and El Molino del Rey contributed an unbroken chain of victories preceding the entrance of our troops into the capital of Mexico.

Successes so brilliant would apparently denote the perfection of military policy, but, paradoxical as it may seem, official documents establish the fact that they were achieved under the very same system of laws and executive orders which in the preceding foreign war had led to a series of disasters culminating in the capture and destruction of our capital.

The explanation of this paradox is to be found partly in the difference of character of our adversaries, but more especially in the quality of the Regular Army with which we began the two wars. For the Mexican War, as for the war of 1812, the Government had ample time to prepare. The admission of Texas into the Union on March 1, 1845, which was ratified by that State on the ensuing July 4, was followed in August by the advance of our Army to Corpus Christi.

On August 6 the Adjutant-General, by direction of the Secretary of War, wrote to the commander, General Taylor:

"Although a state of war with Mexico or an invasion of Texas by her forces may not take place, it is nevertheless deemed proper and necessary that your force should be fully equal to meet with the certainty of success any crisis which may arise in Texas, and which would require you, by force of arms, to carry out the instructions of the Government." . . .

To "meet with the certainty of success" any crisis that might arise in Texas, the commander was given on paper an aggregate of 4,000 men of the Regular Army, with power to call from States, near and remote, such force of volunteers as in his discretion he might judge expedient.

Three days later, August 26, the Secretary of War informed the Governors of Alabama, Mississippi, and Louisiana by letter that General Taylor had been appointed to command the "army of occupation" and requested him to furnish such a force of militia as General Taylor might designate. August 28 similar letters were sent to the Governors of Kentucky and Tennessee. August 30 the Secretary of War wrote General Taylor:

The instructions heretofore issued enjoin upon you to defend Texas from invasion and Indian hostilities, and should Mexico invade it, you will employ all your forces to repulse the invaders, and drive all Mexican troops beyond the Rio Grande. Should you judge the forces under your command inadequate, you will not fail to draw sufficient auxiliary aid from Texas, and, if there be need, from the States, pursuant to your previous instructions. It is not to be doubted that, on your notification, volunteer troops to the number you may require will rally with alacrity to your standard. You have been advised that the assembling of a large Mexican army on the borders of Texas, and crossing the Rio Grande

From Emory Upton, *The Military Policy of the United States* (Washington, 1904), 195–200, 202–203, 221–224.

with a considerable force, will be regarded by the Executive here as an invasion of the United States and the commencement of hostilities. An attempt to cross the river with such a force will also be considered in the same light. . . .

In case of war, either declared or made manifest by hostile acts, your main object will be the protection of Texas; but the pursuit of this object will not necessarily confine your action within the territory of Texas. Mexico having thus commenced hostilities you may, in your discretion, should you have sufficient force and be in a condition to do so, cross the Rio Grande, disperse or capture the forces assembling to invade Texas, defeat the junction of troops uniting for that purpose, drive them from their positions on either side of that river, and, if deemed practicable and expedient, take and hold possession of Matamoras and other places in the country. I scarcely need to say that enterprises of this kind are only to be ventured on under circumstances presenting a fair prospect of success.

The full significance of these orders should not escape our attention. They not only contemplated the possibility of an invasion, but going far beyond, they looked to a bold and aggressive war to be prosecuted by the same class of troops as were called out at the beginning of the War of 1812.

But this was not all. In plain violation of the Constitution, which only authorizes the employment of militia "to execute the laws of the Union, suppress insurrections, and repel invasions," the orders, in case the General saw fit to call out the militia, sanctioned his entrance into a foreign country with troops of this description. As had already occurred in our history, such a force, pleading constitutional limitations, could have abandoned him the moment he crossed the frontier. . . .

In the meantime the necessity for increasing the Regular Army as the only means of insuring economy and safety was not lost sight of by the Government. General Scott, in his annual report in November, 1845, recommended the addition of one regiment of artillery and three of infantry, as also an increase of the number of privates per company in all of the existing regiments. His plan for the increase of the rank and file contemplated the addition of 10 privates to each company of dragoons, and 20 to each company of artillery and infantry, still further qualified by his preference for 100 privates per company. By adopting this plan he added:

Our present skeleton Army may then, without an additional regiment and by the mere addition of privates, be augmented 7,960 men (more than doubled), making a total of noncommissioned officers, etc., of 15,843.

I offer but elements. It is for higher authorities to determine the extent (if any) and mode of augmentation. But I may add that companies with but 42 privates cannot be isolated, as the ordinary service of the frontiers so frequently requires, and hence are often doubled to garrison even some of the smaller posts.

The Secretary of War in his annual report was not less statesmanlike and explicit. After explaining that the concentration of troops in Texas had left the long line of the British frontier guarded by a few posts, that many fortifications on the Atlantic and Gulf coasts were without garrisons, that the troops on the frontier were not more than sufficient to protect the settlements, and that apprehensions and anxiety existed in relation to the abandonment of posts, he continued:

I would respectfully recommend that authority to increase the number of privates in a company, to any number not exceeding eighty should be vested in the President, to be exercised at his discretion, with special reference to what the public interest might suddenly require.

This mode of enlarging the Army, by adding to the rank and file of the present companies, will not, it is believed, impair, but, on the contrary, greatly improve their comparative efficiency, and on that account, as well as on the score of economy, is deemed preferable to that of effecting the same object by raising new regiments at this time.

It is only in view of a probability that a force considerably larger than a permanent peace establishment might soon be required that I should prefer the mode of increasing the Army by raising new regiments, organized on our present reduced scale. This scale is undoubtedly too low for actual service and has nothing to recommend it to a preference under any circumstances but the facility it affords of expanding an army so organized by increasing the rank and file, and of rendering it effective for service in a shorter period than new regiments could be raised, organized, and disciplined.

These reports accompanied the President's message on December 2, 1845. Had Congress acted promptly on their recommendations it would not have been necessary, three months later, to have instructed General Taylor to depend upon raw troops. . . .

By giving each of the 73 companies 100 privates, which might have been done but for a defect in the law, this force could have been raised from 3,554 to 7,300 men, which, with the full quota of officers, noncommissioned officers, and musicians, would have made this force exceed 8,000. This would have given it an effective strength of nearly 6,000 men present for duty.

While these figures are interesting as showing that the needless exposure of our little army had its origin in faulty legislation, the weakness of its numbers in no way daunted its commander. He knew that four-fifths of his officers had received the benefits of professional training at the Military Academy or in the Florida War. Beyond this, he was conscious that the discipline and esprit de corps of his troops had been brought to the highest point by six months of training in the camp of instruction at Corpus Christi. With this preparation and, as has been observed, with practically no authority to increase his force till an invasion should actually take place, the commander was soon destined to confront a large and well-organized Mexican army.

The first collision occurred on April 25, when Thornton's dragoons in a skirmish on the east bank of the river, suffered a loss of 16 killed and wounded. The emergency having come, General Taylor the next day called upon the Governors of Louisiana and Texas for 5,000 volunteers, but, as was to be expected, the call was too late. The enemy had already crossed the river in large force, and was then threatening his line of communication. Loath to abandon his position, he left the Seventh Infantry and two batteries of artillery to garrison Fort Brown, a field work on the left bank of the river, and on May 1 marched with the remainder of the army to Point Isabel. Having replenished his trains and provided for the safety of the depot, he began the return march to the Rio Grande on the evening of the seventh. The next day the crisis arrived. The enemy had invested Fort Brown, and at Palo Alto was drawn up in line of battle to dispute his further advance.

The challenge was promptly accepted. At 2 o'clock our troops moved to the attack, and at dark, after a well-contested engagement, were masters of the field. Though beaten, the enemy was not hopelessly demoralized. The next day he gave battle at Resaca de la Palma, but no longer able to resist the ardor of our troops was again defeated and driven in confusion across the Rio Grande.

The force present at Resaca de la Palma numbered 173 officers and 2,049 men, total 2,222, of whom but 1,700 were engaged.

The losses in the two battles were 170 killed and wounded.

The strength of the enemy was estimated at 6,000, and his losses in killed and wounded at 1,000.

In concluding his official report General Taylor stated:

> Our victory has been decisive. A small force has overcome immense odds of the best troops that Mexico can furnish—veteran regiments perfectly equipped and appointed. Eight pieces of artillery, several colors and standards, a great number of prisoners, including 14 officers, and a large amount of baggage and public property have fallen into our hands. The causes of victory are doubtless to be found in the superior quality of our officers and men.

The effect of this brilliant initiative was felt to the end of the war. It gave our troops courage to fight against overwhelming numbers, demoralized the enemy, and afforded a striking proof of the truth of the maxim, "That in war, moral force is to physical as three is to one." In all of the subsequent battles our troops were outnumbered two or three to one, yet they marched steadily forward to victory, and for the first time in our history temporarily convinced our statesmen, if not the people, of the value of professional education and military discipline. . . .

The report of the first skirmish reached the War Department on Saturday, May 9, 1846. On Monday, May 11, the President sent a message to Congress, then in session, stating that war existed by the act of Mexico, and adding that:

In further vindication of our rights, and defence of the Territory, I invoke the prompt action of Congress to recognize the existence of the war, and to place at the disposition of the Executive the means of prosecuting the war with vigor, and thus hastening the restoration of peace. To this end I recommend that authority should be given to call into the public service a large body of volunteers, to serve for not less than six or twelve months, unless sooner discharged. A volunteer force is beyond question more efficient than any other description of citizen soldiers; and it is not to be doubted that a number far beyond that required would readily rush to the field upon the call of their country. I further recommend that a liberal provision be made for sustaining our entire military force and furnishing it with supplies and munitions of war.

The most energetic and prompt measures and the immediate appearance in arms of a large and overpowering force are recommended to Congress as the most certain and efficient means of bringing the existing collision with Mexico to a speedy and successful termination.

In these few brief lines is to be found the primary cause of all the subsequent delay and extravagance attending the prosecution of the war. Ignoring the experience of the Revolution, of the War of 1812, and later still of the Florida War, whose aggregate duration exceeded sixteen years, without pausing to compute, in the absence of railroads, the time required to transport troops from one to two thousand miles to the scene of hostilities, the President not only expressed his confidence in raw troops, but signified his belief in a formal recommendation to Congress that we could bring a foreign war to a successful conclusion in the brief space of from six to twelve months.

The responsibility for this recommendation cannot wholly be laid upon the President. General Taylor, a witness of the feeble and protracted prosecution of the two preceding wars, in his letter reporting the skirmish of Thornton's dragoons, stated:

"If a law could be passed authorizing the President to raise volunteers for twelve months, it would be of the greatest importance for a service so remote from support as this."

The promptitude with which Congress entertained and complied with the President's unfortunate recommendation finds no parallel in our history. The very day his message was received a bill to raise 50,000 volunteers was introduced, and under the operation of the previous question passed the House of Representatives. The next day it passed the Senate, and on the thirteenth received the President's signature.

The first section of the act read as follows:

Whereas, by the act of the Republic of Mexico, a state of war exists between that Government and the United States, that, for the purpose of enabling the Government of the United States to prosecute said war to a speedy and successful termination, the President be, and he is hereby, authorized to employ the militia, naval, and military forces of the United States, and to call for and accept the services of any number of volunteers, not exceeding 50,000, who may offer their service, either as cavalry, artillery, infantry, or riflemen, to serve twelve months after they shall have arrived at the place of rendezvous, or to the end of the war, unless sooner discharged, according to the time for which they shall have been mustered into service; and that the sum of $10,000,000, out of any moneys in the Treasury, or to come into the Treasury, not otherwise appropriated, be, and the same is hereby, appropriated for the purpose of carrying the provisions of this act into effect.

The second section extended the term of the militia, when called into the service of the United States, to six months; the third section required the volunteers to furnish their own clothes, horses, and equipments, the arms to be furnished by the United States; the fourth section gave to each volunteer, as compensation for his clothing, the cost of clothing allowed to a regular soldier; the fifth section, ignoring the fact that the new force was not militia, authorized the officers to be appointed according to the laws of their several States; the ninth section gave the volunteers the same pay and allowances as regular soldiers, and allowed to those who were mounted a compensation for their horses of 40 cents per day.

It ought not to surprise us if a law passed without debate should have contained many costly, if not dangerous, mistakes. The principal one of these was contained in the brief words "to serve twelve months" or "to the end of the war." Whether this unfortunate alternative may be regarded as evidence of the conviction on the part of Congress that a foreign war could be brought to a speedy and successful end in twelve months—a thing that has never occurred, and probably never will occur under our present system—or as an expression of its confidence in the wisdom and judgment of the President, it is not necessary to discuss.

As might have been foreseen, the sequel proved that our best and only safeguard lies in wise legislation. The provisions of the law, more liberal than those recommended by the President, authorized him, at his option, to accept the services of volunteers "for twelve months" or "for the war." Instead of deciding upon the volunteers for the war, the President permitted the circular calling for the new troops to be couched in the exact wording of the law, thereby enabling each volunteer, at the expiration of twelve months, to elect whether he would receive his discharge or remain in service till the end of the war. . . .

Notwithstanding its unnecessary prolongation the Mexican War marked a great change if not a revolution in our military policy. This result was due to the decay and gradual abandonment of the militia system which up to that time had been regarded as the "great bulwark of national defense." . . .

While in the War of 1812 the combined force of regulars and volunteers of twelve or more months' service was but 12 per cent of the total number of troops employed, the same force in the Mexican War was no less than 88 per cent. The contrast does not stop here. In the first war, relying upon the States instead of appealing directly to the people as intended by the Constitution, Congress became a witness of disasters like those which occurred in the Revolution; in the second, the national troops, organized and supported by Congress, achieved a series of victories unmarred by a single defeat.

In one war, an army of more than 6,000 raw troops, posted in the defense of our own capital, fled with a loss of but 19 killed and wounded; in the other a force of less than 5,000 trained volunteers, supported by a few regular troops, overthrew a Mexican army of four times its number.

In one war, an enemy numbering less than 5,000 men baffled all of our efforts at invasion; in the other our army, with less than 6,000 combatants, entered in triumph the enemy's capital.

But the difference between the results of the two wars is not wholly to be ascribed to the substitution of national volunteers for the militia. In the war of 1812 the Regular Army, which had itself to be created, was unable to furnish a standard of skill and discipline. In the Mexican War, aside from sustaining the principal losses in killed and wounded, it furnished able commanders, and in every field set an example of skill, fortitude, and courage.

As to the influence of military education in producing such diversity of results, General Scott, who, in 1814, was compelled to teach the regular officers of his brigade the elements of squad drill, left his views to the Senate in the memorable words:

> I give it as my fixed opinion that but for our graduated cadets the war between the United States and Mexico might, and probably would, have lasted some four or five years, with, in its first half, more defeats than victories falling to our share; whereas in less than two campaigns we conquered a great country and a peace without the loss of a single battle or skirmish.

Pursuant to the laws increasing the rank and file of the old regiments and raising the new ones, the Army at the close of the war was reduced from 30,890 to 10,320. In effecting this reduction the number of privates per company was fixed at 50 for the dragoons, 64 for the mounted rifles, and 42 for the artillery and infantry. The only trace left by the war on our military organization was the regiment of mounted rifles, the addition of two companies to each regiment of artillery, an extra major to each of the old regiments of infantry, and a slight increase in some of the staff corps. The same fault, it will be perceived, was committed as after the Florida War. We had 2 regiments of dragoons, 1 of mounted rifles, 4 of artillery, and 8 of infantry; in all, 15 regiments, varying in strength from 558 to 800 each, with still no provision for future contingencies.

June 17, 1850, this defect was remedied, and

the principle of expansion recognized by an act, the second section of which authorized the President "by voluntary enlistment to increase the number of privates in each or any of the companies of the existing regiments of the Army, at present serving or which may hereafter serve at the several military posts on the western frontier, and at remote and distant stations, to any number not exceeding 74."

The use of this discretion by the President gave ample proof that he could be trusted in matters of economy. Without availing himself immediately of his authority, he waited until 1853–4, when Indian troubles caused him to order that the 123 companies of cavalry, infantry, and artillery in Texas, New Mexico, Oregon, California, Minnesota, and the country west of the Mississippi be raised to 74 privates each. Without the addition of an officer this order increased the rank and file by 3,489 men, the aggregate of the Army being increased to 13,821. Had the remaining 35 companies been raised to the same standard the increase of privates would have been 4,488, and the aggregate of the Army 14,731.

This feeble increment of 3,489 men afforded but slight protection to the vast territory which by acquisition from Mexico had been so recently extended to the Pacific. Accordingly, by the act of March 3, 1855, the Army was increased by two regiments of cavalry and two of infantry, having the same organization as the regiments already in service. By this and the preceding laws, the Army with 108 companies serving on the frontier could have been raised in the aggregate to 17,861. Had all of its 198 companies been on the frontier, the aggregate would have been 18,349. The actual strength August 1, 1855, was a little over 15,000 men.

From 1855 to 1861 the only law worthy of special notice was the one approved April 7, 1858. The first section authorized the President to receive into the service of the United States a regiment of Texas mounted volunteers, for the defense of the Texas frontier. The second section authorized him "for the purpose of quelling disturbances in the Territory of Utah, for the protection of supply and emigrant trains, and the suppression of Indian hostilities on the frontier," to call for and accept the services of any number of volunteers, not to exceed two regiments, to be organized at the discretion of the President as mounted infantry.

The term of service for all of the above volunteers was fixed at eighteen months. The men were to provide their own horses and horse equipments, for which they were to receive a compensation of 40 cents per day. The fourth section of the law provided that all of the officers should be appointed in the manner prescribed by law in the several States or Territories to which the regiments belonged, except the quartermasters and commissaries, who were to "be detailed from their respective departments of the Regular Army of the United States." This effort to secure economy was undoubtedly a wise step in the right direction, but like so much of our hasty and ill-digested military legislation it began at the wrong end. Had the President been allowed to call for the volunteers by companies, with authority to select the field officers, adjutants, and quartermasters from the Regular Army, not only the economy but the discipline and instruction of the regiments could have been controlled by trusted officers of the Government.

The military operations of 1848 to 1861 were limited chiefly to Indian wars and the Utah expedition of 1858.

The effect of the latter, although bloodless in its termination, was to transfer nearly all the troops of the Regular Army west of the Mississippi.

# Congress versus the President

BY LOUIS SMITH

THE PATTERN OF RELATIONSHIPS between President and Congress in regard to the conduct of the War of 1812 was largely repeated during the War with Mexico. In this conflict, as in the earlier war, the administration was actively opposed by an intemperate and vociferous group in Congress who were critical of the causation, conduct, continuation, costs, and consequences of the war. While some of this opposition was manifested at the outset, its noise and strength grew steadily as the war lengthened and the election of 1848 approached. It became particularly embarrassing in the Thirtieth Congress in which the Whigs had gained a majority in the House of Representatives. The origins of the opposition to Polk's war leadership are complex and obscure. As Albert J. Beveridge has described the situation:

> The assault (on the Polk administration) was largely partisan, somewhat factional, and inspired by the tangled motives of opposition to territorial expansion, antagonism to slavery and its spread into new territory, resentment of Polk's opposition to internal improvements, desire for a high protective tariff, all involved in the very practical and immediate party manoeuvering for the impending Presidential campaign. But the subject of the loudest complaint was the origin of the war; that the President had begun the conflict was the smallest of the practical motives which really inspired the opposition.

The vociferous and indiscriminate hostility to the chief executive on the part of Whig members of Congress was restrained neither by considerations of due respect for the holder of the office of President of the United States nor of the need for wartime unity in the face of a foreign foe. Criticism was unremittingly uninhibited and bitter. On the day that war was declared, Garrett Davis, a Whig representative from Kentucky, cried out in the House, "it is our own President who began this war." Another embittered Whig, Columbus Delano of Ohio, publicly declared that "the war was unholy, unrighteous, and damnable." Senator John P. Hale of New Hampshire said that the war was both a crime and a blunder, and demanded that the "Congress, on whom the responsibility rests, and to whom the country will look in this matter, (should) take the war into their own hands, and declare distinctly and unequivocally to the country what they intend and what they desire." To a resolution honoring General Zachary Taylor for his signal accomplishments in the conflict with Mexico, the House of Representatives, by the narrow margin of 85 to 81, actually adopted an amendment proposed by George Ashmun of Massachusetts, which declared that the war had been "unnecessarily and unconstitutionally begun by the President of the United States." In a speech which it would be difficult to match in the annals of Congress for bad taste, bad temper, and lack of respect for the head of the administration, Alexander Hamilton Stephens of

---

From Louis Smith, *American Democracy and Military Power: A Study of Civil Control of the Military Power in the United States* (Chicago, The University of Chicago Press, 1951), 187–193. Used by permission.

Georgia impugned the competence of the President and his associates to carry on the war.

He wished to say a word about these political managers and intriguers, who had become a curse to the people of the country; who were devoid of character and principle; worms, slimy worms, that crept and crawled, and fawned, and deceived for power; who had not the principle and spirit of men about them. They were all, however, apt in their catechism. There was no question that could be asked that they could not answer, and in a language that had as many readings as the places or sections to which it might reach. They wrote letters that read one way to one class of the people, and another way to another class. And what was it but an attempt to deceive, mislead, humbug the honest yeomanry of this country? Go back, and the history of the past few years would bear him out in the declaration. What was their present Executive? Had he any ability, any character in this country? Had he even been thought of by anybody as a proper person to be head of this Government? No. How was it, then, that he had been intrusted with the important power he had so shamefully abused? It was by nothing but skill in the political catechism, (by which) honest people had been deceived and misled.

Supporters of the President called attention to the unfortunate consequences in the field of these dissensions at home and called upon the Whigs to give up their "war against the administration." Lewis Cass, chairman of the Military Affairs Committee in the Senate, pleaded with his colleagues for unity and patriotic support of the war, declaring that "one unanimous vote in each of these Halls, evincing a determination to prosecute the war with all our strength, would be better than an army with banners." To appeals of this kind Senator Hale had a ready answer:

. . . I want to say a word in regard to a sentiment I have heard avowed here and elsewhere, and it is, that when the country is engaged in war we lose all discretion, we have nothing to do but grant the supplies that are demanded of us, on appeal being made to our patriotism—patriotism can find only rightful action in support of the war; that there is no patriotism anywhere else; and that the Administration, which has been so fortunate or unfortunate as to plunge the country into a war, has only to appeal to the country and expect to receive no other response except hearty and unanimous support. And this doctrine has been carried so far, and in such high places, that the President of the United States has denounced as treason the opposition of Congress, although his mode of prosecuting the war did not accord with their convictions. . . . Sir, I utterly deny the soundness of this doctrine, that Congress ought to have no voice beyond the granting of supplies. If there ever is a time when opposition should be vigilant, scrupulous, watchful, noticing everything that is wrong, it is at a time when, through the acts of the Administration, the country is burdened with an unnecessary war.

Representative Abraham Lincoln, the lone Whig from Illinois in the Thirtieth Congress, who in his own war presidency was to incur congressional criticism and interference in the conduct of war in a more severe and damaging form than has been the lot of any other wartime President, joined in this gadfly attack on Polk. He not only introduced his famous "spot resolutions" demanding proof that the spot on which American soldiers were attacked was on American soil rather than Mexican, but he also supported the Ashmun Amendment which declared that the war had been unnecessarily and unconstitutionally begun by the President. In a subsequent speech defending this vote, he said that he suspected the President "was deeply conscious of being on the wrong side in this matter, that he felt the blood of this war, like the blood of Abel, was crying from the ground against him." In involving the two countries in war, the President had fixed the public eye on military glory, "that rainbow that rises in showers of blood, that serpent's eye that charms but to destroy." "The President," he remarked in a typically Lincolnian figure of speech, "was like a man on a hot shovel, finding no place he could settle down." Moreover, he declared, the President, in his confusion about the war, "talked like an insane man," and

was it not true, as he had said before, that Mr. Polk was lost—that he did not know where he was—that he did not know what to do? He was not satisfied with any position. . . . All this went on to show that he was most completely bewildered, and he (Mr. L.) should be most happy to be assured that there was not something about his conscience that was more harassing than all his mental perplexities.

As is chronically the case in situations of this type, members of Congress were dissatisfied with official reports of the war's policies and progress. They suspected the administration might be withholding from them matters of primary importance. Polk's critics apparently regarded the President's powers as commander-in-chief as instrumental rather than inherent, and assumed that Congress was both entitled to full access to all information about the war and competent to make decisions regarding all phases of it. Therefore, they evinced a jealous solicitude lest the President's conduct of the war encroach upon the policy-making function of Congress and made recurring demands for copies of all presidential orders to generals in the field. When information regarding war plans was forthcoming, it usually became the basis for acrimonious discussion. When it was withheld, there were bitter declamations on the primeval right of legislative bodies to have unimpeded access to all information relevant to their responsibilities.

The viewpoints of Polk's critics were rather fully stated in the lengthy debate which took place in the Senate over resolutions introduced by Senators Mangum and Berrien requesting the President to furnish copies of orders given to Generals Scott and Taylor relative to the conduct of the war in Mexican territory. Since the President is head of a co-ordinate department of the government and therefore not subject to the direction of Congress, the usual formula in such resolutions is that the President is *requested* to furnish the information in question, *if not incompatible with the public interest*. In this discussion, there was an initial tendency to omit the contingency clause *if not incompatible with the public interest* on the ground that the President had no basis either in law or prudence for withholding such information from Congress. Eventually there was a grudging acceptance of the customary formula, but the tenor of the discussion indicated that critics of the chief executive felt that his discretion ought to be exercised on the narrowest basis possible.

Senator Cass of Michigan warned of the military benefits the Mexicans would derive from disclosure of American war plans in the open meeting of Congress and asked his colleagues to accept the obvious fact that "there must of necessity be secrets with regard to the conduct of the war." Senator Willie Mangum of North Carolina, speaking in support of his resolution, disclaimed any intention of embarrassing the conduct of the war by improper disclosures, but expressed fear that the discretion accorded the executive might be improperly used to conceal from the Congress knowledge of the extent and scope of executive purposes, and of the means proposed for the accomplishment of these purposes. Since Congress needed full information in order to act understandingly with reference to the war, he hoped that the President and his associates did not intend to withhold essential information, remarking that "for the sake of the spirit of our institutions; for the sake of the Executive's sense of right, I hope that it may not even be implied that no decent investigation shall be permitted, that no light shall be afforded us." Senator John J. Crittenden of Kentucky declared, "I think it is the right of the Senate to have this information, and that if access to the Executive Departments by the legislative bodies is to be precluded in this way, we must become nothing but the shadow of the legislature." Moreover, he remarked, the Senate could not be satisfied with oral and fragmentary reports from partisans of the administration, but had "a right to the information in its authentic and official form—in that we may see what it contains—no more and no less." Elsewhere in his argument he declared:

> Here is a great subject upon which we are legislating—a question of war and peace—of raising armies; and, when we ask the opinion of our military officers, who are engaged in the war and are acquainted with the country in which the war is carried on, on this great question, it is treated as though it were a State secret, and we are not permitted to appeal to the Executive Department for information, or communications received from these officers. This is most strange and unaccountable. We are subjected to a sort of trial by the ordeal here, and made to walk blindfolded over burning red-hot iron. We want light to guide us. We want all the information that the Government possesses; and are we not entitled to it? . . . The people—Congress—have a right

> to know everything concerning the projects of the Government and the purposes of this war—everything of the least importance. You may keep secret things of no consequence. If you employ an agent, or a spy, or a mercenary, keep his name secret, in God's name, if you have one in your employ; but if the information relates to public affairs—to anything which interests the people of the United States, in any public political aspect and point of view, they have a right to know it. They have set up no department of this Government for the purpose of keeping knowledge, wisdom, and information a secret from them.

But when Crittenden and his colleagues finally conceded that there were limits set by prudence, and that matters might legitimately be kept from the Mexicans, if not from Congress, the resolution was passed with the usual discretionary clause having been added.

Not only did Congress make demands for information which Polk felt the public interest required to be kept secret, but it further embarrassed the administration by proposed resolutions which had important implications for the conduct of the war, as in the one proffered by Toombs of Georgia that Mexico should be assured that none of her territory would be annexed by the United States subsequent to the war, or the one introduced by Representative Botts of Virginia, and in modified form by others later, that we should "withdraw our troops, already covered with glory and surfeited with success, to the true and legitimate boundary of Texas at the time of its annexation to the United States." Another suggestion which was made while the war was still in progress was that new military appropriations should be limited to the amount required to bring our armies home from Mexico by the shortest and cheapest route. Mention has already been made of the Ashmun Amendment which declared that the President had unlawfully and unconstitutionally begun the war with Mexico. And, unlike the other proposals mentioned here, this one was actually adopted by the House. But it remained for David Wilmot of Pennsylvania to introduce the proposal which was the most troublesome of all during the Mexican War, and although it was not accepted by Congress, it was, in one form or another, to agitate that body until the Civil War, being appended to any measure to which it seemed at all relevant. This was the famous "Wilmot Proviso," which stated that neither slavery nor involuntary servitude was ever to be permitted in territory acquired in consequence of the War with Mexico. It was attached as a rider to a bill appropriating two million dollars which had been requested by President Polk for negotiating peace with Mexico. The measure passed the House but was killed by a Whig filibuster in the Senate when the proviso was about to be eliminated by the Democratic majority.

President Polk was vastly surprised and indignant at this outbreak of opposition in Congress, particularly since his election to the presidency had been largely on the issues of "the reoccupation of Oregon and the reannexation of Texas," both being actions which clearly involved the risk of war. He was vexed at Whig members of Congress for seeking always to boost the reputations of Whig Generals Scott and Taylor, and for preventing the authorization of a new top-level military rank to which he had hoped to appoint a general more friendly to the administration. But while Polk failed to get such a place for Thomas Hart Benton, and also failed in other specific matters on which he needed congressional approval, nonetheless, he succeeded in the large objectives to which he had dedicated his administration. Despite this success, he was angered by the procrastination and hostility of the Whigs in Congress. He complained in his diary of "the extraordinary delay of Congress to act upon the war measures which I recommended them," adding:

> The state of things in Congress is lamentable. Instead of coming up to the mark as patriots and sustaining the administration and the country in a foreign war, they are engaged in discussing the abstract question of slavery, and are gravely considering whether it shall exist in a territory which we have not acquired & may never acquire from Mexico. The Presidential election of 1848 has evidently much to do with this factitious state of things.

As has probably been noted in this description of executive-legislative relationships during the conflict with Mexico, congressional committees on the conduct of the war played a negligible role in this period. Such committees were created, but their influence seems to have been insignificant. But there was a continuation of congressional confusion regarding its proper role in the conduct of the war, and likewise a continuation of the controversy between the President and the legislative branch over this matter. Also, it may be correct to say that in the Thirtieth Congress, the House of Representatives, with its Whig majority, frequently functioned as a committee of the whole on the conduct of the war.

Notwithstanding the large significance of the issues under consideration and the presence in Congress of Clay, Webster, Calhoun, Benton, and others who are reckoned among the ablest ever to sit in that body, discussions of the conduct of the war and the relative places of the executive and legislative branches in it seldom attained a profound or edifying level during the time of the Mexican War. Mainly the whole debate was picayune and partisan, with the participants seemingly more concerned with winning the coming election than with defeating the Mexicans.

The discussion developed no new ideas or techniques beyond the precedents established by the end of the War of 1812.

# 7·
# The Civil War

When the Southern states began to secede after Lincoln's election, President Buchanan, who believed their action unconstitutional, could see no constitutional way of preventing it. Nor could Lincoln after he assumed office. Then apathetic Northern opinion was galvanized into action by the firing on Fort Sumter, and the President secured support for coercive methods to preserve the Union.

In waging the war Lincoln stretched his powers under the guise of "necessity." Acting as Commander-in-Chief to direct the war effort, he drew on his constitutional responsibility to see that the laws were executed and to suppress rebellion. Using as his sole criterion the maintenance of the Union, he exercised more jurisdiction over domestic affairs than any other chief executive.

The strategy of the conflict depended in large measure on the resources of the two sections and the geographical imperatives. Theodore Ropp provides a broad overview of these factors and the impact they had on land and sea operations. The choice of military commanders played a significant role in the course of the struggle, and T. Harry Williams assesses the leaders of both sides in the context of their times. The severity and duration of the hostilities demanded a total commitment by both the North and the South, which combined with the impact of technological change to make this what Bruce Catton, in the final selection, calls "The First Modern War."

# Grand Strategy

BY THEODORE ROPP

THE INDUSTRIALIZED NORTH'S DEFEAT of the agricultural South is a familiar theme. But this war can also be thought of as the last of the great wars for North America, one in which the power which commanded the sea defeated a people who were too dependent on water transportation. The South exported agricultural commodities and imported manufactures and even food by water. Its cities were still located on the water, though the Confederacy held only 10 of the 102 American cities of more than 10,000 people. The Confederate seaports, protected by long sandbars, were hard to blockade; all were close to neutral Bermuda or the West Indies. But, as Mahan put it, "The streams that had carried the wealth . . . of the seceding States turned against them, and admitted their enemies to their hearts." To replace these water routes the Southern rebels, like the rebels of 1776, had little land transportation. The North had three east-west railway systems, plus railways leading south to Washington and fanning out from Kentucky into Tennessee, Mississippi, and Georgia. In the Confederacy one line ran from Richmond to Wilmington, North Carolina, and another linked Richmond with the east-west line running from Charleston to Memphis. These lines joined at Chattanooga, a Unionist area open to Northern attack up the valleys of the Tennessee and Cumberland rivers. During the war the Confederates finished a second east-west line from Vicksburg to Charleston. But this road also was to be cut at Atlanta, 125 miles from Chattanooga. There were a few short lines across the Mississippi, but none into Texas or Florida.

In white manpower the Confederates were outnumbered four to one, in total manpower two and a half to one. In industry the North's superiority was overwhelming—at least ten or twenty to one. The South was not well-prepared even for muscle-powered war. Because of her concentration on export crops food for both men and animals was often scanty. "The real conflict was not between factory and field, but between a fairly well coordinated and balanced economy and a distorted, incompetent agriculture." Both governments also failed to deal with many kinds of economic problems—from those of taxation to the kinds of material brought in through the blockade. But if the French government was unable to control the prices of food and fuel in beleaguered Paris, one can hardly blame American statesmen for doing no better. Nineteenth-century Liberal economics was simply unadapted to periods of national emergency. In this respect the men of this age were far less modern than those of the First French Republic.

The rebels of 1861 faced, therefore, somewhat the same difficulties as the rebels of 1776. But they also enjoyed roughly the same advantages. (1) Their armies stood on the defensive in

---

From Theodore Ropp, *War in the Modern World* (Durham, N.C., Duke University Press, 1959), 166–176. Used by permission.

very difficult country, "a wilderness of primeval forest, covering an area twice as large as the German Empire, and as thinly populated as Russia." (2) Britain and France seemed to favor them, a diplomatic advantage which might, as in 1776, prove decisive. (3) They were possibly more united than the Union. The inexperienced Republicans were a minority party even in the North. (4) They were fighting a limited war. They had only to win the independence which many Northerners and the British and French were ready to concede to them. (5) Though they did not enjoy the inestimable advantage of distance, the rebels were almost as well organized as the government. They did not have to face either a large regular army or navy.

Since the United States' military strength was potential rather than actual, much of the credit must go to the political leaders who mobilized this strength and drove their armies to victory. Consciously or not, the Union's over-all strategy was very much like that of the British in 1776: to blockade the Confederacy, capture its seaports, and cut it up along the lines of the great rivers. The United States had also to try to hold the border states and Washington in slave territory, and capture Richmond, a little more than a hundred miles from Washington. Here politics profoundly affected strategy. The loss of Washington or of the Army of the Potomac might well have led to foreign recognition of the Confederacy. For the Confederacy Richmond represented the four Mid-South states which had joined it after Sumter. Without them, the Confederacy could hardly claim to represent a Southern nation; it would indeed have been little more than a cotton planters' conspiracy. Those who criticize this mutual fixation on the two capital cities do not realize how vitally both of them affected the "military forces, the country, and the will" of the contenders.

The Union navy, like the Union army, was created after the war began by Northern industry and trained manpower. The little navy of 1861—with twenty-three steamships and seventy-five hundred officers and men—had not been built to blockade a coast as long as that from Hamburg to Genoa. Its best ships were steam frigates to raid British commerce or to show the flag in distant waters. It had no ironclads or armed river vessels, and many of its higher officers were superannuated. At sixty, David Glasgow Farragut, a Tennessean with a Virginia wife, was only fifty-seventh on the list of captains. The navy's Bull Run was the loss of Norfolk navy yard eight days after the beginning of the war. Its elderly commander did not even do a good job of demolition; about three thousand heavy guns went to strengthen the Confederacy's coast and river defenses. Both sides now rushed to buy, charter, or build ships, and the western armies even rustled up navies of their own, like the Eads gunboats, which were designed by a bridge builder, manned by naval personnel, and owned by the United States Army. These ships were armored with anything that came to hand—railroad rails, boiler plating, chains, oak, coal, hay, and cotton. A Confederate seagoing ironclad, Confederate Secretary of the Navy Mallory believed, could "traverse the entire coast of the United States, prevent all blockades, and encounter, with a fair prospect of success, their entire Navy." Since no Southern machine shop could build marine engines—a report to United States Secretary of the Navy Welles at this time reported thirty-eight such shops in the North, though some of them were small and in bad financial shape—Mallory decided to armor the hull and utilize the engines of the U.S.S. *Merrimac*, sunk in the debacle at Norfolk. The United States replied with three experimental ironclads—a gunboat, an ironclad like the newly completed French *Gloire*, and John Ericsson's "cheesebox on a raft," the *Monitor*.

The *Monitor* combined light draft, armor, and big guns in a movable turret; the guns could be aimed without moving the ship in shallow coastal waters. As Welles pointed out, her "nautical qualities . . . were not a governing object, she was adapted to the shallow waters of our coasts and harbors, and that was what we wanted." The day before the *Monitor* arrived off Norfolk, the *Merrimac* (now the *Virginia*) destroyed two unarmored ships at the cost of two men to two hundred and fifty. The next day the two ironclads fought for four hours.

The *Monitor* fired forty-one heavy shots and was hit twenty-two times. Nobody was killed, though three Yankees and eleven Confederates were wounded. The new ironclads were virtually invulnerable. Their ability to run past all existing coastal defenses was one of the most important factors in the Union's success on Southern waterways. Like all experimental ships, the Union's light draft ironclads had their weaknesses—one whole group of river monitors proved to have "negative flotation"—but they were as remarkable in their day as were the landing craft of the Second World War. After the war one of these "iron sea elephants"—with thirty inches of freeboard for a four-thousand-ton ship—went to Europe and another around Cape Horn. None of the smaller iron-clads built in the Confederacy seems to have reached the open sea. Like the ships of the Continental Navy, they were mostly lost with the ports they were defending. The *Tennessee*, the largest of these ships (her engines were taken from a river steamer) fought a whole Union squadron in Mobile Bay. Her steering tackle was gone, her funnel broken off inside her, and the shutters jammed so that the gun-ports would not open. But she lost only two killed and nine wounded.

It is difficult to estimate the real effects of the Northern blockade. Many Southerners agreed with Lord Wolseley: "Had the ports . . . been kept open . . . by the action of any great naval power, the Confederacy must have secured their independence." As in Germany after 1918, it was easy to exaggerate the effects of this almost impersonal force which had beaten down the men who had fought so long and valiantly. This explanation gained added validity from the belief that the war had been won solely by Northern industry. The effects of blockade are always most apparent at the end of a war; people are more conscious of the hardships of the last few months than of conditions in preceding periods. It was also easier to blame the blockade than to examine certain other factors: the disruption of land transportation, the disastrous cotton embargo, and the Confederacy's failure to control imports and stem inflation. Part of the blame could be shifted to Britain and France, who had so cravenly failed to challenge the North's violations of international law.

During the early phases of the war the Confederate cotton embargo did far more damage than the blockade. Obviously related to the Stamp Act boycott and Jeffersonian Non-Intercourse, the aim of the boycott was to force England and France to break the blockade in order to avoid economic collapse, in a period in which one out of every five Englishmen made his living from the textile industry. Southern agricultural products were the chief sources of foreign exchange for the United States. Without such exports, it was argued, the North could not pay for imported manufactures. "Satisfied that the three great nations England, France, and the United States (the centers of western industrial civilization) could not live without the southern cotton," the South's leaders, with the almost unanimous support of its people, made the blockade temporarily effective. After the embargo had been abandoned, the Confederates were, for revolutionaries, very well supplied with weapons. During the last phases of the war the Confederacy had more arms than men. Its arsenals were running at a third of their capacity because of the shortage of labor. Largely because of poor internal transportation and the lack of purchasing power and credit, food and clothing were always scarcer than munitions. But $200,000,000 worth of goods were run through the blockade, and at least four-fifths of the supplies actually shipped reached the Confederacy. The blockade running system was costly—a point for the blockaders—and too much of the South's foreign exchange was spent on nonessentials, but contemporary French and British studies of the blockade emphasized its ineffectiveness. Steam, close observers believed, had ended the old-fashioned close blockade for good and all.

The only way to plug the leaks in the blockade was to capture the Southern seaports. Less than ten months after Bull Run, seven of the ten Confederate ports with rail connections had been captured or neutralized. No Union iron-clads were involved except at Norfolk. These victories were won by steam rather than by armor and big guns, though the strong forts below New Orleans had been bombarded by big mortars. The real strength of earthworks was not yet appreciated; most of these victories had been won against little more than token resistance. Mobile, Charleston, and Wilmington might possibly have been taken as easily as New Orleans during this stage of the war, but the Confederates strengthened their defenses until it took whole fleets to capture them. Even so, only 3,090 men were lost in all of these operations, more than two-thirds of them in capturing the three remaining seaports. When these losses are compared with Union casualties on land, the value of the Union command of the sea is strikingly apparent.

The most effective Confederate reply to the invulnerable Northern ironclads was the torpedo (a term which was then used for both mines and torpedoes). Torpedoes had been used before, but never as extensively. Floating torpedoes drifted down the rivers. Anchored torpedoes (electrically-detonated "controlled" mines were more successful than contact mines) lurked in the channels. Towed torpedoes were dragged by small boats. Spar torpedoes (mines on the ends of poles) were used by steam launches. Coal torpedoes were hidden in Yankee coal barges. The nature of the coast and the fact that they had little shipping of their own to worry about aided the Confederates, but, considering the state of electricity and chemistry in the 1860's, Confederate torpedo operations were surprisingly successful. They introduced two new elements into naval warfare. For the first time since galley days, a ship could be sunk by attacking her below the waterline. And for the first time a large ship could be attacked by a smaller one. In the 1880's, after the development of the "automobile" torpedo by Robert Whitehead (an Englishman residing in Fiume in Austria-Hungary), a group of French naval officers who called themselves the *Jeune Ecole* based part of their radically new theory of naval warfare on the torpedo.

Land operations outside of Virginia developed along the lines of the great river systems. The most important land operations of 1861 were the civil wars in the border states of Missouri, Kentucky, and West Virginia. Once the Union had secured the heart of the Mississippi system (the area from which the Missouri, Mississippi, Illinois, Ohio, Wabash, Tennessee, and Cumberland rivers fan out like the spokes of a wheel) the Confederacy was open to attacks along the Mississippi, Cumberland, and Tennessee and along the railroad from Louisville. In February, 1862, the Union gunboats and armies broke through at Forts Henry and Donelson on the Tennessee and Cumberland, in the center of the Confederate position. Tennessee was cut nearly in two and the Union forces advanced against the east-west railroad running along its southern border between Chattanooga and Memphis. This led to the decisive battle of Shiloh in April. Two months later New Orleans was lost and the forces pushing down the Mississippi took Memphis. All this had taken place before McClellan's repulse from Richmond. Lee had taken over the command of the Confederates in front of Richmond only five days before the fall of Memphis. One western army was then based on the river and rail lines leading into west Tennessee; a second Union army was based on the rail and river lines to Nashville. In 1863 the first army under Grant opened the Mississippi by capturing Vicksburg and Port Hudson. The second army defeated a Confederate move into Kentucky (in the fall and winter of 1862), captured Chattanooga in September, 1863, was defeated at Chickamauga in Georgia, and finally opened the way for a Union thrust over the mountains in the battles of Lookout Mountain and Missionary Ridge in November.

Sherman's advance to Atlanta in the summer of 1864 was made possible by a combination of rail and water transportation. Sherman used his wagon trains as moving storehouses. They distributed supplies from the railhead to the troops—he later estimated that it would have taken 36,800 six-mule wagons to have hauled supplies for his 100,000 men and 35,000 animals if he had not been able to use the railway—and insured his army against temporary breaks in the railroad. Here the engineering experience of the West Pointers came into play

—their wooden "beanpole and cornstalk" railway bridges were as remarkable for their day as their timber fortifications. The bridge over the Chattahoochie before Atlanta, for example, was eight hundred feet long and one hundred feet high, and was built in four and a half days. After Sherman left Atlanta on November 16 he was able to live off the country because he was certain of getting supplies and reinforcements whenever he hit the seacoast. (The rest of his army, under Thomas, had been sent north to watch Hood, who was beaten in the one really Napoleonic battle of the war at Nashville in December.) Meanwhile Grant had slowly moved the Army of the Potomac (in May and June, 1864) around to the east and south of Richmond. His base and one flank were always on the water. In two months he changed his base of operations four times, finally coming out below Petersburg. The result was to place his army across Lee's communications and in a position to capture both Richmond and Lee's army. When Richmond fell and Lee's army was lost with it, the revolution lost all political vitality. In April, 1865, Lincoln, Grant, Sherman, Lee, and Johnston displayed rare statesmanship as well as great military ability.

The only Confederate naval success of the war was the attack on United States merchant shipping, though the South did not accomplish its long-range objective of forcing the United States Navy to lift the blockade. More than half the American merchant marine was driven from the flag. The raiders destroyed about 110,000 tons and 800,000 additional tons were transferred to foreign owners. This was accomplished by about a dozen ships, five of which were responsible for most of the damage. None of these ships was Confederate-built; in this respect the rebels were much weaker than the rebels of 1776. Like the *Bon Homme Richard*, the Confederate cruisers were not particularly good ships; a rebel government usually has difficulty in purchasing very powerful warships. Their success was due to four factors: (1) the ability of the Confederate cruiser commanders, especially Raphael Semmes of the *Sumter* and *Alabama*, (2) the special conditions of the transition from sail to steam, (3) a rather inept Union system of commerce protection, and (4) foreign aid. The raiders combined the range of sail and the speed of steam. All but two of their 261 captures were sailing ships. The Union's refusal to divert ships from the blockade was sound; convoys organized for the Panama route were successful. But the Union failed to prevent transfer to foreign registries by a system of government war-risk insurance. American trade continued under neutral flags; the failure of the transferred ships to return to American ownership after the war was due to long-term economic factors.

The most successful raiders were purchased in Britain, and repaired, coaled, and partially manned in British ports. An international tribunal later awarded the United States $15,500,000 damages for British violations of international law. But the Confederates never ran a foreign ironclad into a Southern port. Many Americans thought that the British were willing to have Confederate raiders cripple the American merchant marine, but were unwilling to risk war with the United States. The Confederate raiders, it was argued, also showed what United States cruisers might do to the British merchant marine in an Anglo-American war. The British paid damages to prevent precedents which would allow the United States to sell raiders to France or Russia. These Confederate successes and Britain's willingness to pay damages were to be major arguments for the *Jeune Ecole's* theories of naval warfare.

# The Military Leadership of North and South

## BY T. HARRY WILLIAMS

GENERALS AND THEIR ART and their accomplishments have not been universally admired throughout the course of history. Indeed, there have been some who have sneered at even the successful captains of their time. Four centuries before Christ, Sophocles, as aware of the tragedy of war as he was of the tragedy of life, observed: "It is the merit of a general to impart good news, and to conceal the bad." And the Duke of Wellington, who knew from experience whereof he spoke, depreciated victory with the bitter opinion: "Nothing except a battle lost can be half so melancholy as a battle won."

Civil War generals were, of course, not considered sacrosanct—were, in fact, regarded as legitimate targets of criticism for anyone who had a gibe to fling. Senator Louis T. Wigfall was exercising his not inconsiderable talent for savage humor, usually reserved for the Davis administration, on the military when he said of John B. Hood: "That young man had a fine career before him until Davis undertook to make of him what the good Lord had not done—to make a great general of him." One can understand Assistant Secretary of War P. H. Watson's irritation when the War Department could not locate so important an officer as Joe Hooker on the eve of Second Manassas, while also noting Watson's patronizing attitude toward all generals in a letter to transportation director Herman Haupt stating that an intensive search for Hooker was being conducted in Willard's bar. "Be patient as possible with the Generals," Watson added. "Some of them will trouble you more than they will the enemy."

And yet in the final analysis, as those who have fought or studied war know, it is the general who is the decisive factor in battle. (At least, this has been true up to our own time, when war has become so big and dispersed that it may be said it is managed rather than commanded.) Napoleon put it well when he said, perhaps with some exaggeration: "The personality of the general is indispensable, he is the head, he is the all of an army. The Gauls were not conquered by the Roman legions, but by Caesar. It was not before the Carthaginian soldiers that Rome was made to tremble, but before Hannibal. It was not the Macedonian phalanx which penetrated to India, but Alexander. It was not the French Army which reached the Weser and the Inn, it was Turenne. Prussia was not defended for seven years against the three most formidable European Powers by the Prussian soldiers, but by Frederick the Great." This quotation may serve to remind us of another truth about war and generals that is often forgotten: That is that tactics is often a more decisive factor than strategy. The commander who has suffered a strategic reverse, Cyril Falls emphasizes, may remedy everything by a tactical success, whereas

---

T. Harry Williams, "The Military Leadership of North and South," in David Donald, editor, *Why the North Won the Civil War* (Baton Rouge, Louisiana State University Press, 1960), 33–54. Reprinted by permission.

for a tactical reverse there may be no remedy whatever. Falls adds: "It is remarkable how many people exert themselves and go through contortions to prove that battles and wars are won by any means except that by which they are most commonly won, which is by fighting."

If, then, the general is so important in war, we are justified in asking, what are the qualities that make a general great or even just good? We may with reason look for clues to the answer in the writings of some of the great captains. But first of all, it may be helpful to list some qualities that, although they may be highly meritorious and desirable, are not sufficient in themselves to produce greatness. Experience alone is not enough. "A mule," said Frederick the Great, "may have made twenty campaigns under Prince Eugene and not be a better tactician for all that." Nor are education and intelligence the touchstones to measure a great general. Marshal Saxe went so far as to say: "Unless a man is born with a talent for war, he will never be other than a mediocre general." And Auguste Marmont, while noting that all the great soldiers had possessed "the highest faculties of mind," emphasized that they also had had something that was more important, namely, character.

What these last two commentators were trying to say was that a commander has to have in his make-up a mental strength and a moral power that enables him to dominate whatever event or crisis may emerge on the field of battle. Napoleon stated the case explicitly: "The first quality of a General-in-Chief is to have a cool head which receives exact impressions of things, which never gets heated, which never allows itself to be dazzled, or intoxicated, by good or bad news." Anyone who knows the Civil War can easily tick off a number of generals who fit exactly the pattern described next by Napoleon: "There are certain men who, on account of their moral and physical constitution, paint mental pictures out of everything: however exalted be their reason, their will, their courage, and whatever good qualities they may possess, nature has not fitted them to command armies, nor to direct great operations of war." Karl von Clausewitz said the same thing in a slightly different context. There are decisive moments in war, the German pointed out, when things no longer move of themselves, when "the machine itself"—the general's own army—begins to offer resistance. To overcome this resistance the commander must have "a great force of will." The whole inertia of the war comes to rest on his will, and only the spark of his own purpose and spirit can throw it off. This natural quality of toughness of fiber is especially important in measuring Civil War generalship because the rival generals were products of the same educational system and the same military background. As far as technique was concerned, they started equal, and differed only in matters of mind and character. It has been well said: "To achieve a Cannae a Hannibal is needed on the one side and a Terentius Varro on the other." And one may add, to achieve a Second Manassas a Robert E. Lee is needed on the one side and a John Pope on the other.

When Marshal Saxe enumerated the attributes of a general, he named the usual qualities of intelligence and courage, and then added another not always considered in military evaluations—health. It is a factor that deserves more attention than it has received. Clifford Dowdey has recently reminded us of the effects of physical and mental illness on the actions of the Confederate command at Gettysburg. A comparison of the age levels of leading Southern and Northern officers in 1861 is instructive. Although there are no significant differences in the ages of the men who rose to division and corps generals, we note that, of the officers who came to command armies for the South, Albert Sidney Johnston was fifty-eight, Joseph E. Johnston and Lee were fifty-four, John C. Pemberton was forty-seven, Braxton Bragg was forty-four, and P. G. T. Beauregard was forty-three. Of the Union army commanders, Hooker was forty-seven, Henry W. Halleck and George G. Meade were forty-six, George H. Thomas was forty-five, D. C. Buell was forty-three, William S. Rosecrans was forty-two, William T. Sherman was forty-one, U. S. Grant was thirty-nine, Ambrose Burnside was thirty-seven, and George B. McClellan was thirty-four. Hood and Philip H. Sheridan at thirty represent the lowest age brackets. Youth was clearly on the side of the Union, but obviously it cannot be said, with any accuracy or finality, that the generals in one particular age group did any better than those in another. Nevertheless, when Grant thought about the war in the years after, he inclined to place a high premium on the qualities of youth, health, and energy, and doubted that a general over fifty should be given field command. He recalled that during the war he had had "the power to endure" anything. In this connection, it may be worthy of mention that during the Virginia campaign of 1864 Lee was sick eleven of forty-four days, while Grant was not indisposed for one.

The Civil War was pre-eminently a West Pointers' fight. Of the sixty biggest battles, West Point graduates commanded both armies in fifty-five, and in the remaining five a West Pointer commanded one of the opposing armies. What were the men who would direct the blue and gray armies like in 1861? How well trained were they for war? What intellectual influences had formed their concepts of war and battle? A glance at the Point curriculum reveals that it was heavy on the side of engineering, tactics, and administration. The products of the academy came out with a good grounding in what may be termed the routine of military science. They knew how to train and administer a force of troops; or, to put it more accurately and to apply it specifically to the Civil War, they had the technical knowledge that enabled them to take over the administration of a large force without imposing too much strain on them or their men. It should be emphasized, however, that none of the West Pointers had had before 1861 any actual experience in directing troops in numbers. Not a one had controlled as large a unit as a brigade, and only a few had handled a regiment. Except for a handful of officers who had visited Europe, the men who would lead the Civil War hosts had never seen an army larger than the fourteen thousand men of Winfield Scott or Zachary Taylor in the Mexican War.

One subject which was taught but not emphasized at West Point was strategy, or the study of the higher art of war. The comparative subordination of strategy may be explained by the youth of the cadets and the feeling of the school's directors that it was more important to impart a basic knowledge of tactics and techniques to the boys. Nevertheless, many of the graduates enlarged their knowledge of the topic by reading books on military history while stationed at army posts. The strategy that was presented at the Point and studied by interested graduates came from a common source and had a common pattern. It was the product of the brilliant Swiss officer who had served with Napoleon, Antoine Henri Jomini, universally regarded as the foremost writer on the theory of war in the first half of the nineteenth century. Every West Point general in the war had been exposed to Jomini's ideas, either directly, by reading Jomini's writings or abridgments or expositions of them; or indirectly, by hearing them in the classroom or perusing the works of Jomini's American disciples. The influence of Jomini on the Civil War was profound, and this influence must be taken into account in any evaluation of Civil War generalship. There is little exaggeration in General J. D. Hittle's statement that "many a Civil War general went into battle with a sword in one hand and Jomini's *Summary of the Art of War* in the other."

Here it is impossible to attempt more than a summary of Jomini's ideas and writings. Essentially his purpose was to introduce rationality and system into the study of war. He believed that in war rules prevailed as much as in other areas of human activity and that generals should follow these rules. He sought to formulate a set of basic principles of strategy for commanders, using as his principal examples the campaigns and techniques of Napoleon. The most convenient approach to Jomini is through the four strategic principles that he emphasized, the famous principles that many Civil War generals could recite from memory:

(1) The commander should endeavor by strategic measures to bring the major part of his

forces successively to bear on the decisive areas of the theater of war, while menacing the enemy's communications without endangering his own.

(2) He should maneuver in such a way as to engage the masses of his forces against fractions of the enemy.

(3) He should endeavor by tactical measures to bring his masses to bear on the decisive area of the battlefield or on the part of the enemy's line it was important to overwhelm.

(4) He should not only bring his masses to bear on the decisive point of the field but should put them in battle speedily and together in a simultaneous effort.

It is, perhaps, unnecessary to remark that much of this was not new. Xenophon had said about the same thing to the Greeks, and the definition of strategy as the art of bringing most of the strength of an army to bear on the decisive point has been fairly constant in the history of war. But it should be noted that Jomini envisioned the decisive point as the point where the enemy was weakest. This is often true but not always. There are occasions in war when the decisive point may be the strongest one, as Epaminondas demonstrated at Leuctra and the American strategists in the cross-Channel attack of World War II.

To explain how his principles should be applied in war, Jomini worked out an elaborate doctrine based on geometrical formations. He loved diagrams, and devised twelve model plans of battle; some Civil War generals actually tried to reproduce on the field some of these neat paper exercises. In all Jomini's plans there was a theater of operations, a base of operations, a zone of operations, and so forth. The smart commander chose a line of operations that would enable him to dominate three sides of the rectangular zone; this accomplished, the enemy would have to retire or face certain defeat. Jomini talked much of concentric and eccentric maneuver and interior and exterior lines, being the first theorist to emphasize the advantage of the former over the latter.

At times, especially when he discussed the advantage of the offensive—and he always stressed the offensive—Jomini seemed to come close to Clausewitz's strategy of annihilation. But a closer perusal of his writings reveals that he and the German were far apart. Although Jomini spoke admiringly of the hard blow followed by the energetic pursuit, his line of operation strategy allowed the enemy the option of retiring. In reality Jomini thought that the primary objectives in war were places rather than armies: the occupation of territory or the seizure of such "decisive strategic points" as capitals. He affected to be the advocate of the new Napoleonic ways of war, but actually he looked back instead of forward. It has been rightly said of him (in R. A. Preston, S. F. Wise, and H. O. Werner, *Men in Arms*): "By his emphasis on lines of operation Jomini, in effect, returned to the eighteenth-century method of approaching the study of war as a geometric exercise. . . . In emphasizing the continuance of traditional features he missed the things that were new. There can be no doubt that this interpreter of Napoleonic warfare actually set military thought back into the eighteenth century, an approach which the professional soldiers of the early nineteenth century found comfortable and safe."

Jomini confessed that he disliked the destructiveness of the warfare of his time. "I acknowledge," he wrote, "that my prejudices are in favor of the good old times when the French and English guards courteously invited each other to fire first as at Fontenoy. . . ." He said that he preferred "chivalric war" to "organized assassination," and he deplored as particularly cruel and terrible what he called wars of "opinion," or as we would say today, of "ideas." War was, as it should be, most proper and polite when it was directed by professional soldiers and fought by professional armies for limited objectives. All this is, of course, readily recognizable as good eighteenth-century doctrine. This could be Marshal Saxe saying: "I do not favor pitched battles . . . and I am convinced that a skillful general could make war all his life without being forced into one." Eighteenth-century warfare was leisurely and its ends were limited. It stressed maneuver rather than battle, as was natural in an age when professional armies were so expensive to raise and maintain that they could not be risked unless victory was reasonably certain. It was conducted with a measure of humanity that caused Chesterfield to say: "War is pusillanimously carried on in this degenerate age; quarter is given; towns are taken and people spared; even in a storm, a woman can hardly hope for the benefit of a rape." Most important of all, war was regarded as a kind of exercise or game to be conducted by soldiers. For the kings war might have a dynastic objective, but in the thinking of many military men it had little if any relationship to society or politics or statecraft.

Many West Pointers—McClellan, Lee, Sherman, and Beauregard, among others—expressed their admiration of Jomini and usually in extravagant terms. Halleck devoted years to translating Jomini's works, and his own book on the elements of war was only a rehash of Jomini, in parts, in fact, a direct steal. William Hardee's manual on tactics reflected Jominian ideas. But the American who did more than any other to popularize Jomini was Dennis Hart Mahan, who began teaching at West Point in 1824 and who influenced a whole generation of soldiers. He interpreted Jomini both in the classroom and in his writings. At one time Jomini's own works had been used at the academy but had been dropped in favor of abridgments by other writers. In 1848 Mahan's book on war, usually known by the short title of *Outpost*, became an official text. Most of the Civil War generals had been Mahan's pupils, and those older ones who had not, like Lee, were exposed to his ideas through personal relationships or through his book. Probably no one man had a more direct and formative impact on the thinking of the war's commanders.

Mahan, of course, did little more than to reproduce Jomini's ideas. He talked much of the principle of mass, of defeating the enemy's fractions in succession, and of interior lines. But it should be emphasized that his big point, the one he dwelt on most, was the offensive executed by celerity of movement. Mahan never tired of stressing the advantage of rapidity in war—or of excoriating "the slow and over-prudent general" who was afraid to grasp victory. "By rapidity of movement we can . . . make war feed war," he wrote. "We disembarrass ourselves of those immense trains." There was one operation that could change the face of a war, he said. When one's territory was invaded, the commander should invade the territory of the enemy; this was the mark of "true genius." (This passage makes us think immediately of Lee and Stonewall Jackson.) Jominian strategy as interpreted by Mahan then was the mass offensive waged on the battlefield, perhaps with utmost violence, but only on the battlefield. It cannot be sufficiently emphasized that Mahan, like his master, made no connection between war and technology and national life and political objectives. War was still an exercise carried on by professionals. War and statecraft were still separate things.

The Jominian influence on Civil War military leadership was obviously profound and pervasive. But before considering its manifestations, it may be helpful to dispose of a number of generals who do not meet the criteria of greatness or even of acceptable competence. This perhaps too brutal disposal will be performed by means of some undoubtedly too sweeping generalizations. These generals fell short of the mark partly because, as will be developed later, they were too thorough Jominians, and partly because they lacked the qualities of mind and character found in the great captains of war. Of the generals who commanded armies we can say that the following had such grave shortcomings that either they were not qualified to command or that they can be classified as no better than average soldiers: on the Union side—McClellan, Burnside, Hooker, Meade, Buell, Halleck, and Rosecrans; on the Confederate side—Albert Sidney Johnston, Beauregard, Bragg, Joe Johnston, and Edmund Kirby Smith.

McClellan will be discussed later, but here we may anticipate by saying that he did not have the temperament required for command. Burnside did not have the mentality. Hooker was a fair strategist, but he lacked iron and also the imagination to control troops not within his physical vision. Meade was a good routine soldier but no more, and was afflicted with a defensive psychosis. Buell was a duplicate of McClellan without any color. Halleck was an unoriginal scholar and an excellent staff officer who should never have taken the field. Rosecrans had strategic ability but no poise or balance; his crack-up at Chickamauga is a perfect example of Napoleon's general who paints the wrong kind of mental picture. A. S. Johnston died before he could prove himself, but nothing that he did before his death makes us think that he was anything but a gallant troop leader. Beauregard probably was developing into a competent commander by the time of Shiloh, but his failure to win that battle plus his personality faults caused him to be exiled to comparatively minor posts for the rest of the war. Bragg, the general of the lost opportunity, was a good deal like Hooker. He created favorable situations but lacked the determination to carry through his purpose; he did not have the will to overcome the inertia of war. Kirby Smith made a promising start but seemed to shrink under the responsibility of command and finally disappeared into the backwash of the Trans-Mississippi theater. The stature of Joe Johnston probably will be argued as long as there are Civil War fans to talk. But surely we can take his measure by his decision in the Georgia campaign to withdraw from a position near Cassville that he termed the "best that I saw occupied during the war" merely because his corps generals advised retiring. A great general, we feel, would have delivered the attack that Johnston originally planned to make. Johnston undoubtedly had real ability, but he never did much with it. It is reasonable to expect that a general who has sustained opportunities will sometime, once, achieve something decisive. Certainly Johnston had the opportunities, but there is no decisive success on his record.

Of the lesser generals, it is fair to say that James Longstreet and Stonewall Jackson were outstanding corps leaders, probably the best in the war, but that neither gave much evidence of being able to go higher. Longstreet failed in independent command. Jackson performed brilliantly as commander of a small army but probably lacked the administrative ability to handle a large one. In addition, he was never fairly tested against first-rate opposition. Thomas and W. S. Hancock stand out among Union corps generals. Thomas also commanded an army, but his skills were of a particular order and could be exercised only in a particular situation. He excelled in the counterattack delivered from strength. J. E. B. Stuart, Sheridan, N. B. Forrest, and J. H. Wilson were fine cavalry leaders, but we cannot say with surety that they could have been anything else. On the one occasion when Sheridan directed an army he displayed unusual ability to handle combined arms (infantry, cavalry, artillery), but he enjoyed such a preponderant advantage in numbers over his opponent as to be almost decisive. He was never really subjected to the inertia of war. In the last analysis, the only Civil War generals who deserve to be ranked as great are Lee for the South and Grant and Sherman for the North.

We can now turn to an examination of the influence of Jominian eighteenth-century military thought on Civil War generalship, first directing our attention to the first Northern generals with whom Abraham Lincoln had to deal. It is immediately and painfully evident that in the first of the world's modern wars these men were ruled by traditional concepts of warfare. The Civil War was a war of ideas and, inasmuch as neither side could compromise its political purposes, it was a war of unlimited objectives. Such a war was bound to be a rough, no-holds-barred affair, a bloody and brutal struggle. Yet Lincoln's generals proposed to conduct it in accordance with the standards and the strategy of an earlier and easier military age. They saw cities and territory as their objectives rather than the armies of the enemy. They hoped to accomplish their objectives by maneuvering rather than by fighting. McClellan boasted that the "brightest chaplets" in his history were Manassas and Yorktown, both occupied after the Confederates had departed, because he had seized them by "pure military skill" and without the loss of life. When he had to lose lives, McClellan was almost undone. The "sickening sight" of the battlefield, he told his wife after Fair Oaks, took all the charm from victory. McClellan's mooning around the field anguishing over the dead may seem strange to the modern mind, but Jomini would have understood his reactions. Buell argued, in the spirit of Marshal Saxe, that campaigns could be carried out and won without engaging in a single big battle. Only when success was reasonably certain should a general risk battle, Buell said, adding: "War has a higher object than that of mere bloodshed." After the Confederates retired from Corinth, Halleck instructed his subordinates: "There is no object in bringing on a battle if this object can be obtained without one. I think by showing a bold front for a day or two the enemy will continue his retreat, which is all I desire." Meade, who confessed shame for his cause when he was ordered to seize the property of a Confederate sympathizer, thought that the North should prosecute the war "like the afflicted parent who is compelled to chastise his erring child, and who performs the duty with a sad heart."

With an almost arrogant assurance, Lincoln's first generals believed that war was a business to be carried on by professionals without interference from civilians and without political objectives. It is no exaggeration to say that some of the officers saw the war as a kind of game played by experts off in some private sphere that had no connection with the government or society. Rosecrans gave a typical expression of this viewpoint when he resisted pressure from Washington to advance before the battle of Stone's River: "I will not move until I am ready! . . . War is a business to be conducted systematically. I believe I understand my business. . . . I will not budge until I am ready." But, as might be expected, the classic example is McClellan. He refused to retain General Charles Hamilton in his army when Lincoln requested him to, even after, or more accurately, especially after the President emphasized that there were weighty political reasons for assigning Hamilton a minor position. When McClellan conceived his Urbanna plan, he did not tell Lincoln about it for months. He did not seem to know that it was his job to counsel his political superior on his plans; in fact, he did not seem to know that there was any relationship between war and politics. In the winter of 1861–1862 Lincoln implored McClellan to make a move, even a small or diversionary one, to inspire public opinion with the belief that more decisive action was contemplated later. McClellan refused on the grounds that he was not yet completely prepared. That the public might become so discouraged that it would abandon the war impressed McClellan not at all. With him the only question was when the professionals would be ready to start the game.

Lincoln's early generals also accepted blindly the Jominian doctrine of concentration. As they interpreted it, it meant one big effort at a time in one theater. McClellan's proposal to mass 273,000 troops in the eastern department in 1861, a physical and military impossibility at that time, was a typical piece of Jominian thinking. Of course, each commander was convinced that the one big push should be made by him, and each one demanded that other departments be stripped of troops to strengthen his own army. It would be possible to argue that the apparent caution of every Union general in the first years of the war, and the consequent inaction of Union armies, was the result of each commander's conviction that he did not possess enough strength to undertake the movements recommended by Jomini. But this feeling of the generals brought them into conflict with their commander in chief, who was no Jominian in his strategic notions, and their differences with Lincoln will be discussed later.

When we examine the psychology of the Northern generals, the thought immediately occurs that the Southern generals were not like this, and inevitably we ask, why not? Had the Southerners freed themselves from Jomini's dogma? Were they developing new ways of war? The answer to both questions is no. The Confederates were, if possible, more Jominian than the Federals. They simply gave a different emphasis to the traditional pattern of strategic thought. Whereas the Federals borrowed from Jomini the idea of places as objectives, the Confederates took from him the principle of the offensive. Moreover, the Southern generals were fortunate in being able to make enemy armies the object of their offensives because Confederate policy did not look to the acquisition of enemy territory. The influence of Mahan, with his doctrine of celerity and the headlong attack, is also apparent in Confederate strategy, especially as it was employed by Lee. In addition, the poverty of Southern resources had the effect of forcing Southern generals to think in aggressive terms. They could not afford to wait for a big build-up in men and equipment, but had to act when they could with what they had. Paradoxically, the Industrial Revolution, which would have so much to do with bringing about the advent of total war with all its destructiveness, had the immediate consequence of making the Northern generals less inclined to deal out destruction. They could secure material so easily that they refused to move until they had received more than they needed—after which they were often so heavily laden they could not move.

Far from departing from Jomini, the Confederates were the most brilliant practitioners of his doctrine. If we look for successful applications of the principles that Jomini emphasized—the objective, the offensive, mass, economy of force, interior lines, and unity of command—we find them most frequently in the Confederate campaigns and most particularly in the Virginia theater. Lee, the Confederacy's best general, was also its greatest Jominian. Probably it is because Lee embodied so precisely the spirit of traditional warfare that he has been ranked so high by students of war. Military historians are likely to be as conservative as generals. The English writers, who have done so much to form our image of the war, have been especially lavish in their praise. It may be suspected that their attitude stems largely from a feeling that Lee was a gentleman, English style, although for a long while the British, when they faced a possible combination of superior continental powers, studied Lee's strategy because of its application of the principle of interior lines. Cyril Falls said that Lee was a master combination of "strategist, tactical genius, leader of the highest inspiration, and technician in the arts of hastily fortifying defensive positions superbly chosen." Falls added: "He must stand as the supreme figure of this survey of a hundred years of war." Colonel A. H. Burne was more restrained, but spoke admiringly of Lee's audacity, his use of the offensive, and his skill at concentration. The opinions of G. F. R. Henderson and G. J. Wolseley are so well known as not to require quotation.

Let us concede that many of the tributes to Lee are deserved. He was not all that his admirers have said of him, but he was a large part of it. But let us also note that even his most fervent admirers, when they come to evaluate him as a strategist, have to admit that his abilities were never demonstrated on a larger scale than a theater. Cyril Falls, after his extravagant eulogy of Lee, falls on his face in attempting to attribute to his subject gifts for "large-scale strategy": the only example he can find is Lee's redeployment of forces between the Shenandoah Valley and Richmond during the Peninsula campaign! Lee was pre-eminently a field or a theater strategist, and a great one, but it remains unproven that he was anything more or wanted to be anything more. "In spite of all his ability, his heroism and the heroic efforts of his army," writes General J. F. C. Fuller, "because he would think and work in a corner, taking no notice of the whole, taking no interest in forming policy or in the economic side of the war, he was ultimately cornered and his cause lost." For his preoccupation with the war in Virginia, Lee is not to be criticized. He was a product of his culture, and that culture, permeated in its every part by the spirit of localism, dictated that his outlook on war should be local. Nevertheless, it must be recognized that his restricted view constituted a tragic command limitation in a modern war. The same limitation applied to Southern generalship as a whole. The Confederates, brilliant and bold in executing Jominian strategy on the battlefield, never succeeded in lifting their gifts above the theater level.

In many respects Lee was not a modern-minded general. He probably did not understand the real function of a staff and certainly failed to put together an adequate staff for his army. Although he had an excellent eye for terrain, his use of maps was almost primitive. He does not seem to have appreciated the impact of railroads on warfare or to have realized that railroads made Jomini's principle of interior lines largely obsolete. His mastery of logistics did not extend beyond departmental limits. In February, 1865, he said that he could not believe Sherman would be able to move into Northern Carolina. The evidence of Sherman's great march was before him, and yet he was not quite sure it had really happened.

The most striking lack of modernity in Lee was his failure to grasp the vital relationship between war and statecraft. Here the great Virginian was truly a Jominian. Almost as much as McClellan, he thought of war as a professional exercise. One of his officers said admiringly that Lee was too thorough a soldier to attempt to advise the government on such matters as the defense of Richmond. When late in the war a cabinet member asked Lee for his opinion on the advisability of moving the capital farther south, the general replied: "That is a political question . . . and you politicians must determine it. I shall endeavor to take care of the army, and you must make the laws and control the Government." And yet what could be a more strategic question than the safety of the capital? Lee attained a position in the Confederacy held by no other man, either in civil or military life. There was little exaggeration in the statement General William Mahone made to him: "You are the State." But Lee could not accept the role that his eminence demanded. He could never have said as Pitt did: "I know that I can save the country and that no one else can." It has been suggested that Lee did not try to impose his will on the government because of his humility of character, and this may well be true. But it would also seem to be true that he did not know that a commander had any political responsibility.

Lincoln's first generals did not understand that war and statecraft were parts of the same piece. But none of the Confederate generals, first or last, ever grasped this fact about modern war. The most distinguishing feature of Southern generalship is that it did not grow. Lee and the other Confederate commanders were pretty much the same men in 1865 that they had been in 1861. They were good, within certain limits, at the beginning, and they were good at the end but still within the original limits. They never freed themselves from the influence of traditional doctrine. The probable explanation, David Donald has suggested, is that the Confederates won their first battles with Jominian strategy and saw no reason to change and that the Southern mind, civil and military, was unreceptive to new ideas. The North, on the other hand, finally brought forward generals who were able to grow and who could employ new ways of war. Even so doctrinaire a Jominian as Halleck reached the point where he could approve techniques of total war that would have horrified the master. But the most outstanding examples of growth and originality among the Northern generals are Grant and Sherman.

The qualities of Grant's generalship deserve more analysis than those of Lee, partly because they have not been sufficiently emphasized but largely because Grant was a more modern soldier than his rival. First, we note that Grant had that quality of character or will exhibited by all the great captains. (Lee had it, too.) Perhaps the first military writer to emphasize this trait in Grant was C. F. Atkinson in 1908. Grant's distinguishing feature as a general, said Atkinson, was his character, which was controlled by a tremendous will; with Grant action was translated from thought to deed by all the force of a tremendous personality. This moral strength of Grant's may be news to some present-day historians, but it was overpoweringly apparent to all who were thrown into close association with him. Charles Francis Adams, Jr., like all his family not disposed to easy praise, said that Grant was really an extraordinary person, although he did not look it. In a crisis, Adams added, all would instinctively lean on Grant. Lincoln saw this quality in Grant clearly: "The great thing about Grant, I take it, is his perfect coolness and persistency of purpose. I judge he is not easily excited—which is a great element in an officer." But the best tribute to Grant's character was paid by the general who knew him best. In a typical explosive comment to J. H. Wilson, Sherman said: "Wilson, I am a damn sight smarter than Grant. I know a great deal more about war, military history, strategy, and administration, and about everything else than he does. But I tell you where he beats me, and where he beats the world. He don't care a damn for what the enemy does out of his sight, but it scares me like hell." On the eve of the great campaigns of 1864 Sherman wrote to Grant that he considered Grant's strongest feature was his ability to go into battle without hesitation, doubts, or reserve. Characteristically Sherman added "It was this that made me act with confidence."

In this same letter Sherman confessed to a reservation that he had had about Grant: "My only points of doubt were as to your knowledge of grand strategy, and of books of science and history; but I confess your common sense seems to have supplied all this." Common sense Grant had, and it enabled him to deal with such un-Jominian phenomena as army correspondents and political generals. Unlike Sherman, Grant accepted the reporters—but he rendered them harmless. "General Grant informs us correspondents that he will willingly facilitate us in obtaining all proper information," Junius Browne wrote S. H. Gay, then added significantly that Grant was "not very communicative." Unlike McClellan, who would not accept General Hamilton for political considerations urged by Lincoln, Grant took John A. McClernand at the President's request. He could not imagine why Lincoln wanted a command for McClernand but assumed that there must be some reason important to his civil superior. He put up with McClernand until he found a way to strike him down to which Lincoln could not object. In this whole affair Grant showed that he realized the vital relation between politics and modern war.

It was Grant's common sense that enabled him to rise above the dogmas of traditional warfare. On one occasion a young officer, thinking to flatter Grant, asked his opinion of Jomini. Grant replied that he had never read the master. He then expressed his own theory of strategy: "The art of war is simple enough. Find out where your enemy is. Get at him as soon as you can. Strike at him as hard as you can and as often as you can, and keep moving on." After the war Grant discussed more fully his opinion of the value of doctrine. He conceded that military knowledge was highly desirable in a commander. But he added: "If men make war in slavish observance of rules, they will fail. No rules will apply to conditions of war as different as those which exist in Europe and America. . . . War is progressive, because all the instruments and elements of war are progressive." He then referred to the movement that had been his most striking departure from the rules, the Vicksburg campaign. To take Vicksburg by rules would have required a withdrawal to Memphis, the opening of a new line of operations, in fact, a whole new strategic design. But Grant believed that the discouraged condition of Northern opinion would not permit such a conformity to Jominian practice: "In a popular war we had to consider political exigencies." It was this ability of Grant's to grasp the political nature of modern war that marks him as the first of the great modern generals.

The question of where to rank Sherman among Civil War generals has always troubled military writers. He is obviously not a Jominian, and just as obviously he is not a great battle captain like Grant or Lee. Colonel Burne points out that never once did Sherman command in a battle where he engaged his whole force and that he never won a resounding victory. Conceding that in the Georgia campaign Sherman displayed imagination, resource, versatility, broadness of conception, and genuine powers of leadership—all fundamental traits of a great commander—Burne still contends that Sherman exhibited two serious failings: that of pursuing a geographical rather than a military objective and that of avoiding risk. B. H. Liddell Hart, on the other hand, depicts Sherman as the greatest general of the war because more than any other commander he came to see that the object of strategy is to minimize fighting. Part of this evaluation can be written off as an attempt by Liddell Hart to glorify through Sherman the British strategy of the "indirect approach." And yet he is right in saying that Sherman had the most complete grasp of the truth that the resisting power of a modern democracy depends heavily on the popular will and that this will depends in turn on a secure economic and social basis. Sherman, a typical Jominian at the beginning of the war, became its greatest exponent of economic and psychological warfare. Nobody realized more clearly than Sherman the significance of the techniques he introduced. Describing to Grant what he meant to do on his destructive march, he said, "This may not be war, but rather statesmanship." At the same time we must recognize that Sherman's strategy by itself would not have brought the Confederacy down. That end called for a Grant who at the decisive moment would attack the enemy's armed forces. As Burne puts it: "Sherman might help to prepare the ground, but it was Grant who struck the blow." The North was fortunate in finding two generals who between them executed Clausewitz's three objectives of war: to conquer and destroy the enemy's armed forces, to get possession of the material elements of aggression and other sources of existence of the enemy, and to gain public opinion by winning victories that depress the enemy's morale.

It remains to touch on the military leadership of the North and the South at the highest levels where strategy was determined—at the rival Presidents and the command systems they headed. In supreme leadership the Union was clearly superior. Lincoln was an abler and a stronger man than Davis. The Northern President illustrated perfectly the truth of Clausewitz's dictum that "a remarkable, superior mind and strength of character" are the primary qualifications of a director of war. The North developed at an early date an over-all plan of strategy, and it finally devised a unified command system for the entire military machine. The South was unable to accomplish either one of these objectives. But its failure should not be set down as the result of a shortage of brains among its leaders. Here again we need to remind ourselves that ways of making war are always the product of cultures. For the nationalistic North it was comparatively easy to achieve a broad view of war. Conversely, it was natural for the localistic South to adopt a narrow view and to fight a conservative war. Confederate strategy was almost wholly defensive, and was designed to guard the whole circumference of the country. In military jargon, it was a cordon defense. Probably the South's best chance to win its independence by a military decision was to attempt on a grand strategic scale the movement its generals were so good at on specific battlefields—the concentrated mass offensive. But the restrictions of Southern culture prevented any national application of the one Jominian principle that might have brought success.

Just as a cordon defense was the worst strategy for the South, a cordon offense was the best strategy for the North. This was the strategy that Lincoln had pressed upon his generals almost from the beginning of the war—to make enemy armies their objective and to move all Federal forces against the enemy line simultaneously. An offensive along the entire circumference of the Confederacy would prevent the enemy from moving troops from one threatened point to another and would inevitably achieve a break-through. It was an eminently sensible strategy for the side with the greater numbers and the superior lines of transportation and for a war fought over such a vast theater. When Lincoln proposed his plan to general after general, it met with polite scorn. It violated the Jominian principle of concentration in one theater for one big effort. It was the product of a mind that did not know the rules of war.

Not until he found Grant did Lincoln find a general who was original enough to employ his strategy. Grant's master design for 1864 called for an advance of Federal armies all along the line. It was the operation that broke the back of the Confederacy. When Grant explained his plan to the President, he remarked that even the smaller Federal forces not fighting would help the fighting by advancing and engaging the attention of the enemy. We have dealt much with maxims here, and we may fittingly conclude with one. Lincoln grasped Grant's point immediately and uttered a maxim of his own. At least for the Civil War it had more validity than anything written by Baron Jomini. "Those not skinning can hold a leg," said the commander in chief.

# The First Modern War

BY BRUCE CATTON

THE CIVIL WAR was the first of the world's really modern wars. That is what gives it its terrible significance. For the great fact about modern war, greater even than its frightful destructiveness and its calculated, carefully-applied inhumanity, is that it never goes quite where the men who start it intend that it shall go. Men do not control modern war; it controls them. It destroys the old bases on which society stood; and because it does, it compels men to go on and find the material for new bases, whether they want to do so or not. It has become so all-encompassing and demanding that the mere act of fighting it changes the conditions under which men live. Of all the incalculables which men introduce into their history, modern warfare is the greatest. If it says nothing else it says this, to all men involved in it, at the moment of its beginning: Nothing is ever going to be the same again.

The Civil War was the first modern war in two ways, and the first of these ways has to do with the purely technical aspect of the manner in which men go out to kill one another. That is to say that it was a modern war in the weapons that were used and in the way in which these affected the fighting.

On the surface, Civil War weapons look very old-fashioned; actually, they foreshadowed today's battles, and there are important parts of the Civil War which bear much more resemblance to World War I than to the Napoleonic Wars or to the American Revolution. Modern techniques were just coming into play, and they completely changed the conditions under which war would be waged.

Consider the weapons the Civil War soldiers used.

The infantryman's weapon was still spoken of as a musket—meaning a muzzle-loading smoothbore—and yet, by the time the war was a year or more old, nearly all infantrymen in that war carried rifles. These, to be sure, were still muzzle-loaders, but they were very different from the "Brown Bess" of tradition, the weapon on which all tactics and combat formations were still based.

With the old smoothbore, effective range—that is, the range at which massed infantry fire would hit often enough to be adequately damaging—was figured at just about one hundred yards. I believe it was U. S. Grant himself who remarked that with the old musket a man might shoot at you all day, from a distance of one hundred and fifty yards or more, without even making you aware that he was doing it.

The point of infantry tactics in 1861 is that they depended on this extreme limitation of the infantry's effective field of fire. A column of assault, preparing to attack an enemy position, could be massed and brought forward with complete confidence that until it got to comparatively close range nothing very damaging

From Bruce Catton, *America Goes to War* (Wesleyan University Press, 1958), 14–27. Copyright © by Wesleyan University. Reprinted by permission of Wesleyan University Press.

could happen to it. From that moment on, everything was up to the determination and numbers of the attackers. Once they had begun to charge, the opposing line could not possibly get off more than one or two shots per man. If the assaulting column had a proper numerical advantage, plus enough discipline and leadership to keep it moving forward despite losses, it was very likely to succeed.

The assaulting column always went in with fixed bayonets, because any charge that was really driven home would wind up with hand-to-hand fighting. And if the assailants could get to close quarters with a fair advantage in numbers, either the actual use of the bayonet or the terrible threat of it would finish the business.

Artillery, properly massed, might change the picture. The smoothbore field pieces of the old days were indeed of limited range, but they very greatly out-ranged the infantry musket, and if a general had enough guns banked up at a proper spot in his defensive line he could count on breaking up a charging column, or at least on cutting it open and destroying its cohesion, before it got within infantry range. The antidote to this, on the part of the offense, was often the cavalry charge: massed cavalry squadrons could come in to sabre the gunners—which was what the British cavalrymen tried in the charge of the Light Brigade—and make the defensive line something that could be left to the foot soldier and his bayonet.

Up to 1861, all the intricate bits of infantry drill which the recruits had to learn, and all of the professional thinking of the generals who directed their movements, were based on weapons of limited range and tactics of rather personal assault.

Then, suddenly, the whole business went out of date, just because weapons had changed.

The rifled Springfield or Enfield was a very different arm from the old smoothbore. It looked about the same, it was still a muzzle-loader, and today it looks just as much like a museum piece. But it had ever so much more range and accuracy, and it completely changed the way in which men fought.

With the Civil War rifle a good marksman could hit and kill an opponent at somewhere between half a mile and a mile. The weapon's effective range, of course, was a good deal less than that, but an infantry line could still inflict destructive fire on its opponents at two or three times the distance that was possible with the old smoothbore. A decisive engagement could, and often did, take place with the opposing lines more than a quarter of a mile apart. At Antietam, according to an account written after the war, a veteran in the Army of the Potomac said that his unit and a Confederate unit got into action at close quarters; and this, he wrote reflectively, was one of the few battles in all the war in which he actually saw his enemies. Most of the time, "the enemy" was simply a line of snake-rail fence or a grove of trees or a raw length of heaped-up earth, from which came clouds of powder smoke and a storm of bullets. To see the other fellow as a recognizable human being was actually rather unusual—so much so that this veteran noted the fact, when it did happen, in his post-war reminiscences.

All of this meant that the old manner of making an attack was no longer good. To mass an assaulting column and drive it in with the men moving elbow to elbow was simply to invite destruction. It did work now and then, to be sure, if there were especial circumstances to aid the offensive, but under ordinary circumstances it did not work at all. Lee learned this lesson at Malvern Hill, and again at Gettysburg—bear in mind that in the climactic assault of July 3, the attackers outnumbered the defenders at the point of contact by nearly three to one—and Burnside learned it at Fredericksburg; and the lesson was painfully impressed on the mind of U. S. Grant at Cold Harbor.

Things changed for the artillery and cavalry, too. By the middle of the Civil War, artillery that was massed in a defensive line along with the infantry was subjected to killing fire by sharpshooters. Its old advantage was pared down sharply. Many striking things were indeed done by brave gunners who moved their pieces into the front line, and soldiers like John Pelham and Hubert Dilger showed an amazing ability to use their guns at close range; but, in the main, artillery suffered intensely from the infantry's increased range of fire, and the artillerist dreaded infantry fire a good deal more than he dreaded counter-battery fire.

Things were even worse for the cavalry. It became nothing short of suicide for cavalry to attack formed infantry, or artillery with infantry support, and it was rarely even tried. Cavalry became less and less a combat arm, in major battles, although of course it remained extremely important because of its use as a scouting arm and as a means of screening an army's movements.

It took the generals a long time to adjust themselves to the change which had occurred while the war was going on. Many things about Civil War battles which are otherwise inexplicable become clear enough when the sudden modernization in weapons is taken into account. The repeated, disastrous frontal assaults, the frightful toll of casualties, the fact that a hard battle often left the victor too mangled to make an effective pursuit, the final turn to trench warfare—all of these things simply reflect the fact that the weapons which the soldier used in the Civil War had completely changed the conditions under which he could use them. Many of the tragedies and apparent blunders in that war came simply because the generals were trained to tactics which were worse than useless. For all of its muzzle-loaders, its dashing cavalry actions, and its archaic artillery, the Civil War was nevertheless a modern war.

But it was more than just a matter of weapons. Much more important is the fact that the mental attitude of the two governments involved—which of course is to say the mental attitudes of the opposing peoples themselves—had that peculiar, costly, ruthless cast which is the great distinguishing mark of modern warfare.

Neither side in the Civil War was prepared to stop anywhere short of complete victory. In the old days, wars had been formalized; two nations fought until it seemed to one side or the other that it would not be worth while to fight any longer, and then some sort of accommodation would be reached—and, in the last analysis, nothing would have been changed very much. But in the Civil War it was all or nothing. The Southern States wanted absolute independence, and the Northern States wanted absolute union; once a little blood had been shed, there was no half-way point at which the two sides could get together and make a compromise. So the stakes were immeasurably increased, and this too affected the way in which men fought. If you are fighting a total war, the enemy's army is not your sole target. What you are really shooting at is his ability to carry on the fight, which means you will hit him wherever you can with any weapon that comes to your hand.

Probably it is this more than any other single thing that is the distinguishing mark of modern war: anything goes. The old "rules of civilized warfare" which loom so large in the textbooks simply disappear. Making war becomes a matter of absolutes; you cannot stop anywhere short of complete victory. Your enemy's army remains one of your targets, to be sure, but if you can destroy the social and economic mechanism which supports that army, and thereby can cause the army itself to collapse, you have gone a long way toward reaching your goal.

Consider for a moment the logical implications of this attitude. Ultimately, it is nothing less than the road to horror. It obliterates the moralities and the restraints which the race has so carefully built up through many generations. If it has any kind of rational base, the rationale is nothing much loftier than a belief that the end justifies the means. It can—and does—put an entire nation at the mercy of its most destructive instincts. What you do to your enemy comes, at last, to be limited not by any reluctance to inflict pain, misery, and death, and not by any feeling that there are limits to the things which a civilized people may do, but solely by your technical capacity to do harm. Without suffering any pangs of conscience, the group becomes prepared to do things which no single member of the group would for a moment contemplate.

By present-day standards, this process was not carried very far in our Civil War, but the genesis was there. The thing that makes modern war so appallingly frightful is not so much the hideous things which in our sublime innocence we call "weapons" as it is the development of an attitude which makes the unlimited use of those weapons something that is taken for granted. This attitude affected not only the way in which the Civil War itself was fought but the results that came out of the war.

This dawning notion of all-out war changed the way in which the Union soldier, for example, fought. He quickly came to see that anything which hurt the Confederacy's ability to carry on the war brought Northern victory just that much nearer. It "paid," for instance, to tear up railway lines in the South, to destroy iron foundries and textile mills and machine shops, to cut off the sources of raw material which enabled the Confederacy to maintain the fight. It very soon became apparent that it was necessary—using that word in its military context—to cripple the South's ability to feed its civilians and its armies. The farmer's property, in other words, was a military objective; to destroy barns and corn cribs, to drive off herds of cattle and hogs, to kill horses and mules—these acts became definite matters of military desirability. If a state or a section whose pork and corn and cotton enabled the Confederacy to fight were reduced to destitution, the Confederacy was that much weaker and hence that much nearer final destruction.

So we got, in that war, immense destructive raids which had much the same justification that the air raid has today. From sending a Sherman through Georgia, with the avowed objective of destroying that state's productive capacity, or from sending a Sheridan down the Shenandoah Valley under instructions to reduce that rich granary to a condition under which a crow flying across it would have to carry his own rations—from doing that to dispatching a flight of bombing planes to reduce a manufacturing city to smoking rubble is only a step. Modern war began to take shape here in America in the 1860's: and the agonizing uncertainty under which all of us have to live today is, I suppose, a part of our atonement.

In any case, fighting that kind of war leads you to objectives you had not had when the fighting began. This is exactly what happened in the Civil War. The Union soldier, invading the South, had as one of his objectives the destruction of Southern property. The most obvious, easily-removed piece of property in all of Dixie was the Negro slave. Even the Northerner who believed in slavery came to see that, and he came to see it quickly. The mere fact that he thought the black man ought to be a slave led him to understand that this slave, this bit of strangely animate property, was an asset to the government that was trying to destroy the Union. Other kinds of property were to be destroyed. This particular kind could not exactly be destroyed—after all, it was somehow human—but it could be taken away from its owners and thereby rendered useless.

It took the Northern armies only a very short time to learn this lesson. As soon as they had learned it, they began to take the institution of chattel slavery apart, chattel by chattel, not because they had anything against it but because they wanted to win the war.

Bear in mind, now, that most of this work was done by men who had no intention whatever, when they enlisted, of making war to end slavery. Slavery was killed by the act of war itself. It was the one human institution on all the earth which could not possibly be defended by force of arms, because that force, once called into play, was bound to destroy it. The Union armies which ended slavery were led by men like Grant and Sherman, who had profound sympathies with the South and who had never in their lives shown the slightest sympathies with the abolitionists. But they were also men who believed in the one great, fearful fact about modern war—that when you get into it, the guiding rule is that you have to win it. They made hard war, in other words, and hard war in the 1860's meant the end of human slavery.

So Grant and Sherman led armies down through Tennessee into the deep South, striking hard as they went. They struck slavery simply because it was in the way; striking it, they gave it its death blow.

It is interesting to note that along with all of this the Northern soldiers who destroyed slavery came, almost in spite of themselves, to see that the slaves whom they were liberating had claims on their own humanity. The Federal soldier who went South was moving into a hostile land, where he could count on having the enmity of everyone he encountered. Yet in all of this he quickly discovered that he had allies—black folk, who had only the vaguest understanding of what the war was all about but who did somehow see that these heavy-handed young men in blue uniforms were on their side . . . or, if not exactly on their side, at least against their masters, against the system which held them in subjection and numbered them with the ox and the mule as animate chattels. The Federal who wanted to know where Southern armies were and what they were doing had only to ask the nearest Negro; to the best of his knowledge—which usually was pretty limited—the Negro would faithfully tell him. The Federal who had got separated from his command and wanted to find his way back would go to the slave as an ally, and the slave would help him. The Northern boy who had managed to escape from a Southern prison and who, from the bottom of Georgia or South Carolina, sought to tramp the weary miles back to a Federal army camp, knew that the first Negro cabin he came to would be a haven of refuge, a place where he might get something to eat, concealment, a chance to rest, and guidance on his perilous way.

Seeing all of this, the Northern soldier at last came to see that these black folk who were somehow on his side were not just stray bits of property; they were people, people who would do him a good turn if they possibly could, friends on whom he could call in the deepest pit of danger or hardship.

When the Northern government began to fight the Civil War it explicitly disavowed any intention of making war on slavery. By Presidential pronouncement and by specific act of Congress it stated that it was fighting to restore the Union and to do no more than that; the "domestic institutions" of the individual states—meaning slavery—were not involved at all. Yet the mere act of fighting the war killed that program in little more than one year. By the beginning of 1863 the Northern government had proclaimed the emancipation of slaves. The war now was being fought for union *and* for freedom—a most substantial broadening of its base. And this change had come about, not especially because anyone had done a lot of hard, serious thinking about the evils of slavery, but primarily because the change had to come if the war was to be won. The war itself had enforced the change. It had done so because it was, in the strictest sense, a modern war—a war of unlimited objectives and of unpredictable results.

If you are looking for modern parallels they are not hard to find. Consider what happened in World War II—a war which, borrowing a phrase from the very heart of the Civil War itself, we announced would be fought until the enemy had made an unconditional surrender. We went into it for a variety of reasons, I suppose, just as the reasons for any war are very complex, but principally because the driving, expansive force of the Axis nations had become an intolerable threat to our national security. We fought the war and won it—and today we find ourselves compelled to worry about such things as the rights of colonial peoples, about the way in which the teeming millions of Asia and Africa may finally come to have a freer, happier life, about the whole system by which the intricately organized family of man is to order its social and economic relationships, about the true meaning of our ancient ideals of freedom and justice and democracy. We had not bargained for all of this when we began to make war. The war itself, and all that came with it, compelled us to pay heed to it.

So the Civil War, which began as a war to restore the Union, ended as a war to end human slavery. It was fought to a conclusion, the whole fabric of the Southern Confederacy dissolved in smoke, slavery ceased to exist—and it is at this point that we usually fold our hands piously, announce that a great forward step had been taken, and consign the Civil War to the musty ledgers of history. It *ended*—at Appomattox, with the surrender of the last armed Confederate, with the capture of Jefferson Davis, or where you please; after which we would go back and pick up the old threads where they had been interrupted and get on with the business of being Americans.

The only trouble with that point of view is that after a modern war you do not "go back to" anything at all. The mere act of war compels you to face the future, because war always destroys the base on which you have been resting. It is an act of violence which—whatever its dreadful cost, whatever its insane wastage of life and treasure—means that in one way or another you are hereafter going to do something different from what you have done in the past. The Civil War was a beginning, rather than end, simply because it knocked out of existence, forever, one of the things on which American society had been built.

# 8.

# The Army between Wars

Although rapid demobilization took place after the Civil War the army still had a number of important tasks to perform. The presence of French troops in Mexico to support the imported Emperor Maximilian was of vital concern to the American government, and until their removal and the collapse of the monarchy in 1867 the United States maintained a sizable force in Texas. Reconstruction in the South furnished another mission as the subdued states were placed under military control. Order also had to be restored on the Western frontier, where the Indians had exploited the absence of troops engaged in the domestic upheaval. Essentially, however, the army returned to its prewar status and organization in conformity with the mood of a nation satiated with military activity. Yet in the 1870's the nation stood on the threshold of what Walter Millis has called "the managerial revolution in war." Stimulated by the trend toward huge armies, technological advances in weaponry, and the harnessing of the industrial power of the nation to armed conflict, this revolution took form in a drastic realignment of the administrative organization of forces.

Administrative reform in the American services was to lag behind that of European nations. In the United States the professional soldier had never enjoyed the peacetime status that society accorded his European colleagues, and this form of discrimination was reflected in the reluctance to accept the demands of military leaders for the support and authority they deemed necessary to provide the nation with a satisfactory defense structure. Samuel P. Huntington depicts the hostile attitude toward the armed forces and the ways in which certain determined officers sought to overcome this antagonism and provide the nation with an adequate security system.

# The Dark and the Bright

## BY SAMUEL P. HUNTINGTON

THE PREVALENCE OF BUSINESS PACIFISM made the dominant feature of post-1865 civil-military relations the complete, unrelenting hostility of virtually all the American community toward virtually all things military. The military's source of sympathetic conservatism had gone with the South. The blanket hostility of American society isolated the armed forces politically, intellectually, socially, and even physically from the community which they served. Electionwise the military vote was negligible. Military personnel suffered from many disabilities and restrictions which made it difficult for them to vote when they wanted to, and a number of states denied the franchise to those serving in the Regular Army and Navy. Few economic groups had a direct interest in supporting the military. The Army had relatively little need for the products of industry; neither did the Navy before 1881. Even after the construction of an armored, steam navy began in the 1880's, only a small group of business concerns became regular military suppliers. The isolation of the officer corps was enhanced by the manner in which it was recruited. The mounting effects of the congressional system of appointment to West Point and Annapolis hastened the divorce of the military from the South. Both those entering the officer corps and those reaching its highest ranks in the years after the Civil War were a cross-section of middle-class America. As the officer corps became the mirror of the nation, it also became isolated from it. Representative of everyone, it was affiliated with no one.

Socially and physically the services tended to be separated from society. Until 1890 the small Army was strung out along the frontier fighting Indians. After its brief but inglorious role in the Spanish-American War, substantial segments were required overseas in Cuba, Hawaii, the Canal Zone, and the Philippines. Both these missions divorced it from a nation which was rapidly becoming urbanized. Before World War I, in the words of one officer, soldiers "lived apart in their tiny secluded garrisons much after the manner of military monks and they rarely came into contact with the mass of our citizens. . . ." Naval officers likewise had their life apart, spending a large portion of their careers at foreign stations. "The fact that naval officers are separated so much and so long from each other and from other men," one of them commented in 1905, "must tend to lack of unity of purpose, and therefore to lack of influence with the public." Other officers were conscious of their social isolation, highlighted by the absence of military leaders from important social functions, something unheard of in the early days of the country. The United States Army, one officer complained, was virtually

---

From Samuel P. Huntington, *The Soldier and the State: The Theory and Politics of Civil-Military Relations* (Cambridge, Mass., The Belknap Press of Harvard University Press, 1959), 226–237. Used by permission.

"an alien army" existing in "practically complete separation from the lives of the people from which it is drawn." The military were also divorced from the prevailing tides of intellectual opinion. West Point, for example, gradually lost contact with the rest of American education to which it had made such significant contributions, and went its own way.

Congressional military policy accurately reflected the philosophy of business pacifism. Army expenditures were steadily lowered from their Civil War peak of over a billion dollars to thirty-five million in 1871. They hovered about that figure for the next quarter century, varying from a high of forty-six million in 1873 to a low of twenty-nine million in 1880. The strength of the Army averaged about twenty-five thousand officers and men. Naval expenditures were normally about twenty million dollars a year until after 1890, and the strength of the Navy and Marine Corps was about eleven thousand officers and men. The shortage of funds made it impossible for the military to experiment and develop new techniques and weapons of warfare. Both services, for example, continued to use smoothbore cannon long after foreign powers had replaced them with rifled cannon. The Army seldom was able to bring together more than a battalion of troops at a time; the Navy lagged behind other powers in ship design and marine ordnance. Despite the advantages of steam propulsion, the Navy after the Civil War went back under canvas, and the desire for economy made it almost a crime for a naval officer to utilize the engines on his ship. By 1880 the United States Navy was an ill-sorted collection of obsolete vessels incapable of functioning together as a fleet. The United States Army was a far-flung Indian chasing frontier police, skilled at that function but quite unsuited and unprepared for any more serious operations. Business pacifism had reduced the military services to rusty decay.

The isolation, rejection, and reduction of the armed services after the Civil War have left historians to mark this as the low point of American military history. They speak of "The Army's Dark Ages" and the "Period of Naval Stagnation." These phrases are accurate, however, only with respect to the social influence and political power of the military. They describe only one side of the civil-military equation. The very isolation and rejection which reduced the size of the services and hampered technological advance made these same years the most fertile, creative, and formative in the history of the American armed forces. Sacrificing power and influence, withdrawing into its own hard shell, the officer corps was able and permitted to develop a distinctive military character. The American military profession, its institutions and its ideals, is fundamentally a product of these years. No other period has had such a decisive influence in shaping the course of American military professionalism and the nature of the American military mind. The practical work of professional reform, frustrated while the military were associated with the South in the prewar years, became possible once all ties with civilian society had been broken. Universal hostility permitted what limited support prevented. The foundation of this advance was the absence of any significant threat to national security. The isolation of the military was a prerequisite to professionalization, and peace was a prerequisite to isolation. Paradoxically, the United States could only create a professional military force when it was lacking any immediate use for such a force. The dark ages of military political influence were the golden ages of military professionalism.

The withdrawal of the military from civilian society at the end of the nineteenth century produced the high standards of professional excellence essential to national success in the struggles of the twentieth century. If the officer corps had not been rejected, if the Army and Navy had not been reduced to the bone in the 1870's and 1880's, the United States would have had a far more difficult time of it in 1917 and 1942. The military officer who, at the end of the period of isolation, rejoined civilian society in World War I and World War II, was a fundamentally different creature from his ancestor who had withdrawn in the 1860's. When he left, he was a citizen-soldier, an accepted member of the liberal family. When he returned, he was a stranger in his own household. His membership in the national family was no longer free, easy, and relaxed. The years of isolation had remade him into a professional with values and outlook basically at odds with those of the mass of his countrymen. They had interjected steel into his soul which was missing from that of the community. His return marked the beginning of the real problem of American civil-military relations: the tension between the conservative professional officer and the liberal society. While his professionalism thus created intense problems of psychological and political adjustment, it was nonetheless the salvation of his country externally. The ability of the professional officers and their impressive record in leading the forces and conducting the operations of the two world wars were acquired because of, not despite, their rejection at the end of the nineteenth century.

## The Creative Core: Sherman, Upton, Luce

The professionalization of the American military was preëminently the work of a small group of officers in the two generations following the Civil War. The process was begun by Generals William T. Sherman and Emory Upton and by Rear Admiral Stephen B. Luce. The immediate form which American professionalism took was largely of their making. Sherman is the best known of the three, but his popular fame rests almost exclusively upon his Civil War exploits. For almost fifteen years from 1869 to 1883, however, he was the Commanding General of the Army, heading that service for a longer period of time than any other officer except Winfield Scott. He was the leading military personality for an entire generation of soldiers and civilians from the Civil War until his death in 1891. Unlike Grant, whose record became besmirched and disputed by his entrance into politics, as Sherman predicted it would, Sherman retained his military popularity because he would have nothing to do with politics. As Commanding General, he sparked the professional reform movement. Particularly aware of the importance of military education, he vigorously defended the Artillery School at Fort Monroe which had been reëstablished in 1868. The father of the infantry and cavalry school at Fort Leavenworth, Sherman espoused a complete system of military education in which West Point would furnish both the preliminary liberal education required of any professional man and the indoctrination in military values and discipline required of the military man. Advanced schools would then give the officers the specialized knowledge of their profession and prepare them for the higher posts.

More important than the institutional developments in which Sherman had a hand was the tone which he set for the Army. His outlook and thought were thoroughly military, and the professional spirit which he manifested permeated throughout the ranks of the officer corps. Earthy, direct, limited, he was the epitome of all the virtues and vices of the professional officer. A man of simple truths rather than of brilliant concepts, he glorified in the unadorned title of "soldier" and wished to be nothing more or nothing less. Disclaiming other interests, causes, motives, his constantly reiterated motto was: "It is enough for the world to know that I am a soldier." Loyal to the Union, but opposed to abolition and an admirer of the South, he did his duty during the Civil War in the manner of the professional. His single-minded devotion to military ideals led him in the postwar period to object to the use of the Army as a police force—"That should be beneath a soldier's vocation"—and to assert that the Army must always be "organized and governed on true military principles" so as to preserve in peacetime the "habits and usages of war." Civilian control was essential to securing this objective. Democratic procedures were out of place in the Army which should be "an animated machine, an instrument in the hands of the Executive for enforcing the law, and maintaining the honor and dignity of the nation." Sherman was particularly adamant in stressing the divorce of the military from politics. Three of the six Commanding Generals before him had become presidential candidates. With him begins the tradition of political neutrality which, with the sole exception of Leonard Wood, was to be maintained by subsequent Commanding Generals and Chiefs of Staff until after World War II. "Let those who are trained to it keep the office," he wrote of the Presidency in 1874, "and keep the Army and Navy as free from politics as possible, for emergencies that may arise at any time." On party politics, "no Army officer should form or express an opinion." The essential components of the military ethic—hatred of war and avoidance of politics—were succinctly expressed in Sherman's two most quoted phrases: "War is hell" and "I will not accept if nominated and will not serve if elected."

The most influential younger officer in the work of Army reform was Emory Upton. Graduating from West Point in 1861, Upton distinguished himself in the Civil War, rising to become a major general of Volunteers. After the war, he prepared a new system of infantry tactics for the Army, served as Commandant of Cadets at West Point from 1870 to 1875, toured the world in 1876 and 1877 inspecting foreign military institutions, and became superintendent of theoretical instruction at Fort Monroe. His two great works, *The Armies of Europe and Asia* and *The Military Policy of the United States*, were studies of foreign and American military institutions, clearly expressing the fundamental postulates of the professional military ethic and presenting the case for a wide variety of reforms. Although unfinished at the time of his suicide in 1881 and not published until 1904, *The Military Policy of the United States* was a powerful plea for a strong regular military force. It was endorsed by Sherman and subsequently became the Bible of the Regular Army in its disputes with the militia advocates. Throughout the 1870's Upton was in the forefront of the movement for reform. His contemporary, Admiral Luce, was Commandant of Midshipmen at Annapolis between 1865 and 1869, a founder and president of the Naval Institute, and the driving force in the creation of the Naval War College. A tireless proselytizer for naval professionalism, Luce crusaded against politics and technicism, urging naval officers to focus upon their "real business—war." His views were an almost exact expression of the professional ethic, and he exerted a lasting influence throughout the naval officer corps. As Admiral Fiske once truthfully remarked of Luce, "the United States Navy owes more to him than to any other man who was ever connected with it, directly or indirectly." Matthew Maury, Benjamin Isherwood, John G. Walker, A. T. Mahan, Theodore Roosevelt, all made contributions. But none rivaled that of Luce. His achievement was as simple as it was great: "Luce taught the navy to think."

The work of Sherman, Upton, and Luce in the 1870's and 1880's was carried on at the turn of the century by a second generation of reformers: Bliss, Wagner, Young, Carter, and others in the Army; Mahan, Taylor, Fiske, Sims, and their associates in the Navy. Just as Scharnhorst, Gneisenau, Clausewitz, and Moltke set the tone and direction of the German military tradition, these two generations of reformers determined the nature of the professional strand of American militarism. This creative core was a distinctly military group in three ways. (1) They were largely cut off from contemporary American civilian influence. (2) They derived their ideas and inspiration from the American Military Enlightenment and from foreign military institutions. (3) They transcended service boundaries, transmitting ideas and encouragement back and forth between the two services and developing professional institutions applicable to both Army and Navy.

The American military profession differed from those of most other countries in that it was almost entirely the product of the officers themselves. In Europe professionalism was normally the outcome of social-political currents at work in society at large: the Prussian reformers, for instance, were only doing in the army what Stein and his associates were trying to do for the state as a whole. In the United States, however, military professionalism was strictly self-induced. The civilian contribution was virtually nil. Professionalism was the reaction of an inherently conservative group against a liberal society, rather than the product of a general conservative reform movement within society. The military profession was probably unique among significant social institutions in the United States in the extent to which it was created independent of American society. In these origins lie much of the reason for American hostility to the profession as an essentially alien body. Even within the liberal society, some intellectual and political movements existed upon which the officers might have drawn, such as the beginnings of the science of public administration and the civil service reform movement. But little contact existed between these developments and the military. The officers went their solitary way, accomplishing their work without the support and largely without the knowledge of civilian society. Within the narrow limits permitted them by the civilians, they could do more or less as they wished. The creation of a professional spirit, and even of professional institutions, did not require much in the way of money. So long as the Army was kept down to twenty-five thousand men, Congress let the West Pointers run it in accordance with their own ideas. So long as the number of officers was kept low, Congress approved changes in promotion and retirement plans. Sherman, for instance, carefully avoided Congress in setting up the School of Application at Leavenworth; he did not wish it to be "the subject of legislation." Subsequently, he repeatedly pointed out that the schools at both Leavenworth and Monroe required no additional funds beyond "ordinary garrison expenses." And Congress, content with this, shrugged its shoulders and let them be.*

The principal American source of the ideas of the professional reformers was the Military Enlightenment of the 1830's and 1840's. The intellectual grandfather of their work was Dennis Hart Mahan and its father H. Wager Halleck. Sherman, Halleck, and Upton had been students of Mahan; Sherman and Halleck had overlapped at the Academy. All the active figures in the war of reform were graduates of the military or naval academies. From this source flowed the native contributions to the professional reforms. Equally important, however, were what the reformers learned from foreign military institutions. Drawing little help and inspiration from non-military American sources, they turned to non-American military sources. The War of 1870–71 freed the American officers from their reverence for French institutions, and aroused their interest in those of Germany and other countries. Sherman was instrumental in sending Upton on his tour of the world in 1876 and 1877 to inspect foreign military establishments with particular reference to Germany. Upton's report revealed to American officers for the first time in any comprehensive manner the extent to which the United States lagged behind foreign developments. Upton urged the establishment of advanced military schools, the creation of a general staff corps, a comprehensive system of personnel reports by superiors on their subordinates, the compulsory retirement of officers, and the use of examinations as a prerequisite to promotion and to appointment to the staff corps. He was particularly impressed by the military institutions of India which in their clear-cut system of objective civilian control offered many lessons for the United States. "In no free country," he declared, "is the subordination of the military to the civil authority more clearly defined than in the politico-military despotism of India." A decade later Tasker Bliss also traveled through England, France, and Germany studying their military schools.

While the American reformers analyzed the experiences of many countries, Germany was their primary focus of attention. Upton himself expressed great admiration for German military institutions: every Prussian general in 1866, he pointed out, was a graduate of the Kriegsakademie, contrasting this with the backward state of military education in the American forces. Sherman thought the German system of military organization "simply perfect." Wagner echoed these sentiments, extolling the "excellence of the military system of Prussia." Clausewitz was translated into English in 1873, and American professional military journals devoted great

* Five of the six other major advanced schools established by the Army between 1865 and 1914 were first set up by departmental order without prior congressional authorization.

coverage to Prussian affairs.* American officers became fully conscious, indeed overly conscious, of their backwardness in comparison to Germany, and tended to accept German methods as models to be followed without question. By the end of the century American military thinking on organization, stimulated by Spenser Wilkinson's volume on *The Brain of an Army* and by the report of the American officer Theodore Schwan, fully accepted the German general staff theory. The German lessons were frequently misinterpreted and misapplied, but the desire to imitate German institutions was an important force in furthering American military professionalism. Naval interest in German militarism lagged somewhat behind that of the Army officers; attention still focused upon Britain as the classic seapower. Undoubtedly influenced by his father's Gallomania, Alfred Mahan was a warm admirer of Jomini. Nonetheless, by the twentieth century the younger generation of naval officers attempted to espouse German thought on military organization; German methods were introduced at the War College; and Mahan himself eventually was much impressed by Clausewitz.

While separated from civilian influence, the professionalizing core cut across service boundaries. The fundamental institutions and ideas of military professionalism were the same for Navy and Army; consequently, there was much room for mutual interaction and stimulation by the officers of the two services. Having imbibed the basic ideas of professionalism from Dennis Hart Mahan, Sherman, in turn, inspired Admiral Luce to devote his life to the reform of the Navy by demonstrating in practice the meaning of the professional approach to war. In January 1865, Luce, then a lieutenant commander, reported to Sherman at Savannah to plan the cooperation between Navy and Army for the drive northward into South Carolina. Listening to Sherman describe his plan of campaign, Luce had what Mahan was later to call an "illumination," and what was, in truth, a sudden insight into the meaning of military professionalism. In Luce's own words:

> After hearing General Sherman's clear exposition of the military situation the scales seem to have fallen from my eyes. "Here," I said to myself, "is a soldier who knows his business!" It dawned upon me that there were certain fundamental principles underlying military operations which it were well to look into; principles of general application whether the operations were conducted on land or at sea.

This vision enabled Luce to see the need for reorganizing the Navy Department, creating a professional military head for the Navy, and instituting a naval war college. Subsequently Upton became a close friend of Luce and encouraged him in these projects. While Upton was superintendent of theoretical instruction at the Artillery School of Fort Monroe, Virginia, he and Luce exchanged ideas on the means of improving American military education. It was at this time that Luce, citing the Artillery School as a model, first urged the Navy to offer a postgraduate course of instruction "in the Art of War." After securing the establishment of the Naval War College in 1884, Luce brought to it as instructors the son of Dennis Hart Mahan and also an Army lieutenant, Tasker H. Bliss, who at the turn of the century took the lead in organizing the Army War College. Thus, the line of influence ran from D. H. Mahan to Sherman, Halleck, and Upton; from Sherman to Upton and Luce; between Luce and Upton; from Luce to A. T. Mahan and Bliss; from A. T. Mahan to the younger naval officers; and from Bliss back to the Army.

* The March 1884 issue of the *Journal of the Military Service Institution*, for example, contained an article by von der Goltz, correspondence with the Militarische Gesellschaft, and a discussion of von Moltke. This was not atypical.

# 9.

# The Rise of the New Navy

In the years following the Civil War the navy declined to its lowest state since the beginning of the century. The rotting wooden-hulled ships had been rendered obsolete by the armored vessels of European fleets, and the smooth-bore cannon could not compete with the rifled guns carried by more recent craft. Fortunately, during this period the American navy was not called on to perform against any foe, and confusion over the function of the naval arm delayed steps to modernize the fleet. Then, in 1883, a series of factors combined to produce a congressional appropriation for several steel cruisers, which marked the beginning of an extensive building program.

The name most frequently associated with the modern American navy is that of Alfred Thayer Mahan. The son of a West Point professor, Mahan attended the Naval Academy and participated in the Civil War. Although his professional naval career was undistinguished, he became world famous with the publication in1890 of his book *The Influence of Sea Power Upon History, 1660–1783.* In this and subsequent writings Mahan expounded the thesis that national greatness was directly related to an ability to control the sea, which in turn derived from a set of fortuitous circumstances combined with particular traits of character. England, which rose to world prominence through sea power, was his favorite example, and he saw America following a similar path. Until his death in 1914, Mahan wrote on virtually every aspect of American military and foreign affairs, and his influence on defense policy was incalculable. In "The United States Looking Outward" Mahan provides his blueprint for the future, a future dependent on industrial production, trade, a merchant marine, and a powerful navy.

# The United States Looking Outward

BY ALFRED THAYER MAHAN

INDICATIONS ARE NOT WANTING of an approaching change in the thoughts and policy of Americans as to their relations with the world outside their own borders. For the past quarter of a century, the predominant idea, which has asserted itself successfully at the polls and shaped the course of the government, has been to preserve the home market for the home industries. The employer and the workman alike have been taught to look at the various economical measures proposed from this point of view, to regard with hostility any step favoring the intrusion of the foreign producer upon their own domain, and rather to demand increasingly rigorous measures of exclusion than to acquiesce in any loosening of the chain that binds the consumer to them. The inevitable consequence has followed, as in all cases when the mind or the eye is exclusively fixed in one direction, that the danger of loss or the prospect of advantage in another quarter has been overlooked; and although the abounding resources of the country have maintained the exports at a high figure, this flattering result has been due more to the superabundant bounty of Nature than to the demand of other nations for our protected manufactures.

For nearly the lifetime of a generation, therefore, American industries have been thus protected, until the practice has assumed the force of a tradition, and is clothed in the mail of conservatism. In their mutual relations, these industries resemble the activities of a modern ironclad that has heavy armor, but inferior engines and guns; mighty for defence, weak for offence. Within, the home market is secured; but outside, beyond the broad seas, there are the markets of the world, that can be entered and controlled only by a vigorous contest, to which the habit of trusting to protection by statute does not conduce.

At bottom, however, the temperament of the American people is essentially alien to such a sluggish attitude. Independently of all bias for or against protection, it is safe to predict that, when the opportunities for gain abroad are understood, the course of American enterprise will cleave a channel by which to reach them. Viewed broadly, it is a most welcome as well as significant fact that a prominent and influential advocate of protection, a leader of the party committed to its support, a keen reader of the signs of the times and of the drift of opinion, has identified himself with a line of policy which looks to nothing less than such modifications of the tariff as may expand the commerce of the United States to all quarters of the globe. Men of all parties can unite on the words of Mr. Blaine, as reported in a recent speech: "It is not an ambitious destiny for so great a country as ours to manufacture only what we can consume, or produce only what we can eat." In fact of this utterance of so shrewd and able a public man, even the extreme character of the recent tariff legislation seems but a sign of the coming

A. T. Mahan, "The United States Looking Outward," from *Atlantic Monthly*, LXVI (December 1890), 816–824.

change, and brings to mind that famous Continental System, of which our own is the analogue, to support which Napoleon added legion to legion and enterprise to enterprise, till the fabric of the Empire itself crashed beneath the weight.

The interesting and significant feature of this changing attitude is the turning of the eyes outward, instead of inward only, to seek the welfare of the country. To affirm the importance of distant markets, and the relation to them of our own immense powers of production, implies logically the recognition of the link that joins the products and the markets—that is, the carrying trade; the three together constituting that chain of maritime power to which Great Britain owes her wealth and greatness. Further, is it too much to say that, as two of these links, the shipping and the markets, are exterior to our own borders, the acknowledgment of them carries with it a view of the relations of the United States to the world radically distinct from the simple idea of self-sufficingness? We shall not follow far this line of thought before there will dawn the realization of America's unique position, facing the older worlds of the East and West, her shores washed by the oceans which touch the one or the other, but which are common to her alone.

Coincident with these signs of change in our own policy there is a restlessness in the world at large which is deeply significant, if not ominous. It is beside our purpose to dwell upon the internal state of Europe, whence, if disturbances arise, the effect upon us may be but partial and indirect. But the great seaboard powers there do not stand on guard against their continental rivals only; they cherish also aspirations for commercial extension, for colonies, and for influence in distant regions, which may bring, and, even under our present contracted policy, already have brought them into collision with ourselves. The incident of the Samoa Islands, trivial apparently, was nevertheless eminently suggestive of European ambitions. America then roused from sleep as to interests closely concerning her future. At this moment internal troubles are imminent in the Sandwich Islands, where it should be our fixed determination to allow no foreign influence to equal our own. All over the world German commercial and colonial push is coming into collision with other nations: witness the affair of the Caroline Islands with Spain; the partition of New Guinea with England; the yet more recent negotiation between these two powers concerning their share in Africa, viewed with deep distrust and jealousy by France; the Samoa affair; the conflict between German control and American interests in the islands of the western Pacific; and the alleged progress of German influence in Central and South America. It is noteworthy that, while these various contentions are sustained with the aggressive military spirit characteristic of the German Empire, they are credibly said to arise from the national temper more than from the deliberate policy of the government, which in this matter does not lead, but follows, the feeling of the people—a condition much more formidable.

There is no sound reason for believing that the world has passed into a period of assured peace outside the limits of Europe. Unsettled political conditions, such as exist in Haiti, Central America, and many of the Pacific islands, especially the Hawaiian group, when combined with great military or commercial importance as is the case with most of these positions, involve, now as always, dangerous germs of quarrel, against which it is prudent at least to be prepared. Undoubtedly, the general temper of nations is more averse from war than it was of old. If no less selfish and grasping than our predecessors, we feel more dislike to the discomforts and sufferings attendant upon a breach of peace; but to retain that highly valued repose and the undisturbed enjoyment of the returns of commerce, it is necessary to argue upon somewhat equal terms of strength with an adversary. It is the preparedness of the enemy, and not acquiescence in the existing state of things, that now holds back the armies of Europe.

On the other hand, neither the sanctions of international law nor the justice of a cause can be depended upon for a fair settlement of differences, when they come into conflict with a strong political necessity on the one side opposed to comparative weakness on the other. In our still-pending dispute over the seal-fishing of Bering Sea, whatever may be thought of the strength of our argument, in view of generally admitted principles of international law, it is beyond doubt that our contention is reasonable, just, and in the interest of the world at large. But in the attempt to enforce it we have come into collision not only with national susceptibilities as to the honor of the flag, which we ourselves very strongly share, but also with a state governed by a powerful necessity, and exceedingly strong where we are particularly weak and exposed. Not only has Great Britain a mighty navy and we a long defenceless seacoast, but it is a great commercial and political advantage to her that her larger colonies, and above all Canada, should feel that the power of the mother country is something which they need, and upon which they can count. The dispute is between the United States and Canada, not the United States and Great Britain; but it has been ably used by the latter to promote the solidarity of sympathy between herself and her colony. With the mother country alone an equitable arrangement, conducive to well-understood mutual interests, could be reached readily; but the purely local and peculiarly selfish wishes of Canadian fishermen dictate the policy of Great Britain, because Canada is the most important link uniting her to her colonies and maritime interests in the Pacific. In case of a European war, it is possible that the British navy will not be able to hold open the route through the Mediterranean to the East; but having a strong naval station at Halifax, and another at Esquimalt, on the Pacific, the two connected by the Canadian Pacific Railroad, England possesses an alternate line of communication far less exposed to maritime aggression than the former, or than the third route by the Cape of Good Hope, as well as two bases essential to the service of her commerce, or other naval operations, in the North Atlantic and the Pacific. Whatever arrangement of this question is finally reached, the fruit of Lord Salisbury's attitude scarcely can fail to be a strengthening of the sentiments of attachment to, and reliance upon, the mother country, not only in Canada, but in the other great colonies. These feelings of attachment and mutual dependence supply the living spirit, without which the nascent schemes for Imperial Federation are but dead mechanical contrivances; nor are they without influence upon such generally unsentimental considerations as those of buying and selling, and the course of trade.

This dispute, seemingly paltry yet really serious, sudden in its appearance and dependent for its issue upon other considerations than its own merits, may serve to convince us of many latent and yet unforeseen dangers to the peace of the western hemisphere, attendant upon the opening of a canal through the Central American Isthmus. In a general way, it is evident enough that this canal, by modifying the direction of trade routes, will induce a great increase of commercial activity and carrying trade throughout the Caribbean Sea; and that this now comparatively deserted nook of the ocean will become, like the Red Sea, a great thoroughfare of shipping, and will attract, as never before in our day, the interest and ambition of maritime nations. Every position in that sea will have enhanced commercial and military value, and the canal itself will become a strategic centre of the most vital importance. Like the Canadian Pacific Railroad, it will be a link between the two oceans; but, unlike it, the use, unless most carefully guarded by treaties, will belong wholly to the belligerent which controls the sea by its naval power. In case of war, the United States will unquestionably command the Canadian Railroad, despite the deterrent force of operations by the hostile navy upon our seaboard; but no less unquestionably will she be impotent, as against any of the great maritime powers, to control the Central American canal. Militarily speaking, and having reference to European complications only, the piercing of the Isthmus is nothing but a disaster to the United States, in the present state of her military and naval preparation. It is especially dangerous to the Pacific coast; but the increased exposure of one part of our seaboard reacts unfavorably upon the whole military situation.

Despite a certain great original superiority conferred by our geographical nearness and immense resources—due, in other words, to our natural advantages, and not to our intelligent preparations—the United States is woefully unready, not only in fact but in purpose, to assert in the Caribbean and Central America a weight of influence proportioned to the extent of her interests. We have not the navy, and, what is worse, we are not willing to have the navy, that will weigh seriously in any disputes with those nations whose interests will conflict there with our own. We have not, and we are not anxious to provide, the defence of the seaboard which will leave the navy free for its work at sea. We have not, but many other powers have, positions, either within or on the borders of the Caribbean, which not only possess great natural advantages for the control of that sea, but have received and are receiving that artificial strength of fortification and armament which will make them practically inexpugnable. On the contrary, we have not on the Gulf of Mexico even the beginning of a navy yard which could serve as the base of our operations. Let me not be misunderstood. I am not regretting that we have not the means to meet on terms of equality the great navies of the Old World. I recognize, what few at least say, that, despite its great surplus revenue, this country is poor in proportion to its length of seaboard and its exposed points. That which I deplore, and which is a sober, just, and reasonable cause of deep national concern, is that the nation neither has nor cares to have its sea frontier so defended, and its navy of such power, as shall suffice, with the advantages of our position, to weigh seriously when inevitable discussions arise—such as we have recently had about Samoa and Bering Sea, and which may at any moment come up about the Caribbean Sea or the canal. Is the United States, for instance, prepared to allow Germany to acquire the Dutch stronghold of Curacao, fronting the Atlantic outlet of both the proposed canals of Panama and Nicaragua? Is she prepared to acquiesce in any foreign power purchasing from Haiti a naval station on the Windward Passage, through which pass our steamer routes to the Isthmus? Would she acquiesce in a foreign protectorate over the Sandwich Islands, that great central station of the Pacific, equidistant from San Francisco, Samoa, and the Marquesas, and an important post on our lines of communication with both Australia and China? Or will it be maintained that any one of these questions, supposing it to arise, is so exclusively one-sided, the arguments of policy and right so exclusively with us, that the other party will at once yield his eager wish, and gracefully withdraw? Was it so at Samoa? Is it so as regards Bering Sea? The motto seen on so many ancient cannon, *Ultima ratio regum*, is not without its message to republics.

It is perfectly reasonable and legitimate, in estimating our needs of military preparation, to take into account the remoteness of the chief naval and military nations from our shores, and the consequent difficulty of maintaining operations at such a distance. It is equally proper, in framing our policy, to consider the jealousies of the European family of states, and their consequent unwillingness to incur the enmity of a people so strong as ourselves; their dread of our revenge in the future, as well as their inability to detach more than a certain part of their forces to our shores without losing much of their own weight in the councils of Europe. In truth, a careful determination of the force that Great Britain or France could probably spare for operations against our coasts, if the latter were suitably defended, without weakening their European position or unduly exposing their colonies and commerce, is the starting-point from which to calculate the strength of our own navy. If the latter be superior to the force that thus can be sent against it, and the coast be so defended as to leave the navy free to strike where it will, we can maintain our rights; not merely the rights which international law concedes, and which the moral sense of nations now supports, but also those equally real rights which, though not conferred by law, depend upon a clear preponderance of interest, upon obviously necessary policy, upon self-preservation, either total or partial. Were we so situated now in respect of military strength, we could secure our perfectly just claim as to the seal fisheries; not by seizing foreign ships on the open sea, but by the evident fact that, our cities being protected from maritime attack, our position and superior population lay open the Canadian Pacific, as well as the frontier of the Dominion, to do with as we please. Diplomats do not flourish such disagreeable truths in each other's faces; they look for a *modus vivendi*, and find it.

While, therefore, the advantages of our own position in the western hemisphere, and the disadvantages under which the operations of a European state would labor, are undeniable and just elements in the calculations of the statesman, it is folly to look upon them as sufficient alone for our security. Much more needs to be cast into the scale that it may incline in favor of our strength. They are mere defensive factors, and partial at that. Though distant, our shores can be reached; being defenceless, they can detain but a short time a force sent against them. With a probability of three months' peace in Europe, no maritime power would fear to support its demands by a number of ships with which it would be loath indeed to part for a year.

Yet, were our sea frontier as strong as it now is weak, passive self-defence, whether in trade or war, would be but a poor policy, so long as this world continues to be one of struggle and vicissitude. All around us now is strife; "the struggle of life, the race of life," are phrases so familiar that we do not feel their significance till we stop to think about them. Everywhere nation is arrayed against nation; our own no less than others. What is our protective system but an organized warfare? In carrying it on, it is true, we have only to use certain procedures which all states now concede to be a legal exercise of the national power, even though injurious to themselves. It is lawful, they say, to do what we will with our own. Are our people, however, so unaggressive that they are likely not to want their own way in matters where their interests turn on points of disputed right, or so little sensitive as to submit quietly to encroachment by others, in quarters where they long have considered their own influence should prevail?

Our self-imposed isolation in the matter of markets, and the decline of our shipping interest in the last thirty years, have coincided singularly with an actual remoteness of this continent from the life of the rest of the world. The writer has before him a map of the North and South Atlantic oceans, showing the direction of the principal trade routes and the proportion of tonnage passing over each; and it is curious to note what deserted regions, comparatively, are the Gulf of Mexico, the Caribbean Sea, and the adjoining countries and islands. A broad band stretches from our northern Atlantic coast to the English Channel; another as broad from the British Islands to the East, through the Mediterranean and Red Sea, overflowing the borders of the latter in order to express the volume of trade. Around either cape—Good Hope and Horn—pass strips of about one-fourth this width, joining near the equator, midway between Africa and South America. From the West Indies issues a thread, indicating the present commerce of Great Britain with a region which once, in the Napoleonic wars, embraced one-fourth of the whole trade of the Empire. The significance is unmistakable: Europe has now little mercantile interest in the Caribbean Sea.

When the Isthmus is pierced, this isolation will pass away, and with it the indifference of foreign nations. From wheresoever they come and whithersoever they afterward go, all ships that use the canal will pass through the Caribbean. Whatever the effect produced upon the prosperity of the adjacent continent and islands by the thousand wants attendant upon maritime activity, around such a focus of trade will centre large commercial and political interests. To protect and develop its own, each nation will seek points of support and means of influence in a quarter where the United States always has been jealously sensitive to the intrusion of European powers. The precise value of the Monroe doctrine is understood very loosely by most Americans, but the effect of the familiar phrase has been to develop a national sensitiveness, which is a more frequent cause of war than material interests; and over disputes caused by such feelings there will preside none of the calming influence due to the moral authority of international law, with its recognized principles, for the points in dispute will be of policy, of interest, not of conceded right. Already France and Great Britain are giving to ports held by them a degree of artificial strength uncalled for by their present importance. They look to the near future. Among the islands and on the mainland there are many positions of great importance, held now by weak or unstable states. Is the United States willing to see them sold to a powerful rival? But what right will she invoke against the transfer? She can allege but one—that of her reasonable policy supported by her might.

Whether they will or no, Americans must now begin to look outward. The growing production of the country demands it. An increasing volume of public sentiment demands it. The position of the United States, between the two Old Worlds and the two great oceans, makes the same claim, which will soon be strengthened by the creation of the new link joining the Atlantic and Pacific. The tendency will be maintained and increased by the growth of the European colonies in the Pacific, by the advancing civilization of Japan, and by the rapid peopling of our Pacific States with men who have all the aggressive spirit of the advanced line of national progress. Nowhere does a vigorous foreign policy find more favor than among the people west of the Rocky Mountains.

It has been said that, in our present state of unpreparedness, a trans-isthmian canal will be a military disaster to the United States, and especially to the Pacific coast. When the canal is finished, the Atlantic seaboard will be neither more nor less exposed than it now is; it will merely share with the country at large the increased danger of foreign complications with inadequate means to meet them. The danger of the Pacific coast will be greater by so much as the way between it and Europe is shortened through a passage which the stronger maritime power can control. The danger will lie not merely in the greater facility for despatching a hostile squadron from Europe, but also in the fact that a more powerful fleet than formerly can be maintained on that coast by a European power, because it can be called home so much more promptly in case of need. The greatest weakness of the Pacific ports, however, if wisely met by our government, will go far to insure our naval superiority there. The two chief centres, San Francisco and Puget Sound, owing to the width and the great depth of the entrances, cannot be effectively protected by torpedoes; and consequently, as fleets always pass batteries through an unobstructed channel, they cannot obtain perfect security by means of fortifications only. Valuable as such works will be to them, they must be further garrisoned by coast-defence ships, whose part in repelling an enemy will be co-ordinated with that of the batteries. The sphere of action of such ships should not be permitted to extend far beyond the port to which they are allotted, and of whose defence they form an essential part; but within that sweep they will always be a powerful reinforcement to the sea-going navy, when the strategic conditions of a war cause hostilities to centre around their port. By sacrificing power to go long distances, the coast-defence ship gains proportionate weight of armor and guns; that is, of defensive and offensive strength. It therefore adds an element of unique value to the fleet with which it for a time acts. No foreign states, except Great Britain, have ports so near our Pacific coast as to bring it within the radius of action of their coast-defence ships; and it is very doubtful whether even Great Britain will put such ships at Vancouver Island, the chief value of which will be lost to her when the Canadian Pacific is severed—a blow always in the power of this country. It is upon our Atlantic seaboard that the mistress of Halifax, of Bermuda, and of Jamaica will now defend Vancouver and the Canadian Pacific. In the present state of our seaboard defence she can do so absolutely. What is all Canada compared with our exposed great cities? Even were the coast fortified, she still could do so, if our navy be no stronger than is designed as yet. What harm can we do Canada proportionate to the injury we should suffer by the interruption of our coasting trade, and by a blockade of Boston, New York, the Delaware, and the Chesapeake? Such a blockade Great Britain certainly could make technically efficient, under the somewhat loose definitions of international law. Neutrals would accept it as such.

The military needs of the Pacific States, as well as their supreme importance to the whole country, are yet a matter of the future, but of a future so near that provision should begin immediately. To weigh their importance, consider what influence in the Pacific would be attributed to a nation comprising only the States of Washington, Oregon, and California, when filled with such men as now people them and still are pouring in, and which controlled such maritime centres as San Francisco, Puget Sound, and the Columbia River. Can it be counted less because they are bound by the ties of blood and close political union to the great communities of the East? But such influence, to work without jar and friction, requires underlying military readiness, like the proverbial iron hand under the velvet glove. To provide this, three things are needful: First, protection of the chief harbors, by fortifications and coast-defence ships, which gives defensive strength, provides security to the community within, and supplies the bases necessary to all military operations. Secondly, naval force, the arm of offensive power, which alone enables a country to extend its influence outward. Thirdly, it should be an inviolable resolution of our national policy, that no foreign state should henceforth acquire a coaling position within three thousand miles of San Francisco—a distance which includes the Hawaiian and Galapagos islands and the coast of Central America. For fuel is the life of modern naval war; it is the food of the ship; without it the modern monsters of the deep die of inanition. Around it, therefore, cluster some of the most important considerations of naval strategy. In the Caribbean and in the Atlantic we are confronted with many a foreign coal depot, bidding us stand to our arms, even as Carthage bade Rome; but let us not acquiesce in an addition to our dangers, a further diversion of our strength, by being forestalled in the North Pacific.

In conclusion, while Great Britain is undoubtedly the most formidable of our possible enemies, both by her great navy and by the strong positions she holds near our coasts, it must be added that a cordial understanding with that country is one of the first of our external interests. Both nations doubtless, and properly, seek their own advantage; but both, also, are controlled by a sense of law and justice, drawn from the same sources, and deep-rooted in their instincts. Whatever temporary aberration may occur, a return to mutual standards of right will certainly follow. Formal alliance between the two is out of the question, but a cordial recognition of the similarity of character and ideas will give birth to sympathy, which in turn will facilitate a co-operation beneficial to both; for if sentimentality is weak, sentiment is strong.

10.

# The War with Spain

Perhaps the Spanish-American War would not have occurred if it had not been for the modern American Navy, because the movement of troops to Cuba and Puerto Rico would have been hazardous if not impossible in the face of the Spanish ironclads. Moreover, it is unlikely that Dewey would have engaged the Spanish fleet at Manila Bay if he had possessed only wooden ships. In any event, the new vessels provided the means of coercing Spain into granting Cuban independence, and it was both a product of and a catalyst for the brash expansionist spirit that infected segments of the nation as the nineteenth century neared its end. The overwhelming victories at Manila Bay and Santiago brought praise for the modern American Navy and appeared to vindicate its existence. These victories also alerted the other major powers to the existence of a dangerous rival, whose voice promised to be heard more often in world affairs.

Planning for the war with Spain was haphazard and faulty. Fortunately, the United States engaged an inept enemy, whose armed forces operated at great distances from their home base and suffered from governmental neglect. The American war effort, while not equally bad, reflected the attitude toward the army in the previous decades. Frederic Louis Huidekoper, in the following selection, enumerates the "lessons" of the war in a manner reminiscent of General Upton.

# Lessons of the Spanish-American War

## BY FREDERIC LOUIS HUIDEKOPER

HOW SHORT AND DECISIVE A MODERN WAR can be is demonstrated by this struggle which lasted only 109 days from the official declaration of hostilities to the signing of a peace protocol. In certain aspects it was well-nigh unique, and the commander of the American land forces had abundant reason to declare that:

> It is gratifying to record that during the war not a single defeat has been met, and not a prisoner, color, gun or rifle has been captured by the enemy. In this respect the war has been most remarkable, and, perhaps, unparalleled. . . .
>
> While but a small portion of the available forces of the United States—approximately 52,000 men—has been on foreign soil and engaged in fighting a foreign foe, those that have been in the presence of the enemy have fairly demonstrated the character and fortitude of the military forces of the United States.

That a mighty empire in both hemispheres should have been wrested from Spain after four centuries of domination with a loss so infinitesimal on the part of the victorious nation is almost incredible. This was mainly due to the employment by the United States of such a large percentage of Regular troops, to the failure of the Spanish commander at Santiago to concentrate his army, and to the sudden collapse of the war in consequence of the destruction of the Spanish fleets. Credit should also be given to General Garcia and the Cubans who rendered important services.

The principal resistance to our land forces was encountered in Cuba, where the success was achieved by the flower of the American Regular Army. That such a mere handful of trained soldiers was able within twenty-four days and during the worst season of the year to win three actions, to force Admiral Cervera out of the harbour and into certain destruction, to capture Santiago and some 23,000 Spanish troops—a number considerably in excess of their own—and thus in so short a time to end the war, is little less than miraculous. None but an army of highly trained regulars could have accomplished such a result, and the credit belongs rightfully and almost exclusively to them.

History is replete with inaccuracies and omissions, and the campaign of Santiago affords another instance of this fact. Although the rôle played by General Garcia and the Cuban forces after the landing of the American army scarcely redounded to their credit, the fact none the less remains that, prior to General Shafter's arrival, they rendered invaluable assistance by virtually isolating the Spanish in the vicinity of Santiago from those in the rest of the province. With the suggestions made by General Miles on June 2 Garcia complied to such an extent that, out of 36,582 Spanish troops in the province of Santiago, General Linares was reduced to 12,096 soldiers and 1,000 sailors with which to oppose Shafter. That he failed to utilize them as a good general would have done was extremely lucky for the Americans. Thus far historians, almost without exception, have neglected to give to

---

From Frederic Louis Huidekoper, *The Military Unpreparedness of the United States* (New York, The Macmillan Company, 1916), 202–219.

Garcia and his Cubans the proper recognition due for the important services which they rendered in the initial stages of the campaign in Cuba.

The Spanish-American War is notable, not only for the greater percentage of regulars in proportion to the number of troops actually used in active operations than in most of our wars, but for the large number of Regular Army officers employed in the volunteers, no less than 387 serving in the various grades of this force. With the exception of Miles, Wilson and Merritt, none of the general officers had commanded army corps or independent armies during the War of the Rebellion. The first two of these generals were sent to Porto Rico, the last to Manila. General Shafter, while not a brilliant soldier, was by no means devoid of ability—an incompetent commander could not have concentrated 83 per cent of his available forces for the decisive battles as he did on July 1—but he was physically unfitted for campaigning in the tropics and therefore incapable of giving that personal supervision to the operations of his troops which is indispensable to efficient control.

Congress, having neglected to carry out the recommendations of the Endicott Board, found itself in the usual dilemma and sought by an appropriation of $50,000,000 to make reparation, but neither money nor the most strenuous efforts could place our fortifications in an effective state during the short time available. Yet, owing to an absurd construction of the law, the money appropriated could be used for very little else, and preparations indispensable to the efficiency of the several supply departments were much delayed. Once the legal difficulty was overcome and expenditures by the various departments began, one of the most glaring evils of our supply system was carried to its utmost limit, and the duplication of purchases resulted in an enormous surplus of supplies for which there existed no demand and which were disposed of for a trifle by condemnation shortly after the close of the war.

Since we have no general supply department for the Army, and as the supplies of the Engineer, Ordnance, Medical and Signal corps are bought by each one independently of the others and of the Quartermaster Department, and, moreover, as many of the supplies are of the same kind in all the departments, this sort of extravagance will no doubt occur again should the United States be suddenly plunged into war. The consolidation of the Quartermaster, Commissary and Pay departments has to some extent mitigated the evil, but it will not be wholly eradicated until all manufactured articles and raw materials in common use in the Army are provided by a general supply department, fully conversant with the needs of all the branches of the service and how far they can be met by the stores on hand. Until such a change in administration is made, waste and extravagance will inevitably continue to disgrace our absurdly administered Army. . . .

In the Spanish-American War the same piecemeal and hand-to-mouth policy which has marked the military legislation from the beginning of our national career was again apparent. No expansive organization had been instituted in the long years of peace following the close of the War of the Rebellion and, as usual, the increase of the Regular Army occurred after the outbreak of war, with the result that the maximum authorized strength was not attained even at the cessation of hostilities. As this increase came after the creation of the Volunteer Army, the recruits naturally preferred service with the volunteers, just as they have always done and always will do. Moreover, as the governors of the States were empowered to appoint the company and regimental officers, many commissions were obtained in the volunteers by men who were in no respect qualified to lead troops, and the authorities were well-nigh swamped by the applications which poured in upon them. The lack of adequate training on the part of the volunteers rendered them of comparatively small value from the standpoint of a military asset, doubly so since Congress expressly forbade that more than one regular officer should be appointed in any one volunteer regiment. Even so, nearly one-fifth of the regular officers were given volunteer commissions, in spite of the fact that the Regular Army had been more than doubled in size and that many of these officers were needed for recruiting service.

The dearth of trained officers, arising out of the neglect of Congress to make provision beforehand for such an emergency, proved a tremendous handicap. At the battle of Waterloo Marshal Ney appealed to Napoleon for more infantry, which caused the Emperor to retort to Colonel Heymès, who brought the request: "Where does he want me to get them from? Does he expect me to make them?" Congress evidently laboured under the delusion that a sufficiency of trained officers would spring up overnight, but the military authorities knew differently and therefore:

> The War Department requested of Congress authority to issue commissions for active service to retired army officers. This authority Congress denied. From the regular army was taken the maximum number of officers consistent with its efficiency—an efficiency that is the rock upon which this country must build its hope for effective operations during the first few months of any war in which it may be engaged.

As was to be expected, the dearth of trained officers forced the employment of volunteer officers with little or no experience, and the confusion and mismanagement during the course of this war were directly attributable to this cause.

Once again Congress neglected to take full advantage of the national enthusiasm which invariably accompanies the outbreak of hostilities. Instead of requiring all enlistments to be "for the war," it indulged its customary habit of making them too short and limited them to two years. Unless all signs fail, there were unmistakable indications during the summer that, had the war been prolonged until the following year, great difficulty would have been experienced in obtaining the necessary recruits. . . .

To cap the climax Congress expressly stipulated that all volunteers "shall be discharged from the service of the United States when the purposes for which they were called into service shall have been accomplished, or on the conclusion of hostilities." This was tantamount to leaving the question to the adjudication of the volunteers, and scarcely had the Peace Protocol been signed on August 12 than they proceeded to avail themselves of what they deemed to be their privilege. On the eighteenth of that month an order was issued by the War Department for the mustering out of 100,000 volunteers but, as this embraced less than half of that force, any number of officers and men began to clamour for their discharge, using every possible influence to procure it, quite regardless of the fact that the Government was in nowise obligated to grant it until the Treaty of Peace had been definitely signed and ratified. In many cases their demands were complied with in order to reduce military expenditures but, when the regulars were withdrawn from Cuba and Porto Rico, the Government found itself greatly embarrassed by the demands of the volunteers who had to be sent to replace them in order to hold those islands. By the time the Treaty of Peace was signed, the volunteers had in turn been superseded by other regulars, had been brought home and mustered out, so that the terms of the enlistment contracts had been complied with. The exigencies in the Philippines rendered such a course impossible. Allusion has already been made to the declaration of independence by the Filipinos, who were not permitted to participate in the operations culminating in the capture of Manila. Having formed a government, they demanded recognition of it, but this was refused, although no steps were taken to prevent their acquiring control over substantially the rest of the archipelago, partly owing to the paucity of our troops and partly owing to the policy laid down by our Government. This attitude, coupled with a fear that the United States was about to seize the islands, engendered such distrust and enmity that in October the Filipinos began to concentrate their forces, to the number of some 40,000, around Manila and virtually shut up the American army under General Otis in the city, where, apart from guarding 13,000 Spanish prisoners, it was compelled to maintain order among the 300,000 hostile inhabitants. By January, 1899, Otis received a paltry reenforcement of 6,500 men, thus bringing his command up to 20,481, the regulars armed with the Krag-Jörgensen rifle being only 5,372 strong, while the other 15,400 were State volunteers supplied with the obsolete Springfield. On February 4, 1899, began the Philippine insurrection, which was not finally quelled until more than three years later. Congress had not only committed an egregious blunder in the wording of the law of April 22, 1898, instituting the Volunteer Army, but it neglected until March 2, 1899, to create other forces to replace it. In consequence of this failure, not until June 14, 1899—ten months after the necessity had ceased for the use of volunteers called out under the act of 1898—did a sufficiency of regulars reach the Philippines to permit Otis to send home any of his volunteer troops, and not until October 11 did the first of the newly-created force join him. As a matter of fact, the last of these regiments—the 48th Volunteer Infantry—did not arrive at Manila until January 25, 1900. Owing to the lack of a Regular Army large enough to respond to the increased demands in the two hemispheres, the Government was confronted by two alternatives, *namely:* either to abandon the Philippines entirely or to endeavour to hold them by retaining in service such troops as were available. Having determined upon the latter course, it was compelled to break its contract and to hold the men, who had volunteered for the war with Spain only, through a succession of active operations lasting for six months after the period when their term of enlistment had legally expired. A fresh instance was thus afforded of the folly of short enlistments to which the United States has persistently adhered since the beginning of the Revolutionary War.

The causes which brought about these conditions were twofold: first, as we have seen, a conditional enlistment contract—*one of the worst blunders from a military standpoint which can be committed*—and, second, the failure to provide for adequate trained reserves—a defect that has prolonged every one of our wars. Illustrative of the latter are two facts worthy of careful attention. In the haste to get the regular regiments to the front at the outbreak of war, sufficient time was not given to recruit them up to war strength and, moreover, the new material was so raw and untrained that many regimental commanders preferred to leave the new recruits behind. As a result, the returns show that the infantry regiments participating in the attack on San Juan on July first averaged only 556 enlisted men each, whereas their strength should have been 1,272. When it is recollected that the Spanish troops in the province of Santiago numbered over 36,000, the hazardous nature of such a course needs no other commentary. Furthermore, aside from the killed and wounded, the loss by disease in the regulars was such that many of the regiments were reduced to about 300 enlisted men. It thus became necessary to recruit them up to 1,500 and to equip each one anew. "No consideration was given to training, for there was no time for this, only to send the raw material forward as soon as possible, thanking God for the character of our foe." What such a harum-scarum proceeding would have entailed had we been pitted against a great military Power the reader can judge for himself.

The Spanish-American War demonstrated, perhaps as much as in any other respect, the necessity for a General Staff. Had the first plan contemplating an attack upon Havana—which was favoured by the Administration—been carried out, the result could not have failed to end in overwhelming disaster. As a matter of fact, the Spanish fondly hoped that such an attempt would be made. The plan actually executed—which originated with General Miles—was sound in that it was based upon the well-known principle of strategy prescribing that the enemy's force should be broken asunder and the weaker part first overpowered. Cuba, being nearly 800 miles long and from 30 to 120 miles in width, lent itself in an unusually favourable manner to just such an operation. Cervera's entrance into the harbour of Santiago definitely fixed the exact point at which the first stroke should be made, and the fact that it accomplished the desired result is ample proof that in overseas expeditions in time of war the combined efforts of naval and land forces can alone insure decisive success. The method by which Shafter's army eventually achieved victory was haphazard in the extreme, and we have had occasion to glean . . . how readily the lack of proper organization, thoroughly prepared and tested in time of peace, and the absence of a prearranged and comprehensive plan for such an expedition might have ended in irretrievable disaster had we been opposed by an enterprising and powerful foe. Such organization and plans as would obviate the chaos and blunders that characterized Shafter's expedition are the function of a General Staff, which this great country did not possess in 1898.

As has been seen, the Spanish troops in Cuba numbered 198,820 and those in the Province of Santiago 36,582, while Havana was one of the most strongly fortified places in the western hemisphere. Under ordinary circumstances, the chances were not one in a hundred that an army of 17,000, even though its quality were superb, could bring to a successful conclusion all the fighting that might reasonably be expected before the Spanish—who outnumbered it nearly twelve to one—were overcome. Indeed, that so paltry a force was sent on such a mission seems like "flying in the face of Providence." Thanks to the inefficiency of the Spanish commanders in Cuba, the only re-enforcement which reached Santiago was a meagre column of 3,660 under Escario from Manzanillo, and at the crucial moment of the campaign the heights which formed the key to the city were held by a few thousand men upon whom fell the brunt of the American attacks. The apathy and incapacity of Linares, let alone Blanco, were simply incredible. Although the Cubans had isolated the 12,096 troops in the immediate vicinity of Santiago from those in the rest of the province, Garcia's force about the city numbered only some 5,000 and could easily have been brushed aside. The destination of Shafter's expedition was published all over the world for weeks before it reached Siboney and, irrespective of the distances and difficulties of transport, an abler commander would have had ample time to concentrate the bulk of his forces within striking distance. Had Linares attacked with half his troops during the American disembarkation, Shafter would have been driven into the sea. Had he assembled 18,000 on the heights of Santiago at any time within nine days after the Americans landed, the outcome—in the light of the difficulty experienced by our army against only part of that number—can readily be imagined. Napoleon declared that "*In war men are nothing—it is a man who is everything*." Luckily for us, the Spanish did not possess a man in Cuba, but we must carefully refrain from blinding ourselves to the fact that rare indeed in history are the instances in which enormous superiority in numbers have availed a nation so little as was the case in Cuba in 1898. We have already seen that yellow fever made its appearance on July 4; by August first the usefulness of the American army as a fighting force had been greatly impaired by the ravages of that fearful disease, and there was, consequently, grave apprehension among our generals lest Toral would not capitulate promptly. Had the negotiations been prolonged until the Spanish commander learned of the conditions in our army, he would unquestionably have refused to surrender and thereby forced an assault which, it was realized, would necessarily have cost more men than General Shafter dared to lose. Under such circumstances, there is every indication that the Americans would have been compelled to relinquish their position and to abandon Cuba, for the time being at least.

Even after Toral did capitulate, there were more than 163,000 Spanish troops in Cuba, and Havana still defied capture. Notwithstanding the destruction of Cervera's fleet cut off all possibility of re-enforcements, a competent general would have experienced little difficulty in keeping the Americans at bay for months, but difficulties which to a really able commander would have been comparative trifles proved insurmountable to such incapables as Blanco and Linares. And back of them was the weakness, internally as well as externally, of Spain, whose resistance collapsed like a house of cards. Her feebleness is the more incredible if it be compared with another nation, the situation of which is in many respects analogous to that of Spain in 1898. What would have happened had the United States found itself opposed in Cuba by generals and troops in anywise like those of Germany at the present time, the reader can deduce for himself.

One of the most important lessons to be derived from the Spanish-American War is the necessity of such a system as will minimize the length of stay in permanent or semi-permanent camps and will get the troops to the front in the shortest possible space of time. This was fully demonstrated by the fact that out of 223,235 volunteers enlisted during the war, only 289 were killed or died of wounds received in action, whereas no less than 3,848 died of disease; and it must be distinctly remembered that the majority of these volunteers never got into action at all. On April 26 General Miles suggested to the Secretary of War that it was:

of the highest importance that the troops called into service by the President's proclamation be thoroughly equipped, organized, and disciplined for field service. In order that this may be done with the least delay, they ought to be in camp approximately sixty days in their States, as so many of the States have made no provision for their State militia, and not one is fully equipped for field service. After being assembled, organized, and sworn into service of the United States, they will require uniforms, tentage, complete camp equipage, arms, and ammunition, and a full supply of stationery, including blank books and reports for the Quartermaster's, Commissary, Medical, and Ordnance Departments. They will also require complete equipment of ordnance, quartermaster's, commissary, and medical supplies, hospital appliances, transportation, including ambulances, stretchers, etc. The officers and non-commissioned officers will have to be appointed and properly instructed in their duties and responsibilities, and have some instruction in tactical exercises, guard duties, etc., all of which is of the highest importance to the efficiency and health of the command. While this is being done, the general officers and staff officers can be appointed and properly instructed, large camps of instruction can be judiciously selected, ground rented, and stores collected. At the end of sixty days the regiments, batteries, and troops can be brigaded and formed into divisions and corps, and proper commanding generals assigned, and this great force may be properly equipped, molded, and organized into an effective army with the least possible delay.

However, as the Commission appointed by President McKinley to investigate the conduct of the War Department in the war with Spain found, "the War Department had not the officers to send to each State to organize, muster, feed, and equip them, nor had it officers of suffiicent rank to command, drill, and discipline the troops while in State camps."

This insufficiency of officers—for which Congress was responsible—resulted, *faute de mieux*, in the militia and volunteers being concentrated in various camps to which allusion has already been made. During seven and a half months the Quartermaster Department was called upon to transport by rail no less than "17,863 officers and 435,569 enlisted men," a good deal of a tax considering that this particular:

department consisted of fifty-seven officers. It was provided with all necessary clothing, camp and garrison equipage, for the Regular Army of 25,000 men; it was prepared to equip and move an army at least double that size under peace conditions, but was suddenly called upon to furnish within a short period all that was required to fit out an army of 275,000 men for probable operations in an enemy's country.

Moreover, there existed certain statutes—the legality of which could not be questioned—prohibiting it from making any contract "in excess of the appropriations made by Congress for that fiscal year," and that sovereign body saw fit to defer until the beginning of hostilities any appropriation which would permit the approaching situation to be met with any degree of preparedness. Small wonder that the commission reported "that the declaration of war threw upon the Quartermaster's Department an amount of labor and responsibility for which it was neither physically nor financially prepared."

Substantially the same criticism was applied to the Subsistence and Medical departments, the capacities of which were stretched beyond all reason. In the case of the latter, the shortsightedness of Congress resulted in:

the almost absolute lack of any supplies in store when the war broke out. Medicines could be purchased in any quantity and without delay, as could bedding and certain articles of hospital furniture, but other articles of adopted pattern, as surgical instruments or cots of special design, could not. Time was lost in having manufactured standard chests of various kinds to contain drugs, stores, dressings, furniture, etc., and the making of these articles never kept up with the demand for them.

It is therefore not surprising that the Commission found "that at the outbreak of the War the

Medical Department was, in men and materials, altogether unprepared to meet the necessities of the army called out," and "that the shortcomings in administration and operation may justly be attributed, in large measure, to the hurry and confusion incident to the assembling of an army of untrained officers and men, ten times larger than before, for which no preparations in advance had been or could be made because of existing rules and regulations." In the light of what occurred there was abundant justification for the recommendation of the Commission that this department needed "a larger force of commissioned medical officers" and, even more so:

a year's supply for an army of at least four times the actual strength of all such medicines, hospital furniture, and stores as are not materially damaged by keeping, to be held constantly on hand in the medical supply depots.

Whatever difficulties were experienced by the Regular troops in the field in consequence of the shortcomings and the deficiency in the matter of supply on the part of these administrative departments, they were obviously felt to a much greater degree by the volunteers, who had none of the training which would have rendered them sufficiently resourceful to overcome some of these disadvantages. As the largest number of troops in any command throughout the war was concentrated in certain camps—notably in Camp Thomas at Chickamauga, which was not suitable to "accommodate more than 20,000 troops at once for any great length of time" but where 7,283 regulars and 69,459 volunteers were nevertheless sent, and in Camp Alger, which "was very undesirable" but where 31,195 troops were lodged—these conditions ran rampant to a degree that gave rise to a distinctly justifiable scandal. Congress was apparently oblivious to the fact that, although it had set the example by permitting the outbreak of war to find "the country unprepared with any large stock of arms, ammunition, clothing, supplies and equipments," the States would undoubtedly follow in its lead. As a matter of fact, the State legislatures had been even more remiss—as was to be expected—and many of the volunteer regiments reported in a condition positively ludicrous from a military standpoint, being without proper arms, ammunition, uniforms or equipment. "Many sets of such equipments had been issued to the National Guard of the several States. These were reported as serviceable, and when the National Guard was called out as volunteers it was presumed that they would be properly equipped from the stores in the hands of the State authorities. It was found, however, that a large proportion of these stores were not in fit condition for field service, and they had to be replaced."

The instances could be multiplied *ad infinitum* and certainly *ad nauseam*, as is always the case with raw troops. Sickness, culminating in typhoid fever, soon prevailed, especially at Camp Thomas, where the sanitary conditions were "very imperfect and at times decidedly bad." The unvarnished truth is that:

Large bodies of men who are not soldiers, under officers who have had little or no military training, can not be brought together and held for many weeks in camp and remain healthy. If the water supply is not abundant or is not good; if the thoroughly well-established rules of sanitation are not observed; if the discipline of the camp puts little restriction on drunkenness and immorality; if the soldier does not know how to live and his officers do not watch him and teach him; if his food is poorly cared for and badly cooked, and he is permitted to eat and drink anything and everything he can find, sickness will certainly prevail. If, as at Camp Thomas, a regiment can go for ten days without digging sinks; if the sinks dug are not used or they quickly overflow and pollute the ground; if practically no protection is afforded against the liquor sellers and prostitutes of neighboring places; if commands are crowded together and tents seldom struck, or even never during the occupation of the camp; if no one is called to account for repeated violation of sanitary orders, it can not be but that typhoid fever once introduced will spread, rapidly, widely.

How much may be accomplished by intelligent and watchful supervision on the part of surgeons and regimental officers and the observance of the well-established rules of camp sanitation is shown by the record of the Eighth Massachusetts Volunteer Infantry at Camp Thomas. This regiment was for many weeks very healthy, while much sickness was occurring in regiments near by, though the conditions of camp site, of water, and of drill were practically the same. . . .

In conclusion it may be said that it is impossible to bring together a regiment of 1,300 men whose lives and habits have all been different and place them in camp, subject them to its discipline, diet, and duties, without much complaint. They must become acclimated and accustomed to camp life before sickness can be prevented; and until the individual soldier appreciates the necessity of complying fully with the regulations and confines himself to the regular food—and this the soldier never does until experience teaches him the necessity—he will drink polluted water, eat noxious food that disturbs his digestive organs, and will not take care of himself, and no discipline or watching will prevent it. The imprudent acts of the soldiers are the first and greatest cause of sickness in camps.

Another great cause of complaint was the inexperience of officers and surgeons as to proper sanitation, necessity of daily exercises, the camping too long in one place, lack of exercise by marches and other methods to take up the soldier's thoughts. This occurs to all volunteers.

As one war correspondent aptly put the case,

What the country needs to know now is that in actual warfare the volunteer is a nuisance, that it always takes one regular to offset his mistakes, to help him cook his rations, and to teach him to shelter himself and to keep himself clean.

By far the most important lesson to be learned from the Spanish-American War is the necessity for a larger Regular Army than we then possessed. The dearth of trained soldiers prevented a force proportioned to the task that it was expected to accomplish from being sent to Cuba; the same reason caused the retention in the Philippines of the volunteers long after their term of service had legally expired; and a similar cause resulted in our fortifications being most inadequately manned. The strength of the Regular establishment must indispensably be determined by the rôle which it may be called upon to play in the defence of the country or to insure the success of such overseas expeditions as the Government may deem it expedient to undertake. Under any circumstances, it ought to be of sufficient size that the odds that it can accomplish its mission may be on the side of the United States and not overwhelmingly in favour of its enemy, as was the case in 1898. Notwithstanding that General Shafter's command comprised "the finest body of men the country had ever assembled," his expedition to Cuba is almost a by-word among military men. The plain truth is that:

The army was simply disorganized by the working of a system which the very officers who were now called upon to enforce it had time and again endeavored to modernize and bring abreast of the times. And the army bills, which the papers and the political demagogues had combated and defeated, had been drawn up with a view to preventing the occurrence of such a disgraceful spectacle, which these same papers and demagogues now described in such graphic terms and with such indignation, but, of course, without assigning the blame where it belonged—at their own doors.

As the Commission appointed to investigate the conduct of the War Department declared:

*One of the lessons taught by the war is that the country should hereafter be in a better state of preparation for war.* Testimony has been taken on this subject, and suggestions have been made that large supplies of all the material not liable to deterioration should be kept on hand, to be continuously issued and renewed, so that in any emergency they might be available. Especially should this be the case with such supplies, equipment, and ordnance stores as are not in general use in the United States and which can not be rapidly obtained in open market.

*The fundamental responsibility for the majority of these defects rested with that legislative body in which alone is vested the power "to raise and support armies." The demoralization, disorders and incapacity which attended the opening operations were nothing more than the logical outcome of the unwillingness of Congress to prepare for war until the last possible moment. Once again was demonstrated the vicious system to which our legislators have persistently bound us from the beginning of our national career, by neglecting to provide a force of thoroughly trained soldiers either large enough or elastic enough to meet the requirements of war as well as of peace, supported by a militia which has previously had sufficient training to make it, when called out as volunteers, fairly dependable against the regular forces of other nations.*

The whole subject was admirably summed up

in the testimony given before the Investigating Commission by one very distinguished general who declared that:

Congress is chiefly responsible for the bad administration of the army and its organization. They have often been appealed to to reconstruct the army on modern principles, and they have failed to do so, and until this is done the evils we have encountered will recur again, and we will never be able to take our place beside other military nations until we do that.

# 11.

# Between Wars, 1898–1914

As a result of the war with Spain the United States acquired additional defense responsibilities. The acquisition of Puerto Rico, the assumption of a virtual protectorate in Cuba, and the construction of the Panama Canal significantly increased the Caribbean military commitment. The Canal, designed to allow a single fleet to move rapidly from one ocean to the other, created a potentially dangerous link in the defense chain. In the Pacific, American obligations were extended 7,000 miles from the coast to encompass Guam and the Philippine Islands. The navy assumed greater importance as the nation acquired an overseas empire and stressed the doctrines of trade, coaling stations, and colonies. In reply to criticisms that the United States should not procure noncontiguous territories, Senator Albert Beveridge proclaimed that the fleet would make them contiguous. When in 1901 Theodore Roosevelt became President, he vigorously championed the construction of more and larger warships and sent the fleet around the world to demonstrate that America had become a great power. But the navy needed administrative reform, and the following article reveals the factors that affected efforts to achieve a more satisfactory organization.

Though the Dick Act of 1903 finally replaced the Militia Act of 1792 as the basis for a reserve component, the most significant change that took place in the army was the establishment of the General Staff. Modeled after European and especially German structures, the new organization provided for a greater centralization of control and a more effective division of responsibility. Also, profiting from the experience of the recent war, a Joint Army-Navy Board was created to improve liaison and planning between the services.

# The Army General Staff and the Joint Army-Navy Board

## BY ELIHU ROOT

THE IMPORTANT MILITARY EVENT of the year affecting the Regular Army has been the reorganization of the system of military control under the general staff act approved February 14, 1903. . . . This act abolished the separate office of General Commanding the Army, provided for a military Chief of Staff to the President who, acting under the directions of the President, or of the Secretary of War representing him, should have supervision not only of all troops of the line, but of the special staff and supply departments which had theretofore reported directly to the Secretary of War; and it created for the assistance of the Chief of Staff a corps of 44 officers, who were relieved from all other duties. . . .

The regulations which govern the operation of the new corps were adopted on August 3. . . . They divide the corps into the War Department General Staff and the General Staff serving with troops (that is to say, in time of peace with the generals commanding geographical departments), and they prescribe the duties and relations of each of the two classes.

The tenth article of the regulations relating to the Chief of Staff states explicitly the new theory of control inaugurated by the General Staff act. It will be remembered that our old plan of army administration was that there should be a general commanding the Army in peace as well as in war, responsible for the efficiency, discipline, and conduct of the troops, but having no control over finances or the departments of supply and transportation; and that there should be a Secretary of War controlling the finances and the money-spending bureaus, but not commanding the Army, or responsible for the conduct of purely military affairs; and it will be remembered that the result of attempting to work upon that theory of dual and separate responsibility was almost constant discord and a consequent reduction of efficiency. . . .

It will be perceived that we are here providing for civilian control over the military arm, but for civilian control to be exercised through a single military expert of high rank, who is provided with an adequate corps of professional assistants to aid him in the performance of his duties, and who is bound to use all his professional skill and knowledge in giving effect to the purposes and general directions of his civilian superior, or make way for another expert who will do so.

In this way it is hoped that the problem of reconciling civilian control with military efficiency with which we have been struggling for so many years will be solved. . . .

The general plan contemplates that every subject requiring investigation and study shall be worked out first by the officers assigned to the appropriate division and section of the staff, and, when of sufficient importance, shall then be considered by a general staff council composed of the three general officers of the corps

From Report of the Secretary of War, 1903 (Washington, 1903), 328, 330–335.

and the heads of the three divisions, and shall then be acted upon by the Chief of Staff, or laid before the Secretary of War by him with his recommendation. It is gratifying to report that the new system of control has been accompanied by most harmonious effort and cheerful good will on the part of the members of the General Staff, the chiefs of all the War Department bureaus, and the officers of the Army at large. In some cases the intervention of the Chief of Staff and his assistants has resulted in an apparent diminution of the independent authority of other officers. This has been received almost universally with a cheerful readiness to subordinate personal considerations to the good of the service. The exceptions have been so few and unimportant as to justify the belief that they will soon disappear.

Much of the work upon which the General Staff has been employed is of a confidential nature, not to be exhibited in a report which is to become a public document. . . . Of especial importance may be noted the general subject of the distribution of troops, and the location, construction, and enlargement of army posts; the plan for the attendance of militia officers upon military schools and colleges of the Regular Army; the detail of student officers to the General Service and Staff College; the location of military posts in Porto Rico; the reorganization of field batteries; the prevention of desertions; the organization of maneuver divisions and plans for mobilization at West Point, Kentucky, and Fort Riley; the purchase of lands for posts and coast fortifications; the revision of Army Regulations; the revision of Infantry Drill Regulations; the location of a brigade post on the Niagara River; the examination and revision of army appropriation estimates; the details of officers for duty at military academies and colleges; regulations for muster of militia into the service of the United States; reclassification and carding of the professional data on file in the military information division; organization of Alaskan militia; the rearrangement of Territorial departments; the composition, duties, and limits of the principal permanent boards in the Army; the study of the storage and supply depots of all kinds with reference to the prompt and effective collection and distribution of supplies in case of war; the revision of the Articles of War for submission to Congress, adapting them to meet modern conditions and requirements; the study in detail of the supplies necessary for active military operations, including the stock on hand, the productive capacity of Government manufacturers and of private manufacturers, the sources of raw material, and the length of time necessary for production in requisite quantities; and an inquiry into all the elements of cost for seacoast defenses up to this time, and the prospective cost of continuance and maintenance. . . .

Following the same line of policy which led to the organization of the General Staff, the Secretaries of War and the Navy entered into an arrangement, with the approval of the President, which was published to the Army in the following order:

| | |
|---|---|
| General Orders No. 107. | Headquarters of the Army<br>Adjutant-General's Office<br>*Washington, July 20, 1903* |

By direction of the Secretary of War, the following order is published to the Army for the information and guidance of all concerned:

*July 17, 1903*

The Department of War and the Department of the Navy have agreed upon the formation of a joint board to be composed of four officers of the Army and four officers of the Navy, to hold stated sessions and such extraordinary sessions as shall appear advisable for the purpose of conferring upon, discussing, and reaching common conclusions regarding all matters calling for the cooperation of the two services. Any matters which seem to either Department to call for such consideration may be referred by that Department to the board thus formed. All reports of the board shall be made in duplicate, one to each Department. All reports and proceedings of the board shall be confidential. The senior member of the board present will preside at its meetings and the junior member of the board present will act as its recorder. . . .

The common understanding and mutual assistance between the two services, which it is within the power of this board to bring about, may be made to cover a wide range of subjects of great public importance, including the parts to be taken by the military and naval forces, respectively, in case of military operations on the seaboards and on navigable lakes and rivers; artillery defense of naval stations and naval defensive aid to seacoast fortifications; the exchange of information obtained by one branch of the service and useful for both; the manufacture or purchase of cannon, projectiles, explosives, small arms, ammunition, and munitions of war generally available for both services; the purchase and transportation of supplies; the transportation of men upon changes of station; the study and discussion of joint military and naval problems. In all these, and in many other respects, much greater efficiency, at much less cost, can be obtained by cooperation and mutual understanding than by separate services working in entire independence of each other. If the two forces are ever to be called upon to cooperate, the time to determine what each shall do, and the time for each to learn what the other can do, is before the exigency arises. It is hoped that this joint board, which is so constituted as to command the assistance of the General Staff in both arms of the service for the working out of its problems, will contribute materially toward the end desired.

# Origins of the Navy "General Staff"

BY RAYMOND G. O'CONNOR

IN 1951 THE NAVY GENERAL BOARD was dissolved. Established in 1900 and often referred to inaccurately as the Navy "General Staff," the General Board had represented the latest of numerous attempts to provide for more effective professional guidance and administration of the United States Navy. An inquiry into its origins reveals another dimension of the "New Navy" which emerged in the final decades of the nineteenth century.

In its formative years the Navy was controlled and managed entirely by civilians. But in 1815, following the war against Great Britain, a Board of Navy Commissioners was established, consisting of three officers, which was to assist the Secretary of the Navy in the administration of the service. The actual jurisdiction of the Commissioners was restricted to supply and equipment, while policy formulation and control remained with the Secretary. Criticized primarily because it eliminated individual responsibility, the Board was abolished in 1842 and the "bureau system" was inaugurated. This action created five separate bureaus in the Navy Department (increased to eight in 1862), each controlling one branch of naval activity and headed by an officer who was directly responsible to the Secretary. The major defect of the new bureaucratic organization was lack of professional coordination. Each of the autonomous bureau chiefs took his business directly to the Secretary, and thus presented him with but one aspect of the overall problem of naval affairs. No competent career individual or body exercised coordinating jurisdiction or provided the civilian head with the advice and knowledge necessary to administer properly the affairs of the Navy.

The weaknesses of the multifarious bureau system were revealed by its inadequate response to the increased demands imposed on the Navy Department during the Civil War. Yet measures introduced in Congress to establish a Board of Naval Administration and a Board of Admiralty failed to receive Congressional approval. Secretary of the Navy Gideon Welles opposed any permanent body that might deprive his office of control, and he was content to convene informal, temporary boards to resolve the more perplexing questions confronting the Navy.

As successive secretaries made futile efforts to grapple with the complexities of Navy Department administration, a series of incidents exposed the inability of the existing organization to cope with emergencies. When the blockade runner *Virginus* was seized by Spanish officials in 1873 and American members of her crew were executed, the Department was thrown into confusion because war threatened and no staff existed to plot a campaign. The *Baltimore* incident of 1891, which almost brought Chile and the United States to blows, stimulated a burst of activity in Washington. Captain Alfred Thayer Mahan, now acclaimed for his *Influence of Sea Power Upon History* (1890), was ordered to duty in the Navy Department to prepare war plans and to be available for consultation. But this brief emergency, which again laid bare the inadequacies of the bureau system in time of peril, provoked no modification of the prevailing organization.

Serious agitation for a reorganization of the bureau-bound Navy Department was begun in 1878 by Captain Stephen B. Luce, first president of the Naval War College and author of the standard treatise, *Seamanship* (1863). Struck by the failure of the navy to capture Charleston during the Civil War, he concluded that bungling administration was largely responsible and resolved to expose the pitfalls of the bureau system. Luce urged that the Department be divided into two sections, the military and the civilian. A group of naval officers should be "attached to and made a part of" the secretary's office, with the sole responsibility of "preparing plans for naval campaigns and of directing under the Secretary of the Navy the military operations of our fleets and squadrons." Naval administration in France and England demonstrated the wisdom of such a proposal, Luce contended, and he thought it immaterial whether this body be called "a Board of Naval Commissioners, a Board of Admiralty, a Strategy Board, a General Board or a General Staff."

The red-taped inadequacies of the bureau system were also apparent to the Secretary of the Navy, Louisiana lawyer William H. Hunt. In 1881 he felt obliged to convene what was called the First Naval Advisory Board under Rear Admiral John Rodgers, leader of the assault on Korea in 1871, to determine the number and types of vessels needed for the Navy. Surprisingly, the existing organization made no provision for the consideration of such basic requirements. Four years later Secretary William C. Whitney, who was to be one of the architects of the New Navy, complained that the bureau system burdened his office with so many executive duties that he was unable to furnish the counsel and guidance that his position demanded. He therefore asked Congress for a separation of "the work of direction and deliberation from the details of execution," and he was supported by President Cleveland in this unsuccessful effort at reform. The basic need for coordinating bureau activities was being painfully revealed even in the everyday peacetime functioning of the Navy Department. But the preparation of war plans and the direction of the fleet units during time of conflict made it imperative, in the thinking of many naval officers, that a body of professionals be created specifically to handle these problems.

The Navy Department continued its purblind policy of appearing to prepare for all contingencies—except war—until the outbreak of the Cuban insurrection in 1895. Spurred by public clamor, Secretary Hilary A. Herbert telegraphed the Naval War College to begin immediate preparation of plans for a conflict with Spain and the winning of independence for Cuba. The resultant plan of operations was circulated within the Department for criticism and debate for the next three years, but no staff existed to submit alternative proposals. When Congress declared war in 1898, the Navy Department was obliged to adopt the War College plan because it was the only one available. Yet three months before the outbreak of hostilities Secretary John D. Long shortsightedly complained that his energetic assistant, Theodore Roosevelt, did "bore him" with plans of naval and military movement, and the necessity of having some scheme of attack arranged for instant execution in case of emergency.

Dissatisfaction with the existing system became more pronounced as the New Navy emerged during the 1890's. Criticism was concentrated on the lack of an agency to formulate war plans and on the unwieldiness of the bureau system, which required the appointment of temporary boards to find answers to routine questions. Denounced within the service as an "organization of unsurpassed crudity," and from without as "an absence of system," the bureau structure tottered but did not fall. Moreover, in the absence of centralized professional authority, the Bureau of Navigation, which was charged with the control of ship movements and personnel, began to exercise a wider administration of the military functions of the Department.

This encroachment aroused the resentment of other bureaus and made cooperation even more difficult.

The problem of a more centralized professional administration in the Navy Department was attacked by the Naval War College in 1893. Studies were made of patterns business organization, the British Admiralty, and the German army General Staff. A modification of the latter was considered most suitable for the United States, with a nucleus to be formed by combining the Naval War College and the Office of Naval Intelligence. But the proponents of this plan were well aware of the obstacles that lay between them and their objective. Captain Henry C. Taylor, who was president of the College when the studies were begun, reported an "overwhelming opposition" in Washington to the creation of a general staff, which, he thought, "would probably have to grow slowly by a process of natural evolution in the Bureau of Navigation." The officer whom he and Luce thought best qualified to head such a body—presumably Commodore George Dewey—was inclined to favor the innovation but was too busy to take much interest in the project. Assistant Secretary Theodore Roosevelt enthusiastically supported the proposal, but neither he nor Captain Taylor was able to obtain Secretary Long's approval of a staff organization. The plan, Taylor sadly concluded, evidently could be adopted only in the event of war.

The failure to establish a professional body to fill the administrative vacuum that existed between the Secretary and the bureau chiefs is not hard to understand. E. L. Godkin, the redoubtable editor of *Nation*, claimed that it was due to public ignorance of the workings of the Navy Department and the caution of civilian Secretaries who were awed by their own professional incompetence. The lack of unanimity among the naval officers themselves contributed to the inertia. In a lecture before the Naval War College in 1897, Rear Admiral G. E. Belknap contended that "commissions and boards are a snare," and he likened a Navy Department containing an intermediary body between the Secretary and the bureau chiefs to a ship with more than one captain. On the other hand, according to Paullin, "The Secretaries during the period 1881–1897 were jealous of their powers, and naturally opposed any measure calculated to increase greatly the influence and control of naval officers within the department." No doubt all of these factors, as well as "centrifugal forces of the department," contributed to the failure to eliminate what many considered an administrative bottleneck.

As the crisis with Spain over Cuba became more acute, Assistant Secretary Roosevelt urged Secretary Long to appoint a senior naval officer as his "chief of staff" to handle the exclusively military operations. War should be waged by professionals, he maintained, not by amateurs. But Long was not convinced. He believed that the absence of a rival military head was one of the reasons why the Department functioned so smoothly. Although the Secretary was reluctant to place authority in the hands of any individual or group, shortly before the outbreak of hostilities he did ask Roosevelt and three officers to act as a Naval War Board. Roosevelt, who soon dashed off to fight, was replaced as senior member by Rear Admiral Montgomery Sicard, and Mahan was ordered to duty in the Navy Department to serve on the Board. Designed to provide the Secretary with professional advice on strategic, tactical, and technical problems, the Board exercised no authority, and existed only informally under a verbal directive from Secretary Long. Throughout the war the members consulted with Long and prepared dispatches and directives for his approval. Mahan argued vigorously for the appointment of a chief of staff to coordinate and direct military operations, but Secretary Long could not be convinced that such an appointment would be an improvement over the existing organization. Long acknowledged that the service of the Naval War Board "was invaluable in connection with the successful conduct of the war," but when hostilities ceased he dissolved the group. It was strictly an emergency body which was, presumably, neither necessary nor desirable in normal times. In the opinion of Secretary Long, the routine operations of the Navy Department were best coordinated and directed by civil, not naval, authorities.

But the persistent Admiral Luce would not be denied, and he took advantage of the Spanish-American War to accelerate his campaign. Writing to Senator Henry Cabot Lodge, the venerable Admiral criticized the organization of the Navy Department, denounced the civilian administration of affairs, and argued for a general staff. Lodge agreed that "there ought to be a chief of staff in the Navy Department and I have thought so for years." When the war ended a few months later, Luce thought the time ripe to move for the establishment of a permanent professional body along the lines of the Naval War Board. To this end, he suggested that Mahan present his views to Secretary Long, apparently unaware of the earlier clash between the two men over a similar project. A small group of officers, made more acutely aware of existing shortcomings by the inadequate preparations for the recent war and by the valuable work of the now defunct War Board, sought to obtain a staff organization through Congressional action. But they were thwarted by the bitter opposition of the bureau chiefs and Senator Eugene Hale of Maine, chairman of the powerful Senate Committee on Naval Affairs.

Some two years after the clash with Spain, the earlier studies of the Naval War College and the persistent efforts of Admiral Luce and his cohorts began to bear fruit. Captain Taylor, who had commanded the *Indiana* at the battle of Santiago, was more than ever convinced of the need for a reorganization of the Navy Department. In response to a request from Long, Taylor and his colleagues marshalled the arguments for a general staff and presented them in a memorandum to the Secretary. Realizing that the plan would fail if it did not make provision for the bureau that controlled personnel and ship distribution, they suggested that the nucleus of the proposed staff consist of the Chief of the Bureau of Navigation together with representatives from the Naval War College and the Office of Naval Intelligence. But according to Long, "the navy was not quite ready for such a comprehensive change as would occur in case of the adoption of the full general staff system," and he resolved the dilemma by effecting a compromise. In fact, without the perplexing problem of an appropriate assignment for Admiral Dewey, the hero of Manila Bay, a modification of the existing organization probably would not have been made.

The Navy General Board was established by Secretary Long's General Order No. 544, dated March 13, 1900. It was to consist of nine members: Admiral Dewey as president; the Chief of the Bureau of Navigation; the Chief Intelligence Officer and his principal assistant; the president of the Naval War College and his principal assistant; and three other officers of or above the grade of lieutenant commander. "The purpose of the Department in establishing this Board," the order announced, was "to insure efficient preparation of the fleet in case of war and for the naval defense of the coast." The Chief of the Bureau of Navigation was to have custody of war plans, direct the War College and the Intelligence Officer to furnish information desired by the Board, and act as presiding officer in the absence of Admiral Dewey. Meetings were to be held at least once each month, twice a year the sessions should last a week, and a quorum would consist of five officers.

The duties of the Board were then amplified by the Secretary. He directed that it consider the role of the naval reserve and the merchant marine in national defense, consult with the army in order to effect "a full and cordial co-operation of the two services in case of war," and be ready to advise the Secretary on fleet dispositions. Plans should be prepared for the defense of the nation and its dependencies, and for any theater in which war might occur. The selection and preparation of naval bases was to be considered and recommended, foreign navies were to be evaluated, and other topics for investigation were to be determined. Specifically, the Board was to begin an urgent study of plans for the defense of dependencies, the location of naval bases to implement this defense, and the "numbers and kind of ships" needed for this purpose. Members were cautioned to confine their work to a consideration of the broader problems and avoid the "technical questions of material and manufacture," which were handled by the bureaus and the Department. For, Long added, "It is not with the construction, manning, arming and equipping of the ships that the General Board is concerned, but with recommendations as to the proper disposition of the Fleet." While the activities of the Board were limited, it was not to lack for assistance, and officers could be ordered to appear before the Board to give information or advice when required.

At the first meeting, on April 16, 1900, the pertinent directives were read, an Executive Committee was appointed, and it was agreed that sub-committees would be designated as required. The cautious Long, while apparently recognizing the value of this deliberative body, was ever alert to prevent it from exercising authority, and he insisted that all business with the bureaus or other branches of the government be conducted through his office. He was determined that it should remain an advisory body only, directly responsible to the Secretary.

The adherents of the Board regarded it as the nucleus of a general staff that would have the responsibility for planning, coordinating, and controlling the fleet. Admiral Dewey referred to the Board as the "general 'staff'," but Captain Taylor felt that "the reactionary element in the Navy" would prevent an early realization of this objective. The problem was made more difficult by the fear that such a move presaged service encroachment on civilian supremacy. Taylor urged that the General Board be confirmed by act of Congress in order to ensure its permanence, and that steps be taken toward the development of a general staff. But he could get no support for these proposals from the Secretary.

The stubborn Long was out of office scarcely a month when Admiral Dewey presented President Roosevelt with a five page memorandum recommending the formation of a navy general staff. "To assure complete and well-organized preparation for war," he maintained, "experience has shown that the existence of a general staff in any military or naval service is absolutely necessary." The General Board was a start in the right direction, Dewey added, but a general staff, operating under the jurisdiction of a chief of staff as the senior naval officer, would make for an even more efficient and effective navy. President Roosevelt thought that the argument was "conclusive," but his efforts to secure legislation establishing a general staff were not successful.

The creation of the General Board, in the words of Captain John Hood, cast the "first glimmerings of light on a true naval policy" for the United States. Assigned no administrative functions or responsibilities, the Board was able to devote its energies to a consideration of the problems of defense and the implementation of foreign policy within the broad framework of national interests. The Board was a response to a long-felt need for planning and coordination within the Navy Department, for the experience of the war with Spain had emphasized the defects of a system not geared to the exacting demands of modern sea power. Existing largely because of the determined efforts of Rear Admiral Henry C. Taylor, the Board's early success was made possible by his activities as Chief of the Bureau of Navigation during its formative years, and also by the prestige and moderate leadership of the Board's first president, Admiral Dewey, who held the position until his death in 1917. The studies and reports prepared by the Board furnished a guide for the Administration in the formulation and execution of naval policy, and provided the tactical and strategic data necessary to cope with the broadening responsibilities of an America that was sensationally emerging as a major power.

The Navy General Board never became a true general staff, for it did not acquire the status or the authority that was envisioned by its proponents. It did not centralize the control of the Navy Department, eliminate the autonomy of the bureaus, or relieve the Secretary of any responsibilities. Yet the weight accorded the Board's recommendations enabled it to play a major role in the development of American sea power throughout the first half of the twentieth century. Formed at a time when America's commercial and expansionist forces were bursting from their continental barriers, and staffed by the most seasoned officers, the Board was to serve as the "thinking organ" for a navy that was both the first line of defense and a major instrument of foreign policy. Although the Board was a belated and not wholly satisfactory response to the extensive mission that had been assigned the navy, it provided a unity and consistency in planning and policy that marked a new era in naval administration.

12.

# The First World War

Initially, President Woodrow Wilson was considered a virtual pacifist, but he was to employ force to achieve American objectives in Mexico, the Caribbean, and Europe. When the Great War erupted the President declared formal neutrality in the hope that the conflict would not touch the United States. As American rights were violated by the belligerents, a movement swept the nation to expand drastically the size of the armed forces, and Wilson belatedly espoused the cause. Frederic L. Paxson, in the first selection, reveals the movement to prepare in its complexities.

America's entry into the war placed greater demands on the country than any conflict since the Civil War. Though at the outset there was no clear understanding as to what the extent of the commitment would be, it soon became apparent that the allies would be defeated unless the United States furnished huge numbers of men and vast quantities of materiel. Since Germany hoped to win the war before the American influence could be exerted, speed was imperative, and the government organized the productive capacities of the nation to a greater degree than ever before. The massive Army war effort is described by the Chief of Staff in his report for 1919. The Navy effort, confined largely to convoy and escort duty, became the subject of considerable controversy. The testimony of witnesses in the Senate hearings on the subject indicates the nature of the dispute and the elements of naval policy.

# The Rush to Prepare

## BY FREDERIC L. PAXSON

IN THE MIDST OF THE CONFLICTING ARGUMENTS over war, peace, and national policy, Woodrow Wilson reviewed the dreadnaught *Wyoming* as it led out of the Hudson and to sea, on May 18, 1915, the greater part of the American fleet. His hope of traveling with part of it through the Panama Canal had faded. He was soon to announce that public business would keep him from going to San Francisco at all; while the Canal was so persistently blocked by slides that the fleet could not have passed it to the Pacific. The old *Oregon*, now good for nothing but a symbol, functioned at the Exposition. The fleet, even had the Canal been open, would have had to maintain precautionary station in Atlantic waters. The newly created Chief of Naval Operations, Admiral William S. Benson, who took office in that post on May 3, could never have permitted the naval force of the United States to be divided, or to be removed to remote waters in the existing state of international tension. The sinking of the *Lusitania* warned all of the perilous imminence of war. Benson warned the people to get ready; while the President spoke at the review of the Navy as the guardian of peace.

This guardianship of peace had now become a theme of bitter controversy. That it needed to be guarded at all was denied by the pacifist wing of the peace movement; and every effort to guard it was challenged as an act provocative of war. That the United States was nearly defenseless, with every lesson of the war pointing to the helplessness of an unarmed nation, was a counter-theme, pressed with all the devices known to argument and propaganda. The terms pacifist and militarist, freely exchanged, were rarely accepted, and fitted few who took part in the debate. Not many admitted themselves to be conscientious non-resistants; not many openly avowed the decency of the use of military force to conquer national advantage. With a terminology suggesting views more extreme than were often met, the real debate turned upon opinion as to armament; whether it was an insurance for peace and freedom, or whether its very existence was an invitation to war.

Each side of the honest argument was reinforced by recruits who desired not a solution of the major question, but advantage to themselves in the immediate situation in which the United States was placed. On the peace side were many who could better be described as pro-German or anti-British, desiring to reduce armament to its lowest terms so as to lessen the strength of the United States as a potential associate of the enemies of Germany. On the preparedness side were many who hoped for this association, and wanted the United States to come into it well armed. Between the two were groups who feared that an underarmed United States would be in danger should the war leave one of its combatants in a position of victory, with the military hegemony of Europe in its hands, a menace to

---

From Frederic L. Paxson, *Pre-War Years, 1913–1917* (Boston, Houghton Mifflin Company, 1936), 287–307. Used by permission.

the world. There were perhaps as many who were honest in their trust in armaments as the safeguard of peace, as there were those who as honestly held the opposite. Running along through the discussion of preparedness was the tendency of a generation whose finest hate had been big business. It was easy to believe that business and finance wanted armament, and perhaps even war, for the sake of profit. Close to this was suspicion of the munition makers, and confidence that these promoted war.

The battle for preparedness, as old as the period of military reorganization after the Spanish War, entered its World War phase during the autumn of 1914, reinforced now by the public interest in war as a reality. For nearly a year it struggled to catch the public ear, retarded by the persistent confidence of the President that his Administration could do its greatest work for peace if it should refrain from any military gesture. In the summer of 1915, the mind of the President swung to its support, as the *Lusitania* discussions lessened his confidence. He could no longer rely on unarmed peace as either defender of neutrality or guardian of American safety in a world of war. While his Secretary of State, Lansing, became convinced that Germany must not be allowed to break even or to win, Wilson went so far as to be willing to prepare. With increasing earnestness he considered the desiderata of defense in the autumn of 1915. He set Congress to the execution of a program when it met in December, and went on the stump to advocate it in January. His labors with a detailed and novel set of laws were complicated by the emotional pressures from outside and by political obstruction within Congress; but before the end of the session, with many compromises that vexed the extremists of all the agitating groups, he had procured the enactment of a more complete system of defense laws than the United States had known. They covered the Army and the Navy, and reached into the related fields of civilian effort and ocean tonnage. By the time of their signing, his mind had reached definite conclusions, expressed at Cincinnati, October 26, that the business of neutrality was over because it had become too burdensome to be endured, and that the hope for neutrals lay in an association of nations, to give expression and force to the ideal of peace.

Augustus Peabody Gardner of Massachusetts introduced the preparedness debate in its new phase when he proposed, October 15, 1914, his House joint resolution number 372, for the creation of a national security commission. He spoke for an inquiry into the status of defense, inspired by a conviction that it could be shown to be inadequate. The private associations already devoted to military matters, discouraged by the apathy of Congress that fairly reflected the indifference of its constituents, leaped instantly behind him into the fight; too instantly and too earnestly for the immediate advancement to the goal, for their members and directors were often soldiers and therefore suspect, or manufacturers of military material easily vulnerable as having a selfish interest. Financial contributions to the cause, by the latter, did it doubtful service. Little was ever proved, though much could be suspected. Most of the leaders of the progressive movement that had permitted the election of Wilson, and installed his Democratic majorities in Congress, had a harsh belief in the iniquity of big business. Wilson had done much to direct suspicion against the good faith of any lobby. The personnel of the backers of preparedness automatically aroused suspicion, the more intense because American opinion still regarded the war as far removed from American vital interest.

It was a natural professional attitude when members of the military establishment expressed belief in preparedness and deplored the indifference of President, Congress, and people to what appeared to them to be vital. In the existing state of things their mission was to be disregarded in time of peace, and to stand up to be slaughtered in time of war, while the nation armed itself behind their bodies. They knew something of the content of the memoranda on defense prepared by the General Staff of the Army and the General Board of the Navy; but they knew also how little of what was recommended was approved by the secretaries in charge, or accepted by the President, or enacted. The political considerations that the President was bound to respect seemed to military men improper interference with national duty. But their hands and mouths were to a large degree tied by the discipline of the services which forbade them to criticize their official superiors. They were further tied by the obvious desire of the Administration that they should not engage at this time even in advocacy of measures which the President would not support. The reports of the Secretaries of War and Navy in 1914 were held rigidly within the limits of the needs of such forces as had been accepted as proper before the World War started. Garrison, with no interests except as head of the Army, chafed at this. Daniels, journalist and politician before he was administrator, accepted it with more peace of mind. Both had to mediate between generals and admirals who knew about war and an Administration with ideas of its own. The disapproval of the President prevented action upon Gardner's national security inquiry either at the end of the expiring session of 1914, or in the new short session beginning December 7. The election in November had confirmed Administration majorities for the next Congress, but they were too narrow to be tampered with. Gardner refrained from joining the National Security League that was created December 1, but he could rejoice that persons outside of office, and outside the armed forces, were taking up his cause. He and his associates in Congress pressed the danger of unpreparedness wherever opportunity offered, injecting it into all debates upon collateral issues of the war, and reciting what appeared to be the lessons to be derived from the experiences of the combatants. The American League to Limit Armaments gave them additional publicity by attacking them.

The Administration Ship Purchase Bill was blocked in February, 1915, by an opposition running through both parties. It was in a way a measure of preparedness, for the war had taken from service many of the ships that carried United States exports; and without ships there could be no trade. The successful filibuster bore witness to the unwillingness of the country as yet to encourage novel measures.

The troubles of Mexico gave impetus to opinion for preparedness. The troops, after four years on the border, were maintained there only at the cost of stripping from their regular duties men who could not well be spared. In spite of the firmness of the Administration in its attitude of "watchful waiting," and its determination not to intrude too far upon the right of Mexico to adjust its own affairs, there was a possibility that proximity might compel operations for which the existing army would be insufficient. On March 6, 1915, there was incorporated in New York the American Legion, which proposed to enroll volunteers in a reserve available for this work. It was a propaganda gesture, behind which lay enthusiasm for military service and personal conviction of the duty to police America. It gained the full approval of Theodore Roosevelt, who himself coveted command at the head of a brigade. His son, Theodore Roosevelt, Jr., was one of its directors. On its advisory board were Root, Wright, Dickinson, and Stimson, each of whom had been Secretary of War; and its office asserted that twenty thousand applications for enrollment were received during its first fortnight. Colonel Roosevelt allowed himself to draw on his knowledge of the Army, and to check the officers whom he would desire for line and staff. There were few who would not have welcomed him as commander.

The announcement of the American Legion brought immediate inquiries as to its militaristic leaning and its political trend. A distinguished bishop challenged its good faith; General Leonard Wood demanded that insinuations be withdrawn; Secretary Garrison found it necessary to warn his subordinates against taking part in public controversy over defense. General Wood's approval, and the nearness to his office of some of the organizers of the Legion, added to the difficulty of his relations with the War Department. His earnest support of every proposal for defense carried him to the margin of insubordination. Warmly intimate with Roosevelt and his Republican group, he made it impossible for the Administration to escape the belief that he was a political general. The fact that he had come to his generalcy by an unusual route, out of the medical corps and jumping his superiors, was hard for his fellow officers to forgive; and even when they agreed with him, they often disapproved him. Those who were junior to him, and who had served under his command, were quite too devoted. He made his own matters worse when in August, 1915, he arranged for speakers to address the civilian "rookies" in his training camp at Plattsburg, and included Theodore Roosevelt in his list. Roosevelt, now speaking and writing for preparedness on every occasion, addressed the corps August 25. He had already assembled his papers of the preceding year in *America and the World War* (1915), and had still in his mind *Fear God and Take Your Own Part* (1916), and *The Foes of Our Own Household* (1917). He was more than an ex-President, having a political promise brightening since the elections of 1914. His friends hoped that around his name the Republican Party would reassemble its fragments in 1916. He avowed at Plattsburg that he would stand by the President when the latter stood by the United States; but the context suggests that he could not convince himself that Woodrow Wilson would. His bitter attack upon dilatory preparedness stirred the Secretary of War to action. Wood was rebuked by Garrison for permitting the address. Roosevelt could stand up under this censure with indifference; but the episode left Wood outside the confidence of the Administration, which was never again able to make full use of his military ability and enthusiasm.

Even earlier than the Roosevelt-Plattsburg episode the policy of the Administration had shifted its course. Both of the defense departments were now giving their advisers the encouragement long denied, and committees in both services were hard at work, no longer on academic memoranda upon military policy, but upon concrete projects for legislation to be submitted to Congress when next it met. While the Congress was in its short session, ending March 4, 1915, the President showed no sign of departure from his attitude of December, 1914. But during the recess he changed. The accumulating evidence of German misbehavior in the United States hurried the change. The submarine policy indicated a Germany determined upon a course whose only consequence could be submission by neutrals, or war. The British trade restrictions engendered irritation whose intensity the American pro-Germans did not even suspect, though much of the evidence was before them. Before the *Lusitania* correspondence came to an end, a new policy was under way.

The phrase "too proud to fight," picked up and attacked by critics of the Administration after the *Lusitania* sinking, did not carry a true picture of the Wilson mind. A little later in May, at the fleet review, the President struck a different note as he spoke well of the importance of the Navy. While the *Lusitania* correspondence was in progress, it became known that the efforts of the defense officers had been unshackled; and the day after Bernstorff gave his assurance that there should not be another *Lusitania*, the President released the text of memoranda demanding plans that he had sent to the two secretaries on July 21, the very day of the third *Lusitania* note.

While the departments worked to draft what they might hope to get, now that the President was behind them, the forces in politics were shaken into a new alignment. It was rumored that the Democratic leaders in Senate and House, Kern and Kitchin, would refuse to go with Wilson. Republicans saw the fate that might befall them should they oppose, and a war find them in opposition; for the status of the Democratic Party after the Civil War was an object lesson teaching much. The opposition to preparedness became more bitter. Clyde H. Tavenner, an Illinois Representative, attacked "those patriots for profit," asserting that the bankers and munitions makers were leading the United States to war for their own advantage. La Follette inquired, "What do Morgan and Schwab care for world peace when there are big profits in war?" and lamented that "*we are underwriting the success of the cause of the Allies.* . . . We have ceased to be neutral in fact as well as in name." "If," he asserted as Congress met, "if a man dares to intimate that he is unwilling to swallow the whole program for preparedness —*a big army, a big navy, big contracts for munitions of war*—that man is a fool, a coward, or a traitor." La Follette was manifestly none of these; but the movement had reached a phase at which preparedness and patriotism were hard to separate. In October, the President met with and encouraged Edison's Naval Consulting Board. In November, he advocated preparedness before fellow Democrats at the Manhattan Club in New York; while to an admirer of this speech he quoted *Ezekiel*, 33 : 6: "But if the watchman see the sword come, and blow not the trumpet, and the people be not warned; if the sword come, and take any person from among them, he is taken away in his iniquity; but his blood will I require at the watchman's hand."

The new attitude, revealed in the new message, December 7, 1915, dispelled lingering doubts upon the necessity for readjusted positions on preparedness. Some, who had approved the neutral gesture of 1914, now felt themselves abandoned by the President; others, who had criticized it, found it hard to cease criticism and to admit him as one of themselves. Wilson rationalized the change when the Speaker introduced him to the joint session of the houses in the Hall of Representatives. "We have stood apart, studiously neutral," he said, speaking in the name of the United States, and of the other American republics which he was hoping to bring into a Pan-American concord. But the war, he declared, "has extended its threatening and sinister scope until it has swept within its flame some portion of every quarter of the globe. . . . Great democracies are not belligerent. They do not seek or desire war. . . . We regard war merely as a means of asserting the rights of a people against aggression. . . . But we do believe in a body of free citizens ready and sufficient to take care of themselves, and of the governments which they have set up to serve them." With these ideals in mind, he referred to the proposals of the Departments of War and of the Navy, about to be laid before Congress, and to plans for "the purchase or construction of [merchant] ships to be owned and directed by the Government" which were to be renewed. "At least so much by way of preparation for defense seems to me to be absolutely imperative now. We cannot do less."

While Congress worked to its new equilibrium, scrutinizing the concrete proposals, the forces out-of-doors renewed their activity. The Military Training Camps Association prepared its campaign for more and larger camps in 1916; a Junior American Guard, to teach patriotism, was incorporated in New York; a National Society for Patriotic Education started upon its self-selected task, with convictions intensified now that England by its Military Service Act shifted in January, 1916, from the basis of voluntary enlistment toward that of compulsory service; and the National Security League held another of its conferences in Washington, beginning January 20. This League, now reporting ninety-seven branches in operation, and carrying the names of Joseph H. Choate and Alton B. Parker at its head, was still struggling to appear non-partisan. The "fighting wing" of the movement, the American Defense Society, brought out new manifestoes on the minimum needs of preparedness, and had no confidence in reaching them through a Democratic Administration. It was preparing for the private view of a propaganda film, "America Unprepared," and giving endorsement to every military opinion that went beyond the recommendations of the General Board or the General Staff. More violent still, the American Rights Committee, denounced by Viereck as "the same old crowd which has been exposed on former occasions as having intimate relations with the friends of the British Government," was insistent for immediate action, and was prepared for a junction with the Allies.

The Middle West showed itself lukewarm as the discussions ran into January, 1916. In the East there was interest in preparedness; in the Far West the war was little more than an exciting series of news events. The South was suspicious. It soon became clear that the enactment of a program would require more support than the President could command within his own party, and more than the East could bring to his relief. Between Pittsburgh and Denver, on the whole the most American part of the United States, were the constituencies whose Representatives in Congress must be moved if action was to be possible. To these the President gave personal attention. He addressed a group of business associations in New York, Thursday, January 27, urging defense; and the next night he started West, selecting from the hundreds of invitations he received, after the announcement of a speaking tour, those from Pittsburgh, Cleveland, Milwaukee, Chicago, Des Moines, Topeka, Kansas City, and St. Louis. The audiences received him with enthusiasm increasing as he warmed to the task; the addresses were so phrased that they could be accepted by moderates of all groups except the pacifist. They encouraged those who saw in a naval force a means of preventing England from dictating and enforcing its own version of maritime law. The Republican floor leader, James R. Mann, of Chicago, entirely free from the suspicion of being pro-Ally, agreed to their doctrine before they were even delivered. In Missouri, Wilson went with the enthusiasm beyond the doctrine of a navy equal to the second strongest, beyond even a navy equal to any, and asked for a navy unquestionably the strongest. He identified his proposals with the patriotism of the common man, so that opposition in principle became increasingly more difficult; and within the week he was back at his desk, ready for legislative details that were to last for more than seven months.

When on March 6, Hay, of Virginia, introduced the National Defense Act in the House, he did so with the unanimous approval of his Committee on Military Affairs, and was permitted to state that the measure had the endorsement of the White House. The act dealt with the Regular Army, the National Guard, and the volunteer forces, and touched upon industrial preparedness; but before its drafting had been completed to the unanimity he described, the principles underlying it had been fought through the divergent views of those who wished to go all the way to a system of universal military training, and those who were content to continue to rely upon the innate capacity of the American militia.

The Secretary of War, Lindley M. Garrison, resigned during this conflict, February 10. He was discouraged because the President would not stand or fall with him upon his scheme for the use of volunteers, always directly under command of the United States, in place of national guardsmen, recruited out of the militia and functioning as State troops except when specially called into the national service. His kind of army he called a "continental" army; and by the implications of the proposal he brought into focus against it all of the local, personal, and political influences of the National Guard. Determined to get some kind of law, even though not the law he preferred, Wilson let Garrison go, and appointed in his place Newton D. Baker, whom he had desired for a position in the original Cabinet. Major-General Hugh L. Scott acted as Secretary of War *ad interim* until Baker was nominated and confirmed March 7. The issue, settled in principle before Hay spoke for his bill, was vital in the American theory of defense.

So far as the Regular Army was concerned there were no difficulties save those of expediency and cost. This force included 4,572 officers and 88,444 enlisted men at the end of 1914; and was recruited to 4,798 officers and 101,195 men by the next midsummer. It lay within the admitted power of Congress to increase the number at discretion. Since the Root reforms at the beginning of the century, the Regular Army had steadily improved in the effectiveness of its organization and the professional equipment of its officers; but no one expected that it would ever fight a great war. It was a permanent organization, with heavy duties in time of peace, and could be no more than a nucleus around which an enlarged force would be assembled in case of need. The recruiting and training of this enlarged army, calling for high speed in time of emergency, would have been trying enough had there been no barriers of habit and of Constitution.

The Constitution of the United States relies upon the militia, meaning thereby the full man power capable of bearing arms. And the militia is conceived as of the States, liable to be called into Federal service, but to be trained in the States under an organization and discipline that Congress is at liberty to define. But the whole unorganized militia had never been even enrolled. The few young men who from preference took part in the organized units of the

National Guard, some 110,000 in all the States in 1916, treated membership as recreation, and could be driven off the list by stringent discipline. Congress had no share in the raising of this volunteer reserve, and was handicapped in using it. The Constitution enumerates the purposes for which Congress may arrange for calling the militia into the service of the United States: "to execute the Laws of the Union, suppress Insurrections, and repel Invasions." It is silent as to the power of the Union to use the militia outside its borders, or even outside the State of origin. It was the opinion of Attorney-General George W. Wickersham, as recently as 1912, that the enumeration of these purposes forbade all others. Whether he was right or not, the constitutional doubts in the way of using the militia as components of an expeditionary force on foreign soil are such that no Army Act has ever been quite able to reconcile the possible military need of the Union and the rights of the States. The basic Militia Act of 1792 evaded the issue, although it assumed the military obligation of all capable of bearing arms. In the Spanish War the organized militia, called to the State colors, were persuaded by public opinion to enlist as volunteers for the armies destined to Cuba, Puerto Rico, and the Philippines. The Act of 1903 still evaded the issue, but built to a greater uniformity by putting the cost of training upon the Federal Government. The Volunteer Act of 1914 had provided for taking the guardsmen as individuals into the volunteer army. The problem was to secure a peace-time National Guard large enough and well enough trained to be useful to the States; yet free from the limitations as to use that were widely believed to restrict the militia of the States.

Every attempt to restate the law revived the clash between Regular Army opinion that the emergency soldiers should be volunteers from the beginning, trained by professional officers, and always at the command of the United States, and National Guard opinion that the States must not be deprived of their means of local defense and that the identity of State units must not be lost. The hearings on what was to become Hay's National Defense Act were ready to begin when Wilson returned from his speaking trip. Garrison was ready to make his stand for volunteers, to be called a "continental" army, and to include some four hundred thousand men, disregarding the National Guard organization, and governed by the United States. The Regular Army opinion that he adopted objected to the National Guard, not only because of constitutional limitations, but also because it denied the effectiveness of National Guard troops. But the sentimental and local position of the National Guard was too strong to be broken. Wilson accepted the inevitable, Garrison retired, and Hay's bill for the enlargement of the National Guard and for its better training received his countenance.

After a brief debate until March 23, the House accepted the Hay Bill, 403 to 2, although Gardner denounced it as a "joke." In the Senate it was under discussion until summer, with Chamberlain, of Oregon, in charge, preferring compulsory service, or at least the "continental" army scheme, and fighting at every step for a larger Regular Army than the Hay Bill contemplated. When the bill received the assent of the President, June 3, 1916, it was still the Hay Bill in its fundamentals. It was also the earliest of the great measures of preparedness to be enacted, and became a law in the midst of an ostentatious outpouring of public enthusiasm.

The National Defense Act provided for a Regular Army to be gradually enlarged to 175,000 men. This was a compromise between what the House offered and what the Senate wanted. The National Guard remained. But as a sort of substitute for the "continental" army, the bill provided for an Officers' Reserve Corps in which civilians might earn commissions by service in the student battalions at the land-grant colleges, or other colleges accepting them, or by service in volunteer officers' training camps. At this point the experiments launched by General Wood were accepted in the law.

The creation of the Officers' Reserve Corps marked a departure from old practice; for in all the wars of the United States the officers, except those from the Regular Army, had been drawn from the same civilian source as their men, and had come to the duties of command as little selected or informed. Many had done surprisingly well. There is an engaging picture of the young James Abram Garfield, enrolling his college students as volunteers, taking command of them sword in one hand and drill regulations in the other, and growing with his men until he was a general officer of first-class quality. But there is a less engaging picture of many of the untrained officers leading their men to needless death. The Plattsburg idea had the need for officers in mind, for there must be approximately fifty thousand officers for every million men enrolled. The college students' camps of 1913 and 1914 revealed the willingness of many young men to take training even at their own expense. The camps of 1915, some of them for business men, broadened the evidence, so that the War Department in 1915 had recommended that Congress pay the costs of operating the camps. Out of the wrangle over the "continental" army the Officers' Reserve Corps emerged, promising more than merely another method of procuring officers. It promised a break from the old practice of entrusting command to untrained officers, and a barrier to the granting of line commissions to political leaders. The training camps of 1916, whose costs Congress now assumed, gave another measure of the grip of the preparedness movement.

A portion of the federalization scheme for the National Guard, as stated in the National Defense Act, provided that, in emergency and after authorization by Congress, the President might draft into the service of the United States the members of units of the Guard. These would hereafter become soldiers of the United States, subject to order. But before the new federalizing arrangements could be even started, it became necessary to draft, and to enlarge the power of the President by authorizing him to act in anticipation of possible war, instead of having to wait for a specific permission from Congress. During the fortnight after the approval of the National Defense Act, the condition of affairs along the Rio Grande became so ominous that Congress, July 1, gave the President discretion. He had already, in May, called the National Guard of the border States into Federal service for police duties within the United States. On June 18 he had called out the Guard from all of the States. By the end of August there were on duty in the Southern Department or elsewhere 7,003 officers and 133,256 men of the National Guard.

The affairs of Mexico, thus hastening the measures for preparedness, had failed to clear in spite of American patience. The result of the occupation of Vera Cruz in 1914 was indeterminate. Funston was withdrawn from the venture on November 23, but the need for a close patrol of the long border was not lessened. Within Mexico disorder and violence continued to prevail, with consequent destruction of property and loss of life. In proportion as the policies of Diaz had brought foreign capital and managers into Mexico, their presence now was a continuous invitation to pillage and attack. Refugees from all factions congregated in the border towns of Texas, New Mexico, Arizona, and California, while partisan forces acting like brigands ran a guerrilla warfare along the line, fled into the United States for safety, and raided their opponents who had so fled. The recognition of Venustiano Carranza as *de facto* head of the Mexican Government, in October, 1915, brought no peace, but concentrated upon him the efforts of disappointed factionalists.

Just as Garrison resigned and Baker took his place, the border flamed. A peculiarly brutal raid on Americans at Santa Ysabel on January 10, 1916, roused the American opponents of "watchful waiting." Names poured in upon the American Legion, while Roosevelt announced, "We have incurred the contempt of the world; and contempt is the forerunner of aggression." The Senate demanded information of the President, to which Lansing replied, listing 76 Americans killed or disappeared in Mexico in 1913–15 and 128 Americans and Mexicans killed on the border in the United States in the same period. Not all of these were known to have been killed as a consequence of the civil wars; but there were enough clear cases to embitter discussion. The crisis was reached when on March 9 one of the factional leaders, Francisco Villa, raided Columbus, New Mexico, and shot up the town.

The new Secretary of War instantly directed the pursuit of Villa, back into Mexico, until he should be caught. The Carranza Government protested the incidental violation of Mexican territory; while the War Department became acutely conscious of the lack of strategic railroads designed for the protection of the Mexican frontier, and the necessity upon the transport service to replace the army mule with motor trucks. Six days after the Villa raid, under the immediate command of Brigadier-General John J. Pershing, an American column crossed the border in pursuit. Villa was not caught, and as the lines of communication lengthened to four hundred miles between Pershing's outposts and his bases at El Paso and Columbus, the actual safety of the column was endangered. It was more than peace and less than war, with Pershing's freedom of action restricted. The net results included vexatious controversy with the Carranza Government, practical but painful experience in the management of a little mobile army, and a conviction that the Regular Army could not police the border and maintain its intervention without an increase in strength. Pershing and his army were brought back within the United States after eleven months of duty in Mexico, by which time the federalized National Guard was doing border duty. The firmness and discretion with which the pursuit had been executed (for it kept the peace even if it failed to catch the culprit) were rewarded by the promotion of Pershing to the rank of major-general; and when Funston died on February 19, 1917, Pershing took over his command. He had had the largest mobile command and the most serious duties in the field of any of the general officers of the Army.

The summer of 1916 was filled with more excitement than the opening stages of a presidential campaign would have made likely. The National Defense Act became law on June 3; the whole National Guard was called out June 18; and before and after these dates the desire of the advocates of preparedness produced noisy public demonstrations. It was hard for those who disapproved to offer opposition without incurring disrepute; it was easy for those who differed regarding the war in Europe to make common cause for American safety. The demonstrations took the form of mass meetings, and parades that filled the streets. Most of the contending factions took part in them, behind a slogan of "America first," and a denunciation of "hyphenates," although none admitted that the name applied to themselves. "If you gentlemen think that the American people are not in earnest on this question, then you better take a vacation and go back home and consult your constituents," was the warning of an Illinois Republican Representative, who had long been chairman of the Committee on Naval Affairs.

On Flag Day, June 14, the President marched in the most notable of the parades. Most of the large cities arranged them, in a series stretching from spring to summer; but the column in Washington moved along Pennsylvania Avenue just as the Democratic National Convention was assembling in Chicago. To the dismay of his advisers, and of the secret service men responsible for his safety, Wilson led the procession, in summer clothes and shouldering the small flag that was the emblem; and from the base of the Washington Monument he delivered the address of the day. The danger to the life of the President proved to be non-existent; but when a similar parade marched along Market Street in San Francisco, on July 22, the explosion of a bomb spread death and damage. It launched a judicial sequence still to be in the courts after twenty years. Suspicion of guilt fell upon a group of syndicalist labor men, known to believe in sabotage and violence in their controversies. Of these, two, Thomas J. Mooney and Warren K. Billings, were shortly arrested, tried, and condemned to death for murder. There was dual clamor: that they were enemies of society caught red-handed, and that they were innocent victims of conspiracy, railroaded to death in order to make an example. To death they did not go, for presidential urging induced the Governor of California to commute their sentences to life imprisonment. Thereafter, as the convicted men lay in jail at San Quentin and Folsom, they became a rallying theme for marginal labor agitation around the world. And the testimony brought out in the repeated drives for new trial, pardon, or release created suspicion, not only of a perjury plot somewhere, but also of a clumsy system of criminal justice. An immediate consequence of opposition to preparedness demonstrations was the stiffening of the movement. It suggested additional reasons for national armament.

At the crest of the interest, and while the national conventions were preparing the set-up for a presidential campaign, the other measures urged upon Congress in December, 1915, were approaching completion. Alongside the revision of the Army law ran a naval appropriation bill and a shipping bill, making parts of the unified program. Secretary Josephus Daniels recommended that this appropriation act be expanded to carry not only the funds for ordinary Navy use, but the first steps as well in a five-year Navy plan. He refrained from offering a ten-year plan because of his awareness that war experience was modifying Navy thought; he discarded the traditional single-year method because it was haphazard. Daniels urged that during the five fiscal years, 1917–21, ten dreadnaughts be started and six battle cruisers, together with an impressive list of smaller fighting and service craft. He had before him, as he made his report in December, 1915, a recommendation from the General Board, from which he departed, and a consciousness of change that was delaying the laying of the keels of battleships 43 and 44, authorized in March, 1915.

The fleets of the World War were slow in revealing through general engagements the answers to the questions of their effectiveness before aircraft and submarines. It was undetermined whether the capital ship of the future was to be the lumbering and stately dreadnaught battleship, or the swifter battle cruiser, with which only the United States among the major nations was unprovided. There was battle between the naval drafting-rooms, each side reinforced by adherents outside; and this must be compromised before Congress could authorize new units for the Navy. The admirals who testified before the committees were not in agreement among themselves. When Lemuel P. Padgett, of Tennessee, opened the discussion of the Naval Appropriation Bill in the House on May 27, he defended the largest single appropriation that had yet been proposed; but he still had to explain to his colleagues that a chief difference between dreadnaught and battle cruiser was the difference between a maximum speed of twenty-one knots and one of thirty-five. He still relied on the dreadnaught as the "principal fighting ship of the Navy," but he called attention to the twenty-two pre-dreadnaughts still in commission, to the nine dreadnaughts in commission, and to the eight more under construction. His committee recommended the laying down of the keels of five battle cruisers at once, as part of the five-year plan. His bill passed the House June 2, the Senate July 21, and spent more than five weeks in conference before the President signed it, August 29.

Party lines were badly broken as the Senate condensed the five-year plan into three years; but the differences of opinion showed more plainly in the debates than in the voting, for the House accepted the bill 363 to 4 and the Senate 71 to 8. Before the House voted, the debate was illuminated by facts, whose meaning, however, was not clear until the World War was wholly history. On May 31, the German High Seas Fleet came out from its base upon the North Sea, meeting the British Fleet west of Jutland Bank under such conditions that each side, as it defined its mission, claimed the victory. The battle cruisers received a test, satisfying their advocates that they had won the day; the dreadnaughts, coming later into action, convinced their adherents that they determined the outcome. The new bill accepted the necessity for ships of both types, authorizing for immediate construction four dreadnaughts and four battle cruisers, and running up the appropriation to $313,000,000.

The Naval Appropriation Act did more than appropriate for the Navy. To evade the rule that an appropriation bill must not carry general legislation, it was passed under a special rule removing all limitations upon its content. The riders to the bill, thus made legitimate, provided for reorganization in the service. A new precedent was set by a provision for the erection of a Government armor-plate factory. Since part of the opposition to preparedness was a belief in unreasonable profits accruing to manufacturers of equipment, this made the bill more palatable to the opponents of big business. The Army Appropriation Bill, signed also on August 29, carried the funds for the reorganized Army, and carried its riders, too. The conference committee, outside its proper authority, but driven by what it regarded as necessity, added to the bill a revision of the Articles of War. Another rider created a Council of National Defense "for the co-ordination of industries and resources for the national security and welfare."

The Articles of War, being the military laws for the internal discipline and government of the Army, were descended from Revolutionary codes, having been first adapted out of a British code in 1775. They were out of date. For a decade there had been attempts to enact a revision suited to modern conditions. Twice the Senate had passed such a bill, to have it neglected by the House. The Articles now attached to an appropriation bill met an old need, but delayed the final passage of the measure because of one of the articles exempting retired officers from court-martial. Because of this the President vetoed the whole act August 18; and it became necessary to repass it without the offending provision before it could be signed eleven days later.

The Council of National Defense gave body to an idea not new, but brought to new importance by the war experience of the belligerents. Earlier wars had not embraced the whole activity of whole peoples. In the World War the capacity of military man power to consume and destroy supplies was greater than the capacity of the civilian population to produce. The continuous flow of supplies to the front must be adjusted to the minimum needs of the civilian population to continue to live; and no belligerent had possessed machinery for this. It was no longer possible to procure enough military supplies from the open markets; new factories must be built, and new supplies of raw materials reached. Procurement of munitions called for a more penetrating understanding than military men, or politicians, or business men, alone could possess. The various belligerent countries commenced soon after the war began to erect control agencies over food, finance, and essential supplies, and to restrict non-essential industries for the sake of war. These new agencies, mediating between armies and the peoples, became as essential to victory as force itself.

The Naval Consulting Board, with the Committee on Industrial Preparedness preceding it, was an American step leading to the Council of National Defense. The National Research Council, organized in 1916 by the National Academy of Sciences, was another forerunner. The President supported the inclusion of a Council now, rider to the appropriation though it was. Six of his Cabinet (War, Navy, Interior, Agriculture, Commerce, and Labor) were named as council of National Defense, to be a governing board, working through an unpaid Advisory Commission of seven civilian experts, capable in the several fields whose co-operation was essential. The duty of the organization was not administration, but the preparation of plans for action. It was to bear to civil life something of the relation held to the Army and Navy by the General Staff and the General Board. How useful it might be was left to time to tell.

Last of the measures of preparedness, and approved only on September 7, the day before the first session of the Sixty-Fourth Congress adjourned, was the bill creating the United States Shipping Board. "I conceived the idea of a shipping corporation," says McAdoo, in his *Crowded Years: The Reminiscences of William G. McAdoo* (1931), speaking of the disturbed autumn of 1914, when American cargoes crowded the warehouses, waiting the ocean transportation that did not come. As the Ship Purchase Bill, the proposal received the endorsement of the Administration in September, 1914. Opposed by shipping interests, and by both Republicans and Democrats, it was the victim of a harsh filibuster in the next winter. Re-endorsed by the President in December, 1915, it was taken up for debate in the House in the middle of May. The proposals were various. The bill was designed to provide auxiliary merchant ships for the service of Army and Navy in time of war. The hearings on the earlier bills had established the insufficiency of existing American ships for this. It aimed at a better supply of ships for general trade, that an American merchant marine might be revived, and that shippers might be freed from the dictation of foreign owners who enforced the dicta of belligerent Governments as to what freight their ships should carry. A merchant marine, encouraged by direct subsidy, had at various times received strong Republican endorsement. It proposed to establish Government control over the shipping business, in so far as carried on by American ships, and in this it bore resemblance to such designs as had received approval in the Federal Reserve Board and the Federal Trade Commission. The bill had the full support of the Administration, and needed it, for the zeal for preparedness was not strong enough to overcome all of the objections raised against such a Government venture in the preceding Congress. The special rule under which the House considered it was denounced as a gag rule for party purposes. The law failed of the nearly unanimous votes given the Army and Navy bills; receiving only 209 to 61 in the House and 38 to 21 in the Senate, considerably less in each case than either full Democratic strength or actual majority of a full house.

But the bill was driven through. It directed the United States to enter the shipping business through a Shipping Board of five salaried members, who might lease, buy, build, and operate a fleet of merchant ships to the extent of fifty million dollars provided as a working capital. The Board was authorized to set up a Government-owned corporation for the actual work. This last agency, taking form seven months later as the Emergency Fleet Corporation, was something of a novelty in Government procedure; a device to evade the red tape of Government offices and to give the new body an agility in action equal to that of the business corporations against which it should pit itself. The difficulties surrounding the use of such a corporation, however, were small in comparison with the difficulty of procuring the ships themselves. Every shipyard in the United States was busy; every shipway carried a hull building at a high price and often for foreign customers whose need for additional tonnage was even more imperative than that of the United States. There had not been any public statement of the total damage done to Allied shipping by the submarines, but the Allied Governments knew all about it, and were nearly desperate.

No one seems to have been satisfied with the whole of any of the preparedness measures; but in the aggregate they went beyond anything that Congress had attempted in the past, or that American opinion had tolerated. They gave legal shape to the deep conviction developing since 1914. A point of departure, for further development when the emergency should have become more pressing, they were more than partisan and less than technically scientific. They were the bills that could be passed. Their range at least suggested the complexity of any scheme of national defense.

Before Congress completed its session, September 8, the difficulty of holding its attention to the job became extreme. The presidential campaign was under way, so that in the concluding weeks of the session the debates became progressively more partisan. The President was losing the last of his confidence that the neutral pose could be maintained with safety, but had not lost hope that the belligerents might be maneuvered to a peace before all of the new laws had been invoked. Yet no step in this maneuver was prudent or possible until it should be determined whether he or another should make it; no one yet knew what President or which party would become responsible for national safety on March 4, 1917.

# The Army War Effort

## BY GENERAL PEYTON C. MARCH

WAR DEPARTMENT,
OFFICE OF THE CHIEF OF STAFF,
*Washington, June 30, 1919.*

THE SECRETARY OF WAR.
SIR:

At the time of the preparation of my previous annual report existing conditions permitted only a very brief and general outline of the work of the General Staff during the period covered by that report.

The magnitude of the task performed by it, the diversity and the complexity of the problems involved and the nature of the difficulties that had to be overcome during the war, however, render it both desirable and necessary that a more detailed report as to some of the principal activities during this period be made, as time becomes available, in order that some of the more important lessons that have crystallized out of the experience of the war may be indicated.

### Mobilization of entire nation

At the time the armistice with Germany was signed on November 11, 1918, the United States had sent across 3,000 miles of ocean more than 2,000,000 men and a vast quantity of supplies for their support and use. This American activity had been a positive factor in the concluding military actions of the war, culminating in the splendid drive through the Argonne Forest to Sedan.

Considering the distance over which the United States had to operate and the relatively short period of its participation in the war, the achievement is without parallel in the many great performances of the war. Moreover, the organization which made this achievement possible had been developed to such a point that the flow of men and supplies overseas in the ensuing six months would have been a still more impressive accomplishment.

These things were brought about only by the organization of the resources of the whole Nation for the carrying on of the war. This mobilization, not of a national Army merely, but of a whole Nation, was something which has not been seen in any former war. Germany first deliberately planned for war on such a scale and organized for this one purpose her whole national resources. It was necessary for France, England, and the United States to develop under the pressure of actual war conditions the machinery for such universal mobilization.

The declaration of war, on April 6, 1917, found the United States, from a military, industrial, and economic standpoint, thoroughly unprepared for the great task which confronted it.

In connection with the part played by the War Department in this task, I desire in this report to outline, in a general way, the evolution of the plans and the development of the organization of the General Staff, which, under the

Annual report of General Peyton C. March, Chief of Staff, United States Army, 1919, in *War Department Annual Reports, 1919* (Washington, 1920), I, 237–251, 338–347.

Chief of Staff, is charged by the Secretary of War with the planning, development, and execution of the military program. It will not deal with the subject of the manufacture of munitions, which will be covered by the detailed reports of the Director of Munitions and of the chiefs of the bureaus concerned, nor with the operations of the American Expeditionary Force in France, which will be covered by the report of General Pershing.

## Original Tentative Army Program

In the consideration in the spring of 1917 of the military program to be adopted by this country, the amount of tonnage that would be available to transport and to maintain troops overseas was problematical in view of the submarine situation. The sinkings during the months of March, April, and May were very heavy and indicated the serious possibility that Germany's submarine campaign might so reduce ship tonnage that the Allies could not procure the necessary foodstuffs, metals, and supplies required for the successful prosecution of the war.

It was possible that only a comparatively small expeditionary force could be sent overseas, to increase the morale of the Allies and to decrease that of the Germans, reserving the greater part of the available tonnage to carry food and supplies to the Allies. It was, furthermore, considered by some, both in this country and abroad, that the United States would not be able to supply a large land Army and that, therefore, America's chief contribution should be a huge aerial force.

The tentative program adopted at that time accordingly contemplated:

(1) To send overseas promptly a small but complete body of American troops in the form of one tactical division for the purpose of serving as the nucleus for the organization and training of our overseas troops and for the resulting effect upon the morale of the Allies and of the Central Powers. It was essential, in order that the morale of the Germans might be lowered, that some American troops be put into the trenches at the earliest possible date.

(2) To follow this advance detachment by an expeditionary force of sufficient size, if the shipping situation permitted, to make American participation an effective factor in the prosecution of the war. The submarine situation and other conditions made it impracticable at this early date to determine the exact size of this expeditionary force, but in a general way it was contemplated that the capacity of the 16 National Army cantonments and the 16 National Guard camps which were under construction would enable approximately 1,000,000 men to be in France by the end of the year 1918.

(3) In May, 1917, when the plans and policies for our military effort were in a very formulative stage, the French authorities requested that the United States undertake a tremendous part in aerial warfare by sending 4,500 American aviators, and a correspondingly great amount of matériel to France within a year. In the Aviation Section of the Signal Corps there were approximately 35 officers who could fly elementary planes; there were no officers who had had training or experience with fighting ships. Furthermore, there were no fighting ships, no commercial industry for the production of the vast amount of aerial equipment required, and the aeronautical engineers in the country were negligible in number.

Urged by popular enthusiasm, the Aviation Section of the Signal Corps undertook an air program entirely disproportionate to a properly balanced Army and, as events showed, impossible of execution. The history of this transcendental program, which was adopted and undertaken by the Signal Corps practically independently of the rest of the Army, affords an early and a striking example of the necessity for a General Staff to formulate the military program and to coordinate the activities of the various agencies concerned. Such coordination was not, in the case of the air program, effected during the first year of the war.

## The 30-Division Program of October 7, 1917

The original tentative program crystallized into a definite plan when, in the early part of

July, 1917, General Pershing sent back to this country confidential preliminary recommendations covered by his "General Organization Project" of July 10, 1917. This contemplated the shipment overseas during 1917 and 1918 of an American Expeditionary Force of 30 divisions. Under date of September 18, 1917, General Pershing submitted his "Service of the Rear Project" which was approved, and this was followed by his "Schedule of Priority Shipments" of October 7, which was likewise approved. This priority schedule, together with cabled requests received from time to time for special and additional troops, or embodying other minor modifications in the schedule, constituted the program by which priority of shipments overseas was established.

It was divided into six phases and provided for the placing in France by December 31, 1918 of 1,372,399 troops consisting of 30 divisions organized into 5 corps of 6 divisions (4 combat, 1 training, and 1 replacement) each, with the necessary corps troops, Army troops, service of supply troops, and replacements.

This program was the official approved military program when, on March 4, 1918, I assumed the duties of Acting Chief of Staff.

In the early part of 1918 the military situation was most critical. Due to the effectiveness of the steps taken by the British and the American Navies the submarine situation, while, of course, still a matter of great concern, was such as to make clear that the German unrestricted submarine warfare would fail to accomplish the results expected by its proponents, namely, to starve England out and to prevent to a large extent trans-Atlantic and cross-channel shipments of troops and supplies to France.

The situation on the land was, however, much more unfavorable to the Allies. Germany and her allies still maintained a numerical superiority on the western front, and this superiority was being increased daily by the transfer of troops who had been released, for service on the western front, as the result both of the elimination of Russia, during the winter, as an actual factor in the war, and of the defeat of the Italian army by the Austro-Germans in the fall. The German armies also possessed the advantages of shorter interior lines of communication, approximately three millions of Russian and other war prisoners who released soldiers for combatant duty, and trained senior and General Staff officers developed as the result of 40 years of preparation. Furthermore, they possessed the great advantages of unity of command, and of operating on the offensive in enemy territory.

While these advantages were exploited in every way possible in the German propaganda, it was known that the failure of the unrestricted submarine warfare to accomplish the promised results, the failure to capture the channel ports, and, in general the failure, notwithstanding the enormous losses, to terminate the war, were rapidly affecting the German morale. It was inevitable that the German high command would be forced to seek an early and decisive determination of the war by a military victory on the western front before the power of the United States could be developed sufficiently to become a decisive factor. England had reached the limit of her man power; France was exhausted; the necessity for their reinforcement, in the greatest numbers, and at the earliest moment possible was vital to the success of the allied cause.

When I returned to this country in March, 1918, it was with the firm conviction that it was imperative that the shipment of troops to France be vastly increased at the earliest practicable date, and have priority over everything else, and as this policy became effective studies were instituted as to the practicability of putting in France a sufficient number of men to bring the war to an early conclusion.

## The 80-Division Program of July 18, 1918

After a study of the entire situation I came to the conclusion that the war might be brought to an end in 1919, provided we were able to land in France by June 30 of that year 80 American divisions of a strength of 3,360,000 men. On July 18, 1918, I submitted to you a formal memorandum, accompanied by a study of methods by which the men could be obtained, the supplies procured, and an analysis of the shipping which must be obtained in order to accomplish this very large military program. This was accompanied by an estimate of the cost of the proposed program.

In this study I recommended to you the adoption, as the American program, of 80 divisions in France and 18 at home by June 30, 1919, based on a total strength of the American Army of 4,850,000 men. This was approved by you and by the President of the United States and adopted as our formal military program.

The details of this program are shown in tabular form below:

In view of the great length of time required to produce the supplies and equipment required for a possible continuation of this program studies were at once begun on an extension of this program through the year ending June 30, 1920. This extension, which was approved September 3, was given out to the supply departments for their use in preparing estimates. It provided for an Army of 4,260,000, or 100 divisions, in France, and 1,290,000, or 12 divisions, in the United States, or for a total of 5,500,000 men by June 30, 1920.

Up to the signing of the armistice troops were

| Date | During Month Ending on Date Indicated | | | | On Date Indicated | | |
|---|---|---|---|---|---|---|---|
| | | Movement Overseas | | | | | |
| | Men to Be Drafted | Reinforcement Troops | Replacement Troops | Total Troops Shipped | Total in American Expeditionary Forces | Remaining in United States | |
| 1918 | | | | | | | |
| Feb. 28 | ... | ... | ... | ... | ... | ... | ... |
| Mar. 31 | ... | ... | ... | ... | ... | ... | ... |
| Apr. 30 | ... | ... | ... | ... | ... | ... | ... |
| May 31 | ... | ... | ... | ... | ... | ... | ... |
| June 30 | ... | ... | ... | ... | 1,000,000 | 1,450,000 | 2,500,000 |
| July 31 | 345,000 | 200,000 | 50,000 | 250,000 | 1,235,000 | 1,545,000 | ... |
| Aug. 31 | 250,000 | 200,000 | 50,000 | 250,000 | 1,470,000 | 1,545,000 | ... |
| Sept. 30 | 200,000 | 200,000 | 50,000 | 250,000 | 1,705,000 | 1,495,000 | ... |
| Oct. 31 | 155,000 | 200,000 | 50,000 | 250,000 | 1,945,000 | 1,400,000 | ... |
| Nov. 30 | 150,000 | 185,000 | 40,000 | 225,000 | 2,160,000 | 1,325,000 | ... |
| Dec. 31 | 150,000 | 175,000 | 25,000 | 200,000 | 2,350,000 | 1,275,000 | 3,675,000 |
| 1919 | | | | | | | |
| Jan. 31 | 100,000 | 160,000 | 15,000 | 175,000 | 2,515,000 | 1,200,000 | ... |
| Feb. 28 | 200,000 | 160,000 | 15,000 | 175,000 | 2,675,000 | 1,225,000 | ... |
| Mar. 31 | 300,000 | 200,000 | 35,000 | 235,000 | 2,885,000 | 1,290,000 | ... |
| Apr. 30 | 300,000 | 175,000 | 75,000 | 250,000 | 3,060,000 | 1,340,000 | ... |
| May 31 | 300,000 | 100,000 | 100,000 | 250,000 | 3,210,000 | 1,390,000 | ... |
| June 30 | 300,000 | 100,000 | 100,000 | 250,000 | 3,360,000 | 1,440,000 | 4,850,000 |
| | 2,750,000 | 2,155,000 | 605,000 | 2,760,000 | ... | ... | ... |

NOTES. (*a*) The actual wastage of replacements is assumed at 400,000. (*b*) Organization into divisions is as follows:

| Date | American Expeditionary Forces | United States | Total |
|---|---|---|---|
| June 30, 1918 | 24 | 18 | 42 |
| Dec. 31, 1918 | 52 | 18 | 70 |
| June 30, 1919 | 80 | 18 | 98 |

being transported to France in accordance with the program of July 18.

This program, which embodied a material increase in the previous official program (it contemplated 2,350,000 men in France by December 31, 1918, as compared with 1,372,399 contemplated by the program of October 7, 1917), required for its accomplishment a marked intensification of the efforts of all agencies of the War Department and a thorough and effective correlation of their activities.

*Preliminary Steps.* Reference will now be made to some of the steps which were regarded as necessary or desirable in this connection.

As stated in my previous report, shortly after I entered upon the duties of Chief of Staff I adopted the policy of interchanging the officers of the various staff corps in this country and abroad, and pursuant to this policy men were placed at the heads of various bureaus whose experience in France especially equipped them for the handling of the problems pertaining to their respective bureaus in accordance with the methods and principles evolved and practiced during the war.

With your approval I also adopted for the entire Army the principle of promotion by selection, which had already been found by the responsible authorities in France to be a necessary prerequisite to efficiency in the American Expeditionary Forces, and I abolished all distinctions between Regular Army, National Guard, and National Army organizations and personnel, which had previously existed, by consolidating the entire Army into one Army—the Army of the United States. The experience of the war has proved that these steps resulted in a degree of efficiency throughout the Army that would not otherwise have been possible of attainment.

*Extension of Draft Ages.* The studies made in connection with the new program showed that to carry it into effect required the enactment by Congress of legislation extending the draft ages to include men between the ages of 18 and 45 years and would necessitate the creation of a deficit, over the enormous appropriations already made, of approximately $7,000,000,000. The presentation of the program to Congress, accompanied by the statement that this increase in the Army, if legislation were enacted by Congress which would enable it to be effective, would lead to success in 1919, resulted in prompt and favorable action by that body.

*Troop and Cargo Ships.* Perhaps no subject was the cause of more concern in the execution of the accelerated shipping program or in connection with the formulation of the military program than that of the procurement of the vast amount of ship tonnage, especially cargo-carrying tonnage, required for this purpose.

At the outbreak of the war there was operating under the control of the War Department a total of seven transports. The beginning of the great transport fleet under American control which, on the signing of the armistice, aggregated over 600 vessels of a total tonnage of more than three and one-half million dead-weight tons was made when the interned German vessels which had been seized came into service in the fall of 1917 with a tonnage of over 450,000 dead-weight tons.

Subsequent material additions, which were available in connection with the enlarged shipping program which was put into effect after I became Chief of Staff, included the Dutch vessels, aggregating about 300,000 dead-weight tons which were taken over by the United States, and the three great British liners which were assigned to the service of the War Department, in the early months of 1918. A serious deficiency in cargo ships which had developed led to the organization, in February, 1918, of the Shipping Control Committee, which regulated the allocation and distribution of available tonnage, both American and British. Through the cooperation of this committee, and as the result of the urgent representations made to the Shipping Board relative to the necessity of withdrawing additional ships from trade and of the chartering of every available ship that could be secured from any allied or other country, it was practicable to embark, during the months of May, June, July, and August, 1,121,000 men.

On July 9, 1918, there were 75 transports

carrying 171,670 troops en route overseas from the United States. This was the greatest number of troops on the water between the United States and France at any one time during the eastward movement. The embarkation for July exceeded all expectations, 306,000 troops sailing from Atlantic ports.

The department was able to announce to the President and the American people on July 1 that between May 8, 1917, and June 30, 1918, over a million men had either been landed in France or were en route thereto, and by September 22 it was able to announce that a second million had been sent.

Of the 2,082,000 men who had been embarked when the armistice was signed, over a million and a half had been embarked during the last 6 of the 19 months of our participation in the war. Of this number American flag ships carried approximately 44 per cent, the British approximately 51 per cent, the Italians 3 per cent, and the French 2 per cent. It may be stated here that, in the execution of this program, ways were found to increase the normal loading of our own transports without disadvantageous results of any consequence, by almost 40 per cent, and that the American transports surpassed those of the Allies both in the extent to which they were loaded and in the speed of their turn around.

When German submarines appeared off the Atlantic coast with the obvious purpose of delaying our shipping program, pressure was brought to bear on the department, not only from within this country but from our Allies who were cooperating in furnishing the shipping, to modify the program by changing the embarkation points to Canada. Realizing that the German military authorities appreciated the inevitably decisive effect of the continuation of the shipping program and having entire confidence in the effectiveness of the measures adopted by the Navy to protect the convoys of our troops, I declined to accede to the suggestions that any steps be taken which would result in any retardation of our shipment of troops to France. It is of interest in this connection that no United States transport was sunk on an eastward voyage during the period referred to.

A serious difficulty in maintaining this program, by a singularly unfortunate combination of circumstances, was the outbreak at this same critical period of the influenza epidemic which became acute at the time the necessity for the uninterrupted shipment of troops to France was most pressing. Some of the best medical advice at the disposal of the department regarded it as necessary, and so recommended, that the carrying capacity be decreased as much as 40 per cent as a precaution to prevent the ravages of the epidemic. After a most careful consideration of all phases of the situation I declined to approve a decrease of more than 15 per cent in this capacity, believing that this was sufficient reduction to afford every safeguard that was warranted by the urgency of the military situation and that it would afford, in effect, every advantage that was practicable. Events showed this decision to be fully warranted, since the careful observations made at the time showed conclusively that, as a matter of fact, the percentage of deaths from the epidemic on troop transports was actually less than in the camps and cantonments in this country.

The studies made in connection with the formulation of the 80-division program showed that while the troop transport fleet which, as the result of unremitting effort, had been developed by the summer of 1918, could, without great difficulty, be relied upon to meet the requirements of this program so far as the transportation of troops was concerned, a serious deficiency in cargo shipping existed which would require early and radical action. In view of the great demands for cargo tonnage that had already been made on the shipping of this and all other countries in the building up of our transport fleet, the provision of the large amount of additional tonnage required by this program was a difficult and intricate problem. The only possible sources were the United States and England. In July, 1918, the American tonnage not in the War Department service comprised about 550 ships of an aggregate tonnage of about two and one-half million dead-weight tons. The extent to which this tonnage could be withdrawn required very careful consideration especially in the case of that employed in the nitrate, manganese, chrome, sulphur, and New England coal trades. Furthermore, a great part of this tonnage was not suitable for trans-Atlantic service on account of the fact that the ships in question were not of sufficient size to do satisfactory work when bunkered for the round trip, as was necessary in view of the reduced production of coal in Great Britain. As a result of the urgent representations that were made to the Shipping Board and the Emergency Fleet Corporation, however, a program was adopted with which during the period from July to November, inclusive, a total additional tonnage of approximately 2,000,000 dead-weight tonnage was rendered available. This total included approximately 1,000,000 tons which was withdrawn from the trades. It also included approximately 718,000 tons of new vessels (as compared with the Emergency Fleet Corporation estimates of 1,775,699 tons).

After making full allowance for all tonnage that could possibly be supplied from American sources, however, the study showed that the enlarged program would require the provision of additional tonnage amounting to 1,200,000 tons from August, 1918, and reducing month by month to 200,000 tons in February, 1919, and then ending. The only possible source from which this great amount of tonnage could be supplied was England. She had been hardest hit by the submarine warfare and, furthermore, she was at the time already bending every effort to assist in increasing the movement of American troops to France.

The situation, however, required radical steps if the allied cause were to be saved, and in view of this fact the Secretary of War and the Chief of the Transportation Service (then Chief of Embarkation) appeared before the Allied Maritime Council in London on September 30, 1918, and presented the needs of the United States for additional cargo tonnage to carry through the increased military program. The amount of tonnage required would transport about 2,000,000 tons dead-weight of cargo, and its allocation to the supply program of the American Army would result in the accumulation of a deficit of that amount of food and essential commodities for Great Britain and the Allies. Notwithstanding this fact, however, and relying entirely upon the assistance of the United States later as new tonnage became available, England agreed to allocate sufficient tonnage to meet the requirements of the American program subsequent to the date of this conference.

The signing of the armistice on November 11, 1918, left uncompleted the great cargo program. The 80-division program contemplated monthly shipments, increasing by July, 1919, to 1,759,750 short tons; in November, 1918, approximately 825,000 tons were shipped.

The deficiency in shipping rendered it imperative that every possible step be taken to secure the maximum degree of efficiency from the shipping available. Special attention in this connection was paid to plans for still further decreasing the time of turn around. The importance of this is indicated by the fact that a reduction of 10 days in the average turn around of the cargo transports would at this time have been equivalent to an increase in cargo tonnage of approximately 386,000 dead-weight tons. Another important factor in this matter was the action taken to prevent port congestion in France. This was effected in part by the provision of the enlarged terminal facilities at the ports of debarkation and in part by the provision of great quantities of railroad transportation for use in the prompt evacuation of supplies from the ports.

In connection with the formulation and execution of the enlarged program it was also necessary to give consideration to other matters of primary importance.

*Defects of Bureau System.* As the war progressed it became increasingly evident that the organization of the War Department as it existed at the beginning of the war was in many respects entirely inadequate to meet the requirements of the situation.

Under the system of separate and independent bureaus, as organized when we entered the war, a condition of affairs eventually and inevitably developed which threatened the very success of any extensive military program. Each bureau, absorbed in the tremendous expansion of its personnel and in its problems of supply, naturally concentrated every effort upon the development of a program which would meet every possible requirement that might be imposed upon that particular bureau without reference, in general, to the requirements either of other bureaus or services or of the Army program as a whole. With this independent and uncorrelated action of the different bureaus the defects of the existing bureau system soon became manifest. There developed a competition for manufactured articles and for raw materials and for labor which resulted in high prices and in an inefficient distribution of labor, involving a scarcity in certain localities and actual unemployment in others; similarly there resulted a congestion in the placing of contracts and in the location of new manufacturing plants in many localities, irrespective of the labor, fuel, power, and transportation available. Plants and real estate were commandeered or purchased by individual bureaus without consideration of the effect upon the requirements of other bureaus, and no standardized contract procedure obtained to protect either the manufacturers and owners or the United States. The total lack of standardized specifications resulted in a delay in manufacture, a lack of interchangeability, and an increased cost. Nine independent and different systems for estimating requirements were in operation, with a consequent lack of balance in the military program and inefficient utilization of the available manufacturing plants. There were five different sources of supplies for organizations to be equipped and five different and complicated systems of property accountability for the officers charged with equipping these organizations. There were 10 different agencies for handling money accounts in the War Department, with at least five different systems of fiscal accounts, with no adequate supervision of expenditures.

There existed no agency within the War Department for determining questions of priority among the different bureaus for manufacturing articles or for raw materials. Furthermore, there existed no agency for representing the War Department as a whole in its relations with the War Industries Board in connection with the determination of similar questions of priority between the War Department and the other departments and agencies of the Government, although the Army requirements exceeded all others combined; it was impossible for the War Industries Board, in allocating supplies, materials, and manufacturing capacity, to secure adequate information as to the needs of the War Department as a whole. Individual agreements were being made by various bureaus with foreign governments involving obligations as to replacements and deliveries, which were without reference to the military program as a whole or to the tonnage available, and which was impossible of fulfillment. Each bureau had a more or less decentralized system of storage and was proceeding independently with the construction or procurement of new, and in many cases excessive, storage facilities. Each had a different system of property accountability and no practicable means existed for determining accurately and quickly from the records in Washington the amounts of supplies actually available.

There existed no effective means of traffic control for regulating and establishing priorities among the different bureaus as to shipments to ports. The necessity for such a system was especially emphasized by the fact that the relative urgency for different classes of supplies overseas was, necessarily, as indicated by the shipping priority schedule received, subject to frequent and sudden changes as the character of the operations and requirements of our overseas forces changed from time to time. Thus at one time railroad and construction material was most urgently needed, while at other times aviation equipment, medical supplies, motor transportation, and horses and mules were each given priority. It was accordingly impracticable to allocate cargo tonnage to the various bureaus far in advance, and it was essential that a system of traffic control be established which would be responsive, with the minimum of delay, to the changing priority schedules.

The lack of an effective system of traffic control resulted in such a competition for transportation and in such a congestion of railroad equipment, required not only for the shipment of our own supplies but for the shipment of those of the Allies as well, as to result in rendering inoperative a large part of the available railroad equipment of the country. This congestion of railroad equipment was in part contributory to the fuel shortage which at one time threatened seriously to interfere with the sailing of our transports. This lack of an effective system of traffic control also resulted in the filling of the storage facilities at the ports and piers with unessential materials and thereby prevented the shipment of essential materials and supplies. This is instanced by the fact that it became necessary for the authorities in France at one time to protest strongly against the fact that certain bureaus were shipping mahogany desks and other office furniture in space which was urgently needed for food, medical supplies, and ammunition. It was rapidly becoming impossible to load the transports in accordance with the American Expeditionary Forces requirements as shown by the shipping schedules or to furnish adequate shipping lists covering the supplies actually shipped. It was evident that if the storage facilities, the railroad equipment, and the ocean tonnage were to be utilized promptly and to utmost capacity and in accordance with the actual requirements overseas, it would be necessary for a central controlling agency to control every shipment of materials and supplies from its point of origin in the United States to its delivery to the base port in France—to release the shipment from the factory or storehouse, provide the necessary railroad transportation to the terminals at the port of embarkation, collect it at the piers, and load it on the transport, all in accordance with carefully prearranged plans which articulated closely with the plans for organizing, training, and equipping the Army.

It may be noted here that the problem of the shipment, in the great numbers required, of troops from every camp and cantonment to France was closely analogous to that of the shipment of supplies. It involved the same necessity for observing overseas priorities, the same dangers of congestion at the ports of embarkation and the same necessity for a continuous and direct traffic control from the point of origin to the transport.

In order that the War Department might meet the great task and responsibilities imposed upon it by the war it had, during the first year of the war, become increasingly evident that a reorganization was necessary which would provide for:

(1) A redistribution of existing functions of various bureaus in such a manner as to consolidate important similar or identical functions in the one agency best adapted to handle them.

(2) The creation of certain new agencies to handle matter previously handled by existing bureaus but not logically a part of their function, and the creation of certain new services found to be necessary as the result of the developments and experiences of the Army overseas.

(3) The reorganization of the General Staff in such a manner as to enable it to perform its proper functions of an effective central controlling agency to coordinate and to control all existing War Department agencies and services so as to eliminate lost motion and to direct their activities in such a manner as to further to best advantage the development and the execution of the military program as a whole.

The necessity for action along these lines had been recognized by the department and steps had been taken providing for a reorganization of this character to such an extent as was authorized by existing legislation. It was not, however, until the passage by Congress of the Overman Act, which was approved by the President on May 20, 1918, that it was practicable for an adequate and efficient reorganization to be put into effect.

*Reorganization of the General Staff.* One of the most important matters taken up by the department during the earlier part of the war was the reorganization of the General Staff. Prior to the act of February 14, 1903, the United States Army had no General Staff. Since the early history of the country there had been a Commanding General of the Army and a system of semi-independent War Department bureaus which was loosely coordinated either with the line of the Army or with one another. There had long been uncertainty and dispute as to the respective functions and authority of the Secretary of War, the Commanding General, and the bureaus. During the Civil War this War Department organization proved so inefficient that a committee of Congress sat almost continuously to investigate the conduct of the war. The failures of the bureau supply system during the brief War with Spain is a matter of general knowledge. When Mr. Root became Secretary of War on August 1, 1899, he became convinced that there was a fundamental organizational defect in the War Department bureau system as it had grown up through more than a century of history. He pointed out that this system had developed in such a way as largely to tie the hands of the Secretary of War himself and to make it impossible for him to supervise and direct in any effective way the work of his department. After an exhaustive study of the matter he recommended to Congress, and succeeded in securing the enactment of, the organic act of February 14, 1903, which abolished the office of Commanding General of the Army and created a General Staff Corps of 45 officers, having at its head a Chief of Staff, who under the direction of the President and the Secretary of War was charged with the supervision of all troops of the line and of all War Department bureaus.

However, by the act of August 23, 1912, Congress reduced the strength of the General Staff to 36. The national-defense act of June 3, 1916, increased the strength of the General Staff Corps to a maximum of 55, exclusive of the Chief of the Militia Bureau and of the Chief of Coast Artillery, this maximum to be attained, by five annual increments, by 1920. This act, however, in effect still further decreased the strength of the General Staff Corps by providing that "not more than one-half of all the officers detailed in said corps shall at any time be stationed, or assigned to, or employed upon any duty in or near the District of Columbia." It also prohibited the Chief of Staff from attaching to his office for more than 30 days at a time any officers not members of the General Staff Corps.

On April 6, 1917, the date of the declaration of war, the General Staff, which was organized under the provisions of the act of June 3, 1916, had an authorized strength of 41 officers, the first annual increment only having been added. Under the limitations imposed by this act, the General Staff, on the date referred to, consisted of 19 officers stationed in Washington and 22 stationed elsewhere. The task of preparing the plans for creating, mobilizing, organizing, training, equipping, transporting to Europe, and of maintaining and supplying there the future Army of the United States accordingly devolved upon a group of 19 officers, who constituted the General Staff, authorized by law to be stationed in the city of Washington. This personnel was, of course, ridiculously inadequate, not only for the gigantic task confronting it, but for any General Staff work commensurate with the responsibilities of that corps. It is of interest in this connection to note that at the beginning of the war the strengths of the general staffs of Germany, France, and England were, respectively, approximately 650, 644, and 232.

The low ebb to which the General Staff had been brought at the time of the beginning of the war by restrictive legislation is indicated by the fact that on the signing of the armistice of the 1,072 officers on duty on or with the War Department General Staff but 4 had had previous General Staff experience; these 4 were general officers.

The act of May 12, 1917, increased the General Staff to 91 and removed, for the period of the emergency only, the restrictions of the act of June 3, 1916, relative to the number of these officers authorized to be stationed in Washington. This act was followed by the act of May 18, 1917, which authorized the President "to provide the necessary officers, line and staff," for the forces raised under this act, and removed, for the period of the emergency, the legislative restrictions as to the strength and organization of the General Staff Corps.

On June 30, 1919, the strength of the General Staff Corps was 253, including 130 detailed under the act of May 18, 1917, for the period of the emergency. There were at this time 395 officers detailed for duty with the General

Staff, a reduction of 549 since the signing of the armistice.

The evolution and development of the present organization of the different divisions of the General Staff, from the nucleus of 11 officers on duty with the War College Division on the outbreak of the war, is outlined elsewhere in this report in connection with the account of the work of the individual divisions.

The first steps taken to organize the General Staff in such a manner as to enable it to perform its proper function of effecting the coordination of the activities of the various War Department agencies, which was recognized as being necessary to the successful accomplishment of the military program, was the issue on February 9, 1918, of General Orders, as later No. 14. This order organized the General Staff into five main divisions, namely, the Executive, the War Plans, the Purchase and Supply, the Storage and Traffic, and the Operations Divisions. It charged the Chief of Staff with "the planning and development of the Army program," and it provided that the chief of the Purchase and Supply Division should "have cognizance and supervision of the purchase and production of all munitions and other supplies" and should be charged with "the supervision and direction of all purchases, procurement and production activities of the several bureaus, corps, and other agencies of the War Department."

The General Staff was organized under this order on March 4, 1918, when I became Acting Chief of Staff.

The congestion at the ports had, however, become so acute by that time that unless adequate corrective measures had been taken without delay the movement of supplies overseas, both for this country and for the Allies, would undoubtedly within a few months have been practically blocked. Experience had shown that the interior organization of the various bureaus was such as to render an effective supervision of their activities by the General Staff, as contemplated by General Orders, No. 14, impossible. As the result of a careful consideration of the matter I became convinced that a consolidation of procurement, except of certain specialized equipment, of storage, of finance, and of transportation, together with a positive and direct central control of these activities by the General Staff, was essential to the elimination of the unsatisfactory conditions existing and to the rapid, efficient, and economical utilization of the resources of the country to the development of the Army program as a whole. The magnitude of the task, the diversity of conflicting interests, and the intimate correlation required by the different agencies involved permitted no division of responsibility or of effort if the War Department machine was to function with that degree of efficiency which was essential if the urgent and constantly changing needs of our Army were to be met.

On August 26, 1918, with your approval, General Orders, No. 80, was issued. This order provided:

> The Chief of the General Staff is the immediate adviser of the Secretary of War on all matters relating to the Military Establishment, and is charged by the Secretary of War with the planning, development, and execution of the Army program. The Chief of Staff by law (act of May 12, 1917) takes rank and precedence over all officers of the Army, and by virtue of that position and by authority of and in the name of the Secretary of War he issues such orders as will insure that the policies of the War Department are harmoniously executed by the several corps, bureaus, and other agencies of the Military Establishment and that the Army program is carried out speedily and efficiently.

This order definitely charged the Chief of Staff with the responsibility for the execution of the Army program and delegated to him the authority commensurate with this responsibility.

It further consolidated the previously existing Purchase and Supply Division and the Storage and Traffic Division into the Purchase, Storage and Traffic Division, under the Director of Purchase, Storage and Traffic, who was specifically charged with the "control of the . . . procurement and productive activities, including real estate, of the several bureaus, corps, and other agencies of the War Department . . . the storing and warehousing of property for all departments, bureaus, and corps of the Army . . . the movement of all property of the War Department . . . and the transportation of troops and supplies overseas. . . ."

Under the general authority contained in the Overman Act, which had been approved May 20, the Director of Purchase, Storage and Traffic was immediately upon the issue of

General Orders, No. 80, authorized by me to effect a consolidation of the procurement (except in the case of the procurement of certain technical or specialized equipment pertaining to the technical corps) and of the storage functions of the various bureaus and services. The details of the procedure followed in this connection are given elsewhere in this report. In effect the result was to transfer these functions to the Quartermaster Department, already handling about 80 per cent of the procurement and storage activities of the Army, the Quartermaster General, who was designated as the Director of Purchase and Storage, reporting direct to the Director of Purchase, Storage, and Traffic. The transfer of storage functions had, however, progressed much further on June 30, 1919, than had the transfer of procurement functions. The consolidation of procurement rendered necessary a consolidation of financial activities under a Director of Finance, who, together with the chiefs of the previously existing Embarkation and Inland Transportation branches, also reported direct to the Director of Purchase, Storage and Traffic.

Another important change in the organization of the General Staff effected by General Orders, No. 80, was the establishment of the Military Intelligence Division, which had previously been a branch first of the War Plans Division and later of the Executive Division, as a separate and coordinate division of the General Staff. This was necessary in view of the extent and scope of the responsibilities of this division.

A subsequent and important amendment was made in General Orders, No. 80, when, by General Orders, No. 86, dated September 18, 1918, there was established, in the Operations Division, the Personnel Branch, in which there had been effected a consolidation of the handling of the appointments, assignments, and promotions of all commissioned personnel in the Army. This action became necessary as the result of the condition which arose due to the competition among bureaus and services for commissioned personnel and in order that officers might be assigned in accordance with their special qualifications to the arm in which their services could be most useful.

*Other Reorganizations.* In addition to the reorganization of the General Staff and the consolidation of bureau functions above referred to, it was necessary, in the comprehensive and adequate reorganization of the War Department to establish certain new agencies.

At the beginning of the war the Quartermaster Department had, in addition to its other duties, been charged with construction, motor transport, the Transport Service, and the pay of the Army. It had, early in the war, developed that these duties were of such an unrelated character and involved operations on such a scale as to render necessary a separation of these functions from the Quartermaster Corps in order that it might accomplish the tremendous task otherwise devolving upon it. The necessity for this separation of duties was emphasized when, with the consolidation of procurement and storage, the Quartermaster Department developed into the great procuring and storage agency of the Army.

The Construction Division, which was organized as a separate agency from the Quartermaster Department in the early days of the war, was called upon to handle what was probably the greatest construction project ever undertaken, involving expenditures aggregating more than twice the cost of the Panama Canal. The rapid expansion of the Embarkation Service, which was also organized as a separate agency in August, 1917, is outlined elsewhere in this report. These agencies had already been separated from the Quartermaster Department and, following the experiences in the war, a new service, the Tank Corps, had been organized.

This reorganization was continued on my arrival. The development and procurement of material and the handling of the personnel pertaining to gas warfare, which was at that time distributed among four bureaus, was, on June 28, 1918, consolidated into a new service to potential wrongdoers afforded by such a large number of convictions. The duties of this section were ultimately extended to include observation of the disposal of salvage in Europe, estimated to aggregate one and one-half billions of dollars in value.

*Necessity for General Staff Control.* The history of the Revolutionary War, the Civil War, and the War with Spain had shown the necessity of a War Department organization of this character; the experience of the first year of this war had demonstrated clearly that without such an organization the effective accomplishment of the tremendous military program required by a modern war was impossible.

Prior to the war, due to the legislative restrictions imposed upon its organization, no adequate General Staff organization was possible. Neither the bureaus nor the General Staff were, therefore, familiar with the best method of establishing an effective system of General Staff control. It was accordingly necessary for the details of such a system to be worked out, and for the necessary points of contact between the General Staff and the bureaus to be established, under the stress of war.

By March 4, 1918, when I became Chief of Staff, the critical military situation required action, and results, if the imperative needs of our Army overseas, and of the allied cause, were to be met. The existing organization of the various War Department bureaus and services was such that it did not permit the efficient supervision and control of their activities which was imperatively required if the military program were to be carried out. The consolidation of related activities which was necessary to attain this end required a degree of actual administrative control, if results were to be secured with the expedition and effectiveness that was necessary, which, in some cases, was not essentially or fundamentally a General Staff function. Had a proper and adequate General Staff organization and supervision been in existence before the war this degree of administrative control by the General Staff would not have been necessary. Under the existing conditions, however, no other alternative existed if the military program as a whole were to be carried out, and I subordinated all other considerations to the attainment of that end.

*Peace Organization.* Upon the signing of the armistice there was both the time and the opportunity for a clearer definition of the functions and organization of the existing agencies than had been practicable during the active continuation of the war. This work was promptly undertaken, and by June 30, 1919, the end of the period covered by this report, substantial progress had been made in this direction by a reorganization of the Purchase, Storage and Traffic Division which in effect established as four separate and distinct administrative and operating services, the Purchase and Storage Service (a development of the Quartermaster Department), the Transportation Service, the Financial Service, and the Real Estate Service, which, like all other operating bureaus and services of the War Department, are under the control and supervision of the Director of Purchase, Storage and Traffic, as assistant to the Chief of Staff, in all matters which pertain to the supply, transportation, and financial operations of the Army. Such control is essential to the accomplishment of any military program.

The experience of the war has unquestionably demonstrated that this organization is sound in time of war. It is equally sound in time of peace. To revert to a peace organization which must inevitably be disrupted again in time of war would be to discard the costly and invaluable lessons gained from the experience in this war. It is essential that the peace-time organization be such as to require, in time of war, merely the expansion of existing agencies—not the creation and organization of new ones.

*Results Accomplished.* The general nature of the evolution of the War Department organization which was developed to carry into effect its military program has been outlined, and reference has been made to some of the considerations involved in the development of this organization. The results accomplished are indicated by the fact that on November 11, 1918, the date the armistice was signed, the total of the embarkations for France, as stated above, was approximately 2,082,000. Of these more than a million and a half had embarked within the preceding six months.

## Purchase, Storage, and Traffic Division

The United States entered the war with only a partial conception of what it would mean to mobilize the Nation's whole resources for a single purpose, and without having worked out the concrete plans for achieving such an end. It was only by degrees that the country grasped the necessity for the assembling of its entire resources and it was only step by step that there was worked out the mechanism for accomplishing this end.

A few preparatory measures had been taken. The Navy, fortunately, had already achieved unity of organization. It had formerly operated under a bureau system similar to that of the Army, but this had given way to a unified organization which was to prove highly efficient under the strain of war. There was, however, no adequate machinery for coordinating the supply activities of the Army and Navy. Moreover, the carrying on of the war imposed new tasks for the performance of which it presently became necessary to create completely new emergency organizations independent of the existing departments of the Government.

The threat of the submarine to the world's shipping had already led to an appreciation of the necessity for a large shipbuilding program, and the Shipping Board and the United States Fleet Corporation were the agencies which had been created for the accomplishment of this end.

The shortage of tonnage and the necessity for controlling foreign trade, both as a means of directing the restricted flow of raw materials and of making more effectual the economic blockade of enemy countries, led to the establishment of the War Trade Board.

It was the submarine again, with its threat of starvation for England and France, which drove home the need for the United States Food Administration, charged with the control of the food problem as a whole.

The unprecedented war demands upon industry for the production of war supplies caused the creation of the Fuel Administration, which was made responsible for the production, distribution, and conservation of this fundamental of industrial output.

The necessity for operating the railroads of the country as a unified system to insure the uncongested transportation of men and materials led to all important lines being taken over by the Government and the creation of the United States Railroad Administration.

The Council of National Defense, which had been proposed as far back as 1911, was created by the act of August 29, 1916, seven months before the United States entered the war. It was not fully organized, however, until March, 1917, and while it was destined to play an important part in conducting the supply activities of the Government, it had to go through a long course of development before an efficient mechanism was reached for mobilizing national industry and for coordinating the activities of the numerous agencies through which the Government conducted the war. The council itself was composed of a group of six members of the President's Cabinet: The Secretary of War, the Secretary of the Navy, the Secretary of the Interior, the Secretary of Agriculture, the Secretary of Commerce, and the Secretary of Labor.

Provision was also made for a commission "advisory to the Council of National Defense," to be composed of men having special expert knowledge of industrial or natural resources.

During the course of the war the Council of National Defense and the advisory commission established a complex system of subordinate bodies to assist in the carrying out of their functions. It will be sufficient to mention here only three which have a special bearing on the story of the Purchase, Storage, and Traffic Division: The General Munitions Board, the Committee on Supplies, the Committee on Raw Materials.

The General Munitions Board, which functioned during the early stages of the war, developed later into the War Industries Board in July, 1917, and the President by letter of March 4, 1918, to its chairman, made it the great coordinating factor of the Government. The nature of the problems to be solved and the coordinating mechanism which was developed for their solution will be shown later. As the matter of military supplies stood first among those problems, it is necessary at the beginning to describe the supply organization of the Army as it existed in April, 1917, and as it developed during the ensuing months.

*The Army Supply System at the Outbreak of the War.* The supply system of the Army of the United States was, prior to the present war, organized along lines of decentralization and consisted of a number of semi-independent bureaus but loosely coordinated either with the organizations of the line or with the staff of the Army and having practically no relations in common. The absence of correlation was further accentuated by decentralization of activities within the bureaus. Thus, within the Quartermaster Corps, by far the largest agency of this kind, operations were conducted by means of a considerable field force centering around the depot quartermasters, over whom the Office of the Quartermaster General in Washington had general supervision.

At the outbreak of war the supply bureaus of the Army were as follows: Quartermaster Corps, Ordnance Department, Medical Department, Corps of Engineers, Signal Corps.

The expansion of the War Department during the war to meet the need for new services led to the creation of several new bureaus, among which the following served as important supply bureaus: Construction Division, Chemical Warfare Service, Bureau of Aircraft Production. (Most of the purchasing for the Division of Military Aeronautics was done by the Bureau of Aircraft Production.)

A comprehensive statement of the duties and functions of the original supply bureaus, is probably not to be found anywhere. It is safe to say that even the statement of their duties as defined in United States Army Regulations is not complete and that there was considerable overlapping in regard to the procurement of supplies. The following, however, is a general indication of the supply functions of the five bureaus at the outbreak of the war:

(1) The Quartermaster Corps: Subsistence, transportation, animals and vehicles, forage, camp and garrison equipage, clothing, construction of buildings, roads, bridges, ships, etc., retail stores at posts, pay of the Army.

(2) Medical Department: Medical and hospital supplies.

(3) Corps of Engineers: Certain construction, electrical supplies, engineering problems of supply routes.

(4) Ordnance Department: Procured ordnance and ordnance stores, cannon and artillery vehicles, equipment and ammunition, personal and horse equipment and harness, ordnance tools, machinery, and materials, maintained arsenals and depots.

(5) Signal Corps: All supplies connected with signaling, telephones, telegraph, balloons, airplanes.

The supplies needed for the support of the Army during the war were very much larger in amount than for the Navy, the Fleet Corporation, and all other agencies concerned, and the system of Army supply by bureaus was responsible in large degree for the difficult problems of coordination which faced the Government in its task of mobilizing the national resources.

The declaration of war immediately induced the greatest activity in the five supply bureaus and put them under tremendous pressure for the adequate performance of their respective functions on the scale called for by the magnitude of the war. Their personnel was increased with great rapidity. Their structure underwent considerable changes made imperative by the great increase in their tasks. Each bureau felt keenly the duty imposed upon it of obtaining with the greatest speed possible the enormous mass of supplies and material needed for the conduct of military operations. They naturally proceeded along established lines, that is to say, as they were independently constituted, each bureau had its own duties to perform and set about those duties in the main without any adequate coordination with the other bureaus or with other governmental purchasing agencies.

The war, therefore, began with the supply system of the Army organized on the bureau plan, the bureaus being five separate purchasing agencies with separate systems of finance, storage, and distribution, each feeling itself largely independent within its own sphere of action, and accustomed by long habit and tradition to perform its various functions without reference to the activities of the others or of other departments of the Government. Accordingly, when the Army went into the Nation's markets to buy the vast body of supplies needed for the war, it went not as a single agency, seeing the problem of supply as a whole, but as five separate bureaus competing with each other, as well as with the other great agencies of the Government and of the Allies, for manufactured articles, raw materials, industrial facilities, labor, fuel, power, and transportation.

*The Council of National Defense and the War Industries Board.* Some of the disastrous effects of such a system of competitive purchasing by numerous Government agencies in a war of such magnitude are apparent on the surface. In the case of purchases within a given industry, it has been generally recognized that large-scale purchases by the Government might completely disorganize the industry through absurdly high prices both to the Government and to civilians, and might at the same time fail to call forth in full measure the capacity of the country for the production of the particular article. It has been a matter of knowledge also that the process of placing orders for finished articles by bureaus and departments of the Government acting without a common plan tended to stimulate a scramble for raw materials which is equally disorganizing.

There were other aspects of the situation, however, which have not always been considered in connection with these. There was a competition for labor as well as for raw materials, and a resulting disorganization of the labor market, with great scarcity of labor in some regions and actual unemployment elsewhere. Furthermore, the unsupervised placing of war orders resulted in a congestion of contracts, both regional and relative to business firms. The total of contracts placed in a given region would outrun the utmost possibilities of that region in the matter of manufacturing facilities, labor, fuel, transportation, power, etc. This was a corollary of the fact that individual firms would take contracts actually far in excess of their facilities or of their ability to obtain raw materials, labor, transportation, or new facilities. Moreover, the power to commandeer property was originally exercised by individual bureaus and departments without regard to its possibly injurious effect upon the war program of other bureaus.

The responsibility which rested upon each bureau and upon numerous divisions and subdivisions of the bureaus was to procure and deliver in France the particular supplies, materials, or munitions with which it was individually charged. In discharging this obligation each of these numerous agencies played a lone hand. Each naturally wished to show a record of large achievement in getting to France the particular things for which it was individually responsible. It was not an accepted principle early in the war, as it came to be later, that to preempt tonnage space for shipment in excess of actual current needs was, if anything, a greater offense than a failure to provide supplies according to schedule. The carrying capacity of the available ocean tonnage was at all times the neck of the bottle of supply. The system of individual procurement by bureau ignored this fundamental fact, and the natural result was congestion at the ports. This port congestion rapidly developed into a general congestion of railroad facilities, including very serious difficulties in the movement of fuel needed by war industries. An important contributing cause of the fuel shortage was the concentration of contracts in congested districts already referred to as a product of the bureau system of procurement. Other phases of the same problem were shortages of electric power and other power in certain of the congested districts. Moreover, in the carrying out of war contracts placed in the same particularistic way, new manufacturing facilities were frequently created or planned in congested areas which called for raw materials, transportation, and labor when at the same time elsewhere in the country adequate and unused facilities already existed. The outcome of all these difficulties was inevitably such a slowing down in the output of war supplies as resulted, in the worst days of the winter of 1917–18, in conditions approaching partial paralysis of the war machine.

The possible occurrence of such problems had been dimly envisioned in advance. The Council of National Defense had been proposed as early as 1911 with no war anywhere in sight. The council was actually established seven months before the United States declared war with Germany. Its final development was the powerful War Industries Board, which became the great coordinating agency of the Government in the matter of supplies. And within the Army organization the Purchase, Storage, and Traffic Division, with functions dovetailing into those of the War Industries Board, was created in the spring of 1918 for the purpose of effecting the same sort of coordination within the war machine, and came eventually, acting as the agency of the General Staff, to supervise and synchronize the supply activities of the Army bureaus.

But the highly efficient coordinating machinery which finally came into existence was developed only step by step as new phases of the problem of coordination presented themselves.

As to the more general agencies devised as outgrowths of the Council of National Defense or of its advisory commission, reference has already been made to the Committee on Supplies, the Committee on Raw Materials, and the General Munitions Board. The development of these three boards into a nicely articulated organization resulted in the War Industries Board, which stood at the end of the war at the apex of supply coordination. An outline of the development of this organization with which the Purchase, Storage and Traffic Division was closely related as the coordinating factor of the branch of the Government most vitally involved in the prosecution of war, forms a necessary prelude to an account of the latter.

The Committee on Supplies which came into existence on February 12, 1917, was organized to cooperate in an advisory capacity with the purchasing officers of the War and Navy departments in securing requirements of clothing, equipment, and subsistence. In its composition the regular principle was followed of selecting men in close touch with the particular industries concerned and thoroughly informed as to the conditions which would be encountered in the conduct of Government purchasing. The committee was therefore in a position to render service to the Government procuring officers. At the very outset, an order was issued by the Secretary of War under date of April 12, 1917, which suspended the peacetime system of advertising for bids. Under the new system the bureaus were advised by the Committee on Supplies as to the business concerns with which orders could best be placed, and in many instances mills and factories which had never before produced Government goods were induced to place their plants at the disposal of the Government. In these ways the difficult task of procuring clothing, equipment, and subsistence was greatly facilitated at the outset. Within its field of action also the Committee on Supplies endeavored to coordinate the procuring activities of the different bureaus and departments. It performed numerous other services of an advisory character, nearly a billion dollars worth of purchases having been arranged with its advice and assistance. This committee went out of existence in January, 1918.

Under the Committee of Raw Materials was organized a large number of advisory and cooperative committees appointed from the leading industries dealing with raw materials. The committees assisted in assembling trade information for mobilizing the sources of supply of the various raw materials. The Committee on Raw Materials was not a purchasing body, but it gave important advice and assistance in arranging for very large purchases by the Government departments. The committee acted by mobilizing the industries and then recommending to the Government purchasing agencies how best to utilize the facilities so provided.

The General Munitions Board began work on April 9, 1917. Its attention was directed particularly, though not exclusively, to ordnance, ordnance supplies, military vehicles, surgical supplies, optical glass, gauges, tools, and dyes. Its efforts were devoted toward the development of production facilities, the coordinating of Army and Navy purchases, the establishment of storage facilities, and the cantonment construction program, in all of which particulars its services were very useful to the procuring bureaus.

The board performed in a preliminary fashion important functions afterwards turned over to more completely specialized committees. Thus the work of the later Priorities Committee, the Clearance Committee, and Price-Fixing Committee had its beginnings in the early operations of the General Munitions Board.

In July, 1917, the General Munitions Board was transformed into the War Industries Board. This board in turn was completely reorganized by the letter of the President of March 4, 1918, and its powers at the same time were very greatly increased. By Executive order of May 28, 1918, the War Industries Board consisted, in addition to the board members themselves, of a considerable group of commodity sections or divisions and a set of boards and committees, each charged with a general function. Among the most important of the latter were the Priorities Board and the Priorities Committee, the Clearance Committee, the Price-Fixing Committee, and the Requirements Committee. The Commodity Sections were composed of men who had expert knowledge each of a particular commodity, and each section included in its membership representatives of the Government purchasing departments. The machinery thus developed was operating at the end of the war with a high degree of efficiency. The problems of coordination had practically all found adequate solution.

*The Passage of the Overman Act.* The economic embarrassments which confronted the Government during the initial months of the country's participation in the war, have already been mentioned. As cold weather came on, in the latter part of 1917, other difficulties developed. Shortages in clothing, hospital equipment, and other supplies led to hardships in Army camps. An epidemic of pneumonia also developed in the camps which was attributed by some to the shortages in clothing and shelter. About the same time, rumors began to be spread concerning serious failures to realize various parts of the program of supply which had been laid down. The ravages of the submarine were steadily cutting down available ocean tonnage, and great apprehension came to be felt as to the possibility of supplying the Nation's forces and those of our allies with adequate quantities of food and other things highly essential in the conduct of the war. Added to this the uncoordinated procurement activities of the Army bureaus and of the other Government agencies had resulted in excessive and unbalanced railway shipments which first overtaxed the port facilities and finally developed into an extremely serious congestion of the railroad systems. Connected with this was the shortage in fuel which was so widely felt both by the war industries of the country and the civil population. At the same time it became known that a great and final military drive by the Germans was being planned for the spring of 1918, and the whole situation led to a widespread feeling of uncertainty and uneasiness. This led very naturally to inquiry as to the efficiency being shown by the Government in the conduct of the war and to criticism, both destructive and constructive, of methods of production and organization in vogue.

This widespread uneasiness found its center and culmination in a congressional investigation of the conduct of the war, and on December 12, 1917, hearings were begun by the Senate Committee on Military Affairs. Hearings continued until the end of March and during the whole time, in almost daily sessions, the committee heard testimony from the Secretary of War, the heads of the supply bureaus and others whose evidence was regarded as helpful in throwing light on the situation. The investigations served to give definite form to the various criticisms of the Government in its conduct of mobilization and supply, and also to bring out the Government's defense or extenuation of the progress of its program.

During the progress of the hearings a bill was introduced in the Senate providing for a ministry of munitions somewhat along the lines which had been followed in England and France. The proposed new agency would have been charged with the responsibility of supplying the requirements of the Army, Navy, Emergency Fleet Corporation, and the Allies. Another bill was introduced providing for a small war cabinet, to advise with the President and to direct, under a unified plan, the operations of the departments in the conduct of the war. These measures were consistently opposed by the War Department, which held that existing machinery should not be disrupted by such radical and comprehensive reconstruction, but that measures should be taken, and were being taken, for improving the coordination and efficiency of the various boards and departments. To facilitate the carrying out of this process, Senator Overman prepared and introduced the Overman bill, which finally prevailed, although it did not become law until May 20, 1918. This act, in lieu of creating a single agency for the conduct of all supply operations simply gave the President a free hand and complete power to readjust the existing framework of the Government.

During the hearings the chief items under consideration were clothing, hospital conditions at camps, shoes, rifles, machine guns, artillery ammunition, saddles, blankets, and gas masks. The measures taken by the War Department for the supply of these articles were fully discussed, the Secretary of War and other officials explaining difficulties which had been encountered, and claiming for the department on the whole, a high degree of success in meeting the difficulties which had been encountered. The most important phase of the investigation, in the present connection, is the criticism of the machinery which had been provided for carrying on the task of supply, and the official statement by the Secretary of War of organizational plans.

The criticisms of the Senate committee amounted to a vigorous indictment of what may be called the bureau system of supply under which supplies were being independently procured by the various bureaus of the Army and also by the Navy, Emergency Fleet Corporation, and the Allies. Great emphasis was laid upon the evils inherent in a system of procurement by a considerable number of separate agencies and the judgment was forcibly expressed, not only that the task of coordinating the activities of these various agencies was not being adequately performed but that the failure to accomplish this was threatening disaster in the conduct of the war as a whole. In regard to the War Industries Board the main objection was that it did not have legal or adequate powers to bring about effectually the coordination in the supply program which was clearly seen to be necessary, and that there did not exist anywhere under the President any agency armed with adequate power for the achievement of this end.

It was pointed out that at most the War Industries Board could only advise the procurement offices of the various branches of the Government as to where and at what price to buy; that there was no compulsion upon these officers to take the advice offered and that the whole effort of placing orders and making purchases, mobilizing and speeding up industry, taking care of transportation, and planning out in advance, was scattered down through at least a dozen different agencies. It was also asserted that no matter what steps were taken to effect coordination within the War Department no solution of the problem would be reached on account of the necessity that would still exist of coordinating that department with other departments of the Government.

The demand, therefore, was for a war cabinet and also for a ministry of munitions, this ministry to be headed by a civilian who should be a business man of high ability. One phase of the criticism was that the supply program which was essentially a business operation, was being handled by military men whose training did not give them an adequate preparation for the task. The reply of the administration, given through the Secretary of War, was that arrangements had been made for bringing into the War Department, in positions of authority, business men of a high order of ability; that important reorganizations were under way in the Ordnance Department and Quartermaster Corps; that a wide extension of the functions of the War Industries Board was planned; that unified action in the field of transportation and embarkation of supplies had been provided by the appointment of a Director of Storage and Traffic with the Embarkation Service reporting to him; that the General Staff had been reorganized into five main divisions each presided over by an assistant to the Chief of Staff and each charged with the responsibility for a definite part of the war program, and finally that as one of these new divisions of the General Staff, provision had been made for a Director of Purchases and Supplies, whose functions within the War Department should be the coordination of the supply activities of the Army bureaus. A business man of large achievements had been appointed Surveyor General of Supplies to assist the Director of Purchases and Supplies in this task.

The program of the Senate committee was that the supply activities of the great purchasing agencies of the Government should all be combined under one man. The alternative plan of the administration was that the great agencies already in operation should be left undisturbed, but that more adequate mechanism should be provided for supervising and coordinating their activities and rendering them more efficient.

The successful passage of the Overman bill caused the alternative program for coordination to prevail. By means of the authority conferred by the Overman Act, it became possible to carry out without difficulty much that would have been difficult or impossible without such powers. The War Industries Board was developed into the single coordinating body of Government supply agencies and mobilized industries, and out of certain of the measures cited by the Secretary of War before the Senate committee was erected a similar supervisory and controlling agency over the supply affairs of the War Department—the Purchase, Storage and Traffic Division of the General Staff.

# The Naval War Effort

## Letter, Admiral B. A. Fiske to Secretary of the Navy, November 9, 1914

From: Aide for Operations

To: Secretary of the Navy

Subject: The Navy's unpreparedness for war

1. I beg leave, respectfully but urgently, to request the attention of the Secretary to the fact that the United States Navy is unprepared for war. . . .

5. The present condition all over the world is one of general upheaval. The state of unstable equilibrium which the great powers maintained for many years with great skill and care has been at last upset. A conflict is going on, very few results of which can be foretold. One thing probably can be foretold, however. I mean that it can be foretold that the conflict will be violent and also will be long, involving other countries than those now taking part, and followed, even after the war at present outlined has been ended, by a series of more or less violent readjustments of boundaries, insular possessions, treaties, and agreements of every kind.

6. Surely he would be an optimist who would expect that a state of general peace will come in less than five years. During the next five years we must expect a great number of causes of disagreement between this country and other countries, and periods of tension between this Government and others; periods like that preceding the Spanish War, needing only a casualty like the blowing up of the *Maine* to precipitate a conflict.

7. In my opinion, as your professional adviser, and in the opinion of every naval officer with whom I have talked, the United States is in danger of being drawn into war and will continue to be in danger for several years. And when I say war, I do not mean war of the kind that we had with Spain, but war with a great power, carried on in the same ruthless spirit and in the same wholesale manner as that which pervades the fighting in Europe now. It is true that I can not specify the country with which war is most probable, nor the time, nor the cause. But my studies of wars in the past, and my observations of conditions at the present time, convince me that if this country avoids war during the next five years, it will be accomplished only by a happy combination of high diplomatic skill and rare good fortune. . . .

9. Comparing our Navy with the navies which we may have to meet in war, I find that our Navy is unprepared in three ways:

10. First, it has an insufficient number of officers and enlisted men. The number of officers can not be increased—that is, the number of suitable officers—because it takes four years to get a midshipman through the academy and several years afterwards to train him. But the number of enlisted can be increased, and very quickly . . . the fact remains

---

From *Hearings Before the Subcommittee of the Committee on Naval Affairs*, United States Senate, 66th Congress, 2nd Session.

that we want enlisted men right now. To man the ships which should be used in war we need 19,600 more men.

11. The second way in which I find our Navy unprepared is in departmental organization. Our ships are well organized and pretty well drilled; the fleets are well organized, though not very well drilled; but the department itself is neither organized nor drilled in a military way. Perhaps this is nobody's fault, and may be attributed to the fact that our Navy has never had to fight a serious enemy—certainly not in 100 years. The people of the country have naturally devoted their energy along the paths of most obvious profit, and have not been confronted with any obvious military dangers. But in my opinion there is an obvious military danger at present, and the Navy Department should be organized to meet it. The organization which other navies and all armies of great powers employ to meet this danger is known, in English, by the phrase "general staff." In different languages, of course, the words are different, but the meaning is the same. In Great Britain it is called the "Board of Admiralty." This general staff has as its first duty preparation for war, and as its second duty the conduct of war when war comes. In making preparation for war, the general staff makes war plans. These war plans are of two kinds—general and specific. The general plans are simply analyses of what should be the general conduct of the Navy in case of war; and the specific plans are plans in which the general plans are worked out in detail. Besides these general and specific plans, however, the general staff devises means whereby information regarding these general and specific plans shall be given to the various executive bureaus and divisions, corrected up to date, and whereby the various executive bureaus and divisions shall always be compelled to be ready to carry the various parts of those plans into immediate effect. . . .

13. Our Navy Department has no machinery for doing what a general staff does. The closest approach to it is the General Board, which, as part of its numerous duties, "shall devise measures and plans for the effective preparation and maintenance of the fleet for war," and "shall prepare and submit to the Secretary of the Navy plans of campaign," etc. The General Board does carry out these duties but the plans that it makes are general and elementary. It exists entirely as an advisory board to the Secretary of the Navy. It is highly valuable; but, as its name indicates, it is only a "general board." It does hardly 1 per cent of the duties that a general staff would do. Having no executive authority and no responsibility, and being called upon to do a great variety of work, it has not the time to prepare specific plans, and has no means to see that even its general plans are ever carried out. If we compare our General Board with the general staff of any other country or with the Admiralty of Great Britain and when we see what those general staffs have been accomplishing during the past three months, we must become convinced that unless we go on the theory that we shall always have peace we shall be whipped if we ever are brought into war with any one of the great naval powers of Europe or Asia. We shall be like the lawyer who has not prepared his case when pitted against the lawyer who has prepared his case. We shall be as the French were before the Germans in 1870. . . .

15. The third way in which I find our Navy deficient is in training. This deficiency in training is due not to lack of spirit or ability but to a combination of the two preceding causes; that is, to insufficient personnel and lack of departmental organization to which must be added lack of small ships. I mean that, because we have had not enough small ships to do work on the coasts of Haiti, San Domingo, and Mexico, because our ships have been insufficiently manned and because the Navy Department has had no general staff which would devise and carry out a progressive system of training, lack of progressive training has resulted. . . .

16. The subject of the improper organization of our Navy Department was exhaustively analyzed by the Moody Board and afterwards by the Swift Board in 1909. Certain recommendations were made to remedy the evils that they found. These recommendations have not

been carried out. They were, in effect, to establish a general staff, though the words "general staff" were not used. In my opinion, the failure to adopt those recommendations was serious and will invite disaster if a great war comes.

### Testimony of Admiral W. S. Benson

CHAIRMAN. Would you say that the statement in the Secretary's annual report that the navy was from stem to stern ready for war in April, 1917, was justified?

ADMIRAL BENSON. Not from my point of view, no.

CHAIRMAN. Was its personnel adequate?

ADMIRAL BENSON. No.

CHAIRMAN. Were all the ships ready?

ADMIRAL BENSON. No, they were not all ready.

CHAIRMAN. Were they fully manned?

ADMIRAL BENSON. They were not fully manned.

CHAIRMAN. Was the navy mobilized?

ADMIRAL BENSON. It was not. . . .

CHAIRMAN. Was our fleet in 1917 in a condition to meet the German fleet constituted as it was at that time?

ADMIRAL BENSON. Theoretically, no, Mr. Chairman, it could not be.

CHAIRMAN. An admiral or commander-in-chief who would have informed the Department that his fleet was in such condition that he could have met the German fleet on a footing of equality would at least be lacking in a duty, would he not?

ADMIRAL BENSON. I should consider that he was. . . . With the situation as you stated it, I would have no hesitancy in saying so. . . .

CHAIRMAN. Why did you not outline just what his [Sims'] duty should be?

ADMIRAL BENSON. I did not give Admiral Sims his definite and particular instructions. My impression is, although I do not know that, that they were given by the Secretary. . . . I think he had sufficient instructions for the duty he was called upon to perform. . . . I did not give him such instructions, because I did not think it necessary. . . .

CHAIRMAN. Was there a sound, complete and well-defined plan for conducting this particular war?

ADMIRAL BENSON. For this particular war I do not think so; only such general plans or policies as I have already outlined. . . . No definite war plan was drawn up on paper. No, Mr. Chairman, there was not. . . .

CHAIRMAN. What definite plans were drawn up?

ADMIRAL BENSON. I cannot give you that information. I cannot tell you that now. I assume that there were [plans made]. I know that all that was necessary was done and that is all that I do know. . . . The purposes that any plan would have accomplished were accomplished. I assume that as the policies went out to my subordinates, what we had of a planning section drew up the necessary plans or memoranda or instructions or whatever you wish to call them. . . .

CHAIRMAN. Did you formulate any definite operational plans?

ADMIRAL BENSON. I merely outlined general policies and left it to the subordinates to develop any plans that were necessary for carrying them into execution. How many plans were developed at all it would be very difficult or practically impossible for me to state. . . . There must have been plans, but I cannot recall them. . . .

THE CHAIRMAN. Could you have prepared the Navy for war without the consent of the Secretary of the Navy?

ADMIRAL BENSON. No, sir.

THE CHAIRMAN. . . . Did the Secretary ever give you any definite instructions with regard to active preparations for war, in regard to personnel, material or organization, prior to the declaration of war?

ADMIRAL BENSON. Not as a definite preparation for war; I do not think he did. I cannot recollect his having done so.

THE CHAIRMAN. Did he ever hold you up or delay you in any way when you were seeking to make such preparation?

ADMIRAL BENSON. Well, it depends upon how far you mean. I think this: I think that the Secretary was very careful to go over the recommendations that were made to him, and that he gave very careful consideration to matters pertaining to any increases in expenditures and things that might involve unusual outlay, and there were delays in that way; but I do not think there was anything I could state definitely as a hold up, except that there were many things that I felt as a naval officer that we ought to do; that he felt as a politician we ought not to do. But in what we had, with the facilities we had, I do not think that he ever interfered with getting them ready as far as we could, for war.

### Testimony of Admiral C. J. Badger

THE CHAIRMAN. Had any plan been formulated for a war against submarines?

ADMIRAL BADGER. We could not say that, no, sir. . . .

THE CHAIRMAN. Had any plans been formulated, prior to our entrance into the war, for sending anti-submarine craft abroad?

ADMIRAL BADGER. Not that I know of.

THE CHAIRMAN. Was any general plan governing anti-submarine operations ever drawn up in the Navy Department?

ADMIRAL BADGER. I do not know; I do not believe that any such plan was prepared.

THE CHAIRMAN. Was it better, in the opinion of the General Board, to keep the anti-submarine craft on the Atlantic coast or to send them to the war zone?

ADMIRAL BADGER. Now, you are opening a very broad question, Senator, and one that is very controversial.

THE CHAIRMAN. Your report of May 3 recommended sending abroad as much as possible.

ADMIRAL BADGER. As much as the condition of our fleet and the number that we had would permit. Now, I do not object to saying this as one view of the situation. It looked in April and May very much as though peace would have to be declared by the British and the French—the Allies. The reports that we were receiving were most pessimistic here, that they could not hold out. In that case, if the German navy had remained untouched, there was no telling how we in this country might become involved with Germany ourselves, and therefore it was a very doubtful policy whether we should strip ourselves and run the chance of coming in at the last moment and being defeated on the other side as far as prevention of the collapse of the allied powers was concerned, or whether we should look out for ourselves and our own fleet until we could see about it. Therefore, the men who had a responsibility of that kind considered it from that point of view also, that we must look out for our own fleet, in addition to the fleets of the other powers concerned, and not strip our battleships of protection against the submarines that might attack them. We had our fleet here in the Chesapeake. We went to sea for practice purposes, to keep them up, without any real protection, and it was a very dangerous thing, but we had to take the chance, because we had to send all of our other vessels abroad.

### Testimony of Captain W. V. Pratt

. . . The forces did not go over as fast as any of us desired, but the reasons for it do not lie in the failure to accept the recommendations made. The failure to get into the war immediately, in full force, upon the declaration, is not the fault of Operations or the failure to recognize the character of the war, and where it was being waged, but were, for the most part, due to natural causes and to causes which antedated our entry into the war. It was not possible to press a button and move ships, men, and supplies with the rapidity desired either by Sims or by the department. All of the destroyers were not ready to move instantly; navy yards and mercantile ship yards were not ready to undertake the vast amount of work thrown at them. Submarine chasers had to be built. Tugs had to be bought, refitted, and built. Yachts had to be bought, stripped and made ready for war service. The transports, which were the seized German ships, had to be repaired, manned, and put into service. Other transports and supply ships had to be built. Arrangements had to be made with the Army for the transport of its great military force to Europe.

The reorganization and expansion of the Office of Operations and of the bureaus had to be undertaken. The co-ordination of the bureaus with this office had to be developed; the methods of administration had to be divested of their pre-war conservatism, the red tape abolished, and more authority given to subordinates in the matter of detail; habits of quick and accurate thinking and quick decision under the stress of war, had to be developed. The personnel had to be expanded and trained; the task of creating sufficient reserves of war supplies had to be undertaken. The organization of the various bodies which acted as the co-operating agents between the Navy Department and all other departments and with the allied representatives on this side of the water had to be undertaken. Though we knew that the immediate and pressing problem was the suppression of the submarine menace and acted in accordance with the knowledge, we also knew that this problem had to be considered in connection with all the other problems I have outlined. Our country could not afford to make any disjointed effort nor to move forward along any one line of action, without due consideration of all lines. We had to profit, if we could, by any previous mistakes of our allies and we had to prepare for the contingency of a long war. The situation demanded of us that we should make a united, powerful effort, and in this effort the naval establishment had to play its appointed role, in harmony with every other effort our country was putting forth. Every master of military warfare and naval warfare knows that the great general's first concern is with the reserves. The weight of the first blow is ultimately controlled by the strength and co-ordination of the reserves. To build up our reserves was one of our naval problems and had to be considered at the same instant we were called upon to strike at the front.

All of these conditions were difficulties to surmount. They retarded the flow of ships and supplies to Admiral Sims, but the spirit was willing, and the principles he laid down were, in the main, accepted. He always had back of him the loyal support of the office of operations and of the bureaus.

**Letter, President Wilson to Admiral Sims, July 4, 1917**

From the beginning of the war I have been greatly surprised at the failure of the British Admiralty to use Great Britain's naval superiority in an effective way. In the presence of the present submarine emergency they are helpless to the point of panic. Every plan we suggest they reject for some reason of prudence.

In my view this is not a time for prudence but for boldness, even at the cost of great losses. In most of your dispatches you have quite properly advised us of the sort of aid and co-operation desired from us by the Admiralty. The trouble is that their plans and methods do not seem to us efficacious.

I would be very much obliged to you if you would report to me, confidentially of course, exactly what the Admiralty has been doing and what they have accomplished; and added to the report your own comments and suggestions, based on independent thought, as to the whole situation, without regard to the judgments arrived at on that side of the water.

The Admiralty was very slow to adopt the practice of convoy and is not now, I judge, protecting convoys on an adequate scale within the danger zone, seeming to prefer to keep its small craft with the Grand Fleet. The absence of craft for convoy is even more apparent on the French coast than on the English coast and in the Channel.

I do not see how the necessary military supplies and supplies of food and fuel oil are to be delivered at British ports in any other way within the next few months than under adequate convoy. There will presently not be ships enough and our own ship building plans may not begin to yield important results in less than eighteen months.

I believe that you will keep these instructions absolutely and entirely to yourself, and that you will give me such advice as you would give if you were handling the situation yourself and if you were running a navy of your own.

**Letter, Admiral Sims to President Wilson, July 9, 1917**

I have sent by the last mail to the Secretary of the Navy an official paper, dated July, and giving the present British naval policy, the disposition of the vessels of the fleet and the manner and method of their employment.

This will show to what extent the various units of the fleet, particularly destroyers, are being used to oppose the submarines, to protect shipping and escort convoys.

It is hoped and believed that the convoy system will be successful. It is being applied as extensively as the number of available escort cruisers and destroyers will permit. The paper shows also that there remains with the main fleet barely sufficient destroyers and auxiliary forces to meet on equal terms a possible sortie of the German fleet. The opposition to submarines and the application of the convoy system are rendered possible solely by the British main fleet and its continuous readiness for action in case the German fleet comes out or attempts any operations outside the shelter of its fortifications and its minefields.

I am also forwarding by next mail copy of a letter, dated June 27, from the Minister of Shipping to the Prime Minister, showing the present shipping situation and forecasting the results of a continuation of the present rate of destruction. Briefly, this shows that this rate is more than three times as great as the rate of building. A certain minimum amount of tonnage is required to supply the Allied countries and their armies. This letter shows that at the present rate of destruction this minimum will be reached about next January. This is not an opinion. It is a matter of arithmetic. It simply means that if this continues the Allies will be forced to an unsatisfactory peace.

The North Sea is mined by British and German mines for more than a hundred miles north and west of Heligoland up to the three-mile limits of Denmark and Holland. Over thirty thousand mines have been laid and additional mines are being laid.

It is through these neutral waters that almost all submarines have been passing.

A sea attack alone upon German ports or any heavily fortified ports could not succeed against the concealed guns of modern defences.

I have just been informed that preparations are now being made by a combined sea and land attack to force back the German right flank and deny the use of Zeebrugge as a destroyer base, though not yet definitely decided by the War Council; that this would have been done long ago but for disagreements between the Allies.

The German fleet has not left the neighbourhood of Heligoland for about a year.

I am aware of but two plans suggested by our government for preventing the egress of German submarines. These were contained in the Department's dispatches of April 17 and May 11, and were answered in my dispatches of April 18 and May 14, respectively.

These same suggestions and many similar ones have been and continue to be made by people of all classes since the beginning of the war. I have been shown the studies of the proposed plans, and consider them impractical.

It is my opinion that the war will be decided by the success or failure of the submarine campaign. Unless the allied lines of communication can be adequately protected, all operations on shore must eventually fail. For this reason and as further described in my various dispatches, the sea war must remain here in the waters surrounding the United Kingdom. The latest information is available here and can be met only by prompt action here. It is wholly impossible to attempt to direct or to properly co-ordinate operations through the medium of communications, by letter or cable.

Therefore, as requested by you, if I had complete control of our sea forces with the success of the allied cause solely in view, I would immediately take the following steps:

(1) Make immediate preparations to throw into the war area our maximum force; prepare the fleet immediately for distant service. As the fleet, in case it does move, would require a large force of protective light craft, and as such craft would delay the fleet's movements, we should advance to European waters all possible craft of such description, either in service or which can be immediately commandeered and put into service; that is, destroyers, armed tugs, yachts, light cruisers, revenue cutters, minelayers, minesweepers, trawlers, gunboats, and similar craft.

(2) Such a force, while waiting for the fleet to move, should be employed to the maximum degree in putting down the enemy submarine

campaign and in escorting convoys of merchant ships and troops, and would be in position at all times to fall back on our main fleet if it approached these waters.

(3) Prepare the maximum number of supply and fuel ships and be prepared to support our heavy forces in case they are needed.

(4) Concentrate all naval construction on destroyers and light craft. Postpone construction of heavy craft and depend upon the fact, which I believe to be true, that regardless of any future developments we can always count upon the support of the British Navy. I have been assured of this by important government officials.

(5) As far as consistent with the above building program of light craft, particularly destroyers, concentrate all other ship building on merchant tonnage. Divert all possible shipping to supplying the Allies.

(6) As the convoy system for merchant shipping at present affords better promise than any other means for insuring the safety of lines of communication to all military and naval forces on all fronts, we should lend every support possible to insure success to this, and we should co-operate with the British authorities in the United States, and here, who are attempting to carry out the convoy system.

I believe the above advice to be in accordance with the fundamental principles of military warfare. The first step is to establish here in London a branch of our War Council, upon whose advice you can thoroughly depend. Until this is done, it will be impossible to insure that the part which the United States takes in this war, whether it is won or lost, will be that which the future will prove to have been the maximum possible. It is quite impracticable for me, nearly single-handed, to accumulate all the necessary information, and it is not only impracticable but unsafe to depend upon decisions made in Washington, which must necessarily be based upon incomplete information since such information cannot be efficiently communicated by letter or cable.

This can be assured if I be given adequate staff or competent officers of the required training and experience.

I urgently recommend that they be selected from the younger and most progressive types, preferably War College graduate men, of the type of Twining, Pratt, Knox, McNamee, Stirling, Cone, Coffee, Cotton, King, Pye.

I wish to make it perfectly clear that my reports and dispatches have been in all cases an independent opinion, based upon specific and official facts and data which I have collected in the various Admiralty and other government departments. They constitute my own conviction and hence comply with your request for an independent opinion.

### Testimony of Admiral Hugh Rodman

THE CHAIRMAN. Were you given any plans or policy, by the department, before you went over?

ADMIRAL RODMAN. None whatever. I was simply directed to follow a designated route, and I followed that route and found myself amongst the British Grand Fleet.

THE CHAIRMAN. No policy or plan for the conduct of the war?

ADMIRAL RODMAN. No, sir.

THE CHAIRMAN. Did you know any such plan?

ADMIRAL RODMAN. No, sir; I did not need any. I was to go over to splice out the British Grand Fleet.

THE CHAIRMAN. Whom were you to report to over there?

ADMIRAL RODMAN. I do not remember. I will tell you the incident. When I arrived, I reported in the usual naval fashion, my arrival, to the department. That is a cut and dried affair.

THE CHAIRMAN. Did you report to Admiral Sims?

ADMIRAL RODMAN. No, sir. And then I got a telegram from the department: "In future send all your reports and communications direct to Admiral Sims"; so that I was placed under Admiral Sims' command by a telegram from the department.

THE CHAIRMAN. After you had gotten over there?

ADMIRAL RODMAN. Yes, sir. It was explained to me before I left the department, by Operations, that I was going over to splice out the British Grand Fleet. A verbal order is as good to me as any other kind, you know. I knew what I was going for.

THE CHAIRMAN. Did the department give you any instructions to govern your actions after you were on the other side?

ADMIRAL RODMAN. None, whatever.

THE CHAIRMAN. Was that not rather embarrassing to you?

ADMIRAL RODMAN. Not to me. I knew what I went for. Never the slightest embarrassment.

THE CHAIRMAN. Just what did the department tell you to do when you went over there?

ADMIRAL RODMAN. I could not repeat the words. I had an intimate conversation with the Acting Chief of Operations. The chief, I think, was abroad. He simply said, "You are designated to take this command, to go over and splice out—and strengthen the Grand Fleet in their operations against the German main force." Why, Senator, I did not have to have any more instructions than that.

THE CHAIRMAN. And you were told to report to the head of the British Grand Fleet?

ADMIRAL RODMAN. No, sir. I did report to the head of the Grand Fleet, and reported my arrival to the department. I had my orders.

THE CHAIRMAN. What?

ADMIRAL RODMAN. They left it to me to report to the Grand Fleet. That was my object in going. They supposed they could trust my judgment, or they would not have sent me.

THE CHAIRMAN. You were simply told to go over and report to the Grand Fleet?

ADMIRAL RODMAN. Yes, sir.

# 13.
# Naval Disarmament

The magnitude of World War I and its appalling destructive effects produced considerable support for Wilsonian idealism. Then Senate rejection of the League of Nations helped induce a feeling of disillusion in America toward involvement and a belief that participation in the war had been a mistake. The defeat of the Central Powers had altered international power relationships, and national competition was made manifest by the beginning of a naval race between Great Britain, the United States, and Japan. A public bent on peace and a reduction of military expenditures clamored for a halt to this expensive and potentially dangerous situation. Responding to these demands, a conference met at Washington in 1921 to discuss disarmament and Far Eastern problems. In the following selection Harold and Margaret Sprout place the conference in the broad context of international rivalry and assess its results in terms of the aspirations of the powers.

The Naval Limitation Treaty concluded at the Washington Conference placed restrictions on the construction of larger vessels, and succeeding years witnessed a surge of building in cruiser, destroyer, and submarine categories. Efforts to limit these vessels were finally successful in 1930, when the London Naval Treaty was concluded. No agreement was ever reached on land or air armaments in spite of numerous attempts. Naval weapons were simpler and the elements of sea power were more clearly discernible. Yet disagreement over the fighting qualities of warships was keen and deepseated, as is indicated by the testimony of professional experts in the abstract from the hearings on the London Treaty.

# The Washington Naval Conference

## BY HAROLD AND MARGARET SPROUT

THE WASHINGTON CONFERENCE wrote the concluding page of a revolutionary chapter in the annals of sea power and world politics. Broadly speaking, that chapter may be said to have begun with the publication, in 1890, of Captain Alfred Thayer Mahan's famous work, *The Influence of Sea Power upon History*. Mahan traced the steps by which Great Britain in the seventeenth and eighteenth centuries had established a virtually world-wide command of the sea. Under the shelter of dominant naval power, British genius had erected an empire upon which it could be truly said that the sun never set. In the nineteenth century this empire had become the nucleus of a world economic community which, as a result of the combined power of British fleets and finance, had acquired some at least of the attributes of universal sovereignty and a political world order.

The naval sanction of this quasi-world order rested upon a unique combination of geographical, political, and technological conditions. The British Isles lay athwart the ocean portals of northern Europe. Gibraltar, which passed into British hands early in the eighteenth century, dominated sea-borne commerce to and from the Mediterranean. By closing these commercial bottlenecks, the British could blockade or sink most of the naval forces of their Continental enemies, cut them off from their oversea colonies, destroy their maritime commerce root and branch. Before the advent of submarines and aircraft, control of the water's surface in the North Sea and English Channel insured the British Isles against counter attacks or blockade. And as long as there were no important naval Powers in the Western Hemisphere or in the Far East, local dominance over the North Sea, English Channel, Mediterranean, and adjacent waters, automatically resulted in a virtually world-wide command of the sea.

It seems obvious, in retrospect, that the surest way for England to achieve this result was to concentrate superior naval forces in or near these bottlenecks of European commerce, sending to more distant seas only such detachments as were needed to cope with the scattered enemy forces which could not be prevented from slipping through the closely guarded waters surrounding Continental Europe. After generations of trial and error, this finally became the policy and the more or less consistent practice of the British Admiralty. And it was largely upon this record of British experience that Mahan built his sea-power interpretation of history and his strategical doctrine of command of the sea.

Mahan spoke at a critical juncture. In 1890 an explosive compound of resurgent mercantilism, rampant nationalism, rising militarism, and missionary evangelism was brewing in the Old World and in the New. Mahan's sea-power interpretation of history—a strange synthesis of

---

From Harold and Margaret Sprout, *Toward a New Order of Sea Power: American Naval Power and the World Scene, 1918–1922* (Princeton, Princeton University Press, 1940), 278–292. Used by permission.

brilliant strategical analysis and expansionist propaganda—became a flaming standard for this new imperialism, and gave impetus and direction to navalism the world over.

Mahan's doctrines were hailed in many lands as the key which would open for others, as it had previously for Great Britain, the door to world dominion and empire. All that was needed was a powerful fleet of capital ships, surrounded by various kinds of subsidiary craft, and supported by a system of naval bases at home and overseas. Mahan's followers often ignored or belittled the unique geographical and political conditions which had enabled England to reap global dividends from a local concentration of naval power in European waters. They failed in the main to appreciate that about all any other country could hope to achieve with any attainable fleet of capital ships was a purely local or regional command of the sea.

Such regional dominance might very well be the most effective means of insuring certain countries—the United States, for example—against blockade or invasion. But for obvious geographical reasons, no local command of the sea could endow the United States or any other country with a system of colonial defense or with a leverage on world politics even approaching that which British statesmen had long derived from their naval ascendancy in Europe's narrow seas.

Nor could Great Britain herself maintain this historic Pax Britannica in the face of changing conditions and circumstances. The rapid rise of Japanese and American naval Power, attributable in no small degree to the influence of Mahan, undermined British sea power at the periphery. The British Admiralty could thereafter have maintained its global naval dominance only by establishing local superiority, both in the Western Hemisphere and in the Far East, over the steadily growing fleets of the United States and Japan. Any such dispersion of force was contrary in principle to the teachings of Mahan. But it was England's only alternative to surrendering control of those distant seas. And it might well have been seriously attempted, but for the simultaneous and more serious threat to British power at its source, resulting from the accelerating naval pace in Europe, especially in Germany, during the early years of the twentieth century.

Confronted with this new problem for which there was no purely naval solution, British statesmen elected to maintain their historic dominance in European waters, and to seek political substitutes overseas. For this and other reasons, Great Britain entered into a military alliance with Japan, cultivated close relations with the United States, and tacitly recognized America's naval claims in the Western Hemisphere—developments which appear in historical perspective as an important stage in the transition from Pax Britannica toward some new order of sea power.

By and large, however, the broader significance of these events was not recognized at the time. Great Britain was habitually regarded as the senior member of the Anglo-Japanese partnership in the Pacific. With few exceptions, Americans complacently continued to accept England as the world's foremost naval power. And Englishmen themselves still talked as if Britannia actually ruled the waves not only of the North Sea, the English Channel, and the Empire's Mediterranean-Suez life line to India and Australasia, but also of the broad Atlantic and the far broader Pacific as well.

The war of 1914–1918 accentuated this habit of British thought. The British Navy emerged from that conflict stronger in tons and guns than ever before. The war had destroyed or weakened the sea power of every possible European rival. And with the consequent strategic emancipation of British sea power, British discussion of naval matters showed a marked tendency to revert to the historic concept of Pax Britannica.

This trend, however, showed a surprising lack of realism. German air raids and submarine blockade had provided England a foretaste of future perils which threatened the very life of Great Britain. Spread of the European conflict into the Far East had given impetus and opportunity to imperialistic forces within Japan, which were bent on hegemony in eastern Asia and on naval dominance in the western Pacific.

And all this coincided with a portentous increase in the military power of the United States.

These events destroyed the last vestiges of world strategic unity, so long symbolized by the dominant sea power of England. With sentiment, territorial possessions, and established policies at stake in the Far East, the United States in 1918 was driving toward a head-on collision with Japan. After the defeat of Germany, America's wartime association with Great Britain cooled almost overnight into growing suspicion and distrust. And there were ominous signs and portents that the two English-speaking Powers were in grave danger of drifting into a costly and dangerous struggle for world power and dominion.

Against this background of potential anarchy and future conflict, President Wilson projected his famous program of world reconstruction. The cornerstone of his new world order was to be a league of nations, involving arrangements for concerted economic and military coercion to enforce the terms of a just and universal peace. Sea blockade would necessarily bulk large in any system of military sanctions. And there was not the slightest doubt in the minds of American statesmen and their naval advisers that Anglo-American equality of sea power was the most effective, and indeed the only acceptable, basis for American collaboration in the proposed world order.

An Anglo-American command of the seas was at that time both geographically and technically feasible. Despite the rise of submarine and air power, Great Britain still dominated the sea approaches to Continental Europe as well as the Mediterranean-Suez route to India and the Far East. The United States wielded a comparable authority in the Western Hemisphere. And between them, the British and American Navies held the keys to all navigable exits from the Pacific.

Such a Pax Anglo-Americana presented formidable difficulties. To make it effective would require fundamental changes in the British and American thought patterns. There is no denying that British and American interests, while parallel in certain regions and on certain issues, were elsewhere in sharp and seemingly irreconcilable conflict. Whether these and other difficulties could have been overcome, no one can say. For two conditions prevented any attempt even formally to institute in 1919 an Anglo-American command of the seas. One was the utter unwillingness of the British naval class, supported at that time by British statesmanship, to accept the principle of naval parity with the United States. The other was the American Senate's rejection of the League of Nations which, in the view of the Wilson Administration, was the necessary cornerstone of the whole enterprise.

The Administration's alternative to the League of Nations was repeatedly declared to be armed force sufficient, without outside assistance, to defend American territories, interests, and policies throughout the world against any and all possible aggressors. As to what this alternative might ultimately involve, no one could clearly foresee. It all depended on what was to be defended, on the location and strength of potential enemies, and on future developments in naval technology and doctrine.

Characteristically, there is no comprehensive official statement of the political objectives of American naval policy at this critical juncture. Security of the continental United States, of the Panama Canal, and of the sea approaches to North America and the Caribbean, was taken for granted. Defense of our island possessions in the western Pacific was generally accepted as unavoidable. Resistance to Japanese imperialism in eastern Asia was frequently mentioned. And a great deal was said about providing world-wide protection for the American merchant marine which had undergone tremendous expansion during the war, and which was then expected to assume still greater dimensions in the future.

With these objects and others less tangible in view, statesmen and naval experts publicly advocated a "navy second to none." This could be, and was frequently, construed to mean a navy greater than any other—even one "incomparably the greatest" in the world. And we have seen that it was the sense of the General Board, in 1921, that the only safe standard for the United States, as long at least as the Anglo-

Japanese Alliance continued in force, was a navy equal to any two others combined.

Such comparisons, it should be remembered, were always made in terms of the relative strength of fighting fleets. The battleship was considered the index of naval power. The fighting fleet, built around a nucleus of capital ships—battleships and battle cruisers—was the supreme embodiment of military power upon the sea. The fleet's "mission" was to destroy or blockade the enemy fleet. Execution of this mission, according to the accepted doctrine, gave command of the sea which afforded security to one's own coast and commerce, while opening the way for devastating attacks on the seaboard and merchant shipping of the enemy country.

Cruisers, destroyers, submarines, and aircraft, according to the accepted doctrine, were "auxiliaries" to be used primarily, though not exclusively, to protect and assist the capital ships in carrying out their appointed mission. Commerce raiding, even on the grand scale practised by the German submarines in the late war, was officially considered a useful but purely secondary operation. The spirit of Mahan still hovered over the Navy Department. And Mahan's fundamental precept—command of the sea through battle-fleet supremacy—was still the cornerstone of American naval doctrine and policy.

The teachings of Mahan, however, had become after the World War a storm center of doctrinal controversy. It was all but universally conceded that the phenomenal rise of submarine and air power had a bearing on future naval operations. There was respectable opinion to the effect that battle fleets were destined to lose much of their former potency in narrow seas menaced by hostile shore based aircraft. Critics of the Mahan school expressed further doubts as to the feasibility of even attempting, in case of war, to send the American fleet into the western Pacific, where Japan's mandated islands afforded scores of anchorages and lagoons from which submarines and aircraft might operate, possibly with devastating effect, against battleships, and above all against the fleet's extremely vulnerable train of supply and service vessels.

It was generally recognized, moreover, that a fighting fleet of capital ships surrounded by auxiliaries was an instrument of invincible power only so long as it remained within supporting distance of fortified naval bases provided with dry docks, machine shops, stores of fuel and ammunition, and innumerable items of equipment and supply. The American Navy possessed neither bases nor sites for bases anywhere in European waters. In the western Pacific, the United States had sites, but no bases worthy of the name. And the strategic value of those sites had been considerably impaired if not all but destroyed by Japan's wartime occupation of the former German islands north of the equator.

All this pointed toward two general conclusions. The first: that, under conditions prevailing in 1921, the minimum naval standard officially proposed—battle-fleet parity with Great Britain—was certainly adequate to keep any probable combination of future enemies at a safe distance from the continental United States and from the Panama Canal. The second: that, by the same token, the maximum standard publicly discussed—a two-power standard—was just as certainly inadequate to give the United States effective naval dominance in either the eastern Atlantic or the far western Pacific.

Much was said about a Pax Americana; about the destiny of the United States to assume England's historic rôle as mistress of the seas. But such talk ignored the plain facts of political and military geography. It overlooked the total absence of any commercial bottlenecks in the Western Hemisphere that were in any way comparable to Europe's narrow seas. The Panama Canal was a vital waterway for no major Power except the United States. An American fleet based in this hemisphere could never hope to dominate the sea communications of Europe and the Far East, unless overwhelmingly superior to the navies of England and Japan combined.

Any determined attempt on the part of the United States to acquire a position of such commanding advantage would inevitably provoke vigorous counter-measures, especially in the two countries most vulnerable to the pressure of hostile sea power. Such counter-measures would tend to neutralize American efforts, thus stimulating demands for still greater efforts in reply. If earlier experience was any guide, the result would be another cycle of armament competition, with recurring war scares and crises accompanying ever increasing demands for more tons and guns and men to man them.

In the end, the American people, with their immeasurably greater resources, might conceivably succeed in establishing a virtually global dominance. But history offered no precedent for assuming, or even for hoping, that the United States could thus impose a Pax Americana without desperate armed conflict leading to the military defeat of Great Britain and Japan. Whatever the outcome of such a struggle, the appalling costs and world-shaking consequences were fearful to contemplate.

The American people, moreover, were then in no mood for any such enterprise. The idea of war with Great Britain was utterly abhorrent to the vast majority of Americans. A spontaneous reaction against wartime militarism had evolved swiftly into an organized movement for reduction and limitation of armament. There was a spreading conviction that armament competition led inexorably toward universal bankruptcy, ruin, war, and revolution. And as the country slid downhill into the unplumbed depths of the post-war economic depression, this conviction stimulated a rising public demand for relief from the fiscal burden and from the seeming political dangers of the impending struggle for command of the seas.

This growing public demand stiffened congressional resistance to all requests for expanding the Navy. It was impossible to secure appropriations for shore developments desired in Guam and the Philippines. Every proposal to authorize additional ships was rejected or ignored. And there were accumulating indications, in the winter and spring of 1920–1921, that Congress might even order work suspended on the numerous capital ships then in varying stages of construction.

American statesmen were thus confronted with the necessity of making a fundamental choice. They might accept the risks and consequences of an armament race, and strive to whip public opinion into supporting the naval increases which the authorities deemed necessary for the realization of the Government's virtually global objectives. They might conceivably abandon certain of these larger objectives—for example, resistance to Japan's advance in eastern Asia—and thereby bring the ends in view more nearly into line with the military means at hand. Or they might attempt collaboration in an international effort to stabilize the relations of the principal maritime Powers on some basis which included mutual reduction and limitation of naval armaments. For reasons previously analyzed, the Harding Administration chose this third course, and advanced along the road leading to the Washington Conference.

From that body there issued the blueprint of a new order of sea power. The essential feature of this new order was the stabilization of political and naval relations by limitations on the strength and indirectly on the use of battle fleets. To this end the total capital-ship tonnage of the principal naval Powers was reduced, and fixed in approximately the ratio of relative existing strength. Limits were placed on the size and armament of individual ships. And there was to be no further development of insular naval bases and fortifications in the western Pacific.

The practical result was to delimit the areas within which each of the leading naval Powers could individually assert an effective surface command of the seas. For Great Britain, the narrow seas of Europe, the eastern Atlantic, and the Mediterranean-Suez route to India and Australasia were put beyond reach of the Japanese and American battle fleets. The United States was assured uninterrupted sway over the sea approaches to North America and the Panama Canal. And Japan was left in virtually indisputable control of the ocean surface in the far western Pacific as far south perhaps as the equator.

All this was but the recognition and attempted perpetuation of existing facts. Britannia had long since ceased to rule the American seas.

British naval experts had worked out plans for reestablishing a fleet in the Pacific, but they had yet to take the first steps toward putting those plans into execution. No one seriously contended that the threat of Japanese naval power yet extended beyond the western Pacific. The United States had never possessed a fighting fleet strong enough to challenge British sea power in the Old World or Japanese sea power in the Far East. After more than thirty years, the American Navy's shore facilities in the western Pacific still remained substantially as they were when conquered from Spain in 1898. The Navy Department had plans for strengthening the fleet and for building modern naval bases overseas, but political leaders despaired of winning congressional and popular support for efforts in these directions. And there was respectable opinion to the effect that such efforts would be not only politically dangerous but strategically futile as well, in view of Japan's occupation of the former German islands north of the equator.

This freezing of the status quo as to fighting fleets and insular bases, evoked criticism as well as applause. British critics lamented their delegation's bloodless surrender of first rank upon the sea, ignoring both the existing limitations of British sea power and the consequences of a naval race with the United States. Japanese intransigents saw their country condemned to a permanent naval inferiority prejudicial to realization of their asserted destiny in eastern Asia. American critics deplored the limitation of Pacific bases and fortifications which they viewed as tantamount to abandonment of the Philippines and to a general retreat from the Far East.

Actually, there is little or no evidence that the Harding Administration intended any such withdrawal. The Wood-Forbes Report, released in November 1921, envisaged indefinite continuance of American administration in the Philippines. And all available evidence points to the conclusion that the treaties, resolutions, and declarations relating to eastern Asia were officially regarded as a solemn affirmation of long established American principles.

What underwent revision were not so much views of national interest and policy overseas as the methods of supporting them. British statesmen, a generation earlier, had sought political substitutes, under the pressure of necessity, for their previous naval dominance in the Western Hemisphere and in the Far East. Somewhat similarly, American statesmen at the Washington Conference abandoned the struggle for a contested and dubious naval primacy in distant seas, in return for cancellation of the Anglo-Japanese Alliance and for mutual pledges of nonaggression covering island possessions in the Pacific as well as the historic American objectives in eastern Asia.

Whether the gain should be regarded as having balanced the sacrifice depends upon many factors and considerations. If national prestige, diplomatic bargaining power, and the security of far-flung national interests depended solely, or even mainly, on the American Navy's ability to defeat the fighting fleets of Great Britain or of Japan in virtually their home waters, then there was undeniably a strong case against the Washington Treaties. But as we have repeatedly emphasized, formidable obstacles—geographical and technological as well as political—stood between the United States and any such global dominance as that formerly exercised by Great Britain.

Surface battle fleets, however, were by no means the only instruments of national policy overseas. The American arsenal fairly bristled with economic weapons which could be used alone or in combination with military measures. Recognition of British naval dominance in the Old World in no way lessened England's dependence on America for indispensable strategic materials in wartime. Presumptive battle-fleet supremacy in the western Pacific did not free Japan from a still more crucial dependence upon American markets and raw materials.

Furthermore, the Washington Treaties placed no building restrictions on submarines and aircraft. War experience and post-war experimentation with these newer weapons had given some hint of their immense potentialities for local coast defense. A strong shore-based air force could be stationed in the Philippines without violating either the letter or the spirit of the

Treaties. And there were competent experts who believed, even at that early date, that properly constituted submarine and air forces would render America's distant island possessions all but proof against hostile attack by sea.

The Washington Treaties also left open the possibility of a far ranging *guerre de course.* American naval authorities, while concentrating on their fighting fleet of capital ships, had not lost sight of the potentialities of commerce raiding. The Navy Department in 1922 was designing submarines, cruisers, and aircraft carriers with high speed, formidable armament, and great fuel endurance. And the Treaties in no way interfered with these developments.

Thus while the Washington Treaties rendered the main islands of Japan and Japanese communications with eastern Asia secure against an American attack in force, they did not place America's Far Eastern possessions quite at the mercy of Japan or place that country's seaborne commerce entirely beyond the reach of American naval Power.

The British Empire's post-Conference position in the Far East was somewhat comparable to, though considerably weaker than, the position of the United States. The British stake in eastern Asia was far greater than the American. British possessions and dominions stretched all the way from the China coast to New Zealand and beyond. The positive military guarantees of the Anglo-Japanese Alliance had been transmuted into the passive non-aggression pledges of the Four Power Treaty. The reduction of naval tonnage had left England with scarcely enough capital ships for the Home and Mediterranean Fleets, with none whatever for the third fleet which the Admiralty had planned to station in the Far East.

At the same time, Great Britain possessed in that region a number of commanding sites and one partially developed naval base of immense potentialities. This was the base at Singapore, carefully excluded from the fortifications article of the Naval Treaty. Cruiser, submarine, and air forces operating from that base in the Malacca Strait might be sufficient, even without the support of a battle fleet, to disrupt hostile seaborne commerce and to break up attacks aimed at British and other European possessions in the East Indies.

Even though by no means negligible, the naval power which Great Britain and the United States could bring locally to bear in the far western Pacific was potentially far less important than the foundation laid at Washington for Anglo-American cooperation on a much larger scale. Cancellation of the Anglo-Japanese Alliance cleared the way for concentration of American naval forces in the Pacific. A common interest in maintaining peace and the status quo in the Far East seemingly provided the basis for parallel action in that region. And between them, the English-speaking countries held a combination of economic and military weapons, against which Japan's local dominance in the western Pacific lost much of its political significance.

One main artery of Japanese commerce spanned the North Pacific to Canada and the United States. Along this sea route there passed, in 1922, approximately 40 per cent of the merchandise imports and exports of the Island Empire. Another main artery, running southward to the East Indies and beyond, carried an additional 30 per cent of Japan's vital imports. Over these two marine highways moved a large part of the cotton, petroleum, and ores which supported the industry and military power of Japan. Both of these vital trunk lines extended far beyond the zone of Japanese naval control into areas under the indisputable sway of Great Britain or the United States.

The long shadow of Europe, however, fell across this blueprint of Anglo-American cooperation to enforce peace and order in the Pacific. On the balance of power in the Old World depended not only the future security of the British Empire, but also the extent to which Great Britain and the United States could safely divert their naval efforts from the Atlantic to the Pacific. Specifically, the continuance of British naval dominance in the North Sea, English Channel, eastern Atlantic, and Mediterranean-Suez route to India was an essential condition of a Pax Anglo-Americana in the Pacific. And this in turn depended on future developments in war technology and on England's relations with Europe as well as with the United States.

As repeatedly stressed in this volume, the rise of submarine and air power played havoc with the accepted postulates of British naval policy. By 1921 it was at least debatable whether surface fleets organized around a nucleus of capital ships could henceforth execute their historic mission in narrow seas within easy reach of hostile shore-based aircraft. It was still more dubious whether merchant shipping, even under strong naval escort, could successfully weather the perils of aerial and underwater attacks in narrow seas. And Englishmen even then were beginning to voice uneasy forebodings lest Continental air power might ultimately develop into a veritable sword of Damocles threatening destruction to English dockyards, arsenals, and factories—the heart and source of British sea power.

Drastic curtailment of these newer weapons naturally became one of the primary aims of British statesmanship. We have described British efforts at the Washington Conference to secure abolition of submarines and limitation of military aircraft. But there was no separating air power from the problem of land armaments. Until Great Britain was prepared to assume positive responsibility for maintaining European frontiers, French statesmen would entertain no proposals for limiting land armaments. Until such time, moreover, it was quite futile to expect French consent to any limitation of submarines and other auxiliary naval craft, the possession of which gave France some political leverage on Great Britain, as well as added assurance of uninterrupted passage of French troops and supplies from Africa in the event of war in Europe.

British statesmen, however, were unwilling to pay any such price. Instead, they strove to wring what they wanted from France without giving anything substantial in return. The result, as we have seen, was an impasse which prevented any limitation either of military aircraft or of auxiliary naval tonnage. With France, and Italy too, free to build submarines and other torpedo craft without limit, British statesmen and naval authorities would consider no proposal for restricting anti-submarine forces. Cruisers and destroyers were thereby added to the list of unrestricted naval weapons.

This unwillingness, or psychological inability perhaps, of British political and naval leaders to readjust their scheme of statecraft to fit the altered conditions of England's post-war situation, had far reaching implications and consequences. British insistence on all but complete freedom of action with respect to European conditions and crises, helped to undermine the shaky foundations of the League of Nations. The failure to limit auxiliary naval tonnage foreshadowed early resumption of competitive building in the unrestricted classes, a result that could scarcely fail to have unsettling repercussions on Anglo-American relations, and on the new balance of power in the Pacific.

The tragedy of all this is clearer in retrospect than it was in prospect. Renewed naval competition was presently to open a deep fissure in the recently cemented Anglo-American accord, and into this was to be driven the ancient feud over freedom of the seas in war. The future of Occidental interests in the Far East might one day depend in no small degree on Anglo-American cooperation in the Pacific. But the possibility of such a Pax Anglo-Americana would depend not only on the cordiality of British-American relations but also on the security of the British Isles and of the sea routes radiating therefrom. The new order in the Pacific was therefore bound up with the future of British sea power in the Old World. This in turn was inextricably entangled with the balance of land power in Europe, and with the quest for political stability in that war-shattered Continent. Thus in 1922 the problem of sea power was merging with the larger problem of armaments as a whole, which was but one aspect of a gigantic problem of world order and reconstruction. The Washington Conference had taken a step toward a constructive solution of this problem. But much still remained to be done, and some things undone, if the new order of sea power envisaged by Mr. Hughes and his associates was yet to be realized.

# The London Naval Conference

### Objective of Limitation of Naval Armaments

REAR ADMIRAL JONES. In approaching the subject of reduction and limitation of naval armaments, there are two fundamental objectives:

1. Peace objective: Reducing the probability of war and thereby helping to promote universal peace.
2. Economic objective: Materially reducing the burden of taxation.

SECRETARY ADAMS. The prime objectives of the United States delegation to the London conference:

1. To cooperate with other delegations in terminating naval competition by limiting all classes of warships.
2. To assure equality of combatant naval strength for the United States with Great Britain.
3. To arrange a satisfactory relation between our Navy and that of the Japanese.
4. To bring about reduction in tonnage wherever practicable.

ADMIRAL PRATT. The London treaty should be judged on three governing factors:

1. Good will.
2. Naval effectiveness.
3. Costs.

From Abstract of Testimony on the London Naval Treaty of 1930 Given Before the Senate Naval Affairs Committee, Senate Document No. 197, 71st Congress, 2nd session.

The weights to be given the three factors depend upon—

(*a*) Whether a country is faced with immediate need for preparing for war.

(*b*) Whether a country is in a state of peace, with a hope of continuing this state of peace.

### Basis for Determining Parity

#### Parity Means Parity in Combatant Naval Strength

SECRETARY ADAMS. Combatant naval strength seems to be the only means of comparison. If you go outside this and take into account such national assets as merchant marine or military bases; such other balancing assets as fuel, population, wealth, assured food supplies, and raw materials for construction must be considered, and a measure of agreement to stop competitive building would never be reached. Parity is equal fighting force in all cases and can not include the above without giving Great Britain the right to consider many things on our part.

The course of trade in time of war can not be foretold. How supplies are to reach this country in time of war will be a matter to be arranged in some ways which are not strictly naval ways. Our shipping will probably be largely turned over to neutrals. The direction of shipping routes as they exist to-day may not be necessary in war. The problem goes beyond naval knowledge and into other problems.

ADMIRAL PRATT. Supported the view of Secretary Adams and further stated that in effecting actual parity and in securing desirable ratios in combatant ships the problem can be looked at from two viewpoints: (*a*) "naval sea strength in the broad"; (*b*) "fleet combat strength." Naval sea strength in the broad is not permissible, a more restricted view must be taken, and we must view our problem from the angle of fleet combat strength, which is a definite measurable quantity. Naval sea strength in the broad introduces intangible quantities the insertion of which others will easily class as superiority, and which in truth can never be measured accurately.

If during peace we inject the question of trade routes, either of the enemy to be broken down, or our own to be protected, can we hope to secure parity in naval combatant types which are the subjects of limitation? The arguments which can be advanced by one set of claimants, in opposition to the views of another, are so many that the problem becomes too complicated for solution and amicable agreement. An agreement along these lines may be forced, but will probably not be amicable.

The measure of fleet combat strength is a tangible thing; it can be made with reasonable accuracy, and in the endeavor to attain parity between nations in naval strength, it offers probably the best road along which limitation can travel and arrive at agreement. It was the estimate of fleet combat strengths which was used in attempting to arrive at agreement through the instrument of this treaty.

The purpose of the Navy in time of peace is to train for war. Our Navy is one of the best guarantees of peace that we have. The purpose of the Navy in time of war is to destroy the enemy's sea power. If that is accomplished you can maintain your will on the seas.

The cruisers of the United States should not be scattered, but the whole fleet should be concentrated as a combatant unit.

REAR ADMIRAL JONES. Parity in actual combatant tonnage is the only practical basis for agreement. This has always been the attitude of the United States in all conferences between two countries.

## In Determining Parity, Combatant Strength Alone Should Not be Considered

REAR ADMIRAL JONES. United States must have equality of opportunity in areas vital to its physical and economic life. In seeking equality of opportunity where its trade lines and interests lie, United States needs certain types of units because of geographical position or lack of bases. These factors necessitate carrying out unit operations in distant areas, and operations at long distances from own bases and near those of possible enemies. In seeking parity these factors must be considered.

REAR ADMIRAL COONTZ. Combatant strength alone is not all that should be considered. Should be careful to get all we need outside the combatant fleet. Should build ships we can use, not only with the battle fleet, but for other needs, such as defending commerce and keeping open lines of communication.

REAR ADMIRAL PRINGLE. Cruisers are needed outside the battle fleet for exercise of control of sea communications by dispersed operations. In regard to basing equality with Great Britain on combatant equality of the fleets, the most important issue is that the United States preserve to herself the right to build within the imposed limits the ships best suited to her own needs and necessities, and that each nation should have the right to do the same. In arriving at parity we should consult our military needs.

ADMIRAL HUGHES. Only aim of the United States should not be to reach combat equality, but we have to protect our commerce and maintain ourselves at sea. The ships so required are combat ships but not battle line or fleet ships. United States should build as she chooses within allowed tonnage limitations and other nations should be allowed the same privileges.

VICE ADMIRAL COLE. Combat parity between the fleets alone is not all that is essential to parity. Bases in area of operation are important. Nations should be permitted to build as they see fit within the tonnage limitations.

REAR ADMIRAL STANDLEY. Protection of commerce and interests should enter into considerations as well as combat force when seeking parity. A war may be settled without any battle of fleets. During entire life of a war our commerce and trade routes must be protected and war-making material brought into the country. This requires not only a combat force which must be ready at all times, but an additional force to patrol our trade routes. The naval strength of a country is made up of combat ships, merchant marine and bases. Parity in combat units does not give parity in sea power. Parity in merchant marine does not give parity in bases. Parity in everything is essential. Combat parity alone can not bring real parity as far as the domination of the sea is concerned.

REAR ADMIRAL TAYLOR. Parity in sea power can not be acquired by limitation in but one category of sea power. Sea power is made up of navy, merchant marine, and bases. In London treaty parity was based on combat parity and no attention paid to the task thrown on the navy by lack of bases and merchant marine, and need for the protection of trade. Each nation should build as it sees fit within the set tonnage limits.

ADMIRAL NULTON. Combat parity in the combat fleet alone should not be the basis in seeking parity. Ultimate determination is combined resources. Large proportion of war activities are in protection of commerce, destruction of enemy commerce, protection of own lines of communication, scouting, etc. Each nation should have the right to build as it sees fit within the tonnage limitations allotted.

REAR ADMIRAL CHASE. Duplication of ships to obtain parity is fundamentally unsound. Identical ships do not fill the naval needs of two nations equally well, on account of different conditions under which they operate. Fighting strength or naval strength is not susceptible of exact computation. Only equitable means of establishing parity are: (1) Each nation should be allowed equal amounts of tonnage from which to construct its category of ships under consideration; (2) Each nation must be free to utilize its tonnage allotted in the manner it deems will best meet its particular needs. This does not prevent imposition of limits as to maximum size of unit or maximum gun caliber.

REAR ADMIRAL BRISTOL. Combat parity between the two fleets is not the only basis necessary for parity. Our commerce carried in neutral bottoms would require that our cruisers be at different places to see that no advantage was being taken to interfere with our trade in neutral bottoms within the limits established by international law.

### What is the Relative Value of the 6-inch and the 8-inch-gun Cruiser to the United States?

SECRETARY ADAMS. There has been a diversity of naval opinion as to the relative merits of the 6-inch and 8-inch-gun cruisers. The 30,000 tons involved is less than 10 per cent of the cruiser fleet allowed by the treaty, and less than 3 per cent of the total fleet allowed by the treaty. The question is one of expert opinion where there is real doubt. It is wrong to say that the 6-inch-gun ship is not a ship we desire. Naval opinion supports the belief that for many fleet purposes the 6-inch-gun ship is highly desirable. The advantage of the 8-inch-gun ship is possibly for detached duty. The 8-inch-gun ship has not been tried in battle. It has a frail hull not armored in any sense. She is subject to damage by fire from all sorts of guns. The latest design of 8-inch ship has quite an element of armor. It is difficult to evaluate properly between the 6-inch and 8-inch-gun ships. At every different range and condition of visibility the problem changes. To-day when different armaments are likely to be faced, a 6-inch gun is better than an 8-inch gun. The 6-inch gun can be got on the mark quicker, can fire twice as fast as an 8-inch, and is more effective. For many purposes the 6-inch-gun ship is superior. The General Board recognizes the advantage of the 6-inch-gun ship over the 8-inch-gun ship for certain purposes. Inside of 10,000 yards the 6-inch-gun ship is better than the 8-inch on account of rapidity of fire and other reasons. At longer ranges the situation is reversed.

#### Favoring the 6-Inch-Gun Ship

ADMIRAL PRATT. Is not against the 8-inch-gun ship. The 8-inch gun is a better shooting gun than the 6-inch. Would like to have a number of 8-inch-gun ships. The 8-inch gun is no more useful in a night attack than a 12-inch gun; 8-inch gun not as fast shooting as the 6-inch. Must have 8-inch-gun cruisers to send off long distances, but the 6-inch-gun cruisers are needed for night situations and to defend the fleet in a body. In case of a raid the screening ships must fire rapidly. The 8-inch ships can not do it, but must be protected like a battleship. It is not self-protecting. In a long range action between the 6-inch and the 8-inch gun ship, the 8-inch would defeat the 6-inch; but at night the result would go the other way on account of the rapid fire of the 6-inch. The 6-inch-gun ship is superior to the 8-inch-gun ship close in and at long range. If 6-inch guns are mounted in turrets, as should be done, the 6-inch gun will fire twice as fast as the 8-inch. The reason is because the 6-inch gun is hand loaded. The 6-inch-gun cruiser is preferred close in to the fleet.

REAR ADMIRAL YARNELL. Is aware of the fact that the department has a design for putting better armor on our 8-inch-gun cruisers; unfortunately, we have eight ships not so armored, and which could be defeated in close action by ships with 5-inch guns. The present 8-inch-gun ships have practically no armor, while, although the 5-inch-gun ship could not be armored against them, would have the advantage of volume of fire, especially at night or in misty weather. The 8-inch-gun ship would be superior at ranges over 18,000 yards. The 6-inch gun is as effective within 18,000 yards as the 8-inch gun against an unarmored ship, but we are to put more armor on our future 8-inch-gun ships.

REAR ADMIRAL HEPBURN. The injection of the 8-inch-gun cruiser into the armaments of the world is to the distinct disadvantage of the United States. We would be much better off if there were no 8-inch-gun ships in existence. If we had gotten rid of the 6-inch-gun cruisers, the United States should have all 8-inch-gun cruisers, but since there are both, our interests lie in eliminating the 8-inch-gun ship. The 8-inch-gun cruiser is good for only one purpose that the 6-inch-gun cruiser is not, and that is to fight a 6-inch-gun cruiser on her own terms as regards range and visibility. The only reason for 8-inch-gun cruisers is that others have them. Believes that the British see that the 8-inch-gun cruiser is a disadvantage to them. The 6-inch-gun cruiser can fight an 8-inch-gun cruiser if it gets within range. In dispersed operations the 8-inch-gun cruiser is a disadvantage to us. Character of operations in war is such that the 8-inch-gun cruiser is at a disadvantage.

REAR ADMIRAL MOFFETT. Question of 8-inch and 6-inch-gun cruisers was decided at a time when aviation was not considered very much. Under many circumstances the 8-inch-gun cruiser is better than the 6-inch-gun cruiser. We always try to carry the heavier gun, but long-range shooting is dependent on aircraft spotting. The value of the long-range big gun is not as great as it was. Placing landing decks on 6-inch-gun cruisers will make them equal or superior to any 8-inch-gun cruiser without landing decks. The designed 10,000-ton 6-inch-gun cruiser has better defense than present 6-inch-gun cruisers. The design is merely a blue print at present, but thinks that our 8-inch-gun cruisers have little protection.

## Favoring the 8-Inch-Gun Ship

REAR ADMIRAL JONES. Considering the necessity of United States to operate units at long distances from home bases, this country required vessels of great sea endurance, offensive power, and as much protection as possible. The convoy system will probably be necessary in war. The escort of a convoy can not run away. She must fight in order to allow the convoy to scatter and escape, therefore the unit must be powerful enough to meet whatever will be brought against her with some hope of success. Besides the material, we must give the men on those ships a fair chance. In case of a war in the western Pacific our lines of communication west of Hawaii must be kept open for 5,000 miles to the Philippines. This requires the strongest units we are allowed to build under the Washington treaty. Eight-inch-gun ships have the greatest power of survival, particularly in working in distant areas. The use of 6-inch-gun cruisers is in the protective screen for anti-destroyer and submarine attack, in close range where rapidity of fire counts. The 8-inch-gun 10,000-ton cruiser is far superior to the 6-inch-gun cruiser where you have to operate in distant areas, be alone, escort convoys through infested areas.

REAR ADMIRAL PRINGLE. The cruiser with the battle fleet is intended to back up to your own destroyers going in to attack enemy battle fleet, and to break up attacks by enemy destroyers on your own battle fleet. Must be armed to deliver a rapid and well-directed fire. Should carry a gun a little in excess of that carried by the destroyer. Should carry twelve 6-inch guns, and should be handy ships of about 30 knots speed.

Cruisers which act in groups or singly away from the fleet should be 10,000-ton 8-inch-gun ships. They will meet 8-inch-gun ships of other nations. They should have high speed to escape from battle cruisers and speed to overhaul and run down smaller ships with less speed. After satisfying the need of the battle fleet, every ton should be worked into 8-inch-gun cruisers for dispersed operations. Eight-inch-gun cruisers can better perform the duties with the fleet than 6-inch cruisers can perform the duties of 8-inch cruisers in dispersed operations. In dispersed operations the value of the 6-inch-gun cruiser is nowhere nearly commensurate with the value of the 8-inch-gun cruiser.

CAPTAIN SMYTH. Prefers 8-inch-gun cruisers. The cruiser we designate as a fleet cruiser is the one which normally operates where it can drop back on the battleship force if it needs superior power. In a fleet action its normal opponent is a vessel of equal type or a destroyer. Under this condition superiority of gunfire considerably overcomes deficiency in caliber. A 6-inch gun can deliver more shots per gun per minute than the 8-inch gun. At low ranges, 4,000 to 5,000 yards, the 6-inch gun will probably penetrate the armor of any ship which would be the normal target for a light cruiser. Outside that range you enter one where the 8-inch gun will penetrate and the 6-inch gun will not. In the zone 4,000 to 10,000 yards the penetrations are about equal. At the longer ranges, outside of 16,000 yards, the 6-inch gun is inferior to the 8-inch gun, because the 6-inch splash can not be seen from the ship while the 8-inch can. It becomes a matter of fire control and the 8-inch-gun ship can see where its shots are falling and the 6-inch-gun ship can not, and can not control its fire, thus giving the 8-inch-gun ship a 100 per cent advantage. The 6-inch-gun ship loses the effectiveness of its fire control at over about 16,000 yards, while the 8-inch-gun fire control remains effective for about 5,000 yards more. At short ranges, at dawn or dusk, the 6-inch-gun cruiser has the advantage of volume of fire. In a close attack through fog or at night, the 6-inch-gun ship might deliver such a hail of shot as to get in a lucky shot and put the 8-inch-gun ship out of commission, but Captain Smyth prefers the 8-inch-gun ship. That has been obviated in the new design of 8-inch-gun cruiser where the armor protection has been increased. The damage effect of the 8-inch and 6-inch shells after penetrating the armor is in proportion to the weights of the shells, or about $2\frac{1}{2}$ to 1. Prefers the 8-inch-gun cruiser for all operations where the cruiser is not able to fall back on a stronger vessel if the cruiser meets a stronger opponent.

COMMANDER TRAIN. Prefers the 8-inch-gun cruiser to the 6-inch-gun cruiser.

REAR ADMIRAL CHASE. Under the guns of the fleet, the 6-inch-gun cruiser may supply the needs of the fleet a little better than the 8-inch-gun cruiser. Would not build 6-inch-gun cruisers if we were unlimited because he does not believe in two classes of vessels. Would have all 8-inch-gun cruisers. Fleet work is the only duty a 6-inch-gun cruiser can perform with any great degree of efficiency. The 6-inch-gun cruiser would be defeated by the 8-inch-gun cruiser in dispersed operations. Lessons of war show that the larger gun has always won. If a 6-inch-gun ship escorting a convoy met an 8-inch-gun ship the former would be at a great disadvantage; while if the escort ship were an 8-inch-gun ship she could fight with equal chances. The 6-inch-gun ship can not effectively control the fire of her guns at ranges beyond 16,000 yards, while the 8-inch-gun cruiser could control at least 6,000 to 8,000 yards beyond that. The 8-inch gun's splash can be seen farther than the 6-inch can be seen. With the new design of 8-inch-gun cruiser, the 6-inch gun will not be as effective as the 8-inch gun under 16,000 yards range. If the outer line of the fleet screen were composed of 8-inch-gun cruisers, enemy destroyers could not break through, come up to the destroyers, and break through their line. There is always one thing that must redound to the advantage of the 8-inch-gun cruiser—if she sights an enemy she knows that she has a chance. The 6-inch-gun cruiser has not that assurance.

REAR ADMIRAL BRISTOL. Does not believe in any 6-inch-gun cruisers. Would be better off to have all 8-inch-gun cruisers so that they can be interchanged and sent from one duty to another, with the fleet or in distant operations. Knows of no study at the present time which justifies the 6-inch-gun cruiser. During war he would use only 8-inch-gun cruisers for convoy duty.

ADMIRAL HUGHES. In dispersed cruiser operations the 8-inch-gun cruiser has the advantage over the 6-inch-gun cruiser. In such operations the cruiser must be capable of meeting any ship of her own type coming against her, and the 8-inch gun cruiser is the only one that can do it. For dispersed cruiser operations in the western Pacific the 6-inch-gun cruiser would be of little use. She could not get out and get back. They would be of value going out with the battleship fleet, for protective screening. The scout should be the 8-inch-gun cruiser well ahead. The 6-inch-gun cruiser unattached is of little use, for she may meet an 8-inch-gun cruiser. Unattached ships must be strong enough to meet anything sent against them except battleships, then they can run. On detached duty the 6-inch-gun ship is a sort of toy ship. In a night attack the ranges are less and the value of the 6-inch-gun cruiser increases, also in fog. That is a special circumstance. A 6-inch-gun cruiser would probably be a little more efficient against light ships. On a dark night it might be clear and star shell would do away with low visibility. An 8-inch-gun cruiser can do everything that the 6-inch-gun cruiser can do, but the 6-inch-gun cruiser can not do everything that the 8-inch-gun cruiser can do. There are circumstances where the 6-inch-gun cruiser can do better than the 8-inch-gun cruiser with the fleet, but not enough to warrant building many of them.

REAR ADMIRAL REEVES. Commerce can be and it always has been adequately protected only by ships that carry guns superior in power and size to the guns of those ships raiding commerce. The 8-inch-gun cruiser, and not the 6-inch, is the only type that can effectively protect commerce in distant areas where it is fundamentally a single unit operation. If we build only 6-inch-gun cruisers, the value of the merchant ship carrying 6-inch guns, increases automatically. The striking force of a 6-inch gun fired from a merchant ship is the same as that fired from a cruiser. An unprotected 6-inch-gun cruiser can be sunk by a merchant ship carrying 6-inch guns. It is impossible for us to build special types of ships to meet special situations. We would have numerous types. It is uneconomical, and there is no assurance that the special type would be present when you want it. Fog might occur when the "fog cruiser" might not be present. We must build to meet the general situation and the 8-inch-gun cruiser meets the situation. It is effective at night, in fleet action, in repelling destroyer attacks. Our 8-inch-gun cruisers will carry nine 8-inch guns and eight 5-inch guns. The 5-inch gun is as destructive against the destroyer as the 6-inch gun. The 8-inch-gun cruiser can offer in a destroyer attack nine 8-inch guns and eight 5-inch guns, while the 6-inch-gun cruiser has 6-inch guns and a smaller number of 5-inch guns. In a fleet action the destroyers occupy attack positions in the advance of the fleet and on the engaged bow. The 8-inch-gun cruisers will cause the destroyers to occupy a more remote attack position than will the 6-inch-gun cruisers. Therefore as the destroyers come in to attack they must traverse a greater distance and be longer under fire before they reach the point to fire their torpedoes. Only the 8-inch-gun cruiser can form an efficient escort for the aircraft carriers, as the carrier must be protected against destroyers and cruisers. Since the battle cruisers were given up at the Washington Conference, the 8-inch-gun cruiser becomes more important. Keeping up a line of communication is a detached operation, and only 8-inch-gun cruisers can perform such duties.

REAR ADMIRAL HOUGH. A 6-inch-gun cruiser on commercial lanes may be able to give a good account of herself if she meets a 6-inch-gun ship, but if she meets an 8-inch-gun cruiser she is outclassed. The 8-inch-gun cruiser can perform all the functions of the 6-inch-gun cruiser, but the 6-inch-gun cruiser can not perform all the functions of the 8-inch-gun cruiser. He would recommend all 8-inch-gun cruisers. The 6-inch-gun cruiser at very close range has the advantage of rapidity of fire because it has hand loaded guns, but when you mount them in turrets the rate of loading slows up. But the 8-inch gun is so far superior in other respects that it is preferable. The 8-inch-gun cruisers also carry 5-inch guns which can be used at short ranges.

REAR ADMIRAL DAY. The 8-inch-gun cruiser with its 5-inch guns can do fleet work. So can the 6-inch-gun cruiser at less cost. An 8-inch-gun cruiser would have a decisive advantage over a 6-inch-gun cruiser of the *Omaha* type. It would be impossible to armor a ship of the *Omaha* tonnage to resist 8-inch-gun cruisers and have it retain its speed. And if an *Omaha* could be protected with the same armor as an 8-inch-gun cruiser the 8-inch-gun cruiser would tear her to pieces while a 6-inch gun could not pierce the vitals of the 8-inch-gun ship. Outside of 12,000 yards the 8-inch-gun ship would be safe. Inside of that an 8-inch shell would go through anything on the 8-inch ship, but it would go through the 6-inch-gun ship at any range. This is if the 8-inch ship is armored as our last ones will be. Does not believe that in fog or low visibility the 6-inch-gun ship with its high rate of fire would destroy the 8-inch-gun cruisers. The 6-inch-gun cruisers during the battle and during the night following the Jutland action did nothing.

REAR ADMIRAL LEAHY. There is a band of about 13,000 yards where an 8-inch gun will penetrate 4 inches of vertical armor and a 6-inch gun will not. There is a band of about 4,400 yards where an 8-inch gun will penetrate 3 inches of horizontal armor and the 6-inch gun will not. The 8-inch-gun ship can take a range of 15,000 to 20,000 yards from the 6-inch-gun ship and the latter could not penetrate the armor of the former. The 6-inch gun fire would be difficult to control because of the size of the splash. In future all 6-inch guns will be mounted in turrets. The 6-inch shell weighs 105 pounds and has from $2\frac{1}{2}$ to $6\frac{1}{4}$ pounds of high explosive. The 8-inch shell weighs 260 pounds and has from 6 to 11 pounds of high explosive. The 8-inch gun range is 7,000 yards greater than that of the 6-inch. The muzzle velocity of the 6-inch and 8-inch gun is the same. The striking energy of the 8-inch gun is about three times that of the 6-inch gun. In low visibility where the 6-inch-gun cruiser could get within 10,000 yards of the 8-inch-gun cruiser, she would have a good chance. Is not convinced that a 6-inch-gun cruiser is superior to an 8-inch-gun cruiser at short range because of the greater destructive effect of the 8-inch shell. At a range where the 6-inch shells can penetrate the armor of the 8-inch-gun ship, she has a greater advantage than at any other range, and if she has sufficient guns she might be equal to and even superior to the 8-inch-gun cruiser, in the particular situation. This would be an unlikely happening in disperse cruiser operation. It could happen in fleet action or attack on destroyer screen. Can visualize a situation where the 6-inch-gun cruiser might be as good as the 8-inch-gun cruiser, but thinks it unlikely to occur, and under any circumstances would prefer to have the 8-inch-gun cruiser. The Bureau of Ordnance expects to get 4 shots per gun per minute from the 8-inch-gun turrets. At long ranges where the roll of the ship must be given consideration, the fire may be slowed to 3 shots per gun per minute. Six-inch guns in the open fire about eight times per minute, and in turrets about six times per minute. At short ranges the ratio of the fire of the 6-inch gun to the rate of fire of the 8-inch gun is 2 to 1; at long ranges it is about $1\frac{1}{2}$ to 1.

VICE ADMIRAL COLE. Wants 8-inch-gun cruiser for all around work. Arguments for smashing effect of the 6-inch-gun cruiser under conditions of reduced visibility is a special pleading, inasmuch as it provides for those particular cases. The 8-inch-gun cruiser can do the fleet work.

They would alone form an effective defense if the enemy attacked the destroyer screen. In a fleet action the 8-inch-gun cruisers could take care of themselves and prevent enemy destroyers from breaking through the screen. The 8-inch-gun cruiser is superior to the 6-inch-gun cruiser for dispersed operations.

REAR ADMIRAL STANDLEY. Without any limit placed on cost or tonnage, would build all 8-inch-gun cruisers. The 8-inch-gun cruiser can do every possible thing that the 6-inch-gun cruiser can do and do it better. The 8-inch-gun cruiser can do things the 6-inch cruiser can not do. The 6-inch-gun cruiser can not operate in the outer screen because she will have to fight 8-inch-gun cruisers, for this same reason she can not operate on trade routes or protect convoys. Six-inch-gun cruisers are of no use except under the big guns of the fleet. Has conversed with many naval officers and all favor the 8-inch-gun ship. The smaller cruisers should be used with the fleet, because they are of no use against 8-inch-gun cruisers unless they are under the protection of heavier guns. A 6-inch-gun cruiser against a 6-inch-gun cruiser has an equal chance. If you are operating in an area where the enemy has 8-inch-gun cruisers, 8-inch-gun cruisers are necessary. If enemy 8-inch-gun cruisers come out, the 6-inch-gun cruisers will be sunk or must be driven back under the heavy guns again. Eight-inch-gun cruisers are always useful because that is the biggest cruiser except battle cruisers. The 8-inch-gun cruisers will operate on lines of communication and on trade routes. There is no question as to the 8-inch-gun cruiser being able to take care of herself against the 6-inch-gun cruiser.

REAR ADMIRAL MCLEAN. Strongly favors the 8-inch-gun cruiser. There is no doubt but that the 8-inch-gun cruiser can defeat the 6-inch-gun cruiser. It is sound that some 6-inch-gun cruisers are needed with the fleet for work in the destroyer screen where they are under the guns of the fleet. The 8-inch-gun cruiser escorting a convoy could keep off a 6-inch-gun cruiser. One 8-inch-gun cruiser might take care of herself against two 6-inch-gun cruisers. At 15,000 to 20,000 yards the 6-inch gun is hard to control because of the small splash, while at that range the 8-inch splash is visible.

REAR ADMIRAL WILEY. The 6-inch gun fires twice as fast as the 8-inch gun, but the 8-inch shell is heavier, and the gun has a greater range. Control of fire depends upon ability to spot the fall of shot. If you can not spot the fall of shot you can not tell whether you are hitting, and you can not see the splash of a 6-inch-gun salvo to spot it accurately over 16,000 yards, while an 8-inch-gun salvo can be spotted accurately at at least 20,000 yards. Airplane spot improves all spotting. Is in favor of 8-inch-gun cruiser for all purposes, because combatant ships are built to be effective under all conditions under which they will operate in war. The 8-inch-gun cruiser can perform efficiently all the duty that can be assigned to a 6-inch-gun cruiser, but a 6-inch-gun cruiser can not perform efficiently all the duties which may be required of an 8-inch-gun cruiser. This is true in the destroyer screen. The more rapid fire of the 6-inch gun in the destroyer screen does not make it more valuable than the 8-inch gun. Does not consider that the 6-inch-gun cruiser is any better or as efficient as the 8-inch-gun cruiser under any circumstances. They fire more rapidly but have greater dispersion. No 6-inch gun is as effective as the modern 8-inch gun. No improvement can be made in the 6-inch gun which can not be made in the 8-inch gun. The statement that a 6-inch-gun cruiser would "eat up" an 8-inch-gun cruiser if it met it about dark or coming out of a fog sounds very alluring, but you want combat ships to fight under normal conditions and you take your chances if you have not normal conditions. No one but a weak enemy seeks night action. The 8-inch-gun ship and the 6-inch-gun ship may be compared with a man with a rifle and one armed with two revolvers. He may shoot his revolvers from the hip, but if he can not reach the man with the rifle, he is throwing his ammunition away. On the commerce lanes the 6-inch-gun cruiser would be destroyed by the 8-inch-gun cruiser.

REAR ADMIRAL TAYLOR. The 8-inch-gun cruiser is needed to protect commerce. The 6-inch-gun cruiser for that work would be wasted. Our cruisers to protect our commerce have to operate a long way from base, which requires very large radius of action. She has to have defensive and offensive power to fight and defeat her enemy without suffering damage to herself that will force her to come home. If a 6-inch-gun cruiser meets a merchant vessel armed with 6-inch guns, the 6-inch-gun cruiser will win, but with equal batteries the cruiser will sustain so much damage that she will have to come home. With an 8-inch-gun cruiser that will not be the case.

REAR ADMIRAL COONTZ. Wants all of the 8-inch-gun cruisers we can get. We need 8-inch-gun cruisers even if we do not use them in the fleet, on our lines of communication. We want 8-inch-gun cruisers for scouts, steady platforms, long range, and endurance. To have long range guns, the ability to lie on station two or three weeks and do whatever damage is necessary, then rejoin the main body and go to fueling station, is a big asset. The 6-inch gun has not developed any effectiveness over the 8-inch. The 8-inch gun can be developed as much as the 6-inch gun. Wants the 8-inch-gun cruiser for dispersed cruiser operations. If allowed full liberty of action would build all 8-inch-gun cruisers. Instead of the treaty allowance of cruisers, prefers the provisions of the fifteen-cruiser bill for twenty-three 8-inch-gun cruisers.

REAR ADMIRAL NULTON. Security abroad requires vessels with a long cruising radius, and considerable offense and defense, and from the point of national defense the 8-inch gun 10,000-ton cruisers are better suited to the needs of the Navy. If there were no limit, would want some 6-inch-gun cruisers, but if limited, would take all 8-inch-gun cruisers because of their suitability for interchangeability of duty. Every merchant vessel is a potential 6-inch-gun cruiser. The more we come down to the 6-inch-gun basis the less advantageous it is to this country. There are certain phases of fleet work for which the 6-inch-gun cruisers are suited, but if the total number of cruisers is to be limited, the 8-inch-gun cruiser is preferable. The 8-inch-gun 10,000-ton cruiser is the ship for dispersed operations. There has been nothing in the fleet operations to lead him to believe that small cruisers are better than large ones. Practically no naval opinion favors the small cruiser.

REAR ADMIRAL ROBINSON. The high rate of fire of the 6-inch guns is at short ranges only, firing one gun at a time, and not in controlled salvo firing or firing from turrets. The 6-inch guns of the *Omaha* class fire twice as fast as the 8-inch guns of the aircraft carriers. The rates of fire approach equality as the range increases until they are nearly equal at 12,000 yards, due to the time of flight of the projectile. You can not control a shot until you know where the previous one has gone; and if it takes 20 seconds for the shot to travel from gun to target, you can not fire faster than 3 shots per minute. At the range at which the two guns have equality in rate of fire, the 6-inch gun will pierce less than half the armor pierced by the 8-inch gun. This discrepancy increases as the range decreases. It decreases as the range is lengthened. At 6,000 yards the 8-inch gun pierces nearly 10 inches of armor, and the 6-inch gun about 4 inches. At 12,000 yards the chances of hitting with an 8-inch gun and a 6-inch gun are about as 7 to 4 in favor of the 8-inch gun. The damage due to explosion of the shell varies nearly as their weights. The only place a 6-inch-gun ship has the advantage over an 8-inch-gun ship is in a surprise attack where the 6-inch gun can fire faster. The 5-inch anti-aircraft guns of the cruisers are effective against destroyer attack. At night, by using star shells, the 8-inch gun is more effective than the 6-inch gun. A liberal allowance for action in a fog is 5 per cent. We can not afford to build ships for such encounters. A 10,000-ton cruiser can be armored against 6-inch-gun fire without great reduction in speed, but neither it nor one of lesser tonnage can be armored against 8-inch-gun fire without reduction of speed. There is no ship in existence that can bring as many 6-inch guns to bear as the *Salt Lake City* can bring 8-inch guns. In a fleet action against fast wing tactics the 6-inch-gun cruiser is helpless, but the 8-inch gun will pierce the armor belt of any battle cruiser at 11,000 yards and all other armor on the battle cruiser up to 15,000 yards. Neither the Japanese nor the British agree with statements that 6-inch-gun cruisers are to be preferred to 8-inch-gun cruisers, or they would not have taken care to prevent the United

States from building the 8-inch-gun cruisers provided by Congress. The 8-inch-gun cruiser can take care of a destroyer attack attempting to break through the screen as well as a 6-inch-gun cruiser can. For dispersed operations you must have a cruiser that no other cruiser can drive in. You must be able to meet on equal terms anything that can come after you. The 8-inch-gun cruiser is the ship for dispersed cruiser operations.

## Can a 10,000-Ton Ship armed with 6-Inch Guns equal a 10,000-Ton Ship with 8-Inch Guns?

### The 6-Inch-Gun Ship Will Equal the 8-Inch-Gun Ship

REAR ADMIRAL YARNELL. You can put more 6-inch guns than 8-inch guns on the same tonnage. On a 10,000-ton ship you could probably put twelve 6-inch guns and protection against 6-inch shells, which is more protection than the 8-inch-gun cruiser has to-day. The 6-inch gun is as effective as are 8-inch guns against unarmored ships within 18,000 yards range.

REAR ADMIRAL HEPBURN. Intrinsically on a 10,000-ton displacement a ship can be designed with 6-inch guns that is intrinsically better than an 8-inch-gun cruiser.

### The 6-Inch-Gun Ship Will Not Equal the 8-Inch-Gun Ship

REAR ADMIRAL JONES. The 10,000-ton cruiser armed with 6-inch guns is not equal to the 10,000-ton cruiser armed with 8-inch guns.

REAR ADMIRAL PRINGLE. If you assume a 10,000-ton cruiser armed with 6-inch guns and one armed with 8-inch guns and both having the same protection, then as far as fighting value goes, the 6-inch-gun cruiser has no chance with the 8-inch-gun cruiser.

REAR ADMIRAL DAY. There is no advantage in building a 6-inch-gun cruiser of 9,000 or 10,000 tons displacement. They could not operate effectively against 8-inch-gun cruisers. They could carry the same armor, but with their 6-inch guns would have no chance against 8-inch guns.

REAR ADMIRAL LEAHY. It would be exceedingly difficult to build a 6-inch-gun cruiser that would have the same speed, superior armor protection, and more guns in sufficient mounts, to make it equal to the 8-inch-gun cruiser.

REAR ADMIRAL STANDLEY. A 6-inch-gun cruiser with 9,000 or 10,000 tons displacement could not be built which would hold her own against an 8-inch-gun cruiser under any but very special situations. At close range she might have the advantage of rapidity of fire. For general work you cannot conceive of a vessel of that type which could cope with the 8-inch-gun cruiser. The striking force of the 6-inch guns would be less than the 8-inch guns and the 8-inch-gun cruiser would have the advantage.

REAR ADMIRAL COONTZ. The fact that her guns are inferior to the guns of an 8-inch-gun cruiser would make less effective a 9,000 or 10,000 ton cruiser with 6-inch guns.

REAR ADMIRAL ROBINSON. If 6-inch guns are placed on ships of 9,000 or 10,000 tons displacement you could put so much armor on that neither a 6-inch gun nor an 8-inch gun could pierce her, but she would be useless for any purpose. If 6-inch guns were mounted on a ship of exactly the same type, armor, and displacement of an 8-inch-gun ship, she could not compete with the 8-inch-gun ship.

# 14.
# The Concept of Air Warfare

The most dramatic controversy in American military policy was over the role of aircraft. Essentially the debate was between those who believed that planes should be used to support regular army and navy forces and those who felt that air power alone could decide the outcome of war. Thus the dispute centered on the use of the airplane as a tactical weapon or its separate use as a strategic force. Experience in the recent war had proved its value as a supporting vehicle, but there was little evidence to indicate its independent effectiveness.

The leading American exponent of strategic bombing, Colonel William Mitchell, declared that "the airmen regard the air force as being the only element in the Nation's make-up which can fight battles in the air that will result in keeping the enemy out of the air and away from our country; which can sink any battleships or any surface craft that come near in an attempt to violate the territory of the United States with a hostile foot; or smash an enemy's centers of power, manufactories, and means of transportation on land so that he can be conquered." Mitchell, who engaged in heated debate with both military and civil authorities, executed bombing experiments on captured German vessels and provoked a court martial in order to publicize his cause. The following report reveals the extent of government efforts to resolve the problem and the conclusions reached by 1934.

# A Military Aviation Policy for the United States

THE MANY QUESTIONS of vital moment to the efficient development of aviation as an element of national defense have been frequently and thoroughly studied since the World War. There is filed in the records of this committee an analysis of the reports of 14 principal boards and committees which made such studies. In brief, these boards and the scope of their studies were:

(1) The Dickman Board met at Chaumont, France, April, 1919, to consider the lessons to be learned from the present war (World War) insofar as they affect tactics and organization.

(2) The Menoher Board met in Washington, D.C., August, 1919, for the purpose of reporting on bill H.R. 7925, to establish a Department of Aeronautics.

(3) The Military Affairs Committee, House of Representatives, from September, 1919 to February, 1920, studied and reported on a plan for reorganizing and increasing the efficiency of the United States Army, etc. This study resulted in the National Defense Act of June, 1920.

(4) Reorganization Board of Superior Officers which met in Washington, D.C., June, 1920, to define the general plan of organization to be adopted for the Army of the United States under the act of June 4, 1920.

(5) Lassiter Board, which met in Washington, D.C., March, 1923, to determine the proper strength and organization of the Air Service both in materiel and personnel to meet peace and war requirements and the best means for the development of same.

(6) Joint Congressional Committee on Reorganization of the Administrative Branch of the Government, which met in Washington, D.C., February, 1923, to make a survey looking toward the coordination of Government functions and including the specific coordination of the Military and Naval Establishments under a single Cabinet officer.

(7) The Lampert Congressional Committee which met in Washington, D.C., and other places in October, 1924, to investigate contracts, settlements, audits, etc., of the Army-Navy Air Services, etc.

(8) The Eberle Board, which met in Washington, D.C., September, 1924, to consider the policy of the Navy Department with reference to upkeep of the Navy in its various branches.

(9) Morrow Board, which met in Washington, D.C., September, 1925, to study the best means of developing and applying aircraft in national defense and to supplement the studies already made by the War and Navy Departments on this subject.

(10) Committee on Military Affairs, House of Representatives, which met in Washington, D.C., March, 1926, to consider H.R. 10827 which, with amendments, is the Air Corps Act of 1926. The bill H.R. 9044, to create a Department of National Defense, was also apparently considered by this committee.

(11) Committee on Expenditures in the

---

From *Final Report of War Department Special Committee on Army Air Corps*, July 18, 1934.

Executive Departments, H.R. 4742 and H.R. 7012, which met January, 1932 to study the establishment of a Department of National Defense and for other purposes.

(12) The vote in the House of Representatives April, 1932 on the question of establishing a Department of National Defense.

(13) Joint Army-Navy Committee on Duplication of Effort in Army and Navy, which met November, 1932, to ascertain what duplication of effort and expenditures exists in the Army and the Navy and the making of savings by eliminating duplication.

(14) The Drum Board which met in Washington, D.C., August, 1933, to review and revise the air plans for the defense of the United States.

The most important problem under constant consideration throughout this period was the advisability of the creation of a Department of Air and later of a Department of National Defense. Seven of these groups definitely stated, or based their study on the assumption, that aerial activity cannot be carried on independently and that, therefore, the air force of the United States must be an integral part of the ground or naval forces, respectively. Of the other seven groups which considered the specific problem, but one, i.e. the Lampert Committee, made a recommendation for separation through the creation of a single Department of National Defense. On the recommendation of the Committee on Expenditures in the Executive Departments, a clause was inserted in the economy bill, which bill was presented to the Congress in February 1932, for the creation of a Department of National Defense. This provision was not accepted by the House of Representatives. There is some difference of opinion, military and civil, on this subject, but the five Secretaries of War who have occupied that office during and since the World War have each expressed his view as in opposition to separation, as well as General Pershing, who has also emphatically stated his opposition to separating air forces from the Army. . . .

With respect to organization, there has been insistence on the part of many Army Air Corps officers that they should be separate from, and independent of, the rest of the Army. Their chief argument is that they operate in a different medium, i.e., in the air, above the surface of the earth, that their theater of war is or may be separate and removed from that of the ground forces, that the military objectives and character of operations will have normally no great connection with those of the ground forces. Those opposing this theory, which includes for the most part those who have the ultimate responsibility for the national defense, maintain that air forces can operate but for a few hours at a time in the air before they must return to their ground bases, that about 80 to 90 percent of their personnel and maintenance facilities must be in those ground bases, that in war these ground bases must be in friendly territory or be protected by ground forces, that air forces operating from that theater are as definitely tied to it and a part of the theater forces as are any of the other combat arms, and that there must be unity of command over all forces operating in any given theater. . . .

Our national defense policy contemplates aggressive action against no nation; it is based entirely upon the defense of our homeland and overseas possessions, including protection of our sea- and air-borne commerce. Our military policy is founded upon this traditional policy and contemplates offensive operations only when such action is necessary as a defense of our national security. Our existing armaments are less than those required for this purpose. We do not advocate any increase beyond the minimum essential therefor.

It is not a difficult problem for a trained general staff to determine, after review of world conditions, the military forces required to insure the success of our national policy under any conditions that may be considered at any time reasonably likely to arise in the near future. For the Navy the determination is simple—a fleet second to none in the world. For the Army the problem is more complicated. Our traditional policy of relying mainly on a citizen army continues the basis of existing defensive requirements. However, such a policy can be made effective only by maintaining in peace a professional standing army for the following general purposes:

In the continental United States:

(1) A well-balanced, mobile force, to cover mobilization of the citizen army and to perform national domestic missions.

(2) To maintain as overhead the necessary administrative, planning and supply agencies and to form the framework for the expansion required by mobilization.

(3) To keep alive the practice and study of the military art through the operation of schools and by higher training.

(4) To furnish instructors and units for the organization and training of the civilian components.

Outside the continental United States:

(5) To furnish garrisons for our overseas possessions.

While the main missions set forth above are rather fixed and should be based on the continuing congressional mandate for "the immediate and complete mobilization of 1,000,000 men," the variable factor relates to the size, composition, and readiness of the covering (1) and overseas (5) forces. The availability of these covering and overseas forces is as important and vital as the maintenance of adequate naval forces. The ever-changing world situation will bear directly upon this problem. However, there is a minimum below which such forces cannot be allowed to fall under any reasonable circumstances, if our requirements are to be met effectively. The composition of the overseas forces, ground and air, can be definitely determined as concrete local conditions are fixed. In the continental United States the possibilities of hostile invasion are such as to demand a combined ground and air force immediately available and characterized by great mobility and such striking power as to block, on any of our coasts and frontiers, a hostile attempt to invade. The strength and composition of these covering forces should be adequate to hold an invader while the citizen forces are being mobilized.

The development of aviation has increased the power of the offense where the countries at war border upon, or are very close to, each other, and has increased the power of the defense where the contestants are widely separated. This new arm is, therefore, advantageous to our national policy. The idea that aviation can replace any of the other elements of our armed forces is found, on analysis, to be erroneous. The lack of ability to invest or to capture and hold any position, the short period during which aircraft can operate before having to return to its bases, land or floating, the present impracticability of operations on a large scale except in at least fairly good weather, the necessity for protection by other forces except when in the air, and the problems of supply, including replacement of aircraft, are all limitations that should be kept in mind. The fleet, capable of self-maintenance for protracted periods at sea, remains the only entirely dependable force for operations in that element. Since ground forces alone are capable of occupying territory, or, with certainty, preventing occupation of our own territory, the Army with its own air forces remains the ultimate decisive factor in war.

In this connection, attention is called to the following extracts from the latest War Department study (1933). The membership of the committee making this study comprised general officers of the line of the Army, general officers of the War Department General Staff and the Chief of the Air Corps. The principles advocated, the conclusions reached and the recommendations submitted were adopted unanimously and approved by the Secretary of War.

### General Principles for Employment and Organization of the Army Air Corps

(1) In any study of the employment of air forces, it should be realized that said forces cannot operate without bases, land or floating. Furthermore, the facilities associated with such bases must include all those instrumentalities and utilities necessary for operation and maintenance of the air forces. The importance of

these bases may be appreciated by realizing that between 80 and 90 percent of the personnel of an air force is associated with these bases and their supply facilities. While the facilities at such bases may be somewhat limited in temporary emergencies, they will have to be extensive to care for and to permit the operation of any large air force, in fact of any force, that is in excess of 25 to 50 airplanes.

To secure land bases, an enemy would have either:

(a) To seize a suitable harbor on our coast, land his forces, and occupy considerable terrain, then set up the facilities necessary for his air force; or

(b) Establish similar land bases, including air installations near our borders.

In the former case the enemy would have to overcome the harbor defenses and the mobile army and occupy sufficient terrain to establish, and to protect against counter-attack, his land-based aviation, before such aviation could be used. During such operations the only aircraft available to the enemy would be his fleet-borne aviation, and our own air force could concentrate superior forces to interrupt the development.

Proposals are sometimes advanced to the effect that: (1) Land-based bombing airplanes of foreign nations can cross the Atlantic or Pacific, rendezvous at some selected point, deliver a concentrated attack on some vital objective, and then return to home bases. (2) Or with land or floating bases established en route and in territory contiguous to our Nation, an air force superior to our own could launch a decisive attack against some vital area in the United States. These proposals cannot be accepted as a possibility under the present stage of air development. Preparation of adequate bases in peace would be convincing evidence of an intent to attack and would disclose an enemy's proposed plan of operations. Appended hereto is an analysis of General Balbo's flight of 24 Italian planes. For this flight, 8 air bases in foreign countries were established, with 11 surface vessels as agents thereof. The weather services of four nations were utilized. Advance preparations were started in May; the flight was ready in early June, but could not start until July 1. Thirty-three days were consumed between the time of readiness for departure and arrival at destination, 6,063 miles distant, covered in 46 hours of flying in 15 days from start to arrival.

The foregoing indicates the vital importance of bases in all air operations, and, under present air development, shows the unsoundness and fallacy of claims to the effect that the United States is exposed to serious air attacks from land-based air forces which would prove critical to our national defense. . . .

(b) The employment of the units of the Army Air Corps in pursuance of the commander's plan of operations may involve the following:

(1) *Normal mission*—Air operations over the land or the sea, functioning as air units of the Army, in the conduct of land-based operations.

(2) *Special missions*—(a) Joint air operations over the sea with our naval air forces against enemy naval air forces and/or vessels of the enemy fleet.

(b) Joint air operations over the land with our naval air forces against enemy land-based air forces and/or land forces. . . .

[There are a number of important strategic areas in the continental United States.]

These areas will vary in importance due to strategical considerations—possible enemy or enemies and exposure of our own critical industries and resources. Under no conceivable strategical situation will all these areas be exposed to attack at the same time or have the same relative importance. Initial and subsequent strategical considerations will govern the utilization of forces for their defense. Protection of such of these areas as may be involved in operations cannot be accomplished by air forces alone. If our Navy is not available, all elements of our land forces will be required.

While the strategical importance of all these areas demands such peace-time development of ground installations in each area as will make possible their defense in operations, plans contemplating a distribution of our forces (land and air) in all these areas irrespective of possible enemies and consequent relative importance of those areas, would be unsound from a military as well as an economical viewpoint. This would be a cordon defense waste of effort and a false doctrine. . . .

(6) The development of aviation has greatly increased the difficulties of overseas invasion. Both for long-range reconnaissance offshore to detect the approach of enemy expeditions, and for the attack of such expeditions before they reach the shores, there is provided, by a properly constituted Army "G.H.Q. Air Force" a unit heretofore lacking in war.

A properly constituted general headquarters air force will be an especially important unit in land operations. Strategically, this will be used for long-range reconnaissance, for interdicting enemy reconnaissance, for demolition of important installations, and for interdiction of enemy movements. Tactically, the General Headquarters Air Force will be used in support of the ground forces in preparation for battle by combat against enemy air forces engaged in missions of reconnaissance, demolition, and interdiction, during battle by actual participation, and after battle by exploitation of victory or minimizing enemy exploitation in event of defeat.

In the use of the General Headquarters Air Force, as with all other means for waging war, the basic principles of war govern. Of these principles, the concentration of effort, the objective, surprise, the offensive, and security are of primary importance and the mobility of aircraft is such as to permit a skillful leader to apply these principles with especial effect. . . .

The limitations enumerated above show that the ideas that aviation, acting alone, can control the sea lanes, or defend the coast, or produce decisive results in any other general mission contemplated under our policy are all visionary, as is the idea that a very large and independent air force is necessary to defend our country against air attack.

Contemporaneous writers describe aircraft crossing the seas and bombarding with high explosives and gas our cities, with resulting destruction of the entire population. The committee has had computed the quantity of gases of various kinds necessary for effective concentration on areas of given sizes; those computations show the fallacy of the idea presented. To carry sufficient bombs for such a destructive effect would require aircraft in numbers beyond the ability of any nation to maintain, even if a type of plane capable of crossing the ocean with a military load, attacking, and returning to its base, can be developed. The losses inevitable in such an attack and the practical hopelessness of obtaining compensating benefit would condemn such a plan of operations, even if a government, desirous of gaining favorable world opinion and allies or at least friendly neutrals, would authorize an attack directed not only against the military and civilian populations of the enemy, but also against neutrals residing in the city selected as the objective.

The "air invasion of the United States" and the "air defense of the United States" are conceptions of those who fail adequately to consider the effect of ocean barriers and other limitations. Aircraft in sufficient numbers to threaten serious damage can be brought against us only in conjunction with sea forces or with land forces which must be met by forces identical in nature and equally capable of prolonged effort.

In view of the foregoing, our national policy has been to maintain two distinct services for the national defense, the Army and the Navy, with air forces an integral part of each, recognizing said forces as essential and decisive elements.

(a) Our national defense organization comprises the President as Commander in Chief, Congress as the legislative agency, and all the Executive Departments, with their respective forces, as the operating agencies. Aviation is an instrumentality for many of these departments, such bureaus and independent agencies as the Bureau of Air Commerce of the Department of Commerce, the Weather Bureau of the Department of Agriculture, the Coast Guard of the Treasury Department and the National Advisory Committee for Aeronautics being directly involved in aviation questions. It is in the Army and the Navy, the two executive departments which are the fighting arms of the national defense, that this new and powerful instrumentality, aviation, has become of compelling interest. It is now an integral part of each of these two services, the Army and the Navy.

*Has the introduction of aviation as an agent of national defense developed any grounds for a revision in this fundamental organization?*

The Constitution provides that the President shall be Commander in Chief of the armed forces. The introduction of aviation as a new weapon in war affects in no way the soundness of this element of our organization. In the congressional field, the introduction of aviation can have no direct effect from an organizational point of view. Only in the field of the operating agencies, that is the executive departments, have the questions of possible revision arisen.

(b) One proposal looks to a concentration of all Federal, civil, and military aviation in one executive department. This would violate our traditional policy of maintaining as separate functions, civil and war agencies. Such a step would confuse the functional principle of organization with the instruments of operation. It would be no more logical than a consolidation of all other transportation means in a single executive department. Similarly, there would be as much justification for the concentration of all Federal lawyers under the Attorney General, or all chemists under the Bureau of Standards, as to gather all Federal airmen into a single executive department.

(c) Another proposal seeks the concentration of all national defense aviation under one executive department, i.e., a new executive department designed to handle all national defense aviation, or a Department of National Defense with three subdivisions—Army, Navy, and Air.

The considerations and arguments advanced in behalf of such proposals have been discussed in America for the last 16 years as indicated in the foregoing statement on historical background. The analogies in favor of the scheme rest on existing European organization, where national aviation is generally concentrated under one directing head or executive control. Although dissatisfaction is manifested with this plan in some nations, there are many sound reasons why such a policy best accords with the conditions peculiar to these European countries.

First, they promote civil aviation primarily as a national defense asset. Consequently, it appears wise to place the control and direction of commercial aviation (industry and transport) under a war agency rather than a civil one. Second, European war conditions afford special opportunities, peculiar to Europe, for the employment of military aviation to strike powerful blows in advance of any other armed forces. Critical areas are short distances apart with no serious barriers intervening. War industries are generally found in small communities presenting suitable bombing targets. Arteries of travel, roads and railroads, are rather congested and their full capacity would be essential for early war movements. Combat forces are maintained in readiness for immediate action. The comparative speed with which mobilization, concentration and invasion can be effected by land forces, is a vital factor. Under such conditions there will be found many opportunities for employment of military aviation in advance of the time when the large ground forces will be able to strike decisive blows. While such advance aerial operations appear to justify some independence on the part of aviation, they can seldom produce decisive results except in gaining mobilization, concentration and deployment advantages for their own ground forces. As soon as decisive battle between the ground forces approaches, the principles of unity of command and concentration of effort will govern and the air components and ground troops will exert their utmost power in joint actions under one directing head.

The foregoing considerations have application to England as well as to continental Europe—her critical land area is small and her water barrier is not a serious aerial obstacle. In view of her protection by her great fleet England's primary concern is to provide against air attack.

During years of discussion our authorities have consistently declined to accept the European solution. We have followed our traditional policy of keeping civil and war functions separate in peace. Our world supremacy in civil aviation proves the wisdom and soundness of this policy. We have indicated the impracticability of hostile air invasion of our country except as an element of naval or land forces. It must be evident that the peculiar national defense conditions associated with Europe have no general application to America. Our primary needs in military aviation are adequate air forces with our Navy to assist in blocking approaches by sea, and adequate air forces with our Army to assist in repelling an invading force, which the Navy does not overcome, and to participate in land campaigns.

The proponents of the changes under discussion frequently advance the possibilities of economy and avoidance of duplications. Thorough study and analysis of the requirements in overhead establishments (such as superior general staffs, duplications in medical, supply, finance and maintenance services) in the operating organizations and in procurement, development, and issue needs, are convincing that the financial burden would be far greater as a whole under the proposed change than that now entailed. Existing duplication relates mainly to development and procurement. This makes for healthy competition and is minor in comparison to the extra costs involved in the super overhead necessary to the proposal under discussion.

In this connection it should be noted that Japan maintains her air forces organized substantially as does the United States.

(d) A third proposal contemplates leaving our Navy as now organized with its own air component, but consolidating all civil and Army aviation under one head—separate executive department or bureau. The proponents of this change add to the views heretofore discussed the conclusion that such organization would link civil aviation more closely to national defense needs and give aviation such prominence as would insure adequate financial support by the Government. This proposal is really a compromise, with all the attending weaknesses associated with concessions from principle for a temporary advantage. The adherents appear to have less concern for national defense or civil aviation than for the advancement of special interests. Such a change would really result in an executive department of air with the naval air separate, and the views previously expressed in (b) and (c) are applicable.

(e) A fourth proposal relates to the creation of a Federal aviation commission, permanent in character, to regulate national aviation. In some ways this suggestion is an indirect method of accomplishing the major organizational changes discussed in the preceding paragraphs. However, if the proposal relates solely to civil aviation there may be uses therefor.

The Bureau of Air Commerce of the Department of Commerce and the National Advisory Committee for Aeronautics now handle efficiently many of the problems of research, development, coordination, and regulation of civil and military aviation. Except for certain problems of Federal control and regulation, such as rate fixing, the existing agencies appear to be adequate and efficient and are responsible in many ways for our present aviation success. The National Advisory Committee for Aeronautics is an outstanding institution, as evidenced by the testimony presented to this committee and by the pioneering work it has accomplished in aviation research.

(f) Some of the proponents of separating the Air Corps from the Army advance as a reason for this step one important advantage—namely, that the public psychology existing, at least for the time being, would probably secure larger appropriations from the Congress for a separate Air Corps. While realizing the desirability of securing more funds for the Air Corps, the committee feels that it would be unsound to sacrifice the fundamental principles upon which the security of the Nation rests in order to take advantage of a temporary public psychology which may for the moment be willing to spend more on a special arm of national defense because of its popularity. As developed later in this presentation, the committee, after nearly 3 months' study of this question, including an analysis of the latest (1933) War Department report to which previous reference has been had, has recommended an Air Corps of sufficient strength to meet the most serious war threat against our country that can be conceived. Consequently, the committee does not feel justified in advancing a proposal which would place on the taxpayer a further burden.

In the final analysis, the Air Corps has virtually been independent since its inception. In the operations in Mexico in 1916 it was so new a weapon that it really operated independently of Staff control. The overnight expansion required on our entrance into the World War, coupled with the fact that few Regular officers had knowledge of this service, practically exempted it from General Staff control. The results of our attempts to "build a million roads to Berlin" are well known.

In the World War the air arm was a powerful component in the aggregate force on each side. Independent air missions had little if any effect upon the issue of battles and none upon the outcome of the war.

From 1926 to a few months ago the Air Corps has operated primarily under the direct supervision of an Assistant Secretary of War for Air. This committee has studied the present situation and that associated with the air mail operations and is convinced that the time has arrived for the Air Corps to become in all respects a homogeneous part of the Army, under General Staff control, and be subject to military coordination, study, influence, and operation. . . .

The Air Corps units of the Army's covering and overseas forces must be ready at all times for war service. Any great war is now likely to begin with engagements between opposing aircraft, either sea or land based, and early aerial supremacy will be an important factor. This involves many factors but primarily a superior supply of efficient airplanes and of all accessories.

An aircraft industry, therefore, is absolutely essential to the national defense. The size of the air forces for a major emergency would be vastly greater than it would be prudent to maintain in time of peace. Improvements in airplanes are continuous and relatively rapid. Airplanes become obsolete in a few years and, in some cases, are already obsolescent at the time of quantity delivery. Military airplanes cannot in time of peace be stored in large quantities, as can guns for example. This is the premise that leads to the conclusion that there must be maintained in time of peace a satisfactory nucleus of a war-time aviation industry. By a "satisfactory nucleus" is meant a number of aircraft manufacturers distributed over the country, operating on a sound financial basis and capable of rapid expansion to meet the Government's needs in an emergency.

Military aviation in time of war must rely largely upon airplanes built in time of war, and consequently the general condition and productive capacity of the aircraft industry are of national concern.

The preparedness of military aviation for combat may be considered in three stages. During the first, immediate reliance must be placed upon facilities and equipment existing at the outbreak of the war. The second is a longer period of expansion of the existing aircraft industry and delivery of airplanes at a steadily increasing rate. In a major emergency the third period would be the efforts of the Government to speed up the production of airplanes by temporarily drawing into the aircraft industry automobile engine and body manufacturers and other industries whose facilities could be effectively used in the construction of airplanes, parts, or accessories.

For the first few and vitally important months of a war, the permanent aircraft industry would carry the full burden of supplying equipment, and thereafter would also provide for the emergency industry the necessary engineering and supervisory talent.

It is difficult to determine the maximum productive capacity of the American aircraft industry in time of war, and no reliable data are available as to the maximum productive capacities of other nations. It is believed, however, that no other power could exceed in productive capacity the highly industrialized United States.

The development of commercial aviation in the United States has been more rapid than in any other country and has contributed to a great increase in the design and construction facilities of American aircraft manufacturers. The number of civil and commercial airplanes produced is, however, not sufficient to maintain to any appreciable extent a satisfactory nucleus of an aircraft industry.

In the opinion of the committee the major measure to insure the existence of a satisfactory nucleus of an aircraft industry in the United States is the establishment, with the President's approval, of an annual program of procurement for the Army and Navy. If these programs are based on the normal annual replacement of the Army's airplane strength, as recommended herein, plus that of the Navy, the committee believes that the airplane industry of the United States can be maintained on a sound basis and adequate from a national defense viewpoint. The production orders covering this number of airplanes distributed to those firms essential to national defense will assure a continuity of production and stability in the aircraft industry.

The Government should encourage the development of design and engineering staffs in the various airplane factories by a more liberal policy of placing experimental orders for prototypes on a basis on which the Government bears in full the proper cost of development. Such experimental contracts should also provide for changes and additions ordered by the Government, at proper increases in contract prices.

In view of the importance of the aviation industry to the national defense the committee believes that the Government should not enter into competition with private industry by the manufacture of airplanes in Government factories. In the same connection the committee believes that it would be advisable for the Department of Commerce to encourage further the airplane export business. . . .

## General Missions and Methods of Coordination

The Joint Army and Navy Board has made studies on the general missions and methods of coordination of the two services. The conclusions and recommendations of their studies have been approved by the two departments concerned and therefore become governing policy. These actions of the Joint Board are published in "Joint Action of Army and Navy" which defines the general missions of the Army and Navy as follows: "The Army performs functions that normally pertain to land operations; the Navy performs functions that normally pertain to sea operations. Land and sea operations each include air operations over those elements. Sea operations by the Army or land operations by the Navy are proper only when immediately auxiliary to the normal functions."

Since the reorganization of the Joint Board, in 1919, effort, generally successful, has been made to consider every possible operation in which joint action would be required and to establish the basic principles under which unity of command would be established. By this it is expected that controversies between the commanders ashore and those afloat, such as have occurred in past wars, may be avoided. Joint planning committees in oversea departments and in coastal frontiers and sectors have supplemented the Joint Board and its subordinate committees in the War and Navy Departments and have prepared plans fixing responsibility for defensive operations for joint utilization of certain facilities, and the allocation to the Army forces and the naval forces of other facilities. The Munitions Board, operating in connection with the office of The Assistant Secretary of War, recommends the allocation of industry to avoid overlapping of demands and competition in procurement.

Unity of command has been assured in all operations at sea, including those incident to effecting a landing by force on hostile territory. Unity of command has been assured in all operations ashore, including the defense of the coast against actual attack. Studies leading up to these decisions have brought out so strongly the wide divergence in requirements of the Army and the Navy as to equipment, training, organization, and doctrines as to lead the War and Navy Department to oppose every proposal to unite them into a single department, both realizing that it is far better that each should be free to concentrate on its normal and customary missions rather than to adopt a system based upon occasional and short-lived joint operations, especially since these can be met by the adoption of principles insuring coordinated action.

# 15.
# The Lean Years

The revulsion against naval construction that followed World War I was even more evident in regard to the army. The immediate and drastic reduction of the Army was consistent with tradition, for a large standing professional force had never been accepted in America. Furthermore, the non-Wilsonian peace and the reappearance of Old World rivalries led to the feeling that American participation in the recent conflict had been a mistake. The United States, many believed, should never again become involved in a war outside the sphere of its own immediate interests. All that seemed necessary was defense of the Western Hemisphere, and this could best be done by the navy. A small army, designed for rapid expansion in the event of emergency, was deemed adequate even by the majority of military planners.

Unfortunately, even this modest objective was defeated. The meager force permitted by Congressional appropriations was denied funds for the modern weapons that rapid technological advances had produced. The attitude of normalcy and isolation that permeated the 1920's viewed the army as virtually obsolete as the nation moved further away from the notion that war would ever again come to America. The economic depression that began in 1929 increased the pressure for retrenchment in government expenditures, and under a Democratic administration the army found its most important function as administrator of the Civilian Conservation Corps. In the accompanying selection Mark Watson provides a trenchant account of the state of America's land forces during this period.

# The Deterioration of the Army Between Wars

BY MARK S. WATSON

THE ARMED FORCES of the United States underwent an almost continuous weakening from 1918 onward for a decade and a half. The fluctuation in numbers from 1922 to 1936 was small . . . but the deterioration in equipment was continuous in that the 1918 surplus, used up rather than replaced, was not only increasingly obsolescent but increasingly ineffective owing to wear and age. In the mid-thirties the Navy was permitted, by a cautious increase in appropriations, to make a start on a new shipbuilding program which by that time was acutely needed. The Army was less favored, presumably because there was a continuing public confidence, shared by the White House and Congress, in oceans as a bulwark and a belief that the Navy could safely be thought of not merely as the traditional "first line of defense" but as the only really necessary line of defense for the time being. Even the growing reach of the airplane, unmistakably clear on the day of the first trans-Atlantic flight, was not exploited in military form to any such degree as it was in Europe and Japan. The abiding need for trained and equipped ground forces, recognized and continuously recalculated by the Army's General Staff, was generally ignored by the ultimate authority in government.

The majority of Congress is assumed under normal conditions to hold approximately the views of the public which elects it, but it is impossible to say with certainty how accurately the cautious expressions and the reduced appropriations of the prewar Congress with respect to defense measures actually represented the wishes of the public. On the one hand, the newspaper files of prewar years are almost barren of any recorded protest against excessive thrift in money appropriations. On the other hand, a contemporary public opinion analyst maintained both then and thereafter that the public was far ahead of Congress in its ultimate votes to support defense measures. His postwar estimate of the public's attitude during the previous twelve years noted that "one of the first polls we took in this business was on the question of appropriating more money for the Army and the Navy . . . back in . . . 1935. We found in that very early poll that the people were strongly in favor of increasing appropriations . . . at a time when Congress was going exactly in the other direction. . . . During the war years there was no step this country took which the public hadn't approved weeks and months before Congress. . . . In every study we made . . . we found a substantial majority of the people of the country willing and ready to support civilian mobilization or war manpower conscription." It would be difficult to prove, however, that the prewar public, even when willing to express sympathy for defense expenditures, was vigorous in asserting its will unless and until provided with an energizing leader-

From Mark S. Watson, *Chief of Staff: Prewar Plans and Preparations* (Washington, 1950), 15–36. Used by permission of the Chief of Military History, Department of the Army.

ship. Congressmen, and Presidents too, normally responsive to any vigorously expressed wishes of constituents, did not by their speeches or by their votes in those years demonstrate any pronounced change of heart toward a strong defense policy, nor do the records show that they were unseated at ensuing elections because of their lethargy on the rearmament question. It is fair to conclude that the views of office-holders who continued unruffled in office were not in active conflict with the views of the public majority that put them in office. By that test, prewar America was not war-minded, nor even defense-minded to an assertive degree. Even in early 1940 an urgent Army plea to Congress for 166 airplanes was beaten down to 57, and no 4-motor bombers were permitted, an opponent making the explanation that these were not defensive but "aggressive" weapons, the very type against which the American delegates' efforts had been directed at Geneva in 1934.

Appreciation of America's addiction to the defense-only policy is necessary if one is to understand public lethargy in the early days of World War II and the handicaps under which the War Department labored as a consequence. The fact is not appreciated from a mere statement of it so well as from a study of its results. That America was peace-minded for two decades is hardly worth the saying; what matters is that because of this state of mind the nation's military strength was allowed to decrease and decay to the point where it became tragically insufficient and, even more important, incapable of restoration save after the loss of many lives and the expenditure of other resources beyond man's comprehension.

The responsibility for the Army's deterioration between wars was so far from being exclusively that of Congress—although often visited upon Congress because that body was finally responsible for all appropriations—that the Mead committee of Congress in 1946 undertook to lessen public criticism by shifting the onus. The report noted that after 1919 "many persons in the military agencies evidenced an attitude of complacency" and that "largely as a result of this attitude Congressional appropriations for the support of our national defense were reduced to a dangerous minimum." In prompt rebuttal the Under Secretary's office initiated a gathering of typical War Department expressions of a most uncomplacent nature that had been made to or in the hearing of Congress. From the annual reports of Secretary of War John W. Weeks in 1921, 1922, and 1923 were extracted warnings that "our present combat strength will be insufficient to fulfill the functions required by our national defense policy," that "additional cuts would endanger our safety," that "factors which introduce causes for war are now in the making; it is the height of folly to continue the present policy of cutting our financial support of the War Department. . . . We are already cut below our vital needs." Similar complaints of unpreparedness were extracted from the annual reports of Secretary of War Dwight F. Davis in 1925–28, his successors Patrick J. Hurley, George H. Dern, and Harry H. Woodring, and Assistant Secretaries of that period, likewise from reports and speeches of General Pershing and every succeeding Chief of Staff.

General Pershing's pungent remarks on July 4, 1925 noted that "under our very eyes there have already been serious reductions made by Congress" and that "the politician, himself oftentimes uninformed as to his country's history, frequently appeals to the ignorant and unthinking on the score of economy; . . . such demagogues are dangerous." General Douglas MacArthur in 1934 summarized the personnel shortage dramatically, declaring: "In many cases there is but one officer on duty with an entire battalion; this lack of officers (has) brought Regular Army training in the continental United States to a virtual standstill . . . correction is mandatory." Stocks of materiel, he continued, were "inadequate even for limited forces . . . and, such as they are, manifestly obsolescent. The secrets of our weakness are secrets only to our own people." The 1935 report from Mr. Dern predicted that in the event of war "we should find that our so-called economies have in reality been a hideously extravagant waste of money and lives." With less rhetoric Secretary Henry L. Stimson in his 1941 report made the following statement:

"Not until our country saw its former democratic allies and friends struck down in quick succession did our Congress, representing accurately the view of our public, authorize the fiscal appropriations necessary to make any adequate defense. Until such Congressional action, no increased American armies would be raised and paid for and no contracts for munitions could be entered into."

The most spirited defender of the thrifty attitude of a succession of Presidents and Congresses after World War I could hardly deny that the Army's principal spokesmen, military and civilian, had sounded ample warnings. The trouble was that listeners apparently were few, even among those who because of their positions of responsibility might have been expected to listen. Thus when Major General John L. Hines, then Deputy Chief of Staff under Pershing, appeared before the House Appropriations Committee on December 19, 1923 and said bluntly that the 118,000 men asked for were not enough, but that 150,000 were needed, as estimated by Secretary Weeks and General Pershing, a member of the committee demanded of him when those estimates had been made. General Hines said they were in the formal reports. "I had not seen any of those reports," confessed the committeeman.

The routine, disciplined obedience of the Army to the President as Commander in Chief and to such of his agents as the Budget Director was itself a handicap to Army programs, barring any save a refractory officer from demanding more funds than were approved by the White House. This fact was illustrated every year, and often in every year, and the reason for it made clear on November 25, 1924 when Brigadier General K. W. Walker, then Army Chief of Finance, was interrogated by a committeeman on this issue of full acceptance of Presidential directions:

Q. In general, which do you regard as the more important—the President's policy of economy or the actual needs and requirements of the War Department?

GENERAL WALKER. That is a pretty hard question for me to answer. . . . The President's policy is the controlling factor and must be our guide; but that does not prevent the War Department from stating to the President through the Budget Bureau its needs as it sees them.

Q. Would it prevent the War Department from presenting its needs before this committee?

GENERAL WALKER. I think it would. I think when the Budget has once been approved by the President and transmitted to Congress, it is his budget estimate and no officer or official of the War Department would have any right to come up here and attempt to get a single dollar more than is contained in that estimate. . . .

Q. So the final analysis of it is, General, that up to the present the $336,000,000 must suffice, even though that does not meet your requirements at all?

GENERAL WALKER. Insofar as the War Department is concerned, yes, sir. If this committee should develop that more money should be had for any specific purpose, it would be of course its prerogative to give it, just as it is its prerogative to reduce any amount. This prerogative has been exercised time and time again.

A year later, on December 8, 1925, when again the Secretary's plea for an army of 150,000 had been ignored and the Department's reduced estimates were laid before Congress, Major General Dennis E. Nolan, then Deputy Chief of Staff, answered similar questioning from appropriations committeemen in a somewhat tarter manner.

Q. If you do not get all you need that is because you do not ask for it?

GENERAL NOLAN. Oh yes, we ask for it.

Q. Well, you ask the Budget and they do not give you the money, nor does Congress?

GENERAL NOLAN. But we are prohibited by law from asking Congress for anything except the amount that is allowed here in the Budget.

Q. . . . Now, why should you not come up here and frankly tell us that the amount is not sufficient to maintain those activities. . . . ?

GENERAL NOLAN. Because Congress passed a Budget law, in which there is a proviso prohibiting any official of the Government coming before a Committee of Congress and arguing for more money than is permitted under the Budget sent up by the President. That is a matter of law.

Still more directly pointing at the Congressional responsibility, General MacArthur, before the same committee, on November 28, 1932, in his pleas for the Army's miniature armored forces of that day said explosively that "they suffer tremendously from one thing and one thing only—that Congress will not give them enough money to equip them properly with modern tanks." If the Mead committee's postwar judgments found "complacency" about small Army appropriations, it was not in the major public utterances of the several Chiefs of Staff.

In the thirties, when war clouds were mounting both in Europe and Asia, the U.S. Army had ample time to rebuild itself, but no money. When war broke out in Europe late in that decade, the Army was given more and more money, but time, far more precious than money, now was lacking. That eventually the rebuilding took place, and that from the excellence of this performance grew the majestic military successes of 1944–45 is so unforgettable that the radiant last act of the drama (so suggestive of November, 1918) threatens to drive from national memory the gloom and dismay of the first act (so suggestive of 1917).

In their preliminaries, developments, and immediate sequels World War I and World War II followed a cycle whose phases are well-marked: (1) prior to the war, insufficient military expenditures, based on the public's prewar conviction that war could not come to America; (2) discovery that war *could* come after all; (3) a belated rush for arms, men, ships, and planes to overcome the nation's demonstrated military weakness; (4) advance of the producing and training program, attended by misunderstandings, delays, and costly outlay, but gradual creation of a large and powerful army; (5) mounting successes in the field, and eventual victory; (6) immediately thereafter rapid demobilization and dissolution of the Army as a powerful fighting force; (7) sharp reduction of appropriations sought by the military establishment, dictated by concern over its high cost and for a time by the revived hope that, again, war would not come to America. The early phases of the cycle as encountered prior to the arrival of World War II, particularly as they relate to the Office of the Chief of Staff of the Army, can be examined in some detail.

In 1929 President Herbert Hoover instructed the Secretary of War to order an investigation into War Department needs and methods which should "reconsider our whole army program." In accordance with direction from Secretary James W. Good on July 29 this survey was undertaken by the War Department General Staff, resulting in a 165-page report signed by the Deputy and five Assistant Chiefs of Staff. Unfortunately, before the report was completed the stock market collapse of that autumn, heralding the great depression, had doomed any possible program for increasing Army expenditures. The Staff report, however, did not discuss economies. It related a nation's state of preparedness to the respect in which the nation is held and hence to the success with which the nation can make peaceful application of its foreign policies. It reviewed the world situation, noting differences between nations and the existence in America of "certain clearly defined national policies conflicting with those of other countries." It then examined the condition of the Army with regard to personnel and materiel, the reasons for its state and the proposals for remedying it, making two major proposals for that purpose. The 1920 target of 280,000 enlisted strength in the Regular Army, clearly and impressively stated in the National Defense Act of that year, was not dreamed of any more, apparently, for either of the 1929 proposals would have constituted a mean between the strength authorized in the National Defense Act and the strength possible of attainment under the successive appropriation bills. Plan I would have provided 179,000 officers and men in the Regular Army, 250,000 in the National Guard, 116,000 in the Officers' Reserve Corps, 6,000 annually from the Reserve Officers' Training Corps (in colleges), and annual training of 37,500 in the Citizens' Military Training Camps. The Regular Army enlisted strength (excluding Philippine Scouts) was still fixed at 118,750 by the practical limitation of the current annual appropriation. The survey recognized existing shortages in guns and ammunition, in aircraft and antiaircraft equipment, even in tentage and certain clothing items. It reported a surplus of rifles and certain other items useful in case of large mobilization. In plain terms it reproached the Budget Director for making crippling cuts in the Army fund requests without prior consultation with the Army about the relative importance of these requests, with the result that "in effect he and not the responsible head of the Department determines to some degree what . . . shall not be included in the budget." Plan II outlined an organization smaller than that of Plan I. It was opposed as insufficient to Army needs, but what the Army received in succeeding years was much nearer to Plan II than Plan I, and was below both. Personnel was not increased at all.

In 1933 the Army was accordingly at the lowest effectiveness that it had touched since World War I, standing seventeenth among the world's armies by the estimate of the current Chief of Staff. There had been no appreciable drop in personnel but there had been a steady falling off in freshness of equipment and even in the field organization, as a result of continuingly low defense expenditures which themselves were traceable to a conviction on the part of the American public as well as the Congress (comforting in a period of depression) that war was a remote possibility. On June 30 of that year the Army strength stood at approximately 14,000 officers and 122,000 enlisted men, even though the 1920 National Defense Act had authorized a peacetime strength of 280,000 enlisted men. The accompanying concept in the 1920 act had been that a force so small (by 1918 standards) as 280,000 should be capable of rapid and efficient expansion. To that end it would be composed of a maximum number of units in the form of cadres of men highly trained for expansion in emergency. This necessarily meant a minimum number of men per unit in peacetime. The arrangement presupposed a proper balance of units that in emergency, quickly expanded by recruitments, would compose divisions, corps, and field armies complete with headquarters, combat elements, and service organizations. But when the total number in the Army dropped from 280,000 to 125,000 or less it became impossible to maintain even in skeleton form the whole number of units that had been planned originally, and many of them ceased to exist. Hence corps and field army units had to be recreated altogether when the rebuilding of the Army was under way. Instead of a lean, hard organization capable of scientific expansion on short notice, there was from 1920 onward an emaciated organization incapable of expanding directly and automatically into a rounded field force; the skeleton units which had been eliminated would now have to be recreated from the beginning. This problem of recreating whole units, rising in acute form when the Army expansion of 1940 was under way, was referred to at the time by the Chief of Staff (then General Marshall) in an explanation of current personnel needs:

> . . . During the lean years, dating back to 1921, the Army's fight for personnel was a fight for its very life. You will recall that within a year of the passage of the amendments to the National Defense Act of 1920 appropriations for the Regular Army had reduced its strength from the authorized figure of 280,000 to 150,000. . . . By successive stages the strength of the Army was cut and cut until in 1935 it had declined to 118,750.
>
> Let me give you a specific example of the effect of these reductions upon the efficiency of the Army. During this period I commanded a post which had for its garrison a battalion of infantry, the basic fighting unit of every army. It was a battalion only in name, for it could muster barely 200 men in ranks when every available man, including cooks, clerks and kitchen police, (was) present for the little field training that could be accomplished with available funds. The normal strength of a battalion in most armies of the world varies from 800 to 1,000 men. . . .
>
> Part of the reason for this deplorable condition was that, while the new air arm had developed in the latter stages of the World War, no provision for its essential expansion in our Army was made except by emasculation of the basic ground forces. The Air Corps was stripping the Infantry, Artillery, Engineers, and Signal troops. Important headquarters units, essential for battlefield control, were being dropped from the rolls. The Army as a team was gradually being starved into a condition almost comparable to its pre-Spanish-American War condition.
>
> . . . We will be seriously handicapped in our problem of developing skill in handling large units, and keeping them properly supplied in the field, until we are able to organize again at least a limited number of the essential control, supply, and communications units of corps and army troops. Furthermore, and of equal or greater importance, is the pressing necessity for a certain minimum of seasoned, trained units immediately available for service. . . .

The state of the Army in that period of the thirties which General Marshall's letter describes, and the gloomy attitude of its War Plans Division (WPD) at the time, are alike indicated by a notation in one of the contemporary WPD reports that recommendations for increases in Army strength would be presented to President, Congress, and the Budget officer "not with any hope or idea of obtaining immediate action, but so that those responsible would understand the condition and that it should be remedied when possible."

Accordingly consideration was given by the Chief of Staff in 1933, General MacArthur, to means of mobilizing a defense force from each of three stages, (I) with the current strength of 118,000 enlisted men, (II) with a hoped-for 165,000 men, and (III) with the 280,000 men authorized by the Defense Act. Mobilization from stage I, it was pointed out, would be impossible in less than four to six months, there being in existence in continental United States only four incomplete divisions with no supporting force and no cadres for expansion to new divisions. There was no way, at that low stage, to maintain except on paper the four-army establishment which General MacArthur had designed as the target.

Mobilization from stage II, with a force of 165,000, would still provide no immediately available force, but would permit the creation of a more rounded establishment which would permit efficient expansion. In particular, it would furnish one division for each of the four theoretical armies, and also five skeleton brigades. These nine infantry units would thus provide a discernible Regular Army force in each of the country's nine corps areas. The increase to 165,000 would also add slightly to the 14,600-man air force, would create five new antiaircraft regiments, would add men to the Army's incipient tank force, and would permit strengthening the weak garrisons in Hawaii and Panama. The layman is interested in seeing, thus early, the professional judgment on first needs which were to be repeatedly cited, and which long remained unsatisfied.

It was this Mobilization II which General MacArthur urged. The 280,000-man army of Mobilization III, specified though it had been as the peace-strength force as long ago as 1920, now existed only as a planning concept; of the three mobilization plans, Mobilization III alone would provide a balanced army corps for immediate use and, in addition, a framework for later expansion. But, as shown by the WPD notation just mentioned, it was thought of as unattainable, and hence not worth pressing for. General MacArthur and his successor, General Malin Craig, pressed for only what they thought could be obtained, and the 170,000 enlisted strength of 1938 was the result of their pressure. A further 40,000 increase above that point is what General Craig was to seek in February, 1939 when Brigadier General George C. Marshall as his deputy went to Congress to argue for it.

The program under Mobilization II was basic thereafter until the much larger program of 1940 replaced it, and General Staff planning for the Army was pursued with the expectation that a war involving the United States would be, in its first phase, defensive. It looked forward accordingly to the availability of an Initial Protective Force (IPF) made up of only the Regular Army and National Guard in current existence. The 1933–40 concept was of 165,000 enlisted men in the Regular Army and 235,000 in the National Guard, and these made up the 400,000-man total for the IPF, for which the supply branches of the Staff made their computations. (That modest total for the Regular Army was not in fact reached until mid-1937. The figure listed for the National Guard was not reached, even in authorization, until September of that year. Actually the National Guard entered federal service in 1940 and early 1941 with about 200,000 men who had received training of some sort.)

The Initial Protective Force, as its name indicates, was to be the emergency defensive force only. It would be enlarged (as a plan, not a reality) under the 1937 revision to the size specified in General Pershing's 1920 program. This Protective Mobilization Plan (PMP) contemplated a Regular Army of 280,000 enlisted men and a National Guard of 450,000, a total of 730,000. It was assumed that upon declaration of an emergency new recruitments would immediately add some 270,000 men who would be trained as replacements and would bring up the total PMP force to 1,000,000 men.

The General Staff planning of 1933–39 aimed at a provision of weapons and other equipment sufficient for such a force, and it was Congress' failure to supply funds for anything like the PMP total that disturbed the General Staff throughout the period. In 1932 the supply chief of the Staff (G-4) had recognized realistically "the probability of greatly reduced War Department appropriations for Fiscal Year 1934 and succeeding years," and initiated steps toward producing a well-planned and balanced and equipped force at some future time when money should be available. The cumulative value of this 1934 planning of a six-year program was to prove incalculable as World War II drew nearer. The plan itself evidences the realism of General Staff thinking in this realm even in depression days when there was little that is measurable in the way of Staff doing. General MacArthur manifested concern over equipment shortages as early as 1933 in his annual report as Chief of Staff, without result. General Craig, his successor, in his own last annual report summarized his anxiety thus:

> The problem encountered on my entry into office was the lack of realism in military war plans. . . . (They) comprehended many paper units, conjectural supply, and a disregard of the time element which forms the main pillar of any planning structure. . . . What transpires on prospective battlefields is influenced vitally years before in the councils of the staff and in the legislative halls of Congress. Time is the only thing that may be irrevocably lost, and it is the thing first lost sight of in the seductive false security of peaceful times. . . . The sums appropriated this year will not be fully transformed into military power for two years. Persons who state that they see no threat to the peace of the United States would hesitate to make that forecast through a two-year period.

The warning, buried deep in a long official report, passed almost unnoticed in the newspapers of that day and hence by the public and most of the Congress. Not until the alarms of 1940 (when the period of Craig's warning was not yet half over) was there any common grasp of the fact that appropriations could not in fact "be fully transformed into military power for two years. . . ."

The peacetime failure to develop new weapons was in some degree due to the fact that World War I had left on hand a massive surplus of weapons and other equipment, in working condition but in large part obsolescent. The Congressional view was that this surplus should be thriftily used up before anything else of the sort was bought, and newspapers of the period disclose no noticeable expression of disagreement. Hence the slow and ineffective tanks of types little modified from 1918 standards lingered at U.S. Army posts while Germany was building the swift and powerfully armed vehicles that were to make possible Hitler's dazzling successes of 1940. Alongside the 1918 tanks at U.S. Army posts until 1938 lay the 1918-type antitank weapons. Not until 1940 did the American 81- and 60-mm mortars replace the World War I type throughout the Army. The M-1 semiautomatic rifle (Garand), which greatly increased infantry fire power and which was developed by Army Ordnance persistence as a replacement for the pre-1917 Springfield, came from the factories so slowly in 1941 that training plans had to be adjusted to its delivery. The invaluable "bazooka," which for the first time made an enemy tank really vulnerable to assault by a lone infantryman, was issued to troop units while they were deployed in the Tunisian campaign, and to others aboard ship on their way overseas; few of them had ever seen the weapon previously, or heard of it. . . .

This between-wars idea that American armed forces should be designed for defense only, not offense, illuminated as it was by the Washington Treaties for arms limitation (1922) and the Kellogg-Briand Pact (1929), was so completely a national policy imposed upon the Army that it became a guide to Army planning and upon occasion had a particularly crippling effect upon the Air Corps. Thus, in May 1938 a program for acquiring long-range bombers was sent back to the planners by the Deputy Chief of Staff with a sharp restatement of Air Corps limitations. He directed restudy of the program, with the following reminder:

(1) Our national policy contemplates preparation for defense, not aggression, (2) Defense of sea areas, other than within the coastal zone, is a function of the Navy, (3) The Military superiority of . . . a B-17 over the two or three smaller planes that could be procured with the same funds remains to be established, in view of the vulnerability, air-base limitation and complexity in operation of the former type. . . . If the equipment to be provided for the Air Corps be that best adapted to carry out the specific functions appropriately assigned it under Joint Action . . . there would appear to be no need for a plane larger than the B-17.

The Air Corps was still suffering acutely from the two blights thus coupled: the nation's defense-only attitude, plus the still persistent theory that the Navy should be responsible for operations not only upon the ocean but in the air above the ocean. A month after the memorandum just recited the Assistant Secretary of War informed the Chief of Air Corps bluntly that "the unobligated funds set up for two B-15s (a long-range type) will not be used for that purpose, nor for a YB-20 (another long-range type) but will be applied to a portion of the 91 bombers, procurement of which was directed." A further warning against experiment looking toward the long-range bombing fleets which soon were to mature, in spite of 1938 policy, was sent to the Chief of Air Corps by the Secretary of War announcing that "estimates for bombers in Fiscal Year 1940 (must) be restricted to light, medium and attack types." It was not until the next year that the Air Board, appointed March 23, 1939 by the Chief of Air Corps, reported defiantly that the striking forces "will be required to extend the destructive effects of air operations over both land and sea, to great distances beyond their operating bases."

# 16.

# Rearmament and War

The march of events in Europe and the Far East were to provide the stimulus for a rearmament program that restored prosperity, made the United States the "arsenal of democracy," and created the most powerful military force the world had ever seen. The aggressive actions of Japan, Italy, and Germany during the 1930's marked the breakdown of collective security and provoked an arms race that heightened international tensions. President Franklin Roosevelt, fearful that America might once again be drawn into a world conflict, strove to exert moral force to prevent war. But the outbreak of hostilities in China in 1937 and Europe in 1939 ended the hopes for peace. As danger mounted in foreign lands naval appropriations increased rapidly, until in 1940 plans were implemented for the establishment of massive fleets in both oceans. A rapid expansion of the air arm took place and after the fall of France the first peacetime conscription was introduced to implement American defenses. The Lend-Lease Act of 1941 provided for material assistance to victims of aggression as the United States moved from a formal neutrality to the status of a co-belligerent. Modern warfare, to a degree never before in history, demanded the harnessing and regimentation of all the resources of a nation. In the year and a half that followed the defeat of France and the attack on Pearl Harbor, the United States mobilized industry and prepared for the war that finally came. The story of this effort is told in the first of the following selections.

The historians have not agreed on President Roosevelt's responsibility for America's eventual involvement in the war. Were his policies designed to keep the nation out of the conflict or bring it in against the wishes of the majority of the people? The second of the following selections contends that the considerations which dominated Roosevelt's diplomacy during this period were essentially military, designed to protect the national interest as he saw it.

# The Beginnings of Mobilization

IN THE MONTHS that intervened between the invasion of Poland in September 1939, and the national election in November, 1940, legislative foundations were laid for a more adequate system of national defense, but only after thorough debate which spread from the Senate and House chambers to every crossroads. Though creation of administrative machinery for mobilization was necessarily subordinated to the task of obtaining legislation and of promoting public discussion of the issues underlying legislative proposals, by November, 1940, the first steps had been taken in the erection of a governmental machine for defense and for war. . . .

On January 3, 1940, the President, in his annual message, said: "I am asking the Congress for Army and Navy increases which are based not on panic but on common sense. They are not as great as enthusiastic alarmists seek. They are not as small as unrealistic persons claiming superior private information would demand." In reporting the appropriation bill, the House Appropriations Committee recommended 57 new airplanes instead of 496. It eliminated an item of some $12 million for the development of an air base in Alaska. In all, cuts totaling about 10 percent of the requests were made. The Committee's recommendations were accepted by the House without serious protest. By the time the appropriations measures were considered by the Senate, the Nazis had begun moving westward and then all could see that the level of military expenditures proposed in January was far too low. . . .

The German invasion of Denmark and Norway on April 9 appeared to us disturbing but not fatal, but the assault on the Low Countries on May 10 revealed unforeseen methods of making war. Within a week the Army of the Netherlands capitulated. The Belgians surrendered in less than 3 weeks. In little more than 30 days, France, considered to be one of the great land powers of the world, sued for an armistice. The British were driven from the continent. Italy entered the war. Disruption of the pattern of power in Europe had repercussions in the Far East. With the Netherlands and France conquered and with Britain occupied in her defense at home, their Far Eastern possessions became tempting objects of conquest. Even before the French-German armistice was signed in June, 1940, the Japanese militarists began to exert pressure on French Indochina. In July, the British were brought to close the Burma Road. A Germany dominant on the continent and free to develop and utilize its resources could threaten the United States through the economic ties that bound the Latin-American countries to Europe.

The United States was probably in the most precarious position in its history. Yet to many of us the peril seemed remote. Voices proclaimed loudly that all this could never touch us; we had the Atlantic and Pacific for moats. We

---

From Bureau of the Budget, *The United States at War: Development and Administration of the War Program By the Federal Government* (Washington, n.d.), 17, 19–21, 25–27, 29, 35–38, 60–63, 91–95.

continued with unabated zest our political feuds even though these internal cleavages affected our ability to react quickly to changes in the international environment. The coincidence of the crisis with a presidential election further complicated matters. Everything that was done or left undone was open to charges of partisanship. On the other hand, the fact that the crisis occurred during the year of a presidential election insured the most alert and demanding public scrutiny and criticism of governmental policy.

The fall of the Netherlands, Belgium, and France did, however, demolish most of the powerful centers of opposition to the development of industrial facilities for production of defense equipment. By and large, the problem of rearmament, narrowly defined to exclude such questions as the draft, ceased to be one of mobilizing national consensus, and became one of governmental and industrial organization for production. In this, some progress had been made already. Navy expenditures for the year ending June 30, 1940, were 46 percent greater than those for the fiscal year 1937–38. Over the same period, expenditures for the military functions of the War Department increased 54 percent. But this expansion, achieved against fairly strong opposition, was trifling in comparison with what had to be done.

The sweep of German armies over Western Europe also cleared the way for obtaining additional appropriations for national defense. When the President addressed Congress on May 16 to review military developments in Europe, he requested an immediate appropriation of $896,000,000 and additional authority to make contract obligations totaling $286,000,000. In response to this request, funds were made available by acts approved on June 11 and 13. Shortly after the British forces were driven from the continent of Europe, the President made an "urgent and new recommendation" for the appropriation of still more money both for the further expansion of production facilities and for the purchase of additional weapons. Again Congress acted quickly. Including contract authorizations, about $1\frac{1}{3}$ billion dollars were made available by legislation approved on June 26. On July 10, the President went to Congress again for additional appropriations and authorizations of almost 5 billion dollars. Two months later Congress made the necessary authorizations in an act approved September 9, 1940. The delay between the request and the appropriation handicapped the defense program, particularly the construction of training facilities. . . .

It was necessary to induce manufacturers to accept defense contracts. Only recently, businessmen who had manufactured munitions in the first World War had been subjected to investigations, and they were not anxious again to go through that kind of agony. Mr. Knudsen, the advisor on industrial production, Mr. Nelson, Coordinator of Purchases for the Commission, and other businessmen drawn into the Commission's work were able by pressure and persuasion to induce reluctant businessmen to take contracts for the construction of new defense plants and the production of military goods.

The War and Navy Departments, accustomed to small-scale, meticulous, and slow purchasing procedures, had to be shocked into altering their practices to meet the necessities of larger-scale operation. The advice, assistance, and urging of business experts, while not always welcomed by the service departments, brought modifications in their practices. Legislation was required to remove legal limitations on contracting officers and to permit the negotiation of contracts. Congress granted the necessary authority in several acts, but it was not easy for contracting officers, mindful of a reckoning to come for inevitable errors of judgment, to shake off their habitual methods of slow and careful action. The passage in June, 1940 of a statute authorizing the President to order priority for deliveries under Army and Navy contracts gave them further support and strengthened our legislation for defense.

One of the most important blocks to rapid action was the fear that productive facilities, especially for raw materials, would be expanded so much that the Nation would be left with excess capacity. This anxiety colored action within both industry and the Defense Commission. We were not, and we hoped not to be, in the war, but war or no war, the estimates of materials and facilities the crisis would demand to support military production and to maintain the essential civilian economy, were subjects of dispute. Quite apart from the technical problem of estimating quantities of materials and products required to maintain a given military effort over a given period of time, the determination of the new productive facilities we needed had to rest on a correct forecast of the trend of international events. What the trend was became the subject of heated controversy until Pearl Harbor. All sides accepted the proposition that some expansion in capacity was essential to produce commodities which had both civilian and military uses, but they differed about the particular industries to be expanded and about the degree of expansion. Emerging from a period in which our thinking was dominated by the problem of what to do about surpluses, we were cautious in our estimates of the future demands on our industries.

Private enterprise naturally was reluctant to invest its money in plants to produce weapons for a war that might not come, but we were not a nation traditionally disposed to invest public funds in manufacturing establishments. Government ownership of plants and machinery was anathema to many business and financial men, although some plane manufacturers were indifferent about how new factories were financed. After considerable discussion, Congress passed, and on June 25, the President approved, legislation which empowered the Reconstruction Finance Corporation:

(1) To make loans to, or, when requested by the Federal Loan Administrator with the approval of the President, purchase the capital stock of, any corporation (a) for the purpose of producing, acquiring, and carrying strategic and critical materials as defined by the President, and (b) for plant construction, expansion and equipment, and working capital, to be used by the corporation in the manufacture of equipment and supplies necessary to the national defense, on such terms and conditions and with such maturities as the Corporation may determine; and

(2) When requested by the Federal Loan Administrator, with the approval of the President, to create or to organize a corporation or corporations, with power (a) to produce, acquire, and carry strategic and critical materials as defined by the President, (b) to purchase and lease land, to purchase, lease, build, and expand plants, and to purchase and produce equipment, supplies, and machinery, for the manufacture of arms, ammunition, and implements of war, (c) to lease such plants to private corporations to engage in such manufacture, and (d) if the President finds that it is necessary for a Government agency to engage in such manufacture, to engage in such manufacture itself. . . .

Under this legislation, the Rubber Reserve Company and the Metals Reserve Company were established on June 28, 1940, as subsidiaries of the Reconstruction Finance Corporation. Creating of the Defense Plant Corporation and the Defense Supplies Corporation followed on August 22 and 29, respectively. By now the Reconstruction Finance Corporation had become, as large organizations tend to do, fixed in its ways, and it was proud of its record of making "sound" loans. With the encouragement of persons in the Defense Commission who disliked the idea of Government ownership of plants, the RFC wavered for some time before it decided that the Government might own outright a plant essential for national defense but not likely to be built by private investors.

At the same time that steps were being taken to get production of defense articles under way, measures were initiated quietly to mobilize the scientific brains of the country to develop new implements of war. On June 27, through an order of the Council of National Defense, the President established the National Defense Research Committee. The Committee was instructed to "correlate and support scientific research on the mechanisms and devices of warfare, except those relating to problems of flight included in the field of activities of the National Advisory Committee for Aeronautics." The Committee rapidly entered into contracts with universities, industrial laboratories, and other scientific institutions to focus the scientific resources of the Nation on problems relating to the mechanisms and devices of warfare. . . .

Progress in defense production from the fall of France to the end of 1940 was not impressive in terms of defense articles actually manufactured. Instead the period was one in which money was appropriated, contracts were awarded, war plant construction was put in motion, and other preliminaries to actual production were carried out. From June 1 to the end of December, almost $10.5 billion in contracts were awarded. Deliveries under these contracts were very small, of course, and the Government was ridiculed because, for example, it cited the number of planes "on order" as an indication of progress. An impression of the magnitude of total contract awards in the latter half of 1940 may be gained from the fact that these awards were over nine times the total amount spent for military purposes by the War and Navy Departments in the fiscal year ending June 30, 1938. Cash expenditures for all defense purposes in the month of December 1940 slightly exceeded the amount spent for naval purposes during the entire fiscal year ending June 30, 1938. Expansion was under way. . . .

In an age of mechanized warfare a nation cannot "spring to arms." Men must be instructed thoroughly in the care and use of weapons and equipment often requiring great skill. But knowledge of the use of weapons and the operation of complex equipment is not enough; to become an effective team, officers and men must train together in large units under field conditions approximating those of actual military operations. In the spring of 1940, our land forces consisted of a small professional army, the National Guard, and some Reserves. Training of the regular army had been limited severely by the maintenance of the regular army in small groups at scattered posts which made it impossible to conduct field exercises with large bodies of troops. In fact, the first genuine corps and army maneuvers in the history of the Nation became possible in the late spring of 1940. The National Guard required intensive training to be brought to the proper condition, but it represented the most readily available source of additional military personnel.

In his message of May 31, asking for additional armament appropriations, the President recommended that Congress give him authority to call into active service such portions of the National Guard and Reserve as might be necessary. The request was made so that, if Congress adjourned, the President would have authority to meet contingencies which might arise during its absence from Washington. No action was taken immediately to meet the recommendation. Shortly after it was made, Italy entered the war and France surrendered. On July 29, the President reported to Congress that the "increasing seriousness of the international situation" demanded that the national defense structure should be "brought as rapidly as possible to the highest state of efficiency, in training as well as in equipment and materials." He requested Congress to authorize him to order Reserve officers to active duty and to call the National Guard to "active service for such period of intensive training as may be necessary to raise its efficiency to a point comparable with that of our small regular establishment." By legislation approved on August 27, 1940, the President was granted power to call up the National Guard and Reserve officers for 12 months of duty. By order of August 31, effective September 16, the President called into active military service certain elements of the National Guard, and subsequent orders brought other units into service.

Congress did not appropriate until September funds requested by the President early in July for construction of training facilities. The existing shortage of military camps made doubtful the wisdom of calling the National Guard into Federal service in September. Selective Service was, however, under consideration by Congress at the time and it was feared that to delay active duty for the Guard might result in further postponement or defeat of draft legislation.

Induction of the National Guard furnished a large block of personnel which could be trained, conditioned, and disciplined into an important addition to the defensive system. But even with this addition we had insufficient troops for defense. In the summer of 1940, the Administration felt that large numbers of men should be trained for military service. The issue was whether to rely on recruitment of volunteers or to adopt conscription. The introduction of compulsory military training in time of peace presented a grave issue which aroused prolonged debate in Congress and the country at large. The wisdom and necessity of the action were doubted by men of unquestioned sincerity. Thus a distinguished Senator declared—

> . . . Mr. President, were I to be a party to riveting shackles of militarism upon the American people, and superimposing upon the American people in time of peace, the damnable system of conscription which has devastated and ruined Europe, I could not hope for peace with myself hereafter.
>
> Mr. President, this bill is supported by some of the ablest men in the Senate and in the country. When they come to reflect within a few months after their fever has abated and realize that they were hurried beyond necessity and hurried beyond the requirements of the hour, I venture the assertion that many if not most of those who vote for this bill will regret it, because they are men of conscience; and when the last hour comes and the last scene comes for them and they review their careers, they will say, "That is one vote I cast that I would recall if I could."

Our traditional fear of militarism was a major basis of opposition to the proposal. Another objection, which applied also to other issues then under consideration, was the belief that military training was a step toward war:

> More than a year ago—I think it was a year and a half or 2 years ago—I said that I would stand at this desk until the end against war; and I repeat that statement, Mr. President . . . I do not know whether the President wants all the power we are giving him here or not, but I know that we cannot give it to him and convince the American people that we are not ready and resigned and reconciled to the final, inevitable, short step of actually entering the war.

The proposal to draft manpower inevitably suggested the conscription of property. Delays in the execution of defense contracts because of uncertainty about profits added fuel to the flames and brought demands by some members of Congress for the conscription of industry as well as men. With equal vigor others opposed the conscription of factories. For example:

> This is a most extraordinary provision for the confiscation, or at least the appropriation, of property. It modifies every concept of American law we have ever had, as does the draft law. If it were absolutely necessary in time of war, I should be in favor of it; but I do not believe the emergency is one which justifies the drafting of men. I shall refuse to vote for any measure to draft men, and I do not propose to vote for any measure to draft property.

Debate on the issue was by no means restricted to the halls of Congress. Discussion flared throughout the country, but public opinion gradually crystallized in favor of the draft. . . . Opinion became much more favorable after the fall of France, and the upward trend continued during the summer months of 1940. After thorough consideration of every phase of the problem Congress enacted selective service legislation which was approved on September 16; it included provisions permitting obligatory orders upon industry and empowering the Government, if necessary, to seize plants and operate them.

Passage of the Selective Service Act made a huge administrative mechanism necessary for the selection and induction of personnel for military training. Preparatory work by the General Staff of the War Department under way since 1926 included the preliminary training of Reserve officers and National Guard officers for the administration of selective service. As the passage of the bill approached, the President appointed a civilian committee to cooperate with the Joint Army and Navy Selective Service Committee with the consequence that plans which had been developed by the Joint Committee were further revised in the light of the viewpoint of the President's Committee. Once the plans were completed, the rapid creation of machinery for the administration of the legislation was made possible by the collaboration of State and local governments. On October 16, 30 days after the law became effective, more than 16 million men were registered at more than 125,000 registration points in the United States. In the creation of local boards to function in the administration of selective service after the initial listing of registrants, State Governors prepared lists of persons for nomination to the President in whom the power of appointment was vested. In each State a headquarters was established to supervise the work of local boards. Federal-State cooperation and the willingness of thousands of citizens to volunteer their services enabled the rapid erection of a far-flung administrative apparatus which was to function remarkably well in view of the magnitude of its job. . . .

Reorganization of administrative machinery for the guidance of production cleared the way for more vigorous efforts to increase the output of munitions and to speed the construction of factories and shipyards to increase our capacity to produce. On January 3, 1941, the President submitted to Congress the Annual Budget for the fiscal year 1942. Sixty-two percent of the estimated expenditures were to be for defense purposes. Supplemental authorizations and appropriations, however, increased these estimates rapidly. On January 16, the President called to the attention of Congress the necessity for an emergency ship construction program. He requested $350 million for shipbuilding facilities and cargo vessels. A series of additional authorizations and appropriations followed, including the $7 billion fund made available in March for lend-lease purposes. Events abroad made speed more and more urgent. In January the German air force ended British control of the Mediterranean. Early in February the Japanese obtained military concessions in Indo-China. In March Bulgaria joined the Axis. In April Germany invaded Yugoslavia and overwhelmed an heroic but weak resistance.

Although a larger and larger proportion of American resources was diverted to defense production, the acceleration of defense output seemed discouragingly slow. In the press and within the Administration a warm debate was waged over the rate of progress. Industrialists of the Office of Production Management were accused of being insufficiently bold in converting industry to military production and of fearing to enlarge facilities for the production of materials and other components of munitions lest industry be handicapped subsequently by overcapacity. Other groups within the Administration persistently demanded greater speed in the increase of munitions output. Industry was beginning to feel the prosperity flowing from defense spending and was somewhat reluctant to turn to production of war goods. The Administrator of the Office of Price Administration and Civilian Supply demanded heavy cuts in the production of automobiles and other consumer durable goods, and added fuel to the flames of intraadministration debate. The Director-General of the Office of Production Management prodded the War and Navy Departments to raise their sights and to request larger appropriations in order that more adequate production might be initiated. As early as May he also obtained agreement of the automobile industry that a cut of 20 percent would be made in automobile production for the year beginning in August. The Office of Production Management urged the Reconstruction Finance Corporation to expand its program for the construction of synthetic rubber plants and to expedite and enlarge its program for the stockpiling of strategic and critical materials. The President, from time to time, urged greater speed and indicated the direction which the defense production program should take. In May he asked an expansion in the output of critical tools. In July, soon after the German invasion of the U.S.S.R. he sought a prompt and substantial increase in tank output. At the same time, he requested diversion to munitions production of a "substantial part of large durable goods factories in America that are now manufacturing items to meet consumer needs."

In the midst of this discussion, munitions production steadily increased, and the dislocations attendant on diversion of resources to defense purposes began to be felt. Defense production was superimposed upon civilian production, which itself was stimulated by defense expenditures. The slack in the economy was taken up as idle men and industrial capacity were put to work on the defense program. Shortages began to occur as demands for materials increased, and during the first half of 1941 the Office of Production Management put into effect a comparatively mild priorities system. The OPM orders in the first two-thirds of

1941 were designed chiefly to assure that producers of materials gave preference to defense orders.

OPM Order M-1 which became effective March 22, 1941, required that producers of aluminum should give preference to defense orders and specified the sequence in which nondefense orders should be filled. In the following months copper, iron, steel, cork, certain chemicals, nickel, rayon, rubber, silk and other materials were brought under similar control. Exercise of the priority power had the incidental effect of enabling producers of the materials affected to give preference to defense orders without incurring liability for failures to fulfill pre-existing civilian contracts. In addition to requiring that preference be given to defense orders, the OPM in some instances prohibited use of the affected materials for less essential purposes.

Through various orders, the Office of Production Management also developed a ranking of products according to their essentiality. The Army-Navy Munitions Board was empowered by directive to assign specified ratings to military products, while the OPM itself assigned ratings to indirect defense and essential civilian products. Thus, producers of metal-working equipment were entitled to a higher rating than were manufacturers of farm machinery. The priority system developed by the autumn of 1941 was comparatively simple. It did not cover the entire industrial system and its chief effect was to control the sequence in which orders were filled.

Although by the end of the summer no general program for the conversion of entire industries to military production had been effectuated, the diversion of materials to military production through the priorities system made it increasingly difficult for many producers of nonmilitary goods to obtain materials. Small business concerns were affected most seriously. In May the Office of Production Management agreed that the contracting agencies should compel contractors to subcontract parts of their orders so as to utilize existing facilities of industry and to avert "priorities unemployment." In July, following criticism by the Senate Committee Investigating the National Defense Program, the OPM elevated its Defense Contract Service to the status of a Bureau and increased its efforts to bring about the participation of small business in defense production.

Expansion of defense production was accompanied by complex problems in industrial relations. The movement of workers to new industries which were clamoring for additional employees increased the bargaining power of labor and stimulated strikes. Competition of employers for workers placed pressures on wage scales. Long-term measures had to be devised to increase the labor force by training and by bringing additional people into the labor market.

In March the President established the National Defense Mediation Board to settle controversies between employers and employees. The Board consisted of three public members, four representatives of employees, and four representatives of employers. It was instructed to act when the Secretary of Labor certified that a dispute threatening the production or transportation of equipment or materials essential to national defense could not be adjusted by conciliation commissioners of the Department of Labor. In June, the President for the first time used his power to assume control of a plant to prevent disruption of defense production by authorizing the Army to take over the North American aviation plant.

In the summer of 1941, the Office of Production Management inaugurated a program to coordinate and direct the work of Government agencies engaged in training workers for defense employment. New industrial techniques, particularly in the aircraft and shipbuilding industries, required that literally hundreds of thousands of workers should be trained in new skills. Both to make additional workers available and to quell unrest, efforts were inaugurated to prevent discrimination against minority groups by employers in defense industries. "No nation combating the increasing threat of totalitarianism," the President said, "can afford arbitrarily to exclude large segments of its population from its defense industries." This admonition was reenforced in June by creation of the Committee on Fair Employment Practice which was to investigate and redress grievances growing out of departures from the policy against discrimination in employment on grounds of race, creed, color, or national origin. To increase the working force further the Office of Production Management in August urged the employment of more women in industry.

Increasing demands for defense goods created greater demand for raw materials. The prospect of further increases in requirements encouraged speculative operations. The defense boom stimulated increases in wages which, in turn, tended to raise prices. The Office of Price Administration and Civilian Supply cajoled, persuaded, and threatened in an effort to maintain a stable price level, but it was fighting a losing battle and, indeed was not equipped to do much more. In the months since its establishment, however, it had been preparing for more effective price control measures and conducting negotiations within the government to achieve consensus on the general outlines of an economic stabilization policy. On July 30 the President requested Congress to act. He recalled the consequences of failure to control prices in the first World War, traced the alarming increases in prices during 1941, and suggested lines of action. Legislation was needed to control prices, rents, and installment credit. For the maintenance of over-all economic stability, he declared that relatively stable wages also would be necessary and indicated the need for an adequate tax program as part of a general attack on inflation. . . .

The attack on Pearl Harbor both vindicated and condemned the policy of the United States. The predictions that the United States was in danger of attack were fulfilled, but neither foresight nor intelligence had been adequate to foresee with certainty the exact time and place of attack. The voices which had demanded preparation were justified by the turn of events. but we had not been able to mobilize industrial or military strength sufficient to permit quick assumption of the offensive.

The entire policy of the Government had been conditioned by the necessity of maintaining the delicate domestic balance between those who unalterably opposed preparatory measures and those who enthusiastically advocated virtual declaration of war. No substantial body of opinion had been entirely satisfied with the policy of the Government. Those who condemned measures to appease Japan were countered by those in and out of the Government who wanted to play for time. Those who demanded more assistance to Britain were opposed by those who still twisted the lion's tail. Those who urged more rapid mobilization were met with the argument that mobilization inevitably meant war rather than defense. All these shades of opinion were reflected in the Congress and they could not be ignored. Yet the singleness of purpose of the Administration and of like-minded members of both parties in Congress provided sufficient political consensus to permit substantial preparation for what did happen.

Defense measures prosecuted from the middle of 1940 to Pearl Harbor produced a degree of preparedness which was high in comparison with the country's condition upon its entry into World War I. All types of armament actually were coming from the factories in December 1941; in World War I, we depended on our Allies for many types of finished munitions even to the end of hostilities. Expenditures for war in 1941 totaled \$6.7 billions. . . . In December 1941 such expenditures had reached a monthly rate of almost \$2 billions, reflecting the rapid acceleration of the defense program. Munitions production in that month had reached a rate of a billion dollars a year. . . . From January, 1941 to December, 1941 munitions production increased by approximately 225 percent. In November, 1941 2,200 planes and 5,500 plane engines were delivered. Thus plane production was at an annual rate of almost 25,000. Current production, however, was an incomplete measure of accomplishment, for construction was under way on plants and facilities which soon would be ready to add to the flow of war goods. The groundwork had been laid for the rapid rate of increase of output which was to occur in the following year.

We had also a substantial military force inducted and in training. At the end of 1941, the total strength of the Army and Navy exceeded 2 million. . . . An immense program to construct camps and other training facilities was under way. Facilities for training of additional forces were either ready or under construction.

In the matter of the conversion of the Government to the necessities of war, great progress had been made. Although the Government had been criticized consistently for the nature and slowness of its administrative actions, the fact remained that the agencies destined to become the major war agencies had been built up. These organizations could not spring up overnight. Men had to be persuaded to come to Washington and working organizations had to be developed. These men had to acquire or develop a perspective bigger than their company or industry before they could be fully effective. The steps by which we reached the administrative status existing at the time of Pearl Harbor coincided roughly with expansions in the defense program which, in turn, placed different kinds of demands on the Government's administrative system. Further, the evolution of administrative structure had been tangled with the problem of political leadership and with the Presidential problem of maintaining a balance among different elements and different departments within the Administration. The broad issue of public versus military control of the Government repeatedly arose. Although many administrative changes were to be made subsequently, by December 7 a working organization had been established which was staffed by persons who had learned a great deal about how to operate and what needed to be done. This organization could be modified readily as emerging conditions required.

The Nation had the benefit of a year or 18 months of preparatory measures. The advantages of this readiness, imperfect though it was, can perhaps be measured if one speculates on the consequences that might have followed had we been unable to land in Guadalcanal and in North Africa until late in 1943 instead of in 1942 or had we been unable to mount a force adequate to invade Western Europe until the summer of 1945 instead of 1944.

# Did FDR Want War in 1941?

BY RAYMOND G. O'CONNOR

FRANKLIN DELANO ROOSEVELT has furnished posterity with a battery of questions that offer a major challenge to the historian, and controversial though his domestic program may be, both his critics and his apologists are often inclined to judge him on the basis of his foreign policy. In 1941 a confused and divided nation wondered whether peace or war would best serve American interests, and the people sought an answer from the leader who nine years earlier had promised redemption from economic chaos. The sudden attack on Pearl Harbor, which terminated the most intricate and epochal diplomatic negotiations since independence, put an end to speculation and uncertainty. But the solution uppermost in the mind of the President remained a mystery.

Roosevelt was not neutral from the moment that Hitler invaded Poland. Yet it was only with the sudden and unexpected collapse of France that he became fully aware of the real and immediate danger of the Nazi menace. The pressure of events in Europe accelerated his efforts to educate and awaken American public opinion to the threat of Hitlerism and secure support for a policy calculated to insure the defeat of Germany. At the same time the President took steps which led the United States from a professed neutrality to nonbelligerency, cobelligerency, and finally a formal declaration of war. While he maintained that his actions, however far removed from neutrality, were designed to keep the country out of war, the United States exchanged destroyers for bases, patrolled the Atlantic sea lanes, enacted Lend-Lease, tracked German submarines, escorted vessels, occupied British and neutral territory, formulated joint war plans, and coordinated foreign policy with the enemies of aggression. Must we take the President at his word? Must we assume that he meant what he said when he insisted again and again that every move was planned to avoid hostilities? I think not.

In the first place, Roosevelt believed that Nazism was a direct threat to the security of the United States, as well as to that of the rest of the world, and therefore the European conflict could not be considered a "foreign war." Secondly, he was convinced that Britain, and later Russia, could not defeat Germany without American military assistance, and both FDR and Hitler knew that any delay in all-out participation against Germany was to the advantage of the Axis powers. Thirdly, he was confident that an allied victory in Europe would put an end to Japan's aggressive policy in the Far East. And finally, the President felt that the United States must have an equal voice in the formulation and preservation of the peace that followed, which would be possible only in the event that the nation became a full partner in the war effort.

Franklin Roosevelt was never a simple person, and he defied understanding by his friends, his

Based on a paper read at the Pacific Coast Branch meeting of the American Historical Association, December 1958.

associates, and even his family. Yet some conclusions about him are possible and they help clarify his position in 1941. FDR loved a challenge. For him, obstacles, whether polio or politics, were created for the purpose of being overcome, and he was exhilarated by the prospect. Also, he usually knew where he wanted to go but he was not too particular about how he got there. Roosevelt could be, as James M. Burns asserts, both a lion and a fox, varying his means and his tactics in order to attain his objective. Furthermore, he was enough of a realist to settle for less than the ideal and adjust his sights to the possible. These qualities were constantly displayed as the President countered the problems that emerged during the troubled year of 1941.

Roosevelt's peacetime strategy demanded a balance of power both in Europe and in the Far East in order that no single nation or group of nations would be free to threaten the safety of the Americas. He did not regard Japan as a buffer to protect the United States from a hostile China or an aggressive Russia, nor, apparently, did he share Admiral Harold R. Stark's belief that an equilibrium in the Far East was possible only if Japan had a foothold on the continent. The President's opinion was probably influenced by the existence of the Japanese Fleet, which posed the only immediate military threat to the United States in the Pacific.

By 1939 Roosevelt realized that the Atlantic Ocean was no adequate barrier against attack. Meeting with the Senate Military Affairs Committee in January of that year, he warned that America's first line of defense was those buffer states which stood between Hitler and the Atlantic. The French army and the British navy preserved the balance of power in Europe and permitted the United States the luxury of a one-ocean fleet. With the crushing defeat of France in the spring of 1940 the land barrier that protected the Western Hemisphere was eliminated, and the American military buildup shifted from the Pacific to the Atlantic as FDR redoubled his efforts to support America's last line of defense in Europe.

The President pounded home his theme with persistence and skill. At press conferences and in meetings with congressional committees he asked if the United States should defend the Philippines or Alaska, and received a ready affirmative because they were American possessions. He then extended his questions to embrace Canada and Mexico and the countries of South America as he pointedly illustrated the danger of isolationism, and, by clear implication, America's vital interest in the European conflict. In his message to Congress on January 6, 1941, FDR declared: "At no previous time has American security been as seriously threatened from without as it is today," and in May he warned that "the war is approaching the brink of the Western Hemisphere itself. It is coming very close to home," for "the attack on the United States can begin with the domination of any base which menaces our security—north or south." At this time he agreed to occupy the Azores in the event of an attempted German invasion, and he considered a declaration placing West Africa within the compass of the Monroe Doctrine. By September the President was sufficiently sure of his domestic audience to announce that "The Nazi danger to our Western World has long ceased to be a mere possibility. The danger is here now—not only from a military enemy but from an enemy of all law, all liberty, all morality, all religion." Thus FDR finally admitted publicly what he had denied saying or believing a year and a half before—that America's first line of defense was on the Rhine; and now the initial bulwark had been destroyed.

Roosevelt's strategy was clear. All of the hostilities were part of a world conflagration but Hitler was the head and Germany the heart of this force of evil which threatened free institutions and the safety of America itself. Japanese aggression, while jeopardizing allied interests in the Far East, was contingent on Axis success in Europe, which tied the hands of those nations dedicated to the maintenance of the status quo in Asia.

The President responded to the German challenge with all of his resourcefulness and ingenuity. The Lend-Lease Act expressly denied authority for the use of convoys to deliver goods to Britain or the sending of American ships into designated combat areas. FDR merely substituted "patrol" for "convoy" and authorized his cabinet officers to plead publicly for the employment of naval escorts. On April 10, 1941, he circumvented Congress by removing the Red Sea area from those combat zones denied to American vessels by a previous presidential proclamation. In the same month he told a press conference that the naval patrol would extend "as far on the waters of the seven seas as may be necessary for the defense of the American hemisphere." The attack on Russia, although adding a valuable ally to the Nazi resistance, weakened Roosevelt's contention that the conflict was being waged to preserve freedom and probably caused the President to move more slowly in the face of an intensified domestic opposition. But by September he was ready to announce that American warships and planes would protect friendly vessels "in our defensive waters," which included, according to Cordell Hull, "the shipping lanes across the North Atlantic, as well as the waters to the South." In order to bolster Britain's shaky defenses in the Far East, Roosevelt provided navy ships and crews to transport British soldiers to Singapore, and in November he was able to secure the repeal of those sections of the Neutrality Act which prevented the arming of merchant vessels and sending them to belligerent ports. Basil Rauch contends that by this act Congress authorized the President to wage a naval war and did "absolve him of his implied promise to commit no 'act of war' under Lend-Lease." Actually, however, Roosevelt admitted that hostilities already existed in the Atlantic, so this new law was no more than an *ex post facto* authorization at best.

Following the October torpedoing of the destroyer *Kearny*, the President proclaimed that "America has been attacked," and, he added, "We are pledged to pull our own oar in the destruction of Hitlerism." Early in November he declared that "The American people have made an unlimited commitment that there shall be a free world," and "Upon our American production falls the colossal task of equipping our own armed forces, and helping to supply the British, the Russians, and the Chinese. In the performance of that task we dare not fail." Yet at this very time Britain was stripping herself of badly needed armaments to supply Russia, and the previous month she had offered to provide the weapon-starved American army with artillery for target practice. Only two four-engine bombers came from American factories in July, and just over 200 were scheduled for the remaining five months of the year. During 1940 China received $9,000,000 worth of military equipment, and the $7,000,000,000 appropriated for Lend-Lease seemed pitifully inadequate when compared with the estimated need for $150,000,000,000 in supplies by 1943 to support the war effort of the European allies. Nor was the problem merely a matter of funds. Production simply could not even begin to meet requirements until the nation's economy was placed on a war basis. Business was unwilling to convert factories from the manufacture of consumer goods and labor refused to curtail its organizational activities. The spirit of urgency and sacrifice was lacking and only a great national crisis could supply it. In the meantime the self-styled "arsenal of democracy" was not supporting its end of the struggle against the Axis, and the desperate appeals of Britain, Russia and China warned that aid might be too little and too late.

Roosevelt's ultimate objective in desiring a successful conclusion of the European war is revealed by his words and actions in 1941. He announced to Congress on January 6 that "In the future days, which we seek to make secure, we look forward to a world founded upon four essential freedoms," the fourth being, in his words, "freedom from fear which, translated into world terms, means a world-wide reduction of armaments to such a point and in such a thorough fashion that no nation will be in a position to commit an act of physical aggression against any neighbor—anywhere in the world." At a press conference on April 25, he declared himself "agin" dictatorships and said "We will fight for the Democratic process." The following month, in a letter to Harold Vanderbilt, FDR wrote: "It seems so clear that the ultimate choice is between right and wrong that smug inaction on our part is in effect an aid to wrong. Even if our continental limits remain intact I, personally, should hate to live the rest of my days in a world dominated by the Hitler philosophy." During August he joined the British Prime Minister in a statement which called for, after "the final destruction of the Nazi tyranny," the establishment of "a peace which will afford to all nations the means of dwelling in safety within their own boundaries." And in a radio address two days after the attack on Pearl Harbor, he announced: "We are now in the midst of a war, not for conquest, not for vengeance, but for a world in which this Nation, and all that this Nation represents, will be safe for our children. . . . We are going to win the war, and we are going to win the peace that follows." America's entry was an essential step in the attainment of this goal.

In the fall of 1941, as the clouds in Europe darkened, events in the Pacific moved toward a climax. Contrary to the opinion shared by the British and some of his advisers, Roosevelt believed that if Japan were pushed too hard she would fight. He wanted to be firm enough to prevent any action that would threaten Great Britain or Russia and interfere with their struggle against Hitler, but he was reluctant to deprive Japan of an alternative to war.

This, then, was Roosevelt's dilemma. On the one hand he was anxious to avoid a conflict in the Pacific because it would impede the war effort in Europe. On the other hand he had to keep enough pressure on Japan to prevent the collapse of China, the severance of the British Empire lifeline, or an attack on Russia. The President was plagued by the knowledge that the American contribution to the war was falling far short, but a forthright stand in Asia was the equivalent of many divisions and much material.

Following months of tortuous negotiations, a crucial set of proposals was received from Tokyo on November 20. Although Hull considered the offer an ultimatum, the American statesmen began formulating a reply which would delay the clash that many of them believed inevitable. To add to the tension, a Japanese message intercepted on November 22 revealed that if a satisfactory reply to the earlier dispatch was not received by November 29, "things are automatically going to happen." The Secretary of State and the President were agreed that efforts should be made to prevent a break in negotiations, and with this in mind a *modus vivendi* was prepared which offered Japan some raw materials in exchange for certain concessions and guarantees.

In clearing this proposal with the friendly nations Hull received vehement protests from the Chinese and British envoys. He attempted to mollify the former by observing that there was only one chance in three that the Japanese would accept the terms, and to the latter he "pointed out the utter impracticability of requesting a suspension of further (Japanese) military advances in China." That same evening, November 25, a strong telegram arrived from Churchill reaffirming Chiang Kai Shek's objections to the proposed note and stressing the common danger of a collapse of China, which, the Prime Minister asserted, could be hastened by the terms of the *modus vivendi*. After a hasty discussion with his advisers, Hull, on the following morning, recommended to the President that the *modus vivendi* be dropped and a ten point note be substituted containing the basis for a permanent settlement of the Far Eastern crisis. Roosevelt agreed, and on November 26 the Japanese envoys were handed the note which, in Churchill's words, "not only met our wishes and those of the associated Governments, but indeed went beyond anything for which we had ventured to ask."

The controversy surrounding the *modus vivendi* illustrates the two schools of thought concerning the best method of stopping Japan. The British Prime Minister and some of Hull's advisers maintained that a firm and positive warning would be most effective. The President did not share this belief, and he refused to take such a step until November 26. Because of the intercept of November 22, both Hull and Roosevelt knew that the only possibility for continued negotiations lay in the provisions of the *modus vivendi*. By its rejection they knowingly, albeit reluctantly, made the decision for war. Moreover, the moral aspect of the situation was apparently a minor factor in their deliberations. Primarily, they were intent on keeping China in the war because of her restraining effect on the Japanese, whose troops could otherwise be freed for action against the British or the Russians and thereby weaken resistance to Hitler. "We wanted peace," Hull later protested. "We wanted nothing to interrupt the flow of our aid to Britain, Russia, and other allies resisting Hitlerism," and the note of November 26 was designed to promote this resistance. It was a calculated risk and a matter of some controversy as to whether the European war effort would best be furthered by the *modus vivendi* or the ten point note.

A further clue to Roosevelt's intentions is found in his extreme sensitivity to public opinion. Even in his press conferences he was frank in admitting that he could not state publicly certain harsh aspects of the world situation because the people were not ready to accept them. FDR well knew that any public repudiation of his convictions or his policies could jeopardize his entire program of American assistance to Hitler's enemies. When the President warned the Senate Military Affairs Committee in January 1939 of the potential threats to America's safety, he prefaced his remarks with the statement that "it may come as a shock and it should not be talked about out loud because the country would not understand it in those terms." A few days later he branded as a "deliberate lie" the allegation that he had claimed America's first line of defense was on the Rhine, and he denied sharing such an opinion. In April, 1940, he admitted to having been evasive in answering a question as to whether Greenland was included in the Monroe Doctrine because of his fear that the American people would not support such an interpretation. The following month FDR told members of the press that "We have to look ahead to certain possibilities. If I had said this out loud in a fireside talk, again people would have said that I was perfectly crazy," and he followed these prefatory remarks with a warning of the danger of a Nazi victory to the United States.

Both Secretary of War Henry L. Stimson and Secretary of the Navy Frank Knox were openly hostile toward Hitler and outspoken in their pleas for aid to Britain. In their official position as civilian heads of the departments charged with defense, they advocated warlike actions in speeches read and approved beforehand by the President. Obviously they were expressing the opinions of their chief, whose position was much more vulnerable and more open to criticism. These officials and many others in the administration, including the military leaders, were convinced that Hitler could be destroyed only by America's all-out participation in the war. The necessary weapons could not be produced by a peacetime economy, they could not be delivered by the British navy, and the Axis military might could not be defeated by the armed forces of England and Russia alone. Furthermore, time was running out. The Allies needed help immediately to forestall the German successes and prevent a disillusionment that would lead to a negotiated peace. Such a contingency was quite possible in the case of ravaged Russia, and conceivable in the case of battered and war-weary Britain. China had already reached the stage of exhaustion and the Soviets were no longer in a position to provide her with equipment or moral support.

Perhaps Admiral Stark best summed up the attitude of many of FDR's advisers in a memorandum to the President in October, 1941. "I have assumed for the past two years," he wrote, "that our country would not let Great Britain fall; that ultimately in order to prevent this we would have to enter the war and . . . I have long felt and often stated that the sooner we get in the better." According to Robert Sherwood, this memorandum was "highly refreshing to the President," presumably because he agreed with it. Writing of a conference held on the afternoon of the Pearl Harbor attack between the President, Secretary Stimson, Secretary Hull, Secretary Knox, Admiral Stark, and General Marshall, Harry Hopkins observed that "all of us believed that in the last analysis the enemy was Hitler and that he could never be defeated without force of arms; that sooner or later we were bound to be in the war and that Japan had given us the opportunity."

Roosevelt was avowedly dedicated to the destruction of Nazism. At one time he may have believed that this could be accomplished without American intervention, but after the fall of France he realized that Britain alone could not do the job, and his words and his acts soon belied any pretense of neutrality. He moved as fast and as far as he could to help the British within the limits of law and public opinion. He freely interpreted the phrase "aid short of war" to mean "short of declared war," and he stretched his constitutional prerogative as Commander in Chief of the Army and Navy to permit him to wage war without Congressional approval. Yet this was not enough. The American effort was far short of the mark, and, as Sherwood observes, FDR had exhausted his bag of tricks. He could not get the authority to implement his program, or the war spirit to provide the necessary sacrifices. Only the mobilization of America's industrial might and military manpower could do what FDR considered essential for the safety of the Western Hemisphere and the free world.

Other questions occur to the student of this period. Why did Roosevelt refuse to ask Congress for a declaration of war? What made him so sure that he was right? To what extent was he influenced by the experience of his former chief, Woodrow Wilson? No doubt he was haunted by his repeated assertions that he was not going to send American boys to fight in foreign wars, and many people placed the struggle against Hitler in this category in spite of the potential threat to the Americas. Then, too, he feared that debate over the issue would drag out for weeks or months and divide the nation, regardless of the outcome. FDR wanted the support of a united people who could not accuse him of having led the country into war. His profound dedication to the overthrow of Hitlerism was probably associated with his belief in himself as a "man of destiny," placed in the position to exercise a decisive influence at a crucial period in world history. In the fulfillment of this mission he was determined to avoid the mistakes of Wilson, both as a national leader and as the architect of a new world order. Yet the joint objectives of Axis defeat and postwar collective security seemed impossible of realization unless the United States joined in the conflict. Roosevelt's influence on the war or the peace that followed could not be fully exerted unless America's sacrifices and contributions to victory were commensurate with those of other nations.

A president is able to circumvent the constitutional requirement that only Congress can declare war by so conducting foreign affairs that war is unavoidable. No doubt FDR could have pursued a policy that would have postponed hostilities for an indefinite period, but he chose not to do so because the stakes were too high and he believed it would be an unwarranted gamble with national security. If asked whether any responsible statesman ever wants war, Roosevelt, it seems clear, would have answered: "Yes, if he believes that an imperative objective cannot be achieved in any other way." In 1941 there was no alternative consistent with his obligations and his purpose.

# 17.
# The Second World War

Someone once observed that the only thing worse than fighting with allies is fighting without them. Staff conversations between the United States and Great Britain before the attack on Pearl Harbor had led to agreement that Germany was the primary enemy and that operations in Europe would take priority over those in the Far East. This strategy was followed after December 1941, but Russia, reeling under the German attack, complained bitterly about the lack of a second front in Europe. Roosevelt and Churchill also differed about the strategy to be pursued against Germany, and the issue disturbed relations between the military leaders. The compulsions of a common danger and common military objectives, plus the adroit negotiations of the heads of state, produced the compromises that eventually led to victory.

The selections which follow are intended to reveal the problems and complexities of coalition warfare, the extent of military effort in the great theaters of war in Europe and the Pacific, and the considerations that led to the decision to employ the atomic bomb against Japan. The American contribution to victory is, of course, emphasized in these readings. The literature on this subject is enormous and much of it would lead to the conclusion, as one writer has put it, that nothing that anyone did at any time was right. Supporters and detractors exist for every nation, every leader, and every service. But one hopes that agreement may be reached on certain lessons implicit in this greatest of all wars.

# Problems of Coalition Warfare

## BY MAURICE MATLOFF AND EDWIN M. SNELL

THE MILITARY CONVERSATIONS that began in Washington during the last week in December 1941, which accompanied the first wartime meetings of the President with the Prime Minister (the Arcadia Conference), gave the American military staffs the chance at once to reassure and to warn the British staff concerning the military effects of American reaction to the Japanese attack. On December 14 the Prime Minister and his party, which included the British Chiefs of Staff, had set out on H.M.S. *Duke of York*. The War Department's preparations began on December 18, on the receipt of a short message suggesting the agenda for the meetings, sent ahead by the British Chiefs of Staff. The British message listed five principal topics for the conference:

(i) Fundamental basis of joint strategy.

(ii) Interpretation of (i) into terms of immediate Military measures, including redistribution of forces.

(iii) Allocation of joint forces to harmonise with (i).

(iv) Long term programme based on (i), including forces to be raised and equipped required for victory.

(v) Set up joint machinery for implementing (ii), (iii) and (iv).

Several of the War Department planners, working together, hurriedly prepared "notes" on the British message.

Although the Army planners had something to say in their notes about each of the five points raised by the British Chiefs of Staff, the discussions among staff officers that followed and the discussions of the military leaders with the President amounted only to a reserved exchange of views on military dispositions in the near future. The President and the military leaders were extremely cautious and went into the conference without trying to define the American position. The preparations served chiefly to remind the President that the military staffs believed the United States and Great Britain would have all they could do to stop the Japanese and to remind the military staff that the President was anxious to undertake in the Atlantic as strong a demonstration as possible of British and American unity of purpose. The possible movements involving U.S. Army forces fell under five main headings: (1) establishment of an air force based in Australia; (2) strengthening of other positions in the Pacific, especially in Hawaii; (3) reinforcement of British troops in the Middle East; (4) "acquisition" of positions in the South Atlantic—in northeastern Brazil, the Cape Verde Islands, or on the western or northwestern coast of Africa; and (5) relief of British garrisons in Northern Ireland and Iceland (and of the U.S. Marine provisional brigade on duty in Iceland). The Army was most certain of the immediate need

---

From Maurice Matloff and Edwin M. Snell, *Strategic Planning for Coalition Warfare, 1941–1942* (Washington, 1953), 97–102, 113–115, 165–169, 266–278. Copyright 1953 by Orlando Ward. Used by permission of the Chief of Military History, Department of the Army.

to undertake movements under the first heading, and the President was most precise about the immediate need for movements under the last heading.

The exchange of views indicated that the President and Chiefs of Staff were alike uncertain how to proceed with the discussion of strategy until they had had a chance to talk with their British opposites. As the conference was to show, much more clearly than had yet been shown—or could have been shown—the President and the Prime Minister as political leaders in some ways had more in common with each other than either had with his Chiefs of Staff. Likewise, the Chiefs of Staff—particularly those of the same service—might agree with one another more readily on what could be done than they could agree with the heads of their respective governments.

Churchill and his Chiefs of Staff arrived in Washington on December 22; the Prime Minister and the President talked over the situation that evening. On December 23 they began military discussions with the Chiefs of Staff. They held another such meeting on December 26 and, after the Prime Minister's return from Ottawa, two other meetings (January 1 and 4). The Prime Minister then went to Florida for several days to rest. After his return he and the President held two more meetings with the Chiefs of Staff, on January 12 and 14. Mr. Hopkins, Lord Beaverbrook, and (usually) the Secretary of War and the Secretary of the Navy attended along with the Chiefs of Staff and the senior planners. At these plenary sessions at the White House the President and the Prime Minister reached or confirmed their military decisions, after a review of the conclusions of the Chiefs of Staff.

The Army planners apparently expected that, after the preliminary British-American meetings, the scope of military conversations would be extended to include the representatives of Australia, China, and the Soviet Union. But the military conversations at Arcadia—unlike the political conversations, which led to the drafting and signing of the Declaration of the United Nations—involved only the British and American staffs.

The British and American Chiefs of Staff met together twelve times during the conference in an effort to reach agreement on the outstanding military problems so far as possible before presenting them to the President and the Prime Minister. General Marshall and General Arnold represented the Army at these meetings, which were held in the Federal Reserve Building, and the senior Army planner, General Gerow, or his deputy, General Eisenhower, also attended. To help formulate the problems for their meetings, the Chiefs of Staff relied on a committee of British and American planners, who met ten times during the conference and who in turn divided up their work among subcommittees. The War Plans Division, the Air War Plans Division, and (for shipping questions) the G-4 Division furnished the Army members of these subcommittees.

## Grand Strategy

At the opening of the conference it was evident that the British delegation could take for granted American agreement on strategy up to the point to which the British-American staff conversations had gone earlier in the year. It remained the American view, notwithstanding the dangerous situation in the Pacific, that the basis of strategy must be collaboration among the powers at war with Germany, with the primary object of defeating Germany. The powers at war with Germany must increase their production of munitions and raise forces equal to the object and, while doing so, defend themselves at home, hold their strategic outposts as best they could, and weaken German resistance to the extent necessary to prepare for the final assault. The fullest statement of the American view, prepared in the War Department, was an affirmation of American agreement on these propositions, carefully worded so as to introduce no new element.

The British retained their by then familiar view of strategy, looking ultimately to the establishment at various points in Europe of armored forces which, with the help of patriot forces rallying to the cause, would liberate occupied

Europe and defeat Germany. Their theory of these operations, already stated by the British Chiefs in August 1941, the Prime Minister restated at some length for the President, in a document drawn up during the voyage from England. His aim was to make full use of the advantages that the United States and Great Britain could expect to have—command of sea and air, and the aid of the people of occupied Europe. He envisaged landings, perhaps as early as the summer of 1943, "in several of the following countries, namely, Norway, Denmark, Holland, Belgium, the French Channel coasts and the French Atlantic coasts, as well as in Italy and possibly the Balkans." He explained:

> In principle, the landings should be made by armoured and mechanised forces capable of disembarking not at ports but on beaches, either by landing-craft or from ocean-going ships specially adapted. The potential front of attack is thus made so wide that the German forces holding down these different countries cannot be strong enough at all points. An amphibious outfit must be prepared to enable these large-scale disembarkations to be made swiftly and surely. The vanguards of the various British and American expeditions should be marshalled by the spring of 1943 in Iceland, the British Isles, and, if possible, in French Morocco and Egypt. The main body would come direct across the ocean.
>
> It need not be assumed that great numbers of men are required. If the incursion of the armoured formations is successful, the uprising of the local population, for whom weapons must be brought, will supply the corpus of the liberating offensive. Forty armoured divisions, at fifteen thousand men apiece, or their equivalent in tank brigades, of which Great Britain would try to produce nearly half, would amount to six hundred thousand men. Behind this armour another million men of all arms would suffice to wrest enormous territories from Hitler's domination. But these campaigns, once started, will require nourishing on a lavish scale. Our industries and training establishments should by the end of 1942 be running on a sufficient scale.

According to the Prime Minister, the British Chiefs remained in accord with this theory of operations on the Continent and ready to urge the idea of "the mass invasion of the continent of Europe as the goal for 1943," in three phases; first, "Closing the ring"; second, "Liberating the populations"; and third, "Final assault on the German citadel." But the version of British grand strategy that they presented for consideration to the American Chiefs—unlike the version they had presented in August—was not at all explicit on the manner of invading the Continent, although quite explicit about British aims in the Mediterranean. This version, presented by the British Chiefs of Staff on their arrival in Washington, began with a statement of agreed principles, leading to the agreed conclusion "that only the minimum of force necessary for the safeguarding of vital interests in other theaters should be diverted from operations against Germany." The British Chiefs then went on to develop certain corollaries. First they listed the essential features of grand strategy:

> The realisation of the victory programme of armaments, which first and foremost required the security of the main areas of war industry.
>
> The maintenance of essential communications.
>
> Closing and tightening the ring around Germany.
>
> Wearing down and undermining German resistance by air bombardment, blockade, subversive activities, and propaganda.
>
> Maintaining only such positions in the Eastern theatre as will safeguard vital interests while we are concentrating on the defeat of Germany.

In elaborating on these statements the British Chiefs developed their theory of operations against Germany. The first stage was that of "Closing and tightening the ring around Germany," which they defined as "a line running roughly as follows: Archangel–Black Sea–Anatolia–the Northern Seaboard of the Mediterranean–the Western Seaboard of Europe." They explained:

"The main object will be to strengthen this ring, and close the gaps in it, by sustaining the Russian front, by arming and supporting Turkey, by increasing our strength in the Middle East, and by gaining possession of the whole North African coast." They looked forward to limited offensives on the Continent as the next stage, conceivably in 1942 but more probably in 1943, "either across the Mediterranean or from Turkey into the Balkans, or by simultaneous landings in several of the occupied countries of North-Western Europe." They proposed that the allocation of troops and materiel should provide for carrying out such operations as a "prelude" to the assault on Germany, the direction and scale of which would evidently depend on the development of these limited offensives.

It was a foregone conclusion that the British representatives would reintroduce the concept of passing from the defensive to the offensive in the Mediterranean. As late as October, the War Department had had a reminder of the British adherence to this approach from Colonel Bundy, who had talked over future plans with British officers while he was en route to Moscow with the Harriman mission. As he reported they looked forward to using North Africa "as a stepping stone to cutting Italy out, and finally closing in on the continent." As previously instructed by General Marshall, Colonel Bundy had been entirely noncommittal as to the War Department view.

The American planners had remained noncommittal. They did not go so far as to propose that the United States should either accept or reject the British concept of the transition from the defensive to the offensive against Germany. Before December 7 the nearest they had come to stating a principle to govern decisions during the transitional period was to emphasize the need for economy of effort in "subsidiary" theaters. They classified as subsidiary theaters not only the Far East but also Africa, the Middle East, the Iberian Peninsula, and the Scandinavian Peninsula, in accordance with their premise that the plains of northwest Europe constituted the main theater, where "we must come to grips with the enemy ground forces." At the time of the Arcadia Conference the Army planning staff again stated the idea of a great final offensive "with the main effort in Western Europe," which should be "made in conjunction with the strongest possible Russian offensive on the Eastern Front and secondary offensives wherever feasible." The staff was convinced that this must be the final step, seeing "no other area in which it would be feasible from a logistics viewpoint to transport and maintain forces required for an operation of such magnitude." The Army planners were disposed to consider all other operations as strictly holding operations and to regard with disfavor any proposal to establish and maintain in a "subsidiary" theater the favorable ratio of Allied to enemy forces that would be necessary in order to take the offensive there.

It appeared to the Army staff that the United States and Great Britain would in any event be compelled to act in accord with this view of strategy for several months to come. Thus from the American point of view there was no reason for dwelling on the principle for the time being. The staff reached the following conclusions about American and British capabilities:

> It appears that the best which Great Britain can do at the present time is to maintain its position in the British Isles and the Middle East and to attempt to send reinforcements to the Far East. Any British operation, other than those stated, must necessarily be of an opportunist nature, executed with exceedingly small forces and with very doubtful chances of success. . . .
>
> At the present time the United States can only inadequately defend its coasts against air raids, hold Hawaii, the Panama Canal and other existing bases, gradually complete the relief of the British in Iceland, reinforce the Philippines or Dutch East Indies, occupy Natal, and possibly occupy some other base not seriously defended by Axis forces or sympathizers (Cape Verdes or Azores). It will be practicable and may be necessary to send some armored or infantry divisions to the British Isles in the winter or spring. . . . The shortage of United States flag shipping, there being only enough to carry about 60,000 men simultaneously, precludes the possibility of executing more than one, or at most two, of these operations concurrently.

The British Chiefs of Staff, on the other hand, had a specific reason for proposing at once that the American Chiefs of Staff should concur in the British view of the conduct of operations against Germany and specifically that they should accept the conception of "Closing and tightening the ring around Germany." The Prime Minister was hoping for a chance to move soon into French North Africa and wanted American help. He was expecting a favorable American response if the war with Japan did not force the project into the background. He made his proposal at the opening meeting of the conference on December 23 at which he and the President told the Chiefs of Staff what they wanted done. He explained that there were 55,000 British troops and the necessary ships ready to move into Algeria in case Empire forces should gain a decisive enough advantage in the shifting war in the Libyan Desert to push westward to the Tunisian frontier. He therefore "offered for consideration the proposition that at the same time United States forces, assuming French agreement, should proceed to land on the Moroccan coast by invitation. . . ."

The Arcadia study of the North African operation ended inconclusively. On January 10, as a basis for future planning, the British planners reintroduced the estimate for the first three months' force on which the committee had originally agreed to compromise. Except for the first American and the first and second British convoys, they presented even these estimates as "guesses" of what the task force commander might consider necessary, and the guesses included no estimate of air strength. The British did not propose what, for planning purposes, should be taken to be the total strength required for the operation. Their purpose was in fact only to present "a suggested convoy programme" that would fully utilize the limited port capacity of Casablanca. This schedule indicated that the maximum forces that could be landed (including two convoys to Algiers) during the four months following the first sailings would be some 180,000 troops (about half British and half American).

At this point in the conference, planning for troop movements in the Atlantic finally converged with planning for troop movements in the Pacific. It then appeared that—quite apart from the availability of troop shipping and the capacity of the port of Casablanca—the proposed shipping schedule was far too ambitious for any North African operation begun before the latter part of May, 1942. The factor that actually limited American participation in any North African operation begun before that time would be the shortage of cargo vessels in the Atlantic that would result from the desperate effort to contain the Japanese in the South and Southwest Pacific.

During the conference the American planners had been getting impatient with the protracted study of movements in the Atlantic because it was holding up decision on movements to the Pacific. They expected the Japanese might "overextend" themselves until they had isolated the projected American base in northern Australia. By the end of the first week of the conference, the British staff, like the American staff, began to show concern over the danger to the northern and eastern approaches to Australia and New Zealand. The British, quite apart from their dismay at the Japanese advances in Malaya and Burma, were obliged to consider the security of Australia and New Zealand, if they were to keep forces from these dominions in North Africa and in India, as they very much wanted and needed to do. The British planners accordingly began to consider sympathetically the American planners' views. They brought up for discussion the whole question of the defense of the air ferry route from Hawaii to Australia, together with the Navy's project for establishing a refueling station at Borabora (some 2,300 miles south of Hawaii in the Society Islands which, like New Caledonia, were in the hands of the Free French). The American planners agreed that, besides arranging for local defense of Palmyra, Christmas, Canton, Samoa, and Borabora, the United States should consider helping Australia and New Zealand with the defense of New Caledonia and the Fiji Islands, if the Australian and New Zealand Governments could not make adequate provision for it. . . .

On July 8 the War Department operations staff estimated that a decision "on any emergency operations in the European Theater in 1942" could not be long postponed and that it must come "not later than 1 August." On the same day the British War Cabinet made a move toward a decision, a move that resulted almost automatically from its action four weeks before (June 11), when it had declared, with reference to Sledgehammer:

(a) We should not attempt any major landing on the Continent this year unless we intended to stay there;

(b) All plans and preparations for "Sledgehammer" should be pressed forward with the greatest vigour, on the understanding that the operation would not be launched, except in conditions which held out a good prospect of success;

(c) The Chiefs of Staff should have authority to ask for the necessary shipping to be taken up for "Sledgehammer" on July 1, without further reference to the War Cabinet.

The Prime Minister in June had further defined the conditions for launching Sledgehammer in a statement of two principles, "generally approved" by the War Cabinet:

No substantial landing in France in 1942 unless we are going to stay; and

No substantial landing in France unless the Germans are demoralized by failure against Russia.

In view of these declarations (the basis of the Prime Minister's eloquent appeal to the President), the British Chiefs of Staff found themselves, by July 1, in the curious position of having authority to mount an operation that their government evidently did not intend to launch. To prepare themselves against this situation they had on June 24 asked the Minister of War Transport to submit by July 1 an estimate of the cost of withdrawing ships for use in Sledgehammer. On June 30 they received the report, which estimated that it would mean tying up some 250,000 tons of shipping and analyzed the consequences for the British shipping program. At the same time the British Chiefs received a report they had requested from Admiral Mountbatten, who pointed out that to mount Sledgehammer would tie up all landing craft in the British Isles and all his instructors trained in landing operations. It would thus not only rule out large-scale raids on the French coast but also suspend amphibious training for all forces not assigned to Sledgehammer. The result would be to slow down preparations for landings in 1943. The one justification for mounting the operation, in the judgment of Mountbatten, would be a fixed intention of actually carrying out Sledgehammer.

Against the disadvantages of mounting an operation so very unlikely to be launched, the British Chiefs of Staff weighed the advantages: "In the first place, our preparations are bound to keep the Germans guessing. They may not force them to withdraw troops from their Eastern Front, but they are unlikely to weaken their Western Front, particularly in air forces. Secondly, the mounting of 'Sledgehammer' will be a useful dress-rehearsal for 'Round-up,' especially for Commanders and Staffs."

But they concluded that beyond question the disadvantages outweighed the advantages, and declared: "If we were free agents, we could not recommend that the operation should be mounted." They ended by stating the limitations on British freedom of action—the cautious declaration on Sledgehammer given in May to Molotov, and the compromise directive on future plans worked out in Washington in June. They pointed out that if the War Cabinet should decide not to mount Sledgehammer, the Soviet Government would soon discover that preparations were not going ahead, and that, whatever the decision, it would be necessary to reopen the question at once with the U.S. Government.

The British Government soon acted on the recommendation of its Chiefs of Staff. On July 8 the Joint Staff Mission in Washington received notification of the decision taken not to mount Sledgehammer and of the hope expressed by the War Cabinet that the United States would agree to the invasion of North Africa.

The stated British objections to Sledgehammer had a great deal of force. The heavy odds against successful landings in France in 1942 and the great cost of mounting a purely contingent operation were indeed fundamental objections, which could have been urged with telling effect against it when Marshall first proposed it. The risks and costs were obviously great. Had the British in April refused, therefore, to plan for a contingent operation, as part of the whole scheme General Marshall proposed, it would of course have been open to the War Department to join the Navy Department and the Pacific commands in advising the President that the United States should not assume the risks involved in diverting available forces from the Pacific. The War Department operations staff had so recommended. In the words used by General Eisenhower to conclude his exposition of the manifold reasons for singleminded concentration of Army forces in the British Isles: "WPD further believes that, unless this plan is adopted as the eventual aim of all our efforts, we must turn our *backs* upon the Eastern Atlantic and go, full out, as quickly as possible, against Japan!"

In July the alternative to go "full out, as quickly as possible" against Japan still remained. It would greatly lessen the dangers perpetuated and the tensions created by Army deployment policy in the Pacific. On July 10 Marshall proposed this alternative. When the JCS met that afternoon he read the dispatch from the British War Cabinet announcing the decision not to mount Sledgehammer. He did not touch on the reasons given by the British for the decision but passed at once to the two questions raised by the decision: (a) should the United States agree to invade North Africa? (b) did the British really want to invade the continent in 1943? Marshall repeated his objections to Gymnast as an operation "expensive and ineffectual" and his conviction "that it was impossible to carry out Sledgehammer or Roundup without full aggressive British support." He then proposed a momentous change in strategy, which would at once rule out the North African operation and settle the basis for future collaboration with the British: "If the British position must be accepted, he proposed that the United States should turn to the Pacific for decisive action against Japan." He went on to list the military and political advantages that (as MacArthur had already pointed out) would attend this course of action:

"He added that this would tend to concentrate rather than to scatter United States forces; that it would be highly popular throughout the United States, particularly on the West Coast; that the Pacific War Council, the Chinese, and the personnel of the Pacific Fleet would all be in hearty accord; and that, second only to Bolero, it would be the operation which would have the greatest effect towards relieving the pressure on Russia."

Admiral King, of course, was ready to make common cause with Marshall. He repeated his own objection to Gymnast—"that it was impossible to fulfill naval commitments in other theaters and at the same time to provide the shipping and escorts which would be essential should that operation be undertaken." Admiral Towers supplemented the case against Gymnast by declaring that the transfer of aircraft carriers from the Pacific to the Atlantic for Gymnast would result in a "most unfavorable" disposition of forces. King also expressed doubt of the British intentions, declaring: ". . . that, in his opinion, the British had never been in wholehearted accord with operations on the continent as proposed by the United States. He said that, in the European theater, we must fight the Germans effectively to win, and that any departure from full Bolero plans would result in failure to accomplish this purpose." Lieutenant General Joseph T. McNarney in turn observed that "in his opinion, the R.A.F. was not enthusiastic over Bolero."

Admiral King readily agreed to join Marshall in submitting to the President (with minor modifications) a memorandum that Marshall had already drawn up expounding his case. It first presented the argument against Gymnast: "Our view is that the execution of Gymnast, even if found practicable, means definitely no Bolero-Sledgehammer in 1942 and that it will definitely curtail if not make impossible the execution of Bolero-Roundup in the Spring of 1943. We are strongly of the opinion that Gymnast would be both indecisive and a heavy drain on our resources, and that if we undertake it, we would nowhere be acting decisively against the enemy and would definitely jeopardize our naval position in the Pacific."

The memorandum passed to a recommendation that the President should urge the Prime Minister "that we go through with full Bolero plans and that we attempt no other operation which would detract from this major effort." The memorandum stated the consequences of British unwillingness to go ahead with Bolero: "Neither Sledgehammer nor Roundup can be carried out without full and whole-hearted British support. They must of necessity furnish a large part of the forces. Giving up all possibility of Sledgehammer in 1942 not only voids our commitments to Russia, but either of the proposed diversions, namely Jupiter and Gymnast, will definitely operate to delay and weaken readiness for Roundup in 1943."

Finally, the memorandum offered an alternative course to be followed should the President fail to persuade the Prime Minister: "If the United States is to engage in any other operation than forceful, unswerving adherence to full Bolero plans, we are definitely of the opinion that we should turn to the Pacific and strike decisively against Japan; in other words assume a defensive attitude against Germany, except for air operations; and use all available means in the Pacific. Such action would not only be definite and decisive against one of our principal enemies, but would bring concrete aid to the Russians in case Japan attacks them."

At the same time General Marshall independently drew up a more informal summary of his reasoning, which concluded with a plain statement of his aim: "I believe that we should now put the proposition up to the British on a very definite basis and leave the decision to them. It must be made at once. My object is again to force the British into acceptance of a concentrated effort against Germany, and if this proves impossible, to turn immediately to the Pacific with strong forces and drive for a decision against Japan."

Marshall's reasoning was a consistent extension of the very reasoning that had led the War Department to propose the concentration of Army forces in the British Isles. The War Department's aim was to commit the bulk of United States Army forces to one main front at a time, and thereby to realize the advantages of long-range planning over a single main line of overseas communication. The War Department had adopted this approach on the assumption that in order to defeat either Germany or Japan it would probably be necessary to defeat very large German and Japanese forces on their home soil. For the War Department, the danger in opening an additional front was to be measured, not in terms of the combat units initially committed, but in terms of the ultimate effect on the employment of manpower, and specifically on the Army troop basis. "Concentrating" Army forces in the Pacific was in every way an inferior line of play to concentrating them in the British Isles (for all the reasons that the staff had listed in February and March), but the military staffs assumed it must be done sooner or later, and it was hence a development more desirable than the opening of a main offensive front in the Mediterranean—a development that the War Department (and the Navy Department) hoped entirely to avoid.

Upon receiving the proposal, the President, who was then at Hyde Park, telephoned to ask General Marshall and Admiral King to prepare a full exposition of "your Pacific Ocean alternative" and send it to him that afternoon by plane. He wanted: ". . . a detailed comprehensive outline of the plans, including estimated time and overall totals of ships, planes, and ground forces. Also, any proposed withdrawal of existing or proposed use of ships, planes, and ground forces in the Atlantic." Finally, he wanted to be advised of the probable effect of the change on the defense of the Soviet Union and the Middle East.

The answer, signed by all three members of the JCS, began by acknowledging that there was no plan to cover the case, adding that though the staffs were at work, it would take them some time to draw one up. After alluding to the projected landings in the Solomons, the hope of extending the operation into New Guinea and the Bismarck Archipelago, and the limitations that had affected these plans, the memorandum traced the lines of advance from the South and Southwest Pacific—either "northward along the Truk-Guam-Saipan line" or "northwestward through the Malay barrier and Borneo to the Philippines" or along both lines—and mentioned the possibility of operations from China and (in case of war between Japan and the USSR) from Siberia.

The memorandum then explained, in simple terms, the effect on the disposition of forces and shipping. The effect on naval strength in the Atlantic would be small, mainly to allow for "some strengthening of anti-submarine measures." The effect on Army deployment would be great. The only ground forces to be moved across the North Atlantic would be two divisions to the British Isles and 15,000 troops to Iceland, to fulfill commitments made at the Arcadia Conference. The air forces set up for Bolero would be cut back by two thirds, leaving only eighteen out of fifty-two groups due to be sent to the British Isles. There would be a correspondingly great reduction in service forces.

The shift to the Pacific would cut the rate of Army deployment. Even if all the shipping allocated to Bolero—half of which was British shipping—were made available for use in the Pacific, the number of troops that could be transported (with equipment) each month would be cut from 100,000 to about 40,000. The greater distance, any withdrawal of British shipping, and the lack of developed Pacific bases would all limit the rate at which forces could be put into action in the Pacific. Accordingly, some air units would be held in the United States and Alaska in readiness for operations in Siberia. It was as yet too soon to plan long-range ground force deployment. The short-term plan was to divert at once to the Pacific airborne and parachute units and the three trained amphibious divisions set up for Bolero, and additional troops as necessary to garrison positions seized from the Japanese.

The memorandum concluded with a statement of the effect of the shift on the active fronts. On the Eastern Front it would be unfavorable, but might be counterbalanced by a favorable effect on the Far Eastern Front, in case of war between the USSR and Japan. The effect of the shift on the position in the Middle East would be small, although the change was likely to have some indirect effect by drawing the attention of the Japanese away from India.

Early in the morning of the next day (Monday, July 13) General Marshall asked the War Department for an analysis of what Gymnast might cost and what it might accomplish, and for the answer to several questions concerning the Pacific alternative:

What is there in the outline of the Pacific plan prepared on Sunday, July 12, that might be compromised in favor of providing more means to the United Kingdom?

What would be the effect of the Pacific plan on allocation of landing craft? What has already gone to England? What can or should be sent to the Pacific including Alaska?

What was the effect of the cut in the estimated production of landing craft for vehicles? Is that cut definite and final or could the situation be improved?

Is the landing craft already sent to England sufficient for commando operations?

If the British give us tonnage, can we afford to send them more divisions? If so, how many?

What changes in schedule of airplane deliveries would be effected by a change in the Pacific plan? Figure out on a time basis what the schedule of delivery of airplanes would be to England and to the Pacific area.

Marshall wanted the answers before Thursday, July 16. The planning staff of SOS went to work at once to prepare a statement of requirements and resources for a major deployment against Japan over the remaining nine months covered by the Bolero plan (July 1942–March 1943). The statement, submitted by Somervell on July 14, was calculated on the diversion from Bolero to the war against Japan of all but thirteen air groups (out of fifty-three), all but two divisions (out of fourteen) and most of the service troops:

| | Air Groups | Divisions | Service Troops |
|---|---|---|---|
| Siberia and Alaska | 15 | 1 (Alaska) | 19,500 |
| Hawaii | 5 | 1 | 3,600 |
| Fijis | 2 | – | 1,400 |
| New Caledonia | 2 | 2 | 19,400 |
| Australia | 14 | 5 | 74,400 |
| India | 2 | 3 | 46,400 |
| Totals | 40 | 12 | 164,700 |

Somervell measured roughly how far it would be possible to carry out the shift to the Pacific with the statement that the backlog of units built up in the United States, for lack of ships to move and supply them, would require an additional construction program for approximately 400,000 troops. Under the Pacific alternative, as under the Bolero plan, the limiting factor was likely to be the amount of cargo shipping available. He estimated that the lack of cargo shipping during the period might cut back, by perhaps 100,000 men, deployment for which troop shipping would be available, although, as he remarked in closing, no forecast of available cargo shipping for so many months ahead could be very accurate.

As it turned out, General Marshall had no occasion to go into the details of the Pacific plan with the President, or to reargue the case against Gymnast, of which the operations staff, as instructed, prepared a new version. On July 14 the President sent word to Marshall that he did not approve the Pacific alternative, that he would confer with him on Wednesday morning (July 15) and probably with all the members of the JCS in the afternoon, and that he had "definitely" decided to send him with Admiral King and Mr. Hopkins to London "immediately" (if possible on Thursday, July 16). At the meeting of the JCS on the afternoon of July 14 Marshall read the message. General Wedemeyer took notes on the discussion that followed: ". . . it was indicated that unquestionably the President would require military operations in Africa. The relative merits of operations in Africa, in Northwest Africa, and in the Middle East were discussed. All agreed to the many arguments previously advanced among military men in the Army and Navy that operations in the Pacific would be the alternative if Sledgehammer or Bolero were not accepted wholeheartedly by the British. However, there was an acceptance that apparently our political system would require major operations this year in Africa."

The President objected to the very idea of delivering an ultimatum to the British. He made this perfectly clear to Stimson and Marshall upon his return to Washington on the fifteenth. He also held that it would be a mistake to try to defeat Japan first. He thought it would be impracticable until the United States Navy had been greatly strengthened. He also held it would be uneconomical to try to defeat Japan first, for much the same reason that the War Department held a Mediterranean offensive to be uneconomical—that it would not contribute to the defeat of Germany and would be unnecessary after the defeat of Germany. On July 16 he stated this view formally in his instructions to Hopkins, Marshall, and King on their mission to London:

> 9. I am opposed to an American all-out effort in the Pacific against Japan with the view to her defeat as quickly as possible. It is of the utmost importance that we appreciate that defeat of Japan does not defeat Germany and that American concentration against Japan this year or in 1943 increases the chance of complete German domination of Europe and Africa. On the other hand, it is obvious that defeat of Germany, or the holding of Germany in 1942 or in 1943 means probable, eventual defeat of Germany in the European and African theatres and in the Near East. Defeat of Germany means the defeat of Japan, probably without firing a shot or losing a life.

The President, on his return to Washington on July 15, indicated that, as the JCS had inferred, he would require operations of some kind in Africa in case the British would not agree to carry out Sledgehammer. Of the various alternatives the JCS had discussed, he was apparently rather inclined to favor the reinforcement of the Middle East by several American divisions. On July 15 he gave General Marshall a preliminary statement of points to govern the negotiations in London. The first page of the President's outline read as follows:

> 1. Proceed with Sledgehammer and stay in France if we can.
> 2. Get all United States troops in action as quickly as possible.
> 3. Proceed in all other theaters as now planned.
> 4. Keep up aid to Russia but via Basra.

The second page read:

> 1. Abandon Sledgehammer 1942.
> 2. Slow up Bolero 1943 for the coming three months.
> 3. Take all planes now headed from United States to England and reroute them to (a) Middle East and Egypt (majority) (b) S.W. Pacific (minority).
> 4. Send 5 divisions to England slowly.
> 5. Send 5 divisions to Middle East fast.
> 6. Speed up Bolero preparations by October —so that Bolero Roundup will be ready April, 1943.
> 7. Keep up aid to Russia, but via Basra.

Some of these points the War Department staff incorporated in a draft of instructions for the conference, which Major General Thomas T. Handy and General Marshall in turn revised. The draft was addressed to Marshall and King (not Hopkins). The effect of the instructions proposed by the War Department, had the

President adopted them, would have been simply to rule out any change in American commitments, or any action by American ground forces (aside from raids) across the Atlantic in 1942, except in case a collapse of Soviet resistance seemed imminent. The effect would also have been, in any event, to rule out operations against French North Africa. In short, the War Department proposed to stand pat.

The President was willing to give his representatives in London one more chance to persuade the British to undertake a cross-Channel operation in 1942, but not to put off a decision on an alternative operation across the Atlantic in case the Prime Minister held his ground. The President appreciated the doubts of his military leaders that the Prime Minister might not be any more willing to undertake an American-style cross-Channel operation in 1943 than in 1942, whatever his present professions. But he was not disposed to resolve these doubts by means of an ultimatum, which would indeed have been ill-adapted to the purpose of securing the "full," "whole-hearted" collaboration of the proud leader of a great people. Besides, he agreed with the Prime Minister that a diversion to the Mediterranean would not rule out a cross-Channel operation in 1943. Finally, his willingness to take a chance on future British intentions and on the consequences of a diversion from Bolero was reinforced by his own determination to get "action" across the Atlantic, which he asked for in his instructions to Hopkins, Marshall, and King: "It is of the highest importance that United States ground troops be brought into action against the enemy in 1942."

Even these instructions did not in so many words "require military operations in Africa." Instead, the President simply required that his emissaries in London should reach a decision. The inclusion of Mr. Hopkins as a member of the mission itself indicated that the mission had plenary powers, and the President inserted after the formal opening sentence a second paragraph, which explicitly stated the theme of decision:

"2. The military and naval strategic changes have been so great since Mr. Churchill's visit to Washington that it becomes necessary to reach immediate agreement on joint operational plans between the British and ourselves along two lines:

(a) Definite plans for the balance of 1942.
(b) Tentative plans for the year 1943 . . .

The President then proceeded to eliminate the central idea of the draft instructions—that decisions should be left contingent on the outcome of operations on the Eastern Front. The first step in making the change was to introduce at once (as paragraph 3) the statement of principles that had appeared in the draft instructions as a basis for investigating the courses of action open "in the event Russian collapse becomes probable":

"3. (a) The common aim of the United Nations must be the defeat of the Axis Powers. There cannot be compromise on this point.

(b) We should concentrate our efforts and avoid dispersion.

(c) Absolute coordinated use of British and American forces is essential.

(d) All available United States and British forces should be brought into action as quickly as they can be profitably used.

(e) It is of the highest importance that United States ground troops be brought into action against the enemy in 1942."

A second step was to rephrase the policy to be followed in supplying the USSR. In place of the bare reference to the continuation of shipments via the Persian Gulf and the suspension of the northern convoys, the President introduced a statement of good hopes and good intentions:

"4. British and American materiel promises to Russia must be carried out in good faith. If the Persian route of delivery is used, preference must be given to combat materiel. This aid must continue as long as delivery is possible and Russia must be encouraged to continue resistance. Only complete collapse, which seems unthinkable, should alter this determination on our part."

A third step was to restate the draft provision with reference to Sledgehammer, which the American representatives were still to urge, but not as a contingent operation; they were instead directed (in paragraph 5): "You should strongly urge immediate all-out preparations for it, that it be pushed with utmost vigor, and that it be executed whether or not Russian collapse becomes imminent." A fourth change was in the provision for discussions in London in case the American representatives should conclude (and inform the President) that Sledgehammer was "impossible of execution with reasonable chances of serving its intended purposes." The President's own statement of his views was not that the two nations in that case should go ahead with plans for Roundup so long as it looked as if the Red Army could contain large German forces, but instead:

"7. If Sledgehammer is finally and definitely out of the picture, I want you to consider the world situation as it exists at that time, and determine upon another place for United States Troops to fight in 1942."

The passages that followed did not explicitly limit the choice of "another place" for an operation in 1942. Instead, the President simply passed to the point that a cross-Channel operation in 1943 would apparently depend on the outcome of operations on the Eastern Front, and thence to the declaration (in paragraph 8): "The Middle East should be held as strongly as possible whether Russia collapses or not." After calling attention to the numerous consequences of the loss of the Middle East, he concluded:

"(8) You will determine the best methods of holding the Middle East. These methods include definitely either or both of the following:

(a) Sending aid and ground forces to the Persian Gulf, to Syria and to Egypt.

(b) A new operation in Morocco and Algiers intended to drive in against the back-door of Rommel's armies. The attitude of French Colonial troops is still in doubt."

The President then made his formal declaration of opposition to the Pacific alternative, and closed with the following admonitions:

"10. Please remember three cardinal principles—speed of decision on plans, unity of plans, attack combined with defense but not defense alone. This affects the immediate objective of United States ground forces fighting against Germans in 1942.

11. I hope for total agreement within one week of your arrival."

The President's representatives arrived in London on Saturday, July 18. They first conferred with the Americans stationed there—Admiral Stark, Lieutenant General Dwight D. Eisenhower, and General Spaatz. During the first three days of their meetings with the British in London (July 20–22) they tried to persuade the British Chiefs of Staff of the merits of a revised version of Sledgehammer that had been hurriedly worked up by General Eisenhower's staff—an operation to secure a foothold on the Cotentin (Cherbourg) peninsula. They urged in its favor the good effect at the very least of heartening the Soviet Government by giving concrete evidence of an intention to engage a part of the German Army at the first moment, and the advantage of having a starting point for operations in 1943. By accepting the objective of securing a "permanent" lodgment on the Continent, on which the British Government had insisted, they evaded the chief political objection of the Prime Minister only to run directly into the most forcible objections of his Chiefs of Staff. In short, they had at last to face the fact that the British Government, in requiring permanent landings, had set a condition that the British Chiefs of Staff believed to be impossible to satisfy. On July 22, at a conference attended by the Prime Minister and his principal military leaders and advisers, the American representatives acknowledged defeat.

They reported the impasse to the President, who owned that he was not altogether surprised and agreed that the matter might as well be dropped. He directed them to settle with the British on one of five alternatives, listing them in order of preference: (1) a British-American operation against French North Africa (either Algeria or Morocco or both); (2) an entirely American operation against French Morocco (Gymnast); (3) combined operations against northern Norway (Jupiter); (4) the reinforcement of Iran. . . .

The President first introduced the subject of a division of responsibility among theaters by the two countries on February 18 (1942) in a communication to the Prime Minister. He wrote: "It seems to me that the United States is able because of our geographical position to reinforce the right flank (Australia and New Zealand) much better than you can and I think that the United States should take the primary responsibility for that immediate reinforcement and maintenance, using Australia as the main base. . . . Britain is better prepared to reinforce Burma and India and I visualize that you would take responsibility for that theater. We would supplement you in any way we could, just as you would supplement our efforts on the right flank."

A few days later the British Chiefs of Staff indicated that they were thinking along similar lines.

On March 7 the President proposed that the world be divided into three general areas for the prosecution of the war against the Axis: (1) the Pacific area, (2) the Middle and Far East area, and (3) the European and Atlantic area. The first region would be an American responsibility, the second British, and the third combined American and British. On the next day General Marshall discussed the issue at the White House.

General Eisenhower meanwhile prepared a study along the lines of the President's proposal. Eisenhower defined the three areas of strategic responsibility as follows: (1) The Pacific area, which included the American continents, China, Australia, New Zealand, and Japan, but excluded Sumatra and the Malay Peninsula, was to be an area of American responsibility. (2) The Indian Ocean and Middle East area—the Indian Ocean and all land areas contiguous thereto west of Singapore, and the Middle and Near East—was designated an area of British responsibility, with American assistance limited to material aid from surplus production. It was stipulated that the United States should have access to bases in India and routes to China within this area. (3) Europe and the Atlantic, in which the major effort against Germany was to be made, was to be an area of British-American joint responsibility.

Eisenhower further proposed, following the sense of the March 7 White House meeting, that the CCS exercise general jurisdiction over grand strategy and the allocation of war material in all areas, in addition to direct supervision of all strategic and operational matters in the European and Atlantic area. In the Indian Ocean and Middle East area the British Chiefs of Staff were to exercise jurisdiction; in the Pacific area the United States Chiefs of Staff were to exercise jurisdiction.

On March 9 the President sent a personal message to the Prime Minister asking him, in view of the developments in the Southwest Pacific area since the Arcadia Conference, to consider the operational simplification that had been proposed in Washington. The operational responsibility for the Pacific area would rest on the United States, with decisions for the area being made in Washington by the United States Chiefs of Staff in consultation with an advisory council representing Australia, New Zealand, the Netherlands Indies, China, and possibly Canada. The supreme command in the Pacific area would be American. The middle area—extending from Singapore to and including India, the Indian Ocean, Persian Gulf, Red Sea, Libya, and the Mediterranean—would be a British responsibility, but the United States would continue to allocate to it all possible munitions and vessel assignments. The third area—Europe and the Atlantic—would be a joint British-American responsibility and would include definite plans for establishment of a new front on the European Continent. "I am becoming more and more interested in the establishment of this new front this summer," the President added.

The Prime Minister replied on March 18, generally concurring in the President's proposals and stating that he and the British Chiefs of Staff saw "great merits in simplification resulting from American control over Pacific sphere and British control over Indian sphere and indeed there is no other way." The Prime Minister implicitly accepted the postponement of a combined North African operation and movements of American troops to the United Kingdom as a necessary corollary to the use of shipping for deployment to the Southwest Pacific and movement of British troops to the Middle East. With the understanding that British and American efforts everywhere could be directed by "machinery of the Combined Chiefs of Staff Committee acting directly under you and me," the Prime Minister also approved the President's proposals for "executive conduct" of the war.

In regard to the Pacific theater, Churchill wrote: "On supreme and general outlook in Pacific we are both agreed on the paramount importance of regaining the initiative against Japan. . . . We assume that any large-scale methods of achieving this would be capable of being discussed by combined Chiefs of Staff Committee in Washington. . . ."

And in summing up: ". . . I feel that your proposals as I have ventured to elaborate and interpret them will achieve double purpose, namely (a) integrity of executive and operational action and (b) opportunity of reasonable consultation for those whose fortunes are involved."

### Creation of SWPA and POA

While the President and the Prime Minister were reaching agreement on the world-wide division of strategic responsibility, the JCS were considering the subdivision of the Pacific theater, which they assumed would become a responsibility of the United States. The Navy was primarily concerned with the "threat to the line of communications between the Americas and Australia–New Zealand," and Admiral King had made the first formal proposal for revision of command arrangements in the Southwest Pacific immediately after the fall of Singapore. The War Department planners considered various alternatives suggested by Admiral King. At the same time the War Department informally told Brett of its agreement with the principle expressed by the New Zealand and Australian authorities meeting in Melbourne that operations in the South and Southwest Pacific based on Australia should be under unified command.

The JCS, after studying the recommendations of the Australian and New Zealand Governments, adopted instead the Navy's view that New Zealand belonged with the line of communication, and proposed the establishment of a new "Australian area" that would include only "the Australian continent and the direct enemy approaches thereto, a strategic entity appropriate for unified command." Eisenhower pointed out that since Australia had to serve as a base for all military operations in the Southwest Pacific there were obvious disadvantages in setting up an Australian area which would not include New Zealand, New Caledonia, and the Philippines. Accordingly the War Department recommended extending the area to include these islands and proposed giving the area, so extended, the "more descriptive designation" of "the Southwest Pacific Area." General Marshall proposed to the Joint Chiefs that the "Southwest Pacific Area" be established as a subarea command in the Pacific theater "to comprise all land areas in the Pacific for which the United States is made responsible, southwest of the line Philippines–Samoa (both inclusive), thence south along the meridian of 170° W." The participating governments—Australia, New Zealand, the Netherlands Indies, and the United States—would select a supreme commander whose directive would be prepared by the United States Joint Chiefs of Staff in collaboration with representatives of these governments. The sea and island areas in the Pacific Ocean northeast of the Southwest Pacific Area would be known as the North Pacific Area and "placed under the command of a United States Navy officer."

The JCS, acting "in anticipation of final approval of the division of the world into three major theaters," thereupon modified their proposal by extending the boundary of the area northward to include the Philippines and renaming the area the Southwest Pacific Area. But they retained the separation of Australia from New Zealand and New Caledonia, ruling that the defense of these islands, as the Navy insisted, was essentially a part of the defense of the lines of communication from the United States.

On this basis the JCS proceeded to set up commands in the Pacific theater, in effect making the Army responsible for operations in Australia and to the north and northeast, to and including the Philippines—the Southwest Pacific Area—and making the Navy responsible for operations in the rest of the Pacific theater—the Pacific Ocean Area—except for a small Southeast Pacific area (for which no command was established). . . . General MacArthur was to be Supreme Commander, Southwest Pacific Area (SWPA). Admiral Chester W. Nimitz, who was in command of the Pacific fleet, was to become Commander in Chief, Pacific Ocean Area (POA), directly controlling the South Pacific subarea through a deputy whom he would designate.

# War in the Pacific

## From the War Reports of Fleet Admiral Ernest J. King

ON FEBRUARY 1, 1941, command afloat in the high echelons was vested in three Commanders in Chief, one of whom commanded the Asiatic Fleet, one the Pacific Fleet, and one the Atlantic Fleet, provision being made whereby one of these three, depending on the circumstances, would act as Commander in Chief, United States Fleet, chiefly for purposes of standardization. In case two or more fleets operated together, he would coordinate their operations. At the time Pearl Harbor was attacked, the Commander in Chief of the Pacific Fleet was also Commander in Chief of the United States Fleet.

Almost immediately after our entry in the war it became apparent that for the purpose of exercising command all oceans must be regarded as one area, to the end that effective coordinated control and the proper distribution of our naval power might be realized. On December 20, 1941, therefore, the President changed this organization by making the Commander in Chief, United States Fleet, separate and distinct and in addition to the other three Commanders in Chief, and ordered the Headquarters of the Commander in Chief, United States Fleet, established in the Navy Department in Washington.

As of January 1, 1942, Admiral H. R. Stark was Chief of Naval Operations, Admiral E. J. King was Commander in Chief of the United States Fleet, Admiral T. C. Hart was Commander in Chief of the Asiatic Fleet, Admiral C. W. Nimitz, who relieved Admiral H. E. Kimmel late in December, was Commander in Chief of the Pacific Fleet, and Vice Admiral (now Admiral) R. E. Ingersoll was Commander in Chief of the Atlantic Fleet.

In March, 1942 (coincident with my appointment as such), the duties of the Chief of Naval Operations were combined with the duties of the Commander in Chief, United States Fleet. Admiral Stark, who had so ably performed the duties of Chief of Naval Operations during the vital period preceding the war, became commander of United States Naval Forces in Europe. This move was accompanied by a number of adjustments in the Navy Department organization, calculated, among other things, to facilitate the logistic support of the forces afloat by providing for its coordination. Except for the fact that the Asiatic Fleet ceased to exist as such in June, 1942, that basic organization of the United States Fleet and supporting activities is still in effect. In the spring of 1942, however, and from time to time thereafter, independent commands were established directly under the Commander in Chief, United States Fleet. . . .

The war in the Pacific may be regarded as having four stages:

(1) The defensive, when we were engaged almost exclusively in protecting our shores and our lines of communication from the encroachments of the enemy.

(2) The defensive-offensive, during which, although our operations were chiefly defensive in character, we were able nevertheless to take certain offensive measures.

(3) The offensive-defensive, covering the period immediately following our seizure of the initiative, but during which we still had to use a large part of our forces to defend our recent gains.

(4) The offensive, which began when our advance bases were no longer seriously threatened and we became able to attack the enemy at places of our own choosing. . . .

During the year 1944, the whole of the United States Navy in the Pacific was on the offensive. My previous report, summarizing combat operations to 1 March 1944, showed the evolution by which we had passed from the defensive, through the defensive-offensive and offensive-defensive stages, to the full offensive. To understand the significance of our operations in the account which follows, the reader must be aware of the basic reasons behind them.

The campaign in the Pacific has important elements of dissimilarity from the campaign in Europe. Since the "battle of the beaches" was finally won with the landings in Normandy last June, the naval task in Europe has become of secondary scope. The European war has turned into a vast land campaign, in which the role of the navies is to keep open the trans-Atlantic sea routes against an enemy whose naval strength appears to be broken except for his U-boat activities. In contrast, the Pacific war is still in the "crossing the ocean" phase. There are times in the Pacific when troops get beyond the range of naval gun support, but much of the fighting has been, is now, and will continue for some time to be on beaches where Army and Navy combine in amphibious operations. Therefore, the essential element of our dominance over the Japanese has been the strength of our fleet. The ability to move troops from island to island, and to put them ashore against opposition, is due to the fact that our command of the sea is spreading as Japanese naval strength withers. As a rough generalization, the war in Europe is now predominantly an affair of armies, while the war in the Pacific is still predominantly naval.

The strategy in the Pacific has been to advance on the core of the Japanese position from two directions. Under General of the Army MacArthur, a combined Allied Army-Navy force has moved north from the Australian region. Under Fleet Admiral Nimitz, a United States Army-Navy-Marine force has moved west from Hawaii. The mobile power embodied in the major combatant vessels of the Pacific Fleet has, sometimes united and sometimes separately, covered operations along both routes of advance, and at the same time contained the Japanese Navy.

In November, 1943 South Pacific forces secured a beachhead on Bougainville, on which airfields were constructed for the neutralization of the Japanese base of Rabaul on New Britain. Simultaneously Southwest Pacific forces were working their way along the northern coast of New Guinea.

In November, 1943 Pacific Ocean Areas forces attacked the Gilbert Islands, and at the end of January, 1944 the Marshall Islands—the first stepping stones along the road from Hawaii. To control the seas and render secure a route from Hawaii westward, it was not necessary to occupy every atoll. We could and did pursue a "leap frog" strategy, the basic concept of which is to seize those islands essential for our use, by-passing many strongly held intervening ones which were not necessary for our purposes. This policy was made possible by the gradually increasing disparity between our own naval power and that of the enemy, so that the enemy was and still is unable to support the garrisons of the by-passed atolls. Consequently, by cutting the enemy's line of communicating bases, the isolated ones became innocuous, without the necessity for our expending effort for their capture. Therefore, we can with impunity by-pass numerous enemy positions, with small comfort to the isolated Japanese garrisons, who are left to meditate on the fate of exposed forces beyond the range of naval support.

This strategy has brought the Navy into combat with shore-based air forces. It has involved some risks and considerable difficulty, which we have overcome. However, as we near the enemy's homeland, the problem becomes more and more difficult. During the first landing in the Philippines, for example, it was necessary to deal with the hundred or more Japanese airfields that were within flying range of Leyte. This imposed on our carrier forces a heavy task which we may expect to become increasingly heavy from time to time. While shore-based air facilities are being established as rapidly as possible in each position we capture, there will always be a period following a successful landing when control of the air will rest solely on the strength of our carrier-based aviation.

The value of having naval vessels in support of landings has been fully confirmed. The renewed importance of battleships is one of the interesting features of the Pacific war. The concentrated power of heavy naval guns is very great by standards of land warfare, and the artillery support they have given in landing operations has been a material factor in getting our troops ashore with minimum loss of life. Battleships and cruisers, as well as smaller ships, have proved their worth for this purpose. . . .

Within the past twelve months the character of our operations has increasingly necessitated a free and rapid interchange of forces of the several services, so that the greatest possible strength can be brought to bear against the enemy at the place and the time that will do the most good. It is a matter of basic policy to freeze the smallest possible number of forces in permanent assignment to any single area, and to leave the major portion of the fleet as a mobile unit that is ready for service where it is most vitally needed. As an example, during the past year Admirals Halsey and Spruance, in turn commanding major units of the Pacific Fleet, have been moving back and forth between the Central and Southwest Pacific in support of the westward advances of Fleet Admiral Nimitz in the Pacific Ocean Areas and of General of the Army MacArthur in the Southwest Pacific Area. As a general principle, all naval forces are placed under a naval commander of the nation that has the primary naval responsibility in the area of operations. During the invasion of Normandy and in the Mediterranean, United States naval forces operated under British naval commanders, while British and Australian naval forces are under our operational control in the Pacific.

The harmonious integration within and between the services has been particularly essential in amphibious operations, where personnel of one service have served under the command of another. In any amphibious operation, command of all forces engaged rests in the hands of the naval commander until the troops have been put ashore and have established their command organization. At this point the landing force commander advises the naval commander that he has assumed command of his troops ashore.

The function of the Navy in an amphibious operation falls into four main phases. During the "approach" phase, the Navy commands passage to the area of landings for the invasion forces, bombards shore batteries, landing beaches and supporting areas, conducts mine sweeping operations, and removes beach obstacles. Frequently the bombing of landing beaches and shore defenses is a joint function of Army and Navy aircraft. In the "landing" phase, the Navy, by employment of special landing craft, puts the invasion forces and all their equipment ashore, under cover of ships' guns and carrier aircraft. In the "support" phase, after the consolidation of the beachhead, the Navy continues to provide artillery and air support to the forces ashore for as long a time as they remain within range of ships' guns, and until shore-based aviation can relieve our carriers of the task of air support. In the "supply" phase, the Navy guarantees the security of the supply lines of the invasion forces and obstructs the enemy's efforts to reinforce his troops by sea.

The extent and varied character of naval participation in amphibious operations have required vast quantities of ships, men and material. Consider, for example, the Lingayen Gulf landings on January 9, 1945. The naval attack and covering forces for this operation consisted of 1,033 ships, ranging in size from battleships and carriers on down through landing craft. The naval personnel in this force numbered upwards of 273,000. The Army forces put ashore on D-day and during the following four days were slightly more than two thirds of this number. Similarly, in the landings on Iwo Jima, approximately 800 naval vessels were involved, with a total personnel of over 220,000. Approximately 60,000 Marines were landed in the first three days of the operation, a ratio of ships' personnel to troops landed of slightly less than 4 to 1.

The experience of more than three years of war has demonstrated the soundness of our concept of a "balanced fleet," in which aircraft and ships work together as a coordinated team. There has been no dispute as to "carriers versus battleships." Aircraft can do some things that ships cannot do. Ships can do some things that aircraft cannot do. Working together, surface ships, submarines, and aircraft supplement each other so that the strength of the unified team is greater than the sum of the parts.

Given the conditions under which naval war is now fought, it is impossible for a fleet to operate effectively without air power of its own. Our superiority in carrier strength has enabled us to take giant's strides across the Pacific in spite of the enemy's island network of air bases. The fast carrier task forces of the Pacific Fleet, consisting of carriers, battleships, cruisers, and destroyers, have repeatedly made bold offensive thrusts into distant waters, inflicting significant damage on the enemy's shipping and installations. They have supported amphibious operations, controlling the air both before and after landings and until airstrips could be completed. They have equally proved their worth in the two major actions with the Japanese fleet that have taken place during the past year. The clearest evidence of their effectiveness is seen in the box score of damage inflicted upon the enemy by Admiral Halsey's Third Fleet between August 24, 1944 and January 26, 1945. During these five months, while the Third Fleet was engaged in supporting the Western Carolines and Philippine Island operations, 4,370 enemy aircraft were destroyed, 82 enemy combatant ships sunk, and 372 enemy auxiliaries and merchant ships sunk (excluding small craft), against a loss in combat by the Third Fleet of only 499 of our own planes and the light carrier *Princeton*.

The amphibious landings of the past twelve months have repeatedly shown the value of naval gunfire in gaining victory and in saving the lives of our assault troops. Shore bombardments in preparation for landings, during the landings, and for as long after as troops are within range of ships' guns, have been carried out on a scale not contemplated in the past. New methods, joint procedures, and new materials have been developed. A sufficient volume of fire is laid down to knock out the shore and beach defenses and to drive off the beach defense personnel. Initially fire is carried out by heavy ships and support aircraft. Battleship fire provides the only gun (or weapon for that matter) that is sufficiently powerful and accurate to knock out reinforced concrete pillboxes eight to ten feet thick, and other similarly strong land gun emplacements. Just prior to landing, destroyers, gunboats, and rocket ships lay down heavy barrages of fire; ships and aircraft continue to give support as the troops move in. Although ships are designed primarily to fight other ships, their effectiveness against heavy shore batteries has been well-proven in this war, as in the past. The risk of so exposing ships is justifiable if the object sought is sufficiently important, more especially when command of the sea is not in jeopardy. The Normandy landing was an especially convincing demonstration of the value of naval gunfire in support of troops, not only as they land but also as they move inland off the beaches. The new applications of naval gunfire in amphibious operations, as well as in fleet actions, have demonstrated that the battleship is a versatile and essential vessel, far from obsolete.

We have heard much of things being ahead of schedule in the Pacific. Actually we have had no schedule, except to go as far and as fast as the means in hand would permit. It can be said that the war today is ahead of our expectations of last year. This should stimulate rather than sap our determination to carry on with every means we can muster. I have said before, and I repeat —a quick and easy Pacific victory cannot be taken for granted, even after the European war is over. While we rejoice in the reoccupation of Guam and of the Philippines, from which our forces were driven three years ago, we must constantly realize that we are only now gaining a position from which we can assault the heart of the Japanese strength. That is our goal, and the enemy is welcome to know that we shall continue to press him with every means at our command. But the very speed of our advance has created new production problems. Our accelerated operations are placing a heavy strain upon reserves of certain vital items, while production of certain necessities is falling behind mounting requirements. It is only by unrelenting support and effort on the home front that our advance can continue. . . .

The major strategic decision of the war provided first for the defeat of Germany and then for the defeat of Japan. Both of these tasks have now been accomplished and we can view in clearer perspective the two major campaigns which led to victory. The contrast between them is at once apparent. The war in Europe was primarily a ground and air war with naval support, while the war in the Pacific was primarily a naval war with ground and air support.

In the European war, sea power was an essential factor because of the necessity of transporting our entire military effort across the Atlantic and supporting it there. Without command of the sea, this could not have been done. Nevertheless, the surrender of the land, sea, and air forces of the German Reich on May 8, 1945 was the direct result of the application of air power over land and the power of the Allied ground forces.

In the Pacific war, the power of our ground and strategic air forces, like sea power in the Atlantic, was an essential factor. By contrast with Germany, however, Japan's armies were intact and undefeated and her air forces only weakened when she surrendered, but her Navy had been destroyed and her merchant fleet had been fatally crippled. Dependent upon imported food and raw materials and relying upon sea transport to supply her armies at home and overseas, Japan lost the war because she lost command of the sea, and in doing so lost—to us—the island bases from which her factories and cities could be destroyed by air.

From the earliest days of the war our submarines, operating offensively in the farthest reaches of the Pacific, exacted a heavy toll of Japanese shipping. At a conservative estimate, they sank, in addition to many combatant ships, nearly two thirds of the merchant shipping which Japan lost during the war.

Our surface forces—fast task forces composed of aircraft carriers, fast battleships, cruisers, and destroyers—carried the war to the enemy homeland and destroyed impressive numbers of naval vessels and merchant ships. Our amphibious forces, operating initially behind air offensives and under air cover launched from carriers, seized the island bases which made possible the achievements of land-based aircraft in cutting enemy lines of communications and in carrying devastation to the Japanese home islands.

Thus our sea power separated the enemy from vital resources on the Asiatic mainland and in the islands which he had seized early in the war, and furnished us the bases essential to the operations of shore-based aircraft from which the atomic bombs finally were despatched, and on which troops and supplies were being massed for the invasion of Kyushu and of Honshu. The defeat of Japan was directly due to our overwhelming power at sea.

The destruction of the Japanese Navy followed the Nelsonian doctrine that naval victory should be followed up until the enemy fleet is annihilated. Of 12 battleships, 11 were sunk; of 26 carriers, 20 were sunk; of 43 cruisers, 38 were destroyed; and so on throughout the various types of ships, which collectively constituted a fleet considerably larger than ours was before the war began. The few ships that remained afloat were for the most part so heavily damaged as to be of no military value.

In striking contrast is the record of our ships. Although 2 old battleships were lost at Pearl Harbor, 8 new battleships have since joined the fleet. Against 5 aircraft carriers and 6 escort carriers lost, we completed 27 carriers and 110 escort carriers. While we lost 10 cruisers, 48 new cruisers have been commissioned. We lost 52 submarines and built 203. The capacity of the United States to build warships, auxiliary ships and merchant ships, while supporting our forces and our Allies all over the world, exceeded all former records and surpassed our most sanguine hopes. . . .

In the successful application of our sea power, a prime factor has been the flexibility and balanced character of our naval forces. In the Atlantic the German Navy was virtually limited to the use of submarines, without surface and naval air support. In the Pacific, Japanese sea power was hampered by army control, and Japanese naval officers lacked the freedom of initiative so necessary to gain and exercise command of the seas. On the other hand, while ours was a vast fleet, it was also a highly flexible and well-balanced fleet, in which ships, planes, amphibious forces, and service forces in due proportion were available for unified action whenever and wherever called upon.

It is of interest to note, in connection with formulation of plans for the future strength of our Navy, that our fleet in World War II was not solely engaged in fighting enemy fleets. On numerous occasions a large part of the fleet effort was devoted to operations against land objectives. A striking example is the capture of Okinawa. During the three months that this operation was in progress our Pacific Fleet—the greatest naval force ever assembled in the history of the world—was engaged in a continuous battle which for sustained intensity has never been equaled in naval history; yet at this time the Japanese Navy had virtually ceased to exist—we were fighting an island, not an enemy fleet.

With the possible exception of amphibious warfare, which covers a field of considerably broader scope, the outstanding development of the war in the field of naval strategy and tactics had been the convincing proof and general acceptance of the fact that, in accord with the basic concept of the United States Navy, a concept established some 25 years ago, naval aviation is and must always be an integral and primary component of the fleet. Naval aviation has proved its worth not only in its basic purpose of destroying hostile air and naval forces, but also in amphibious warfare involving attacks in support of landing operations, in reconnaissance over the sea, and in challenging and defeating hostile land-based planes over positions held in force by the enemy. . . .

The epic advance of our united forces across the vast Pacific, westward from Hawaii and northward from New Guinea, to the Philippines and to the shores of Japan, was spearheaded by naval aviation and closely supported by the power of our fleets. In these advances, some of the steps exceeded 2,000 miles and the assaulting troops often had to be transported for much greater distances. The Navy moved them over water, landed them, and supported them in great force at the beaches, kept them supplied and, particularly at Okinawa, furnished air cover during weeks of the critical fighting ashore.

The outstanding development of this war, in the field of joint undertakings, was the perfection of amphibious operations, the most difficult of all operations in modern warfare. Our success in all such operations, from Normandy to Okinawa, involved huge quantities of specialized equipment, exhaustive study and planning, and thorough training as well as complete integration of all forces, under unified command. . . .

In connection with the matter of command in the field, there is perhaps a popular misconception that the Army and the Navy were intermingled in a standard form of joint operational organization in every theater throughout the world. Actually, the situation was never the same in any two areas. For example, after General of the Army Dwight D. Eisenhower had completed his landing in Normandy, his operation became purely a land campaign. The Navy was responsible for maintaining the line of communications across the ocean and for certain supply operations in the ports of Europe, and small naval groups became part of the land army for certain special purposes, such as the boat groups which helped in the crossing of the Rhine. But the strategy and tactics of the great battles leading up to the surrender of Germany were primarily army affairs and no naval officer had anything directly to do with the command of this land campaign.

A different situation existed in the Pacific, where, in the process of capturing small atolls, the fighting was almost entirely within range of naval gunfire; that is to say, the whole operation of capturing an atoll was amphibious in nature, with artillery and air support primarily naval.

This situation called for a mixed Army-Navy organization which was entrusted to the command of Fleet Admiral Nimitz. A still different situation existed in the early days of the war during the Solomon Islands campaign where Army and Navy became, of necessity, so thoroughly intermingled that they were, to all practical purposes, a single service directed by Admiral William F. Halsey, Jr. Under General of the Army Douglas MacArthur, Army, Army aviation, and the naval components of his command were separate entities tied together only at the top in the person of General MacArthur himself. In the Mediterranean the scheme of command differed somewhat from all the others.

All these systems of command were successful largely because each was placed in effect to meet a specific condition imposed by the characteristics of the current situation in the theater of operations.

## From the War Reports of General of the Army George C. Marshall

It had always been the concept of the United States Chiefs of Staff that Japan could best be defeated by a series of amphibious attacks across the far reaches of the Pacific. Oceans are formidable barriers, but for the nation enjoying naval superiority they become highroads of invasion.

Japan's attack on our fleet at Pearl Harbor gave her a tremendous but, nevertheless, temporary advantage. The Japanese had reckoned without the shipyards of America and the fighting tradition of the United States Navy. Even before parity with the Japanese fleet had been regained, the Navy successfully maintained communications with Australia and had undertaken limited offensives in the Solomons to halt the enemy advance. A desperate courage stopped the Japanese before Australia in the now historic battle of the Coral Sea and then shortly afterward utterly smashed the Japanese advance toward the United States itself in the decisive action at Midway.

The broad strategic allocation of resources among the theaters was controlled by the Combined Chiefs of Staff, but the actual control of operations in the Pacific had been retained by the United States Chiefs of Staff. At the Casablanca Conference, the Combined Chiefs agreed that Japan must be prohibited from further expansion and from consolidating and exploiting her current holdings. This resolution was agreed upon even though we were at the very moment having great difficulty in concentrating sufficient resources to defeat the European Axis.

It has been declared axiomatic that a nation cannot successfully wage war on two fronts. With a full appreciation of the difficulties and hazards involved, we felt compelled to wage a war not only on two fronts, but on many fronts. Thus we arrived at the concept of global war in which the vast power of American democracy was to be deployed all over the earth.

At the Trident Conference of May, 1943 in Washington when the specific strategy of the global war was conceived, it was determined to step up the pace of the advance on Japan. Then a few months later, in August, 1943, at the Quadrant Conference in Quebec, the specific routes of the advance on Japan were laid out. General Douglas MacArthur was directed to continue his operations up the New Guinea coast to reach the Philippines by the fall of 1944. Operations in the Gilberts, the Marshalls, and the Marianas were agreed to, and it was forecast that by the spring of 1945 we would be able to secure a lodgment in the Ryukyus on the threshold of the Japanese homeland.

Admiral King was confident that somewhere during these advances, probably during the Marianas or the Philippine campaigns, the United States fleets would meet and decisively defeat the Japanese Navy. No long-range military forecast could have been more accurate.

At the Quadrant Conference General Arnold proposed an air plan for the softening of Japan. It was later approved and carried into execution. It called for the establishment of bases in China, in the Marianas, and other Pacific islands from which would operate the huge B-29 Superfortresses then only just going into production.

At the turn of the year 1943 Army forces in the South Pacific area were added to General

MacArthur's strategic command. It was the intention of the Joint Chiefs of Staff to maintain the initiative, advancing by amphibious flanking actions on the Philippines and the Japanese islands from the south and from the east. The advance across the tremendous reaches of the Central Pacific was placed under command of Admiral Chester W. Nimitz. There were two axes of the operations on the southern flank—one in New Guinea commanded by Lieutenant General Walter Krueger, the other in the Solomons under Admiral William F. Halsey.

It was General MacArthur's intention to proceed by a series of envelopments up the coast of New Guinea and into the Philippines. We now enjoyed superiority both on the sea and in the air. He was therefore able to land his troops where the Japanese were weakest and confine their stronger forces in pockets from which, because of incredibly difficult terrain and our air and sea superiority, they could never break out. As a result there were at the time of surrender hundreds of thousands of Japanese troops isolated in the jungles of the Pacific islands, dying on the vine and of no further use to their Emperor. As General MacArthur reported toward the end of 1944:

> The enemy garrisons which have been bypassed in the Solomons and New Guinea represent no menace to current or future operations. Their capacity for organized offensive effort has passed. The various processes of attrition will eventually account for their final disposition. The actual time of their destruction is of little or no importance and their influence as a contributing factor to the war is already negligible. The actual process of their immediate destruction by assault methods would unquestionably involve heavy loss of life without adequate compensating strategic advantages.

Even with the intense preoccupation in the campaigns in Europe during the past two years, this great nation had been able steadily to increase the resources available in the Pacific until at the moment of German collapse General MacArthur and Admiral Nimitz were established on the threshold of the Japanese homeland and the industries and cities of Japan were crumbling under our aerial bombardment. The United States Navy dominated the Pacific. The Commonwealth Government, under President Osmena, had been re-established in power and in residence in the Philippines.

On July 1, 1943, General MacArthur had four American divisions and six Australian divisions under his control. His air force had less than 150 heavy bombers. Admiral Nimitz had nine Army and Marine divisions. Yet in the spring of 1945 these two commanders were ejecting the Japanese from the Philippines and the Ryukyus—already on the home stretch to Japan. . . .

By direction of the Joint Chiefs of Staff, General MacArthur assumed command of all United States Army Forces in the Pacific on April 6. Both he and Admiral Nimitz, Commander of Naval Forces in the Pacific, were directed to prepare for the final operations against Japan. By June General MacArthur had created a new command known as the United States Army Forces in the Western Pacific under Lieutenant General W. D. Styer to replace the old Southwest Pacific Area. General Richardson was redesignated Commander of the Army Forces of the Middle Pacific.

On July 10 the Joint Chiefs of Staff ordered another revision of the Pacific Command.

The formerly China-based 20th and 21st Bomber Commands were deactivated. The 21st became the Twentieth Air Force and the personnel of the 20th Bomber Command was transferred to the Eighth Air Force, which had been redeployed from Europe. General Twining, who had started in the Pacific war with the Thirteenth Air Force in the Solomons, later moved to command of the Fifteenth Air Force in Italy, was given command of the new Twentieth Air Force. General Doolittle retained command of the Eighth.

Both air forces which now controlled the mightiest fleet of superbombers ever assembled, were combined into the United States Strategic Air Force, the Command which controlled the American air assault on Germany. General Spaatz retained command of USSTAF in the Pacific. General Giles became his deputy. General LeMay, who once had commanded the B-29 fleet in China, then built up the Superfortress attack in the Pacific, became his Chief of Staff.

Strategic control of the Superfortress fleet remained with the Joint Chiefs of Staff with General Arnold as their agent.

During July the superbombers had steadily increased the scale of their attacks on the Japanese homeland. From the Marianas bases, the B-29's averaged 1,200 sorties a week. Okinawa airfields which now occupied almost all suitable space on the island began to fill with heavy bombers, mediums, and fighters which united in the aerial assault on the Japanese islands, her positions on the Asiatic mainland and what was left of her shipping. Fighters from Iwo Jima swept the air over the Japanese islands, strafed Japanese dromes and communications and gave the superbombers freedom of operation. The Third Fleet augmented by British units hammered Japan with its planes and guns sailing boldly into Japanese coastal waters. The warships repeatedly and effectively shelled industries along the coasts.

These mighty attacks met little opposition. Terrific air losses during the fierce battles of Japan's inter-defenses had made the enemy desperate. Knowing that invasion was not long off, he husbanded his now waning resources for the final battle. Defending the homeland the enemy had an army of 2,000,000, a remaining air strength of 8,000 planes of all types, training and combat.

General MacArthur was massing troops and planes in the Philippines and in Okinawa and in bases to the south of the Philippines for the showdown. He, in cooperation with Admiral Nimitz, was preparing to execute two plans for the invasion of Japan: the first, known as operation Olympic, provided for a three-pronged assault on Southern Kyushu in the fall of 1945 by the Sixth United States Army, consisting of the I and the XI Army Corps and the V Marine Amphibious Corps. The three groups were to land in the order named at Miyazaki, Ariaka Wan, and on the beaches west of Kagoshima to isolate the southernmost Japanese island and destroy the defending forces there. Preceding the main assault were to be preliminary operations in Koshiki Retto and a divisionary feint off Shikoku by the IX Corps.

The second phase of the Japanese invasion, operation Coronet, was to be carried out in the early spring of 1946. The Eighth and Tenth Armies, consisting of nine infantry divisions, two armored divisions and three Marine divisions were to assault the Kanto or Tokyo plain of Eastern Honshu. These two veteran Pacific Armies were to be followed ashore by the First Army which had spearheaded our victory in Europe and was now to be redeployed for the final battle of the Pacific. In this attack the First Army would have contained 10 infantry divisions. The three armies had the mission of destroying the Japanese Army on the main home island and of occupying the Tokyo-Yokohama area. On Kyushu we would have held a one-corps reserve of three infantry divisions and one airborne. From here the plan was to fan out to the north and clean up the remainder of the Japanese islands. Supporting the cleanup would ultimately have been an air garrison equivalent to 50 groups.

These were our plans for final victory in World War II should Japan fight to a last-ditch national suicide. But we had other plans which we anticipated might bring a much speedier end to the war. For years the full resources of American and British science had been working on the principle of atomic fission. By the spring of this year we knew that success was at hand. While President Truman was meeting with the British Prime Minister and Generalissimo Stalin at Potsdam, a new and terrible bomb was taken to a deserted area of New Mexico and detonated. The results were even more terrifying than was anticipated. A report was rushed to the Secretary of War and the President at Potsdam, Germany, and it was decided to use this weapon immediately in an effort to shorten the war and save thousands of American lives. From Potsdam General Spaatz received orders to drop the atomic bomb on the industrial installations of one of four selected cities from which he could make his own selection according to weather and target any time after August 3. He chose the military base city of Hiroshima.

On August 6 the bomb was dropped. The results are well known.

Two days later the Soviet Union declared war on Japan and within a few hours the Red

Army was again on the march, this time driving with powerful blows into the pride of Japanese military power, the Kwantung Army of Manchuria. The first Red offensives were across the Manchuria borders and southward on the island of Sakhalin. The advance by the Red divisions was swift. They struck first to isolate Manchuria and then Korea. In rapid thrusts from Outer Mongolia and Trans Baikal, the Soviet forces drove deep into Manchuria and struck the Khinghan Range, captured the communications center and bases at Hailar and crossed the Khinghan barrier into Harbin, key city of Central Manchuria. To the south strong mobile forces crossed the desolate Gobi Desert toward Southern Manchuria.

Then, on August 9, the Strategic Air Forces loosed a second atomic bomb on Nagasaki, which displayed greater destructive blast and fire than the Hiroshima bomb. The smoke of the Nagasaki detonation rose 50,000 feet into the air and was visible for more than 175 miles.

The week of August 6 had been one of swift and sudden disaster to the nation which fired the first shot in the series of conflicts that led to World War II. Japan was being made to pay in full for her treacheries at Mukden and at Shanghai, at Pearl Harbor and at Bataan. The enemy situation was hopeless. On August 10 the Japanese Government sued for peace on the general terms enunciated by the Allied powers at the Potsdam Conference.

## From the War Reports of General H. H. Arnold

On August 14, Japan, still the military ruler of half a billion people and a land area of nearly 3,000,000 square miles, admitted complete defeat. This admission had been forced on her as the result of a vast and well-coordinated effort on the part of all arms of the United States services, the forces of our fighting Allies, and the enormous industrial resources of our country. It is the province of this report to sum up the part played by air power in the coordinated effort.

Fully recognizing the indispensable contributions of other arms, I feel that air power's part may fairly be called decisive.

The collapse of Japan has vindicated the whole strategic concept of the offensive phase of the Pacific war. Viewed broadly and simply, that strategy has been to advance air power, both land- and carrier-based, to the point where the full fury of crushing air attack could be loosed on Japan itself, with the possibility that such attack would bring about the defeat of Japan without invasion, and with the certainty that it would play a vital role in preparation for, and cooperation with, an invasion. No invasion was necessary.

The war fought against Japan fell into three general phases. First was a "defensive" phase, from the attack on Pearl Harbor and other Allied bases to the Battle of Midway. This was followed by the "holding" phase, preventing the Japanese from extending their stolen empire until our men and materiel could be deployed over the wide expanse of the Pacific for offensive operations. As Germany came first on most priority lists, an immediate offensive was not possible. The third, or "offensive" phase came during 1944 and 1945. . . .

The harnessing of atomic energy and its application at the climax of the Pacific war have tended to overshadow a most important point. Even before one of our B-29s dropped its atomic bomb on Hiroshima, Japan's military situation was hopeless. Without attempting to minimize the appalling and far-reaching results of the atomic bomb, we have good reason to believe that its actual use provided a way out for the Japanese government. The fact is that the Japanese could not have held out long, because they had lost control of their air. They could not offer effective opposition to our bombardment, and so could not prevent the destruction of their cities and industries.

A modern industrial nation such as Japan would never have admitted defeat unless her industrial potential had been hopelessly weakened, the morale of her people seriously affected, and her isolation from the essentials necessary to wage war rendered virtually complete by blockade and the destruction of her Navy and merchant fleet. The fanatical Japanese would never have offered to accept the crushing terms of the Potsdam ultimatum merely because of the odds against them. The Japanese Army was still capable of inflicting heavy casualties on an invading force. The Kamikaze Corps had shown its capabilities in the Philippines and Okinawa campaigns and was preparing for an even greater effort against our invasion. Yet the Japanese acknowledged defeat because air attacks, both actual and potential, had made possible the destruction of their capability and will for further resistance.

It should be emphasized that the many phases and separate operations of those sustained air attacks were closely and carefully related to each other and had as a primary objective the defeat of Japan without invasion.

Let it be clearly understood that the blockade of Japan was by no means exclusively an air blockade. Since early in the war the Japanese merchant fleet had been a primary target of our sea, air, and submarine forces. To the submarines goes the chief credit for reducing the Japanese merchant fleet to the point where, on V-J Day, that fleet consisted of about 300 ships —a little more than a million gross tons or 20 per cent of the shipping afloat when the war began. Nevertheless, aircraft sank over a million tons of shipping in 1944, and in spite of the dwindling number of targets, continued attrition at the 1944 rate until the end of the war. By the end of the war, the sea-air blockade was, to all intents and purposes, complete.

Meanwhile, our B-29s were making Japan bleed internally. A necessarily candid report was given on September 4, 1945 by the then Premier Prince Naruhiko Higashi-Kuni to the Japanese Diet. "The general conditions of the country," he said, "began to show marked signs of impoverishment and exhaustion . . . so much so that in the days just preceding the termination of the war it seemed almost impossible to carry on modern warfare further for any long period of time. The manufacture of modern war materials, principally aircraft, by mass production methods such as we had adopted before would shortly have to face insurmountable difficulties as a result of the destruction of transportation and communications facilities caused by air raids. . . . Our losses in naval and aerial strength were so enormous as to obstruct seriously the prosecution of the war. . . . Moreover, various industries suffered directly from air raids which caused huge damages to plants and lowered the efficiency of the workmen. . . . Frequently air raids together with depreciation of rolling stock and equipment brought about a steady lowering of its capacity and a tendency to lose unified control. Despite the exertion of all possible efforts the carrying capacity of railways . . . would have to be reduced . . . to less than one half as compared with last year."

Experts now on the scene confirm this summary. What were in some circles regarded as "over-optimistic" claims of the damage we were doing have turned out to be conservative.

By the end of 1944, our Twentieth Air Force had only begun its assaults on the sources of Japanese industrial, economic, and political strength. In 1944 not more than 100 bombers attacked Japan in a single operation; in early August, 1945, 801 Superfortresses attacked in a single night's operation.

This increase in the numbers of bombers is not the whole story. Bomb load per aircraft increased from 2.6 tons in November, 1944, to 7.4 tons in July, 1945. During the entire period of operations the XXI Bomber Command flew nearly 90,000,000 miles to and from the Japanese mainland, with an accident loss rate of slightly more than one aircraft for every 1,000,000 miles flown. The percentage of airborne aircraft lost on bombing missions dropped from a high of 5.7 per cent in January to 0.4 per cent in July. The B-29 airmen became steadily more independent of weather or natural vision, more a day-or-night air force, until in July, the record month of B-29 effort, more than 75 per cent of all bomb releases were by radar.

In March, Major General LeMay, then commanding the XXI Bomber Command, made one of the important decisions of the war—to attack Tokyo with incendiaries at low level at night with his full force.

In no previous operation, night or day, had our B-29s bombed from altitudes of less than 24,000 feet; but on the night of March 9, Tokyo was attacked by 279 B-29s at a mean bombing altitude of 7,050 feet. The Japanese defenses were confused, and only 14 B-29s were lost to all causes. Some 15.8 square miles of the heart of Tokyo were burned out in what was, prior to the use of the atomic bomb, the most destructive air attack in history. The Tokyo attack was followed by devastating night incendiary attacks on Nagoya, Kobe, and Osaka in quick succession, and thereafter the air campaign to destroy urban industrial areas vital to Japan's ability to carry on the war continued by night and by day until the day of capitulation.

In all incendiary attacks over 100,000 tons of bombs were dropped in the course of more than 15,000 sorties, against 66 Japanese cities ranging in population from Tokyo, with its teeming millions, to the fish-processing city of Tsuruga, with a population of 31,000. Nearly 169 square miles were destroyed or damaged in the 60 cities for which photographic reconnaissance is available, with more than 100 square miles burned out in the five major cities attacked. The destruction, including that caused by the two atomic bombs, amounts to over 42 per cent of the urban industrial areas involved. The 68 Japanese cities attacked with incendiaries and atomic bombs had in 1940 a total population of over 21,000,000—almost exactly equal to our twelve largest American cities. We can imagine the effect on our capacity to continue the war if the tables had been turned, and Japanese airmen had destroyed nearly half of any group of our industrial cities having a population of 21,000,000.

Premier Prince Naruhiko Higashi-Kuni admitted that by June, 1945, when all of the major cities of Japan had been attacked with incendiaries, Japan's ability to carry on modern warfare was "disastrously undermined," and that the destruction of the medium and small cities in rapid succession thereafter had "calamitous consequences." In addition to the destruction of industrial installations, the casualties caused had significant effects on the dislocation of industrial manpower and on enemy morale. The Japanese have stated that air attacks killed 260,000, injured 412,000, left 9,200,000 homeless, and demolished or burned down 2,210,000 houses.

Never in the history of aerial warfare has such destruction been achieved at such moderate cost. The combat efficiency of the B-29s was such that we were able to reduce Japan more economically than Germany. We needed fewer bases than had been required by us in Europe. In all the attacks on urban industrial areas, the loss ratio, due to all causes, was only 1.22 per cent of attacking aircraft. In the group of cities under 100,000, three and one-half square miles of urban industrial area were destroyed for each B-29 lost to any cause. The smaller cities were, generally speaking, attacked during the months of July and August, and the low loss ratio reflects the steadily increasing operational efficiency of the B-29s, the decline in scale of attacks and aggressiveness of the Japanese Air Force, and the total ineffectiveness of the antiaircraft defenses of the smaller cities.

In the last months of the Pacific war we had, as previously stated, the benefit of interim reports of the United States Strategic Bombing Survey, which had been evaluating damage in Europe. Survey teams including specially qualified men visited the bombed targets, studied the damage on the ground, interviewed German personnel, and examined German records. Their findings supported the value of attacks on the enemy's key industries.

In the Japanese aircraft industry total serious damage amounted to 30.6 per cent of the estimated 89,500,000 square feet of plan area devoted to that industry. It has been estimated that the combination of attacks on the aircraft industry and on urban industrial areas denied to the Japanese some 7,200 combat airplanes which, in the absence of bombing, would have been produced by August, 1945. The attacks on urban industrial areas were responsible for substantial losses, especially because of the destruction of propeller plants. The two most important plants, which together were responsible for 70 per cent of the output of propellers for combat aircraft, were rendered useless. It is thought that the damage to the propeller plants alone without further attack on the aircraft industry would have reduced Japanese airplane production by November, 1945, to a rate equivalent to 41 per cent of January, 1945, production.

Prior to the cessation of hostilities, Japanese

Home Island rates of production of petroleum products had been reduced to 65 per cent of requirements at the July, 1945, monthly rate of consumption.

The synthetic oil industry was a material sufferer—it has been estimated that air attacks in 1945 against synthetic-oil plants cost Japan thousands of barrels of petroleum products. By the end of hostilities, air attack had at least temporarily put out of operation 100 per cent of Japan's high grade lubricating oil capacity. Tetraethyl lead production was down to 28 per cent of capacity. While the Japanese had a considerable surplus of refining capacity at the end of the war, B-29 attacks during 1945 against 11 of the largest and most modern refineries in the Home Islands had, nevertheless, rendered these refineries useless. Likewise, although Japan's inability to ship oil from the southern areas had given her a large excess oil storage capacity, that capacity had been reduced by nearly 6,000,000 barrels by air attack.

There were other important phases of the integrated over-all plan of air warfare.

For instance, the story of B-29 mining operations and the part these operations played in the blockade of the Home Islands has for security reasons never been fully told. This was the first use of aerial mines as a truly strategic weapon. Concerning the B-29 mining operations, Admiral Nimitz cabled General LeMay, "The planning, operational and technical operation of aircraft mining on a scale never before attained has accomplished phenomenal results. . . ."

By combining the four basic types of influence mines, each with a wide range of adjustments, 200 different mines could be produced, each tailored for a special job.

The mining program was divided into five major phases. The first phase, started on March 27, 1945, involved the mining of the vital but narrow Shimonoseki Straits between Honshu and Kyushu, and certain naval bases out of which Japanese naval units were likely to steam to the defense of Okinawa. In the second phase, B-29s ranged from Shimonoseki Straits to Tokyo Bay, the plan being to interdict the shipping lanes between the great industrial cities, which depended on water transportation for 75 per cent of their requirements. In the third phase, attention was turned to the secondary ports along the western and northern coasts of Honshu, on which Japan was becoming more and more dependent for any commerce from Manchuria and Korea across the Sea of Japan. The fourth phase involved intensified mining of the ports of Northern and Western Honshu and Kyushu, Kobe and Osaka. In phase five, every port of consequence used by the Japanese on the southern and eastern coasts of Korea was mined, and re-mining of other ports was continued. Mining the port of Rashin, Korea, only 125 miles from Vladivostok, involved a round trip of 4,160 miles, using Iwo for staging purposes. Throughout the mining campaign, nearly half the mines dropped were reserved for Japan's shipping bottleneck, Shimonoseki Straits. All mines were dropped by radar at night.

Accumulating evidence points to the fact that this mining campaign achieved greater success than was anticipated. More than half a million tons of shipping were sunk, damaged or immobilized. The blockade as a whole was so complete that only the thinnest trickle of raw materials flowed from the Asiatic continent, shipments of food were a fraction of that required to keep the Home Islands above a starvation diet, and the Japanese were unable to supply their vast forces in "Greater East Asia" with adequate equipment.

These were the principal operations against the Japanese Home Islands.

# War in Europe

## From the War Reports of General of the Army George C. Marshall

IN GOOD CONSCIENCE this Nation can take little credit for its part in staving off disaster in those critical days. It is certain that the refusal of the British and Russian peoples to accept what appeared to be inevitable defeat was the great factor in the salvage of our civilization. Of almost equal importance was the failure of the enemy to make the most of the situation. In order to establish for the historical record where and how Germany and Japan failed I asked General Eisenhower to have his intelligence officers promptly interrogate the ranking members of the German High Command who are now our prisoners of war. The results of these interviews are of remarkable interest. They give a picture of dissension among the enemy nations and lack of long-range planning that may well have been decisive factors of this world struggle at its most critical moments.

As evaluated by the War Department General Staff, the interrogations of the captured German commanders disclose the following:

The available evidence shows that Hitler's original intent was to create, by absorption of Germanic peoples in the areas contiguous to Germany and by the strengthening of her new frontiers, a greater Reich which would dominate Europe. To this end Hitler pursued a policy of opportunism which achieved the occupation of the Rhineland, Austria, and Czechoslovakia without military opposition.

No evidence has yet been found that the German High Command had any over-all strategic plan. Although the High Command approved Hitler's policies in principle, his impetuous strategy outran German military capabilities and ultimately led to Germany's defeat. The history of the German High Command from 1938 on is one of constant conflict of personalities in which military judgment was increasingly subordinated to Hitler's personal dictates. The first clash occurred in 1938 and resulted in the removal of von Blomberg, von Fritsch, and Beck and of the last effective conservative influence on German foreign policy.

The campaigns in Poland, Norway, France, and the Low Countries developed serious diversions between Hitler and the General Staff as to the details of execution of strategic plans. In each case the General Staff favored the orthodox offensive, Hitler an unorthodox attack with objectives deep in enemy territory. In each case Hitler's views prevailed and the astounding success of each succeeding campaign raised Hitler's military prestige to the point where his opinions were no longer challenged. His military self-confidence became unassailable after the victory in France, and he began to disparage substantially the ideas of his generals even in the presence of junior officers. Thus no General Staff objection was expressed when Hitler made the fatal decision to invade Soviet Russia.

When Italy entered the war Mussolini's strategic aims contemplated the expansion of his empire under the cloak of German military success. Field Marshal Keitel reveals that Italy's declaration of war was contrary to her agreement with Germany. Both Keitel and Jodl agree that it was undesired. From the very beginning Italy was a burden on the German war potential. Dependent upon Germany and German-occupied territories for oil and coal Italy was a constant source of economic attrition. Mussolini's unilateral action in attacking Greece and Egypt forced the Germans into the Balkan and African campaigns, resulting in over-extension of the German armies which subsequently became one of the principal factors in Germany's defeat.

Nor is there evidence of close strategic coordination between Germany and Japan. The German General Staff recognized that Japan was bound by the neutrality pact with Russia but hoped that the Japanese would tie down strong British and American land, sea, and air forces in the Far East.

In the absence of any evidence so far to the contrary, it is believed that Japan also acted unilaterally and not in accordance with a unified strategic plan.

Here were three criminal nations eager for loot and seeking greedily to advance their own self-interest by war, yet unable to agree on a strategic over-all plan for accomplishing a common objective.

The steps in the German defeat, as described by captured members of the High Command, were:

1. *Failure to invade England.* Hitler's first military setback occurred when, after the collapse of France, England did not capitulate. According to Colonel General Jodl, Chief of the Operations Staff of the German High Command, the campaign in France had been undertaken because it was estimated that with the fall of France, England would not continue to fight. The unexpectedly swift victory over France and Great Britain's continuation of the war found the General Staff unprepared for an invasion of England. Although the armistice with France was concluded on June 22, 1940, no orders to prepare for the invasion of Britain were issued prior to July 2. Field Marshal Kesselring stated that he urged the invasion since it generally was believed in Germany that England was in a critical condition. Field Marshal Keitel, Chief of Staff of German Armed Forces, however, stated that the risk was thought to be the existence of the British fleet. He said the army was ready but the air force was limited by weather, the navy very dubious. Meanwhile, in the air blitz over England the German Air Force had suffered irreparable losses from which its bombardment arm never recovered.

2. *The Campaign of 1941 in the Soviet Union.* In the autumn of 1941 after the battle of Vysma, the Germans stood exhausted but apparently victorious before Moscow. According to Jodl, the General Staff of the armed forces considered that one last energetic push would be sufficient to finish the Soviets. The German High Command had neither envisioned nor planned for a winter campaign. A sudden change in the weather brought disaster. The Red Army defense, a terrific snowstorm, and extremely unseasonable cold in the Christmas week of 1941 precipitated the strategic defeat of the German armed forces. Impatient of all restraint, Hitler publicly announced that he had more faith in his own intuition than in the judgment of his military advisers. He relieved the Commander in Chief of the Army, General von Brauschitsch. It was the turning point of the war.

3. *Stalingrad.* Even after the reverse before Moscow in 1941, Germany might have avoided defeat had it not been for the campaign in 1942 which culminated in the disaster at Stalingrad. Disregarding the military lessons of history, Hitler, instead of attacking the Soviet armies massed in the north, personally planned and directed a campaign of which the immediate objectives were to deprive the Soviet Union of her vital industries and raw materials by cutting the Volga at Stalingrad and seizing the Caucasian oil fields. Beyond these concrete objectives was evidently the Napoleonic dream of a conquest of the Middle East and India by a gigantic double envelopment with one pincer descending from the Caucasus through Tiflis and the other from North Africa across Egypt, Palestine, and the Arabian desert. The campaign collapsed before Stalingrad with the magnificent Russian defense of that city and in the northern foothills of the Caucasus, where a break-down of German transport to the front left the German armor stalled for 3 weeks for lack of fuel in the critical summer months of 1942. Field Marshal Keitel in reviewing this campaign remarks that Germany failed completely to estimate properly the reserve of Russian industrial and productive power east of the Urals. The statement of both Keitel and Jodl is

that neither was in favor of the Stalingrad campaign, but that the recommendations of the High Command were overruled by Adolf Hitler.

4. *Invasion of North Africa.* Allied landings in North Africa came as a surprise to the German High Command. Field Marshal Kesselring, who, at the time, was commanding all German forces in the Mediterranean except Rommel's desert task force, states that his headquarters did expect a landing and had requested reinforcement by a division. However, Kesselring's fears were not heeded by Hitler and Goering. Allied security and deception measures for the landing operations were found to have been highly effective. Only when the Allied fleets and convoys were streaming through the Straits of Gibraltar did the Germans realize that something very special was under way, and even then false conclusions were drawn: either that the Allies intended to land in rear of Rommel in the Middle East, or that these were British reinforcements en route to the Far East, or supplies for starving Malta. Since no advance preparations had been made by the Germans to repel such an Allied invasion of North Africa, all subsequent efforts to counter the Allies suffered from hasty improvisation. Defense continued, however, because, as Field Marshal Keitel now states, since evacuation was impossible, the Germans had only the choice of resisting or surrendering.

5. *The Invasion of France.* All German headquarters expected the Allied invasion of France. According to Colonel General Jodl, both the general direction and the strength of the initial assault in Normandy were correctly estimated; but Field Marshal Keitel states that the Germans were not sure exactly where the Allies would strike and considered Brittany as more probable because of the three major U-boat bases located in that region. Both agree that the belief of the German High Command that a second assault would be launched, probably by an army under General Patton, held large German forces in the Pas-de-Calais area. Both Keitel and Jodl believed that the invasion could be repulsed or at worst contained, and both named the Allied air arm as the decisive factor in the German failure.

Prior to the invasion, important divergencies of opinion developed between Field Marshal von Rundstedt, Commander in Chief West, and Rommel, commander of the threatened army group. Rundstedt desired to hold his armored forces in a group around Paris and in Eastern France; Rommel to push them forward to positions in readiness close to the coast. The Rommel view prevailed. Von Rundstedt was subsequently relieved by Colonel General von Kluge.

Soon after the Allied capture of Cherbourg, dissension again broke out in the High Command. Von Kluge and Rommel wished to evacuate all Southwestern France, blocking or destroying its usable ports. They believed that a continuation of the fight in Normandy could only end with the destruction of their Western armies and that they should withdraw before disintegration began. Von Kluge recommended defense on the general line: lower Seine-Paris-Fontainebleau-Massif Central. Hitler refused to accept this recommendation, relieved Kluge from command, and reappointed von Rundstedt as Commander in Chief West. Under direct instructions, Rundstedt continued the battle of Normandy to its final denouement. Hitler himself ordered the Avranches-Mortain counterattack and was much surprised when it completely failed. Keitel expressed further surprise at the audacious exploitation of the American break-through at Avranches during this counterattack, and particularly of the thrust toward Brest.

6. *The Ardennes Counterattack.* The German offensive in December, 1944 was Hitler's personal conception. According to Jodl, the objective of the attack was Antwerp. It was hoped that overcast weather would neutralize Allied air superiority, and that an exceptionally rapid initial break-through could be achieved. Other German officers believe that this operation was reckless in the extreme, in that it irreparably damaged the comparatively fresh armored divisions of the Sixth Panzer Army, the principal element of Germany's strategic reserve, at a moment when every available reserve was needed to repulse the expected Soviet attack in the east.

7. *The Crossing of the Rhine.* Even after the failure of the German counteroffensive in the Ardennes, the Germans believed that the Rhine line could be held. The loss of the Remagen bridge, however, exploded this hope. The entire Rhine defensive line had to be weakened in the attempt to contain the bridgehead, and the disorderly German retreat in the Saar and Palatinate rendered easy the subsequent drive eastward of the Allied armies toward Hamburg, Leipzig, and Munich.

Not only were the European partners of the Axis unable to coordinate their plans and resources and agree within their own nations how best to proceed, but the Eastern partner, Japan, was working in even greater discord. The Axis, as a matter of fact, existed on paper only. Eager to capitalize on the preoccupation of the Western Powers in Europe, Japan was so greedy for her own immediate conquests that she laid her strategy, not to help Germany defeat Russia and Great Britain, but to accumulate her own profit. Had the way been open Germany and Japan would have undoubtedly joined their armies in Central Asia, but to Japan this objective was secondary to looting the Far East while there was no real force to stop her.

## From the War Reports of General H. H. Arnold

Prior to the uncovering of many facts after V-E Day, it was popularly supposed that the Nazis were a ruthlessly efficient organization, with a system cleansed by purges, rallied by a deified leader, spoon-fed with propaganda, spied on by secret police, and forced by grim necessity to present a solid front to the enemy. Actually, policy, decisions, and strategy of the highest importance were often dictated by personal ambition, Nazi party feuds and pressure politics.

Germany began the war with a great numerical superiority in aircraft, and succeeded against little opposition. Consequently, the Germans delayed in making needed changes, and then made far too many. A substantial share of these changes were due to parts shortages caused by bombardment. For instance, after our attacks on plants producing ball bearings, the Daimler Benz 603 engine was modified for sleeve bearings, and was unreliable from then on—engine failures caused many accidents.

Dr. Albert Speer, Reichminister for Armaments and War Production, said, "We had blueprints every few months and then had to change or tear down the buildings. If a program lasted longer than three months it was a miracle. It was the fault of the Luftwaffe General Staff." When Speer had taken over the industry in March, 1944, there had been 50 different types of fighters being produced. And even in the drastic emergency, faced with rebuilding and dispersing the shattered industry, he could not reduce the number of types below 38.

Generalleutnant Werner Kreipe, in command of all flying training, stated that Hitler, Goering, and the General Staff never understood the significance of air power because of the ease of early German conquests. They did not, at any rate, analyze the combinations of power, and it was not until March 1, 1944, after our effective attacks on the fighter aircraft industry, that fighters were given priority over tanks, U-boats, flak guns, and V-weapons. Kreipe said that the Wehrmacht and Luftwaffe General Staffs became loaded down with Party fanatics, whose belief that quick victory could be had on the ground thwarted a pre-war Luftwaffe plan for a strategic air force.

In April, 1944, the High Command faced our bombing threat realistically and decided to go all-out for defensive fighter production. Generalleutnant Adolf Galland, commanding the fighter arm, pushed a plan calling for an eventual production of 5,000 fighters a month to combat Allied bombers and regain control of the air. He was opposed by Goering, who clung to the belief that Germany could have a great bomber force as well, despite inadequate manpower and training facilities, and a shortage of aviation fuel. The amended plan called for a reduced fighter figure and for bombers, a scheme which Galland termed "entirely unrealistic."

However, if the plan was unrealistic, upon seeing it Hitler projected it to fantasy. The ME-262 jet plane, Germany's great hope, and, we must state frankly, the greatest threat to continued bomber operations, was then in production. Under no circumstances, Hitler declared, would the ME-262 be used as anything but a bomber. Messerschmitt had promised him that it would carry a 1,000-kilogram bomb. Actually, it never carried more than a 500-kilogram bomb, but the Nazis were obsessed with the idea of retaliation bombing at any cost.

Hitler named the ME-262 the "Blitzbomber," and vetoed the scheme of Goering and Galland to compromise by equipping it with a bomb rack and using it as a fighter-bomber. Hitler persisted in this amazing decision from April until October, a period which saw the invasion and the sweep across France. As a bomber, the ME-262 did nothing. The ME-262's which our airmen fought during that period were a few Galland had secured, despite Hitler's edict, for an "Experimental Unit." In October, when Hitler relented, only a handful were released to the fighter arm, and it was 1945 before the bomber idea was finally discarded.

## Some Results of Allied Bombardment

Speer estimated that he could have made from 30 to 50 per cent more fighter planes, but for our bombing.

The Reich had a labor shortage despite millions of imported slave workers. The repair and reconstruction of bomb damage, defensive measures, and labor wastage in dispersing industry, digging underground factories, building railroads and power lines and living quarters at dispersal sites—every effort to combat or escape air attack drew upon manpower. Speer said between 250,000 and 300,000 men were employed in the removal of bomb damage in the chemical industry (including oil), and in all industry about one million men. This figure was for clearing away bomb damage, and did not include those engaged in reconstruction or in manufacturing materials for replacement.

Bomb damage multiplied.

The first attack on an oil plant was relatively easy to repair. Subsequent bombings compounded the damage; pipe joints sprang leaks far from any bomb strike, valves failed to work, linings fell out of furnaces, distillation units had to be overhauled. There was not enough manpower to go around. Even so, Speer was never able to stop the use of men and materials for expansion of basic production, which cost manpower and enormous amounts of critical materials for planned future schedules at the cost of armament production in existing plants. Despite military necessity, Germany was never able to allot more than approximately 60 per cent of its raw materials to armament production. The demand for consumer goods remained inordinately high because of air attacks.

By February, 1945, Germany's transportation system was overstrained as the result of air attack.

Every move of the dispersal program for industry put an added load on transportation. Machinery had to be shipped, building materials transported, plus everything required by the workers. When factories had been established, one part made here, another there, a third somewhere else, there was a constant shuttling of components before the final assembly was ready to ship. General Jodl said: "It was most annoying to have to route artillery from Essen to central Germany to equip and test fire, and then to ship it to an Army camp up front."

Putting factories underground in the effort to escape bombing created new problems.

In June, 1944, the Junkers aircraft engine factory at Magdeburg had been moved because of air attack. The main body of the plant was put underground at the notorious Mittlewerk at Niedersachswerfen, near Nordhausen. The supercharger and small components section was put in a former chocolate factory at Hasserode. The injection pump section went to Lengefeld, while the propeller section went to Ebersbach. And these were temporary moves until a new underground installation near Woffleben was completed.

At Mittlewerk, because of bad ventilation, workers had headaches. It was necessary to work three eight-hour shifts instead of two twelves, as formerly. Metal dust lay an inch thick on the floor of the polishing shop, and workers wore masks. Temperature had to be too cold for comfort, or the limestone roof would fall. Two roof falls killed several workers and injured others. Following these accidents the compressor rotor polishing shop was moved outside to a former flour mill. The local water was unfit to drink and a supply had to be hauled in. Sanitation problems were left unsolved; employees had to walk out of the long tunnels to latrines at the foot of the hill outside. Food difficulties arose in the area from the influx of workers.

Speer himself summed up the production end of dispersal underground: "One cannot win aerial warfare through cement and tunnels."

## Our Attacks on Nazi Transportation Continue

The bombing of oil production had all but eliminated civilian trucking. The German Armies had discontinued the use of trucks in large measure except on the battle fronts, and the air threat was such that they no longer kept big supply dumps near the front but required the railroads to bring supplies from the rear as needed.

The industrial burden on the railroad system was graphically described by Franz Hayler, Secretary of State, Economic and Political Counselor to Field Marshal Kesselring, who said that in February, 1945, Germany's entire war production for a month and a half was loaded on railroad cars in transit—components going here, assemblies going there, raw materials somewhere else.

The Germans had a large repair organization. They could run a line through a bombed marshaling yard, and get trains running, but that left the marshaling yard useless to do its job. Another switch yard, farther away, had to take its place.

The bombing of railroads was cumulative in effect.

By the summer of 1944 the Germans were unable to deliver stocks of coal to war factories in preparation for winter. Most coal came from the Ruhr, and normally much of it was shipped to Northern and Central Germany via the Dortmund-Ems and Mittelland canals during the summer (the canals were iced over in the winter). The RAF had repeatedly bombed strategic points on these canals, the Gland by-pass of the Dortmund-Ems, and the Gravenhorst embankment of the Mittelland, with the result that these important water routes were open to traffic scarcely a fortnight during six months. The railroads could not take the added burden. It was either more coal or less armaments. The Germans made a gamble. They didn't ship coal in the summer to store for next winter's factories. Perhaps they saw the end, or perhaps they could do nothing about it. They didn't store coal.

Daily shipments of Ruhr coal by the end of 1944 had dropped from 14,000 tons to 6,000. In November, Speer had ordered stocks of coal on hand to be used up for armament manufacture, regardless of where the next lump was coming from. By February, 1945, the coal shortage was paralyzing the German armament industry. The Russian drive had cut off coal from Silesia, which had furnished more than half the coal to run the railroads themselves. Germany depended on the harassed railway system to get coal from the Ruhr and Saar. In mid-winter the *Reichsbahn* was faced with getting and distributing coal for industry, totally reorganizing the complex system of shipment priorities, and redistributing locomotives and rolling stock. This in itself was a tremendous task.

## One of the Largest Missions of the War

Such was the situation on February 22, 1945 when the Allied Air Eorces flew Operation Clarion. The target: German transportation.

On the morning of February 22, 1945, more than ten thousand Allied planes were airborne from their bases in England, France, Holland, Belgium, and Italy. The 200 individual targets covered an area of nearly a quarter of a million square miles. The object was to paralyze the *Reichsbahn.*

Instead of bombing from 25,000 feet, the heavies were to glide over the targets as low as 5,000 feet. Instead of operating in huge formations, they were to break up over Germany into groups and squadrons, and fan out for the many targets, with and without fighter escort.

The Luftwaffe was still potent, and our Operations men paced the floor the night of the twenty-first. They studied the skies next morning, when the mission was airborne. Major General Orvil Anderson, Eighth AF Chief of Operations, said: "We could lose three hundred planes today, but we won't." He gambled on the German inability to improvise quickly to meet a new situation. He said: "By the time that Gauleiter gets through thumbing the pages of his manual, the boys will be coming home."

And, true enough, Operation Clarion was a "milk run." All over Germany bombs exploded on signal control points, marshalling yards, main lines, level crossings, embankments, bridges, viaducts, round-houses, over-passes, small junctions. Fighters and fighter-bombers attacked rolling stock. Herr Dorpmuller's rail repair organization was swamped. Immediately, according to General Buhl, war production was cut in half. Generalmajor Peters said traffic was reduced 90 per cent.

Operation Clarion marked the end of large scale mobility for the German Armies.

### The Nazi Defense of the Ruhr

Hitler's last chance to hold his Western front was the Ruhr, one of the world's great arsenals. The heart of the Ruhr consists of an industrial belt east of the Rhine running east and west, some forty miles long and from ten to fifteen wide, lying mainly between the Ruhr River and the Rhine-Herne Canal. The area is built up, and had a normal population of three and a quarter million. In the Ruhr were coal mines, steel plants, armament works, chemical plants, and many other industrial installations.

Paced by the Ninth Air Force, Allied air power began sealing off the Ruhr, as it had the Normandy battle front in 1944. The Germans used all their ingenuity to keep traffic moving with armaments and supplies. The railroad repair system was highly organized, with concentrations of foreign labor and prisoners of war in reserve at likely points of attack to run lines through bombed marshaling yards, and throw up replacement bridges.

In the Ruhr campaign, as in Operation Clarion, air power set out to swamp the repair facilities.

In addition to the Dortmund-Ems and Mittelland canals, there were five main rail lines and a number of subsidiaries fanning out from the Ruhr. The plan called for isolating the Ruhr district and smashing the extensive transportation system within it. Air attacks began in late February on the bridges in a line from Bremen south to Marburg, thence southwest to Coblenz on the Rhine. This was called a line of interdiction; nothing was to cross that line if air power could prevent it. There were 16 bridges on this line of interdiction. In 40 attacks by 1,800 heavy and medium bombers, 14 were destroyed, or made impassable. Of the two still standing on March 24, bombs had cut approaching rail lines. The line of interdiction was maintained. Transport inside the line was hammered continually.

### Allied Ground Troops Advance

Meanwhile Allied Ground Forces made a splendid drive forward early in March. The Rhineland was lost to the Germans, along with the flower of three armies. An Allied column thrust down the natural corridor from Euskirchen, broke the German 74th Corps, reached the Rhine at Remagen, and crossed to make a bridgehead. The Fifth Panzer Army was pocketed and cut to ribbons, and the German Seventh Army had collapsed in the southern Eifel.

For the Germans, the war from here on was chaos.

On March 1, 1945 an order had come that under no circumstances could any Nazi staff officer cross back over the Rhine. Two days later the order came to retreat across the Rhine. When the American ground forces gained the Remagen bridgehead, General Model ordered Bayerlein to plan an attack to wipe it out. Next day Model rejected the plan. Two days later Field Marshal Kesselring arrived as Commander of the West, saw the plan, and was furious that it had not been carried out.

In a rage, Model dressed Bayerlein down, and turned 1,500 reinforcement troops intended for Bayerlein to a commander of a Volksgrenadier Division named Tollsdorf, an incompetent whose "Division" consisted of 200 men with practically no arms. Eight swimmers tried to go down river to bomb the bridge, and were never heard of again. Hitler ordered the bridgehead wiped out with V-2's. Nothing came of the order. Five officers were shot because of the Remagen affair, and a bridge complex swept over the officer corps, causing the blowing of many bridges without regard to military necessity. Because of the bombardment of railroads, tanks had to be driven from railheads far to the rear; of 42 new King Tigers sent to reinforce Bayerlein, 34 were worn out on the way and never reached him. The Eleventh Panzer left its entire supply column in a wood near Altenkirchen for want of gasoline.

### Air's Role in the Crossing of the Rhine

At 0600 hours on the morning of March 24, the 21st Army Group, British and Americans, began crossing the Rhine north of the Ruhr River. At 1000 hours, troops of the First Allied Airborne Army, carried in heavily escorted aircraft and gliders of the United States 9th Troop Carrier Command and the RAF 38th and 46th Groups, began landing on the opposite side of the Rhine.

In seventy-two hours preceding the airborne landing, AAF heavies and mediums flew 2,090 sorties in 56 attacks against small towns and villages in the area, which had been turned into strongpoints. More than 8,500 tons of bombs were dropped on communication centers. On March 21 and 22, some 1,200 Eighth AF heavies pounded ten airfields in the area. Escorting fighters knocked 53 enemy fighters out of the sky and destroyed 116 on the ground. Fighter-bombers and fighters of Second British Tactical Air Force and U.S. Nineteenth Tactical Air Command joined in the assault.

On the day of the landing, Allied aircraft flew more than 7,000 sorties over the battlefield and the area bounded by the line of interdiction stretching from Bremen to Coblenz. Ninth AF mediums and the Second British Tactical Air Force hit twenty-three flak positions. Fighter-bombers joined the task of silencing enemy flak before the airborne trains arrived. Throughout the day the Air Forces gave direct cooperation to the landing, hitting communication centers and defense points, gun and mortar sites, forward positions and strongpoints. Fighter-bombers flew armed reconnaissance against the enemy lines of communication. From Italy, the Fifteenth Air Force sent 150 heavies escorted by five groups of fighters on a 1,500-mile round trip to Berlin. A tank factory was bombed, and this attack drew off enemy fighters in Central Germany who otherwise would have gone to the Rhine.

Despite ground haze and smoke, all but two per cent of the paratroopers and three per cent of the gliders made successful landings, settling down 14,365 men, 109 tons of ammunition and explosives, 695 vehicles, 113 artillery weapons, 765 pieces of equipment and supplies. And Eighth Air Force Liberators dropped 582 tons of supplies and equipment that day.

The airborne landing was successful. Ground troops began closing a great pincer around the Ruhr and the German armies in it.

The enemy counted on supplying himself within one of the world's greatest arsenals. Hopes were high at first among the 17 German divisions. There was food for a month and a half. Motor fuel would be available because of the many benzol producers in the Ruhr. Ammunition production could be continued and deliveries made on the spot.

### The Luftwaffe's Final Effort

During the Ruhr campaign, the Luftwaffe was heard from once more.

Goering had begun plans for this last try in March. In a special Order of the Day Luftwaffe pilots were asked to volunteer for a secret, dangerous duty. Some 300 were selected and sent to Stendal for a ten-day course in ramming training, most of which consisted of getting them into the right frame of mind by lectures, films, and Nazi indoctrination. They were taught ramming technique—the technique of flying out of the sun on a line astern of the bombers, opening fire at extreme range, and holding it until the final sharp ramming dive aimed just forward of the bomber's tail. Unlike the Japs, the pilots were allowed to bail out if possible. Eighty pilots were equipped with FW-190's and sent to Prague to operate against the Fifteenth Army Air Force heavies. The remainder were given ME-109's and organized into a unit of four *Gruppen* known as *Sonderkommando Elbe* and given such fancy names as *Falken* and *Raubvogel*, or birds of prey.

On April 7 these groups were ready. At 0930 hours they were alerted; the Eighth AF was forming. Thirteen hundred heavies and 850 fighters were in the air. At 1116 hours *Sonderkommando Elbe* rose to do and/or die. In their ears were dinned patriotic music and exhortations, and the pilots' radio transmitters had been removed from their planes so that they could not talk back.

When it was over, 65 German planes had gone down before our fighters; the bombers' guns brought the total to 104, and there is no estimate of how many enemy planes were destroyed by our 22 bombers and 3 fighters which were lost. The final "Big Blow" had failed. And we went on. In the two-week period of April 5–19, the Eighth and Ninth Air Forces almost annihilated the Luftwaffe, between them destroying 3,484 planes in the air and on the ground.

As for the Ruhr pocket, it vanished in the 18 days from April 1 to 18. German commanders blamed the breakdown of distribution on air attack. It was impossible to supply the ammunition factories or ship the finished product. An ammunition dump was useful only if a unit happened to be alongside it. The artillery regiment of the 59th Volksgrenadier Division had plenty of food, but there was no way of sending it to the infantry regiments of the same division, some of which had been without food four days upon surrender. Rear echelons were stripped of weapons. Even so, infantrymen of the 176th Volksgrenadier Division were captured unarmed. Tanks, being mobile, could get fuel and ammunition from the dumps, but they ran out of spare parts. Fighting units on the front had no fuel to send trucks back to the dumps. Dump staffs found their trucks overburdened with the necessity of constantly shifting location, and could spare few vehicles to deliver to the front. And as with tanks, there were no spare parts. Dump crews burned their gasoline, unable to evacuate it, while front line crews destroyed tanks and artillery because there was no fuel to move them.

The air interdiction of the Ruhr was complete. On April 16, General Carl A. Spaatz, Commanding the United States Strategic Air Forces in Europe, announced the end of the strategic air war as such. Our big job was done; there remained only the mopping up.

The AAF's organization for these successive steps in aerial conquest of Germany had undergone many changes since the early days of August, 1942. For the final phase we were formed into a series of air armies working in close and constant cooperation, with flexibility of operations as the keynote. The United States Strategic Air Forces in Europe, under General Spaatz, comprised not only the Eighth Air Force of Lieutenant General James H. Doolittle, with three air divisions, but also the Mediterranean-based Fifteenth Air Force under Lieutenant General Nathan F. Twining and the Twelfth Air Force, under the command of Major General John K. Cannon. In addition to these powerful Air Forces was the tactical Ninth Air Force, under Lieutenant General Hoyt S. Vandenberg, comprised of medium and attack bombers, fighters, and fighter-bombers. Directly under SHAEF was the First Allied Airborne Army, commanded by Lieutenant General Lewis H. Brereton.

Although our air organization was adjusted to meet the needs of a changing strategic and tactical situation, we held steadfastly, despite early discouragement and temporary setbacks, to our over-all objective of fatally weakening from the air the enemy's will and ability to continue the war. We achieved that objective.

This does not mean that we won the air war alone. We must never forget that the air war over Europe was a case of the closest joint effort with the RAF, from beginning to end. At times the AAF and the RAF employed different tactics and their secondary objectives differed, but at all times it was done with complete understanding of each other's capabilities and limitations. A case in point is the coordinated efforts of RAF night bombing and AAF daylight bombing of Nazi industry: each complemented the other.

Another notable example of cooperation is the use of Soviet bases by the AAF for shuttle bombing. Under this arrangement, at a critical stage of the air war, Mediterranean-based and England-based heavies were able to extend their range greatly and to strike at vital industrial targets the Nazis believed they had placed beyond the reach of air attack.

With the D-Day invasion, another partner, the Ground Forces, joined the all-out battle against Germany proper. Nazi war industry had been shattered by air attack, the Luftwaffe had been crippled, but there still remained huge and powerful Nazi Ground Armies to be crushed before final victory. The magnificent job done by Allied Ground Forces is a matter of record. But again it was a case of cooperation, this time between Allied Ground and Air Forces. Strategic bombing continued as before, whereas tactical air operations shifted from the role of softening up for invasion to cooperation with the invasion forces in battle.

The flexible organization of the AAF was suited to this dual role. Our based-in-Britain heavies could at a moment's notice turn from a strategic mission to such tactical roles as bridge destruction. When bases were gained in France, our medium and attack bombers, fighters and fighter-bombers became more deadly; and as airfields were secured closer and closer to Germany, and even within Germany itself, they could more and more effectively combine strategic strikes with their tactical operations.

It was at this point, with distance no longer a factor in differentiating strategic from tactical operations, that the air war reached its ultimate objective.

This objective reached, we could look back almost with amazement to those dozen Fortresses pioneering daylight strategic bombing on August 17, 1942, through the long uphill fight of 1943; the bombing of rubber production; the shock of losing 60 bombers in the attack on the Schweinfurt ball-bearing works; the fight against weather as the Luftwaffe grew in potency in 1943; the development of long-range fighters that could give us escort all the way; the fine days in February, 1944, which permitted our all-out offensive against the German Air Force; the assault on V-weapon sites months before the first buzz bomb hit London; the pounding of airfields and transportation along the "invasion coast"; the opening of the strategic oil campaign on April 5, 1944 from Italy and on April 11 from England; D-Day on June 6; the sealing off of the battlefield on the Seine-Loire triangle; carpet bombing for the break-through at St. Lo, July 25; the sweep across France, the Ardennes, the Rhineland; Operation Clarion; the Ruhr; and finally, Germany prostrate under nearly a million and a half tons of bombs. Our total aircraft losses on combat missions were 18,418; the enemy lost 32,921. Some 284,000 airborne troops had been transported by 9th Troop Carrier Command, 210,000 casualties from all services evacuated. Millions of propaganda leaflets had fluttered from the skies.

We saw that mistakes had been made. Strategic bombing was a new military weapon, and we had had to learn many things as we went along, but we took pride in the job as a whole. Nazi ground commanders, Luftwaffe generals, manufacturers, politicians, transportation men saw our air domination as the root of their disaster, particularly the incessant bleeding of industry by strategic bombing, especially the oil campaign and the cumulative dislocation of transportation. And it was the air threat, according to Speer, the certainty that the bombers would keep coming, day after day, week after week, that brought the final collapse.

# The Decision to Use the Atomic Bomb

BY HARRY S. TRUMAN

THE HISTORIC MESSAGE of the first explosion of an atomic bomb was flashed to me in a message from Secretary of War Stimson on the morning of July 16. The most secret and the most daring enterprise of the war had succeeded. We were now in possession of a weapon that would not only revolutionize war but could alter the course of history and civilization. This news reached me at Potsdam the day after I had arrived for the conference of the Big Three.

Preparations were being rushed for the test atomic explosion at Alamogordo, New Mexico, at the time I had to leave for Europe, and on the voyage over I had been anxiously awaiting word on the results. I had been told of many predictions by the scientists, but no one was certain of the outcome of this full-scale atomic explosion. As I read the message from Stimson, I realized that the test not only met the most optimistic expectation of the scientists but that the United States had in its possession an explosive force of unparalleled power.

Stimson flew to Potsdam the next day to see me and brought with him the full details of the test. I received him at once and called in Secretary of State Byrnes, Admiral Leahy, General Marshall, General Arnold, and Admiral King to join us at my office at the Little White House. We reviewed our military strategy in the light of this revolutionary development. We were not ready to make use of this weapon against the Japanese, although we did not know as yet what effect the new weapon might have, physically or psychologically, when used against the enemy. For that reason the military advised that we go ahead with the existing military plans for the invasion of the Japanese home islands.

At Potsdam, as elsewhere, the secret of the atomic bomb was kept closely guarded. We did not extend the very small circle of Americans who knew about it. Churchill naturally knew about the atomic bomb project from its very beginning, because it had involved the pooling of British and American technical skill.

On July 24 I casually mentioned to Stalin that we had a new weapon of unusual destructive force. The Russian Premier showed no special interest. All he said was that he was glad to hear it and hoped we would make "good use of it against the Japanese."

A month before the test explosion of the atomic bomb the service Secretaries and the Joint Chiefs of Staff had laid their detailed plans for the defeat of Japan before me for approval. There had apparently been some differences of opinion as to the best route to be followed, but these had evidently been reconciled, for when General Marshall had presented his plan for a two-phase invasion of Japan, Admiral King and General Arnold had supported the proposal heartily.

The Army plan envisaged an amphibious landing in the fall of 1945 on the island of Kyushu, the southernmost of the Japanese home

---

From Harry S. Truman, *Memoirs*, I, *Year of Decisions* (New York, Doubleday and Company, 1955), 415–421. 

islands. This would be accomplished by our Sixth Army, under the command of General Walter Krueger. The first landing would then be followed approximately four months later by a second great invasion, which would be carried out by our Eighth and Tenth Armies, followed by the First Army transferred from Europe, all of which would go ashore in the Kanto plains area near Tokyo. In all, it had been estimated that it would require until the late fall of 1946 to bring Japan to her knees.

This was a formidable conception, and all of us realized fully that the fighting would be fierce and the losses heavy. But it was hoped that some of Japan's forces would continue to be preoccupied in China and others would be prevented from reinforcing the home islands if Russia were to enter the war.

There was, of course, always the possibility that the Japanese might choose to surrender sooner. Our air and fleet units had begun to inflict heavy damage on industrial and urban sites in Japan proper. Except in China, the armies of the Mikado had been pushed back everywhere in relentless successions of defeats.

Acting Secretary of State Grew had spoken to me in late May about issuing a proclamation that would urge the Japanese to surrender but would assure them that we would permit the Emperor to remain as head of the state. Grew backed this with arguments taken from his ten years' experience as our Ambassador in Japan, and I told him that I had already given thought to this matter myself and that it seemed to me a sound idea. Grew had a draft of a proclamation with him, and I instructed him to send it by the customary channels to the Joint Chiefs and the State-War-Navy Co-ordinating Committee in order that we might get the opinions of all concerned before I made my decision.

On June 18 Grew reported that the proposal had met with the approval of his Cabinet colleagues and of the Joint Chiefs. The military leaders also discussed the subject with me when they reported the same day. Grew, however, favored issuing the proclamation at once, to coincide with the closing of the campaign on Okinawa, while the service chiefs were of the opinion that we should wait until we were ready to follow a Japanese refusal with the actual assault of our invasion forces.

It was my decision then that the proclamation to Japan should be issued from the forthcoming conference at Potsdam. This, I believed, would clearly demonstrate to Japan and to the world that the Allies were united in their purpose. By that time, also, we might know more about two matters of significance for our future effort: the participation of the Soviet Union and the atomic bomb. We knew that the bomb would receive its first test in Mid-July. If the test of the bomb was successful, I wanted to afford Japan a clear chance to end the fighting before we made use of this newly gained power. If the test should fail, then it would be even more important to us to bring about a surrender before we had to make a physical conquest of Japan. General Marshall told me that it might cost half a million American lives to force the enemy's surrender on his home grounds.

But the test was now successful. The entire development of the atomic bomb had been dictated by military considerations. The idea of the atomic bomb had been suggested to President Roosevelt by the famous and brilliant Dr. Albert Einstein, and its development turned out to be a vast undertaking. It was the achievement of the combined efforts of science, industry, labor, and the military, and it had no parallel in history. The men in charge and their staffs worked under extremely high pressure, and the whole enormous task required the services of more than one hundred thousand men and immense quantities of material. It required over two and a half years and necessitated the expenditure of two and a half billions of dollars.

Only a handful of the thousands of men who worked in these plants knew what they were producing. So strict was the secrecy imposed that even some of the highest-ranking officials in Washington had not the slightest idea of what was going on. I did not. Before 1939 it had been generally agreed among scientists that it was theoretically possible to release energy from the atom. In 1940 we had begun to pool with Great Britain all scientific knowledge useful to war, although Britain was at war at that time and we were not. Following this—in 1942—we learned that the Germans were at work on a method to harness atomic energy for use as a weapon of war. This, we understood, was to be added to the V-1 and V-2 rockets with which they hoped to conquer the world. They failed, of course, and for this we can thank Providence. But now a race was on to make the atomic bomb—a race that became "the battle of the laboratories."

It was under the general policy of pooling knowledge between our nation and Great Britain that research on the atomic bomb started in such feverish secrecy. American and British scientists joined in the race against the Germans. We in America had available a great number of distinguished scientists in many related fields of knowledge, and we also had another great advantage. We could provide the tremendous industrial and economic resources required for the project—a vastly expensive project—without injury to our war production program. Furthermore, our plants were far removed from the reach of enemy bombing. Britain, whose scientists had initiated the project and were contributing much of the original atomic data, was constantly exposed to enemy bombing and, when she started the atomic research, also faced the possibility of invasion.

For these reasons Roosevelt and Churchill agreed to pool the research and concentrate all of the work on the development of the project within the United States. Working together with the British, we thus made it possible to achieve a great scientific triumph in the field of atomic energy. Nevertheless, basic and historic as this event was, it had to be considered at the time as relatively incidental to the far-flung war we were fighting in the Pacific at terrible cost in American lives.

We could hope for a miracle, but the daily tragedy of a bitter war crowded in on us. We labored to construct a weapon of such overpowering force that the enemy could be forced to yield swiftly once we could resort to it. This was the primary aim of our secret and vast effort. But we also had to carry out the enormous effort of our basic and traditional military plans.

The task of creating the atomic bomb had been entrusted to a special unit of the Army Corps of Engineers, the so-called Manhattan District, headed by Major General Leslie R. Groves. The primary effort, however, had come from British and American scientists working in laboratories and offices scattered throughout the nation.

Dr. J. Robert Oppenheimer, the distinguished physicist from the University of California, had set up the key establishment in the whole process at Los Alamos, New Mexico. More than any other one man, Oppenheimer is to be credited with the achievement of the completed bomb.

My own knowledge of these developments had come about only after I became President, when Secretary Stimson had given me the full story. He had told me at that time that the project was nearing completion and that a bomb could be expected within another four months. It was at his suggestion, too, that I had then set up a committee of top men and had asked them to study with great care the implications the new weapon might have for us.

Secretary Stimson headed this group as chairman, and the other members were George L. Harrison, president of the New York Life Insurance Company, who was then serving as a special assistant to the Secretary of War; James F. Byrnes, as my personal representative; Ralph A. Bard, Under Secretary of the Navy; Assistant Secretary William L. Clayton for the State Department; and three of our most renowned scientists—Dr. Vannevar Bush, president of the Carnegie Institution of Washington and Director of the Office of Scientific Research and Development; Dr. Karl T. Compton, president of the Massachusetts Institute of Technology and Chief of Field Service in the Office of Scientific Research and Development; and Dr. James B. Conant, president of Harvard University and chairman of the National Defense Research Committee.

This committee was assisted by a group of scientists, of whom those most prominently connected with the development of the atomic bomb were Dr. Oppenheimer, Dr. Arthur H. Compton, Dr. E. O. Lawrence, and the Italian-born Dr. Enrico Fermi. The conclusions reached by these men, both in the advisory committee of scientists and in the larger committee, were brought to me by Secretary Stimson on June 1.

It was their recommendation that the bomb be used against the enemy as soon as it could be done. They recommended further that it should be used without specific warning and against a target that would clearly show its devastating strength. I had realized, of course, that an atomic bomb explosion would inflict damage and casualties beyond imagination. On the other hand, the scientific advisers of the committee reported: "We can propose no technical demonstration likely to bring an end to the war; we see no acceptable alternative to direct military use." It was their conclusion that no technical demonstration they might propose, such as over a deserted island, would be likely to bring the war to an end. It had to be used against an enemy target.

The final decision of where and when to use the atomic bomb was up to me. Let there be no mistake about it. I regarded the bomb as a military weapon and never had any doubt that it should be used. The top military advisers to the President recommended its use, and when I talked to Churchill he unhesitatingly told me that he favored the use of the atomic bomb if it might aid to end the war.

In deciding to use this bomb I wanted to make sure that it would be used as a weapon of war in the manner prescribed by the laws of war. That meant that I wanted it dropped on a military target. I had told Stimson that the bomb should be dropped as nearly as possible upon a war production center of prime military importance.

Stimson's staff had prepared a list of cities in Japan that might serve as targets. Kyoto, though favored by General Arnold as a center of military activity, was eliminated when Secretary Stimson pointed out that it was a cultural and religious shrine of the Japanese.

Four cities were finally recommended as targets: Hiroshima, Kokura, Niigata, and Nagasaki. They were listed in that order as targets for the first attack. The order of selection was in accordance with the military importance of these cities, but allowance would be given for weather conditions at the time of the bombing. Before the selected targets were approved as proper for military purposes, I personally went over them in detail with Stimson, Marshall, and Arnold, and we discussed the matter of timing and the final choice of the first target.

General Spaatz, who commanded the Strategic Air Forces, which would deliver the bomb on the target, was given some latitude as to when and on which of the four targets the bomb would be dropped. That was necessary because of weather and other operational considerations. In order to get preparations under way, the War Department was given orders to instruct General Spaatz that the first bomb would be dropped as soon after August 3 as weather would permit. The order to General Spaatz read as follows:

JULY 24, 1945

TO: GENERAL CARL SPAATZ
COMMANDING GENERAL
UNITED STATES ARMY STRATEGIC AIR FORCES

1. The 509 Composite Group, 20th Air Force will deliver its first special bomb as soon as weather will permit visual bombing after about 3 August 1945 on one of the targets: Hiroshima, Kokura, Niigata and Nagasaki. To carry military and civilian scientific personnel from the War Department to observe and record the effects of the explosion of the bomb, additional aircraft will accompany the airplane carrying the bomb. The observing planes will stay several miles distant from the point of impact of the bomb.

2. Additional bombs will be delivered on the above targets as soon as made ready by the project staff. Further instructions will be issued concerning targets other than those listed above.

3. Dissemination of any and all information concerning the use of the weapon against Japan is reserved to the Secretary of War and the President of the United States. No communique on the subject or release of information will be issued by Commanders in the field without specific prior authority. Any news stories will be sent to the War Department for special clearance.

4. The foregoing directive is issued to you by direction and with the approval of the Secretary of War and the Chief of Staff, U.S.A. It is desired that you personally deliver one copy of this directive to General MacArthur and one copy to Admiral Nimitz for their information.

/s/ Thos. T. Handy
General, GSC
Acting Chief of Staff

With this order the wheels were set in motion for the first use of an atomic weapon against a military target. I had made the decision. I also instructed Stimson that the order would stand unless I notified him that the Japanese reply to our ultimatum was acceptable.

A specialized B-29 unit, known as the 509th Composite Group, had been selected for the task, and seven of the modified B-29's, with pilots and crews, were ready and waiting for orders. Meanwhile ships and planes were rushing the materials for the bomb and specialists to assemble them to the Pacific island of Tinian in the Marianas.

On July 28 Radio Tokyo announced that the Japanese government would continue to fight. There was no formal reply to the joint ultimatum of the United States, the United Kingdom, and China. There was no alternative now. The bomb was scheduled to be dropped after August 3 unless Japan surrendered before that day.

On August 6, the fourth day of the journey home from Potsdam, came the historic news that shook the world. I was eating lunch with members of the *Augusta*'s crew when Captain Frank Graham, White House Map Room watch officer, handed me the following message:

TO THE PRESIDENT

FROM THE SECRETARY OF WAR

Big bomb dropped on Hiroshima August 5 at 7:15 P.M. Washington time. First reports indicate complete success which was even more conspicuous than earlier test.

I was greatly moved. I telephoned Byrnes aboard ship to give him the news and then said to the group of sailors around me: "This is the greatest thing in history. It's time for us to get home."

# Lessons of World War II

## From the War Reports of Fleet Admiral Ernest J. King

IN DECEMBER, 1941 the United States faced seasoned enemies, who not only had long been preparing for war but who had actually been waging it for several years. Within the limited facilities and means available throughout the years of peace, the United States Navy had, however, equipped itself with weapons the equal of, or superior to, those of other navies and had laid the groundwork for still further development. During the war the science and industry of this country and our Allies were mobilized to apply existing scientific knowledge to the perfection of these weapons and the development of new and more deadly means of waging war. As a result the United States Navy was able to maintain the technical advantage over the navies of our enemies, which contributed so materially to the outcome of World War II.

The means of accomplishing this were not so much directed toward making new discoveries, as toward the exploitation of the skills and techniques which civilian scientists had already cultivated in years of peace. When war appeared imminent, the War and Navy Departments and the National Academy of Sciences gave close attention to the most profitable manner of utilizing the strength of American science in military and naval research. It was decided to attempt a solution involving the maximum flexibility and initiative, in which the fundamental principle would be cooperation between science and the armed forces, rather than to bring the scientists into military and naval laboratories, as was done in England. The principle proved thoroughly sound. The arrangement adopted was the establishment by executive order of the Office of Scientific Research and Development, which had as its scientific and technical working bodies the National Defense Research Council, the Medical Research Council, and later the Office of Field Service. To assure full integration of the potentialities of these organizations with the Navy's own research and development program and the needs of the service, the late Secretary Knox, in July, 1941, established the office of Coordinator of Research and Development. Throughout the war, the development of new weapons and devices has been accelerated by the teamwork between the users, the scientists, the engineer-designers and the producers.

The devices and weapons resulting from the research and development program have been put to use in every phase of naval warfare. Particular examples, cited because of their complexity and diversification, are amphibious warfare, carrier warfare, submarine and antisubmarine warfare. In each of these cases, our combat effectiveness has been materially increased by improvements in communications, navigational devices, fire control, detection equipment, firepower, aircraft performance (range, speed, armament, handling characteristics) and by advanced training methods and equipment.

Perhaps the greatest technological advances of the entire war have been made in the field of electronics, both within the naval laboratories and in collaboration with the Office of Scientific Research and Development. Pre-existing radar sets were developed and new models created for ship- and air-borne search, fire control, and for accurate long-range navigation. Identification and recognition equipment were developed for use in conjunction with radar systems. New and highly efficient short-range radio telephones were used for tactical communication. In the successful antisubmarine campaign in the Atlantic, small radio-sono-buoys were used; these, when dropped from aircraft, listened for the noise made by a submarine and automatically relayed the information to the searching plane. Great strides have been made in electronic antisubmarine detection equipment. Underwater echo-ranging gear and listening equipment have been improved in quality and extended in function since the outbreak of the war. Countermeasures have been developed for jamming enemy radar and communication systems, disrupting the control signals for his guided missiles, and counteracting his measures to jam our own equipment.

The foundation for our shipboard radar systems had been laid before the war. The earliest observations or radio phenomena of the kind that are exploited by radar were made at the Naval Research Laboratory by groups working with Dr. A. H. Taylor and Dr. R. N. Page, and the military possibilities were immediately grasped by these scientists and by Rear Admiral H. G. Bowen, then Director of the Laboratory. Because of this, at the outset of the war, our Navy alone had on its ships a search radar specifically designed for shipboard use. We had already incorporated in these radars the technical development of using a single antenna for transmission and reception. Radar of this type contributed to the victories of the Coral Sea, Midway, and Guadalcanal. Over 26,000 sets of air-borne radar equipment were produced from the Naval Research Laboratory's redesign of British air-borne equipment. Ours was the first navy to install radar in submarines. Similarly a highly efficient super-sonic echo-ranging gear for submarine and antisubmarine warfare had been completely developed, and was installed before the war began. The success of all these electronic devices can be traced back to intensive early development of new types of vacuum tubes.

Initially, from want of experience against an enemy attacking with the persistence demonstrated by the Japanese, our antiaircraft batteries were inadequate. Particularly was this true in the case of automatic weapon batteries, consisting at that time of the .50-caliber and 1.1-inch machine guns. The main antiaircraft batteries in the fleet, consisting of 5-inch and 3-inch main batteries were controlled by directors employing optical range information. Although antiaircraft fire-control radar was under development, no installations were operative in the fleet.

By the time Japan surrendered, our defenses had been revolutionized. The fleet was equipped with accurate antiaircraft fire-control radar. Our antiaircraft gun defenses consisted of multiple power-driven 40-millimeter mounts, 20-millimeter mounts, and 5-inch twin and single mounts, many of which were controlled by small intermediate-range radar-fed gun directors. The VT, or proximity influence fuse, initially sponsored by the Navy and by the Office of Scientific Research and Development, marked a radical change from previous methods of detonating a projectile and vastly increased the effectiveness of antiaircraft defenses.

At the end of the war, the 8-inch rapid-fire turret had been developed and was ready for introduction to the fleet. Completely automatic in action, it can be used against ship, aircraft, or land targets. The guns are loaded from the handling rooms automatically and are automatically laid.

When the threat of the German magnetic mines became known in 1939, the Navy immediately mobilized scientific talent and industrial capacity to produce a countermeasure. Several methods of demagnetizing our ships were developed. These were applied before Pearl Harbor to all combatant vessels, and later to all other vessels, and were of material assistance in maintaining the safety of our vital shipping lanes. At the same time, acoustic and magnetic firing devices were developed and produced in quantity for our mines and depth charges. Electric torpedoes were developed to supplement the air-stream torpedo, which at the outbreak of war was our weapon of underwater attack.

Rockets and rocket launchers were developed, with the assistance of California Institute of Technology and other agencies, for use on board ships and aircraft. Appropriate types of rockets were developed for use against submarines, for the support of amphibious landings, and for aircraft. These allowed heavy firepower to be concentrated in light craft.

Fighter-plane speed was greatly increased during the war. At the end an experimental model ready for combat use had a speed of over 550 miles per hour. This plane was powered with turbo-jet engines, little known before 1941. Development of the conventional aircraft engine had also progressed; whereas initially the maximum size was 1,000 horsepower, improved types of 3,000 horsepower are now in use. Torpedo bombers, scout bombers, patrol bombers, and scout observation planes have all been rapidly developed during the period. Carrier-borne aircraft with increased speed, range, and armament carried the battle to the Japanese homeland, and patrol aircraft with high speed, long range, and greater offensive power aided in supplying the information necessary to the success of those operations. Developments of the arresting gear, launching catapults, and handling equipment of our surface ships kept pace with the increasing weights of planes, and allowed more planes per ship to be carried than had been possible in peacetime.

Our aircraft were a focus for developments in many fields. Radar opened new possibilities for search, night combat, and operations under poor visibility conditions. Aircraft guns were increased in size from the .30-caliber World War I weapon to 20-millimeter, 37-millimeter, and 75-millimeter guns. Air-borne rockets up to 11.75 inches in diameter radically increased the striking power of conventional aircraft, with little penalty on performance. Rocket power was also used on seaplanes for assistance in take-off with heavy loads and in high seas, making possible the rescue of many downed aviators and thereby reducing our combat losses. Development of the "fire bomb" further extended the tactical versatility of aircraft.

Training was enormously expedited by the introduction of a great variety of synthetic training devices. These endeavored to offer trainees an approximation of battle experience and to develop the reactions of a veteran before actual combat. As an example, it is now possible for the entire crew of a submarine to rehearse approaches and torpedo attacks against enemy task forces in trainers on dry land, which provide simulated visual observation of the enemy, simulated radar and sonar information, and in which all of the complex battle gear and fire-control mechanisms operate as they do in a real submarine.

Certain developments, whose progress was most promising, were not completed in time for extensive combat use. These are primarily guided missiles and pilotless aircraft, utilizing remote control by electronic apparatus. These new developments will play a major role in warfare of the future, carrying new explosives over greatly increased ranges.

In the early days of research leading toward the application of atomic energy for military purposes, the Naval Research Laboratory was the only government facility engaged in this type of work. At the Laboratory there was developed a liquid thermal diffusion process for separation of uranium isotopes. Enriched chemicals, as well as basic designs and operating practices, were later supplied to the Army and used in one of the Oak Ridge plants manufacturing the atomic bomb.

The complexity of modern warfare in both methods and means demands exacting analysis of the measures and countermeasures introduced at every stage by ourselves and the enemy. Scientific research can not only speed the invention and production of weapons, but also assist in insuring their correct use. The application, by qualified scientists, of the scientific method to the improvement of naval operating techniques and material, has come to be called operations research. Scientists engaged in operations research are experts who advise that part of the Navy which is using the weapons and craft—the fleets themselves. To function effectively they must work under the direction of, and have close personal contact with, the officers who plan and carry on the operations of war.

During the war we succeeded in enlisting the services of a group of competent scientists to carry out operations research. This group was set up as a flexible organization able to reassign personnel quickly when new critical problems arose. Fiscal and administrative control of the group was originally vested in the Office of Scientific Research and Development. The group as a whole was assigned to the Navy for functional control, and in the course of time was attached to my Headquarters.

The initial impulse toward the formation of such a group arose in April, 1942, during the early days of the antisubmarine war. With the cooperation of the Antisubmarine Division of the National Defense Research Committee, seven scientists were recruited by Columbia University and assigned to the Antisubmarine Warfare Unit, Atlantic Fleet.

During the year 1942 the group was considerably increased in size, and in July 1943, at a strength of approximately forty members, it was incorporated into the staff of the Tenth Fleet as the Antisubmarine Warfare Operations Research group. Subsequently the administrative responsibility for the group was transferred from Columbia University to the Office of Field Service, without alteration in relationships with the Navy. In October, 1944, with the decline of the submarine menace, the group was transferred to the Readiness Division of my Headquarters and renamed the Operations Research Group. At the close of the war it consisted of seventy-three scientists, drawn from a wide variety of backgrounds. Many of the members were attached, as the need arose, to the staffs of fleet and type commanders overseas, and at operating bases in war theaters. So far as possible they were afforded the opportunity of observing combat operations at first hand.

Operations research, as it developed, fell into two main categories: theoretical analysis of tactics, strategy, and the equipment of war on the one hand; and statistical analysis of operations on the other. Each type of naval operation had to be analyzed theoretically to determine the maximum potentialities of the equipment involved, the probable reactions of the personnel, and the nature of the tactics which would combine equipment and personnel in an optimum manner. Action reports, giving the actual results obtained in this type of operation, were studied in a quantitative manner in order to amplify, correct, and correlate closely the theoretical analysis with what was actually happening on the field of battle. The knowledge resulting from this continued cross-check of theory with practice made it possible to work out improvements in tactics which sometimes increased the effectiveness of weapons by factors of three or five, to detect changes in the enemy's tactics in time to counter them before they became dangerous, and to calculate force requirements for future operations.

The late war, more than any other, involved the interplay of new technical measures and opposing countermeasures. For example, the German U-boats had to revise their tactics and equipment when we began to use radar on our antisubmarine aircraft; and we, in turn, had to modify our tactics and radar equipment to counter their changes. In this see-saw of techniques the side which countered quickly, before the opponent had time to perfect the new tactics and weapons, had a decided advantage. Operations research, bringing scientists in to analyze the technical import of the fluctuations between measure and countermeasures, made it possible to speed up our reaction rate in several critical cases.

Likewise, in their struggle to counteract our improved convoy escort tactics, the U-boats introduced the acoustic torpedo, which steers for a ship by listening to the sound it makes under water. Our development of countermeasures was based on studies by the Operations Research Group into the pattern of sound produced in the sea by ship's propellers and on the probable reaction of the torpedo to various decoy devices. In this and other cases, information derived from intelligence sources was interpreted by the members of the group in the light of their own scientific knowledge and utilized to devise improved countermeasures.

Submarine and antisubmarine operations are closely complementary. Methods developed for attack have as a counterpart methods for defense based on the principles underlying both. In the subgroup devoted to submarine warfare, theoretical and operational studies were carried out on coordination of attack by groups of submarines; torpedo fire control; effectiveness of rescue of downed aviators; causes of loss of United States submarines; the relative merits of various types of torpedoes under differing circumstances; and enemy countermeasures to our radar search equipment.

Research on air problems has been devoted in the main to perfection of tactics designed to minimize flak hazard to naval aircraft attacking gun-defended targets, and to analysis of accuracy and effectiveness of aerial weapons, primarily against sea-borne targets. Bombs, rockets, and torpedoes are designed for distinct uses, conditioned by the accuracy of launching and by their lethal effectiveness. Studies of the peculiarities of these weapons have led to recommendations for tactics and training procedures.

Studies were carried out by other subgroups on defense of task forces against suicide attacks, on the effectiveness of antiaircraft fire, and on problems of naval gunfire as a support for amphibious landings.

The Operations Research Group, to be renamed the Operations Evaluation Group as more closely descriptive of its function, will be continued as part of the naval organization at an appropriate peacetime strength.

The assistance and cooperation of industry and science have been indispensable. Without this assistance, many of the weapons which have come into being as the result of intensive wartime research and development otherwise never would have been completed and introduced into the fleet.

It had often been predicted that in a national emergency the totalitarian countries would have a great technical advantage over the democracies because of their ability to regiment scientific facilities and manpower at will. The results achieved by Germany, Italy, and Japan do not bear out this contention. Studies made since the close of the war indicate that in none of these countries was the scientific effort as effectively handled as in the United States. The rapid, effective and original results obtained in bringing science into our war effort are proof of the responsiveness of our form of government to meeting emergencies, the technical competence of American scientists, and the productive genius of American industry.

It would be unfair to others to single out by name individual scientists who made important scientific and technical contributions to the improvement of old or the development of new weapons. There were thousands of such contributions. It is generally conceded that with respect to originality of ideas and individual resourcefulness the scientists in the Axis countries were as competent as our own. Where American science outdistanced the Axis powers was in the superior administration of the over-all effort so that the available scientific manpower of the country could function with the maximum effectiveness. The leadership for what may be broadly termed the civilian emergency scientific effort was provided by the same individuals during the entire war period. These individuals deserve special mention among those responsible for the superb administrative efficiency which characterized the American conduct of the war throughout. Dr. Vannevar Bush as the Director of the Office of Scientific Research and Development carried the over-all administrative and technical responsibility for that organization. Under him Dr. James B. Conant as Chairman of the National Defense Research Committee, Dr. Alfred N. Richards as Chairman of the Committee on Medical Research, and Dr. Karl T. Compton as the head of the Office of Field Services administered the scientific and technical activities of the Office of Scientific Research and Development. Dr. Frank B. Jewett as the President of the National Academy of Sciences and of its working body the National Research Council, and Dr. Jerome C. Hunsaker as the Chairman of the National Advisory Committee for Aeronautics directed the activities of these organizations during this period. The coordination of the work of these groups with the Navy was handled by the Office of the Coordinator of Research and

Development headed by Rear Admiral J. A. Furer.

I wish to pay particular tribute to the group of scientists, industrialists and officers of the Army and Navy who, under the direction of Major General L. R. Groves, USA, achieved the final outstanding technical success of the war—the development of a practical atomic bomb and the method of using it from aircraft.

Sufficient progress in the technical development and use of improved weapons and associated equipment has been made during the war to emphasize the necessity for continued progress. Working under the stress of an emergency, the factor of primary importance was immediate effectiveness against the enemy. This resulted in "crash designs" and production that required considerably more personnel, weight and space, than the more seasoned designs that might have been produced had time been available. Thus, the rapid expansion and development of new weapons and devices during the war was often at the cost of factors of major importance, such as the reserve buoyancy and stability of the ships in which they were installed. Those wartime designs, while they have well served their purpose against the enemy, have nevertheless created problems of refinement and improvement in the ultimate design of equipment, which must be so resolved that a minimum of personnel, weight and space will be required to attain the desired effect. These problems must be energetically attacked in the coming years of peace. Only by continuing vigorous research and development can this country hope to be protected from any potential enemies and maintain the position which it now enjoys in possessing the greatest effective naval fighting force in history.

## From Maurice Matloff, 'Strategic Planning for Coalition Warfare', 1943–1944*

In 1943 the debate over European strategy entered a new stage. Though the strategic ideas of each partner in the Allied coalition remained essentially the same as in 1942, the circumstances of their application changed. The mid-war period—roughly from January, 1943 to the establishment of a foothold in Normandy in the summer of 1944—was the period of increasing plenty. The power to call the turn on strategy and to choose the time and place to do battle passed to the Allies. The United States, along with its partners, had to come to grips with the offensive phase of the coalition war. United States troops and supplies flowed out in ever-increasing numbers, and the full impact of American mobilization and production was felt not only in the theaters but also in Allied Councils. Similarly, the ability of the Russians not only to survive the German assault but also to launch a series of counteroffensives lent weight to Soviet ideas on Allied strategy. The balance of power within the coalition steadily shifted to the United States and the Soviet Union.

As the new year opened, the Western Powers and the Soviet Union were still linked by the bond of danger, but had not yet found a common ground of agreement. Between the United States and the United Kingdom, fundamental war strategy and planning for the immediate future were unsettled. Into this vacuum and state of uncertainty the President, at the Casablanca Conference in January, 1943, introduced the principle of unconditional surrender—a concept that was to have important consequences for the Allied coalition as well as for the American military staff for the remainder of the war. . . .

It appeared at the time to the American staff that the thoroughness of British preparations and the long experience of the British in international negotiations had a decisive influence at the conference. In retrospect, the pains taken by the British seem to have been somewhat unnecessary, given the uncertainties of the situation and the unreconciled views on the American side. Despite his forceful presentation of the American military case, General Marshall succeeded in making no real change in the direction Allied strategy had taken in the second half of 1942. The Casablanca Conference merely recognized that the initiative would be maintained by the Allies both in the Pacific and in the

* From Maurice Matloff, *Strategic Planning for Coalition Warfare, 1943–1944* (Washington, 1959), 19, 38–42. Used by permission of the Chief of Military History, Department of the Army.

Mediterranean, and defined short-range objectives in those areas in terms of operations in the South-Southwest Pacific and against Sicily. No real long-range plans for the defeat of the Axis Powers emerged. The questions of Asiatic and cross-Channel operations were simply left open for future negotiation. Agreement on a round-the-clock combined bomber offensive was reached but it was not tied in precisely with Mediterranean or cross-Channel operations. Nor were the relationships among these operations and Pacific and Asiatic undertakings clearly defined.

The Casablanca Conference was thus indecisive on basic strategic issues. The indecisiveness appeared to the United States staff to be a victory for the British. If Casablanca marked essentially the reaffirmation of the old in strategic planning, it was also a foreshadowing of the new. The simple terms in which War Department planners had tried to solve the problem of limiting operations in subsidiary theaters had failed. The problem had become so complex—in the new phase of the war—that they would have to start out all over again and find new formulas. However far apart the two nations appeared to be on operational strategy, there was a hopeful sign for the future in the staff's agreement at last on a general system of command to govern combined British and United States operations. The Americans, especially, could take comfort from the incorporation in the set of guiding principles adopted of the conception of unified command—under a supreme commander—that Marshall and his staff had been urging from early in the war.

Significant portents emerged in the American staff's stress on enlarging the scope of the war against Japan and, above all, in the President's announcement of the unconditional surrender concept. So important did the President regard this statement of purpose that he suggested to the correspondents that they might call the Casablanca Conference the " 'Unconditional Surrender' Meeting." In the final analysis, his announcement of the unconditional surrender formula was the most significant contribution of the conference—one that, for better or worse, was to have profound influence on the subsequent conduct of the war.

The President had actually informed the JCS of his intention to support this concept as the basic Allied aim in the war in a meeting at the White House on January 7, one week before the conference. No study of the meaning of this formula for the conduct of the war was made by either the Army or the Joint Staff before or during the conference—a striking illustration of the want of understanding between the White House and the military staffs. Nor did the Combined Chiefs of Staff discuss the significance of the concept to which the President and Prime Minister committed themselves publicly at Casablanca and thereby raised issues long to be debated in the war and postwar periods.

Leaving aside its external effects, this principle was to have important internal consequences for the coalition. It is significant that the President did not set forth as his war aim the objective of restoring the European or Asian balance of power—although, to some observers at least, the United States had been drawn into the global and coalition struggle because the balance of power on the opposite shores of both the Atlantic and the Pacific had been upset. Nor was his concern here with the terms of settlement. What the President appeared to be offering at the time was a simple formula of common and resolute purpose—a slogan that would rally the Allies for victory and drive home to friend and foe alike that this time there would be no negotiated peace and no "escape clauses" offered by another Fourteen Points. In particular, it might serve to reassure the Russians—who were bound to be disappointed by the continued failure of the Western Powers to open the second front in Europe—of the uncompromising determination of the Western Powers to wage a fight to the finish with Germany. It was vague enough to permit general agreement on the planning for the defeat of Germany and yet specific enough to prevent internal dissension over the terms of surrender. But, in retrospect, this concept, which the other partners came to accept, served to conceal the divergent national objectives back of the common strategy eventually worked out by the Western Powers with the Soviet ally. It is, of course, still a moot point whether anything more or less than the single-track idea of unconditional surrender would have succeeded in this "strange alliance."

For American staff planning, the President's announcement was to prove no less important. To date the President had asserted control over the United States military strategy on grounds of policy. The specific objectives of the President, for which he was prepared to run serious political and military risks, even against the better judgment of his military advisers, were the traditional defensive objectives of United States policy—essentially the security of the Atlantic and Pacific Oceans. These were all reflected in the politico-military policies he had actively supported in 1942—establishing the line Australia—Hawaii, keeping China in the war, maintaining the lines of communication to the United Kingdom, invading North Africa. Beyond these limits the United States had no well-defined objectives. It may be conjectured that at this point in the war, when these objectives were secured, the President passed at once in his mind, impatiently, to the peace conferences that would follow a clear-cut victory, at which he could appear—uncommitted and disinterested—to emulate the purposes, while avoiding the mistakes, of President Wilson. Indeed, from the beginning of the war he had shown a strong disposition to postpone territorial and political settlements until after the war. Whatever he may have thought, his apparent reluctance to spell out his political objectives discouraged, though it did not entirely prevent the United States military authorities from expecting and requesting guidance on the questions of national policy that would in fact be influenced —or simply settled—by future operations.

The strategic planners, who had been concerned in 1940, 1941, and 1942 over the President's apparent indifference to military expediency, were doubtless pleased to have a freer hand to work out their problems in strictly military terms. But it was by no means a coincidence that, as the war progressed, they would begin to note, and even to insist, that there were really no "strictly military" problems in grand strategy and to keep closer relations with the White House and the State Department in the hope of getting guidance (and, doubtless, of exercising some influence) on the "political" decisions.

Indeed, the principal political decisions that the President made during the midwar years with reference to military operations were made by default. For this reason, of course, they cannot be documented and dated in the same way that active decisions can be documented. This fact is all the more true because the CCS and the JCS, the only bodies that had any standing on military operations, were reluctant to raise political questions.

For the United States military staff, unconditional surrender was to serve essentially as a military objective, reinforcing their own notions of a concentrated, decisive war. To them unconditional surrender provided a definable goal that was to be attained as expeditiously as possible. Winning the war decisively would obtain top priority, just as it had in the war games held in peacetime. A convenient handle had thus been provided to the military that could be used in formulating their plans. Henceforth the basic premise of all planning to defeat Germany and Japan would be the accomplishment of unconditional surrender.

At the same time, the formula complicated the task of the United States military staff in midwar. It meant that they would now—largely without consistent Presidential guidance—have to work out the precise terms of the offensive phase of the war through negotiation with the Allies. The President's concern in 1943–44 would be primarily that of meeting the contractual relations with the Allies. With the British, the close partner, this would mean seeing to it that somehow their notion of a cross-Channel operation was reconciled with the American. With the Russians, with whom relations were not so close, it signified continuing to bolster the Soviet war effort with lend-lease and the earliest possible establishment of a second front in Europe. In the President's view, a firm alliance with the USSR and Great Britain must be sedulously cultivated. He himself would be serving as a mediator among the Allies—essentially a Wilsonian position.

The great debate on European strategy between the Americans and the British—opened by the decision for Torch—endured down to the summer of 1944. It is not surprising that the American strategists, left largely on their own to resolve the problems of offensive warfare with the Allied staffs, should take refuge in their conventional view of war as a big engagement. But only gradually did the Americans—with Marshall as the foremost spokesman—win their way back to the notion of waging a war of mass and concentration on the Continent. Their task was to secure agreement of the President, the British, and eventually the Russians. In the debate with the Allies, the trump card held by the United States staff was the fresh, flexible military power of the United States—the forces it had built up and still had not committed. The series of decisions reached at the great international conferences of 1943 and 1944—from Casablanca through the Second Quebec—reflect the compromises worked out by the British and Americans—between the principles of opportunism and long-range commitments, between a war of attrition and a war of mass and concentration. In the meantime, old fronts were being expanded and new fronts were being opened all over the world. Significant as the signs and portents of Casablanca proved to be in the final analysis, more significant for the immediate future was the prospect that the advances already begun in the Mediterranean and the Pacific would be carried on in the two areas in which United States deployment had been especially heavy in 1942.

### From the War Reports of General H. H. Arnold

One of the lessons that the war has driven home to the Nation is the necessity for continuing research and development, not only in engineering, but in all phases of military activity. The battle of the laboratories and factories and test bases has not been an easy one. Men have been killed and wounded in its campaigns, but that we are winning is evident in the reports which come back daily from our forces scattered over the world. It cannot be too strongly emphasized that our superiority is due not only to the weight of our production, but also to the *kind* of our production.

First of all, I should like to mention our work with planes which fly by jet propulsion and to set down something of their history.

During a stay in England early in 1941 I had occasion to examine various research and development projects on gas turbines and jet propulsion for aircraft. The possibilities of this new means of aircraft power led to the decision that we must initiate a similar gas-turbine and jet-propulsion program in this country without delay. To accelerate such a program from the start it was thought advisable to procure from England the production rights as well as the physical article of an engine which had already been successfully test flown—this was the Whittle engine.

Therefore, on Thursday, September 4, 1941, an initial conference was held in AAF Headquarters to determine the feasibility and desirability of going into immediate production in this country on the English Whittle engine project, as well as to determine which airplane manufacturer was at that time best qualified to carry out the jet propulsion development in conjunction with the General Electric Company, which had had extensive experience with steam turbines and turbo superchargers. Present at this conference were (the then) Major General Carl Spaatz, Major General O. P. Echols, and other members of the Air Staff as well as Messrs. Muir, Shoults, Stevenson, Jr., and Puffer of General Electric. After an examination of the preliminary data and drawings received from England, General Electric agreed that it would be possible to produce a duplicate engine in 6 months with two more engines in an additional 2 months, the latter two engines to be flight articles. The vital necessity for absolute secrecy was stressed. A cable was dispatched to England to obtain complete information. It was further decided to invite Mr. Bell, of the Bell Aircraft Corporation, to Washington the following morning.

On Friday, September 5, 1941, Mr. Bell and his chief engineer, Mr. H. M. Poyer, reported to my office, together with Mr. Shoults of General Electric and the AAF officers present the day before. The proposition was presented to Mr. Bell and after a brief discussion he stated his desire to participate in the project. It was then decided to build 15 engines, and 3 twin-engined airplanes designated as XP-59A. The Bell and General Electric companies were to work in close collaboration. The contracts, under absolute secrecy, were prepared by (the then) AAF Materiel Command. Colonel D. J. Keirn was project officer.

Never has a plane been built in this country under greater secrecy. At both General Electric and Bell, the men who worked on the project were investigated even as to their personal habits, so that not even through careless conviviality could mention of the project leak out. The workers were segregated in blacked-out, heavily guarded buildings; even so, some of the workers were unaware of what they were doing. For instance, the men at Bell who were fabricating the wing sections were never allowed to see the fuselage. A year later the first jet plane was disassembled, crated, and sent west with military police riding on the train with it. On the bed of a dry lake in the Western desert it was put together, ground tested and flown.

The plane was a success.

We have learned many things since then about jet propulsion. The absence of vibration and engine noise makes for less pilot fatigue. It appears that the planes are outstandingly safe—the use of kerosene as a fuel greatly reduces the fire hazard, and the low center of gravity facilitates braking and minimizes ground looping. The jet engine is of simple construction—it has only about 10 percent of the moving parts of the usual reciprocating engine, it has no ignition system, no carburetor, no automatic throttle control and since there is no propeller, there is no need for prop controls and instruments. No warm-up of the engine is needed—a highly desirable feature militarily.

Since that first P-59 many other jet planes have been projected, built, flown. So rapid has been our advance that the P-59 is today classed as a trainer. . . .

As a nation we were not prepared for World War II. Yes, we won the war, but at a terrific cost in lives, human suffering, and material, and at times the margin of winning was narrow. History alone can reveal how many turning points there were, how many times we were near losing, and how our enemies' mistakes often pulled us through. In the flush of victory, some like to forget these unpalatable truths.

Our enemies' blunders, not likely to be repeated in the future, contributed materially to Allied victory. Among them were the following:

(a) Germany's underestimate of the power, technological resources, and the determination of the Royal Air Force in the Battle of Britain.

(b) The failure of Germany to invade England, which would have been possible after Dunkerque.

(c) Underestimation of the temper and power of the United States.

(d) The failure of Germany to appreciate the threat of the United States heavy bombers, and to understand and adopt the strategic uses of Air Power.

(e) Germany's incapacity to understand the Soviet Union's determination to maintain its integrity, and to realize the power with which it would back that determination.

(f) The failure of Japan to invade Hawaii after the Pearl Harbor attack.

(g) The failure of Japan to secure bases in Australia.

Although we were woefully unprepared as a nation, we still had the time so essential to build a military force, time given us by our Allies fighting with their backs to the wall, and by the distance of oceans. That precious time without doubt will not be given us again.

Today many modern war devices of great destructive power can be built piecemeal and under cover. Sub-assemblies might be secretly made in underground laboratories, and assembled into an annihilating war machine. War may descend upon us by thousands of robots passing unannounced across our shorelines—unless we act now to prevent them.

Today, Japanese and German cities lie in ruins, but they merely suggest the vast destruction that can be done with the weapons of tomorrow. The first target of a potential aggressor might well be our industrial system or our major centers of population. If the United States is to be secure in the future, we must never relinquish the means of preventing such a blow.

The AAF's size and power have been achieved only by tremendous efforts and expenses which, to a large extent, might have been unnecessary if as a nation we had been realistic about war from 1930 to 1940.

What we shall lose in size as a peacetime Air Force, we must compensate for in the lessons we have learned in two world wars. Equally with the problems of today, the problems which may have to be faced in 1975 or 1985 will require imagination, boldness, and the utilization of available skills, manpower, resources.

It is recalled that at the outset of this war, some of the leading aircraft manufacturers in the country stated that they could not make the necessary number of airplanes in the time set. They also believed that only aircraft companies could manufacture aircraft because of the precision methods required. As it turned out, automobile, refrigerator, radio and other manufacturers quickly learned to produce aircraft and related equipment with precision methods.

Certain strategic and critical materials necessary to the AAF might be difficult to procure in time of war. Such materials must be procured in time of peace and a sufficient stockpile maintained.

The training of personnel in time of war, like the production of materials, can only be done in a wholesale manner by utilizing all available facilities and experienced operators wherever found. While we trained men in new skills, we also went to the shops, garages, laboratories, and factories of the Nation and adapted old skills to new military jobs. Ingenuity of this kind kept us going through a very critical period.

As we think of the future, we would do well to remember that any United States preparation for preserving the peace would be incomplete without participation by other nations of this hemisphere. The American Republics must work together in ever closer unity. To this end, military equipment, training and indoctrination should be standardized as much as possible among these nations, especially in the technical field of aviation.

Since the birth of this Nation, the people of the United States, peaceloving and hoping for world-wide acceptance of our concept of democracy, have never sponsored a strong peacetime military organization. History has demonstrated that we have thereby neither avoided war nor deterred others from going to war.

We cannot measure the price which we have paid in lives and effort for the wars in which we have participated. We cannot know for certain to what extent the maintenance of a strong peacetime military organization would have reduced the price we have paid in past wars, or to what degree such an organization would have worked toward the maintenance of world peace. We do know, however, that the course which we have followed in the past has not achieved the goal which we sought. Might it not now be wise to try the alternative course of action in the hope that it will bring us what we seek—world peace and our own security?

Air Power includes a nation's ability to deliver cargo, people, destructive missiles and war-making potential through the air to a desired destination to accomplish a desired purpose.

Air Power is not composed alone of the war-making components of aviation. It is the total aviation activity—civilian and military, commercial and private, potential as well as existing.

Military Air Power—or Air Force—is dependent upon the air potential provided by industry which, in turn, thrives best in an atmosphere of individual initiative and private enterprise. Government can do much to increase this air potential by judicious use of its coordinating and planning powers.

An Air Force is always verging on obsolescence and, in time of peace, its size and replacement rate will always be inadequate to meet the full demands of war. Military Air Power should, therefore, be measured to a large extent by the ability of the existing Air Force to absorb in time of emergency the increase required by war together with new ideas and techniques.

National safety would be endangered by an Air Force whose doctrines and techniques are tied solely to the equipment and processes of the moment. Present equipment is but a step in progress, and any Air Force which does not keep its doctrines ahead of its equipment, and its vision far into the future, can only delude the nation into a false sense of security.

# 18.

# The Postwar Dilemma

The vision of a peaceful world under the collective security of the United Nations contributed to a repetition of America's customary hasty and extensive demobilization. All but skeleton police forces were returned from abroad as the temporary warriors resumed their civilian pursuits. Exclusive possession of atomic weapons further lulled the nation into a sense of security, and President Truman found himself conducting diplomatic negotiations without the support of conventional forces. Though such a problem had not been anticipated, growing Russian intransigence cast doubts on the efficacy of the United Nations or the prospect of justice prevailing in affairs between nations. The totalitarian Soviet Union appeared to be following the Fascist pattern of aggression as it sought to extend its influence and the doctrines of Communism throughout the world.

In the United States a dispute raged over the kind of defense structure that should be adopted. Each service vied for a larger share of appropriations as the nation tried to determine the mission of the armed forces. In the first of the following selections, Samuel P. Huntington analyses the course of military policy during the early years of peace. In the second selection Walter Millis describes the new defense organization established by the National Security Act of 1947. It was to provide a more effective, though not wholly satisfactory, administrative arrangement for the planning and unification of military effort. As the United States became committed to the leadership of the Free World in its struggle against Communism the strains on the defense establishment increased proportionately, and the North Atlantic Treaty, the nation's first peacetime military alliance, added a new dimension to America's security obligations.

# The Interim Years: World War II to January, 1950

## BY SAMUEL P. HUNTINGTON

### Cold War and Demobilization, 1945–1946

DURING THE EIGHTEEN MONTHS after V-E day, the World War foreign policy of great power unity gave way to the Cold War foreign policy of containment. During the same period, military policy changed fundamentally in scope but not in content: in classic fashion it simply shifted from the feast phase of a mobilization strategy to the famine phase. Foreign policy adjusted to the rise of a new opponent, military policy only to the defeat of old ones.

The change in foreign policy began before the end of World War II. On April 2, 1945, the Secretary of State advised the Secretaries of War and the Navy "of serious deterioration in our relations with Russia." A few days later Ambassador Harriman warned by cable from Moscow that we "must clearly realize that the Soviet program is the establishment of totalitarianism, ending personal liberty and democracy as we know and respect it". The Soviets, he said, were simultaneously pursuing three lines: collaboration with the United States and Great Britain in establishing a world security organization; creation of their own security system by extending their sway over their neighbors; and extension of their influence into other countries through local Communist parties and the opportunities offered by economic chaos and democratic freedoms. Arguing that the Soviets interpreted the "generous and considerate attitude" of the United States as a sign of weakness, he urged that the United States follow a tough policy, "that we should maintain positions that would be hard for the Soviet authorities if they maintained positions hard for us; and that we should hurt them if they hurt us."

The cables from Harriman represented the first effort to assess the overall nature of the Soviet problem and to spell out an approach for dealing with it. Significantly, the initiative came from the Moscow embassy, that part of the government most exposed and most sensitive to the actions of the Soviets. In Washington, Forrestal, Leahy, and others accepted the Harriman analysis. The new President made it clear in the spring and summer of 1945 that he intended to bargain toughly with the Soviets on specific issues. He refrained, however, from formally endorsing the Harriman retaliation thesis and declined to utilize American forces in Europe to stop the extension of Soviet influence westward. Nevertheless, the controversies with the Soviets over Poland, the Balkans, UN procedures, Iran, the Dardanelles, and the Italian peace treaty underwrote the validity of Harriman's thesis, and in September, 1945, for the first time, the United States allowed a high-level conference (the Council of Foreign Ministers) to break down without agreement rather than make further concessions to Soviet demands. Throughout the last six months of 1945, American policy-makers gradually came to agree on the need for

From Samuel P. Huntington, *The Common Defense: Strategic Programs in National Politics* (New York, Columbia University Press, 1961), 33–47. Used by permission.

a tougher line with the Soviets. The wartime image of postwar great power unity was slowly replaced by a new image of Soviet-American rivalry.

The expectations of conflict were formally confirmed on February 9, 1946. In a grim speech, which Justice Douglas labeled "The Declaration of World War III," Generalissimo Stalin argued that a peaceful international order was "impossible under the present capitalistic development of world economy" and announced a five-year plan for massive industrial expansion. Almost simultaneously, in an eight-thousand-word cable from Moscow, George F. Kennan furnished the first overall postwar explanation of Soviet behavior and suggested a course for dealing with it. The Soviet leaders, he declared, had inherited "the traditional and instinctive Russian sense of insecurity," which reinforced their adherence to Marxist dogma and their view of the inevitability of conflict between the capitalist and communist worlds leading to the victory of the latter. Russia, he warned, would expand its influence through every possible means and attempt to fill every power vacuum. At times tactical considerations might lead the Soviets to appear more friendly and amenable, but such moves were only temporary maneuvers. In Kennan's words:

> We have here a political force committed fanatically to the belief that with the United States there can be no permanent *modus vivendi*, that it is desirable and necessary that the internal harmony of our society be disrupted, our traditional way of life be destroyed, the international authority of our state be broken, if Soviet power is to be secure. This political force has complete power of disposition over the energies of one of the world's greatest peoples and the resources of the world's richest national territory. . . . The problem of how to cope with this force is undoubtedly the greatest task our diplomacy has ever faced and probably the greatest it will ever have to face.

To meet this force Kennan urged "cohesion, firmness, and vigor" on the part of the West. His cable furnished the preliminary rationale for a policy of firmness which was reflected immediately in the sterner tones of Secretary Byrnes' February 28 speech to the Overseas Press Club, the decision to send the *Missouri* to Turkey, and the successful resistance to Soviet demands upon Iran.

Firmness, however, was presumably more than a matter of attitude. At the same time that American policy toward Russia was hardening, the armed forces which might, in the final analysis, have to underwrite that policy were melting away. Harriman, Kennan, Forrestal, and others could fairly easily reassess Soviet intentions. To reverse or even to redirect the disintegration of American military strength was quite a different matter. Initial plans for postwar demobilization had been drawn up in the midst of the war: the Joint Chiefs approved a system of individual rather than unit demobilization in September, 1943. Two years later the last and greatest postwar demobilization of the American armed forces got under way. Only war justified the maintenance of large military forces. The war was over. Hence there was no reason to keep men in the armed services against their will. Such was the logic of demobilization prevalent among the troops, Congress, and a large and articulate minority of the public. Congressmen were reluctant to undertake the responsibility for establishing demobilization policies themselves, but with a few exceptions they did not hesitate to flail the War and Navy Departments for their slowness in discharging their men.

The pressure to "bring the boys home" produced one of the most rapid demobilizations in world history. On V-J day the Army had 8,020,000 men. By January 1, 1946, it had been cut almost in half to 4,228,936 men. By July, 1946, ten months after the end of the war, it was down to 1,889,690 men. On V-J day the Army Air Forces had 218 effective combat groups. By January 1, 1946, there were only 109 effective groups. The strength of the Navy on V-J day was 3,400,000 men. In March, 1946, it was less than half this size, 1,600,000 men. The decline in the military effectiveness of the armed forces, moreover, far exceeded the decline in their personnel strengths. The rapid loss of men affected almost all units. Frequently it was impossible to replace individuals with critical occupational specialities. It became difficult to maintain equipment. Turnover was huge. Replacements often were not properly trained. One month after the end of the war, the Joint Strategic Survey Committee reported that " . . . a year or more would be required to reconstitute our military position at a fraction of its recent power." The same month an Air Force general declared that the point was rapidly being approached when "the Army Air Forces can no longer be considered anything more than a symbolic instrument of National Defense." On November 15, the European and Pacific theater commanders estimated that their troops could operate at only about 50 percent of their wartime efficiency. "By the Fall and Winter of 1945–1946 the armies and the air forces that had been victorious in Europe and in the Pacific were no longer a closely integrated military machine, but rather had disintegrated to little more than large groups of individual replacements."

As the leaders of the government were well aware, foreign policy and military policy were moving in opposite directions. Stimson, Marshall, and Forrestal, all warned against too rapid demobilization. Their words, however, did little to stem the tide, and the disintegration of American military forces inevitably affected American diplomacy. The public and congressional pressure to speed up demobilization in September and October, 1945, probably encouraged the Soviets in their stringent demands at the London Council of Foreign Ministers. In November Secretary Byrnes expressed concern to the Secretaries of War and the Navy that the reductions underway and contemplated would reduce American influence. On January 11, 1946, after the overseas riots and demonstrations of American servicemen, Under Secretary of State Acheson declared that demobilization "was a matter of great embarrassment and concern to his own Department in their conduct of our foreign affairs." Still later, at the Paris Peace Conference in September, 1946, the Secretary of State expressed concern and "almost alarm" at proposed further reductions in American forces in Europe. Subsequently, Byrnes argued that he consciously felt it necessary to refrain from speaking out vigorously in the fall of 1945 because of American military weakness. Only when General Eisenhower assured him in February, 1946, that the reorganization of the Army was progressing satisfactorily did Byrnes feel that he could publicly espouse a stronger line.

Demobilization obviously affected what American diplomats felt they could say and the results they were likely to achieve in international bargaining. What could be done to ease this constraint and close the gap between foreign and military policies? To stem the tide of demobilization would have required the President and the Administration bluntly and dramatically to warn the nation of the threat from the Soviet Union. It was just exactly this, however, which the Administration was reluctant to do during the winter of 1945–1946. Reversing the disintegration of American military strength would require a denunciation of Soviet Russia which would undermine completely our ultimate objective of arriving at an appropriate agreement with her. But, on the other hand, agreement was impossible without the strength to compel it. To speak out would reveal fully our military weakness; to remain silent would perpetuate it.

These issues were raised many times during the winter of 1945–1946. In the middle of October Forrestal argued that the President should fully reveal to the people "the details of our dealings with the Russians and with the attitude which the Russians have manifested throughout." Byrnes, however, opposed this on the grounds that it would justify to the Russians their hostile attitude toward us. In January Forrestal suggested that the President contact leading newspaper publishers and radio commentators and explain to them the seriousness of the situation, and Secretary Ickes urged that the State Department make a nationwide broadcast portraying the debilitating effects of demobilization on foreign policy. The following month, in his lengthy analysis of the nature of the Soviet threat from Moscow, Kennan similarly demanded that the truth be told to the American people:

> We must see that our public is educated to the realities of the Russian situation. I cannot over-emphasize the importance of this. . . . I am convinced that there would be far less hysterical

anti-Sovietism in our country today if realities of this situation were better understood by our people. There is nothing as dangerous or terrifying as the unknown. It may also be argued that to reveal more information on our difficulties with Russia would reflect unfavorably on Russo-American relations. I feel that if there is any real risk here involved, it is one which we should have the courage to face, and the sooner the better.

No dramatic presentation of the type desired by Forrestal, Ickes, and Kennan was made. Demobilization moved into its final stages as the policy of firmness hardened into a more explicit policy of containment. The issue which was raised, however, returned at each subsequent major reconsideration of American strategy, in 1950, 1953, and 1957. Should the Administration present to the American people the grim facts about unpleasant developments in international politics? The negative answer of the Truman Administration in 1946 foreshadowed similar responses in later crises.

Critics later lamented the rapidity and scope of the demobilization of 1945–1946 and the unfortunate effects it had upon American foreign policy. They deplored the irresponsibility of the troops, the pressures from Congress and the public, the ineffectuality of the Administration. They argued that stronger and more courageous leadership would have prevented the disintegration of America's armed might. To be sure, the rapid demobilization did weaken the support for American diplomacy in the first eighteen months after the end of the war. It is a mistake, however, to think that any other course was possible. Demobilization was the last phase of World War II. As such, it was not the alternative to a wiser and more effective policy but rather a prerequisite to it. The citizen-armies mobilized to fight World War II were ill-adapted to the requirements of the Cold War. Military support of diplomacy is not just a matter of numbers; it is also a question of purpose and organization. The decks had to be cleared, the World War II force dissolved, before new armies could be brought into existence shaped and trained for the radically new needs of the Cold War. Delayed demobilization would simply have meant delayed adjustment. This sober truth was recognized by at least some military men. The Navy and the Air Force, which completed their demobilization in 1946, were able to develop the forces required for the Cold War faster than the Army, which did not complete its demobilization until June, 1947. Demobilization, with its uproar and chaos, the 80,000 letters a week to congressmen, the speeches and editorials denouncing brass and militarism, the soldier committees and "I wanta go home," was the final violent swing of the pendulum of the old order, total peace to total war to total peace, an indispensable prelude to the somber greyness of the Cold War dawn.

## Policy Conflict, 1947–1949

Demobilization of the World War II military system was a necessary but not sufficient cause for the creation of a Cold War military system. The foreign policy upon which that system presumably would be based was succinctly and publicly expressed by George Kennan in the spring of 1947:

> [T]he main element of any United States policy toward the Soviet Union must be that of a long-term, patient but firm and vigilant containment of Russian expansive tendencies. . . . Soviet pressure against the free institutions of the western world is something that can be contained by the adroit and vigilant application of counterforce at a series of constantly shifting geographical and political points, corresponding to the shifts and maneuvers of Soviet policy, but which cannot be charmed or talked out of existence.

In late 1947 or early 1948 this policy was elaborated in one of the first papers, NSC 20, processed through the new national security policy machinery. Early in 1947 the Truman Doctrine revealed some of the political and economic implications of containment. What, however, were the military requirements of containment? What sort of strategy was needed to support this policy?

The State Department furnished one answer in a June, 1948, paper on Soviet actions "affecting the nature of the U.S. defense arrangements." This analysis argued that "war is not a probability but is always a possibility." It did not emphasize the need to shape the military system to the requirements of a future war. Instead, the paper held that the main reason it was "necessary that the United States maintain armed strength" was to furnish "support for our political position." The other purposes of American forces were to act "as a deterrent," to serve "as encouragement to nations endeavoring to resist Soviet political aggression," and, lastly, to "wage war successfully in case war should develop." This hierarchy of purposes implied that the United States would have to maintain strong military forces to support policy for an indefinite period. A policy, the report said, "based on the maintenance of a permanent state of adequate military preparation is better than an effort pointed toward a given peak of danger." The paper, in short, outlined most of the military requirements of a strategy of deterrence to support a policy of containment. It was, perhaps, a landmark in the evolution of American strategic thought from the old strategy of mobilization for general war to a new strategy of deterrence. Significantly, it was produced by the State Department, not the Joint Chiefs of Staff.

At that time a strategy for containment appeared to have two principal implications. First, it seemed to require stronger military forces than were then being maintained. American foreign policy was constantly brought up short by the inadequacy of American military forces. As General Marshall later recollected:

> I remember, when I was Secretary of State I was being pressed constantly, particularly when in Moscow (Fourth Meeting of Council of Foreign Ministers, March–April, 1947), by radio message after radio message to give the Russians hell. . . . When I got back, I was getting the same appeal in relation to the Far East and China. At that time, my facilities for giving them hell—and I am a soldier and know something about the ability to give hell—was $1\frac{1}{3}$ divisions over the entire United States. That is quite a proposition when you deal with somebody with over 260 and you have $1\frac{1}{3}$rd.

Similarly, at a White House meeting in February, 1958, General Gruenther warned of the dangers of trouble in Greece, Italy, Korea, and Palestine. At that time those were the "geographical and political points," in Kennan's phrase, where the "adroit and vigilant application of counter-force" might be necessary. The forces available, however, were minimal. The total general reserve for emergencies consisted of some 70,000 Army and Marine troops. The employment overseas of anything more than a division, Gruenther emphasized, would require partial mobilization. As Marshall succinctly pointed out: [W]e are playing with fire while we have nothing with which to put it out."

The problem for containment was not just the inadequacy of American military strength but also the nature of that strength. Two of Forrestal's three key components of American military power, exclusive possession of the atomic bomb and productive capacity, were almost irrelevant to current "support for our political position," and the useful scope of the third, predominant sea-power, was limited. The atomic bomb was of little help in preserving the integrity of Iran, suppressing guerillas in Greece, or deterring an attack in Korea. Ground troops were needed for containment, and in July, 1949, the author of containment warned the Joint Strategic Survey Committee that the United States was limiting its choice, in the event of Soviet aggression, either to replying with the atomic bomb or to doing nothing. He urged the desirability of having two or more mobile and mechanized divisions, trained and ready for instant use in "brush fire" wars. Other State Department officials thought that even larger forces were necessary and that American nuclear retaliatory power also needed strengthening. Two factors, however, prevented the military requirements of containment from being realized.

First, domestic political considerations limited the size of the military effort. The logic of foreign policy might require larger military forces. Inevitably, however, the President and the Administration also thought in terms of the domestic environment. President Truman fought a continuing battle over taxes with the Republican majority in the 80th Congress. In January, 1947, he explicitly declared his opposition to a general tax reduction. Congress responded by passing H.R. 1, providing significant cuts in individual tax rates. The President vetoed the bill. Within a month Congress passed a revised version of the bill. The President vetoed that. Early in 1948 President Truman again declared that tax revenues should not be decreased but also recommended a tax credit of $40 for each individual taxpayer to be compensated for by enactment of a modified excess profits tax. This was election year politics to the Republicans. Congress approved a general reduction in individual income tax rates and an increase in individual exemptions which, it was estimated, would decrease revenues by about $5 billion. The President vetoed this bill, and Congress passed it over his veto. Despite the Democratic majority the following year, the President's recommendations for a $4 billion increase in taxes were ignored by Congress. No other significant change in tax rates was made until after the start of the Korean War.

The Administration thus faced a definite ceiling on its income. Federal revenues in FY 1946 and FY 1947 were $39.8 and $41.5 billion, respectively. Following the passage of the 1948 act, they dropped to $37.7 billion in FY 1949 and, under the impact of the recession, to $36.5 billion in FY 1950. President Truman, moreover, as Forrestal said, was "a hard money man if ever I saw one," who has "determined not to spend more than we take in taxes." With this high priority for a balanced budget, expenditures had to be severely limited. Yet interest costs, which varied from $5 billion to $5.8 billion from FY 1947 through FY 1950, were unavoidable. Economic assistance to Greece and Turkey, interim aid to western Europe, the European Recovery Plan, and related activities were obviously of the highest priority. They took from $4.6 billion to $6.5 billion. The costs of domestic programs varied from a low of $11.6 billion in FY 1948 to a high of $16.1 billion in FY 1950. On the average, for the four years, the picture was:

| | | |
|---|---|---|
| Revenues | | $38.9 |
| Interest | $ 5.4 | |
| Foreign aid | 5.5 | |
| Domestic programs | 14.0 | |
| Total | | 24.9 |
| Available for security | | $14.0 |

In actuality, from FY 1947 through FY 1950 security expenditures were: $14.4, $11.7, $12.9, and $13.0.* The subtraction of other expenditures from estimated revenues was exactly the means which the Administration used, with variations, to set the level of security expenditures. In May, 1946, the President decreed that in FY 1948 military activities could have one-third of the funds remaining after the fixed charges had been met. This was the initial appearance of the "remainder method" of calculating security expenditures which was to become a familiar feature of both Truman and Eisenhower peacetime budgets. In all four fiscal years from FY 1947 through FY 1950 the Truman Administration set and maintained reasonably firm ceilings on military appropriations and expenditures. In FY 1950, for instance, despite the initial high requests of the services and Forrestal's efforts to secure a $17 billion budget, the President established and held to a ceiling of $14.4 billion on new appropriations for the Defense Department. Actual military spending during that year came to only $11.9 billion. Early in FY 1950 the President set the ceiling for the FY 1951 budget at $13 billion. As he declared at the time:

> The budget policy on which my ceiling determinations for 1951 are based is that of (a) holding governmental expenditures as closely as possible to present levels and, in particular, (b) preventing the prospective large rise in the military area by adjustments in present plans. Even under this stringent policy the outlook is for sizable deficits, at least in the next two years, under present tax rates.

* *Expenditures* are actual disbursements of funds from the Treasury. *Appropriations* are the principal form of *new obligational authority* by which Congress authorizes expenditures. *Military expenditures* are those made by the Department of Defense and its predecessor agencies for military defense. *Major national security* includes spending for military defense, military assistance, atomic energy, stockpiling, and defense production. *International affairs and finance* includes funds for the conduct of foreign affairs, economic and technical assistance, and information activities. These are official budget terms. In this volume the phrase *total foreign policy expenditures* will also be used to refer to expenditures for major national security and international affairs and finance.

This statement concisely revealed the implications for military spending of the desire of the Administration to balance the budget and the desire of Congress to reduce taxes.

These constraints upon the size of the military effort were one factor in preventing the development of the forces required for deterrence. They were not the only one. Even with an $11 billion budget, conceivably, as Kennan argued, it would have been possible to create the ground forces necessary to maintain some situations of strength if this need had been given sufficient priority. The second constraint on strategy was not civilian and budgetary but military and doctrinal. American military thinking was preoccupied not so much with the maintenance of forces-in-being with which to deter war but rather with the preparation of forces to win a major war if one should occur. The most probable and most serious danger was a Soviet attack on western Europe. Military planning was oriented toward this contingency. The overwhelming strength of the Red Army in Germany and eastern Europe made it unlikely that western Europe could be successfully defended on the ground without a major increase in the forces there. Consequently, American policy was directed to making clear the American commitment to defend Europe (North Atlantic Treaty, 1949), developing the nuclear weapons and airpower capabilities which would wreak havoc upon an aggressor, and making preparations to mobilize the industrial, manpower, and maritime strength of North America to rescue western Europe in the event of attack. Many military leaders, of course, were aware of other potential threats. The development of Soviet power would eventually require a continental defense system; the policy of containment, as Gruenther pointed out, required a readiness to use ground forces in many places about the globe. Nonetheless, given the budgetary limitations, the main emphasis of military policy was on preparation for general war with the Soviet Union.

This preoccupation was reinforced by the natural tendency to identify war with total war. "We can be certain [General Marshall declared in his final report as Chief of Staff in 1945] that the next war, if there is one, will be even more total than this one." Two and a half years later, General Eisenhower, in *his* final report as Chief of Staff, echoed these sentiments and urged more extensive preparation for the total mobilization which would be required in the future. The other services shared similar expectations. The World War II experience, so recent and so compelling, furnished the basis for postwar requirements. "All advocates of every theory of American security," commented the House Armed Services Committee in 1950, "turn back to the experiences of World War II for historical examples—for illustration—to prove the soundness of their own arguments." For the Army, in particular, the future total war would be World War II with additions. "Armed forces and the nature of war, if war comes during the next few years," declared the Army's leading planner in 1947, "will in general be similar initially to the closing phases of World War II." Agreeing that the next war would be a total war, the Air Force and the Navy, however, were more reluctant to identify it with World War II. The Air Force, in particular, emphasized that the weapons of World War II were obsolete. Its image of total war assigned the initial and decisive role to airpower, with the surface services playing secondary and supporting parts. Navy opinion was hesitant about defining exactly what a new world war would be like. The Army view that it would be World War II over again implicitly held that it would be World War II in Europe over again. The Air Force view also left little room for the Navy. "I just feel that World War III," Admiral Radford argued, "is going to be different, and I would hate to see our new organization patterned after the organization of World War II." Nonetheless, the principal goals of all the services—UMT for the Army, 70 groups for the Air Force, the flush-deck supercarrier for the Navy—had been set before the end of World War II. Whatever relevance they had to the needs of the Cold War was fortuitous.

All the services recognized that American military forces would have to maintain an unprecedented degree of readiness in the future. For the Army, however, this meant not the abandonment of mobilization but its improvement. General Marshall admitted that the atomic bomb made it necessary to be ready to fight immediately and that the United States would not have time, allies, or oceans to protect it in World War III. Nonetheless, he also strongly argued that American security would be assured if it were possible to mobilize four million men within one year after an emergency developed. In a similar vein General Eisenhower interpreted "preparedness" to mean "a state of organized readiness to meet external aggression by a timely mobilization of public opinion, trained men, proved weapons and essential industries, together with the unmatched spiritual resources of America. . . ." Such a concept was a far cry from the readiness which later became commonplace in the Cold War. The Air Force view was somewhat more advanced. "The first requirement of the peacetime Air Force," General Spaatz said, "is a combat force-in-being; ready for immediate employment; thoroughly trained; well equipped; wisely disposed on strategic bases; and capable of rapid concentration anywhere over suitable airways and connecting bases."

In the immediate postwar years the concept of deterrence by forces-in-being had little place in military planning. The Joint Chiefs did accord a deterrent role to the atomic bomb, but deterrence was seen as a peculiar function of the bomb and strategic airpower, not of the armed forces as a whole. Army leaders maintained their prewar faith in industrial potential despite warnings that a revolution was taking place in military affairs. In 1946 in a remarkably prescient volume, five social scientists outlined the future effects of nuclear weapons and the requirements of a policy of "determent." Our military authorities, Bernard Brodie complained "continue to think in terms of peacetime military establishments which are simply cadres and which are expected to undergo an enormous but slow expansion *after* the outbreak of hostilities." Nevertheless, two years later the Army Chief of Staff endorsed Bernard Baruch's World War I views that war would require "a mobilization" of all the country's resources, "industrial, agricultural and financial," and the following year, after the Soviet atomic bomb, another Chief of Staff declared that "if there is any single factor today which would deter a nation seeking world domination, it would be the great industrial capacity of this country rather than its armed strength."

Continued Army reliance on the industrial and manpower potential reflected in part the budgetary limits on the armed forces. As Eisenhower pointed out, the Army's M-Day requirement was 1,300,000 men. The Regular Army, he held, could never be this large. Ready reserve forces were necessary. Conditioned by the lean years of the 1920s, the military found it difficult to conceive of a situation in which American peacetime military force might decisively influence the behavior of foreign powers. In 1950 both Generals Bradley and Collins agreed that if war did come the budget was too little, and if war did not come the budget was too much. If we were sure, General Collins said, that there would be a war, we ought to be spending $50 billion a year on defense instead of $13 billion. The Joint Chiefs, he continued, did not advocate this, because if the war did not come, such a level of spending would unduly upset the economy. The probability of a future war and the likely character of that war, in short, were the two factors which should determine the level and nature of military programs. Elsewhere Collins did state that it was necessary to begin thinking more about preventing war than preparing for war, but this axiom had not been integrated into the military planning process. In contrast, the State Department at the same time was taking the lead in developing a program estimated to cost up to $35 billion on the quite different assumption that such a program was necessary to deter war. The military, however, found it difficult to grasp the constructive, creative role which military force could play in peace to maintain peace.

Thus, from 1946 through 1949 the United States followed several different strategies, none of which it was willing to pay for. A foreign policy of containment demanded not only airpower and nuclear weapons but ground forces to repulse local aggressions. The support for these forces came largely from the professional elements in the State Department and a few people, such as Gruenther, in the Pentagon. In general, however, the Army espoused an improved version of the prewar mobilization strategy. Necessarily, this limited the ability of the diplomats to develop high-level support for limited war forces. During 1947 and 1948, moreover, the most ardent and respected advocate of a mobilization strategy was the Secretary of State. General Marshall's great concern was with neither brush-fire war divisions nor nuclear airpower but universal military training. On the other hand, the Air Force was certain that strategic airpower and nuclear weapons would not only deter a future general war but also would provide the easiest and most effective way of winning one. The implications of neither limited war, nor mobilization, nor nuclear airpower were fully spelled out. An inadequate balance existed but no overall strategic plan. Budgetary policy gave domestic needs priority and left the country without the military forces to implement either the foreign policy of the diplomats or the strategy of the soldiers. The Army did not get UMT. The Air Force did not get the 70 wings it wanted. The State Department did not get its limited war divisions. The two great constraints on effective military planning, the doctrinal heritage from the past and the pressure of domestic needs, combined to produce a serious gap between military policy and foreign policy.

# The National Security Act

BY WALTER MILLIS

WITH THE NATIONAL SECURITY ACT the post-war reorganization of the American military, diplomatic and political system was substantially complete. It was a reorganization which, of course, included many other elements—the Atomic Energy Act; the military appropriation acts which sought to establish a sound level of peacetime military expenditure; the proposals for universal military training and their failure; the reorganization of the civil government; the substitution of civil for military control in the occupied areas, and the Truman "loyalty" order, issued only nine days after the enunciation of the Truman Doctrine and for the first time establishing in the United States in peacetime a large-scale system of testing persons not for their acts but for their political beliefs. But of all these measures the Security Act was the most comprehensive and most conscious in its intent. It put the capstone, so to speak, on the new governmental structure deriving from the experiences of the Second World War. Subsequent developments were to flow, not from the experiences of the war but from the harsh lessons of the post-war period to which it led.

The National Security Act represented a kind of basic charter of civil-military relations and of security policy formation. The core of the new system was the National Security Council, with the President as chairman and a membership including the Secretary of State, the Secretary of Defense, the three service Secretaries, the chairman of the new National Security Resources Board and such other department or agency heads as the President might from time to time add to it. The Central Intelligence Agency was placed directly under the Council. While it retained some responsibilities in the "cloak and dagger" field, CIA's major function was to collect and "coordinate" (a distressingly frequent word) all intelligence coming into other branches of the government, to analyze it and make the distillate available to the President and the National Security Council.

The theory was that NSC, composed of the highest civilian officials responsible for diplomatic, military and industrial planning, and informed by CIA, would generate the basic policy recommendations in all matters affecting the national security. Accepted by the President, these recommendations would define the national policy and provide a clear, consolidated guide to action by the planning and operating agencies. With policy thus defined, the State Department would know how to conduct its international negotiations; it would also know the military potentials available to it. The now unified Military Establishment would devise the strategic and logistic plans necessary to support the agreed policy, or ensure (through its civilian representatives in NSC) that no policies were adopted making demands beyond the available military capabilities. The new National Security

From *Arms and the State: Civil-Military Elements in National Policy*, by Walter Millis with Harvey C. Mansfield and Harold Stein (New York, The Twentieth Century Fund, 1958), 178–185. Used by permission.

Resources Board, charged with all problems of industrial, manpower and raw material mobilization, would prepare mobilization plans to support the military strategy or (at least inferentially) keep the strategic planners within the bounds which the national resources would sustain.

### The Military Establishment

The Military Establishment itself was composed of three Departments, each independently administered by its civilian Secretary and each sustaining a military service under the command of its Chief of Staff. These were, however, now linked together by a whole series of "joint" and "coordinating" agencies. A common military direction was provided by the Joint Chiefs of Staff, where the three service chiefs (and the Chief of Staff to the President when there was one) would sit together. The Joint Chiefs of Staff, however, was much more than four (or three) eminent officers sitting around a table; it was an agency, provided with its secretariat, its Joint Staff, its many joint committees and groups and its intricate organization charts, all directed toward providing a structure of common planning and command. They would, theoretically, serve as advisers to both the Secretary of Defense and the President, and transmit Presidential decisions to the affected services.

Military administration, as distinct from military command, was in theory to be coordinated by the Secretary of Defense. His authority had been limited. He was given only "general direction, authority and control" over the departments; he was expressly forbidden to maintain a military staff and was allowed to appoint not more than three special assistants from civil life. To advise him, he was given a War Council, composed of the three Secretaries and the three service Chiefs of Staff. He was given two other agencies of common action: a Munitions Board to coordinate military procurement and a Research and Development Board to coordinate military research. Both were under civilian heads, responsible to the Secretary of Defense, but neither was well insulated from the military command authority embodied in the Joint Chiefs.

The Office of the Secretary of Defense (he had no Department) was thus kept to a minimum. But he was given one significant power—to "supervise and coordinate" the budget estimates. The new system quite plainly recognized the budget as not only the clearest expression of military policy but the controlling factor over its course and development. It sought carefully to mesh the military with the civilian responsibilities for the budget. With the policy decisions of NSC and the President as their guide, the Joint Chiefs would, in theory, prepare the strategic plans necessary to support them. They would then assign to the respective services both their strategic and their logistic responsibilities for fulfillment of the plans. The service departments would then independently make their own estimates of what they required in the way of weapons and force levels to enable them to meet the assigned responsibility. The result would be embodied in three departmental budgets. These would go back to JCS for review and consolidation. The result, with duplications and wastes eliminated, was supposed to represent a strictly military estimate of the minimum requirements for support of the policies received from NSC and the President.

But the civilian departmental Secretaries had already had a commanding voice in the preparation of the departmental estimates. The civilian Secretary of Defense was required to "supervise and coordinate" the whole process of military budget-making; and the civilian Comptroller in the Office of the Secretary of Defense was soon to become one of the most powerful officials in government. He (and the Secretary of Defense) reviewed the JCS budget before finally presenting it to the President and the Budget Bureau. In theory, military appropriations originated in the policy determinations of NSC and the President, these were translated into military terms by JCS, these were translated into money by the departments, this was reviewed by JCS and revised by the Secretary of Defense, to return to the White House and its Budget Bureau for final integration into the total national policy. There is a certain beauty in the theory. It is hardly necessary to say that it was seldom to appear in the practice.

Civil and military control had been intermingled all along the line. There was no point in the whole budget process at which the soldiers were not being ridden by the civilian budget-makers, and no point at which the civilian budget-makers were not being ridden by the soldiers, with neither in a position of clear responsibility for the results. It may be that such a situation is inescapable; at any rate, neither of the two obvious avenues of escape is attractive. One is to put the civilians in complete control, through the budget, of all questions of military plan and policy; the other is to put the military in complete control, through their estimates of the requirements of military plan and policy, over the budget. In the decade after 1947 the country was to wrestle with both ideas and was to accept neither. The budget, though a powerful regulator of civil-military relationships, is not a final nor altogether adequate one.

### Weak Points in the System

While one must leave the question of the efficacy and success of the 1947 National Security Act to the later history, it may be useful to indicate here some of the ways in which it was to fail to meet the expectations entertained for it. The National Security Council proved the first weak point in the mechanism. This was due partly to Truman's disinclination to make full use of it; but mainly, perhaps, to the inherent difficulty of its assigned role. While it was to produce "policy papers" by the hundred over the next few years, they were not often to deal with the really big issues, and when they did, they lacked the precision and decisiveness necessary if they were to serve as guides to action. It may be that in a democratic society effective operating policy simply cannot be generated by a group of non-elected administrators passing in secret, in the light of secret information, on the secret productions of an anonymous planning staff. Or it may be that in our difficult and fluid world the very concept of a long-range, fixed "national policy" is defective and that it is impossible to arrive at policy determinations (or predictions) capable of providing a firm foundation for continuing military policy and military preparation. Whatever the reason, the soldiers have never ceased to complain since 1947 that they never receive the policy directives which would enable them to return clear military answers for the problems presented to them. Eisenhower reactivated NSC and infused into it a greater responsibility than it enjoyed under Truman. It is not clear that the net results have been much better.

If JCS received inadequate guidance from NSC, it also suffered under handicaps of its own. JCS had worked with rather remarkable though imperfect success in the conduct of a colossal war effort, and it was to work well again in the conduct of the Korean War, but it was not well suited to meeting the different and in some ways more difficult, because more uncertain, problems of an uneasy peace. After 1947, the nation looked to JCS to provide militarily sound answers for two broad and basic questions: How much of the nation's total resources should be devoted to military preparation? How should the determined amount be allocated among the services, the various weapons systems, the rival strategic theories? These questions were inherently unanswerable. There is no way of knowing how much should be given to preparation against a peril which can never be estimated with precision and which may never appear at all. And there is no way of deciding finally between weapons systems for each of which there are compelling arguments, none of which can be put to practical test, and all of which are highly uncertain in their probable effects.

It is asking too much of any military body to return technically "sound" replies to questions such as these; it was certainly asking too much of JCS. The Joint Chiefs were composed of the three service commanders (in addition to the Chief of Staff to the President, who at that time was not even *primus* among *pares*), each with his first loyalty to the service which he headed and passionately engaged as a partisan in the issues on which the JCS was supposed to give a corporate judgment. By their composition, the Joint Chiefs were almost constitutionally incapable of resolving the major problems which the National Security Act had confided to them. Since there appeared to be no other agency, in existence or imaginable, which could be relied upon to resolve these problems rightly, there was something to be said for leaving them to an agency which, rather than resolve them wrongly, would not resolve them at all. It is certainly better to leave unanswerable questions unanswered than to provide specious answers clothed in an appearance of technical authority. But this was not appreciated in the earlier years of the peacetime JCS, and the chiefs were to come in for much bitter criticism of their inability to arrive at a "sound" and unified strategic system.

Without clear policy guidance and unable to resolve the technical differences, JCS could hardly distribute to the three services their basic strategic and logistic responsibilities with much exactitude. Lacking such directives, each continued to build its budget requests around what it would like to have (and thought that it could get) rather than around clearly calculated "needs." When these requests were submitted to JCS for review, the Joint Chiefs (three of whom were the men making the requests) could do little more than "cut the pie" with approximate equality. The Secretary of Defense could do little more (aside from insisting on certain operating economies, generally of a minor kind) than cut the totals further to what he thought the Budget Bureau would stand for. The Budget Bureau's responsibility was to squeeze the whole thing under a pre-determined "ceiling"; this it could do only by hunting out what to its civilian mind looked like military "non-essentials." So it happened in the Truman years; so it happened again under Eisenhower. Out of this process there has never emerged a long-range, self-consistent military policy, clearly adequate to the military "need" and clearly consonant with the economic and political base. That such a policy could emerge is perhaps only another illusion. When real needs have in crises imposed themselves the plans have been revised drastically upward to meet them; when they have passed, the pressures of economy have revised drastically downward all estimates of their possible recurrence.

NSC and JCS were the key elements in the reorganization, and both, with the later Department of Defense, have survived. The other agencies of unification were at best only partially successful. The National Security Resources Board was essentially an agency for stand-by planning against a possible future "emergency." As the realization slowly grew that our problems were not those of the future but of the present, NSRB tended to lose its significance and was never able to establish the prestige intended for it. It was ultimately abolished, and its powers transferred to the Office of Defense Mobilization. The Munitions Board and the Research and Development Board, while useful, tended to develop into service "log-rolling" agencies, and had difficulty in establishing satisfactory relationships with JCS. Robert A. Lovett, Truman's last Secretary of Defense, was critical of them, and the Eisenhower Administration superseded them with individual Assistant Secretaries of Defense. Little was heard of the War Council. Louis Johnson, when he succeeded Forrestal as Secretary of Defense, endeavored to revive it under a different name, but its achievements were not notable, and it appears to have been buried under the massive accretion of power in the Department of Defense. The "coordination" system envisaged in 1947, with the Secretary of Defense no more than a moderator among inter-service disputes, had yielded slowly but steadily to a centralization of power in the hands of the Defense Secretary.

Even the Central Intelligence Agency has fallen somewhat short of expectations, and it may be that the concept of "intelligence," like those of "policy" or "strategic plan," is a concept unable to carry all the burdens popularly assigned to it. It may be that nations, like men, will never be all-knowing, all-wise and all-powerful; and that the trinity of intelligence, policy and strategy, the one proceeding from the other, will never find any very valid counterpart in the real world of desperate expedient and stratagem in the face of the unexpected and the unprepared-for—the world which we seem normally to inhabit.

The National Security Act, at any rate, could not transform the real world into one of order and precision. It was to fail to fulfill many of the hopes which had been entertained for it. Stimson's approving comment upon its enactment: "When the civilians and the soldiers are in cordial and sympathetic agreement, each conscious of his proper function and his proper relation to the other, there are few limits to the advances that can be made," was not to be fully borne out. Indeed, it reflected a misconception; it echoed the great days of half a century before, when Elihu Root, a civilian, had forced a rational military organization upon the reluctant soldiers of 1900. It was not too relevant to the real issues of 1947. The underlying problem in the writing of the National Security Act was never to secure agreement between the military and the civilians; it was to secure agreement among the military men (and their civilian supporters), and this problem received little more than formal solution. But the signature of the act completed the post-war reorganization. We had constructed our new system. Almost immediately it was to be put to severe test.

# 19.

# The Challenge of Korea

The first instance of Communist military aggression occurred in Korea. Caught by surprise, the entire world anxiously watched the United Nations and the United States to see the nature of their response. President Truman, convinced that the Second World War had resulted from the failure of the League of Nations to provide collective security, was determined that a third World War should not occur through a similar default. At his instigation, the Security Council first denounced the aggression, and then called on all members to lend support to South Korea. Acting through the United Nations, the President committed air, land, and naval forces to what became a collective resistance to a unilateral action.

The uniqueness of the Korean experience raised a number of questions regarding American defense policy. Many felt that the President, as Commander-in-Chief, had no authority to wage war without the consent of Congress. Also, America's military posture was based on the prospect of all out war with heavy reliance on the strategic use of nuclear weapons delivered by aircraft. The relative shortage of conventional forces found the nation unprepared for the kind of fighting that took place in Korea. Moreover, the initial objective of resisting aggression was succeeded, following General MacArthur's brilliant tactical victories, by the objective of unifying North and South Korea through force of arms. The subsequent Chinese intervention and eventual stalemate in the war led to violent disputes over the method of waging war and the role of civilians and military men in policy formulation. In the following selection Morton H. Halperin analyses the controversial aspects of the limiting process in the Korean War.

# The Limiting Process in the Korean War

## BY MORTON H. HALPERIN

THE NORTH KOREAN ATTACK on South Korea suggested the willingness of the Communists to seek a limited objective by a limited use of force. The Soviets probably intended to seize South Korea with the use of North Korean forces and then to halt their military operations. When the United States intervened, they recognized their miscalculation of American intentions, while proceeding on the assumption that American intervention need not lead to world war. The attack upon South Korea, moreover, seems to have been motivated by the Soviet compulsion to fill power vacuums. In view of the specific United States declaration that South Korea was outside its defense perimeter, the Soviets could have reasonably counted on a quick and easy victory by the North Koreans. But, while Communist conduct during the war reflected a doctrine that included the limited use of military force, and limited objectives, neither the Chinese nor the Russians seemed to have any idea of the optimum methods of communicating intentions and capabilities to the other side in the course of such a war.

American doctrine, on the other hand, seems to have been much less hospitable to the limitation of warfare. It would appear that the United States had not foreseen the possibility of Soviet military action in South Korea or any other local area unconnected with a general Soviet military offensive. The result was the American decision not to prepare for the defense of South Korea in view of the low estimate of its value in a general war. Thus, the decision of June of 1950 to defend South Korea was not based on a re-estimate of South Korea's military importance, but on a recognition that something had occurred for which American military doctrine had not been prepared. It is important to note that, in its policy decisions throughout the war, the United States was operating without any general theoretical notions of the nature of limited war in the atomic age, and its decisions were probably affected by the lack of such theory.

Each side's image of the other's doctrines and intentions influenced its decisions. The Soviets clearly underestimated the likelihood of American intervention. In the Soviet view, the American declaration that it would defend South Korea only as part of its United Nations obligations had meant that the United States would not in fact defend South Korea. The Soviets failed to anticipate the partly moral and partly political American reaction to aggression. They were insensitive to the importance that the United States would attach to repelling "illegal" aggression, as opposed to less clear-cut violations of international law.

The American decision to intervene in Korea and the subsequent decisions were also based on and influenced by estimates of Soviet doctrine and intentions. In assessing the motives and operating doctrine of the North Korean attack, American policy-makers gave consideration and,

From Morton H. Halperin, "The Limiting Process in the Korean War." Reprinted with permission from *Political Science Quarterly*, Vol. 78, No. 1, March 1963, pp. 20–39.

to some extent, credence to five different interpretations, as follows:

(1) The "diversionary move" interpretation. In view of the number of other areas, particularly Western Europe, that appeared more militarily significant than South Korea, the South Korean attack was seen as a diversionary move, aimed to draw American resources away from the areas where they were most important. Truman reports that he shared this view in part and was determined not to leave Europe vulnerable to Soviet aggression.

(2) The "soft-spot probing" interpretation. By this image of Soviet doctrine, the Soviet compulsion to fill power vacuums had led to the attack on South Korea which had been abandoned by the United States and which was clearly incapable of defending itself.

(3) The "testing" interpretation. This was the view that seemed most to influence Truman's image of the North Korean attack. It recalled the progress of Hitler's aggressive moves and asserted that the North Korean attack should be seen as a prelude to attacks in other areas if that aggression were allowed to succeed. This view differed from the "soft-spot probing" interpretation in its assumption that the Communists' success in Korea would encourage them to attempt aggression in the other areas where Western defense capabilities were far stronger. In short, the purpose of the Korean attack was to probe the firmness of Western intentions, and not simply to fill a power vacuum.

(4) The "demonstration" interpretation. By this interpretation, the Soviets were mainly concerned with demonstrating their own strength and American weakness in order to promote, on a long term basis, important shifts in political allegiance throughout the world.

(5) The "Soviet-Far-East-strategy" interpretation. This interpretation put emphasis on the idea, discussed above, that the Soviets hoped to prevent the entrance of Japan into the Western Camp and to pave the way for further Communist expansion in the Far East.

As George has pointed out, the inclination of American policy-makers toward the "testing" interpretation of Soviet doctrine—in which the Korean attack was equated with Hitler's early expansionist moves—may have reinforced the likelihood that the United States would intervene in Korea. If the "soft-spot probing" interpretation of Soviet conduct had been accepted instead, the United States might have been more prone to cede South Korea while taking steps to prevent the existence of power vacuums elsewhere. It was the belief that successful aggression would embolden the Soviets that made the defense of South Korea seem so crucial.

### The Fear of General War

In an analysis of the limiting process, it is important to say again that the Korean War was fought before the era of intercontinental ballistic missiles and fusion weapons. Thus, while both sides could have expanded the war quickly and decisively, there was not the danger that now exists of a sudden unleashing of nuclear missiles which within an hour could destroy a large part of both the United States and the Soviet Union.

Even without this threat of a mutually devastating strategic exchange, the danger of a world war was nevertheless present, and it is significant that both sides seem to have been determined to avoid its occurrence. Truman has reported that the major American aim in Korea was to prevent a third world war; the United States was determined not to give the Soviets any "excuse" to initiate global war. The Russian decision to remain out of the war seemed to be partly motivated by a fear of igniting a global war. In this situation where neither side could gain a decisive advantage by going first, both sides seemed to recognize that, no matter who started the global war, both would suffer major losses. While the United States could have attacked the Soviet Union with its relatively limited stockpile of atomic weapons, it could probably not have prevented a Soviet ground attack in Western Europe which might result in Communist domination of the European continent. The Soviets had no capacity to attack the United States and could not have prevented an

American attack on the Soviet Union. While both sides avoided forcing the other into starting a global war, neither was preoccupied with the possibility of "pre-emption" by its adversary.

The United States was, however, concerned that the Korean War should not lead it to expend those military capabilities which were considered an important deterrent to general war. Whereas today there is a somewhat clearer distinction between the main forces to deter and fight a general war and forces primarily designed for local war, in Korea the United States was, in fact, using the troops and the material which it felt were necessary to deter general war. At the MacArthur hearings, Air Force General Vandenberg rejected a Senator's suggestion that the United States should commit a major part of the American Air Force to the Korean War effort. He argued instead that the United States must get a cease-fire

> without endangering that one potential that we have which has kept the peace so far, which is the United States Air Force; which, if utilized in a manner to do what you are suggesting, would [sic.], because of attrition and because the size of the Air Force is such and the size of the air force industry is such that we could not still be that deterrent to [general] war which we are today.

## Domestic Political Pressures

During the Korean War, the Truman Administration continued to pursue its domestic political goals. Despite the war, it was "politics as usual" on both sides of the political fence. The President was busily engaged in promoting his Fair Deal program, consolidating the position of the Democratic Party, strengthening his Northern and Western liberal support in Congress, and calming the political crises raised by such men as Senator McCarthy. Nor was the Administration immune to criticism from the Republican Party which felt it possible, necessary, and desirable to attack the Administration's conduct, as well as to question the basic concept of limited war.

After the MacArthur hearings, a Republican minority report declared: "We believe that a policy of victory must be announced to the American people in order to restore unity and confidence. It is too much to expect that our people will accept a limited war. Our policy must be to win. Our strategy must be devised to bring about decisive victory."

These few sentences suggest a number of important assumptions about the nature of wartime politics. The first is the notion that the unity of the American people can be achieved only with a declaration that victory is the goal. A further implication is that, after such a declaration, the method of achieving a battlefield victory becomes a "military" problem, that is, beyond the realm of partisan domestic politics. On the other hand, once the government admits that there are other political considerations that affect and moderate the goal of a strictly military victory, then, according to this Republican statement, it is legitimate to criticize the particular policy adopted. Unity will come only when the country is asked to back an absolute goal. If there is no such goal, then it is the duty of the opposition to examine and critically appraise the war effort.

Congress, as a whole, also felt itself free to criticize. The inquiries into the firing of General MacArthur were striking in that they required the Administration, *during the war*, to justify its conduct and to explain publicly what it hoped to accomplish in the war and how it was conducting the war, as well as to explicate a host of particulars which must have been of as much interest to the Communists as they were to the Senators across the table.

The quotation from the Republican Senators also reflects the then still strong American opposition to limited war. The Senators stated flatly that the American people would not accept the strategy of limited war, and indicated their rejection of the strategy as well. The implication is that during a limited war the American government will be subjected to attacks from the political opposition, from Congress, and from public citizens on two grounds: on the legitimacy of fighting a limited war, and on the particular tactics employed in the war.

The general public seems to have shared the Republican Senators' dissatisfaction with the course of the Korean War, at least in its later stages. On the other hand, the public apparently approved the decision of the Eisenhower Administration to end the war short of victory. The public's disapproval of the Korean campaign probably added to the margin of Eisenhower's victory in 1952; his ending the war enhanced the Republican image as the party of peace and increased the Eisenhower plurality in 1956. On the other hand, at least according to the results of the Michigan Survey Research Center voting studies, the Korean War did not have a major or lasting impact on popular political attitudes.

American political leaders seem to have overestimated the effect of the war on the voting public. Korea is taken as demonstrating—as to some extent it did—that local wars are not popular with the American public. Leading the United States into one or expanding it is likely to be perceived as a political liability; ending one on almost any terms may be a political asset.

All these domestic pressures undoubtedly influenced the manner in which the Truman Administration conducted its Korean operations, both by hampering its freedom of action and by increasing the costs of various actions.

## The Great Decisions

The remainder of this essay will explore several of the major decisions to limit or expand the Korean War and the general nature of the Korean War limiting process.

### Atomic Weapons

As was noted above, the most dramatic limit on the Korean War was the failure of either side to use its atomic weapons. According to Brodie,* there were four reasons why nuclear weapons were not used by the United States:

(1) The Joint Chiefs of Staff and civilian policy-makers continued to feel that the war in Korea was basically a Soviet feint. There was, therefore, a strong case for conserving the then relatively limited stockpile of atomic weapons for the principal war which, they thought, would come in Europe. Their fear was not that the employment of nuclear weapons would lead to an expansion of the war and a Soviet attack on Europe, but rather that Korea was deliberately designed as a decoy to get us to exhaust our nuclear stockpile and our conventional military resources, so that the Soviets could later attack with impunity in Europe. It was the desire, then, to save resources and not the fear of provoking the enemy that was one of the main causes of the American decision not to use nuclear weapons in Korea.

(2) American policy was also affected by the reports of local commanders that there were no suitable targets for nuclear weapons in Korea. While the impact of this view was considerable, it apparently reflected an uninformed attitude about the possible uses of nuclear weapons. Commanders in the field came to think, for example, that atomic bombs were of little use against bridges, a belief which Brodie explained as follows:

> This odd idea probably resulted from a misreading of the results at Hiroshima and Nagasaki. Some bridges were indeed badly damaged at those places and some were not, but for the latter it was generally forgotten that a bridge only 270 feet from ground zero at Hiroshima was actually 2,100 feet from the point of explosion, and also that it received its blast effect from above rather than from the side.†

Nuclear weapons were still relatively new and had not been extensively tested, and it is probable that commanders in the field were too busy to search out potential targets for nuclear weapons.

(3) Our allies, particularly the British, were strongly and emotionally opposed to the use of nuclear weapons in the Korean War. This pressure from our allies strengthened our own anxieties and moral doubts about again using these terrible new weapons.

(4) A subsidiary reason for the failure to use nuclear weapons in the Korean War was the fear of the retaliatory employment by the Soviets of the few atomic weapons in their possession against Pusan or Japan, despite the American near-monopoly over these weapons.

* Bernard Brodie, *Strategy in the Missile Age*, (Princeton, 1959), 319–321.

† *Ibid.*, 319n.

Brodie doubts, however, if this fear played a conscious part in the relevant decisions.

The United States, then, was concerned with the vulnerability of Europe and with co-ordinating policy with her allies. It was also determined not to be drawn in by a Soviet feint in Korea. But it is important to note that the first and second factors will not obtain in the future. The American stockpile of tactical nuclear weapons is now so great that military commanders may urge their use precisely because they are a non-scarce military resource, and certainly no argument can be made that they should not be used because they are scarce. Military officers now have a much better understanding of the capabilities of nuclear weapons, which, moreover, now come in much smaller sizes. Thus, it will be clear to military commanders that there would be suitable targets for their use in any conceivable future major limited war. While we can expect continued pressure from our allies against the use of nuclear weapons, it is possible that certain allies might advocate their use in some situations. There will, however, be other international political pressures—for example from the uncommitted or neutral states—against nuclear weapons, and the possibility of a Soviet nuclear response will be a much more important determinant of the decision.

We know much less about the details of the Russian decision not to use atomic weapons in Korea. The Russians seemed determined not to supply any materiel to the forces fighting in Korea which could clearly be labeled as having been supplied by them after the war began. This would certainly be the case with atomic weapons. In addition, the Soviet stockpile of such weapons was so small that its use in a localized military encounter might have seemed wasteful.

Here again, the limit observed by both sides seems not to have resulted from an attempt—or even an awareness of the need—to bargain with the enemy. However, the Soviets were probably more restrained than the United States by the fear that the initiation of nuclear attacks would be met by a response in kind.

The Chinese Communists seem genuinely to have feared the possibility of the American use of nuclear weapons when they intervened in the Korean War. According to Whiting, the Chinese felt that a nuclear response was a real possibility; intervention was considered risky; and every effort was made to delay it and to minimize its consequences. The extent of this Chinese concern was reflected both in its shelter-building program and in domestic Chinese Communist propaganda. But Peiping was reassured by the three-week testing period of relatively small Chinese intervention which revealed that United States aircraft, although authorized to bomb the Korean ends of the Yalu bridges, were forbidden to venture into Chinese territory.

The background of the limit on the use of atomic weapons in the Korean War, then, suggests a failure of both sides to understand what the other side was likely to do and what the other side's fears and goals were. It also suggests that, to a large extent, the determination of limits is based on considerations other than those that result from the battlefield interaction. Some of the other limiting points established in the war reveal the same pattern.

### Chinese Intervention

One of the major expansions of the Korean War was the decision of the United Nations Command to cross the thirty-eighth parallel. This decision was based partly on the military consideration that one could not stand by and allow the enemy forces to regroup for renewed attack just beyond the border. It was also made on political grounds. When the battlefield conditions changed in its favor, the United States decided to pursue the unification of Korea by military means. In crossing the parallel the United Nations Command was aware of the risk that it might trigger Chinese Communist intervention, and tried by reassuring statements to prevent it. But, it apparently underestimated the Chinese reaction, and, at the same time, it failed to develop a concurrent strategy which, by retaliatory threats or other sanctions, could succeed in preventing Chinese intervention. As Whiting has suggested,* the threat to use atomic

* Allen S. Whiting, *China Crosses the Yalu: The Decision to Enter the Korean War* (New York, 1960), 162.

weapons on the Chinese mainland, if the Chinese intervened, might have been a much more effective deterrent than the attempt to reassure them that a march to the border did not presage an attack on mainland China. The threat to use atomic weapons would have involved major political costs for the United States, and it is not clear that the American government would have warned of a possible atomic attack, even if it recognized its likely effect. Had it been aware that the fear of greater expansion might have deterred Chinese intervention, an alternative course might have been to threaten to expand the war to China with conventional weapons. But even this was not done. In fact a decision was made that Chinese intervention would not lead to conventional bombing beyond the Yalu. MacArthur reportedly believed that this decision had been leaked to the Chinese.

In choosing, instead, to inform the Chinese of its limited objectives, the United States also considered it important to reassure the Chinese that their hydroelectric plants would not be jeopardized by a march up to the Yalu. But, as Whiting has pointed out:

> It was widely believed in Western circles that a determining factor in Chinese Communist concern over North Korea was the reliance of Manchurian industry upon power supplies across the border as well as along the Yalu River. This belief prompted explicit reassurances from Western spokesmen, both in Washington and at Lake Success, concerning "China's legitimate interests" near the frontier. Yet we have seen that Peking ignored this issue completely in its domestic as well as its foreign communications. The absence of propaganda about the protection of the hydroelectric installations, despite the need to maximize popular response to mobilization of "volunteers," suggests that this consideration played little if any role in motivating Chinese Communist intervention.*

In its advance through North Korea, then, the United Nations Command was attempting to communicate two points to the Chinese Communists: first, that it was prepared to go up to but not beyond the Yalu, and second, that it was prepared to respect China's legitimate interests in the northern regions of North Korea. It sought, therefore, to establish its limited objectives: that United Nations forces would take all North Korea, that the North Korean government would cease to exist, but that China's legitimate industrial interests would be protected. And it sought to assure the Chinese that the capture of North Korea would not be used as a springboard for an attack into China. It assumed that these were the limits in which the Chinese were interested, and that these would serve to keep the Chinese out of the war. But Chinese interests were different and could only be satisfied by different boundary conditions to the war.

Neustadt argues that the Chinese were not in any way affected by the announcement of the United Nations aim to destroy the North Korean government:

> To judge from what the Chinese said, and later did, Peking's concern was with MacArthur's military progress, never mind its foreign policy objective. Chinese concern was not confined to anything so simple as a buffer zone along the border; an entity called North Korea, not the border, was at stake (perhaps in roughly the same sense that South Korea, under reverse circumstances, was for Washington). Even had the United Nations promised restoration of an independent North once all resistance ceased—which, naturally, no one proposed—I know of nothing to suggest that Peking would have withheld intervention. The Communist world does not take kindly, it appears, to the dismantling of the member state's facilities for government: the party and the army. MacArthur's military progress threatened both, no matter what came after. In short, the military risks and the diplomatic dangers usually associated with MacArthur's march across the parallel existed independent of the words used in the UN resolution. MacArthur's march was authorized before the words were seen, much less approved, at Lake Success.†

Even if we assume that Neustadt was attempting to justify the policy of an Administration with which he was connected, it seems clear that Washington was convinced in retrospect that its declarations did not influence the Chinese decision to enter the war and that no other declara-

* Whiting, 151–152.

† Richard E. Neustadt, *Presidential Power: The Politics of Leadership* (New York, 1960), 125; see also 123–124.

tory policy could have altered the Chinese decision. American policy-makers have concluded that once the decision was made to cross the thirty-eighth parallel, nothing could be done to affect the Chinese decision. In fact, the State Department reportedly argued in December of 1950 that the Chinese decision to intervene was made prior to the crossing of the thirty-eighth parallel. In one sense, at least, this conclusion may be wrong: the Chinese position might have been altered by threats to expand the war with the use of atomic weapons against China. Moreover, it is by no means certain that the Chinese were interested in preserving the total territorial integrity of North Korea. It is possible, as Whiting suggests, that an American commitment to advance only part way up the peninsula —that is, to permit the maintenance of the North Korean government in some part of its territory—might have been sufficient to deter the Chinese entrance into the war:

> Neither before [n]or during the first three months of war [Whiting wrote] did the degree of interest in Pyongyang evinced by Peking warrant acceptance at face value of its concern for a "just" peace, based upon the status quo ante.
>
> This is not to say that the Chinese Communist leadership was prepared to accept with equanimity the total defeat of North Korea. As a minimal goal, intervention must have been attempted to preserve an entity identifiable as the DPRK, and to prevent unification of all Korea under U.N. supervision. The late date of Chinese Communist entry into the war suggests that it was the political importance of the North Korean government, rather than its territorial integrity, that was at stake. Although intervention was officially predicated upon U.N. crossing of the thirty-eighth parallel, no Chinese People's Volunteers and Democratic People's Republic of Korea defense lines were established during the August–October period, not even to protect Pyongyang. To Peking, a "just" Korean peace was not an end in itself but rather a means towards fulfilling other related goals of policy.*

Thus, even after the crossing of the thirty-eighth parallel, Chinese intervention might have been prevented, had the United States acted differently. Although it tried to impose limits on expansion, the United States failed to grasp adequately either the reasons that the Chinese felt intervention was necessary or the threats that might have deterred their intervention. Both sides expanded the war, the United Nations by crossing the thirty-eighth parallel and the Chinese by entering the war. Both sides failed to convey to each other the kind of counteraction to be expected which might have deterred expansion. China attempted to prevent the crossing of the thirty-eighth parallel by declaring her intention to intervene, but this intention, relayed by the Indian Ambassador, was not taken seriously by the United Nations Command. The United Nations sought to prevent the Chinese entrance, not by threatening a further expansion, but by attempting to satisfy the Chinese security interests that, it was assumed, might lead her to enter the war.

Despite these two major acts of expansion which followed closely on each other, the war remained limited, and this fact suggests the fallacy of the proposition that the limitation of a war depends on neither side drastically expanding the war at any point. These were major expansions, but neither seems to have brought the sides close to decisions to initiate global war or to expand very substantially the area or intensity of the local war.

### Ports and Troops

Despite the fact that United States planes taking off from airfields in South Korea and Japan, and from aircraft carriers, consistently bombed targets in North Korea, the Communists engaged in almost no bombing south of the thirty-eighth parallel. This was one of the major asymmetries of the war both from a legalistic point of view and in terms of interfering with the military operations of the enemy. Both sides apparently devoted considerable attention to the question of what targets to attack, and a variety of motives affected the relevant decisions.

The American decision to bomb targets in North Korea was made prior to the commitment of American ground troops in June 1950. A month later permission was given to bomb industrial targets in North Korea, but the use of incendiary bombs was not permitted because of the civil damage that would have resulted. The Air Force was not allowed to bomb the areas

* Whiting, 155–156.

close to the Soviet and Chinese borders. Rashin was the single industrial center within the forbidden area and it was the only industrial target in North Korea which was not destroyed by mid-September when an end to industrial bombing was ordered by the Joint Chiefs. With this task completed, the bombing of the North Korean halves of the Yalu bridges was authorized. Because of the restrictions imposed, the operation was only partly successful and came to a halt with the freezing of the Yalu in late November. It was not until June 1952 that attacks on the hydroelectric plants in North Korea were authorized; within two weeks almost ninety per cent of the North Korean power capacity was destroyed.

American attacks on targets in North Korea steadily expanded. The attacks were aimed at affecting the immediate military situation. The restraints observed had several motives: (1) to avoid extensive civilian destruction considered undesirable on both humanitarian and propaganda grounds; (2) to avoid a spill-over of the war into China or the Soviet Union—the spill-over into China prior to her entry into the war probably did not have a major impact on Chinese policy, but it did create propaganda and political difficulties; (3) to avoid damaging, in the case of the hydroelectric plants, targets considered vital to the Chinese, so as to avoid their entrance into the war, presumably in retaliation.

The Communists exercised far greater restraint on their air forces. Except for a few night "heckling" attacks from small biplanes in the spring of 1951, no air attacks were made on any targets in South Korea. The Communist restraint was not the result of the absence of inviting military targets. The port of Pusan was an extremely inviting target for bombardment and mining. It was the key to the American logistic effort and frequently was lighted up all night. American logistic convoys and troops in the field also could have been hampered by air attacks. A number of factors seem to have influenced the Communist decision not to respond in kind to United Nations air attacks on North Korea:

(1) The Communists may have believed that it would have been very difficult, if not impossible, for the United Nations to continue its operations in Korea if Pusan came under heavy attack. It might also have been obvious that, once the United Nations committed itself to the defense of South Korea, it was no longer in a position where it could afford to accept complete withdrawal. Therefore, if attacks on its logistic lines made impossible its continued conduct of an effective ground war in Korea, the United States might have been forced to engage in strategic strikes against the Chinese, if not the Russian, homeland. If the Communists found this supposition credible, they may have concluded that, once their initial grab for South Korea failed, they could not afford to do anything that would lead to their complete control over South Korea.* They may have recognized that American confinement of the war to the Korean peninsula was dependent on her ability to fight there effectively.

(2) In order to avoid attacks on Chinese air bases just north of the Yalu, Red airmen were not allowed to attack United Nations positions from these bases. Although the Communists were permitting the United States the sanctuary of bases in Japan and on aircraft carriers, they apparently were afraid that they would not be granted a similar sanctuary for bombing operations. United States planes managed to keep the North Korean airfields out of commission throughout the war. Thus, given that the Chinese limited the use of their fields to staging operations and to fighter planes, they were incapable of bombing operations.

(3) There is some evidence to suggest that Soviet pilots constituted a significant part of the "Chinese" air force during the Korean War. If this is true, the explanation for target restraint may have been the desire to avoid the capture of Soviet airmen. This proof of direct Soviet involvement in the war would at the least have been politically damaging and, from a Soviet point of view, might have created an intolerable risk of American retaliation.

* This thesis implies that the Chinese would not have driven the United Nations forces off the Korean peninsula by ground action even if they had the capability. There is no evidence to substantiate or invalidate this point.

By the end of the war the United States was exercising almost no target restraint in North Korea and the Communists were doing no bombing in South Korea. Each side was guided by a complex series of motives and incentives. However, despite the asymmetry of the actions there is nothing to suggest that either side treated its decisions on targets as being closely related to, affected by, or likely to affect, the opponent's decisions on these questions.

## Conclusions

The development of the limiting process in the Korean War seems to have been the work, on the whole, of the civilian decision-makers, at least on the American side, in rejecting or approving requests by the military to engage in military operation which would have the effect of expanding the war. In some cases, particularly on the question of using atomic weapons, the military never made the request, and so, in some sense, no decision was made. On three occasions, General MacArthur was refused his requests: to employ Chinese Nationalist troops, to impose a naval blockade on China and to bomb bases and supply lines in China. But a number of MacArthur's requests for permission to expand the war were approved. These included the commitment of American ground forces, the Inchon offensive, and the crossing of the thirty-eighth parallel.

In deciding whether to go on the offensive in the war, Truman reports that the National Security Council recommended the consideration of three factors: action by the Soviet Union and the Chinese Communists, the views of friendly members of the United Nations and the risk of general war. It is clear that this and other decisions were also influenced by American objectives and doctrine, as well as by domestic political pressures. The balancing of the factors varied from decision to decision, but all played a role in the major decisions to limit or expand the war.

Much less is known about the Communist decision-making process or the factors which influenced their decisions to limit or expand the war. The initial decision to keep the Chinese out of the war seems to have been based largely on domestic conditions in China, particularly the desire of the Chinese to implement their program of economic growth and development, and their desire to avoid military entanglements at a time when they had not yet consolidated their hold over their own country. The reasons for the Russians' abstention from open intervention in the war are less clear. It is apparent that Russia was determined not to do anything that directly labeled her as a participant. She did not publicize the participation of any Russian "volunteers" in the war, nor provide any atomic capability, although she did supply large amounts of conventional military equipment. One likely explanation is the Russian fear that her intervention would lead to total war, and, it should be remembered, the strategic balance at this stage was one that drastically favored the West. The United States had the capability of inflicting great destruction on the Soviet homeland with its stock of atomic weapons, while the Soviets had no capability of directly attacking the United States, although they might have been able to take a large part of Western Europe with ground forces. Thus, the Soviets, aware of their inferior strategic position, were probably determined to keep out of the war and to provide no excuse for a direct American attack on the Soviet Union.

It should be noted that both sides apparently arrived at their decisions to limit the war for different reasons and with minimal attention to the battlefield interaction. In addition, they observed very different limits: that is, both did not abstain from the same actions. What we did in North Korea was quite different from what the Communists did in South Korea, but the Chinese used a much greater percentage of their gross national product than we did. Nevertheless, while we used naval vessels and airplanes to bomb troops and airfields beyond Korea, they did not. The United States engaged in logistical interdiction, the Communists did not. Each side, then, observed its own series of limits and restraints only in some general way related to, and dependent on, the limits of the other side.

At least a few of the limits were symmetrical.

Both sides restricted their military operations almost entirely to Korea, and neither used nuclear weapons. There was lack of symmetry in that all the military targets in North Korea were attacked but some in South Korea were not. The United States attacked the Chinese points of entry—the Yalu bridges—but the Chinese did not attack ours—the ports. Both sides observed a number of what Schelling has called "legalistic" limitations. The United Nations carefully observed both the Chinese and Russian borders and tried to avoid crossing them inadvertently. There was symmetry in the absence of official declarations of war. The United Nations troops participated in the war in a "police action" capacity, and none of the countries involved, including the United States, declared war. The Chinese used "volunteers," and the Russians supplied equipment and, presumably, technicians but little manpower for the battle.

In some cases, the limits represented a recognition of the battlefield interaction—if one side did something the other was likely to reciprocate—which would result in expansions of the war benefiting neither side. But the origin of many of the limits observed, and part of the explanation for others, lay not within the dynamics of the war itself, but within the domestic and international context in which the war was fought.

# 20.

# The "New Look"

Defense policies were subjected to a vigorous attack during the Presidential campaign of 1952. Waste and unnecessary expenditures were stressed as the Republican candidate demanded "more bang for the buck." The election placed in the White House a man who had spent a major portion of his life in the military profession, and who had compiled a distinguished record. By his own admission Eisenhower knew more about the subject of defense than almost anybody, and reduced the military budget by paring conventional forces and emphasizing the deterrent effect of overwhelming strategic airpower. The doctrine of "massive retaliation" adopted by his administration is spelled out in the address by Secretary of State John Foster Dulles.

The shortcomings of an all-out war approach were revealed in 1954 when the United States government reluctantly refrained from committing troops to the conflict in French Indochina. In 1957 the vaunted American technological superiority in weapons systems was shattered by the launching of the Russian Sputnik, which ushered in the missile age. As the nation frantically sought to prevent the Russians from achieving complete ascendancy in this new dimension of warfare, the budget climbed drastically and debate raged over the amount and allocation of defense expenditures. The Report of the Committee on Appropriations of the House of Representatives contains a summary of the testimony, quotations from witnesses, and a comprehensive assessment of American military policy in 1960.

# The Doctrine of Massive Retaliation

## BY JOHN FOSTER DULLES

IT IS NOW NEARLY A YEAR since the Eisenhower administration took office. During that year I have often spoken of various parts of our foreign policies. Tonight I should like to present an overall view of those policies which relate to our security.

First of all, let us recognize that many of the preceding foreign policies were good. Aid to Greece and Turkey had checked the Communist drive to the Mediterranean. The European Recovery Program had helped the peoples of Western Europe to pull out of the postwar morass. The Western powers were steadfast in Berlin and overcame the blockade with their airlift. As a loyal member of the United Nations, we had reacted with force to repel the Communist attack in Korea. When that effort exposed our military weakness, we rebuilt rapidly our military establishment. We also sought a quick buildup of armed strength in Western Europe.

These were the acts of a nation which saw the danger of Soviet communism; which realized that its own safety was tied up with that of others; which was capable of responding boldly and promptly to emergencies. These are precious values to be acclaimed. Also, we can pay tribute to congressional bipartisanship which puts the nation above politics.

But we need to recall that what we did was in the main emergency action, imposed on us by our enemies.

Let me illustrate.

1. We did not send our army into Korea because we judged in advance that it was sound military strategy to commit our Army to fight land battles in Asia. Our decision had been to pull out of Korea. It was Soviet-inspired action that pulled us back.

2. We did not decide in advance that it was wise to grant billions annually as foreign economic aid. We adopted that policy in response to the Communist efforts to sabotage the free economies of Western Europe.

3. We did not build up our military establishment at a rate which involved huge budget deficits, a depreciating currency, and a feverish economy because this seemed, in advance, a good policy. Indeed, we decided otherwise until the Soviet military threat was clearly revealed.

We live in a world where emergencies are always possible, and our survival may depend upon our capacity to meet emergencies. Let us pray that we shall always have that capacity. But, having said that, it is necessary also to say that emergency measures—however good for the emergency—do not necessarily make good permanent policies. Emergency measures are costly; they are superficial; and they imply that the enemy has the initiative. They cannot be depended on to serve our long-time interests.

### The Need for Long-Range Policies

This "long time" factor is of critical importance.

---

*Department of State Bulletin*, Vol. XXX, No. 761, January 25, 1954. Made before the Council on Foreign Relations, New York, N.Y.

The Soviet Communists are planning for what they call "an entire historical era," and we should do the same. They seek, through many types of maneuvers, gradually to divide and weaken the free nations by overextending them in efforts which, as Lenin put it, are "beyond their strength, so that they come to practical bankruptcy." Then, said Lenin, "our victory is assured." Then, said Stalin, will be "the moment for the decisive blow."

In the face of this strategy, measures cannot be judged adequate merely because they ward off an immediate danger. It is essential to do this, but it is also essential to do so without exhausting ourselves.

When the Eisenhower administration applied this test, we felt that some transformations were needed.

It is not sound military strategy permanently to commit United States land forces to Asia to a degree that leaves us no strategic reserves.

It is not sound economics, or good foreign policy, to support permanently other countries; for in the long run, that creates as much ill will as good will.

Also, it is not sound to become permanently committed to military expenditures so vast that they lead to "practical bankruptcy."

Change was imperative to assure the stamina needed for permanent security. But it was equally imperative that change should be accompanied by understanding of our true purposes. Sudden and spectacular change had to be avoided. Otherwise, there might have been a panic among our friends and miscalculated aggression by our enemies. We can, I believe, make a good report in these respects.

We need allies and collective security. Our purpose is to make these relations more effective, less costly. This can be done by placing more reliance on deterrent power and less dependence on local defensive power.

This is accepted practice so far as local communities are concerned. We keep locks on our doors, but we do not have an armed guard in every home. We rely principally on a community security system so well equipped to punish any who break in and steal that, in fact, would-be aggressors are generally deterred. That is the modern way of getting maximum protection at a bearable cost.

What the Eisenhower administration seeks is a similar international security system. We want, for ourselves and the other free nations, a maximum deterrent at a bearable cost.

Local defense will always be important. But there is no local defense which alone will contain the mighty landpower of the Communist world. Local defenses must be reinforced by the further deterrent of massive retaliatory power. A potential aggressor must know that he cannot always prescribe battle conditions that suit him. Otherwise, for example, a potential aggressor, who is glutted with manpower, might be tempted to attack in confidence that resistance would be confined to manpower. He might be tempted to attack in places where his superiority was decisive.

The way to deter aggression is for the free community to be willing and able to respond vigorously at places and with means of its own choosing.

So long as our basic policy concepts were unclear, our military leaders could not be selective in building our military power. If an enemy could pick his time and place and method of warfare—and if our policy was to remain the traditional one of meeting aggression by direct and local opposition—then we needed to be ready to fight in the Arctic and in the Tropics; in Asia, the Near East, and in Europe; by sea, by land, and by air; with old weapons and with new weapons.

The total cost of our security efforts, at home and abroad, was over $50 billion per annum, and involved, for 1953, a projected budgetary deficit of $9 billion; and $11 billion for 1954. This was on top of taxes comparable to wartime taxes; and the dollar was depreciating in effective value. Our allies were similarly weighed down. This could not be continued for long without grave budgetary, economic, and social consequences.

But before military planning could be changed, the President and his advisers, as represented by the National Security Council, had to take some basic policy decisions. This has been done. The basic decision was to depend primarily upon a great capacity to retaliate, instantly, by means and at places of our choosing. Now the Department of Defense and the Joint Chiefs of Staff can shape our military establishment to fit what is *our* policy, instead of having to try to be ready to meet the enemy's many choices. That permits of a selection of military means instead of a multiplication of means. As a result, it is now possible to get, and share, more basic security at less cost.

### The Far East

Let us now see how this concept has been applied to foreign policy, taking first the Far East.

In Korea this administration effected a major transformation. The fighting has been stopped on honorable terms. That was possible because the aggressor, already thrown back to and behind his place of beginning, was faced with the possibility that the fighting might, to his own great peril, soon spread beyond the limits and methods which he had selected.

The cruel toll of American youth and the nonproductive expenditure of many billions have been stopped. Also our armed forces are no longer largely committed to the Asian mainland. We can begin to create a strategic reserve which greatly improves our defensive posture.

This change gives added authority to the warning of the members of the United Nations which fought in Korea that, if the Communists renewed the aggression, the United Nations response would not necessarily be confined to Korea.

I have said in relation to Indochina that, if there were open Red Chinese army aggression there, that would have "grave consequences which might not be confined to Indochina."

I expressed last month the intention of the United States to maintain its position in Okinawa.* This is needed to insure adequate striking power to implement the collective security concept which I describe.

All of this is summed up in President Eisenhower's important statement of December 26.† He announced the progressive reduction of the United States ground forces in Korea. He pointed out that United States military forces in the Far East will now feature "highly mobile naval, air and amphibious units"; and he said in this way, despite some withdrawal of land forces, the United States will have a capacity to oppose aggression "with even greater effect than heretofore."

The bringing home of some of our land forces also provides a most eloquent rebuttal to the Communist charge of "imperialism."

* *Bulletin* of Jan. 4, 1954, p. 17.

† *Ibid.*, p. 14.

### Nato

If we turn to Europe, we see readjustments in the Nato collective security effort. Senator Vandenberg called the North Atlantic Treaty pledges "the most practical deterrent and discouragement to war which the wit of man has yet devised." But he said also that "if the concept and objective are to build sufficient forces in being to hold the Russian line . . . it presents ruinous corollaries both at home and abroad."

In the first years of the North Atlantic Treaty Organization, after the aggression in Korea, its members made an emergency buildup of military strength. I do not question the judgment of that time. The strength thus built has served well the cause of peace. But the pace originally set could not be maintained indefinitely.

At the April meeting of the Nato Council, the United States put forward a new concept, now known as that of the "long haul."‡ That meant a steady development of defensive strength at a rate which will preserve and not exhaust the economic strength of our allies and ourselves. This would be reinforced by the striking power of a strategic air force based on internationally agreed positions.

We found, at the Council of last December, that there was general acceptance of the "long haul" concept and recognition that it better served the probable needs than an effort to create full defensive land strength at a ruinous price.§

‡ For a report on the April meeting of the Nato Council, see *ibid.*, May 11, 1953, p. 673.

§ For a report on the December meeting of the Nato Council, see *ibid.*, Jan. 4, 1954, p. 3.

## European Defense Community

One of the emergency aspects of Nato is that it was begun before there was a solid foundation.

For example, Western Europe cannot be successfully defended without a defense of West Germany. West Germany cannot be defended without help from the Germans. German participation is excluded by the armistice arrangements still in force.

The West German Republic needs to be freed from the armistice; and new political arrangements should be made to assure that rearmed Germans will serve the common cause and never serve German militarism.

The French produced a plan to take care of this matter. It was to create a European Defense Community, composed of France, Italy, Belgium, the Netherlands, Luxembourg, and West Germany. They would have a European army, including Germans, but there would be no national armies in West Europe.

A treaty to create this defense community was signed in May, 1952. But when the Eisenhower administration took office last January, no government had sought parliamentary ratification, and the project was nigh unto death.

President Eisenhower is deeply convinced that there can be no long-term assurance of security and vitality for Europe, and therefore for the Western World including the United States, unless there is a unity which will include France and Germany and end the disunity which has led to recurrent wars, and in our generation to two world wars. As Nato's Chief Commander, and now as President, he continues to make clear the importance which the United States attaches to the consummation of the European Defense Community and, we would hope thereafter, a political community.

Until the goals of Edc are achieved, Nato, and indeed future peace, are in jeopardy. Distrust between France and Germany is inflammable, and already Communist agents are looking to it as a means for international arson.

There are of course immense difficulties in the way of the final consummation of Franco-German unity. But we have confidence that peace will soon have the indispensable foundation of the Edc.

New collective security concepts reduce non-productive military expenses of our allies to a point where it is desirable and practicable also to reduce economic aid. There was need of a more self-respecting relationship, and that, indeed, is what our allies wanted. Trade, broader markets, and a flow of investments are far more healthy than intergovernmental grants-in-aid.

There are still some strategic spots where the local governments cannot maintain adequate armed forces without some financial support from us. In these cases, we take the judgment of our military advisers as to how to proceed in the common interest. For example, we have contributed largely, ungrudgingly, and I hope constructively, to end aggression and advance freedom in Indochina.

The technical assistance program is being continued, and we stand ready to meet non-recurrent needs due to crop failures or like disasters.

But, broadly speaking, foreign budgetary aid is being limited to situations where it clearly contributes to military strength.

## The Hope

In the ways I outlined we gather strength for the long-term defense of freedom.

We do not, of course, claim to have found some magic formula that insures against all forms of Communist successes. It is normal that at some times and at some places there may be setbacks to the cause of freedom. What we do expect to insure is that any setbacks will have only temporary and local significance, because they will leave unimpaired those free world assets which in the long run will prevail.

If we can deter such aggression as would mean general war, and that is our confident resolve, then we can let time and fundamentals work for us. We do not need self-imposed policies which sap our strength.

The fundamental, on our side, is the richness—spiritual, intellectual, and material—that freedom can produce and the irresistible attraction it then sets up. That is why we do not plan ourselves to shackle freedom to preserve freedom. We intend that our conduct and example shall continue, as in the past, to show all men how good can be the fruits of freedom.

If we rely on freedom, then it follows that we must abstain from diplomatic moves which would seem to endorse captivity. That would, in effect, be a conspiracy against freedom. I can assure you that we shall never seek illusory security for ourselves by such a "deal."

We do negotiate about specific matters but only to advance the cause of human welfare.

President Eisenhower electrified the world with his proposal to lift a great weight of fear by turning atomic energy from a means of death into a source of life.* Yesterday, I started procedural talks with the Soviet Government on that topic.

We have persisted, with our allies, in seeking the unification of Germany and the liberation of Austria. Now the Soviet rulers have agreed to discuss these questions. We expect to meet them soon in Berlin. I hope they will come with a sincerity which will equal our own.

We have sought a conference to unify Korea and relieve it of foreign troops. So far, our persistence is unrewarded; but we have not given up.

These efforts at negotiation are normal initiatives that breathe the spirit of freedom. They involve no plan for a partnership division of world power with those who suppress freedom.

If we persist in the courses I outline we shall confront dictatorship with a task that is, in the long run, beyond its strength. For unless it changes, it must suppress the human desires that freedom satisfies—as we shall be demonstrating.

If the dictators persist in their present course, then it is they who will be limited to superficial successes, while their foundation crumbles under the tread of their iron boots.

* *Bulletin*, Dec. 21, 1953, p. 847.

Human beings, for the most part, want simple things.

They want to worship God in accordance with the dictates of their conscience. But that is not easily granted by those who promote an atheistic creed.

They want to think in accordance with the dictates of their reason. But that is not easily granted by those who represent an authoritarian system.

They want to exchange views with others and to persuade and to be persuaded by what appeals to their reason and their conscience. But that is not easily granted by those who believe in a society of conformity.

They want to live in their homes without fear. But that is not easily granted by those who believe in a police state system.

They want to be able to work productively and creatively and to enjoy the fruits of their labor. But that is not easily granted by those who look upon human beings as a means to create a powerhouse to dominate the world.

We can be sure that there is going on, even within Russia, a silent test of strength between the powerful rulers and the multitudes of human beings. Each individual no doubt seems by himself to be helpless in this struggle. But their aspirations in the aggregate make up a mighty force.

There are signs that the rulers are bending to some of the human desires of their people. There are promises of more food, more household goods, more economic freedom.

That does not prove that the Soviet rulers have themselves been converted. It is rather that they may be dimly perceiving a basic fact, that is that there are limits to the power of any rulers indefinitely to suppress the human spirit.

In that God-given fact lies our greatest hope. It is a hope that can sustain us. For even if the path ahead be long and hard, it need not be a warlike path; and we can know that at the end may be found the blessedness of peace.

# An Overview of American Defense Policy

THE COMMITTEE ON APPROPRIATIONS submits the following report in explanation of the accompanying bill (H.R. 7454) making appropriations for the Department of Defense for the fiscal year ending June 30, 1960.

## Appropriations and Estimates

The estimates considered by the Committee are based on the President's budget submitted in January and an amendment to that budget transmitted by the President on March 26, 1959 as reflected in House Document No. 102. The items provided for in the accompanying bill embrace the cost of all regular military functions for 1960 except construction. Requirements for military construction will be provided for in a subsequent appropriation bill.

The table on page 332 lists in summary form appropriations for fiscal year 1959, estimates for the fiscal year 1960, and the resultant net effect of Committee action on the 1960 requests.

## Summary of the Bill

The bill as reported by the Committee is $399,861,000 below the President's budget request. Over a period of four months the budget programs have been thoroughly reviewed. As a result of these studies the Committee has determined that a number of changes should be made. Some of the recommended changes provide for increases in appropriations, some for decreases. The changes made, it is believed, will increase, over the next few years, the overall deterrent power of United States military forces.

We continue to live in a period of rapid change and new concepts. The budget presented to Congress was formulated in large measure during the latter part of last year. Budget planners must of course have a cut-off date in order to put the budget in final form for presentation to Congress. After the budget is presented and while it is being considered by Congress it is not practical for the Executive Branch to seek numerous modifications. If the Executive Branch were to submit a new budget today there would no doubt be many modifications of the programs submitted in January. It should be said, however, that the great majority of the programs which were presented in the budget have been provided for.

Major Committee changes are summarized at this point. All changes are explained in detail throughout the body of the report. Increases provided for by the Committee's action total $779,800,000, including (a) $152,500,000 for maintaining the National Guard at a strength of 400,000 and the Army Reserve at a strength of 300,000; (b) $200,000,000 for Army procurement to advance the NIKE-ZEUS anti-ICBM missile and to continue modernization of Army

*House of Representatives Report 408.* Department of Defense Appropriation Bill, 1960. 86th Congress, 1st Session. To accompany H.R. 7454.

*Summary of appropriations*

| Title | Appropriations, 1959 | Budget estimates, 1960 | Recommended in bill, 1960 | Bill compared with— Appropriations, 1959 | Bill compared with— Budget estimates, 1960 |
|---|---|---|---|---|---|
| Title I—Military Personnel | $11,809,409,000 | $11,624,924,000 | $11,614,624,000 | −$194,785,000 | −$10,300,000 |
| Title II—Operation and Maintenance | 10,055,281,800 | 10,502,978,000 | 10,403,367,000 | +348,085,200 | −99,611,000 |
| Title III—Procurement | 15,263,563,000 | 13,347,963,000 | 13,003,013,000 | −2,260,550,000 | −344,950,000 |
| Title IV—Research, Development, Test, and Evaluation | 2,759,953,300 | 3,772,335,000 | 3,827,335,000 | +1,067,381,700 | +55,000,000 |
| Total, Titles I, II, III, and IV | 39,888,207,100 | 39,248,200,000 | 38,848,339,000 | −1,039,868,100 | −399,861,000 |
| Distribution of appropriations by organizational component: | | | | | |
| Army | 9,051,701,200 | 8,985,000,000 | 9,206,905,000 | +155,203,800 | +221,905,000 |
| Navy | 11,480,310,400 | 11,107,775,000 | 11,025,103,000 | −455,207,400 | −82,672,000 |
| Air Force | 17,982,276,800 | 17,767,200,000 | 17,228,506,000 | −753,770,800 | −538,694,000 |
| Office of the Secretary of Defense | 1,373,918,700 | 1,388,225,000 | 1,387,825,000 | +13,906,300 | −400,000 |
| Total, Department of Defense | 39,888,207,100 | 39,248,200,000 | 38,848,339,000 | −1,039,868,100 | −399,861,000 |

equipment; (c) $255,300,000 for Navy anti-submarine warfare capability; (d) $85,000,000 as a down payment on an additional 8 squadrons in the projected Air Force ATLAS ICBM program; and (e) $87,000,000 for acceleration of the Air Force MINUTEMAN ICBM.

Offsetting these increases are a number of sizable decreases totaling $1,179,661,000, which a majority of the Committee felt would have no substantial effect on our defense capability. Among these were reductions in the amount of $83,000,000 in military personnel offset to the extent of $81,000,000 by an additional transfer from Army stock fund cash; $163,911,000 in the Operation and Maintenance appropriations for the respective services; a reduction of $260,000,000 by elimination of the proposed Navy super aircraft carrier; a reduction of $127,500,000 in the Air Force MACE missile program; a reduction of $162,700,000 in the Air Force BOMARC anti-aircraft missile program; reductions totaling $101,400,000 in the proposed Air Force aircraft procurement of passenger-type jet aircraft; a reduction of $100,000,000 in contingencies for aircraft modification; a reduction of $50,000,000 in radar improvement procurement programs; and a $131,150,000 across the board one percent reduction in all procurement for the purpose of enforcing competition in military contracting and improved procurement practices generally.

Should these actions be approved, the Congress will place a significant imprint upon the fiscal year 1960 defense program in a way which should improve our defense posture. The Committee in effect is saying to the Department of Defense you can do a better defense job for less by eliminating or cutting back or otherwise modifying certain programs and by tightening up on operations generally. At the same time the Committee is also saying that more should be done in certain areas. The $38,848,339,000 recommended for appropriation is $399,861,000 less than the $39,248,200,000 requested for appropriation by the President and is $1,039,868,100 less than the $39,888,207,100 appropriated for the same purposes in fiscal year 1959.

The amounts above do not include $1,563,200,000 requested in the President's Budget for military construction which will be included in a separate bill, to be reported later.

Committee action on the Defense budget results in a net increase in funds for the Army totaling $221,905,000; a net decrease in funds for the Navy totaling $82,672,000; and a net decrease in funds for the Air Force totaling $538,694,000.

## The Challenge we are Attempting to Meet

Any attempt to reach a determination on total defense requirements necessitates a thoroughgoing evaluation of the world-wide situation which we are now facing and the probabilities with which we must be prepared to cope. Such an evaluation naturally involves some knowledge of our latest intelligence appraisals. The Committee received extensive briefings in this regard. It was on the basis of these intelligence evaluations that the President's Budget was originally prepared and that the Committee action has been taken. There is, of course, always room for differences of opinion in the evaluation of intelligence data.

Many decisions pertaining to the military budget depend a great deal upon the accuracy of intelligence information and its evaluation. Wrong information or an incorrect evaluation in this regard could cost billions of dollars and endanger the security of the Nation. The importance of proper intelligence and evaluation cannot be overstated. To be on the safe side the Nation must always be prepared for the worst.

It is agreed that the military threat as posed by the Communist bloc is the major element of concern to our national security. However, there are additional and serious threats to our position of world leadership in economic, scientific and technological areas. All these areas are inter-related.

Last year the Committee stated: "... the world is moving rapidly into a period of increasing danger—danger to ourselves, our possible enemies, and for that matter, to all peoples of the world." The intercontinental ballistic missile era is now upon us. It is estimated that during this calendar year the U.S.S.R. and the United States will have ICBM's ready for operational deployment with troops. The predominant weapons carrier today is the manned aircraft but missile predominance is definitely on the way. Nevertheless, during this transition period we must continue to rely in considerable degree on the old while perfecting the new. Military planning and decisions on military procurement are extremely difficult at this point. Obviously, the old is still necessary and may continue to be necessary for some time to come. The difficulty comes in trying to determine the extent to which the old should be carried forward. Indications are that a mix of old and new weapons may be required for a long time. Many military men of unquestioned ability are reluctant to give up the old reliable and familiar weapons for new weapons untested in actual armed conflict. It is during a period of transition such as the present that the expense of maintaining a balanced military force is the greatest. As the newer weapons become more reliable a clearer picture of our long range military requirements should come into focus.

As it stands today, both sides in the great power struggle between the East and the West already have the capability to inflict upon one another tremendous damage. It is believed, however, that the edge still rests with the strategic air capability of the United States.

The threat is expected to worsen. As Secretary of Defense Neil H. McElroy stated to the Committee last January: "My opinion is that as the long range ballistic missile comes into the arsenals of the two countries, the peril to those countries will be greater than it is now when the delivery of the strategic weapon must be done by aircraft. I say this because we have some defense against aircraft. We are still developing a defense against long-range ballistic missiles."

### Limited vs. General War

A great deal of study has been devoted to the question of the proper relationship between preparation for limited war and preparation for general war. It is doubtful that this issue can ever be fully resolved. Decisions made in this regard will always be a matter of judgment based upon an appraisal of the threat confronting us. Much testimony was taken upon this subject. However, no advocate on either side ever seriously questioned the idea that global war is still and will continue to be the most serious and immediate danger to our national security. In this regard, Secretary McElroy stated to the Committee:

> Our number one requirement is to be prepared for general war in order that we may deter it. I do not think there could be the slightest question about that being our number one requirement, ... of course, that can not be the only requirement on us. We must also be in a position to apply whatever forces are needed in a situation of local conflict and apply them promptly so that we either deter such a conflict from breaking out or, if it does break out, can contain it so it does

not expand into something which could become big. So we do not think of one as being exclusive of the other, but if there is a single thing we have as a positive first responsibility, it is the deterrence of general war.

In considering the horrible results which would ensue from a general atomic war, General Nathan F. Twining, Chairman of the Joint Chiefs of Staff, was asked a question as to the effect of a surprise atomic attack upon the United States. In response he said: "It would be beyond one's imagination to know how bad it would be. Whether the people will crack, or go crazy or not I don't know. There would be a lot left, I think, who would get back together again but it would be a different kind of a world, a different life."

The question naturally arises, has this emerging picture of the unthinkable consequences of all-out atomic warfare diminished the possibility of general war and conversely increased the possibility of limited wars. This particular question was raised a number of times in the course of the hearings. At one point, when it was put to Secretary of Defense McElroy, he responded as follows:

> I must believe that, Mr. Chairman, or I think we are in bad shape. If we have a general war, as discussed this morning, not much of the world will be left. So I have to believe, if I think we are doing anything right in this country militarily, that we will succeed in restraining the people who might otherwise start a general war. So I would have to answer that I believe a limited war is more likely than a general war.

Both Secretary of the Army Wilber M. Brucker and Army Chief of Staff General Maxwell D. Taylor stressed particularly the greater probability of limited war. Secretary Brucker said at one point; ". . . limited war is the more likely form of war or aggression." General Taylor also stated that he considered limited wars were "certainly much more probable" than general war. However, General Taylor acknowledged:

> . . . our overall strategic deterrent strength is always present as a political factor throughout the world regardless of what is happening, and when I stress the importance of limited war I certainly recognize the continuous requirement for this umbrella of protection represented by the deterrent weapons.

Admiral Arleigh Burke, Chief of Naval Operations, when asked about this question, stated to the Committee:

> I think there is always a possibility of general war. I think that possibility is becoming more and more remote, because both countries realize that we can suffer severe damage now and we can destroy Russia now. That will continue, I believe.

In further testimony later on, he stated:

> The people in this country in general, I believe, are very much concerned about general nuclear war, so there is a tendency to think only in terms of general nuclear war as being the only war that we have to take care of. That is not true. We have not fought a general nuclear war and we may not, and we probably will not.

It is apparent from the preceding quoted testimony that top civilian and military officials in the Department of Defense agree that general war still represents the most deadly threat to the survival of this nation, and any other nation becoming so involved. Furthermore, it is evident that these officials agree that because of this deadly threat the occurrence of such a war is somewhat improbable. Nevertheless, it is also evident that this will be true only so long as the United States maintains retaliatory forces of such unquestioned power as to deter any possible enemy from resorting to an all-out attack upon this country. It was with this ever in mind that the Committee acted upon the accompanying bill. Everyone apparently is in agreement that as long as we are well prepared for general nuclear war, such a war is much less likely. However, it does not necessarily follow that limited wars involving the direct interests of the United States are therefore made much more likely than they would be otherwise. Since a general war very definitely might develop from a limited war this ever present threat acts as a major deterrent to the possibility of limited war. In fact, the very threat of general war growing out of a single incident acts as a real deterrent to any aggressive military adventures by the Communist bloc. We must, however, maintain a capability of coping quickly with any incidents which may develop as an additional assurance against a small affair growing into a much larger one.

It is not so much a matter of mobilizing immediately available manpower to handle a limited war as it is the capability of the necessary manpower to get quickly to the spot, adequately equipped and supported. General Taylor has made it clear that the major problems in this regard arise from inadequate planning and lack of coordination between the respective services. He lists a five point program which he considers necessary to meet the possible challenges posed by future limited war situations. These are:

> First, the modernization of military equipment applicable to limited war situations; secondly, the improved strategic mobility of limited war forces; third, the pre-planned use of air and sealift necessary to move these forces; fourth, an expanded program for joint planning and training of the elements of limited war forces; and finally, the public recognition of our increased capability in coping with the challenge of limited war.

Appropriating additional funds can help with the modernization of military equipment, resulting in improved mobile capability. Improving strategic mobility of limited war forces seems to be largely a matter of the type of equipment to be carried with the troops and proper planning so that sufficient airlift and sealift is readily available to these forces without question, when the need arises. The Committee has provided more than was asked for in the budget toward equipment modernization. Funds for Army procurement have been increased by $200,000,000, to provide for advances in the NIKE-ZEUS Anti-ICBM program and equipment modernization. This program is discussed at length under the heading Army Procurement. The rest of the program for limited war preparation, as outlined by General Taylor, appears to be a job for the coordinated efforts of the Joint Chiefs of Staff.

In dealing with the question of limited versus general war, it should be kept in mind that military power alone, of any type, cannot solve all problems of conflicting international interests. Certainly United States military strength is not likely to prevent local wars in various parts of the World which do not directly involve United States interests. It is doubtful that even if the United States had had military power many times greater than it actually has had over the past fourteen years, many of the eighteen so-called limited wars which have occurred since the end of World War II could have been avoided. It should be recognized that there are limitations on the use of military force in solving our international problems. Communist subversion or penetration resulting from military and economic aid or political intrigue will not be stopped by military strength alone.

### Adequacy of United States Forces

Except for the reservations held by some military leaders regarding the degree of our preparation for limited war, the general consensus among Department of Defense officials is that the nation is prepared today to meet the military threat it faces. To get a clear understanding of the relative positions taken by the witnesses it is necessary to look at their testimony before the Committee. At one point in dealing with this subject Secretary of Defense McElroy stated: "Our forces are fully capable of carrying out their assigned missions and will continue to have this capability during the period covered by this budget."

To the direct question, "Is our military strength today sufficient to deter a major war?", both Secretary McElroy and General Twining replied with an unqualified "Yes".

With respect to the future, Secretary McElroy stated: "I think our position will still be one in which we will have adequate force to retaliate against an attacker, with the result that the effectiveness of that force will be sufficient to deter him from starting a general war."

General Twining also concurred in this judgment.

The views of the Joint Chiefs of Staff on the 1960 Defense Budget were incorporated in a signed statement to the Secretary of Defense which reads as follows:

> The Joint Chiefs of Staff consider that the fiscal year 1960 proposed expenditure figure is

adequate to provide for the essential programs necessary for the defense of the nation for the period under consideration. They find no serious gaps in the key elements of the budget in its present form, but all have reservations with respect to the funding of some segments of their respective service programs.

It should be pointed out, however, that each of the Services requested funds for the financing of programs which were not included in the Budget.

The question of the forces we should have and whether or not we have too much in one area or too little in another is a particularly difficult problem. In this connection the Chief of Staff of the Army and the Chief of Naval Operations both stated that, in their opinion, the retaliatory forces considerably exceeded the requirements. Along this line, General Taylor told the committee:

> I consider that we have an excess number of strategic weapons and weapons systems in the atomic retaliatory force. . . .
>
> I refer to the aggregate of bombers of the Air Force, of the Navy, and of our oversea commands and our allies; of the ICBM's and the IRBM's that are coming along in the hands of the Air Force. I see in the future the POLARIS system, a very promising system, coming forward. When I add together all those vehicles capable of delivering the atomic retaliatory attack, in my judgment the aggregate is excessive to the requirements.

Along the same line, Admiral Burke stated categorically: "I think there is a rate of building up retaliatory capability which is greater than that which is necessary. . . . I think we do have too much retaliatory power, and I think that we should put more money into limited capability."

Both General Taylor and Admiral Burke felt that the total defense budget proposed for fiscal year 1960 was adequate, but that a greater portion of the total should be devoted to limited war capabilities.

This point of view was not shared by the Chief of Staff of the Air Force, General Thomas D. White, or by a number of other ranking officers who appeared before the Committee. General White stated to the Committee:

> Our present capability to react to limited war situation is good. It includes the forces of the United States Army, the Navy, the Air Force, and the Marine Corps. The Air Force contributes tactical fighter bombers, troop carrier, and support forces, many of which are already overseas. Any units of the Strategic Air Command that may be required are also available.
>
> In addition, allied forces must be considered. They also possess a real capability for limited war situations. The United States Military Assistance program, combined with the efforts of our allies has resulted in allied ground, naval, and air forces of substantial size and growing effectiveness. These world-wide forces, supported as necessary by United States forces, present potential local aggressors with a formidable obstacle.

General Thomas S. Power, Commanding General of the Strategic Air Command, was even more emphatic in his opinion. He stated to the Committee: ". . . I maintain that we have sufficient armed forces to tailor a force to handle any small war."

In response to a direct question as to whether we have placed too much emphasis on deterrent power, General Power answered with a categorical "No". In his judgment, ". . . our deterrent posture is deteriorating."

Earlier he said: "The force which is now programmed . . . is not adequate because it is not coming fast enough."

General Lauris Norstad, Supreme Allied Commander, Europe, also expressed his judgment that, with respect to the retaliatory forces, ". . . we certainly do not have too much."

These are honest differences of opinion regarding the adequacy of the forces which we now have. They must be evaluated in the light of the special hopes and plans of each of the services. Fortunately, all are reasonably in agreement that the retaliatory forces now in existence are sufficient, for the present. It must be kept in mind, however, that the concept of massive retaliation as a deterrent is invalid unless enough of the retaliatory force is invulnerable to surprise attack so that it is able to retaliate effectively, even after such surprise attack. This poses a serious problem in the evaluation of Soviet ICBM capability. The problem will become increasingly more important in future months as the Soviet missile arsenal increases. It was with this in mind that the Committee decided to step up our own ICBM program over the next few years, and provide special funding authority for undertaking an airborne alert of our SAC forces, should the President consider such action desirable.

### Attaining a Balanced Force

Achieving a proper balance between general war and limited war capabilities without greatly increasing the burden upon the taxpayer and the economy, is one of the most difficult problems confronting the President, the Department of Defense, and the Congress. The President said in his budget message that the 1960 Defense Budget contains such a balance. Both Secretary McElroy and General Twining from their overall viewpoints expressed the opinion that the 1960 Budget represents such a balance. However, it is obvious from testimony of the respective members of the Joint Chiefs of Staff and other military officers throughout the hearings, previously quoted, that there is considerable difference of opinion in this regard. Differences of opinion are natural and understandable, but the testimony clearly indicates that there is something wrong in our present military planning. It seems quite apparent that in this regard the Joint Chiefs of Staff, as a corporate body, is not providing the kind of advice and leadership which this country requires. The individual members of the Joint Chiefs of Staff are able and experienced military men. It is not with these individuals but rather with the organization and system of operations that the Committee is concerned.

General Maxwell Taylor, the Army Chief of Staff made this situation quite clear in his testimony before the Committee this year. At one point in speaking of the work of the Joint Chiefs of Staff, he stated the problem in very definite terms when he said:

> I think that our weakness is in not determining standards of sufficiency—how much is enough for the atomic retaliatory force, for air defense, for limited warfare forces, for strategic airlift and sealift, for reserve-type forces—all of those categories to which several services contribute. We never look at the problem horizontally and determine whether each function is properly supported by the appropriate forces of all contributing services.

This is a most serious indictment of the inner workings of our military organization. It makes it easier to understand why there is so much confusion and duplication with resultant waste in the military establishment. The President, the Secretary of Defense, the Congress, and the American people have a right to expect a better job from the Joint Chiefs of Staff in the way of military guidance. As a corporate body, the Joint Chiefs of Staff must set up plans for the guidance of the various commands and the respective services. Hard decisions are required, and the President, the Secretary of Defense and the Joint Chiefs must assume the major responsibility for tailoring military forces to requirements. Each year the question which confronts us of "who gets what" is becoming more difficult to cope with.

The Joint Chiefs of Staff should look at what is available for what purposes and attempt to match it with the needs. As an example, the Joint Chiefs should take a look at the combined forces of the Marine Corps and the Army. It is not a question of combining the Army and Marine Corps. It is merely a question of looking at the combined strength and the combined capability of these two great forces in making the final determination as to what our ground force should be in providing for our commitments throughout the world. The Joint Chiefs should take a similar look at the combined air power capabilities of the Air Force and Navy. Such an approach should be the function of the Joint Chiefs of Staff in connection with preparation of plans for the 1961 budget request. The costing out of such determinations can be done by the respective services and through the usual budgetary process.

Many of the basic military questions which confront the Congress and the country are apparently never discussed by the Joint Chiefs of Staff. For example, the hearings reveal that the Joint Chiefs did not discuss specifically in connection with the 1960 military budget whether the Army should be maintained at 870,000 or

900,000, whether funds should be sought for a Navy carrier, and what should be done with reference to the B-52 bomber program.

### Committee Action on the 1960 Defense Bill

The national defense scene is fast moving. We are in a period of drastic change and new concepts. Advances in technology keep us in a continual state of uncertainty regarding the extent to which we should go in investing in a particular weapons system. As was pointed out earlier in this report, the military budget before the Committee was prepared many months ago. Considerable change with respect to plans for certain programs have already been suggested by military sources.

The Committee, in preparing the Defense bill for 1960, has tried to take action in the light of the situation as it exists today. As an example of the changing situation, when Secretary of the Air Force Douglas and Chief of Staff White were before the Committee in February, they argued against any further expansion in the program for ATLAS missiles. Today, however, their position is changed. It is understood that they have now asked the Department of Defense for approval of a larger program.

Considerable flexibility is required if we are to deal effectively with the fast-moving military picture. Accordingly, the budget is set up on a flexible basis. Within the vast appropriations provided, the Department of Defense has great flexibility to meet changing situations. Committee action on the 1960 budget request is also tailored toward this end.

The detailed changes made in specific programs are discussed under the respective appropriation headings in the report. However, a number of these changes are of such significance that they warrant specific separate treatment along with a discussion of the defense policies involved. What has been done toward providing for limited war was discussed previously in the report under that heading. What is proposed for other major defense programs is discussed in the paragraphs which follow.

### The Missile Gap

The intercontinental ballistic missile is a military weapon of prime importance and also a psychological weapon of first magnitude. The Committee made a special effort to explore all aspects of this problem, and to establish the facts as to where we stand in relation to the U.S.S.R. Hundreds of pages of testimony were devoted to this subject. A number of special presentations, on and off the record, were studied.

Estimates of Soviet ICBM capability were of necessity presented on the basis of what the Russians would be able to do, not necessarily what they will do. It seems obvious, however, that the Russians will do everything they are capable of doing in this field. They have demonstrated great pride in their accomplishments in rocketry. They are not unaware of the great military and psychological potential of the ICBM weapon.

It would appear from the estimates presented to the Committee that the Soviet Union could have three times as many ICBMs in position and ready to fire in anger as the United States will have during the period of the early 1960's. Exact numbers and dates are necessarily classified. Both the United States and the U.S.S.R. are expected to have a limited number of operational ICBM missiles during the current calendar year.

The 1960 Defense Budget does not provide for immediate matching of Soviet production capability in long-range ballistic missiles. This was a studied position of the Department of Defense, it being reasoned that: ". . . there is no particular logic in trying to match everything it is estimated our opponent might do."

The Department preferred to rely on the position that: ". . . the manned bomber is still the principal means of striking a decisive retaliatory blow and will continue to be a most important element of the retaliatory forces for some years to come."

From intelligence evaluations there seems little doubt that the United States has an overwhelming superiority in strategic bombing forces represented by our B-52 and B-47 aircraft. However, reliance upon such retaliatory force depends upon the avoidance of a surprise attack which might destroy it on the ground, thus rendering it incapable of counterattacking. This is one of the special threats incident to a significant ICBM capability in the possession of an adversary—especially during the period when we will have no anti-ICBM weapon and no effective system to detect the approach of the ICBM. This raises a question regarding the feasibility of providing for a continuous airborne alert of our bomber forces as discussed on page 341 of the report.

The Secretary of Defense proposed what he termed a balanced defense posture for the United States at this time. This would include principal reliance for quite some time on the manned bomber and a gradual and somewhat modest introduction into our inventory of the ICBM. As already indicated, the Secretary does not propose that we try at this time to match Soviet ICBMs missile for missile. There is considerable reluctance to accept fully the cumbersome and expensive liquid propellant ATLAS and TITAN intercontinental ballistic missiles. Yet, these missiles offer us our only hope of an early operational capability in quantity. The proposed solid propellant MINUTEMAN ICBM is expected to be much more reliable, much cheaper and more desirable than the ATLAS and TITAN, but the MINUTEMAN simply has not been perfected and will not be available for several years. If we are to have an early and significant ICBM capability, we must attain it through the ATLAS and TITAN programs, principally through the ATLAS, which is more advanced in time. Not to be overlooked, of course, is the proposed Navy POLARIS Fleet Ballistic Missile. This is a very promising system and must be considered as a part of this broad picture. The POLARIS missile system is discussed briefly hereafter.

The Committee realizes that it would not be wise to rely wholly, now or in the near future, on the ICBM as the only prime weapon in our arsenal. Its reliability has not been fully established. There must be a period of growth and experience before there can be reasonably adequate assurance in this regard. Also, proper balance in defense capability is necessary. Despite these considerations the Committee, at this critical period in world history, is not happy over the prospect of being in second place to the U.S.S.R. in the highly significant ICBM field. The Committee feels that a missile gap exists and does not wish to see it widened.

In an effort to improve our ICBM capability above and beyond actions proposed in the budget the Committee has taken steps to provide for an expansion of the ATLAS missile program. It has also undertaken, insofar as possible, to provide for the acceleration of the more advanced type solid propellant MINUTEMAN missile. This was done by adding $172,000,000 to the budget request. Committee action provides $85,000,000 for the ATLAS and $87,000,000 for the MINUTEMAN missile programs. The amount for ATLAS missiles will provide a down payment on eight additional squadrons, costing substantial additional funds in subsequent years. However, to fully implement this program during fiscal year 1960, the Air Force states that an additional $195,000,000 should be made available for military construction. The plan is for all of these squadrons to be of the so-called hardened type, thus providing protection from atomic attack, except for a direct hit. Because specific authorization of construction is required prior to appropriation, the responsibility of providing for this phase of the expanded ICBM program rests primarily with other Committees.

### Polaris Fleet Ballistic Missile

In acting on the 1959 Defense Appropriation estimates last year, the Committee added funds for an additional four POLARIS fleet ballistic missile submarines. By this action, the authorized number of POLARIS type submarines was increased from five to nine. Funds have been released by the Administration for construction of only one of the additional POLARIS type submarines. The remaining monies are being held in reserve for release early in fiscal year 1960. In addition, the 1960 Budget includes funds for advance procurement of long lead-time items for three additional POLARIS submarines, to be fully funded in the fiscal year 1961 program.

Even though the Administration has not permitted this program to move forward as fast as provided for last year, the Committee action, supported by the Congress, has nevertheless paid off. Development of the fleet ballistic missile weapons system appears to be moving ahead at a gratifying pace. With continued development success, by next year progress should be such that it may be possible and reasonable again to accelerate this program.

The POLARIS fleet ballistic missile weapons system, because of its basic mobility and the expected capability of launching its weapons while concealed beneath the surface of the seas, holds great promise as being one of the most effective deterrent weapons systems yet conceived. The Committee insists that everything possible be done to bring about its successful development at the earliest possible date.

### Air Defense

A primary objective of the defense program is to deter war. All facets of our defense program, the capabilities of each service down to the last man, play a role in this great effort. Inasmuch as a complete defense against a potential foe is practically unattainable, and that is especially true today, there is common agreement that an overwhelming offensive capability is the best defense. Our military program has been patterned in that direction for years. This is not to say that no effort has been made or should be made to attain a good defensive posture. Indeed, our offensive power must never be left open to destruction from surprise attack. Protection against such an eventuality is the primary role of our air defense forces.

In an effort to protect our offensive retaliatory forces, as well as the population centers of the nation, we have spent over the past ten years in the area of $29 billion. This includes radar warning networks, fighter aircraft and antiaircraft missiles—the entire air defense package. Proposals have been made and are under study within the Defense Department which could increase this total spending to about $49 billion by 1963. A detailed listing of what the system entails would be of little value for our purposes here. Generally, however, the system now in being can be described as encompassing (a) early warning radar networks and radar coverage of most of the United States tied into the electronic computer control centers of the semiautomatic ground environment system known as SAGE, (b) hundreds of supersonic fighter aircraft stationed throughout the nation, and (c) NIKE antiaircraft batteries surrounding most major target areas. The so-called BOMARC antiaircraft missile defense system, and ability to combat the ICBM or even to detect its approach, is yet to come.

By the end of fiscal year 1959, we will have expended or committed for expenditure nearly $3,700,000,000 for Nike-Ajax and Nike-Hercules air defense missile systems. By the end of fiscal year 1959, we will have expended or committed for expenditure approximately $1,900,000,000 on the BOMARC air defense missile system. The above figures for both missiles are all inclusive, including direct assignable costs for military personnel and operating expense. The NIKE is an Army program; the BOMARC is an Air Force program. In addition, the 1960 budget contains estimates amounting to nearly $1 billion for these two missile systems. This, of course, is only a part of the total overall air defense budget, and if all programs are approved the cost curve is projected to rise sharply. Coupled with the air defense program is the increasingly important anti-ICBM program, including an ICBM early warning system. This will add additional billions to the expense involved.

The question naturally arises—wherein lies the greater threat, and what is to be done about it? Systems are under construction to provide for early warning of intercontinental ballistic missile attack. Actual defense presents a much more difficult problem. This problem is being attacked and the Committee is providing additional funds for advance procurement in order to speed along the NIKE-ZEUS anti-ICBM missile program. Development takes time and there is little more that can be done for the present. We have a number of competing systems, however, for defense against aircraft. Great progress has been made in aircraft warning systems, in fighter interceptor aircraft armed with air-to-air missiles and in the development of ground-to-air missiles, such as the BOMARC and the NIKE-HERCULES. The problem in this area may well be that we have too many possibilities, or too many services involved. Competing systems supported by enthusiastic industrial and service advocates tend to create confusion and uncertainty. Great promises, often somewhat nebulous but calculated to get support and contract awards, are held out by the advocates of all systems.

The availability of more than one promising possibility frequently makes it necessary to pick and choose, often an extremely technical and difficult process. In the air defense area, we have a very definite problem of this type in the competing concepts behind the BOMARC and the NIKE-HERCULES ground-to-air missiles.

The BOMARC air defense missile system has been under development for many years. The first missile was test fired in 1952 and still none are in operational units. This missile is designed to intercept attacking aircraft at much greater distances from the target area than the NIKE-HERCULES missile. The greater range capability which is sought for the BOMARC has added complexity and additional cost to the missile. However, because of the greater range planned for the BOMARC over the HERCULES missile, and therefore the fewer number of missiles required to defend a given target area, it is not definitely known which system would be the more expensive in the long run. The Committee, in the light of all the uncertainties, is unable to make such a cost determination at this time.

The official position of the Department of Defense is that we need both the NIKE-HERCULES and the BOMARC missiles. This conclusion may be correct but the entire issue is clouded by the claims and counter claims of representatives of the individual services. Billions of taxpayers' dollars are involved in this controversy. It is believed that a final decision in this area can only be made after a careful military analysis. Admittedly the issues involved are extremely complex and difficult to resolve. An immediate re-examination of the whole problem at the highest level is urgently required. The Committee requests that such action be taken.

The Committee in a further effort to focus attention upon the necessity for an early decision on the air defense missile controversy has made a sharp reduction in funds requested for the BOMARC missile system. The budget request for the BOMARC missile for production, development, test and evaluation totaled $447,300,000. Of this amount, $84,600,000 is for test and evaluation. The Committee has reduced funds for production by $162,700,000. This is not claimed as a long-range saving. The Committee would be willing to appropriate the full budget estimate and more if it had full confidence in the proposed BOMARC missile—if it had the assurance that the system would actually work. The contractor for this missile has already received over a period of years commitments in excess of $1,100,000,000. Before further commitments and expenditures pile up, a new hard look should be given to the proposed BOMARC and the whole air defense problem.

The so-called Furnas Committee, at the request of the Department of Defense, has recently completed a study of the BOMARC. The Committee gave the BOMARC approval with certain important reservations. By the terms of its directive from the Department of Defense, the Furnas Committee did not give full consideration to NIKE-HERCULES, fighter aircraft, and other important air defense factors in making the study. The study as a result is inadequate and not conclusive with respect to the overall air defense picture.

It should be observed that neither the NIKE-HERCULES nor the proposed BOMARC are capable of combatting the ICBM or even missiles of the Hound Dog type launched at targets from distant aircraft. We are spending vast sums on air defense. It is time to re-examine what we are getting for our money.

### Airborne Alert

The Committee gave consideration to the question of whether or not an airborne alert is required at this time or may be required at a later date. The Committee is pleased that the

Air Force has undertaken exercises calculated to test and improve our airborne alert capabilities.

We now have the ability to detect the approach of aircraft but we are not yet able to detect the approach of attacking intercontinental ballistic missiles. It is fair to assume that the U.S.S.R. will move forward as rapidly as possible with the development and deployment of the ICBM. During this period of expansion and improvement and prior to our development of a reliable ICBM detection system, we must make sure that necessary precautions are taken to maintain our deterrent power.

The Committee feels that an airborne alert may be necessary as a means of protecting our Strategic Air Command forces and increasing our deterrent position. Such an operation would of course be extremely costly in wear and tear on men and machines. The budget contains no funds specifically programmed for a continuous airborne alert. The Committee has provided no specific funds for such purposes but has taken steps to make an airborne alert immediately possible in the event the President feels it necessary.

The Committee has provided language in Section 612 of the general provisions of the bill giving the President authority to incur a deficiency in Air Force funds at any time he feels it necessary to maintain an airborne alert.

### Anti-Submarine Warfare

The growing Soviet submarine fleet is an unprecedented threat to our control of the seas. It can not be minimized. It must be contained if there is to be assurance that the sealines of communication are to be available, in the event of war, to the oceanic confederation which is the free world. Of even greater concern is the threat of surprise attack from missile firing submarines lying hidden off our coasts. The primary responsibility for containing this threat rests with the United States Navy. That it is a matter of deep concern to the Navy was made clear by Admiral Burke the Chief of Naval Operations when he stated to the Committee:

The Russian Navy is second only to ours in size. Most of their ships have been built since World War II. Of greatest concern to the Navy is their submarine force numbering about 450. The Russians are capable of building nuclear powered submarines.

Progress has been made in the anti-submarine warfare capability of the Navy, but the submarine has progressed faster than anti-submarine capabilities. Admiral Burke described the situation as follows: "We need to improve our capability to combat submarines. Since World War II, the submarine has progressed faster than the anti-submarine warfare capability to combat it."

This last factor together with the number of Soviet submarines constitutes a shocking and dangerous situation. At the beginning of World War II Germany had about 48 submarines, and it will be recalled that during subsequent months the German U boats almost swept Allied shipping from the seas and threatened to become a decisive factor in the war. We are now told that relatively speaking we have lost ground since World War II in anti-submarine warfare. In effect, Admiral Burke warns that we are now confronted with a situation which is a vastly greater potential threat than faced us in this area of warfare in World War II. An inability to meet and destroy this threat will, in the event of general war, expose not only the vital sealines of communications to the Soviet undersea fleet, but will make this country exceedingly vulnerable to missile firing submarines.

The budget estimates submitted by the President contain certain funds for anti-submarine warfare. The Committee does not feel, however, that these funds will provide for the progress needed to increase our capability in this area. A major effort is required. It has, therefore, increased the estimates for anti-submarine warfare by $255,300,000 as shown in the following tabulation:

| Appropriation | Funds |
|---|---|
| Operation and Maintenance, Navy | $4,500,000 |
| Aircraft and related procurement, Navy | 39,000,000 |
| Shipbuilding and Conversion, Navy | 97,200,000 |
| Procurement of Ordnance and Ammunition, Navy | 69,600,000 |
| Research and Development, Navy | 45,000,000 |
| Total | 255,300,000 |

Details of the increases are discussed in this report under the various appropriation headings. In summary, however, these funds provide for additional and sorely needed effort in the research and development field; for essential ammunition and fire control equipment including missiles, mines and torpedoes; as well as for additional anti-submarine warfare aircraft and helicopters. Funds are also provided for the construction of a guided missile destroyer and an additional nuclear submarine with primary anti-submarine capability.

# 21.

# The McNamara Mix

During the Presidential campaign of 1960 the Democratic candidate, John F. Kennedy, denounced the Eisenhower defense policy for allowing the Soviet Union to surge ahead of the United States in the number of intercontinental ballistic missiles and for allowing the conventional forces to deteriorate. On taking office, President Kennedy discovered that the alleged missile-gap was nonexistent. However he did urge and secure financial support for the expansion and reorganization of the ground forces. In the first selections, Charles H. Donnelly reviews the defense proposals of the new administration, and McGeorge Bundy describes the operations of the National Security Council.

Among the many disputes that prevailed during the Kennedy years were those over the quasi-military involvement in South Vietnam, the production of the B-70 bomber, the value of atomic-powered aircraft carriers, and the furnishing of nuclear weapons to Nato allies. Perhaps most vexatious of all was the storm that raged over the way that Secretary of Defense Robert McNamara ran the Defense Department. In the third of the following selections, the Secretary explains his methods and the basis for the policies instituted by the Kennedy administration.

For years the United States had attempted to reach some agreement on the limitation or reduction of nuclear weapons. An apprehensive public watched hopefully as delegates labored through numerous "disarmament" conferences without results. In the fourth selection, President Kennedy, speaking only a few months before his assassination, presented his formula for a peaceful world. The test-ban treaty to which he referred was eventually signed and ratified by the participating nations. It, too, is still a subject of controversy, though many previous opponents have changed their minds since.

On January 18, 1965, President Lyndon B. Johnson presented to Congress the first comprehensive Defense Message since 1961. Emphasizing the pacific nature of American military power, he described the awesome force at the nation's disposal, revealed the correlation between capabilities and commitments, and indicated guidelines for the future. This final selection sets forth the multiple dimensions of defense policy as viewed by the Johnson administration.

# United States Defense Policies in 1961

BY CHARLES H. DONNELLY

## Introduction

THE ELECTION OF A PRESIDENT from a political party other than the one which had controlled the White House for 8 years was, in itself, assurance that national defense policies would receive a thorough reexamination and reevaluation in 1961. The leaders of the free world and the Communist bloc awaited the outcome of this review with understandable interest.

Basic national goals and the broad strategy for attaining these goals have been the result of many years of bipartisan collaboration, hence no sweeping changes in either goals or strategy were expected. National goals and national strategy are of such importance that they tend to transcend partisan politics, but strong differences of opinion often arise over tactics and administrative procedures for implementing national strategy, and it is significant that these differences often occur between members of the same political party, as well as between parties. It was to be expected, however, that there would be changes in emphasis on some strategic details and administrative practices by the new administration.

National defense policies are courses of action by which the Government seeks to meet problems and situations, existing or anticipated, concerning the security of the Nation. As has been said in previous studies in this series, defense policies are designed to help attain foreign policy goals and the desideratum is a defense status adequate to make foreign policy objectives attainable, rather than tailoring these objectives to the levels which existing defenses can support.

Defense policies can generally be separated into two groups: those which are concerned with initiation of actions by the United States for the attainment of its national objectives, and those which result from the initiation by other countries of actions which our Government considers to be threatening toward the United States or its allies. The policy of trying to attain a workable plan of disarmament is an example of the first group, while any plans the Government may have for action in the event our physical access to Berlin is jeopardized would be an example of the second group of policies.

United States defense policies may become more meaningful if they are considered in the light of the various factors with which policymakers must contend. Aside from the more obvious and better known situations, such as the long-range, unceasing, and aggressive efforts of Soviet leaders to achieve their ultimate goals, United States planning and policymaking officials have been increasingly concerned with some circumstances of more recent nature.

One of these factors has been the growing tendency on the part of Soviet leaders to indulge in "brinkmanship." While Communist ideology does not approve the taking of inadmissible risks—actions jeopardizing the security of the "revolutionary base"—the Communists have

From *United States Defense Policies in 1961*, House Document No. 502, 87th Congress, 2nd Session, 1–9.

been increasingly bold in pressing cold war actions which might lead to war. It is important for the West to evaluate correctly the significance of these actions. Has the confident—sometimes cocky and even arrogant—attitude of the Soviets been based on a belief that they actually hold a substantial superiority over the West, especially in military, political, and space activities, or has it been a cover to mislead the free world while giving the Communist bloc time to strengthen and consolidate its position? If the former is true and the will of Americans to fight to defend their rights has been underestimated, the danger of general war may be serious, especially if the Communist leaders believe that the time needed to reach their goal can be shortened materially, at a cost which they can afford to pay, by resorting to all-out military measures.

Another important factor is the attitude of the unalined nations. During the early years of the United Nations, the Western powers could almost always depend upon a substantial majority vote in the General Assembly in support of measures which they put forth, with the Soviet Union usually resorting to vetoes in the Security Council to block measures which it did not like. With the emergence of more than a score of newly sovereign nations from colonial status, the Western nations can hardly hope to retain the favorable position in the General Assembly which they have held in the past.

A third situation which the United States must face is the erosion of its foreign base situation. Whenever the United States has maintained a military base in a foreign country for an extended period, regardless of how friendly may have been our relations with that country, our occupation of the base has almost invariably led to some degree of bad feeling between the two countries at one time or another. Even though they may welcome the protection, sovereign states do not like the presence of foreign troops within their boundaries, no matter how friendly these forces may be.

Many countries face the problem realistically and make the best of it but the trend has been to invite United States forces to leave, as in Iceland in 1956 (until the Hungarian situation caused the Icelandic Government to reverse itself), and more recently in Morocco. Even when the host government refuses to heed local opposition to a United States base, as at Holy Loch, Scotland, there is a question of the lengths to which the United States should go in asking a friendly government to risk its life with its voters over an issue involving our foreign bases.

One of the most complex environments affecting defense policies, and one of the most difficult with which the military has to cope, is that of dealing with defense industry. For one and three-quarters centuries no sizable munitions industry held a foothold in the United States for very long because of the traditional aversion of Americans to large standing armies. Without a big military force to provide a steady market year after year, there was not enough incentive for industry to build up a permanent munitions business. When war came, industry loyally converted its production to an all-out war effort, and it quickly reconverted to civilian production as soon as the war was over. The mass production methods of the twentieth century were generally adaptable to the production of both consumer goods and weapons, so conversion and reconversion were not too difficult. The complexity and intricacy of modern "super" weapons have introduced some hard problems in engineering and management for industry to deal with and the high precision work demanded often means that the mass production methods which were so successful in the past are no longer always adequate. Many weapon systems are hardly more than a gleam in the eye at the initial contracting stage. As one observer has put it, at the outset of a missile program the final product has not even been invented. This means that the military must seek a large supply of scientific, engineering, and management skills of the highest quality—commodities hard to find. The result has been wide changes in contracting procedures, increasing pressures from industrial concerns for shares of the $25 billion annual defense procurement expenditures, and raids on the services for the trained personnel which industrial firms need in order to qualify for defense contracts.

Finally, military planning is done in an arms race environment, calling for constantly increasing efforts to design more effective weapon systems and find better ways of using them. As long as this situation exists, planners realize that they cannot rest upon their oars even briefly, lest the Communist powers overtake us. In the absence of anything indicating that this situation is likely to change in the immediate future, the race for weapons advantage can be expected to grow in intensity.

## Major Defense Problems at the Beginning of 1961*

As in previous studies in this series, at this point the major problems facing the Department of Defense at the beginning of the year are listed. Problems rather than policies are listed because the solution of problems—or the necessity to live with them until they are solved—leads to the formulation of policies, and a policy is more meaningful if one is conversant with the situation which created the need for the policy. It should also be noted that this list has been compiled on Capitol Hill; therefore it may not coincide with the opinions of Defense officials.

*Problems Related to Foreign Policy.* (1) Arms control and reduction—restrictions on nuclear testing: Following the quick collapse of the May 1960 summit meeting in Paris, Premier Khrushchev made it plain that any serious negotiations between the United States and the Soviet Union over major issues would have to wait until a new administration came into the White House. Some progress had been made, however, toward agreement on a treaty to ban nuclear weapons testing before the conference adjourned its meeting on December 5, 1960. President-elect Kennedy was on record as being opposed to the United States resuming testing as long as there was any reasonable hope of reaching agreement on a treaty.†

(2) Berlin: Soviet pressures to get the allies out of Berlin and the concomitant problem of the future of Germany were, like the question of disarmament, put aside by Mr. Khrushchev for the time being, pending installation of a new administration in Washington. Khrushchev indicated, however, that his patience was wearing thin and that he could not wait beyond April 1961 to get an agreement with the West on Berlin and a German peace treaty.‡

(3) Collective defense activities: (i) Congo: The United States policy has been to let the United Nations handle this difficult problem. To this end, we have furnished logistical and financial support to the United Nations armed forces in the Congo but have refrained from furnishing any police or combat forces. The negative and even antagonistic attitude of the Soviet Union toward United Nations efforts to reach an ultimate solution here has intensified the problem.

(ii) Cuba: The United States took its problem of deteriorating relations with the Castro government to the Organization of American States for support. The breaking off of diplomatic relations by the United States, following orders by the Cuban Government that American Embassy personnel in Havana must be reduced to a skeleton force, made the Cuban situation one of the most active problems facing the new administration.

(iii) Laos—Southeast Asia: The deterioration of the Laotian situation toward the end of 1960 threatened the security of all of southeast Asia and made this one of the most urgent problems facing President-elect Kennedy.

(4) Defense against guerrilla and paramilitary operations: The use of guerrilla and undercover personnel to subvert the government of a country which is a Communist target poses a difficult problem—not only for the country which is being attacked but for the United States in coming to the assistance of that country. Such operations often precede open military aggression, as has occurred in southeast Asia. The United States is seeking an effective means of dealing with this kind of threat.

(5) Deterrence to war: The prospective effectiveness of the United States Armed Forces as a deterrent to war was a campaign issue in 1960, with particular attention to whether or not a missile gap existed. The question of deterrence was high on the list at the beginning of 1961.

* Charles H. Donnelly, *United States Defense Policies in 1960*, House Document No. 207, 87th Congress, 1st Session (Washington, 1961), pp. 113–116.

† *New York Times*, Oct. 10, 1960, p. 19.

‡ *Ibid.*, Oct. 23, 1960, p. 1.

(6) Future of outer space: The policy of the United States that space activities should be devoted to the benefit of all mankind has been thwarted by the Soviet refusal to join in an effective control of space activities. As long as the Soviet Union refuses to join in a system of international control, the United States must continue a program of military operations in space or run the risk of imperiling its national security.

(7) Nuclear weapons for allies: Although President Eisenhower, in February 1960, recommended liberalization of United States laws with respect to supplying nuclear arms to allies, this matter was still under consideration at the beginning of 1961.*

(8) Oversea bases: The intense efforts over the years by the Soviet Union to make the United States give up its foreign bases, and the nervousness of some allies over permitting American forces to be based on their territory, make this a long-range problem for American planners. At the beginning of 1961, the future basing of American troops in Berlin was the most serious item in this category. The whole matter of foreign bases is so closely allied to other matters that it is difficult to consider bases as a problem apart. Seapower, strategic airpower, military airlift, nuclear weapons for allies, collective defense arrangements, strategic intelligence, the advantages of "showing the flag," and the cost of quid pro quos to host countries are some of the factors entering into consideration of basing arrangements.

*Domestic Problems with Military Implications.* (1) Civil defense: the civil defense program was still on dead center at the beginning of 1961. The Symington committee on the Defense Establishment proposed to President-elect Kennedy that the problem be moved to the Defense Department.

(2) Closing military installations: The evolution of weapons systems and of the military organization to meet changing conditions is largely responsible for the closing of some installations and the opening of others. When conflicts with the Indians abated in the last century, many frontier posts were closed but this had little effect on the national economy. Today, the closing of an airbase or an arsenal in a labor surplus area is likely to have repercussions. This is one area in which the Defense Department, in trying to conduct its business economically, often runs head on into the economic and social problems of civilian localities. This is a perennial problem but one which is becoming more important as strategies and weapon systems change.

(3) Government policymaking machinery: Some overhauling of our Government machinery at the policymaking level appeared to be desirable in order that decisions could be taken in time to cope with the accelerations of the jet-rocket age. The Senate Subcommittee on National Policy Machinery stood ready to help the new President.

(4) Growing influence of the military-industrial complex on American life: The emergence of the munitions business as a major part of United States industry and the resulting wide increase in military-industry contacts have inevitably led to marked influences upon almost every phase of American life. The question is whether the trend of these influences is good or bad. Various warnings have been intimated in past years, but the problem was emphasized by President Eisenhower in his farewell address to the Nation on January 17, 1961.†

Obviously this situation should not be allowed to develop in a manner adverse to public interest: at the same time unwarranted attacks against the military and industry based upon this relationship could have a dangerous effect upon national security.

(5) Civilian-military relationships: The significant shift in power in national defense matters from military to civilian leaders, a shift which is still expanding, started after World War II through the efforts of civilian leaders and culminated in the National Security Act. (It might be remarked here that some older observers have been frankly surprised at the relative calmness with which the military have accepted the situation, together with the loss of a certain amount of prestige which goes with power). The smooth-

* *Ibid.*, Feb. 4, 1960, questions 8 and 16, p. 12.

† *Ibid.*, Jan. 18, 1961, p. 22.

ness of this shift has been disturbed to some extent by the rapid turnover in civilian authorities at the policymaking level and the existence of certain instances where civilians have held authority but without responsibility. Broadening of the base of national strategy which came about as a result of the cold war has also brought civilians into the field of strategic planning, an area which traditionally was attended to by the military.

Whether justified or not, the increase in authority and activity in military matters by civilians has aroused dissatisfaction on the part of some military officials, and of civilian officials who have not always been pleased with the degree of military cooperation which they received. One source of dissatisfaction on the part of the military was the manner in which restraint was sometimes exercised against public expressions of opinion by the military. While this situation did not appear to be a major problem at the beginning of 1961, there were evidences that it was deteriorating.

(6) Labor problems: The large number of man-hours lost in the construction of missile bases during 1960 made it important, in the interest of national security, that some solution to work stoppages be found.

(7) Conservation of foreign exchange: The need to halt the outflow of gold led the previous administration to reduce drastically the number of dependents accompanying the military abroad. This had a bad effect on morale.

*Military Problems.* (1) Antisubmarine warfare: The combination of nuclear power for submarines, missiles which can be fired from submerged positions, and a greatly increased knowledge of oceanography, make protection from hostile submarines a major problem.

(2) B-70 program: The B-70 program, from its inception, has see-sawed from development of the bomber as a complete weapon system to a curtailed program for the development of a Mach 3 airplane without the bomb-navigation, defensive, and traffic control subsystems which would make the plane a complete weapon system. At the end of 1960, the Defense Department made another shift in policy and put the program back on a basis of the development of a complete weapon system. There was enough dissent to this position among scientific and military planning circles to insure that this was not a closed matter, however.

(3) Defense against hostile missiles—AICBM program: In the opinion of many, development of a truly effective defensive system against ballistic missiles is not only the most difficult but the most important defense problem facing the Nation. The question at the beginning of 1961 was still whether or not the Nike-Zeus system had shown enough promise to warrant the expense of undertaking procurement of long lead-time items in order to advance the date of possible operational use.

(4) Defense procurement: Military procurement has regularly received a major degree of attention both in Congress and in the executive branch. While the huge expenditures for present-day weapon systems have come to be accepted as necessary to national defense, many Members of Congress are far from satisfied with the fact that a relatively small percentage of military procurement is obtained through advertised bidding.

(5) Defense reorganization: The issue of further reorganization in the Department of Defense rested quietly in Congress during 1960, pending the certainty that there would be a new president who, whether a Republican or a Democrat, would undoubtedly have some convictions as to the wisdom of bringing about further unification of the military services. The report of the Committee on Defense Establishment (Senator Symington, Chairman) to President-elect Kennedy was one of several indications that the issue would be more active in 1961.

(6) Limited warfare forces: There was a growing feeling that the forces for dealing with limited warfare situations were still not adequate to cope with nonnuclear warfare situations if threats developed in several parts of the globe at one time, and that insufficient attention had been paid to dealing with intrusion through guerrilla and related actions. Airlift, tactical air support of the Army, and modernization of the ground forces were all involved in this question.

(7) Nuclear war deterrent forces: (*i*) *Bombers versus missiles*. The debate here was largely over the question of the rate at which long-range ballistic missiles and space operations could be expected to replace the manned bomber as the principal deterrent against nuclear attack.

(*ii*) *Reliability*. The urgent need to maintain the status of our deterrent weapon systems has led to efforts to compress the research and development period in some cases and also to telescope development and production phases where possible. As several automobile manufacturers can testify, the practice of putting a new car into production before the "bugs" have been eliminated can be costly. Meeting the requirements of reliability and at the same time getting new weapons into operational use quickly have raised a major problem for both Defense and industry.

(*iii*) *Survivability*. The importance of the quality of survivability to a deterrent force or weapon can hardly be overestimated. Hence the arguments between the backers of mobile weapon systems and those who put their faith in hardened launching sites. This argument has involved, particularly, the Minuteman mobile and hardened base concepts and the Polaris fleet ballistic missile, as well as the manned bomber.

(8) Personnel matters: There are, of course, always problems where people are concerned. At the end of 1960 some of the more pressing problems concerning personnel had to do with retention, pay, and housing, and several matters of concern to retired personnel, such as dual employment and dual compensation, also pay equalization for those retired before June 1, 1958.

(9) Reserve Forces—Future status: For several years the Department of Defense has sought to cut the strength of paid drill attendance of both Army Reserves and Army National Guard. Just as regularly, Congress has refused to accept these cuts. Presentation of the President's budget request for fiscal year 1962 showed that the Pentagon had not given up its efforts toward reducing these Reserves. The question is important as to just how Reserve units can be expected to meet the requirements of modern warfare in view of the training required to handle modern complex weapons and the time needed to mobilize a substantial number of Reserves in an emergency.

(10) Roles and missions: (*i*) *Military space activities*. At the beginning of 1961 the policy as to how space responsibilities would be divided between the services had not been decided.

(*ii*) *Reserve Forces*. Although the Joint Chiefs of Staff had reported that, in their opinion, existing roles and missions for the Reserves were suitable and adequate, the matter was far from settled, especially in light of the recommendation put forth by the Symington committee and other sources that a strong civil defense mission be assigned to the Reserves.

(*iii*) *Tactical air support*. This matter was officially settled by Secretary of Defense Wilson's memorandum of November 26, 1956 and the directive which emanated from the memorandum (DOD Directive 5160.22, March 18, 1957).* Nevertheless, the Army has never been satisfied with the weight limitation placed on its tactical aircraft under this order, and a substantial number of both military and civilian experts believe that there is strong justification for placing close air support units under the control of ground force commanders.

## National Objectives and Basic Defense Policies

The national objectives of the United States are substantially the same as those which the Founding Fathers put in the Preamble to the Constitution: "form a more perfect Union, establish Justice, insure domestic Tranquillity, provide for the common defence, promote the general Welfare, and secure the Blessings of Liberty to ourselves and our Posterity."

Today, the American goal is also to see these benefits spread globally, in a world of law and order where war is no longer resorted to as a way of settling international differences. It must be conceded that attainment of this latter goal appears to be some distance away.

Basic defense principles or policies are guidelines for officials and planners who are charged

* Charles H. Donnelly, *United States Defense Policies in 1957*, House Document No. 436, 85th Congress, 2nd Session (Washington, 1958), pp. 113–119.

with responsibility for the defense aspects of national strategy. Based upon these guidelines, national concepts are formulated for the broad implementation of defense policies; military plans are prepared in accordance with these concepts; the forces and munitions needed to carry out the plans are calculated; and the budgetary requirements for obtaining these forces with equipment and weapons are established and presented to Congress for decision.

President Kennedy, in his budget message to Congress on March 28, 1961, listed eight basic defense principles or policies, as follows:*

1. The primary purpose of the Armed Forces is to preserve peace, not to make war, by deterring the start of wars of all kinds and dimensions, by providing backing for diplomatic settlement of disputes, and by insuring adequate bargaining power bringing about an end to the arms race.

Our military posture must be sufficiently flexible and under control to be consistent with our efforts to explore all possibilities and to take every step to lessen tensions, to obtain peaceful solutions, and to secure arms limitations. Diplomacy and defense are no longer distinct alternatives, one to be used where the other fails—both must complement each other.

2. The United States will never threaten, provoke or initiate aggression, nor will its Armed Forces be used to strike a first blow in any attack; but if aggression should come, the U.S. response will be swift and effective.

3. The U.S. Armed Forces must be adequate to meet national commitments and to insure national security, unfettered by arbitrary budget ceilings.

4. The Armed Forces must be subject to ultimate civilian control and command at all times, in war as well as in peace.

5. Our strategic arms and defense must be adequate to deter any deliberate nuclear attack on the United States or our allies by making clear to any potential aggressor that sufficient retaliatory forces will be able to survive a first strike and penetrate his defense in order to inflict unacceptable losses upon him.

6. The strength and deployment of our forces in combination with those of our allies should be sufficiently powerful and mobile to prevent the steady erosion of the free world through limited wars; and it is this role that should constitute the primary mission of our oversea forces.

7. The U.S. defense posture must be both flexible and determined. Any potential aggressor contemplating an attack on any part of the free world with any kind of weapons, conventional or nuclear, must know that our response will be suitable, selective, swift, and effective.

8. The U.S. defense posture must be designed to reduce the danger of irrational or unpremeditated general war—the danger of unnecessary escalation of a small war into a large one, or of miscalculation or misinterpretation of an incident or enemy intention.

* House Document 123, pp. 2–4 [4]. Also, Congressional Record, daily ed., Mar. 28, 1961, pp. 4717–4718.

# The National Security Council

## Exchange of Letters between Senator Henry M. Jackson and Mr. McGeorge Bundy

UNITED STATES SENATE
SUBCOMMITTEE ON NATIONAL
POLICY MACHINERY
*July 13, 1961*

MR. MCGEORGE BUNDY
*Special Assistant to the President for National Security Affairs*
*The White House, Washington, D.C.*

DEAR MR. BUNDY:

As you know, our subcommittee will shortly hold hearings bringing to a close its nonpartisan study of how our Government can best staff and organize itself to develop and carry out the kind of national security policies required to meet the challenge of world communism.

As you also know, we have been deeply concerned from the outset with the organization and procedures of the National Security Council, its subordinate organs, and related planning and followthrough mechanisms in the area of national security.

Early in our study, the previous administration was kind enough to make available to the subcommittee a series of official memorandums describing the functions, organization, and procedures of the National Security Council and its supporting mechanisms. These memorandums, which were printed by the subcommittee in our Selected Materials, proved of great interest and value to our members, to students and interpreters of the policy process, and to the wide general audience which has been following our inquiry.

The purpose of this letter is to ask whether the present administration could now furnish us with official memorandums which would be the current equivalent of the above documents given us by the Eisenhower administration.

I presume that this material is readily at hand, and that it could be made available to us by August 4, so that we could profit from its study during the final phase of our hearings and make it a part of our permanent record.

Sincerely yours,
HENRY M. JACKSON
*Chairman, Subcommittee on National Policy Machinery*

THE WHITE HOUSE
*Washington, September 4, 1961*

HON. HENRY M. JACKSON
*United States Senate, Washington, D.C.*

DEAR SENATOR JACKSON:

I have thought hard about your letter of July 13, which asks for official memorandums that would be the current equivalent of memorandums submitted by the previous administration.

From *Organizing for National Security*, "Inquiry of the Subcommittee on National Security Policy Machinery of the Committee on Government Operations," United States Senate, 87th Congress, 1961, Vol. 1.

I find that this is not easy to do, but let me try. The previous administration wrote out of many years of experience in which it had gradually developed a large and complex series of processes. This administration has been revising these arrangements to fit the needs of a new President, but the work of revision is far from done, and it is too soon for me to report with any finality upon the matters about which you ask. It seems to me preferable, at this early stage in our work, to give you an informal interim account in this letter.

Much of what you have been told in the reports of the previous administration about the legal framework and concept of the Council remains true today. There has been no recent change in the National Security Act of 1947. Nor has there been any change in the basic and decisive fact that the Council is advisory only. Decisions are made by the President. Finally, there has been no change in the basic proposition that, in the language of Robert Cutler, "the Council is a vehicle for a President to use in accordance with its suitability to his plans for conducting his great office." As Mr. Cutler further remarked, "a peculiar virtue of the National Security Act is its flexibility," and "each President may use the Council as he finds most suitable at a given time."* It is within the spirit of this doctrine that a new process of using the NSC is developing.

The specific changes which have occurred are three. First, the NSC meets less often than it did. There were 16 meetings in the first 6 months of the Kennedy administration. Much that used to flow routinely to the weekly meetings of the Council is now settled in other ways—by separate meetings with the President, by letters, by written memorandums, and at levels below that of the President. President Kennedy has preferred to call meetings of the NSC only after determining that a particular issue is ready for discussion in this particular form.

I know you share my understanding that the National Security Council has never been and should never become the only instrument of counsel and decision available to the President in dealing with the problems of our national security. I believe this fact cannot be overemphasized. It is not easy for me to be sure of the procedures of earlier administrations, but I have the impression that many of the great episodes of the Truman and Eisenhower administrations were not dealt with, in their most vital aspects, through the machinery of the NSC. It was not in an NSC meeting that we got into the Korean war, or made the Korean truce. The NSC was not, characteristically, the place of decision on specific major budgetary issues, which so often affect both policy and strategy. It was not the usual forum of diplomatic decision; it was not, for example, a major center of work on Berlin at any time before 1961. The National Security Council is one instrument among many; it must never be made an end in itself.

But for certain issues of great moment, the NSC is indeed valuable. President Kennedy has used it for discussion of basic national policy toward a number of countries. He has used it both for advice on particular pressing decisions and for recommendations on long-term policy. As new attitudes develop within the administration, and as new issues arise in the world, the NSC is likely to continue as a major channel through which broad issues of national security policy come forward for Presidential decision.

Meanwhile, the President continues to meet at very frequent intervals with the Secretary of State, the Secretary of Defense, and other officials closely concerned with problems of national security. Such meetings may be as large as an NSC meeting or as small as a face-to-face discussion with a single Cabinet officer. What they have in common is that a careful record is kept, in the appropriate way, whenever a decision is reached. Where primary responsibility falls clearly to a single Department, the primary record of such decisions will usually be made through that Department. Where the issue is broader, or where the action requires continued White House attention, the decision will be recorded through the process of the National

* Robert Cutler, "The Development of the National Security Council," *Foreign Affairs*, April 1956 ("Organizing for National Security," reprinted in "Selected Materials," committee print of the Committee on Government Operations of the Senate, GPO, 1960).

Security Council. Thus the business of the National Security staff goes well beyond what is treated in formal meetings of the National Security Council. It is our purpose, in cooperation with other Presidential staff officers, to meet the President's staff needs throughout the national security area.

The second and more significant change in the administration of the National Security Council and its subordinate agencies is the abolition by Executive Order 10920 of the Operations Coordinating Board. This change needs to be understood both for what it is and for what it is not. It is not in any sense a downgrading of the tasks of coordination and followup; neither is it an abandonment of Presidential responsibility for these tasks. It is rather a move to eliminate an instrument that does not match the style of operation and coordination of the current administration.

From the point of view of the new administration, the decisive difficulty in the OCB was that without unanimity it had no authority. No one of its eight members had authority over any other. It was never a truly Presidential instrument, and its practices were those of a group of able men attempting, at the second and third levels of Government, to keep large departments in reasonable harmony with each other. Because of good will among its members, and unusual administrative skill in its secretariat, it did much useful work; it also had weaknesses. But its most serious weakness, for the new administration, was simply that neither the President himself nor the present administration as a whole conceives of operational coordination as a task for a large committee in which no one man has authority. It was and is our belief that there is much to be done that the OCB could not do, and that the things it did do can be done as well or better in other ways.

The most important of these other ways is an increased reliance on the leadership of the Department of State. It would not be appropriate for me to describe in detail the changes which the Department of State has begun to execute in meeting the large responsibilities which fall to it under this concept of administration. It is enough if I say that the President has made it very clear that he does not want a large separate organization between him and his Secretary of State. Neither does he wish any question to arise as to the clear authority and responsibility of the Secretary of State, not only in his own Department, and not only in such large-scale related areas as foreign aid and information policy, but also as the agent of coordination in all our major policies toward other nations.

The third change in the affairs of the NSC grows out of the first two and has a similar purpose. We have deliberately rubbed out the distinction between planning and operation which governed the administrative structure of the NSC staff in the last administration. This distinction, real enough at the extremes of the daily cable traffic and long-range assessment of future possibilities, breaks down in most of the business of decision and action. This is especially true at the level of Presidential action. Thus it seems to us best that the NSC staff, which is essentially a Presidential instrument, should be composed of men who can serve equally well in the process of planning and in that of operational followup. Already it has been made plain, in a number of cases, that the President's interests and purposes can be better served if the staff officer who keeps in daily touch with operations in a given area is also the officer who acts for the White House staff in related planning activities.

Let me turn briefly, in closing, to the role of the Presidential staff as a whole, in national security affairs. This staff is smaller than it was in the last administration, and it is more closely knit. The President uses in these areas a number of officers holding White House appointments, and a number of others holding appointments in the National Security Council staff. He also uses extensively the staff of the Bureau of the Budget. These men are all staff officers. Their job is to help the President, not to supersede or supplement any of the high officials who hold line responsibilities in the executive departments and agencies. Their task is that of all staff officers: to extend the range and enlarge the direct effectiveness of the man they serve. Heavy responsibilities for operation, for coordination, and for diplomatic relations can be and are delegated to the Department of State.

Full use of all the powers of leadership can be and is expected in other departments and agencies. There remains a crushing burden of responsibility, and of sheer work, on the President himself; there remains also the steady flow of questions, of ideas, of executive energy which a strong President will give off like sparks. If his Cabinet officers are to be free to do their own work, the President's work must be done—to the extent that he cannot do it himself—by staff officers under his direct oversight. But this is, I repeat, something entirely different from the interposition of such a staff between the President and his Cabinet officers.

I hope this rather general exposition may be helpful to you. I have been conscious, in writing it, of the limits which are imposed upon me by the need to avoid classified questions, and still more by the requirement that the President's own business be treated in confidence. Within those limits I have tried to tell you clearly how we are trying to do our job.

Sincerely,

McGeorge Bundy

# Decision Making in the Defense Department

BY ROBERT S. McNAMARA

WHAT I WANT TO talk to you about is the problem of decision-making in the Defense Department, and the way we are trying to approach the problem.

The Department of Defense is responsible for spending nearly 10 per cent of the national income of this country. It employs 3.7 million Americans directly, in and out of uniform, and millions more indirectly in every aspect of our economic life. It absorbs over half of every tax dollar, as it has done for over a decade.

All of this is well enough known. If anything, the potential dangers of this so-called "military-industrial complex" have been overstated rather than understated in recent months. But at the risk of repeating the obvious, let me point out once again that this unavoidably vast establishment exists for one purpose and one purpose only: to act as the servant of United States foreign policy. Our responsibility is to provide this nation with the means to safeguard its legitimate interests and to meet its commitments at home and around the world. The Defense Department exists to serve that purpose, and to serve none other.

Yet, although it is easy enough to say in a few words what our purpose is, the translation of this purpose into decisions on force levels, on contingency war planning, on weapons developments—and cancellations—on reorganizations, on all the range of decisions which shape our defense establishment, cannot be readily or easily deduced from the general principles. You probably remember General Marshall's shrewd remark: "Don't ask me to say we agree in principle; that just means we haven't agreed yet."

What I want to do is to outline, as best I can in a single talk, how we are trying to translate these general principles, on which all Americans would agree our defense policy should be based, into specific decisions that will effectively carry through those general principles. These specific decisions will inevitably and properly remain the subject of searching, even harsh, criticism. We are, after all, dealing with issues which could affect the very life of this nation, indeed the life of a great part of this planet. We cannot and do not claim infallibility. Only the future can tell when and where we have been right, when and where we have been wrong. We can only do our best to approach these problems as sensibly and realistically as we know how.

Let me start with two points which seem to me axiomatic. The first is that, at least within any range of defense spending that is likely to appear at all desirable in the foreseeable future, the United States is well able to spend whatever it needs to spend on national security. The second point is that this ability does not excuse us from applying strict standards of effectiveness and efficiency to the way we spend our defense dollars.

Last fall, while we were preparing for the fiscal 1964 budget decisions, the separate requests for funds of the three military depart-

---

*Vital Speeches of the Day*, June 1, 1963, 508–512. Delivered before the American Society of Newspaper Editors, Washington, D.C.

ments totalled over $67 billion. The budget as finally submitted to the Congress totalled nearly $54 billion, a cut of over $13 billion. This was still $2 billion more than the current defense budget, and $10 billion more than when we took office in 1961. We have been criticized both for overruling the military in cutting the Service requests, and for spending too much money, presumably in failing to cut the Service requests far enough. Sometimes, to my continuing surprise, we are criticized on both counts by the same people.

The fact is that we could, as a nation, afford to spend more than we are proposing if that were judged to be in our national interest. Our national security does not need to be compromised to keep defense spending down. Where we have cut, the cuts have not represented decisions to compromise national security in the name of frugality. For our children will hardly admire us for our frugality if it is achieved at a price they will have to pay in blood and suffering. And where we have added to defense spending, those additions have not been based on the naive notion that the bigger our defense budget is, the safer we will be. National security in this age of hydrogen bombs and intercontinental missiles is more complicated than that.

The facts are that national security in these times cannot be purchased by military spending alone, however generous a scale, and that the task of assuring that our military spending truly serves the national interest is more complicated than it has ever been in the past. And more urgent. The test we have to apply, over and over again, is whether a particular expenditure for a specific purpose is really in our national interest.

Every dollar we spend inefficiently or ineffectively is not only an unnecessary addition to the arms race which threatens all mankind, but an unfair burden on the taxpayer, or an unwise diversion of resources which could be invested elsewhere to serve our national interests at home or abroad, or a dollar that could, even if kept in the military budget, be invested in something that would better strengthen our military posture. The fact that we cannot be poor enough to grudge the price of our own survival does not mean we are rich enough to squander our resources in the name of national security.

I do not mean to suggest that we can measure national security in terms of dollars—you cannot price what is inherently priceless. But if we are to avoid talking in generalities, we must talk about dollars: for policy decisions must sooner or later be expressed in the form of budget decisions on where to spend and how much.

When we took office, we saw three major tasks before us. First, we had to accelerate the strengthening of our strategic nuclear force, a task which involves not merely increases in the size of the force, but major improvements in its survivability and in the provisions to maintain responsible command and control at all times. We had a firm base from which to work. My predecessor, Tom Gates, had already given strong support to such programs as Minuteman and Polaris, which are designed to ride out any conceivable attack, so that they do not have to be launched on short or ambiguous warning. But we felt further impetus was needed. We have, for example, increased by 50 per cent the programmed rate of Polaris procurement, and doubled our production capability for Minuteman. We have increased by 50 per cent the portion of B-52 bombers on 15-minute ground alert. The kind of flexibility that these programs provide is absolutely vital. Overall, in the last 24 months we have doubled the number of warheads in our strategic alert forces. And during the same period we have increased by 60 per cent Nato's tactical nuclear forces in Western Europe.

Second, major increases in our non-nuclear capabilities were urgently needed. Accordingly, we increased the number of combat-ready Army divisions by 45 per cent. We augmented by 30 per cent the Air Force capability for tactical air support of combat operations. We have increased our procurement of combat supplies and equipment, to correct serious imbalances and inadequacies that had developed over the years. We have increased nearly six-fold our special forces, made up of highly trained men who can not only deal with guerrilla warfare, but more important, can train the peoples under terrorist attack to defend themselves.

The third major effort cannot be so easily defined. What it involves is a broad effort to improve the effectiveness and efficiency of the defense establishment. It is this effort that I want to talk about most, partly because it is the most controversial—really the only one of these three efforts which has been widely controversial—partly because it is, by its nature, very diffuse, involving a wide variety of largely independent efforts, which cannot properly be summed up in a few sentences.

The first two of our major objectives—the improvement of our strategic retaliatory forces and the buildup of our non-nuclear forces—commanded wide support by the time we took office.

The importance of additional effort to assure that our strategic retaliatory nuclear forces were both adequate and subject to effective control at all times was widely accepted. Consequently, it was clear that a number of major and expensive steps were needed in the strategic retaliatory area. It would have been national folly to allow any question to arise in the mind of a potential attacker that United States forces were not capable of absorbing a surprise attack and striking back with devastating fury.

It was equally clear that we could not either effectively or sensibly count on the threat of massive retaliation to deter the whole range of political and military aggression open to an ingenious and determined adversary. It is doubtful whether such a threat was ever a universal deterrent. It did not deter the attack on Korea, the pressure on Berlin, or the attempt to subvert Southeast Asia. Still less is it likely to be a universal deterrent in an age when nuclear superiority, even though substantial in terms of numbers, cannot guarantee a victory in any meaningful sense.

No one in a position of responsibility seriously believed that a decision to employ our strategic nuclear forces could make sense except in the face of massive aggression—such as a large-scale attack on Western Europe—and consequently it was clear that, unless we were willing to live under a constant threat of having to choose between nuclear holocaust and retreat, we required major improvements in our less-than-all-out war capabilities. It remained for us to translate these general notions into specific programs, to fill in the details, to carry the programs through vigorously and expeditiously. But on the general aims, there was little quarrel.

It is only in the third area, the problem of increasing the effectiveness and efficiency of our military establishment, that controversy has developed. Not that there was much disagreement about the need: for years everyone who has thought seriously about the Department of Defense has felt that major improvements were needed. The solutions offered ranged from drastic proposals for complete unification of the armed forces to vague suggestions about "cutting the fat out of the military budget."

Thus, there was a national consensus here that reforms were in order. But there was no consensus on just what should be done. And there was an additional and inevitable human problem. For these reforms would necessarily take the shape of changes in the traditional ways of doing things, and limitations on the customary ways of spending defense money. It is inevitable that people will take more easily to suggestions that they should have more money to spend, as in the improvement of our nuclear and non-nuclear capabilities, than to suggestions that they must spend less, or that they must abandon established ways of doing things. Yet the very substantial increases in the budget which we felt necessary added a further strong incentive, if any were needed, to move ahead on these problems of increasing efficiency and effectiveness.

The first and most important thing to notice about the effort in this area is what it is *not*. It is *not* an effort to save dollars at the expense of military effectiveness. What we are trying to do can be divided into two parts: the first is essentially a series of management reforms of the kind you will find in any well-run organization, an effort which is in large part covered by the formal Five Year Cost Reduction Program we set up in July 1962. The common characteristic of reforms in this part of the effort is that they have very little, if anything, to do with military effectiveness, one way or the other. They neither increase nor decrease our military effectiveness;

they merely save money by introducing more efficient methods of doing things.

To give a small example of what I mean, we found that the various elements of the Department were using slightly different forms for requisitions—16 in all. As a result, nearly every time a piece of property was transferred from one part of the Department to another, a new requisition form had to be typed out, tens of thousands of forms per year. By establishing a common requisition form and system, we eliminated tens of thousands of man-hours of labor formerly wasted in having clerks retype the forms. This will save us about $20 million a year when the change becomes fully operative.

The creation of the Defense Supply Agency to handle the purchase of common supplies for the Department saved $31 million this year in overhead costs alone, and these annual savings will grow in succeeding years. I need not dwell on such colorful, but relatively minor accomplishments as the consolidation of the 18 different types and sizes of butcher smocks, the 4 kinds of belt buckles, and the 6 kinds of exercise bloomers.

We estimate that actions initiated this year will ultimately save nearly $300 million through increased use of competitive, as opposed to non-competitive procurement; over $300 million through shifts from cost-plus-fixed-fee contracts to fixed or incentive price contracts; over $300 million through better management of inventories; nearly $300 million through closing or reducing operations at 330 installations, freeing 45,000 men and 280,000 acres of land, and so on down the line. The total savings which will ultimately be realized from actions taken so far in the cost reduction program will be over $1.9 billion.

Our target by fiscal year 1967 is saving $3.4 billion a year, each year, every year, through reforms in the procurement and logistic areas alone. So we are not talking about trivial sums of money. And my own judgment is that we are still only scratching the surface. I believe that we should eventually be able to surpass our own present goal of $3.4 billion annual savings, and I emphasize that we are talking about *annual*, not one-time savings. Several years ago there was talk of saving $8 billion per year by unifying the Armed Services. I think that through vigorous pursuit of the cost reduction effort we can save the same kind of money that had been envisaged through unification of the Services without the serious disadvantages of a single Service.

As I have said, most of this formal cost-reduction program has little or nothing to do with military effectiveness, one way or the other. It merely saves large sums of money.

The second, and really the more important, part of the effort does bear directly on military effectiveness. Although dollar savings are sometimes an important by-product, here the essential point is to increase military effectiveness. For example, we found that the three military departments had been establishing their requirements independently of each other. I think the results can fairly be described as chaotic: the Army planning, for example, was based primarily on a long war of attrition, while the Air Force planning was based, largely, on a short war of nuclear bombardment. Consequently, the Army was stating a requirement for stocking months of fighting supplies against the event of a sizable conventional conflict, while the Air Force stock requirements for such a war had to be measured in days, and not very many days at that. Either approach, consistently followed, might make some sense. The two combined could not possibly make sense. What we needed was a coordinated strategy seeking objectives actually attainable with the military resources available.

We are moving with all reasonable speed towards a properly balanced force structure. I say with all reasonable speed because there would be enormous practical difficulties in trying to get this job done overnight. But we are moving as fast as we sensibly can to balance men against supplies; deployable divisions against sea and airlift capability to handle those divisions; ground combat units against tactical air squadrons to support those units.

A realistic reappraisal of our needs resulted in a reduction of stated requirements by $24 billion, but also in a doubling of the division-months of combat equipment actually on hand. The fact is that in the past so-called requirements bore almost no relation to the real world: enormous requirements existed on paper, often almost entirely disembodied from the actual size and nature of the procurement program. There were gross inventory imbalances: the Army, for example, while in general far short of its stated requirements, had 270 per cent of its requirement for 105 mm. towed howitzers, 290 per cent of the requirements for 4.2 inch mortars; we had ten times as many 2.75 inch rockets as were required. By taking a more realistic look at the whole requirements picture, we were able, for example, to save $150 million on Sparrow missiles for the Navy and Air Force, $163 million on Army .50 caliber machine guns.

The new form of budget for the first time grouped together for planning purposes units which must fight together in the event of war. The Navy strategic force, the Polaris submarines, are considered together with the Air Force Strategic Air Command; Navy general purpose forces are considered together with the Army and Marine divisions and the Air Force Tactical Air Command. This kind of reform provides substantial improvement in the effectiveness of our military establishment. Even where it does not lead directly to lower expenditures, it is economical in the true sense of the word; that is, it gives us the maximum national security obtainable from the dollars we do spend. We can imagine many different kinds of wars the United States must be prepared to fight, but a war in which the Army fights independently of the Navy, or the Navy independently of the Air Force, is not one of them. Quite obviously, the coordination of the planning of the four Services makes eminently good sense on the narrowest military grounds.

So I would repeat: it is a mistake to equate our efforts towards improving effectiveness and efficiency solely with a desire to save money. That is very important. But military effectiveness is even more important. Money savings are what is easiest to talk about: for it is easy to explain something in terms of saving X hundreds of millions of dollars, and complicated to get into the details of planning and logistics, and the like. But the fact is that the total effort is aimed *both* at saving money and improving military effectiveness. And it is the latter, improving the effectiveness of our military establishment, which is the first priority, for it is the latter which directly affects national security.

Where the situation becomes more complicated is when decisions must be made on requested force level increases or development or procurement of new weapons.

The first thing to remember is that adding a weapon to our inventory is not necessarily synonymous with adding to our national security.

The second thing to remember is that even if we were to draft every scientist and engineer in the country into weapons development work, we could still develop only a fraction of the systems that are proposed. We must pick and choose very carefully among the proposals to get the ones on which we should actually proceed. This process of choice must begin with a requirement for solid indications that a proposed system would really add something to our national security. Even then, we still have to pick and choose, but we cannot even seriously consider going ahead with a full-scale weapons system development until that basic requirement has been met.

The whole subject of Research and Development management deserves a separate speech. Development costs alone on typical major weapons systems today average upwards of $1 billion. Over a billion dollars was spent on the atomic airplane, which was little closer to being a useful weapon when we cancelled it, shortly after taking office, than it had been half a dozen years earlier. Eighty million was spent on the Goose decoy missile, essentially a pilotless aircraft that the enemy would confuse with our B-52s. But the device, once launched, could not be recalled. Since the B-52s have to be launched on ambiguous warning to avoid being destroyed on the ground, the non-recallable decoys were obviously incompatible with the B-52s. These are a few examples of the sort of thing we hope will happen less often in the future.

The RS-70 is an example of a weapon which, it seems to me, fails to meet the basic requirement for a major systems development: a solid indication that the weapon, if developed, would add significantly to our national security. It happens to be a particularly expensive weapon: to develop, procure, and operate a modest force of these planes would cost us at least $10 billion. Yet considering the weapons we already have, or will have by the time the RS-70 could be operational, it is very hard to see how this weapon would add to our national security.

The whole debate on the RS-70, in fact, has tended to be conducted in terms which have very little to do with the facts of the situation. There is a lot of talk about missiles versus bombers. I have no feeling about missiles versus bombers as such. If bombers serve our national interest, then we should be interested in bombers; if missiles, then we should be interested in missiles; if a mix, then we should be interested in the mix. As General LeMay observed: "If kiddie cars will do the job, we will use them." But the question is really not about bombers versus missiles, because the RS-70 is not a bomber in anything like the traditional meaning of the term. The RS-70 would carry no bombs. It would attack its target with a very complex air-launched missile system from distances of hundreds of miles. Now there are various platforms from which to launch missiles. We can launch them from hardened silos in the ground; we can launch them from submarines under the sea; we can launch them from aircraft. The question is not bombs versus missiles. We are all agreed it must be missiles. The debate is about alternative launching platforms and alternative missile systems. And the particular launching platform and missile system proposed in the RS-70 program just is not an effective means to accomplish the missions proposed to be assigned to it.

Skybolt was a somewhat different story. The Skybolt development was begun in 1959 to meet a very specific need. This was to clear a path for our bombers by knocking out the enemy's air defenses. The defense suppression role is vital: unless it is performed, the bombers cannot get through to their targets. One reason that it is now agreed that by the 1970s the traditional manned bomber will be obsolete is that by then we anticipate it will be more costly to suppress air defenses in order to carry out an effective bombing attack than it will be to attack the target directly with missiles. Even now, bombers are of limited value unless we have something that can go in ahead and clear a path for them. That means a missile.

The Hound Dog had been developed for that job, but the Skybolt, it was planned, would do it much better. Two important things have happened during the Skybolt development that changed this judgment: First, the development itself fell far short of its goals: Skybolt turned out to be much more expensive than had been anticipated; it would be less accurate than had been anticipated; it would take longer to achieve acceptable levels of reliability than had been anticipated. Second, we had been successful in developing other weapons that were still on the drawing board when Skybolt was proposed. What all this added up to was that while the defense suppression role remained vital, Skybolt was no longer vital. In fact, it became clear that by using the already developed Hound Dog plus some additional Minutemen, already developed, we could do the defense suppression job for about $2 billion less than we could by continuing to go ahead on Skybolt as if nothing had changed since 1959.

These two illustrations, the RS-70 and Skybolt, point up some of the fundamental considerations that must enter into defense policy decisions. Does the proposal really add something significant to our national security? If the proposal does serve an important need, does it do so as well as other alternative means of reaching the same end? Do the assumptions on which you based your preliminary decisions several years ago still hold true?

Let me note also another reason for restraint in pushing ahead uncritically on proposed new weapons of doubtful importance. As weapons systems grow more complex, more expensive, and more difficult to maintain in a high state of military readiness, it is essential that we limit as far as possible the number of new systems that we bring into operation; for we want to be as sure as possible that we can depend on every system to operate when it is really needed. A basic fact of life is that under the chaotic conditions of combat you do not get anything like the efficiency of weapons systems that you get on a test range. Relative simplicity is a most desirable characteristic of a weapons system, or of a combination of systems.

One of the difficulties in the past has been the tendency of planners, concentrating on a particular proposed system, to forget that every additional bit of complexity you add to your operation tends to degrade the overall efficiency of the operation. Eventually you reach a point where the advantage of adding a new system is outweighed by the effect of the additional complexity. We have accumulated some disturbing evidence about the effect of proliferation of weapons systems in the recent past on the operational dependability of those systems. We don't want to put ourselves in the position of the camera bug who weights himself down with so much specialized equipment for every contingency that he actually gets poorer results than a more lightly equipped competitor. And let me add that not only do the proliferation and complication of weapons reduce dependability, but they are also major factors contributing to enormous excess inventories of parts and equipment —excesses which today amount to over $12 billion.

These considerations had a great deal to do with the TFX decisions. On that issue, the really difficult decision was not the choice of contractor, but the cancellation of the Services two-plane program and the substitution of a single aircraft to serve both the Air Force and the Navy. After extended discussion and great controversy, both the civilian and military leaders now agree such a program will meet the military requirements. It will yield a saving of approximately $1 billion. The choice of a contractor for such an aircraft was a subsidiary decision. Both contractors presented acceptable designs, each capable of meeting the military requirement, and with little to choose between them on the basis of performance. The choice of contractor, therefore, could be determined by the civilian authorities who are charged by law with making such decisions, on considerations of ultimate cost and program risk.

What I have been suggesting in these illustrations is that the question of how to spend our defense dollars and how much to spend is a good deal more complicated than is often assumed. It cannot be assumed that a new weapon would really add to our national security, no matter how attractive the weapon can be made to seem, looked at by itself. Anyone who has been exposed to so-called "brochuremanship" knows that even the most outlandish notions can be dressed up to look superficially attractive. You have to consider a very wide range of issues—the missions our forces must be prepared to perform, the effects of a proposed system on the stability of the military situation in the world, the alternatives open to us for performing the missions required.

You cannot make decisions simply by asking yourself whether something might be nice to have. You have to make a judgment on how much is enough.

I emphasize judgment because you can't even be sure yourself, much less prove to others, that your decision was precisely right to the last dollar—even to the last billion dollars. But the decision has to be made.

There is an important difference between the way we make these tough decisions today, and the way they used to be made. Formerly, an arbitrary budget ceiling was fixed for national defense, and funds were then apportioned among the Services. Today we examine all our military needs, and then decide at what point our military strength is in balance with the requirements of our foreign policy.

There are, of course, sharp differences of opinion on where we should spend our marginal defense dollars. And here is where the responsibility most clearly falls on the Secretary of Defense, because here is where it must fall not only constitutionally but under any rational system. For these decisions can only be made from the point of view of the defense establishment as a whole, not from the point of view of the individual Services. Indeed the very biggest decisions—such as the basic kinds of forces we need, and the occasions on which we might want to commit those forces—must be made at an even higher level: for they involve basic questions of national policy which transcend the interest of the Defense Department, or the State Department, or indeed any part of the government, and must be made at the Presidential level.

Earlier, I described the chaotic situation that resulted from the individual Services deciding unilaterally what kind of defense preparations were most urgently needed. Each of the Services had a different concept of what kinds of wars we should be prepared to fight, with the result that the forces under the Army, Navy and Air Force simply did not fit together in the way they must to maximize their combat effectiveness. Now this same problem comes up when the Services recommend weapons systems. There is nothing wrong with that. It is inevitable. The Services properly fight hard for their viewpoints. This is probably the greatest single advantage of having separate Services, instead of one unified Service. But as a practical matter, although it is important to consider a variety of alternative policies, at the end we must have one defense policy, not three conflicting defense policies. And it is the job of the Secretary and his staff to make sure that this is the case, just as it is the job of the President to see that we have one national security policy, and not a series of conflicting policies in the State Department, the Treasury, the Defense Department, and so forth.

There is nothing innately desirable about centralization. But the fact remains that when national security decisions affect broad interests they must be made from a central point, not from subordinate points each specially concerned with one part of the forest—and not even by a committee made up of representatives of the different parts of the forest. For the nature of committees is to compromise their special interests, which is not the same as making the decision from the point of view of the national interest.

The Secretary of Defense—and I am talking about any Secretary of Defense—must make certain kinds of decisions, not because he presumes his judgment to be superior to his advisors, military or civilian, but because his position is the best place from which to make those decisions.

This same kind of argument applies when economic interests affected by defense decisions generate, as they inevitably will, political pressures on defense officials. Such pressures are an intrinsic and necessary part of a democratic political process. There are a good many advantages in forcing public officials to listen to people outside of their own staffs who do not share their views and assumptions. But it is the duty of government officials, representing the national interest rather than any smaller interest, to stand up to these pressures where what is asked cannot be reconciled with the national interest.

No single speech can do justice to the full complexity of defense decision-making. But at heart the problem comes down, always, to the same questions: What is really in our national interest? What will help this country to play the role we want it to play in this terribly critical period of the world's history? We are interested in saving money, in alleviating economic hardships from base closings and the like, in sound military-civilian relations, in the whole range of issues which tend to dominate the headlines. But the national interest towers above them all; and it is the national interest, above all, that we seek to serve.

# The Strategy of Peace

## BY JOHN F. KENNEDY

I HAVE . . . chosen this time and place to discuss a topic on which ignorance too often abounds and the truth is too rarely perceived—and that is the most important topic on earth: peace.

What kind of peace do I mean and what kind of peace do we seek? Not a Pax Americana enforced on the world by American weapons of war. Not the peace of the grave or the security of the slave. I am talking about the genuine peace—the kind of peace that makes life on earth worth living—and the kind that enables men and nations to grow and to hope and build a better life for their children—not merely peace for Americans but peace for all men and women—not merely peace in our time but peace in all time.

I speak of peace because of the new face of war. Total war makes no sense in an age where great powers can maintain large and relatively invulnerable forces and refuse to surrender without resort to those forces. It makes no sense in an age when a single nuclear weapon contains almost ten times the explosive force delivered by all the Allied air forces in the second world war. It makes no sense in an age when the deadly poisons produced by a nuclear exchange would be carried by wind and water and soil and seed to the far corners of the globe and to generations yet unborn.

Today the expenditure of billions of dollars every year on weapons acquired for the purpose of making sure we never need them is essential to the keeping of peace. But surely the acquisition of such idle stockpiles—which can only destroy and can never create—is not the only, much less the most efficient, means of assuring peace.

I speak of peace, therefore, as the necessary rational end of rational men. I realize the pursuit of peace is not as dramatic as the pursuit of war—and frequently the words of the pursuer fall on deaf ears. But we have no more urgent task.

Some say that it is useless to speak of peace or world law or world disarmament—and that it will be useless until the leaders of the Soviet Union adopt a more enlightened attitude. I hope they do. I believe we can help them do it.

But I also believe that we must re-examine our own attitudes—as individuals and as a nation—for our attitude is as essential as theirs. And every graduate of this school, every thoughtful citizen who despairs of war and wishes to bring peace, should begin by looking inward—by examining his own attitude toward the course of the cold war and toward freedom and peace here at home.

First: Examine our attitude towards peace itself. Too many of us think it is impossible. Too many think it is unreal. But that is a dangerous defeatist belief. It leads to the conclusion that war is inevitable—that mankind is doomed—that we are gripped by forces we cannot control.

We need not accept that view. Our problems are man-made. Therefore, they can be solved by

---

*Vital Speeches of the Day*, July 1, 1963, 558–560. Delivered at Commencement, American University, Washington, D.C.

man. And man can be as big as he wants. No problem of human destiny is beyond human beings. Man's reason and spirit have often solved the seemingly unsolvable—and we believe they can do it again.

I am not referring to the absolute, infinite concepts of universal peace and goodwill of which some fantasies and fanatics dream. I do not deny the value of hopes and dreams but we merely invite discouragement and incredulity by making that our only and immediate goal.

### Concrete Actions Needed

Let us focus instead on a more practical, more attainable peace—based not on a sudden revolution in human nature but on a gradual evolution in human institutions—on a series of concrete actions and effective agreement which are in the interests of all concerned.

There is no single, simple key to this peace—no grand or magic formula to be adopted by one or two powers. Genuine peace must be the product of many nations, the sum of many acts. It must be dynamic, not static, changing to meet the challenge of each new generation. For peace is a process—a way of solving problems.

With such a peace, there will still be quarrels and conflicting interests, as there are within families and nations. World peace, like community peace, does not require that each man love his neighbor—it requires only that they live together with mutual tolerance, submitting their disputes to a just and peaceful settlement. And history teaches us that enmities between nations, as between individuals, do not last forever. However fixed our likes and dislikes may seem, the tide of time and events will often bring surprising changes in the relations between nations and neighbors.

So let us persevere. Peace need not be impracticable—and war need not be inevitable. By defining our goal more clearly—by making it seem more manageable and less remote—we can help all people to see it, to draw hope from it, and to move irresistibly towards it.

And second: let us re-examine our attitude towards the Soviet Union. It is discouraging to think that their leaders may actually believe what their propagandists write.

It is discouraging to read a recent authoritative Soviet text on military strategy and find, on page after page, wholly baseless and incredible claims—such as the allegation that "American imperialists circles are preparing to unleash different types of war . . . that there is a very real threat of a preventative war being unleashed by American imperialists against the Soviet Union . . . (and that) the political aims," and I quote, "of the American imperialists are to enslave economically and politically the European and other capitalist countries . . . (and) to achieve world domination . . . by means of aggressive war."

Truly, as it was written long ago: "The wicked flee when no man pursueth." Yet it is sad to read these Soviet statements—to realize the extent of the gulf between us. But it is also a warning—a warning to the American people not to fall into the same trap as the Soviets, not to see only a distorted and desperate view of the other side, not to see conflict as inevitable, accommodation as impossible and communication as nothing more than an exchange of threats.

No government or social system is so evil that its people must be considered as lacking in virtue. As Americans, we find Communism profoundly repugnant as a negation of personal freedom and dignity. But we can still hail the Russian people for their many achievements—in science and space, in economic and industrial growth, in culture, in acts of courage.

Among the many traits the peoples of our two countries have in common, none is stronger than our mutual abhorrence of war. Almost unique among the major world powers, we have never been at war with each other. And no nation in the history of battle ever suffered more than the Soviet Union in the second world war. At least 20,000,000 lost their lives. Countless millions of homes and families were burned or sacked. A third of the nation's territory, including two-thirds of its industrial base, was turned into a wasteland—a loss equivalent to the destruction of this country east of Chicago.

Today, should total war ever break out again—no matter how—our two countries will be the primary targets. It is an ironic but accurate fact that the two strongest powers are the two in the most danger of devastation. All we have built, all we have worked for, would be destroyed in the first 24 hours. And even in the cold war—which brings burdens and dangers to so many countries, including this nation's closest allies—our two countries bear the heaviest burdens. For we are both devoting massive sums of money to weapons that could be better devoted to combat ignorance, poverty and disease.

We are both caught up in a vicious and dangerous cycle with suspicion on one side breeding suspicion on the other, and new weapons begetting counter-weapons.

In short, both the United States and its allies, and the Soviet Union and its allies, have a mutually deep interest in a just and genuine peace and in halting the arms race. Agreements to this end are in the interests of the Soviet Union as well as ours—and even the most hostile nations can be relied upon to accept and keep those treaty obligations and only those treaty obligations, which are in their own interest.

So, let us not be blind to our differences—but let us also direct attention to our common interests and the means by which those differences can be resolved. And if we cannot end now our differences, at least we can help make the world safe for diversity. For, in the final analysis, our most basic common link is that we all inhabit this small planet. We all breathe the same air. We all cherish our children's future. And we are all mortal.

Third: Let us re-examine our attitude towards the cold war, remembering we are not engaged in a debate, seeking to pile up debating points.

We are not here distributing blame or pointing the finger of judgment. We must deal with the world as it is, and not as it might have been had the history of the last eighteen years been different.

We must, therefore, persevere in the search for peace in the hope that constructive changes within the Communist bloc might bring within reach solutions which now seem beyond us. We must conduct our affairs in such a way that it becomes in the Communists' interest to agree on a genuine peace. And above all, while defending our own vital interests, nuclear powers must avert those confrontations which bring an adversary to a choice of either a humiliating retreat or a nuclear war. To adopt that kind of course in the nuclear age would be evidence only of the bankruptcy of our policy—or of a collective death-wish for the world.

To secure these ends, America's weapons are non-provocative, carefully controlled, designed to deter and capable of selective use. Our military forces are committed to peace and disciplined in self-restraint. Our diplomats are instructed to avoid unnecessary irritants and purely rhetorical hostility.

For we can seek a relaxation of tensions without relaxing our guard. And, for our part, we do not need to use threats to prove that we are resolute. We do not need to jam foreign broadcasts out of fear our faith will be eroded. We are unwilling to impose our system on any unwilling people—but we are willing and able to engage in peaceful competition with any people on earth.

Meanwhile, we seek to strengthen the United Nations, to help solve its financial problems, to make it a more effective instrument for peace, to develop it into a genuine world security system—a system capable of resolving disputes on the basis of law, of insuring the security of the large and the small, and of creating conditions under which arms can finally be abolished.

At the same time we seek to keep peace inside the non-Communist world, where many nations, all of them our friends, are divided over issues which weaken Western unity, which invite Communist intervention or which threaten to erupt into war.

Our efforts in West New Guinea, in the Congo, in the Middle East and the Indian subcontinent have been persistent and patient despite criticism from both sides. We have also tried to set an example for others—by seeking to adjust small but significant differences with our own closest neighbors in Mexico and Canada.

Speaking of other nations, I wish to make one point clear. We are bound to many nations by alliances. These alliances exist because our concern and theirs substantially overlap. Our commitment to defend Western Europe and West

Berlin, for example, stands undiminished because of the identity of our vital interests. The United States will make no deal with the Soviet Union at the expense of other nations and other peoples, not merely because they are our partners, but also because their interests and ours converge.

Our interests converge, however, not only in defending the frontiers of freedom, but in pursuing the paths of peace.

It is our hope—and the purpose of allied policies—to convince the Soviet Union that she, too, should let each nation choose its own future, so long as that choice does not interfere with the choices of others. The Communist drive to impose their political and economic system on others is the primary cause of world tension today. For there can be no doubt that, if all nations could refrain from interfering in the self-determination of others, the peace would be much more assured.

This will require a new effort to achieve world law—a new context for world discussions. It will require increased understanding between the Soviets and ourselves. And increased understanding will require increased contact and communication.

One step in this direction is the proposed arrangement for a direct line between Moscow and Washington, to avoid on each side the dangerous delays, misunderstanding, and misreadings of the other's actions which might occur in a time of crisis.

We have also been talking in Geneva about other first-step measures of arms control, designed to limit the intensity of the arms race and reduce the risks of accidental war.

Our primary long-range interest in Geneva, however, is general and complete disarmament—designed to take place by stages, permitting parallel political developments to build the new institutions of peace which would take the place of arms. The pursuit of disarmament has been an effort of this Government since the 1920's. It has been urgently sought by the past three Administrations. And however dim the prospects are today, we intend to continue this effort—to continue it in order that all countries, including our own, can better grasp what the problems and the possibilities of disarmament are.

The only major area of these negotiations where the end is in sight—yet where a fresh start is badly needed—is in a treaty to outlaw nuclear tests. The conclusion of such a treaty—so near and yet so far—would check the spiraling arms race in one of its most dangerous areas. It would place the nuclear powers in a position to deal more effectively with one of the greatest hazards which man faces in 1963—the further spread of nuclear weapons. It would increase our security—it would decrease the prospects of war.

Surely this goal is sufficiently important to require our steady pursuit, yielding neither to the temptation to give up the whole effort nor the temptation to give up our insistence on vital and responsible safeguards.

I am taking this opportunity, therefore, to announce two important decisions in this regard:

First: Chairman Khrushchev, Prime Minister Macmillan and I have agreed that high-level discussions will shortly begin in Moscow towards early agreement on a comprehensive test ban treaty. Our hopes must be tempered with the caution of history—but with our hopes go the hopes of all mankind.

Second: To make clear our good faith and solemn convictions on the matter, I now declare that the United States does not propose to conduct nuclear tests in the atmosphere so long as other states do not do so. We will not be the first to resume. Such a declaration is no substitute for a formal binding treaty—but I hope it will help us achieve one. Nor would such a treaty be a substitute for disarmament—but I hope it will help us to achieve it.

Finally, my fellow Americans, let us examine our attitude towards peace and freedom here at home. The quality and spirit of our own society must justify and support our efforts abroad. We must show it in the dedication of our own lives—as many of you who are graduating today will have an opportunity to do, by serving without pay in the Peace Corps abroad or in the proposed National Service Corps here at home.

## Peace and Freedom Related

But wherever we are, we must all, in our daily lives, live up to the age-old faith that peace and freedom walk together. In too many of our cities today, the peace is not secure because freedom is incomplete.

It is the responsibility of the executive branch at all levels of government—local, state and national—to provide and protect that freedom for all of our citizens by all means within our authority. It is the responsibility of the legislative branch at all levels, wherever the authority is not now adequate, to make it adequate. And it is the responsibility of all citizens in all sections of this country to respect the rights of others and respect the law of the land.

All this is not unrelated to world peace. "When a man's ways please the Lord," the scriptures tell us, "he maketh even his enemies to be at peace with him." And is not peace, in the last analysis, basically a matter of human rights—the right to live out our lives without fear of devastation—the right to breathe air as nature provided it—the right of future generations to a healthy existence?

While we proceed to safeguard our national interests, let us also safeguard human interests. And the elimination of war and arms is clearly in the interest of both.

No treaty, however much it may be to the advantage of all, however tightly it may be worded, can provide absolute security against the risks of deception and evasion. But it can—if it is sufficiently effective in its enforcement and it is sufficiently in the interests of its signers—offer far more security and far fewer risks than an unabated, uncontrolled, unpredictable arms race.

The United States, as the world knows, will never start a war. We do not want a war. We do not now expect a war. This generation of Americans has already had enough—more than enough—of war and hate and oppression. We shall be prepared if others wish it. We shall be alert to try to stop it. But we shall also do our part to build a world of peace where the weak are safe and the strong are just.

We are not helpless before that task or hopeless of its success. Confident and unafraid, we labor on—not toward a strategy of annihilation but toward a strategy of peace. Thank you.

# Peace Through Power

BY LYNDON B. JOHNSON

## To the Congress of the United States

One hundred seventy-five years ago, in his first Annual Message, President Washington told the Congress:

> Among the many interesting objects which will engage your attention that of providing for the common defense will merit particular regard. To be prepared for war is one of the most effectual means of preserving peace.

For the Eighty-ninth Congress—as for the First Congress—those words of the first President remain a timely charge.

In the twentieth year since the end of mankind's most tragic war you and I are beginning new terms of service. The danger of war remains ever with us. But if the hope of peace is sturdier than at any other time in these two decades, it is because we—and free men everywhere—have proved preparedness to be "the most effectual means of preserving peace."

Arms alone cannot assure the security of any society or the preservation of any peace. The health and education of our people, the vitality of our economy, the equality of our justice, the vision and fulfillment of our aspirations are all factors in America's strength and well-being.

Today we can walk the road of peace because we have the strength we need. We have built that strength with courage. We have employed it with care. We have maintained it with conviction that the reward of our resolution will be peace and freedom.

We covet no territory, we seek no dominion, we fear no nation, we despise no people. With our arms we seek to shelter the peace of mankind.

In this spirit, then, I wish to consider with you the state of our defenses, the policies we pursue, and—as Commander-in-Chief—to offer recommendations on our course for the future.

## The State of our Defenses

I am able to report to you that the United States today is stronger militarily than at any other time in our peacetime history.

Under our free and open society, the American people have succeeded in building a strength of arms greater than that ever assembled by any other nation and greater now than that of any combination of adversaries.

This strength is not the handiwork of any one Administration. Our force in being and in place reflects the continuity and constancy of America's purpose under four Administrations and eight Congresses—and this responsible conduct of our system is, of itself, a source of meaningful strength.

For the past four years, the focus of our national effort has been upon assuring an indisputable margin of superiority for our defenses. I can report today that effort has succeeded.

Our strategic nuclear power on alert has increased three-fold in four years.

---

White House press release on President Johnson's Defense Message to Congress, January 18, 1965.

Our tactical nuclear power has been greatly expanded.

Our forces have been made as versatile as the threats to peace are various.

Our Special Forces, trained for the undeclared, twilight wars of today have been expanded eight-fold.

Our combat-ready Army divisions have been increased by 46 percent.

Our Marine Corps has been increased by 15,000 men.

Our airlift capacity to move these troops rapidly anywhere in the world has been doubled.

Our tactical Air Force firepower to support these divisions in the field has increased 100 percent.

This strength has been developed to support our basic military strategy—a strategy of strength and readiness, capable of countering aggression with appropriate force from ballistic missiles to guerrila bands.

Our forces are balanced and ready, mobile and diverse. Our allies trust our strength and our adversaries respect it. But the challenge is unceasing. The forms of conflict become more subtle and more complex every day. We must—and we shall—adapt our forces and our tactics to fulfill our purposes.

If our military strength is to be fully usable in times requiring adaptation and response to changing challenges, that strength must be so organized and so managed that it may be employed with planned precision as well as promptness.

The state of our defenses is enhanced today because we have established an orderly system for informed decision-making and planning.

Our planning and budgeting programs are now conducted on a continuing five-year basis and cover our total military requirements.

Our national strategy, military force structure, contingency plans and defense budget are all now related in an integrated plan.

Our orderly decision-making now combines our best military judgment with the most advanced scientific and analytical techniques.

Our military policy under the Secretary of Defense is now more closely tied than ever to the conduct of foreign policy under the Secretary of State.

Thus, we now have the ability to provide and maintain a balanced, flexible military force, capable of meeting the changing requirements of a constantly changing challenge.

### Basic Defense Policies

1. *Four years ago, President John F. Kennedy stated to the Congress and the world: "The primary purpose of our arms is peace, not war." That is still their purpose. We are armed, not for conquest, but to insure our own security and to encourage the settlement of international differences by peaceful processes.*

We are not a militaristic people, and we have long denounced the use of force in pursuit of national ambition. We seek to avoid a nuclear holocaust in which there can be neither victory nor victors. But we shall never again return to a world where peace-loving men must stand helpless in the path of those who, heedless of destruction and human suffering, take up war and oppression in pursuit of their own ambitions.

2. *The strength of our Strategic Retaliatory Forces must deter nuclear attack on the United States or our Allies.*

The forces we now have give that capability.

The United States has:

More than 850 land-based Intercontinental Ballistic Missiles

More than 300 nuclear-armed missiles in Polaris submarines

More than 900 strategic bombers, half of them ready at all times to be airborne within 15 minutes.

These strategic forces on alert are superior—in number and in quality—to those of any other nation.

To maintain our superiority, the immediate future will see further increases in our missile strength, as well as concentration on further technological improvements and continuing vigorous Research and Development.

We are:

Requesting more than $300 million to continue our program for extending the life and improving the capabilities of our B-52 strategic bombers, while eliminating two squadrons of B-52Bs, the earliest—and least effective—model of this plane.

Continuing development of engines and other systems for advanced aircraft to retain our option for a new manned bomber, should the need arise.

Continuing deployment of the SR-71, the world's fastest airplane, which will enter the active forces this year.

Continuing installation of the new over-the-horizon radars, giving us almost instantaneous knowledge of ballistic missiles launched for attack.

Continuing procurement and deployment of our latest strategic missiles, Minuteman II and Polaris A-3, greatly extending the range, accuracy, and striking power of the strategic forces.

Replacing older, more costly, and vulnerable elements of our strategic forces. The out-dated Atlas and Titan I missiles will be retired this year and the remainder of the B-47 forces will be phased out during Fiscal Year 1966.

All this is part of a continuing process. There will always be changes, replacing the old with the new.

Major developments in strategic weapon systems we propose to begin this year are:

A new missile system, the Poseidon, to increase the striking power of our missile carrying nuclear submarines. The Poseidon missile will have double the payload of the highly successful Polaris A-3. The increased accuracy and flexibility of the Poseidon will permit its use effectively against a broader range of possible targets and give added insurance of penetration of enemy defenses.

A series of remarkable new payloads for strategic missiles. These include: *penetration aids*, to assure that the missile reaches its target through any defense; *guidance and re-entry vehicle designs*, to increase many-fold the effectiveness of our missiles against various kinds of targets; and methods of reporting the arrival of our missiles on target, up to and even including the time of explosion.

A new Short Range Attack Missile (SRAM) that can, if needed, be deployed operationally with the B-52 or other bombers. This aerodynamic missile—a vast improvement over existing systems—would permit the bomber to attack a far larger number of targets and to do so from beyond the range of their local defenses.

3. *The strength, deployment, and mobility of our forces must be such that, combined with those of our allies, they can prevent the erosion of the Free World by limited, non-nuclear aggression.*

Our non-nuclear forces must be strong enough to insure that we are never limited to nuclear weapons alone as our sole option in the face of aggression. These forces must contribute to our strategy of responding flexibly and appropriately to varied threats to peace.

I have already cited the increases achieved during recent years in the strength and mobility of our Army, Navy, Marines, and of our air transport which gets them to the scene of battle and the tactical aircraft which support them there. These forces, furthermore, are now better balanced, better integrated, and under more effective command and control than ever before. We shall maintain our present high degree of readiness.

We must further improve our ability to concentrate our power rapidly in a threatened area, so as to halt aggression early and swiftly. We plan expansion of our airlift, improvement of our sealift, and more prepositioned equipment to enable us to move our troops overseas in a matter of days, rather than weeks.

To this end, we will:

Start development of the C-5A Cargo Transport. This extraordinary aircraft capable of carrying 750 passengers will bring a new era of air transportation. It will represent a dramatic step forward in the worldwide mobility of our forces and in American leadership in the field of aviation.

Build fast deployment cargo ships, capable of delivering military equipment quickly to any theatre. This represents a new concept in the rapid deployment of military forces. These ships will have a gas turbine engine propulsion system, a major advance in marine engineering for ships of this size. Such vessels will be deployed around the globe, able to begin deliveries of heavy combat-ready equipment into battle zone within days or even hours.

Increase our Forward Floating Depot Ships stationed close to areas of potential crisis.

Begin large-scale procurement of the revolutionary swept wing F-111 and the new A-7 Navy attack aircraft.

We will also begin construction of four new nuclear-powered attack submarines, and ten new destroyer escorts. And we will continue to develop a much smaller, more efficient, nuclear power plant for possible use in our future aircraft carriers.

4. *While confident that our present strength will continue to deter a thermonuclear war, we must always be alert to the possibilities for limited destruction which might be inflicted upon our people, cities, and industry—should such a war be forced upon us.*

Many proposals have been advanced for means of limiting damage and destruction to the United States in the event of a thermonuclear war. Shifting strategy and advancing technology make the program of building adequate defenses against nuclear attack extremely complex.

Decisions with respect to further limitation of damage require complex calculations concerning the effectiveness of many interrelated elements. Any comprehensive program would involve the expenditure of tens of billions of dollars. We must not shrink from any expense that is justified by its effectiveness, but we must not hastily expend vast sums on massive programs that do not meet this test.

It is already clear that without fall-out shelter protection for our citizens, all defense weapons lose much of their effectiveness in saving lives. This also appears to be the least expensive way of saving millions of lives, and the one which has clear value even without other systems. We will continue our existing programs and start a program to increase the total inventory of shelters through a survey of private homes and other small structures.

We shall continue the research and development which retains the options to deploy an anti-ballistic missile system, and manned interceptors and surface-to-air missiles against bombers.

5. *Our military forces must be so organized and directed that they can be used in a measured, controlled, and deliberate way as a versatile instrument to support our foreign policy.*

Military and civilian leaders alike are unanimous in their conviction that our armed might is and always must be so controlled as to permit measured response in whatever crises may confront us.

We have made dramatic improvements in our ability to communicate with and command our forces, both at the national level and at the level of the theater commanders. We have established a National Military Command System, with the most advanced electronic and communications equipment, to gather and present the military information necessary for top level management of crises and to assure the continuity of control through all levels of command. Its survival under attack is insured by a system of airborne, shipborne and other command posts, and a variety of alternative protected communications.

We have developed and procured the Post Attack Command Control System of the Strategic Air Command, to assure continued control of our strategic forces following a nuclear attack.

We have installed new safety procedures and systems designed to guarantee that our nuclear weapons are not used except at the direction of the highest national authority.

This year we are requesting funds to extend similar improvements in the survivability and effectiveness of our command and control to other commands in our overseas theaters.

6. *America will continue to be first in the use of science and technology to insure the security of its people.*

We are currently investing more than $6 billion per year for military Research and Development. Among other major developments, our investment has recently produced antisatellite systems that can intercept and destroy armed satellites that might be launched, and such revolutionary new aircraft as the F-111 fighter-bomber and the SR-71 supersonic reconnaissance aircraft. Our investment has effected an enormous improvement in the design of anti-ballistic missile systems. We will pursue our program for the development of the Nike-X anti-missile system, to permit deployment of this anti-ballistic missile should the national security require. Research will continue on even more advanced anti-missile components and concepts.

About $2 billion a year of this program is invested in innovations in technology and in experimental programs. Thus, we provide full play for the ingenuity and inventiveness of the best scientific and technical talent in our nation and the Free World.

American science, industry, and technology are foremost in the world. Their resources represent a prime asset to our national security.

7. *Our soldiers, sailors, airmen, and marines, from whom we ask so much, are the cornerstone of our military might.*

The success of all our policies depends upon our ability to attract, develop fully, utilize and retain the talents of outstanding men and women in the military services. We have sought to improve housing conditions for military families and educational opportunities for military personnel.

Since 1961, we have proposed—and the Congress has authorized—the largest military pay increases in our history, totaling more than $2 billion.

To ensure that the pay of military personnel, and indeed of all government employees, retains an appropriate relation to the compensation of other elements of our society, we will revise their pay annually. The procedures for this review will be discussed in my budget message.

It is imperative that our men in uniform have the necessary background and training to keep up with the complexities of the ever-changing military, political, and technical problems they face each day. To insure this, the Secretary of Defense is undertaking a study of military education to make certain that the education available to our service men and women at their Academies, at their War Colleges and at the Command and Staff Colleges, is excellent in its quality.

In recent years large numbers of volunteers have been rejected by the military services because of their failure to meet certain mental or physical standards, even though many of their deficiencies could have been corrected. To broaden the opportunity for service and increase the supply of potentially qualified volunteers, the Army is planning to initiate an experimental program of military training, education and physical rehabilitation for men who fail at first to meet minimum requirements for service. This pilot program, which will involve about 10,000 men in 1965, will establish how many of these young volunteers can be upgraded so as to qualify for service.

8. *Our citizen-soldiers must be the best organized, best equipped reserve forces in the world. We must make certain that this force, which has served our country so well from the time of the Revolution to the Berlin and Cuban crises of recent years, keeps pace with the changing demands of our national security.*

To this end, we are taking steps to realign our Army Reserves and National Guard to improve significantly their combat-readiness and effectiveness in times of emergency. This realignment will bring our Army Reserve structure into balance with our contingency war plans and will place all remaining units of the Army reserve forces in the National Guard. At the same time, by eliminating units for which there is no military requirement, we will realize each year savings approximating $150 million. Under our plan, all units will be fully equipped with combat-ready equipment and will be given training in the form of monthly week-end drills that will greatly increase their readiness. Under the revised organization, both the old and the new units of the National Guard, as well as individual trainees who remain in the Reserves, will make a much greater and continuing contribution to our national security.

We shall continue to study our reserve forces and take whatever action is necessary to increase their combat effectiveness.

9. *The Commander-in-Chief and the Secretary of Defense must continue to receive the best professional military advice available to the leaders of any government in the world.*

The importance of a strong line of command running from the Commander-in-Chief to the Secretary of Defense and the Joint Chiefs of Staff to the Unified and Specified Commanders in the field has been repeatedly demonstrated during recent years.

The Secretary of Defense will present to you certain recommendations to strengthen the Joint Staff.

10. *We will strengthen our military alliances, assist freedom-loving peoples, and continue our Military Assistance Program.*

*It is essential to continue to strengthen our alliances with other free and independent nations.* We reaffirm our unwavering determination that efforts to divide and conquer free men shall not be successful in our time. We shall continue to assist those who struggle to preserve their own independence.

The North Atlantic Treaty Organization is a strong shield against aggression. We reaffirm our belief in the necessity of unified planning and execution of strategy. We invite our NATO allies to work with us in developing better methods for mutual consultation and joint strategic study. We shall continue to seek ways to bind the alliance even more strongly together by sharing the tasks of defense through collective action.

*We shall continue our program of military and economic assistance to Allies elsewhere in the world and to those nations struggling against covert aggression in the form of externally directed, undeclared guerrilla warfare.* In Southeast Asia, our program remains unchanged. From 1950, the United States has demonstrated its commitment to the freedom, independence, and neutrality of Laos by strengthening the economic and military security of that nation. The problem of Laos is the refusal of the Communist forces to honor the Geneva Accords into which they entered in 1962. We shall continue to support the legitimate government of that country. The Geneva Accords established the right of Laos to be left alone in peace.

Similarly, the problem of Vietnam is the refusal of Communist forces to honor their agreement of 1954. The North Vietnam regime, supported by the Chinese Communists, has openly and repeatedly avowed its intention to destroy the independence of the Republic of Vietnam through massive, ruthless, and incessant guerrilla terrorism against Government and people alike.

Our purpose, under three American Presidents, has been to assist the Vietnamese to live in peace, free to choose their own way of life and their own foreign policy. We shall continue to honor our commitments in Vietnam.

## Principles of Defense Management

1. *To carry out our strategy and enforce our policies requires a large budget for defense.*

The world's most affluent society can surely afford to spend whatever must be spent for its freedom and security. We shall continue to maintain the military forces necessary for our security without regard to arbitrary or predetermined budget ceilings. But we shall continue to insist that those forces be procured at the lowest possible cost and operated with the greatest possible economy and efficiency.

To acquire and maintain our unprecedented military power, we have been obliged to invest more than one-half of every dollar paid in taxes to the Federal Government. The Defense budget has grown from $43 billion in Fiscal Year 1960 to more than $51 billion in Fiscal Year 1964. I now estimate the Defense expenditures for Fiscal Year 1965 to be about $49.3 billion, or approximately $2 billion less than in Fiscal Year 1964. I further estimate that Defense expenditures for Fiscal Year 1966 will be reduced still another $300 million.

There are two main reasons for this leveling-off in Defense expenditures:

First, we have achieved many of the needed changes and increases in our military force structure;

Second, we are now realizing the benefits of the rigorous Cost Reduction Program introduced into the Defense establishment during the past four years.

As I have stated—and as our enemies well know—this country now possesses a range of credible, usable military power enabling us to deal with every form of military challenge from guerrilla terrorism to thermonuclear war. Barring a significant shift in the international situation, we are not likely to require further increments on so large a scale during the next several years. Expenditures for Defense will thus constitute a declining portion of our expanding annual Gross National Product, which is now growing at the rate of 5 percent each year. If, over the next several years, we continue to spend approximately the same amount of dollars annually for our national defense that we are spending today, an ever-larger share of our expanding national wealth will be free to meet other vital needs, both public and private.

Let me be clear, however, to friend and foe alike. So long as I am President, we shall spend whatever is necessary for the security of our people.

2. *Defense expenditures in the years ahead must continue to be guided by the relentless pursuit of efficiency and intelligent economy.*

There is no necessary conflict between the need for a strong defense and the principles of economy and sound management. If we are to remain strong:

Outmoded weapons must be replaced by new ones,

Obsolete equipment and installations must be eliminated,

Costly duplication of effort must be eliminated.

We are following this policy now, and so long as I am President, I intend to continue to follow this policy.

We have recently announced the consolidation, reduction, or discontinuance of Defense activities in some 95 locations. When added to those previously completed, these actions will produce annual savings of more than $1 billion each year, every year, in the operations of the Defense Department, and release about 1,400,000 acres of land for civilian purposes. These economies—which represent more prudent and effective allocation of our resources—have not diminished the strength and efficiency of our Defense forces, but rather have enhanced them.

We are the wealthiest nation in the world and the keystone of the largest alliance of free nations in history. We can, and will, spend whatever is necessary to preserve our freedom. But we cannot afford to spend one cent more than is necessary, for there is too much waiting to be done, too many other pressing needs waiting to be met. I urge the Congress to support our efforts to assure the American people a dollar's worth of Defense for every dollar spent.

3. *While our primary goal is to maintain the most powerful military force in the world at the lowest possible cost, we will never be unmindful of those communities and individuals who are temporarily affected by changes in the pattern of Defense spending.*

Men and women, who have devoted their lives and their resources to the needs of their country, are entitled to help and consideration in making the transition to other pursuits.

We will continue to help local communities by mobilizing and coordinating all the resources of the Federal Government to overcome temporary difficulties created by the curtailment of any Defense activity. We will phase out unnecessary Defense operations in such a way as to lessen the impact on any community, and we will work with local communities to develop energetic programs of self-help, calling on the resources of state and local governments—and of private industry—as well as those of the Federal Government.

There is ample evidence that such measures can succeed. Former military bases are now in use throughout the country in communities which have not only adjusted to necessary change, but have created greater prosperity for themselves as a result. Their accomplishments are a tribute to the ingenuity of thousands of our citizens, and a testimony to the strength and resiliency of our economy and our system of government.

4. *We must continue to make whatever changes are necessary in our Defense establishment to increase its efficiency and to insure that it keeps pace with the demands of an ever-changing world; we must continue to improve the decision-making process by those in command.*

The experience of several years has shown that certain activities of the Defense establishment can be conducted not only with greater economy, but far more effectively when carried out on a Department-wide basis, either by a military department as executive agent or by a defense agency. The Defense Communications Agency, established in 1959, and the Defense Supply Agency and the Defense Intelligence Agency, established in 1961, have all eliminated duplication of effort, improved management, and achieved better fulfillment of their missions, In addition, we have recently announced:

Consolidation of the Field Contract Administration offices of the Military Department under the Defense Supply Agency;

Formation of the Department of Defense Contract Audit Agency, to increase the efficiency and lower the cost of Government auditing of Defense contracts;

Formation of the Traffic Management and Terminal Command, under the single management of the Department of the Army, to regulate surface transportation of military cargo and personnel within the Continental United States.

Each of these actions will lead to better performance, surer control, and less cost. Most important, these actions are informing and expediting the decision-making process. We will continue to seek out opportunities to further increase the effectiveness and efficiency of our Defense establishment.

## Conclusion

The Secretary of Defense will soon come before you with our detailed proposals for the coming year. He will have recommendations for further strengthening of our strategic forces and our conventional forces. He will have additional suggestions for achieving greater efficiency, and therefore greater economy.

As you consider the state of our defenses and form your judgments as to our future course, I know that you will do so in the knowledge that today we Americans are responsible not only for our own security but, in concert with our Allies, for the security of the Free World. Upon our strength and our wisdom rests the future not only of our American way of life, but that of the whole society of free men.

This is an awesome responsibility. So far, we have borne it well. As our strength rose—and largely as a consequence of that strength—we have been able to take encouraging steps toward peace. We have established an Arms Control and Disarmament Agency. We have signed a limited nuclear test ban agreement with the Soviet Union. We have, at the same time, met the challenge of force, unflinchingly, from Berlin to Cuba. In each case, the threat has receded and international tensions have diminished.

In a world of 120 nations, there are still great dangers to be faced. As old threats are turned back, change and turmoil will present new ones. The vigilance and courage we have shown in the last twenty years must be sustained as far ahead as we can see. The defense of freedom remains our duty—twenty-four hours a day and every day of the year.

We cannot know the future and what it holds. But all our experience of two centuries reminds us that: "To be prepared for war is one of the most effectual means of preserving peace."